The Lost Civil War Diary of JOHN RIGDON KING

The Lost Civil War Diary of JOHN RIGDON KING

The Story of an American Civil War Hero

DONALD B. JENKINS

AMERICA
THROUGH TIME®
ADDING COLOR TO AMERICAN HISTORY

America Through Time is an imprint of Fonthill Media LLC
www.through-time.com
office@through-time.com

Published by Arcadia Publishing by arrangement with Fonthill Media LLC
For all general information, please contact Arcadia Publishing:
Telephone: 843-853-2070
Fax: 843-853-0044
E-mail: sales@arcadiapublishing.com
For customer service and orders:
Toll-Free 1-888-313-2665
Visit us on the internet at www.arcadiapublishing.com

First published 2018

ISBN 978-1-63499-070-7

Typeset in 10.5pt on 13pt Sabon
Printed in the United States of America

Contents

Acknowledgments

Numerous people contributed their advice, time, skills and materials in making this book possible. First and foremost, I would like to thank both Fonthill Media and Arcadia Publishing. They exhibited a great deal of patience and expertise in guiding a novice writer through the publication process.

I wish to thank Elizabeth Foster and her family for their early support of my project. They provided invaluable photographs, newspaper clippings from the King family album, letters and John Kings' personal papers.

I would also like to thank the Newtown History Center of the Stone House Foundation for their assistance with the Nisewanger family genealogy and for their encouraging words in support of my project.

In addition, I wish to thank my wife, Beverly, for proofreading many chapters of my manuscript and offering suggestions for changes. Likewise, I owe a note of thanks to my daughter, Jennifer, who despite her very busy schedule took helped me with computer issues that were beyond my capabilities. She also constantly encouraged me to complete the manuscript. She was the only person who from day one who repeatedly told me that it would be published one day.

Special thanks to Stacy Mason of the Collections Center for Media Services at Harper's Ferry Center for providing a copy of John R. King's speech of January 7, 1915, given at the Hotel Belvedere in Baltimore before the Military Order of the Loyal Legion. Stacy also provided several early photographs of Captain King.

I also wish to express a word of gratitude to Stefanie Basalik, Executive Director of the Washington County Historical Society for referring me to

Fonthill Media. In addition, I thank Robyn Sumner for assisting me with finding and scanning several early photographs of Hagerstown from their collection.

I am very much indebted to Barbara Stricklin of the Baltimore Polytechnic Institute for sending me much appreciated biographical information and photographs of the school's past Dean and President, William R. King.

Joseph Berger of the Washington County Free Library assisted me numerous times in locating and sending me a large number of old Hagerstown newspaper articles.

I also give thanks to the following individuals and institutions who kindly offered illustrations from their collections: Jill Craig of the Washington County Regional Library, Terre Heydari of the DeGolyer Library at Southern Methodist University, Roberta Fairburn of the Abraham Lincoln Presidential Library, Kyna Hamill of the Medford Historical Society, Arthur House at the National Archives and the Joint Archives Committee of the Handley Regional Library and Winchester-Frederick County Historical Society.

Special thanks to Nathan Ensminger for the photographs he took at Manassas National Battlefield Park.

A special nod goes to Martin Brotsky of Dominion Camera for his painstaking work restoring many old photographs.

Without the generosity of the above persons in submitting written documents as well as photographs and illustrations, my manuscript would never have been published.

Editorial Note

The diary has been transcribed as it was written to include errors in grammar, punctuation and spelling. Detailed endnotes are at the end of the book.

Prologue

On a clear and sunny Saturday morning during July, my brother and I ventured to a farm auction in the Shenandoah Valley. The estate of ninety-eight year old Hazel R. Hillyard (also spelled Hilliard) of Broadway, Virginia, was up for sale to the highest bidder because she had moved into a retirement home. Miss Hillyard taught school in Rockingham County her entire life. She had resided on the small farm where the auction was being conducted since birth. She was the last in a long line of Hillyards who had lived and worked on that same piece of property.

The auction advertisement listed numerous early pieces of American 19th century pottery. Since I was an avid collector, here was an opportunity to obtain some more pieces. For many years, I had a marginal interest in Civil War artifacts and antiques. Although the advertisement also listed *carte de visite* photographs of Robert E. Lee and Stonewall Jackson, I really did not expect to find much in the way of Civil War artifacts even though the auction was being held in the heart of old Virginia.

The pottery sold early and brought strong prices as numerous pottery dealers and collectors were present. Hence, I was only able to purchase small cream pitcher. Later in the sale, the auctioneer pulled out a tray of 19th century ambrotypes and daguerreotypes along with the aforementioned Lee and Jackson CDV's. Among the group was a rare ambrotype of an unidentified Confederate soldier posed in a chair. He was holding a large bowie knife in his left hand and an old flintlock musket in his right. The young man wore a grim and determined expression on his face. Because I knew that his soldier was most likely a local man, I bid heartily and won the ambrotype. Later in the sale, I asked around and found a distant nephew to Miss Hillyard. I asked him if he knew who was pictured in my image. He said, "Why, that is grandpa Jimmy." Jimmy was Hazel's grandfather. I later learned that James D. Hillyard enlisted in the Confederate Army at the age of eighteen years on April 3, 1864. Like other local boys, Jimmy served in Company A, 3rd Battalion, Virginia Mounted Rifles, also known as the White Horse Cavalry, also known as Chrisman's Boy Company. In May of 1864, these boys and young men joined Brigadier General John D. Imboden's cavalry brigade.

Later in the auction, my brother and I discovered a large number of cardboard boxes filled with old books waiting to be sold. Since Hazel was a schoolteacher, that was not surprising. What was eye opening was the sight of a handwritten daily diary that covered the years 1861 to 1862. This book was not mentioned in the auction advertisement and no one, including the auctioneer paid any attention to it. It was simply mixed in with other fairly worthless old textbooks. After spirited bidding on the diary, I won the lot. I did not really have time to look at it until I got home late Saturday evening. I later discovered that it had been written by a man named John Rigdon King of Hagerstown. I wondered how and why his Civil War diary ended up in Broadway, Virginia, ninety-two miles away from his hometown. I was also curious why the diary was in Miss Hillyard's possession. After an initial reading, I noticed one possible connection. According to a diary entry, one of John King's best friends in Hagerstown was Tom Hilliard. Were the Hillyards of Broadway related to the Hilliards of Hagerstown? The mystery began. What had initially seemed like an easy puzzle to solve turned into a lengthy transcription, research, and writing project that took years to complete.

The Extended King Family for 1860 and 1870

HAGERSTOWN 1860
Samuel Liles King Sr.
Eliza Lane King (first wife of Samuel L.)
Children:
Mary Adelaide "Addie" King
Harrison Eader King
John Rigdon "Rig" King
William "Willie" R. King
Virginia King
Lilly King

HAGERSTOWN 1870
Ann R. King (second wife of Samuel, Sr.
Children:
Laura Cornelia King
Samuel Liles King, Jr.

Charles G. Lane (father of Eliza Lane King—John's father in law)
Maria Lane
Children:
John C. Lane
Sophia Lane
John H. King (brother of Samuel L. King, Sr.—John R. King's uncle)
Mary King

Oliver King
George H. King
Arthur King

HAGERSTOWN 1870
Samuel Z. McLaughlin (brother-in-law of Samuel L. King Sr.
Adelaide "Addie" King McLaughlin
Children:
Emma McLaughlin
Richard McLaughlin
Lula McLaughlin
Rigdon C. McLaughlin

HOWARD COUNTY, MARYLAND 1880
John Rigdon "Rig" King
Annie M. King—wife
Children: Mary E. King
Children: Mary Elizabeth King Adams

ALLEGHENY COUNTY, PENNSYLVANIA 1880
James King (brother of Samuel L. King, Sr.)
Eliza King—wife
Harrison E. King—(nephew)
Children of James: Lizzie, Jennie, Susan, Mattie

I

The Early Life of John Rigdon King and Family June 24, 1844 to October 21, 1861

In his memoirs, John R. King traced his family roots back to the Reverend John King, a Scottish covenanter who thwarted King James II and his ally, John Graham (Viscount Dundee) of Claverhouse.[1] Reverend King was executed August 14, 1679, after being defeated and captured at Bothwell Bridge. However, Reverend King had seven sons who emigrated to Ireland, one group eventually moving to England and settling in Yorkshire. John R. King then told the following story of his grandfather, John King:

> My grandfather married Polly Sutton, daughter of Lord Sutton; this union proved offensive to the Sutton family. Resenting the prejudices of Caste, John and Polly Sutton King, with scant belongings set sail for the "Golden West," where industry and right living alone mark the crown of nobility. They cast their lot in Frederick County, Maryland.
>
> Being highly educated, John King taught school five days in the week and on Saturdays followed his profession of Civil Engineering and became the first land surveyor of Frederick County, Maryland. This was before Washington County was formed.
>
> My father, Samuel Lysle King, often told us how his father tramped, barefoot over those rugged Mountains, making his surveys. He (i.e. John King) died at the age of 104 years.[2]

My father was "a Virginian who never got away from the idea that the Lord made Virginians a little better than others," said John R. King, son of Samuel Lysle King.[3]

According to John, Samuel was born in Virginia though it is not known how he came to be born in that state if his parents resided in Maryland. Nothing is known of the childhood or early adolescent days of Samuel's life.

On October 15, 1833, Samuel L. King and Eliza Lane were married, in Hagerstown, Washington County, Maryland.[4] Just twelve days before he was married, Samuel L. King placed the following advertisement on the front page of the *Torch Light*, a local Hagerstown newspaper, on October 3, 1833.[5]

COACH MAKING
Samuel L. King
Would respectfully inform the citizens
of *Hagerstown*, and the adjoining
country that he has taken the shop oc-
cupied by Mr. D. L. Armstrong, in South
Potomac street, *Hagerstown,* a few doors
from the Lutheran Church, where he is
prepared to make to order, all kinds of *Coa-
ches, Hacks, Gigs, Buggies, Etc.*
in the best manner, and most fashionable
style. *Having* on hand, a quantity of well
seasoned *timber*, the public may be assured
that his work will be strong and durable.
He will also repair all vehicles which may
be entrusted to him, with neatness and du-
rability.
A *Coach Maker*, will meet with constant
employment and good wages, if immediate.
October 3

The advertisement ran in the paper on November 7 and probably in other issues. Apparently, Samuel had a specialized profession prior to marriage and wanted to inform the town folk that he was now open for business. According to the advertisement, he was also seeking another coach maker for his new coach shop.

Samuel L. King

Samuel L. King was a well-known and well-respected member of the Hagerstown community. Throughout his years, he was a member of numerous charitable, patriotic, civic and business associations, organizations and committees. For instance, he was a lifelong member of St. Paul's Methodist Episcopal Church and served in numerous capacities within the church. As early as January 9, 1836, he was elected to position of "hose guard" of the First Hagerstown Hose Company, a local firefighting unit, along with George A. Bender, Daniel F. Little, John Marr and James Zwisler.[6] John R. Key was elected President while George Fechtig was voted in as Vice President.[7] As it is today, it was quite an honor to be a member of the First Hose Company in 19th century Hagerstown. The Hagerstown branch of the First Hose Company has been in existence for over two hundred years, is still active and is situated at 33 South Potomac Street.

Samuel also served in a local militia company. On August 27, 1846, the Hagerstown newspaper, *Torch Light*, announced the results of the recent military elections. While Isaac S. Hershey was elected captain of the 3rd Company of the 24th Regular Maryland Militia, Samuel L. King was selected as First Lieutenant with William Biershing as Second Lieutenant.[8] According to an article that appeared in *Herald Freedom & Torch Light* newspaper on January 3, 1855, the patrons of the public schools of Hagerstown met at C. F. Gelwicks' school room to elect, by ballot, three trustees.[9] Samuel L. King, George Fechtig, and Martin King were selected. Charles Gelnicks was one of John Kings' school teachers. As if he were not busy enough with his coach and plough making businesses, Samuel L. King was also a member of the Independent Order of the Odd Fellows, Potomac Lodge No. 31, which is now housed at 301 West Howard Street. An announcement that appeared in the *Herald Freedom & Torch Light* April 14, 1852, by a committee of S. L. King, R. Sheckles and C. Sheppard urged the public, Sister Lodges and friends to attend the Order's anniversary meeting to be held at Lyceum Hall on April 23.[10] The guest speaker was to be Jervis Spencer, Esquire.

Samuel King's business enterprise seemed to do well initially. However, a Bill of Sale recorded February 1, 1837, in the land records book for Washington County shows that he sold the following to John McCurdy:

> 3 Barouch Bodys, 3 Buggys, 3 Sets of Wheels, 8 Carriage parts, 1 ditto ditto ironed,
> 3 Benches and Tools, 1 Set of poplar boards, 1 ditto ash plank, ditto Hickory ditto,

> 1 ditto of Oak Spokes, 1 Steam box and kettle, 1 second hand Baroch, 4 setts of
> Harness, 2 plated dashes, 3 setts of black japaned harness mounting, 2 ditto Brass
> ditto, 2 ditto of Silver ditto, 2 Stoves and pipe, Paints, Brushes, Cups, Paint Stores, 3 Varnish Cans and Varnish, Harness trimmers tools, 3 Sets Steel C. Springs, 2 Eliptic ditto, 1 Set different sized augers, 1 Sleigh and harness, 3 Blacksmith tools, 4 sets of stock and dies, 1 drill press and tools.[11]

John McCurdy was a store owner in Hagerstown. Included in the sale were unfinished carriages, wood, parts, paints and varnishes and tools of Samuel's trade. It appears that he was liquidating his coach making business. An owner of such a trade would necessarily have had a great of capital tied up in parts, materials, tools and other equipment. Perhaps he was obligated to sell most of or part of it in order to pay taxes or outstanding debts. It is not known for certain what happened. In any case, Samuel did not run another newspaper advertisement for "coach making" until 1845. In addition, Samuel King's complicated business and financial history, as evidenced by bills of sale and judgments recorded in Washington County's land record books along with mortgages and deeds, shows a variety of sales and debts owed and paid. Besides selling just ploughs and handmade horse driven vehicles, he also dealt in furniture and household furnishings. A Bill of Sale recorded on February 7, 1837, shows that he sold his brother-in-law, John C. Lane, the following for $250.00:

> Twenty yards figured carpeting, two feather beds, eight quilts, wash kettles, three wash tubs, Kitchen spoons, Sadles, pots, pans, knifes and forks, two meat skewers, one kitchen table, one thousand lb. pork, fifteen bushel potatoes, one cow, one hog, one two horse wagon and harness, six sleigh baskets, three willow carriages.[12]

It is apparent that Samuel King had branched out into other pursuits, now becoming a retailer of a wide variety of goods. As noted by another Bill of Sale also recorded February 7, 1837, Samuel sold a large lot of furniture and household items to Elizabeth Jordan for $276.00:

> 1 Bureau $20, 1 Ditto 16.50, 1 Safe 6.00, 6 chairs .75 $4.50, 1 Ditto $1.00, 1 Ditto 1.25 $7.50, 2 Ditto small size at 75 cts. chair $1.50, 1 Dining table $6.00, 2 breakfast Ditto at $4.00 $8.00, 1 ten plate stove $18.00, 1 Bed and Bedstead $25.00, 1 Ditto $17.00, 1 Ditto $10.00, 1 Looking

glass $7.00, 1 Eighteen days clock $25.00, 20 yds. carpet at 50 cts ft., 1 Settee $8.00, 1 Copper Kettle $7.00, 1 set silver tea spoons $6.00, 3 Hogs at $3.00 $9.00, 1 Cow $18.00 = $226.00. [13]

In this particular instance, Samuel may have been a broker or middleman for the sale. On March 18, 1836, he purchased the exact same set of goods from John Frame of West Franklin Street in Hagerstown and seems to have simply resold them for a $50.00 profit to Elizabeth, widow of Martin Jordan of Lancaster.[14] Perhaps, the widow had recently moved to Washington County and needed furniture and household furnishings in her new home. Perhaps the transaction also included the transport of the large set to goods to Mrs. Jordan's residence.

If Samuel had sold most or all of his coach making materials and tools to John McCurdy February 1, 1837, he purchased some more by February of 1845. In an advertisement that appeared in February 12, 1845, issue of the *Herald Freedom*, he referred to his new venture, which included not just making ploughs and coaches, but also repairing them. This is second advertisement he put in the local newspaper following the initial one which had appeared twelve years earlier. According to this new ad, sometime two years earlier in 1843, he had changed the name of his business to S. L. King & Company as evidenced by the following newspaper advertisement:

OFFICIAL

The undersigned thankful very much for the very liberal patronage extended to him, for the last two years, as one of the firm of Samuel L. King & Co., would respectfully beg leave to inform the public and his friends generally, that he has taken the Shop lately occupied by Samuel L. King & Co. known as Davis' old stand South Potomac street, Hagerstown, where he is prepared to make and repair all kinds of PLOUGHS to order, which will be warranted to perform or no sale.

Also Wagon and Blacksmith work of all kinds made and repaired at short notice, and upon the most accommodating terms. All orders from a distance promptly attended to.

In connection with the above he has, at the warm solicitation of his friends in this and other parts of the county, fitted up a neat and commodious Coach-Shop in South Potomac Street, opposite the Lutheran church, where he will hold himself in readiness to make and repair all kinds of

COACH WORK

for neatness and durability unsurpassed by any in the county. From his long experience in this branch of his business he has no hesitation calling on his old customers to give him a call and have their Carriages tip't off in a style not equalled by any in this place. He shall have an eye to the very depressed state of the times in fixing his prices, and most respectfully solicits a share of the public favor.

All kind of Country produce taken in payment for work, at market prices.[15]

Samuel L. King

The public land liber books for Washington County show no more transactions involving Samuel L. King until a deed transfer made May 5, 1849, and recorded May 25, 1849. Priscilla Redburn, Samuel's aunt, gave him 88⅞ acres of land, building and improvements known as the "Redburn Farm" which had previously been "conveyed to a certain Lydia Redburn, since deceased and the said Priscilla Redburn by Henry Redburn, by his deed bearing date on or about the 17th day of May 1820…"[16] The Redburn family was well-known in the state of Maryland. Henry Lillie Redburn was born 1735 in Newchurch, Lancaster, England and immigrated to the United States where he settled in Maryland. Henry died after 1830 and left his estate to his nine children, two of which included Lydia, born *c.* 1784 and died before 1849, and Priscilla, born in 1790 and who died in 1855.[17] The "Redburn Farm" that was a gift to him from his aunt Priscilla, was the first piece of property that Samuel King owned in Washington County and would be the only land that he would ever own. Previously, he probably rented his home and workshop on South Potomac Street in Hagerstown.

Although no records exist, Samuel King apparently did well in his business of making and repairing both coaches and ploughs and as serving as a general blacksmith. However, beginning in 1849, a number of financial setbacks began to occur. These reversals may have been due to a lot of competition in Hagerstown from other coach and plough makers and also may have been caused, in part, by the "very depressed state of the times" Samuel referred to in his advertisement. Whatever the causes, things did not go well for him beginning in 1849 and continuing throughout the 1850s.

Just after he received the "Redburn Farm," Samuel and his wife, Eliza, signed a promissory note with attorneys Henry K. Tice and David C. Hammond for $600.00 on May 16, 1849. He borrowed using the "Redburn

Farm" as collateral and promised to make payments, which included interest, with the last one of $159.00 due May 17, 1853. The total amount that he would repaid would be $690.00 if all payments were made according the schedule. This mortgage was recorded in the Washington County liber books.[18]

Next, the following Bill of Sale was recorded November 27, 1849:

> I, Samuel L. King, of Washington County, Md. for and in consideration of the sum of five dollars to me in hand paid, by Jervis Spencer... and in consideration of two judgments in Washington County Court, against me, one at the suit of J. Parsons, J. Murray, and Saml. McMurray for the sum of $90 with int. and costs; the other one at the suit of Jas. Murray and Saml. McMurray for the sum of $150, with int. and costs, in which said cases, the said Spencer is Attorney and Agent for the Plaintiffs... do grant, bargain and sell the said Jervis Spencer... the following property, to wit, one new coach, just being finished, and ready to set on the wheels, and four buggies, being all carriages owned by me and which are now on my premises in Hagerstown...[19]

The attorney, Jervis Spencer, would sell the coach and buggies in order to pay the Plaintiffs. Once that was done, the Bill of Sale would be released. Mr. Spencer probably assisted Samuel King in setting up this payment arrangement as both he and Samuel were both Odd Fellows in Lodge 21. This transaction, although called a Bill of Sale, was really a forfeiture of property.

In a probable attempt to raise some needed capital, Samuel King placed a lengthy advertisement in the Hagerstown *Herald Freedom* on May 15, 1850, offering to sell at public auction his "entire livery of horses, carriages and buggies. The advertisement ran as follows:

> Public Sale
>
> The subscriber will sell at a public sale, at his residence on South Potomac St. Hagerstown, on Saturday the 1st day of June next, the following property embracing his entire Livery of Horses, Carriages and Buggies, viz: Four Head of Young & Gentle Harness Horses among which are Thee FINE MARES, suitable for family or farm purposes. One Fine Large Family CARRIAGE, entirely new, 1 new and 1 second-hand iron AXLE, two-seated BAROUCHES 2 new Leather top Buggies and 1 second-hand do., 1 Eliptic Spring Wagon nearly new, 1 new one horse Wagon, 2 double

> sets Brass Mounted Harness, 1 new single set Brass do., 3 sets plain single Harness, 3 Riding Saddles and Bridles. –ALSO At the same time and place he will offer for sale, a number of his Superior Challenger Ploughs; and also a number of DOUBLE SHOVEL PLOUGHS. Sale to commence at 10 o'clock A.M.
>
> Terms.—A credit of six months will be given on all sums over $10, the purchase giving his
> note will approved security; all sums under $10 must be cash.20
> May 15, 1850
>
> Samuel L. King

Samuel was also in debt to Stickney Beatty for $96.55 plus interest and again a Judgment was obtained and recorded October 20, 1851. This time, however, Samuel did not forfeit coaches or buggies but instead furniture and household goods which included the following:

> Four stoves and pipe, 3 feather beds, bedsteads and bedding, 60 yards of figured Carpeting, 3 dozen chairs, 1 pr. mahogany Card Tables, together with all the household kitchen furniture of the said Samuel L. King.[21]

Since 1838, when Samuel and Eliza's first child, Mary Adeline (nicknamed Addie) was born, his family had rapidly grown in size. His second daughter, Virginia L. was just one year old. His sons Harrison and John, eleven and seven years old respectively, were already in private schools. Hence, Samuel had three children to feed and clothe; a house and farm some distance from Hagerstown, which meant he still had to pay rent in the city, increased tuition costs, and a retail business that was doing poorly. In addition, per the 1850 promissory note with attorneys Tice and Hammond, he was required to pay $177.00 May 17, 1851, $168.00 May 17, 1852 and $159.00 May 17, 1853. As if all of that were not bad enough, at the end of the year 1851, three more Judgments were recorded on December 11, 1851. John D. Ridenour, Richard Sheckles and James Mason brought suit against Samuel L. King for their clients in the amounts of $98.51, $51.78 and $55.46 plus interest of $0.83 interest each, for a total of $208.24.[22] This time he had to forfeit:

> 1 sorrel horse, 1 new carriage, 2 iron axle tree buggies and one two horse Spring Wagons agreed that John Ridenour etc. are authorized to sell the above mortgaged goods & chattels by public auction to the highest bidder or bidders for cash or credit ... after first giving notice by advertisement

> by hand bills for ten days of the time place manner and terms of the sale... shall be paid over to the said King all such surplus over and above the aforesaid sums of money.

During 1852, Samuel King and David Brumbaugh engaged themselves in an accusatory exchange regarding the efficacy of their respective ploughs. The heated discourse took place in the local newspaper, the *Herald Freedom & Torch Light*. King had heavily advertised the superiority of his "Challenger" plough while Brumbaugh espoused the originality and efficiency of his "Washington County Regulator" plough. Mr. Brumbaugh even went so far as to publish certified statements from Samuel Wilk, William M. Kuhnes, "plow maker," I. Conrad, and Abraham Elshaman supporting his claims. Finally, in a Letter to the Public dated February 25, 1852, Mr. Brumbaugh suggested that King enter his Challenge plough in the next Washington County Agricultural Fair and declared that "I shall decline future, to notice any further communication through the papers from Mr. King on the subject.[23]

In yet another agreement made three years later on January 25, 1854, and recorded the same day, Samuel King was indebted on an earlier note to the Hagerstown Savings Institution in the amount of $350.00 and another four Judgments were filed against him totaling $281.00.[24] This time, he had to give up quite a bit more to satisfy his debts:

> one bay horse, one Cow, seven shoats, one Carriage, three Buggies two Spring Wagons, five bedsteads, beds and bedding, eighty yards Carpeting, one pair Card Tables, six Stoves, and one Clock.

Seemingly, Samuel King's financial situation improved over the next several years. His name did not appear on any more judgments in 1855 or 1856. He even placed an announcement in the *Herald Freedom & Torch Light* declaring his candidacy for Sheriff of Washington County on June 12, 1855, for the upcoming 1855 to 1857 term, but lost the election to Benjamin A. Garlinger.[25] Then, on February 28, 1857, he sold "all that parcel or tract of land called 'Redburn Farm' of 88⅞ acres plus buildings and improvements for $400.00 to the aforementioned attorneys, Henry K. Tice and David C. Hammond. Whether this sale was the result of financial concerns may or may not have been the reason for the sale of Samuel's only known piece of property.

One more entry appeared in the Washington County land records for Samuel L. King before the Civil War. According to a Bill of Sale recorded

January 20, 1859, he sold to his brother, John H. King of Martinsville, Virginia (now West Virginia), the following for $225.00.[26]

One Bugie	$80.00
1 old Carriage	30.00
1 unfinished Rocheway*	75.00
1 Secondhand Wagon	25.00
1 Bugie boddy	15.00
	$225.00

* A type of carriage.

One more auction appeared prior to the Civil War, but it was not placed by Samuel King. On February 29, 1860, Samuel Eichelberger placed the following advertisement in the *Herald Freedom and Torch Light* newspaper.[27]

PUBLIC SALE

Will be sold at public sale, at the late residence of S. L. King, opposite the Lutheran church, on Friday 9th day of March next, the following property to wit:

BEDSTEADS AND BEDDING

Tables, Chairs, Carpets, Stores, &c-Also Kitchen Furniture, including a COOKING STOVE and a number other articles not necessary to mention.

Terms:—a credit of 8 months will be given on all items of $5 and upwards, purchasers giving notes with approved security, and if not paid within 30 days of becoming due, interest will be charged from date; sums under $5 the cash will be required. No property removed until settled for.

Also-at the same time and place, a very Handsome and well finished

Rockaway and a Second-hand CARRIAGE
Said carriage will be sold on a good credit or will be disposed of in trade.
Sale will commence at 10 o'clock A.M. on said day.
I have Three Houses for Rent from the first day of April next.
Feb. 20, 1860

SAMUEL EICHELBERGER

This was the same Samuel Eichelberger, who was probably an attorney and friend of the court, who drew up the agreement made and recorded January 25, 1854, that enabled Samuel King to satisfy his debts to Hagerstown

Savings Institution and to others. In the present instance, as noticed by Mr. Eichelberger's reference to the "late residence" of Samuel King, it appears that the latter was planning to sell his furniture and household belongings on March 9th preparatory to relocation. In fact, that is what happened. The U.S. Census for Hagerstown, taken June 7, 1860 at the Charles G. Lane home, showed that the Kings were now residing with Charles G. Lane, a wealthy and well-known resident who also was Samuel L. King's father-in-law.[28] The Kings had vacated their former home and Samuel's workshop across from St. John's Lutheran Church where they had lived for many years. The King family was staying with the Lanes temporarily until they could relocate in Baltimore. The census listed Samuel, age 45, his wife, Eliza, age 44 along with their five children, Adeline or "Addie" age 22, Rigdon (John) age 16, Virginia age 7, William or "Willy" age 5 and Lilly age one.[29] Their oldest son, Harrison, was not shown. Samuel still gave his occupation as a "Coachmaker" and Addie was employed as a "Mantua Maker" or dress maker. Also living in the same dwelling house were Charles G. Lane, a "Cabinet Maker," his wife, Maria, and two children, John C. Lane, a "clerk," and Sophia Lane.[30] Charles G. Lane's real estate was valued as $7,000 and his personal estate was stated to be worth $8,000.[31] Sometime between June 7 and July 3, 1860, Samuel King moved his family to Baltimore, Maryland. He probably left Hagerstown to improve his business prospects. In Washington County, he had not done well financially and probably sought better opportunities. In addition, he wanted his son, John Rigdon, to enter the printing business with an old acquaintance of his. On the 1860 16th Ward Baltimore U.S. Census, the same five children were listed, but now a sixth child, Harrison, was present.[32] Samuel's occupation was now shown as a "Travelling Agent" or traveling salesman. The only other person listed as working was Harrison, age 19, who was a baker. One non-relative was also shown on the census, John Coon, a "machinist," age 21. More than likely, John Coon was helping Samuel King manufacture his "Challenger" ploughs. Oddly, although John R. King is not listed as a printer on either of the 1860 censuses, he would later state that he entered the printing business in 1859 and left it when the Civil War began. Perhaps his occupation was inadvertently omitted from both censuses or possibly John had his date wrong and did not serve as a printer's apprentice until after the 16th Ward Census was taken on July 3, 1860. Officially, a family was not supposed to be counted twice on two different censuses since doing so defeated the entire purpose of the effort.

Samuel L. King had lived in Hagerstown most of his life and had supported his growing family by crafting buggies, coaches and carriages for nearly thirty years. He supplemented his income by also making "Challenger" ploughs and by buying and selling both furniture and household goods. Hence, he was very much aware the wholesale and retail costs of goods. While he spent some time in Baltimore with his entire family before the Civil War, once the Civil War began, he soon realized a new business opportunity and soon returned to Hagerstown with his family. The business acumen he now had would serve him well in his next endeavor, one in which he would partner with his son-in-law, Samuel Z. McLaughlin. Samuel King would also share his vast knowledge wholesale and retail purchasing with second oldest son, John R. King, who would also use it to favorable advantage.

John Rigdon King

In contrast to the paternal side of his family, John King often mentioned the maternal Lane branch of his family history. At one point he stated that "My mother was a Lane, who had three Brothers, Charles, Samuel who located in Little Rock, Ark., and John C. who lived and died in Fredk Co., the father of Colonel Billie."[33] Colonel Billie was also known as Colonel William P. Lane. In a long letter to Lenore Hamilton, daughter of deceased Governor William T. Hamilton, John went on to say:

> My Mother's Grandfather was a Woltz—three Brothers, Dr. George, Peter and Samuel, their name appears in the first U.S. Census—Dr. George, according to a paper read before the Wash. Co. Medical Society by the late Dr. Reichard, was a Medical Officer on the staff of General Washington and Peter joined Capt. Mantz' Co. in the Flying Camp on the first day of July 1776.[34]

Dr. V. Milton Reichard began a medical practice in his hometown of Fairplay, Washington County, Maryland, in 1882.[35] According to an article that appeared in the *Herald Mail* newspaper, he was "one of the original members of the Washington County Medical Association and one of the signatories to the incorporation of the Washington County Historical Society."[36] At one medical society meeting, Dr. Reichard presented the Woltz or Waltz family genealogy. How Dr. Reichard obtained the Woltz genealogy and why he presented it are not known. However, the data John King recited regarding his ancestors is generally correct. Peter Woltz (Waltz) of Wayne County, Pennsylvania, joined Captain Mantz's Company, 1st Maryland Battalion as a private and fought in the American Revolution.[37] He served from April of 1775 until September of 1780 and "was in 14 hard fought battles."[38] The son of John Reinhardt and Catherine Woltz, he married first to a Miss Moon and in 1790 to Eva Milliron in Westmoreland County, Pennsylvania. Peter had five children: John, Catharine, Christiana, Peter and David. On April 26, 1832, he died at the age of eighty-three years and was buried at High Church, Summit County, Pennsylvania.[39]

John George Adam Woltz, son of Peter Woltz, Sr., was born October 16, 1744 in York, Pennsylvania.[40] On Friday, February 10, 1744, he married Charlotte Shugars who bore him eight children.[41] He was a cabinet maker from Hagerstown. During the American Revolution, he served as a Lieutenant Colonel with the Maryland Militia from Frederick, Maryland. In 1811, Lieutenant Colonel Woltz died and was buried in St. John's Lutheran Church. This was the same church that was across the street from where the Kings would later reside. However, when the cemetery was later moved, Mary Eliza Walling (Woltz) Long paid to have the heavy oak caskets of Lieutenant Colonel and Charlotte carried to Williamsport, Maryland, and reinterred in Riverview Cemetery, where they remain today.[42] Although his father, Peter, Sr., was a physician, there is no evidence that George was a doctor or that he served on General George Washington's staff.

Of Major John George Adam Woltz's eight children, one daughter was named Catherine Woltz, who was born *c.* 1777.[43] Catharine married Seth Lane. This is the tie between the Woltz and Lane families. Samuel King's wife's father, i.e., Eliza's father, was the wealthy Charles G. Lane, as mentioned earlier. Charles was born March 17, 1804 and died January 4, 1873. Charles's father was Seth Lane, born *c.* 1774 and died *c.* 1824.[44] Hence, Seth and Catherine Woltz Lane were Eliza's grandparents. Therefore, Seth and Catharine were John R. Kings' great-grandparents. Colonel John George Adam and Private Peter Woltz were both Johns' great-great-grandparents.

While residing in Hagerstown, Samuel and Eliza King had six children. In order from oldest to youngest, they were: Mary Adeline "Addie" King born *c.* 1838, Harrison Eader King born July 25, 1840, John Rigdon King, born June 24, 1844, Virginia Lilies King, born *c.* 1850, William "Willie" Richard King, born December, 1852, Virginia Liles King, born in 1858 and Lillie C. King, born *c.* 1859. Lillie did not survive her childhood years and Virginia died at the age of nineteen in 1869.

In his advanced years, John R. reminisced about his early life and education in Hagerstown, Washington County, Maryland.

> I was born June 24th 1844, in the house still standing, directly opposite the St. John's Lutheran Church, the son of Samuel L. and Eliza Lane King. My

first school teacher was Miss Susan Norris, who kept a private school for very young children in a small log house at the foot of Eichelbergers Hill.[45]

Free public schools in the State of Maryland did not come into being until an act of the General Assembly, known as the Van Bokkellen system was passed in 1865.[46] The historical records show that "under this act the free public schools of Washington County was organized July 11, 1865, with Thomas A. Boult as president."[47] Thus, during John Kings' school age years of the eighteen fifties and early eighteen sixties, his parents had to send him to one of the many private schools. As John later admitted, he did not fare so well with the second teacher that his parents found for his primary education.

My next school was Mr. Hoffman's located just where the Y.M.C.A. are now building, (opposite the Zion Reformed Church) and there is where I distinguished or disgraced myself. Mr. Hoffman was cruelly severe; It was in this school that I learned to write, goose quill pens were used. It was before the advent of steel pens. Ellen Hoffman, daughter, was assistant, quite as cruel as her father. Mr. Hoffman used a hickory stick like an old fashioned ram rod with an iron ferrule on the end. My mother who went to school with him told me he used it in her day and entertained no love for him—Ellen's favorite method while sitting at one end of the school to aim a ruler at an offending pupil and her aim was so unerring that she could shoot that ruler from one end of the room to the other and hit the mark every time. I had been rather lax in my lessons, so one day the old man gave me a lesson, two columns of words out the old Walker dictionary with the injunction that if I missed spelling one word of failed in the definition he would thrash me. I knew he meant business, and there was no playing on the street that evening. I remained in doors studying my dictionary. My sister Addie helping me; I went to bed that evening knowing my lesson perfectly, at ease, but when I was called up before that desk to recite, I got "buck fever" and missed one word that old tyrant laid down the book took off his specks, reached for that old hickory caught me and laid me across his knee and whaled me. I caught a good hold on the fat part of his leg with my teeth and closed with all my force I could, he dropped me quick, I ran behind my desk and the teacher after me. I picked up my ink stand and let it fly at him, he caught it in his hand, the ink went all over him. He ordered me out, never to return again—as I went down the stairs he was at the pump washing, he said you rascal you have ruined my clothes, as I turned the corner of the house, I called back: "I am glad of it."

> I was a hero among the boys that day, but when my father did to me—o mama; that incident occurred nearly 70 years ago, it was so unjust that I have never had any compunctions of conscience for what I did and I fear, if the question of sorrow and regret for my part in it will come up before the Great Searcher of all hearts, my prospect of future felicity, if it so depends will not be bright.[48]

As John King also later recalled:

> My next school was the old red brick building which stood about where the new post office stands (the southwest corner of Antietam Street and Summit Avenue) . William Allen was the teacher, brother of Jim Allen in Williamsport, he in turn was succeeded by Charles Gelwicks, he was a bird; every morning he laid in a lot of nicely trimmed Quince sticks and he wore them out during the day. One of the boys was Dorsey Campbell who had a large hump on his back, Gelwicks was thrashing him one day and a piece of the stick broke off and struck Ben Butter in the eye destroying his sight. Miss Ella Taggert was the assistant principal, we used to go downstairs to her room and sitting before the large map would lustily sing our geography lesson.[49]

Charles Gelnick and his wife, Catharine, appear on the 1860 U.S. Census for Hagerstown, Maryland. His occupation is listed as a "teacher." At that time, at age fifty, Charles and his wife had four children, including Luther, age twenty-two, whose trade was given as a "painter."[50]

Late in life, John King also mentioned that after school in the "old red brick building," he "then (went) to the Old Academy, where (I was) among many of my age" and that "Buck Schley was my chum and this friendship lasted through life."[51] The "Old Academy" John referred to was the Hagerstown Academy, an all-male, private high school in town. In 1974, a reporter for *The Daily Mail,* Ora Ann Ernest explained that "in the era preceding public high schools, it (the Hagerstown Academy) was patronized by boys who sought education beyond the primary schools known variously as common schools, subscription schools, country schools, singing schools or old fashioned pay-schools which were often located on one room log buildings in many spots throughout the county."[52] Due to its excellence, "the institution was liberally patronized by persons in the District of Columbia and some of the counties of Virginia, bordering the Potomac, besides Washington and other counties in Maryland."[53]

Founded in 1810, the Hagerstown Academy prominent instructors of the Classics, Messrs. Roscoe W. R. Abbott, Andrews, and others and featured

Mr. Thomas Curtis as head of the English Department and was said to be "outstanding."[54] A Hagerstown atlas of 1877 shows the location of the school as between the railroad tracks on the outskirts of town near South Walnut Street. In fact, it was the only building on Academy Hill Street with an address of 100. Today, although the building is gone, it was "located in the middle of what is now the 100 block of South Prospect Street."[55] Based upon the 1877 atlas and the location of John King's boyhood home across from St. John's Lutheran Church, it seems that he could have walked only about twelve hundred feet to get to the Academy. Unfortunately, John never mentioned his curriculum or how many years he attended the Academy. Nevertheless, judged from his thoughtful and flowing diary with its exceptional handwriting, John King must have received a good education in the primary schools and in Hagerstown Academy despite his self-described disciplinary problems. Remarkably, John King was only seventeen years of age when he wrote the diary.

Aside from John R. King, many other distinguished men of nineteenth century Maryland graduated from the Hagerstown Academy. They include John's "chum" Colonel Buchanan "Buck" Schley, Sr., one of John's childhood friends, Maryland Governor William T. Hamilton, Alexander Armstrong, Dr. John McPherson Scott, Dr. Otho Holland Williams Ragan, John Nicholas Brambaugh, William Updegraff, Jacob R. Stockslager, Luther M. Bovey, Dr. Edwin M. Schindel and many other well-known doctors, lawyers and businessmen of the era.[56] According to one source, the school continued to function as a private academy until 1876 when it was purchased by the Washington County Board of Education and began to be used as a boys' high school.[57] In 1907, the county built and opened Surrey High School and the Hagerstown Academy was then used for the lower grades. Finally, once the school system stopped using it, the Western Maryland Railroad took it over as an office building until it burned in a fire of 1918.[58]

John King mentioned that he was friends with Buck Schley throughout his life. The only surviving son of Frederick Augustus Schley and Barbara Hall Schley, his third wife, Buchanan Sr. was born August, 1848, in Frederick County, Maryland. Hence, he was four years younger than John. After his mother died when he was eighteen months old, Buck was taken and was brought up by his older brother, George, who lived in Hagerstown.[59] After attending Hagerstown Academy, Buchanan or "Buck" enrolled in St. John's School, then Princeton University, and finally the University of Virginia.[60] Upon the completion of a study of law with his brother, George, Buchanan was admitted to the bar in 1871. Colonel Buchanan Schley was employed by the Western Maryland Railway as an attorney, the same railroad that had one of its depots near his old school and which later would utilize the Hagerstown Academy for an office.[61] Buck was very prominent in the Maryland Democratic Party and later held several political appointments including Surveyor of the Port of Baltimore, State Census Superintendent and State Tax Commissioner.[62] He died in April of 1916 and his obituary appeared in the *New York Times*.

Likewise, although John did not attend the Hagerstown Academy at the same time as Governor William T. Hamilton (born September 8, 1820 and died October 26, 1888), they became friends when John was a boy in Hagerstown. Later in life, John, in a long letter to Governor Hamilton's daughter, Lenore, recalled:

> My association with your Father began as a boy-his law partner George W. Smith and he were great Fishermen, and every Saturday in season they went up to the Conococheague near Leiter's Mill-Charlie Smith and I always went with them. Those were the happy days.[63]

William Thomas Hamilton was governor of Maryland from January 14, 1880 until January 9, 1884. John King helped him with an issue that arose when Hamilton had been elected a U.S. Senator in 1869. Also, during his tenure as governor, he went to John King's farm in Howard County for a visit.

Another of John's boyhood friends from Hagerstown was David Stuart Gordon. Although born in nearby Franklin County, Pennsylvania, David Gordon spent his youth in Hagerstown. As John later reminisced:

> David Stuart Gordon was born 97 years ago just over the line in Pennsylvania, but his boyhood and early manhood were spent in Hagerstown, which he always regarded as his home town. I first knew him as a clerk in Armstrong's Dry Goods Store, located on Washington street, west of the Square, adjoining Victor Thompson's Drug Store. Gordon was one of the most popular young men of the town. Possessed of a beautiful tenor voice, he belonged to a group of singers including Nannie Fechtig, Emma Kepler, contraltos; Addie King (John's sister-Ed.), soprano; Gordon, tenor, and Bushnel, bass. They all belonged to the old Methodist church. They met weekly (at the King home) for practice and gave many charity concerts in the old Lyceum Hall. When the Missouri-Kansas border trouble became acute, threatening civil war, Gordon, moved by a spirit of adventure, quit the dry goods business and located in Kansas. It was not long before he was commissioned a lieutenant in the Second Dragoons, later the Second U.S. Cavalry.[64]

John King would see no more of his friend, David S. Gordon, until May of 1862, when they met again at the entrance to a Confederate prison in Salisbury, North Carolina. Well after the Civil War, John King met with David at the latter's home in Chevy Chase, Maryland, and was told by David that "I am going to start at the Square, go west on Washington street as far as the Catholic church and name every business place and resident."[65] John then says that he was impressed as David "did the remarkable feat."[66] Like David Gordon, John King was very fond of Hagerstown and its residents. He sometimes said that there were four thousand citizens in Hagerstown and he knew them all. Also, while he did not name all the businesses, he attempted to list all the residents of the street where he grew up, on South Potomac Street. The following list contains the names John provided.[67] Next to each is information about these households taken from the 1860 U.S. Census for the City of Hagerstown.[68] Unfortunately, 1860 Census data was not available for all the names John mentioned.

Armstrong–Alex, a wealthy merchant, age 62, his wife Susan, age 50 and two children: William, 15 and Alex 13.

Chrissinger–George, a coach maker, age 44 his wife Sarah, age 34 and four children: Lent 9, Clarence 4, Aysey 1 and Kate under 12 months old.

Gumbert–John, a baker, age 48, his wife Christiana age 39, and five children: Mary 15, William 13, David 10, John 7 and Lillian 3.

Gumbert Confectionary and Ice Cream–"three cent glasses of ice cream with real cream".

Mcliheny Rouskulp.

Snively, Miss Lida.

Biershing–George, age 40, his wife S. A. 43 and five children: John W. 13, Elizabeth R. 11, George F. 8, Sarah 4 and Charles E. 1.

Biershing–William, age 37, his wife E. C. 43 and three children: Kate 13, Annie M. 11 and Rachel 9.

Seibert–Samuel, a merchant, age 47, and his wife Lydia age 45.

Small–Peter B., a shoe dealer, his wife Sarah age 43 and seven children: William L., a clerk, age 22, Albert, student, age 20, Charles 17, Melville Rench 14, Mary 11, Peter 8, and Harry 5.

Bouts.

Benter.

Frieze.

Schner–age 62 and Ann, age 24.

Schner–Nathaniel, age 27, his wife Amanda, age 25 and two children: Frederick 2 and Annie less than one year old.

Hershey–Barbara, age 48, Lydia M. 42, Frances 40 and Savilla M. 39.

Blake–Catharine, age 50, and four children, John H., a painter, age 20, George, age 17, Kate, age 21 and Emma, age 10.

Harris–Benjamin, a shoemaker, age 46, his wife, Eliza, age 49 and six children: Charles E., a shoemaker, age 21, Mary E., age 18, William B., a clerk, age 16, John C. 13, Ezra 10 and Emma 7.

Clark, Z. B.–a shoemaker, age 43, his wife Sarah, age 38 and five children: Laura 17, Alice 15, Amelia 13, and Elizabeth 11.

Squire Handy–also known as M. H. Handy, no occupation given, and his wife, Catharine, age 62.

Clark–William "Billy," no occupation listed, his wife, Elizabeth C., age 32 and two children: James 13 and William 11. Billy lived "in a large Rough Cast house" on the southeast corner of the pike, according to John King, a house later occupied by John's uncle, John H. King.

Gelnicks–Charles, John King's "school teacher of painful memory," age 50, his wife, Catharine, age 42 and four children: Luther, a painter, age 22, Mary 18, Olivia 16 and James 9.

The above people were John Kings' friends and neighbors on South Potomac Street. He was close to two of the Gumbert boys, David "Davey" and William "Ril." Also, he was close to Rench Small. Some of this other boyhood friends who did not live on South Potomac, but who also resided in town were John Gray, Charley Poffnberger, Charley Smith, and Dan Waltz. Without a doubt, his best friend was Tom Hilliard, who John mentions time and time again in his diary. Growing up in antebellum Hagerstown must have been a wondrous experience in the eighteen fifties and early eighteen sixties. They had the best of both an urban and a rural environment. The town itself, being the "Hub" of Western Maryland had a constant flow of travelers, tradesman, homesteaders, adventurers, and farmers. The railroad from Baltimore and Philadelphia brought in the latest fashions, products and newspapers from all over the country. One could order anything from the latest French dresses, cigars, the newest farm implements to India Pale Ale. Also, there were many good private schools and tutors available. Community activities were numerous. The Lyceum was a grand public hall for meetings, lectures, music, and other local events. The Lyceum would later be employed as a hospital for the sick and the wounded during the Civil War. In the mid-nineteenth century, Hagerstown was anything but a backwoods country stop. At the same time, the countryside was just outside town and in a few minutes, the boys could go fishing, horseback riding, climb the nearest mountain, or travel by wagon or carriage to one of the nearby towns, such as Williamsport or Chambersburg. As teenagers, the Hagerstown boys could seek employment in any one of a number of shops and stores. For instance, David Gordon worked in Armstrong's Dry Goods store and John King, as stated in his diary, found a job in Abraham Levi's store in town. Other boys could apprentice with their father or one of the many tradesmen in town including cabinetmakers, shoemakers, machinists, blacksmiths, tailors, clothiers, liverymen, tinners, and wheelwrights.

In his diary, Rig King often cited his travels in Washington County and beyond, running errands and meeting young women his age. As with most young men he soon became fond of women and enjoyed various activities with them. Specifically, he spoke of going to dances in Williamsport. In his later years, he again recalled the experience:

> I mentioned Williamsport, ah, how as a youngster of the adolescent age I went with other boys and girls, to that old Town to dances at Andersons Hotel to the tune of Williamsport Gals Can't your come out tonight"-those old dances, how the memory of them thrills-the old fiddler calling out the figures Hands round," Swing your partners," "Ladies to the centre," etc.—to the old tune of "Turkey in the Straw."[69]

Perhaps because of lack of family finances, John King did not attend a college or university. By the age of fifteen, however, he was ready to learn a trade. His father, Samuel, was well-acquainted with James Young, Sr. an established "book and job printer" in Baltimore, who had his shop at 114 West Baltimore Street.[70] Apparently, Samuel visited Baltimore often, sometimes taking his entire family and staying for some time. In a biographical article which appeared in the *Baltimore Sun* in 1913, the following was noted:

> (John King) is the product of the printing office. It was there that he gained the greater part of his early training after going through the public and private schools of Hagerstown. His first employment was in the office of James Young, Sr. That was in 1859.[71]

In 1859, James Young, Sr., was forty-eight years old. His large family was composed of this wife, Elinora, and eight children to support: Sarah R., Ella, Mary E., Emma, Laura, Annie, James Jr., and Fanny.[72] Most likely, he sought young men to apprentice because his only son, James Jr., was too young to be of much assistance in his shop in 1859, being only twelve years old. In 1921, John King recalled:

> After I tired of school, I went to the old Mail office to learn to be a printer, my father thought that (the) boys in that office, Gid Shirey, foreman, were too bad so he made arrangements for me to go to Baltimore to his old friend James Young, to finish my trade where I remained until the Civil War broke out. I caught the war fever and went back to Hagerstown.[73]

By an Ordinance of Secession adopted by the state of South Carolina on December 20, 1860, by a vote of 169-0, the first Southern state left the Union.[74] By February 1, 1861, Alabama, Florida, Georgia, Mississippi, and Louisiana had seceded as well. Jefferson Davis, a former Secretary of War under President Franklin Pierce and U.S. Senator from Mississippi, was elected President of the Confederate States of America on February 4, 1861. After the Battle of Fort Sumter, four more states, including Arkansas, North Carolina, Tennessee and Virginia also joined the Confederacy. The remaining border states of Delaware, Kentucky, Maryland and Missouri would never leave the Union.

Due to its strategical importance, Hagerstown and Washington County were soon in the throes of war. Hagerstown's location as "The Hub" of transportation lines and its border position on the Potomac River made it sought by both the Union and the Confederacy. The Union army would eventually have ten thousand soldiers based along the Potomac from Washington D.C. to its headwaters. The Confederates soon set up camp in Harper's Ferry and placed soldiers along the Virginia side of the river. Also, the fields close to Hagerstown and Williamsport would become camps for the largest army the world had ever seen. Hagerstown itself and its environs would become one immense supply depot for the Union Army. As Williams mentions, "before the beginning of May, armies were on both borders of Washington County, four thousand Federals in Chambersburg, Pennsylvania and a similar number in Harper's Ferry."[75] Williams also reported:

> Companies were forming in Washington County in late May, the Sharpsburg Rifles, Union Guards of Williamsport, Home Guards organized in Hagerstown and one by the same name in Clearspring ... while this was going on a number of young men from Washington County joined the Confederates at Harper's Ferry and at other points.[76]

People were rapidly taking one side or the other based upon their sentiments and sympathies. There were numerous public and private meetings, heated political speeches at rallies, and a great deal of voting for this candidate or that. Some people supported the Union Party while others agreed with the tenets of the Peace Party. Neighbors disagreed with one another. Families took different sides and members of families chose different parties. The local newspapers took sides with the *Herald and Torch Light* becoming the voice of the Union Party while the *Hagerstown Mail* was aligned with Peace Party. Again from Williams, based upon comments of the population at the time:

> The excitements of the war were more lively and the feelings of animosity were necessarily much more bitter here than elsewhere. This County was a battle field. It was overrun by both armies. Vast quantities of property were destroyed. The population were divided in sentiment and each ascribed to the other the losses and indignities they suffered. It was literally a fratricidal strife and a fratricidal strife is always the most embittered... No trust could be placed in a friend, no confidence in a guide and it was well for a man to keep the doors of his mouth from her that lay on his bosom, for the son rose against the father, the daughter-in-law against the mother-in-law and a man's enemies were often those from his own house. There was strife and division within the family circle. In some instances the father would side with one side, the mother with the other. Some of the sons would join the Northern army and some the Southern or it might be the father arrayed against his sons and not unfrequently would brothers be brought into direct conflict in opposing forces.[77]

The King family circle had no strife within its ranks, as all members were decidedly pro-Union. However, they lived in the midst of a chaotic atmosphere which took place at their front door on South Potomac Street in Hagerstown. In addition, they lost many friends and acquaintances to the conflict. As he would later note in his reminiscences, many of Johns' boyhood friends crossed the Potomac River in the quiet and darkness of night and joined the Confederate Army at Harper's Ferry.

Although a small body of fifty Federal troops had entered Hagerstown on April 19, 1861, then quickly departed, the first real appearance of a large number of Union soldiers was not until Saturday morning, the 15th of June.[78] On that day, one-thousand men of the 1st Pennsylvania Regiment under Colonel Yhoe "who marched through Hagerstown with drums beating and flags flying, out the Baltimore pike and encamped on Ranney Hunter's farm below Funkstown."[79] Next came the 2nd, 7th, 8th, and 10th Pennsylvania Regiments and the "Scott legion under Colonel Gray passed down Potomac street to the College of St. James."[80] General Alpheus S. Williams, Brigadier General of the 3rd Brigade which included the 7th, 8th, 10th and 20th

Pennsylvania Regiments, and his staff rode with Colonel Emly of the 8th. The following day, Sunday, June 16, 1861, another large body of troops composed of the 14th and 15th Pennsylvania Regiments arrived and marched out to Jonathan Hager's farm on the Baltimore Pike where they encamped in a large field about one and a half miles from Hagerstown.[81] If that were not enough, on that same Sunday, still another Pennsylvania regiment, one from Connecticut and one from Wisconsin also joined the mass of bodies on Hager's land.[82] Apparently, Messrs. Hunter and Hager were paid for the use of their land by the Federal Army as neither name appears on the list of claims filed with the Southern Claims Commission after the war. Finally, a large force under Brigadier General George Cadwallader, commander of the 1st Division, Department of Pennsylvania, came down the Greencastle Road and went out to nearby Williamsport to make their camp.[83] The citizens of Hagerstown and Washington County were in absolute awe of the plethora of flags, men, horses, artillery caissons and wagons. Never had such a large military body been seen like the one that camped all over Washington County for most of the Civil War. Williams, in his book, *History of Washington County,* described the scene of those three days in the middle of June when the Union Army first arrived in force in Hagerstown:

> The Northern Army began to pour into Hagerstown, and until Monday evening (June 17) the heavy tramp of heavy of the soldiers, the beating of the drums and the martial music of the military bands, the sound of the heavy baggage wagons and the trains of the artillery did not cease. Here was the army with banners, the pomp and circumstance of war in the streets of Hagerstown. People left their usual avocations to gaze upon the unusual sight. The streets were filled with long lines of bristling bayonets; at every corner guards were stationed; companies paraded the streets. The brightness of the arms of the men had not yet been dulled nor their uniforms soiled by active service and the scene was very inspiring. All day Sunday the clangor of military movements continued and the roll of the drum mingled in confused sound with the peals of the church going bells. The congregations who attended church that day were small and inattentive. The army occupied all minds. Some considered merely the glittering show of the hour. Others saw with prophetic sight the dogs of war that were unloosed. Many fearfully anticipated that havoc in our midst because Maryland was a border state and it seemed probable that the hostile forces would meet right here. The troops were well received by the people. The Union people were loud in their expression of loyalty while the secessionists generally kept discreetly quiet.[84]

At this time, the population of Hagerstown itself was only about four-thousand souls. Hence, some may have felt overwhelmed by the vast numbers of Union soldiers from other states confronting them. The total number of Union officers and enlisted men in the area easily exceeded the population of the county's largest town. While the majority of the troops were well-behaved, in large part by the presence of the Provost Marshal and his men, occasionally fights broke out. The visiting men had access to spirits and displays of public drunkenness were not rare. In addition, some crops, soon ready for harvest, were destroyed by marching troops. Horses were stolen. Fence rails were taken by soldiers for the building of camp fires. After the Civil War, eighty-eight claims were filed by citizens of Washington County with the Southern Claims Commission to seek compensation for losses. At the same time, a lot of the local people were making money on the presence of the Union Army. Washington County was primarily agricultural. Farmers like Messrs. Ranney and Hager rented out their large fields for camps. Others sold grain and produce to the army. Shops, stores and taverns in Hagerstown saw their sales greatly increase.

As mentioned previously, Samuel L. King had previously worked as a craftsman, constructing and selling carriages, wagons and ploughs. As a businessman and entrepreneur, Samuel quickly realized that he, too, could profit from the war. Although he had had some financial difficulties with his businesses in the past, the Civil War raging in Western Maryland and nearby western Virginia presented new opportunities and the potential to make a great deal of money in a short period of time. In 1861, he and his new son-in-law, Samuel Z. McLaughlin, went into the business of selling goods in the camps of the Union Army. On October 10, 1861, Reverend James Curns performed the ceremony to marry Samuel L. King's daughter, Addie, to Samuel Z. McLaughlin in Mercersburg, Pennsylvania, at the Methodist Parsonage.[85] The two Samuels, like many other retailers who followed the movements of the army, were known as sutlers. A sutler is a civilian merchant who followed an army to sell provisions to soldiers from a tent, back of a wagon, or from store on or near the camp. The two Samuels hauled wagonloads of goods into the Union camps of Maryland and into the Shenandoah Valley of Virginia. Samuel's two oldest sons, Harrison Eader King and John Rigdon King, would also support the war effort, but in a much more dangerous way than their father or brother-in-law. On September 30, 1861, Harrison enlisted as a private in Company E of First Regiment, Potomac Home Brigade. His brother, John Rigdon King, only seventeen years old in 1861, was too young to enlist. Instead, John or "Rig" as he was nicknamed, followed in his father's footsteps and became not only a sutler, selling provisions to Union Army, but then worked as a Civil War photographer. In later life, John never mentioned either of these professions. In fact, he never mentioned the diary at all. Hence, there is no record of any part of the diary in the newspaper biographies of him or in his written reminiscences. His very unusual diary begins Tuesday, October 22, 1861, in Hagerstown, Maryland.

II

The Lost Diary of John Rigdon King

Tuesday October 22th 1861

I had a big quarrel with one beautiful neighbor (Mr. Rasset), and at one time thought it would result in bloodshed, when he said that my Ma was not a lady which made me draw a deadly weapon in the shape of a "Zou're knife" which had the desired affect, has asked pardon and said he did not mean it. I was out and dug some horse-radish for Ma; I then went and laid out one dollar and thirty one cents ($1.31) for this book, for one Sargents 4th Reader, and a Montieth 3rd Geography for Bro. Willie. About 7 o'clock in the evening there was an alarm of Fire, I ran with the First Hose in the direction of the light, which proved to be a Brick Kiln. After the fire I received $5 from Ed Mobley.

Thus closed Tuesday the 22d of October 1861.

October 22, 1861

"Willie" or William was John King's younger brother. In 1860, the King family resided in Baltimore Ward 16 (Independent City) Maryland, according to the 1860 U.S. Census.[1] The head of the household was Samuel King, age 45, his wife Eliza, age 37, and six children. Mary (nicknamed Addie) was 20, Harrison was 19, John was 16, William (nicknamed Willie) was 12, Virginia was 10, and Lillie was 3. Another male, John Coon, occupation "machinist," age 21 was also shown in the household. Samuel King's occupation was listed as a "Travelling Agent." This census was taken July 3, 1860. John is infuriated with a neighbor for making a disparaging remark and pulls out a "Zou're knife." A Zoave knife was carried by soldiers of the same name and resembled a Bowie knife in that it was a large-bladed knife with a long handle.

When John says that he "… ran with the First Hose," he literally means that he is running to a fire with the local fire company, the First Hagerstown Hose Company, but more about that later. In the nineteenth century, many towns and cities had brick kilns, usually at the rear of the property, for use by potters to fire their "greenware" at high temperatures. Both stoneware and redware were manufactured right in town and the wares were sold locally. The kilns, as well as home fireplaces, could be fire hazards. Sometimes, the exiting sparks from the kiln or from the homes would ignite neighboring roofs. Hagerstown is known to have several

Wednesday October 23d 61

I arose from sweet slumber about five O'clk. to go to Hancock on business for Darby Co., I started about 6 ½ O'clk., stopped at Newcommers, about 4 miles from town to see my Sister Addie McLaughlin, the morning being very cold and inclement I took a small drink of Life itself, with a little sugar, which had the affects of warming me up a little, stopped a while at Clearspring and seen Cousin Oliver King, who is a refuge from Martinsburg and a Union man, leaving Clearspring we walked up the Mountain to "Fair View," and then after a wearisome ride arrived at Hancock; after dinner I attended to some business and bought half a dozen chickens at 12 ½ a piece. Thus closed Wednesday Oct. 23rd 1861

October 22, 1861 conitnued

such potteries with kilns. The First Hose was the local fire brigade of which he was a volunteer member. Ed Mobley was an official of the fire company who was apparently paying John for services rendered.

Martin W. Happel, a 19th century potter in Hagerstown, immigrated to the United States along with his wife and two children from Hesse-Darmstadt, a region of Germany.[2,3] He was only twenty-seven years old, but undoubtedly had already apprenticed as a potter in his native country. On December 24, 1868, Happel purchased "a portion of a lot situated on South Locust Street in Hagerstown together with buildings and outbuildings fronting fifty-two feet and running back eighty-two feet to the lot of Joshua Wilson together with the use of water in the adjoining lot said Martin Happel to pay half the cost for a pump" for nine-hundred dollars.[4] A plentiful amount of water was needed to operate a pottery. On September 8, 1870, Martin Happel, Philip Fleigle and John Beckman, trading as Feigle, Happel and Co., bought from A. James Weise, Trustee, for two-thousand and seven-hundred dollars, a lot fronting on E. Washington Street forty-five feet and running back one-hundred and ninety feet with Locust Street.[5] This land and buildings, known as "Weise Pottery Property," consisted of a dwelling house and pottery store and adjoined the land previously purchased by Happel in 1868. The Fleigle-Happel Pottery was located at 75 East Washington Street.

October 23, 1861

John's sister Addie was married to Samuel (Sam) McLaughlin, who was in business with John's father. Clear Spring, Maryland is 11.3 miles almost due west of Hagerstown. Hancock, Maryland is 13.5 miles northwest of Clear Spring. Therefore, the total miles one way of the trip to Hancock is 24.8 miles, a pretty good ride by horseback or wagon.

Oliver King was one of John H. Kings' sons. Oliver's occupation in Martinsburg was a machinist while that of his brother, George H., was a telegraph operator.[6] Telegraph operators were exempt from military service and, perhaps, that is why George is not shown on any regimental list. Oddly, Oliver also could not be found on any roster of Maryland Union soldiers. Their father and John King's uncle, John H. King, was a fairly wealthy merchant of Martinsburg. Like much of West Virginia, Martinsburg's residents were deeply divided over the Civil War, with some fighting for the South and some for the North.

John mentions that he "... walked up the Mountain to Fair View" in his diary. That peak is known as Fairview or North Mountain which is 1,656 feet high and can be seen just beyond Clear Spring traveling west on the old National Road (Route 40). John ate his dinner at Fair View Inn atop the mountain and which would have had a magnificent view of the Great Valley below. During the Civil War, the Union Army Signal Corps used the summit as an observation post during and after the battle of Antietam in September of 1862 and again after the battle of Gettysburg in July of 1863 in attempting to observe the crossing of Lee's army over the Potomac River.[7] On October 20, 1862, as part of the raid on Chambersburg, four regiments of General J. E. B. Stuart's cavalry along with four cannons crossed the Potomac from Virginia into Maryland at McCoy's Ford unnoticed by the soldiers atop the mountain due to a dense fog.[8]

Thursday Oct. 24th 61

After a pleasant nights rest I arose about 7 o'clk, and after a hearty breakfast, and prepared for another tiresome ride back to Hagerstown, stopping at "Fair View" for dinner, arrived at Hagerstown about 6 O'clk. So ended Thursday

Friday Oct 25th 61

I was husking corn all day at Uncle Chas. Lane's, and felt very tired at night. Nothing more of importance transpired on Friday Oct 25 1861

Saturday Oct 26th 61

Was husking corn a while, and went down St. but nothing of importance transpired
through the day.

Sunday Oct 27th 1861

Was at the M. E. Church and heard a very sensible sermon from the Paster (Mr. Sears) from St. Mark 40th to the 42th verse 12th chap. Quarterly collection was taken. I attended Sabbath School in the afternoon. Nothing more of importance transpired on Sunday Oct. 27th 61.

October 23, 1861 conitnued

The officer in charge of the Fairview Station, Lieutenant W. W. Rowley noted that he and his men were attacked by about twenty Confederate cavalrymen "… about 8 o'clock a.m. … and were so nearly surprised by at their station as to lose 2 privates, taken prisoners and nearly all of their signal equipments."[10] After being driven from their station, Lieutenant Rowley and another officer who escaped rode hard to Clear Spring, only three miles away, and "… reported the facts to Captain Russell, of the First Maryland Cavalry, who immediately sent the dispatch to Colonel Kenly, commanding at Williamsport."[10]

October 25, 1861

Charles G. Lane was John's maternal uncle. Perhaps because the King family had just moved from Baltimore, Samuel L., his wife Eliza and their five children were residing with the Lanes on June 7, 1860, when the census came to the Lane home.[11] On that census, John's father gave his occupation was a "coachmaker" while Charles G. Lane reported his as a "cabinet maker." Mr. Lane must have been successful with his profession as evidenced by real estate said to be worth $7,000 and personal property valued as $8,000. Much of the personal property may have been wood and other materials for building furniture.

Monday Oct 28th 1861

Arose rather early to go to Chambersburg, Pa., where I arrived about 8 O'clock and stopped at the "Franklin Hotel," I went to see one of my customers on Main St. and took a glass of "Lager" at his expense which warmed me up a little. I left the Place about 4 ½ o'clk. and arrived in H.T. (Hagerstown) about 6 ½ o'clk, and so ended Monday Oct 28th 61 _

Tuesday Oct 29th 1861

I commenced to husk corn about 9 O'clock at Uncle Charles Lane's, and kept at it all day, and felt very tired in the evening. Nothing more of importance to note. Oct 29th 61

Wednesday Oct. 30th 1861

I was husking corn again all day and in the evening I bought a pair of Boots from Chas. Harris for Five dollars and a half ($5 ½) cash. Nothing more of importance to note.

October 27, 1861

The "M.E. Church" that John attended is St. Paul's Methodist Episcopal Church in Hagerstown, Maryland. The pastor at this time was Samuel W. Sears. Reverend Sears was born in Maryland about 1834. Sears entered itinerant ministry in 1855. Sometime after 1860, the Sears family moved to Hagerstown. Items from the Hagerstown newspapers show that Pastor Sears performed twenty-two marriages between January 8, 1862 and January 9, 1863. Sometime in 1863, Reverend Sears moved to Cumberland in Allegany County, Maryland. Overall, he served a full forty years as a pastor in various churches in Maryland and Pennsylvania.[12]

October 28, 1861

Unfortunately, the Franklin Hotel would not be standing much longer. On July 30, 1864, under orders from Confederate Lieutenant General Jubal Early, Brigadier General John McCausland burned much of Chambersburg, Pennsylvania,for not meeting a ransom of $100,000 in gold. McNulty's Franklin Hotel was within the downtown area that was destroyed by fire.[13] This destruction was said by the Rebels to be in retaliation for the burning of Shenandoah Valley, including the Virginia Military Institute. The proprietor of the hotel was Brigadier-General William C. McNulty of the Fifth Brigade of Pennsylvania Militia for the counties of Fulton, Bedford, Somerset, Blair, and Cumbria. From 1860 to 1863, Brigadier-General McNulty also served as property registrar, recorder and clerk of the courts of Fulton County.[14]

October 30, 1861

Charles H. Harris had a boot store located at 20 West Washington St., Hagerstown.[15] He is listed on the 1860 census for Hagerstown as a twenty-one year old shoemaker who was residing at home with his father, Benjamin, also a shoemaker.[16]

Thursday Oct 31st 1861

I took Ma along to Williamsport and up to John Coutons, returned about 6 O'clock and Tom Hilliard and me took a ride, and met two certain "Girls," and took them along and we had a most glorious time with them in the night, the Union candidates were treating at Capt. Heist and of course I was about. So end the last of Oct. 1861

Friday November 1st 1861

I had my favorite employment to-day, that of working about the House, I was making shelves and fitting "Stove Pipe," in the course of which my "Angry Passions" rose very often, but I never did any harm. Nothing more of importance transpired on the first of November

Saturday Nov. 2nd 1861

The weather is very stormy and disagreeable. I thought the wind would blow the House away last night. About 12 O'clock last night, the 39the Illinois Regmt Col. Lyon arrived and left about 11 O'clock to-day for Williamsport to join Gen. Lamon's Brigade; they were fine looking set of men. To-night Lt. Frank Gallagher of the "Union Rangers" 4th reg. "Potomac Home Brigade" will speak in the Junior Hall and I am bound to hear him. Nothing more of importance to note.

November 2, 1861

Our diarist errs when he mentions a Colonel Lyons of the 39th Illinois Regiment as the regimental history makes no mention of a Colonel Lyons. The Union army had a Brigadier General Nathaniel Lyon, who was the first general killed in the Civil War. However, the colonel of the 39th Illinois was Colonel Austin Light, who received his commission July 22, 1861.[17] Colonel Light had been in the regular army and had seen service in the Florida and Mexican Wars. Hence, at the time of this diary entry, Colonel Light was in command of the regiment. But, on November 25, 1861, Colonel Light was dismissed from further service by order of the War Department. The reasons for his departure were due to "… charges connected with his former army experiences,"[18] His replacement was Lieutenant-Colonel T. O. Osborn, who was immediately promoted to the colonelcy. According to the regimental historian, "It had been intimated and we had reason to believe that we were to be sent to General Sigel's division, but while waiting for transportation, Colonel Ward H. Lamon, Marshall of the District of Columbia, arrived on the 26th day of October with an order from General Fremont for us to proceed to Williamsport, Maryland, to join Ward H. Lamon's brigade.[19] Ward H. Lamon had been a law partner of Abraham Lincoln in Illinois. Lamon remained a close friend of the new President and, at times, acted as his unofficial bodyguard. After being appointed as a U. S. Marshal, Lamon decided that he would like to be a brigadier general. During May of 1861, Lamon was allowed by Lincoln to recruit and command a regiment of volunteer infantry, and later his command was increased to a brigade.[20] Although Lamon had no prior military experience, that fact did not deter Lincoln from allowing the appointment. Handbills were distributed in Virginia announcing the formation of a new regiment called the "First Regiment (Oregon Rifles) Virginia" and seeking recruits with Union sentiments.[21] Lamon's new brigade would be called "The Virginia Brigade." It would also include the 39th Illinois Infantry

Regiment and Captain James Thompson's Independent Battery C, Pennsylvania Volunteer Light Artillery. The former regiment, having journeyed from St. Louis, arrived in Hagerstown at midnight by train and had to remain in the cars until morning due to pounding rain and high winds.[22] The next day, November 2, the 39th left for their final destination, Williamsport, and arrived there about 3 o'clock and took "quarters in several vacant warehouses on the banks of the canal" due to the weather.[23] Finally, on the next day, the regiment marched about one mile from town and set their tents in an area which was called Camp Lamon. Colonel Leonard of the 13th Massachusetts regiment was in command of the new camp. While Lamon's original desire was to recruit a full brigade of infantry, cavalry, and artillery, his wish was never realized. According to the regimental historian of the 39th Illinois, "The brigade that was to have been organized by Ward H. Lamon and to which it was to have been assigned was never more heard of after reaching Williamsport"[24] Recruitment efforts were not successful and in November of 1861, Colonel returned to Washington, D.C. and resumed his duties as U. S Marshall until the end of the war. Lamon's brigade was broken up and reassigned to other Virginia units. The infantry companies were merged into the Third Maryland Infantry; the artillery units became part of the Pennsylvania Light Artillery and the cavalry companies of what had become the First Virginia Union Volunteers joined the First Maryland Cavalry.[25]

The "Union Rangers" were the troopers of Company D of Cole's Cavalry, formally known as the First Potomac Home Brigade Cavalry. Pearce K. Curll was captain of this company initially. Francis Gallagher was a forty-four year who hailed from Baltimore and who helped organize this company. He is listed in Baltimore city directories for 1849-50, 1851 and 1860 as an attorney at law with an address at 4 Law Buildings, St. Paul Street.[26,27,28] Gallagher also had been a prominent Democratic leader in Baltimore before the war.[29] Born in Donegal, Ireland, Gallagher enlisted August 31, 1861 at Frederick, Maryland, as second lieutenant in Company D.[30] He was taken prisoner September 2, 1862 and exchanged December 18, 1862. On January 29, 1862, the following Letter to the Editor, titled "Temperance-A Good Movement," appeared in the *Herald of Freedom & Torch Light* newspaper:

> Seven of the soldiers at "Camp Bradford," belonging to Captain Pearce A. Curll's Cavalry company, made their appearance at "Headquarters" a few evenings since and made their solemn oath on the Holy Evangely of Mighty God to abstain from the use of all intoxicating liquors for the space of one year. The oath was by administered Lieutenant F. Gallagher, who expressed to the men the great satisfaction the officers would feel if every man in the Company, who drank at all, would follow their example,—No soldier can serve King Alcohol and his country at the same time. Columbia's defenders should be men of steady nerve who trusty rifles could not tremble in the hands that grasp to uphold our country's honor; "Then water, bright water, give water to me, And wine to the trembling debauchee."[31]

It is not known if the sobriety of some of his company's soldiers contributed to increased performance, but on October 31, 1862, Gallagher was promoted to first lieutenant and on June 13, 1863, he was given the rank of captain. Companies A, B, D and I of Cole's Cavalry were "… assigned to General Banks' Division encamped near Frederick City during fall and winter of 1861 and 1862."[32] When spring came in 1862, the regiment went with General Banks to Winchester, but they were eventually reassigned to guard the Baltimore and Ohio Railroad in Maryland and Virginia.[33] Under cover of a cloudy sky and darkness, in October of 1863, Captain Gallagher led a squad of twenty troopers into Confederate-held Berryville, Virginia. There were hundreds of General Imbodens' force of two thousand soldiers scattered about in town and it was soon learned that they intended to advance upon Union Colonel Simpson at Charlestown, West Virginia.[34] Brazenly trotting into town on horseback, clad in rain slickers which masked their uniforms, the group went down main street. The captain entered the hotel and found the proprietress, an old acquaintance, while the other cavalrymen waited outside.[35] Additional intelligence regarding troop strength and intended actions was obtained by Captain Gallagher and the squad quickly left Berryville as openly as they entered. Unfortunately, the captain was kicked by a horse on the way to Charlestown to warn Colonel Simpson and broke his leg near the ankle on Friday, October 17. Captain Gallagher had a lengthy recuperative period and was unable to return to military service. On December 2, 1864, he was mustered out. Sometime after this date, he was promoted to Lieutenant-Colonel. In a Baltimore City directory for 1865–1866, he lists himself both as an attorney at law and as a lieutenant-colonel with an address on 149 Aisquith Street.[36] However, at this point in time, the war hero and well-known speaker and lawyer Francis Gallagher seems to disappear as he no longer listed on any Baltimore city directory, U.S. Census nor is he mentioned in the Baltimore newspapers. He may have died or he may have returned to Ireland.

Sunday Nov. 3rd 1861

This, the morning of the Lords Day we see the clear blue Sky, and the Sun shining in all His brilliancy, not like yesterdays dark, gloomy and rainy day. I heard Hon. Frank Gallagher speak last night, and was a most powerful and eloquent address, coming as it did from and old "War Horse" of Democracy. I attended Church this morning and Mr. Sears preached from Pauls first Epistle to the Corrintheons 15th Chap. 58th verse after which the Sacrament of the Lord Supper was administered ; I attended S. (Sunday) School in the Afternoon, and was mad-Teacher of Class No. 6

Monday Nov. 4th 1861

I arose about 6 O'clock to go to Hancock but Alas! U was doomed to disappointment, for the stage had gone and left me. I had most disagreeable job of fixing and moving two stoves

Tuesday Nov. 5th 1861

I was awakened early in the morning by the noise of the Hagerstown & Clearspring Companies coming up from Frederick to vote. H. E. King was in the Hagerstown Company. At night there was a grand Rally and Union speeches were made by the Quantity, the Band of the 13th Mass. Regiment was in attendance. I was pretty lively Until 12 ½ O'clock, then I went home and took Ril Gumbert along, and we laid down on the Parlor floor and slept 'till morning. I had my old 6 barrel 'Iron Sides' on hand all the while-and would give a salute every now and then.

November 5, 1861

John R. King's older brother, Harrison E. King, volunteered for Union service in the First Regiment of the Potomac Home Brigade Infantry and was mustered in August 1, 1861, as a private in Company D.[37] He was promoted to Corporal then later to First Lieutenant March 1, 1865 of Company E of the 13th Maryland Infantry on March 1, 1865, and was discharged May 29, 1865.[38] The First Regiment, Potomac Home Brigade, Maryland Volunteers, was organized at the City of Frederick, Maryland, from August 15 to December 13, 1861, to serve three years. Companies A, B, D and I were recruited in Frederick County, Company C in Baltimore City; Companies E, F and H in Washington County; Company G in Baltimore, Carroll and Frederick Counties and Company K in Baltimore City and Frederick County. William P. Maulsby, Sr., a lawyer and state senator from Frederick, Maryland, was colonel of this regiment. Colonel Maulsby's regiment "... was assigned to General Banks' Division, which was encamped in the vicinity of Frederick City, Maryland, during the fall and winter of 1861-62.[39] Veterans of the First Potomac Home Brigade Regiment and new recruits would organize to form the 13th Maryland Infantry Regiment as of March 1, 1865.

Wednesday Nov. 6th 1861

This is the day of the State election, the day in which Maryland is to prove her loyalty To the Federal Government, she is to elect a full slate and County Ticket. Old Maryland has this day in thunder tones, that the Union must and shall be preserved, the Union Ticket was elected in Hagerstown by almost 330 Majority and the County will be almost 3000; the(re) was a great deal of excitement up (the) street at the Polls, especially whe(n) the Rebels came up to vote, a good many was rejected at night. I was lively and sallying around, the returns have not all came in. I remitted to B. F. Darby tho, ninety dollars $90 o/". In the morning I purpose go to Hancock and expect to return on Saturday the 9th.

Thursday Nov 6th 1861

To-day I am very sore and horse, caused by hallowing so much yesterday and last night, the election's returns have not as yet all came in from the County. Yesterday afternoon about 3 O'clock there was a splendid silk Company Flag presented to Co. E, 1st Reg. Potomac Home Brigade, Capt. Wm/" Yance, it was presented by Judge Danl/" Weisel, and was received in behalf of the Company by Peter Neglig, Capt. Geo. Heysers Band was in attendance. At night the newly elected Sheriff has all his friends at house treating them and of course I considered myself one of his friends. I took care of one of my friends that was there and took a little too much "Old Rye."

November 5, 1861 continued

John King's brother, Harrison, would serve with the 13th until he was mustered out of service May 29, 1865. Harrison's family nickname was "Harry."

The 1860 U.S. Census shows only one Gumbert family residing in Hagerstown. The head of the household was John Gumbert, age forty-eight years and originally from Bavaria.[40] His occupation was given as a "baker." One of his sons, William, may have been nicknamed "Ril." William was only thirteen years old in 1860 and was only about age fourteen at the time of this diary entry, depending on whether his birthday was before or after the date the 1860 Census was taken. Also, a William Gumbert, age sixteen, was a musician for Company A of the 7th Maryland Infantry, enlisted August 18, 1862 and who was mustered out May 31, 1865.[41] Undoubtedly, this is the same William Gumbert and is most likely John's friend who slept with him on the floor. One source notes that Private Gumbert was a drummer from Hagerstown.[42]

November 6, 1861

At this point, we have no idea who B. F. Darby is and why John is sending him $90.00.

November [6] 7, 1861

John King erred in dating this entry. Thursday was the 7th of November, not the 6th.

Captain William H. H. Yontz enlisted in First Regiment of the Potomac Home Brigade Infantry on August 23, 1861. He was mustered out October 1, 1864. Also, this is John's first mention of Judge Daniel Weisel.

Friday Nov 8th 1861

I laid on the floor all night and got up about 3 O'clock to get ready to go to Hancock, started about 6 ½ O'clock, stopped a few minutes at Newcomers and drank a cup of coffee, arrived at Hancock about 12 O'clock.

Saturday Nov. 9th 1861

This day the Stars & Stripes float in P.(?) C. I had a very good breakfast this morning Of my favorite dish "Buck-wheat cakes,"

November [6] 7, 1861 continued

It is no surprise that Company E's flag was received by Peter Negley. At this time, he was one of the most prominent men of Hagerstown and had served as Cashier of the Hagerstown Savings Institution since 1854. On July 6, 1864, Hagerstown was visited by Confederate Brigadier General John McCausland, nicknamed "Tiger John," and 1,500 of his cavalry troopers. They sought $200,000 in ransom from the citizens as retribution for the burning of the Virginia Military Institute and other sites in the Shenandoah Valley by Union General David Hunter. McCausland reduced the amount to $20,000 and all three banks in Hagerstown came up with the money. Peter Negley would have been involved in gathering the amount provided by the Hagerstown Savings Institution. In 1865, Negley's bank was re-chartered as the First National Bank of Hagerstown and he remained as cashier until 1870.[43] On September 23, 1865, Peter Negley, Samuel L. King, our diarist's father, and eighteen other men were elected as delegates from District No. 3 to the County Convention.[44] In addition, on October 18, 1865, the President of the Central Committee of Washington County appointed Peter Negley as one of five gentlemen from District No. 3 to serve his committee.[45] Perhaps seeking some diversion, in 1866, Mr Negley purchased part of the local *Herald & Torch Light* newspaper and together with his son, Charles, who would also become a lawyer, ran it until they sold it to James G. McDonald in January of 1883.[46] In 1870, President Ulysses S Grant named Mr. Negley as First Assistant Treasurer of the new United States Sub-Treasury in Baltimore until President Garfield appointed F. M. Darby, Esq., to replace Negley in 1881[47] Finally, while completely alone at his residence in Hagerstown on June 7, 1884, Peter Negley died of a heart ailment. The following obituary titled "Death of a Maryland Patriot," appeared in a newspaper from his wife, Priscilla's hometown:

> The Hon. Peter Negley, of Hagerstown, Md., who died suddenly of heart disease at this his home, Sunday, was one of those true and patriotic men of the South whom Northern soldiers remember with gratitude. A Southerner by birth, he remained loyal to the Union, and gave frequent discomfiture to its opponents and aid to its defenders. An editor and publisher of the Hagerstown newspaper, he was able to deal heavy blows. He was for 12 years Assistant United States Treasurer at Baltimore. When Hagerstown was compelled to contribute for rebel support Mr. Negley preserved the funds of the bank, of which he was Cashier, by cleverly concealing them on his wife's person. The latter was a native of Worchester, and many a Worchester soldier was indebted t her for kindness during the War, and preserves a tender memory of them to-day.[48]

Other contemporary accounts of the ransom of July 6, 1884, mention the amount paid by the city as $20,000, but do not confirm the report of Mrs. Negley hiding money from the Confederates.

Captain George Frederick Heyser was the leader of a Hagerstown band called Captain Heyser's Silver Coronet Band. It was so-called because the members presented Captain Heyser with a silver coronet. Some called it Hagerstown First Band, but several other bands also played at special events. However, the Silver Coronet Band, for thirty years played at political rallies, community events, free concerts for the poor, picnics, and other special occasions. The band was a regular participant in numerous gatherings in Hagerstown in the 1850s and 1860s.

and rest assured I done justice. I started for Home about 1 o'clock and arrived there at 6 O'clock.

Sunday Nov. 10th 1861

I attended church and heard a most forcible sermon from Mr. Sears from the 13th Chap 9th verse of Isah (Isaiah); attended School in the Afternoon, the Teachers took a vote whether or not we would have an exhibition, it was defeated.

Monday Nov. 11th 1861

Bro. H. E. King went to Frederick this morning to join his company which went on Friday last. I went and helped John Lane with his corn, when it rained and then we stopped

Tuesday Nov. 12th 1861

I was husking Corn all day and at night, feel pretty tired, I went to Church at night.

Wednesday Nov. 13th 1861

I again went to work husking corn by myself, John Lane having gone Soldiering and the Negro sick, at night. I feel very tired.

Thursday Nov 14th 1861

I again resumed my job of husking Corn, stopped about 4 O'clock went home and dressed and went up street. At night there was

---

November 10, 1861
Rev. Samuel W. Sears served the Methodist Episcopal Church in Hagerstown for several years. He performed numerous marriages during the Civil War throughout the year 1862 and to the beginning of 1863.

November 11, 1861
The distance from Hagerstown to Frederick, Maryland is about 23 miles.

November 13, 1861
Lane was the maiden name of John's mother, Eliza Lane King. Eliza Lane King's brother and John King's maternal uncle, was Charles G. Lane. Charles' son, John C. Lane, aged 16, was living with his father in Hagerstown. John C. would have been either age 17 or 18 in the fall of 1861. No records of a John Lane who enlisted in the Union Army in 1861 could be located.

a grand Illumination and "Torch Light" Procession. I went home about 11 ½ O'clock.

Friday Nov 15th 1861

It was raining all day and consequently can't go to work, "More Rain, More rest" Sayeth the old proverb.

Saturday Nov 16th 1861

It is very cold this morning and the wind is high. The "Union Rangers" stationed at the Fair Grounds left this afternoon for Frederick.

Sunday Nov. 17th 1861

I was at Church this morning and heard a splendid discourse from the Rev. Dr. McCreedy, Chaplain of the 39th Illinois Regiment, he preached from the 1st Chap Corrin. 31st verse coming from Church I met Mr. Imidor of Balto. a coal oil dealer on Liberty St. Yesterday I was made acquainted with two young Ladys from Beaver-Creek named Mifs Lane and Susan Fishock and received a very pressing invitation to pay them a visit my old confidential Tom Hilliard and me were together.

November 17, 1861

The Rev. Dr. McCreedy referred to was Chaplain Charles S. McReading of the 39th Illinois Regiment. Reverend McReading hailed from Channahon, Illinois and was commissioned October 9, 1861.[49] He was nicknamed Chaplain "Mack" and

> "while in the service he was active and devoted to his duties, although but seldom with the regiment on account of it being continually on the move, and his health did not permit of his sharing the privations and exposures that were encountered up to the date of the regiment going into winter quarters at Suffolk, Va., in September, 1862."[50]

One regimental historian felt that this chaplain's spiritual comfort was "almost nil" but that he was helpful assisting soldiers with sending money home at paydays.[51] John King said he "heard a splendid discourse" from the reverend. Perhaps Rev. McCreedy's oratory in the pulpit made up for his lack of being able to provide comfort in his personal ministrations. Chaplain Mack resigned his commission August 9, 1862 and never returned to the regiment.

This is the first time John mentions this boyhood friend. Thomas (Tom) E. Hilliard, was also born and raised in Hagerstown. Born September 23, 1843, he may have served in the Confederate army, but no official records of his service are known. From 1873, Tom was Register of Wills for Washington County and served in that capacity until his death April 15, 1918. He is buried in Rose Hill Cemetery.

The Fishach family lived in Beaver Creek as John cites, but were within the Boonsboro District. Henry Fishach was a farmer, fifty-six years of age when the 1860 U.S. Census was taken July 23.[52] Included in the household were his wife, Polly, aged fifty-seven, a son Joseph, a daughter, Susan, aged nineteen, and Magdaline, aged sixteen.[53]

Monday Nov 18th 1861

I again went at husking corn and finished, tomorrow we will haul in fodder.

Tuesday Nov 19th 1861

Went to work hauling in Fodder and finished about 1 O'clock and went to Shippenburg Pa. for John Gumbert.

Wednesday Nov 20th 1861

I laid over night in Chambersburg and 4 ½ O'clock in the morning I went to Shippensburg, left there about 10 ½ O'clock for Hagerstown, where I arrived at 12 O'clock.

Thursday Nov 21st 1861

I received to-day from Mefs B. F. Darby & Co., Baltimore, Two-Thousand (2000) "A La Wana" cigars costing me $4.50 for 1000, I sold one thousand five-hundred (1500) for $6-for 1000. I have 500 left.

November 17, 1861 continued

Susan Fishach would have been about twenty years old at this time while Polly would have been about seventeen. Perhaps he enjoyed having older "lady friends. Throughout his diary, Mr. King frequently attended Sunday church services and invariably cites both and verse of the scriptures that were read during the service. Beaver Creek, Maryland is about 6 miles from Hagerstown, an easy ride.

November 19, 1861

As previously mentioned, John Gumbert is mostly like the father of John's good friend and companion, "Ril" or William Gumbert. The father's occupation as shown on the 1860 U.S. Census was "butcher," but he later may have owned a Confectionary and Ice Cream shop in Hagerstown. Our diarist does not provide the reason for his trip to Shippensburg.

November 20, 1861

Chambersburg, Pennsylvania is 20.7 miles north of Hagerstown. Shippensburg, Pennsylvania is about 11 miles northeast of Chambersburg.

November 21, 1861

We now know that B. F. Darby was a company in Baltimore, Maryland. According to Wood's Baltimore City Directory for 1860, Benjamin, Franklin and David Darby were all part of a company called Kephart, Darby & Sons.[54] The company is shown at 296 W. Baltimore (Street) and specialized in selling whole fruit and confections. They are listed as "Fruiterers and Confectioners." Apparently, as did some of similar companies in Baltimore, Kephart, Darby & Sons also sold cigars wholesale.

Friday Nov 22nd 1861

This as a very dull day in Town, yesterday it was a little lively, a good many of the 13th Mass. Regt. was in Town, it being thanksgiving day in Massachusetts. Sister Addie and husband is in Town, and took Supper with us.

Saturday Nov 23rd 1861

It rained all night-very hard but cleared up very nice about 9 O'clock in the afternoon. My old confidential (Tom Hilliard) and me went down to Beaver-Creek at Mr. Henry Fishach's to pay them a visit, as we had promised the Ladys; at night we went to Benwold Chapel to a meeting, and heard as I thought a very poor Sermon. We had a very lively time going and coming.

Sunday Nov 24th 1861

I stayed up pretty late last with the Ladys, and Tom and me had fine fun, went up stairs To bed and had a little fun up there, with John Gray; we woke pretty early the next morning and cut up a little before we got out of bed. After breakfast we prepared for Church, we had lots of fun on the road, we put the Ladys out at the Church and started for Boonsboro, but the most important feature of our ride to the Church was just as we were about to start for Boonsboro, I gave the Horse a cut, he jumped a little and out went poor old Tom backwards out of the Wagon, but did not hurt himself; we went to Town and got a little "You know what" and then returned to Church.

November 22, 1861

At this time, there was no National Day of Thanksgiving. Prior to President Lincoln's Proclamation of October 3, 1863, which set the last Thursday of November "as a day of Thanksgiving and Praise," each state set its own Thanksgiving holiday at different times, specifically New England and other Northern states. Massachusetts apparently had their date of Thanksgiving as November 21st prior to Lincoln's Proclamation.

November 24, 1861

In 1860, John Gray was a twenty-one year old farm laborer who resided in Boonsboro, Maryland, with his mother, Mary, and three sisters.[55] John F. Gray, from Beaver Creek, would later join Company H of the 3rd Regiment of the U.S. Maryland Cavalry and served from September 28, 1863 to September 5, 1865.[56] This soldier was probably the same John Gray that John mentions here.

Our diarist is a bit hesitant in mentioning that he and his friend, Tom, consumed some alcohol on the Sabbath.

Monday Nov 25th 1861

I could not finish on the other page the history of our days proceeding yesterday and will finish on this. We got back to Church just as it was leaving out, we loaded up the Girls and made for Home (presumably Boonsboro—Editor), we got there about dinner time, we done justice at the Table. We left there about 4 ½ O'clock for Hagers Town, but got very cold before we got there, thus closes the history of our visit to Beaver-Creek. This morning I met with Joe. Hines of England and now enlisted in the "Union Rifles" N.Y. he is a very lively fellow, took dinner with him at Knode Hotel, after that we got a Horse and Buggy and went to Leitersburg. Tom Hilliard was Pilot, we had a most lively time, we were "Gay and Happy"

Tuesday Nov. 26th 1861

This day the new Sheriff (Henry Gantz) enters into the discharge of his dutys, he takes possession of the Jail . Tom and me went round to the Jail and helped the Ladys, he introduced me to Mifs Shoop sister-in-law to the Sheriff, and she is very good company, we had a very nice dinner went down street-stopped a while in Court, the new Judge presiding (Judge Weisel), from there we went to John Gumberts, who had the Ill. Band there to dinner, it was reported he was married, but such was not the case, the Band played at Recher's Saloon, and again went to Gumberts here they played again, and was treated.

November 25, 1861

"Union Rifles" was a nickname for a Union regiment. However, it became part of the 51st New York Infantry which was not stationed anywhere near Hagerstown and which did not have a soldier named Joseph Hines on its regimental roster.[57] Perhaps another New York also used the sobriquet "Union Rifles."

November 26, 1861

Henry Gantz was born in Maryland in March of 1826. As a young man, he worked on his father, John's farm in District No. 1 of Washington County.[58] He was already married to Catharine Shoop. As a Republican, he was elected to Sheriff and served during the first years of the Civil War from 1861 to 1863. By 1870, Henry Gantz and his wife were residing in Montgomery County, Maryland, where he was employed as a railroad contractor and his son, William, was a "railroad boss."[59] His other three sons were Jacob S., Frederic M., and John F. By 1880, Henry was back in Hagerstown now employed as a banker and all of his children had left his household.[60] By 1900, now seventy-four years old he had moved to Columbus, Ohio, was renting a room with his wife and stated that he was working as a "contractor".[61] Henry Gantz died in 1908, his wife Catharine passed away in 1917 and both are buried in Rose Hill Cemetery, Hagerstown.

The Miss Shoop our diarist mentions was presumably Christiana, age twenty in 1860, who was residing with John and Sarah Shoop of Boonsboro, Maryland. In the 1860's, the Shoops operated a pottery business in Boonsboro which was composed of John, aged sixty and the patriarch, Benjamin F, aged twenty-five, Benjamin F. Lancaster, aged thirty-two and an apprentice, Daniel Jacobs, aged seventeen years.[62] These potters probably made redware vessels. Apparently, none of their ware was marked.[63]

Wednesday Nov 27th 1861

This morning it commenced hailing and it is very disagreeable, I was up to see Aunt Maria Lane who has been very sick. I found her to be a great deal better, and was sitting Up. Bro. Willie is at present very sick with "Billious Fever" and is out of his mind most all the while, he has been sick for a week. I sold five-hundred cigars to Geo. House for $2.80.

Thursday Nov. 28th 1861

This day is set forth by the Governor of the State, as a day of Thanksgiving and Prayer. Willie is very poorly this morning and afraid he wont live long. I met with Lt. Lord T. Nickolson of the 39th Ill. Regiment, and received an invitation to a Dance at Williamspt.

Friday Nov. 29th 1861

Which I got home this morning at 6 O'clock from the Dance at Williamsport. I enjoyed Myself very much, went over in a two horse Hack, the dance commenced about 8 O'clock and continued until 5 in the morning. We had a splendid Supper at 1 O'clock, and at 3 O'clock we had some more very nice refreshments. Bro. Willie is just about the same, as he was yesterday, this is a very disagreeable day and I feel very bad and sleepy.

November 27, 1861

Maria Lane was the wife of Charles G. Lane. John King's younger brother, William, was about twelve old at this time. Bilious fever refers to any fever that exhibits symptoms of nausea and vomiting in addition to an increase in internal body temperature and strong diarrhea. The term is no longer used, but in the 18th and 19th centuries it was commonly cited as a cause of death. John King only made a profit of $2.80 on his purchase of 2,000 cigars.

November 28, 1861

The only Lieutenant Nicholson shown on the roster of the 39th Illinois Infantry Regiment was Daniel A. Nicholson of Company K from Marseilles, Illinois.[64] Lord T. may have been a nickname. However, in the regimental history, his name is given as Donald A. Nicholson. However, this is an error as his actual first name was actually Daniel.[65] Mr. Nicholson joined the Union Army October 11, 1861, as a 2nd lieutenant, was promoted to 1st lieutenant March 15, 1862, and then resigned his commission June 14, 1862. The regimental historian added the following history regarding this officer:

> Was born in Canada. He proved a good officer and soldier up to the time he forced by the enemy to ford the Potomac river January 4, 1862. After this he became disabled by rheumatism and left the service. In December, 1864, he again entered the service, being commissioned First Lieutenant of Company E 153rd Illinois Infantry; was mustered out to said organization as Captain, October 25th, 1865. He is now living at Marseilles, and is occupied as a stone-mason.[66]

Saturday Nov. 30th 1861

I feel much better this morning after a good sleep, poor Willie is very ill with "Typhoid Fever" and is very weak. In the afternoon Tom and I went to Williamsport with Cigars, Tobacco and Gloves but done very poor, we brought 1st Lt. Lord with us to Town.

Sunday Dec. 1st 1861

This is the first of December and it is clear and cool. Lt. Lord and I went to the M.E. Church and heard a sermon from a strange Preacher. I attended School in the afternoon; In the evening went visiting with Lt. Lord. Bro. Willie is very poorly, we thought he was dead.

Monday Dec 2nd 1861

I was with Liut. Lord all morning, he went home at noon. Willie is about same as he was yesterday.

Tuesday Dec. 3rd 1861

I went to Williamsport with Charly Poffenbager to sell things to the Soldiers, but did not do very well.

December 1, 1861

The "M.E. Church" that the diarist refers to is St. Paul's Bethel Methodist Episcopal Church in Hagerstown.

December 3, 1861

This is the first time John mentions that he peddled goods to the Union troops stationed in the general area. He apparently loaded some goods upon a wagon and traveled to Williamsport, Pennsylvania, which is 153 miles away. Merchandisers who followed the armies and sold items to the soldiers were generally called "Sutlers." Sutlers offered food, clothing, personal items, metal ware such as tinware, photographs and about anything else a soldier might need while in the field. Charles A. Poffenberger, aged fourteen, is listed on the U.S. 1860 Census for Washington County taken June 5, 1860.[67] Hence, John's assistant in sales was sixteen years old at the time of this diary entry. He is shown as residing with Louisa Poffenberger, presumably his mother, who was forty years old and who stated that her occupation was a "seamstress." Charles would see Union service under Colonel Edward Mobley. At the age of seventeen, he enlisted on August 13, 1862, as a private in Company A of the 7th Maryland Infantry Regiment and was mustered out after the end of the war, i.e., May 31, 1865[68,69] Mobley raised a company called the Bradford Guards in about ten days in Hagerstown and it left for Baltimore August 18, 1862.[70] Two companies, A and I, of the 7th Regiment recruited in Washington County while Companies B, E, and G were raised in Frederick. On September 16, 1864, Private Poffenberger was taken prisoner and was sent to Libby Prison in Richmond, Virginia where his health deteriorated.[71] After the war, Charles was residing in the Ward 4 of the District of Columbia with his mother, sister, wife Julia and two children was employed with the Capitol Police.[72]

Wednesday Dec 4th 1861

Charly and me went again to the Camps but did not do very well again, we bought a Barrel of Apples which we paid Six Dollars ($6) for, and we just about made out.

Thursday Dec.5th 1861

We again went to the Camps peddling and to-day we done very well. At night there was going to be a little fight between a Soldier and a Citizen, but passed off without bloodshed.

Friday Dec. 6 1861

We again went to the Camps, but done most miserably, didn't make out expenses.

Saturday Dec. 7 1861

I didn't go to Camp to-day and about 10 O'clock Cousin Kate Lane and Sue Weast, from Boonsboro came to Town in a nice Buggy and Horse which we (Tom & me) took charge of and went out to Newcomers to see Sister Addie and all, and had a good Dinner and a nice time. There was considerable excitement in Town this afternoon caused by the report of heavy cannonading not very far off, there was various rumors as to where it was.

Sunday Dec. 8th 1861

A crowd of us went to Wm/" pt.(Williamsport, Maryland) to-day to ascertain the cause of the firing heard yesterday, and found it was the Rebels trying to destroy Dam No. 5, but had not succeeded when we left at 5 O'clock.

December 7, 1861

This is John's first mention of cannon fire heard by the citizens of Hagerstown. At this point, no one seems to know from what direction or locality the cannonading is coming from. "Kate" may have been a nickname for John's first cousin, Sophia Lane. "Sue" or Susan Weist from Boonsboro was about twenty years old at this time. She resided with her mother, also named Susan, aged forty-five in 1860 and three siblings.[73]

Monday Dec. 9th 1861

It is very warm and pleasant to-day, which is more like a summer day than a day in December.

Tuesday Dec 10th 1861

It was a little cloudy early this morning but cleared up very nice during the day. Mrs. Welk her son and Julia Lane was in Town to-day.

Wednesday Dec 11th 1861

To-day it is very windy and I fell (feel) very bad halving bee (been) with two friends of mine, Lieuts. Brucker & McEntash of the 39th Ill.(Illinois) Regts. and stayed up pretty late.

December 8, 1861

On December 6, 1861, a portion of General Stonewall Jackson's army struck Dam No. 5, located on the Potomac River. Union troops were already stationed along vital points of the waterway and had soldiers posted at Dam No. 5. Two companies of the Stonewall Brigade were sent to wade waist high in the water to break the dam and drain a large section of the canal. Union forces sent out snipers which forced the waders back to shore.[74]

An article regarding an earlier attack on Dam No. 5 appeared in the Hagerstown newspaper *Herald of Freedom & Torch Light* on June 12, 1861:

> Information reached here that an attempt was made by the Virginia rebels, on Saturday and Sunday nights last, to destroy Dams No. 4 and on the Chesapeake and Ohio canal. At No. 5 they were met by the brave Guards of Clearspring, who, after considerable skirmishing, succeeded in repulsing them, killing one their men. The rebels endeavored to blow up the dam by means of a blast, for which purpose they had procured four kegs of powder, but were driven off before they were able to injure it. At Dam No. 4 some damage was done to the Canal, but we learn none to the Dam itself. It is clearly the duty of every local citizen in the county to rally to the defence and protection of the property of the Canal Company.—The Canal cost the State of Maryland many millions of dollars, its trade and commerce are the life arteries of our people, and they must defend it at all hazards and every cost until the Government can relieve them. We understand the firing was resumed at Dam No. 5 on Monday, but have not learned particulars.[75]

In this instance, the local newspaper is urging its citizens and local militia to take up arms to protect these Dams since the taxpayers paid for them and since they are considered vital to the local economy. Apparently, Union troops had not yet arrived to carry out this task.

Throughout the Civil War, Union troops were positioned all along the Potomac River, its adjacent canals, dams and fords and along the Chesapeake & Ohio Railroad which ran west of Washington, D.C. The railroad served as an important transport for troops and supplies westward. The fords had to be protected to prevent Confederate forces from crossing into Maryland and Southern Pennsylvania. Washington D.C. was constantly fearful of a large Rebel force crossing the Potomac River and attacking the city from the west.

December 10, 1861

The 1860 U.S. Census shows Julia Lane, age nineteen, living with her mother, Elizabeth, and four siblings in Boonsboro, Maryland.[76] There is no husband shown and no occupation is given for Mrs. Lane.

Thursday Dec. 12th 1861

I went out to Newcomer's to help to Butch and had a nice time.

Friday Dec. 13th 1861

Sam McLaughlin (my Bro-in law) and me went hunting but had very bad luck. I left the country about 2 O'clock for Town. Addie is in with me.

Saturday Dec. 14th 1861

This is a very pretty day but is very dull with me. Last night a friend, and me had Oysters at Kolklessers Saloon.

Sunday Dec. 15th 1861

I attended the M. E. Church to-day and heard a very good sermon from Mr. Sears.

Monday Dec. 16th 1861

This morning I got up very early to help Uncle Charles to Butcher, he had four very large ones, the largest of which weighed 462 lbs; this evening I feel very tired. The streets are lively to night with various War Rumors caused by a big fight in Western Va. and from the belligerent news from England, she wants our government to beg pardon for the arrest of the two Rebel envoys, Mason & Slidell on board of a British vessel.

December 11, 1861

Simon S. Brucker was from Pontiac, Illinois, and was mustered into service October 11, 1861, as a 2nd lieutenant. He was promoted to 1st lieutenant May 26, 1862 and later resigned April 20, 1864. His friend, John W. McIntosh, hailing from Bloomington, was mustered into the Union army also on October 11, 1861, as a 1st lieutenant and was later promoted to captain August 7, 1862. However, Captain McIntosh was cashiered out March 30, 1863, for unknown reasons.[77] These officers, like Lieutenant Nicholson had just joined the U.S. Army. In fact, this regiment departed from St. Louis and arrived in Hagerstown at midnight, November 2, and went to the market house at 6 o'clock the next morning.[78] They did not reach their intended camp at Williamsport until November 7 after having had to wait for the baggage trains and ambulances to catch up.[78] The 39th Illinois stayed in camp at Williamsport until they departed for Hancock, Maryland, on December 15, arriving at that place the next day.[79] Their orders were to guard the Baltimore and Ohio Railroad. Hence, the regiment had a short stay in Williamsport, only about six weeks.

December 13, 1861

Addie is John King's older sister and is married to Sam McLaughlin.

Tuesday Dec. 17th 1861

There was some Boonsboro Folks up to-day Ed. Welk came with them, and him and me was to-gether all day.

Wednesday Dec. 18th 1861

This is a beautiful morning, like a spring morning. The Town was enlivened about 12 O'clock by the passage of the 5th Conn. Regt/" through Town to Williamsport.

Thursday Dec. 19th 1861

Town is lively to-day caused by the presence of two Cavalry Companys from Gen. Banks division, they go to Williamsport.

Friday Dec. 20th 1861

The weather looks very uncertain this morning, with indications of rain. I walked out to Newcomers to-day and stayed some time and rode back with Mr. Miller (of Jones & Miller)

Saturday Dec 21st 1861

Nothing of importance transpired to-day, but a night about 7 O'clock an alarm of fire was sounded which proved to be Wm/" Hager's Barn I ran and worked very hard until 11 O'clock when we came home, and went to Capt. Heists and had Ale.

December 16, 1861

John was probably referring to the Battle of Camp Allegheny, also called the Battle of Allegheny Mountain, which began at sunrise on December 13, in Pocahontas County, Virginia, now part of West Virginia. Brig. Gen. Robert H. Milroy led an assault against Confederate forces led by Colonel Edward Johnson. Confederate artillery roused Union troops occupying a dense woods and Milroy retreated to his camps at Green Spring Run close to Cheat Mountain. The result of the actions was inconclusive.

December 21, 1861

According to the 1860 census for Funkstown, Maryland, William H. Hager, aged fifty-two, was a very wealthy farmer and miller.[80] His real estate and his personal property were valued at $60,000 and $20,000 respectively on the census. The Millers were doing very well financially at this time. Mr. Hager lived with his wife, five sons and two daughters on a large plot of land near Hagerstown. It is not known if Mr. Miller had fire insurance to cover the loss of his barn.

Sunday Dec. 22nd 1861

This is a bitter cold morning and overcoats are resorted to. I attended the M. E. Church and heard a good sermon from the 22nd/" Chap Gen. 1 & 2 Verse. At 12 O'clock Capt. Howes (regular) Battery of Guns passed through Town on their way to Washington, they came from Romney Va. and about 1 ½ O'clock there was another Battery of 4 Pieces passed through, on their way to the same place, which makes one think there will be an important move by Gen McClellan towards Manassas.

Monday Dec. 23rd 1861

This is a very disagreeable morning hailing, raining, and freezing. Through the day it began to Snow and snowed very hard, but blowed clear in the evening.

Tuesday Dec. 24th 1861

This is the day before Christmas, and the streets presents quite a lively appearance, business is brisk. I bought a Turkey for 60 cts.

Wednesday Dec 25th 1861

This is Christmas, a day celebrated is the birth of our Lord and Saviour Jesus Christ. I arose at the usual time this morning ate a

---

December 21, 1861 continued

Captain Lewis Heist was a prominent retail merchant, i.e., grocery store owner, and saloon keeper/ brewer in Hagerstown. He was born February 17, 1811, in Hesse-Darmstadt, Germany.[81,82] Born about 1810, his wife, Margaret, also was born in Germany and the she probably immigrated with him. Margaret Heist had, at least, three children: Levis, Martin, William. One son, William, followed in his fathers' footsteps and became a brewer. Along with the family's financial success came several prestigious elective offices for Lewis. He was chosen as President of the Hagerstown Building Association in 1870.[83] Then, in 1872, he was elected as one of the Directors of the Citizens' National Bank.[84] In 1873, Captain Heist won election to the town council for Ward 2, the only Republican to obtain a seat.[85] Lewis Heist is listed twice on the 1875 Business Directory for Hagerstown, as a brewer and as a grocer, with and address of 9 and 11 South Potomac Street.[86] On January 18, 1877, Captain Lewis Heist died and was buried in Rose Hill Cemetery, Hagerstown, Maryland.[87]

December 22, 1861

Romney, Virginia, now West Virginia, was fortified by a fairly large contingent of Federal troops. The area around the town of Romney was an important hub because it was located in the South Branch Valley. Here crossed the road from Winchester to Grafton on the Baltimore & Ohio Railroad and the road from Monterey, Virginia, to Cumberland, Maryland, on the Potomac River. Therefore, whoever held this town had control of the northwest valley.

light Breakfast, and started out, I made calls at Mifs Garmberts, Mifs Sheckels and Miss Carson, I (had) several others to make but in the afternoon Tom Hilliard his Bro and me went to Williamsport got Ale Old Rye and "Tom and Jerry", and then left for home.

Thursday Dec. 26th 1861

This is styled the second day of Christmas, but I shall not. I made a few calls to-day among them was Cousin Annie Powles, and spent part of the evening with Miss Gumbert.

Friday Dec. 27th 1861

This morning I had the very unpleasant job of helping haul ins two loads of Fodder for Uncle Chas. Lane. The weather is very cold and windy.

Saturday Dec. 28th 1861

To-day is a bitter cold day and very dull. Sister Addie & Saml. McLaughlin her husband is in Town.

Sunday Dec. 29th 1861

I this morning attended the German Reformed Church and heard a very good Sermon preached by their Pastor Rev. Wagnor, his text

---

December 25, 1861

John King, typical for a young man of his age, certainly enjoyed "courting" the young ladies of the city and county. The Miss Garmbert mentioned is probably Miss Mary Gumbert, the daughter of John Gumbert, who was aged seventeen. Miss Sheckels, also a resident of Hagerstown, was most likely the seventeen year-old daughter of Richard and Marie Sheckels.[88] Mr. Sheckels was a well-known auctioneer in the city. Ads for sales by auctioneer Sheckels of real estate, estates, livestock, farm equipment, horses, carriages, sleighs, buggies, furniture and other various items appear in numerous issues of Hagerstown newspapers from February 12, 1851 to January 5, 1865. According to the U.S. Censuses for 1860 and 1870, there was no family with the surname of Carson residing in Hagerstown. However, the young lady cited may have been either Alice Carson or her sister, America, daughters of George and Malida Carson of Funkstown, Maryland.[130]

December 26, 1861

Ann or Anna Powles appears on both the 1860 and 1870 U. S. Censuses for Hagerstown with her husband Jacob H., a "saddler" or harness maker.[89,90] On the 1870, she is thirty-nine years of age and he is forty-one and they have two young children, Joshua and Harry K. as well as a saddler's apprentice, Rossir Maddox, in their household.

was from the 2nd/' Chap 9 verse of St. Mathew. I attended S. (Sunday) School in the afternoon, and received a new scholar.

Monday Dec. 30th 1861

This is a beautiful day, very pleasant and warm, but very dull with me. I laid out 40 cents in Dry Goods, I have my Friend Wm/" B. Harris up in my Parlor with, and intend taking a smoke.

Tuesday Dec. 30th 1861

This is the last day of the Year 1861, it has been a year in the History of our Country. Civil War has begun in this year, and we may see the end of another, and it may be two before we see this war of Treason ended, but we pray to God that before the end of another Year, we may see that "glorious emblem of National freedom, the "Star Spangled Banner" float from Maine to the coasts of Florida: in this Year (1861) we became nearly involved with a difficulty with England, a Country that has always held a deceitful love for this county, it grew out of the arrest and imprisonment of four Rebel emiseraries, (emissaries) Slidel, Mason and their private secretaries from on board a British Ship, by Capt. Wilks, of the "San Jucinte" the proceeding was not done altogether with accordance with the international laws, with regard to the right of search, he should seize the vessel and taken it into port, but allowed it to proceed; the prisoners were released.

Wednesday January 1st 1861

To-day ushers in the Year 1862, the old year having passed away and been numbered among the things that were. The year was one

---

December 29, 1861

The pastor mentioned is most likely Reverend S. G. Wagner, who was associated with the German Reform Church in Hagerstown.

December 31, 1861

John erred by giving Tuesday a diary entry of a second December 30, but Tuesday was December 31. He did not correct it later.

Once again, John shows his strong sense of patriotism as well as his considerable knowledge of current events. He offers that the boarded British ship should have been taken to port instead of the arrest of the Confederate emissaries. Whether he read about this incident in the local paper or came up with on his own is unknown of sad experience, and will be remembered with sorrow by most of those who now dwell in the land extending from the St. Lawrence to the Rio Grande. The appearance of the war-cloud put a sudden check to all the industrial pursuits in this Country, and a more general dearth than ever before known prevailed, sowing broadcast, want and desolation in many hitherto happy households. But the new year is a new era in the calendar of the world, and it may be hoped that the clouds which have gathered so thickly may disperse and the bright sun of peace and prosperity again

Wednesday Jany. 1st/" 62 (continued)

gladden the hearts of the people. It may have its share of vicissitudes, sorrows, and trials, but it may also have its pleasures bestowed with less niggard hand than in the past. About 9 O'clock last night an alarm of fire was given, it proved to be a stack of Fodder at the Alms House. Today a party of us left Town, on a pleasure excursion and went to Boonsboro, ran around there a little and then started for Sharpsburg, and got there in time to see the dress parade of the 12" Indiana Regt./", and while there came across two Hagerstown Lady Friends, and walked around with them awhile, and then we started for home, which we reached about 6 ½ O'clock, very well satisfied with the way in which we celebrated the 1st/" of January 1862.

Thursday Jan. 2nd 1862

This morning it is very cold and very dull with me. I got my hair cut and paid 11 cts. The Cars did not come at usual time this evening, and was delayed on account of the transportation of Troops, and of course we did not get the Balto, N. Y & Phila. Papers.

Friday Jan. 3rd 1862

It is bitter cold this morning. The Cars did not arrive until 1 O'clock last night. About 3 O'clock this morning the 110 Pa. Regt. came to

January 2, 1862

John King gives the price of a haircut in Hagerstown in 1862. He also indicates that the city papers from Baltimore, New York and Philadelphia come by rail. The "Cars" referred to by him are railroad cars. John, most likely, reads these papers and this may explain, in part, why he is so knowledgeable of events pertaining to the war.

Town and they were a hard set. About 4 O'clock this afternoon there was a riot among them, it appears that there are four Company of Irish among them and they got to fighting the 6 Compys, of Cavelry and Capt. Welsh Co. was called out to quell the riot, some were killed.

<u>Saturday Jan. 4th</u> 1862

This morning we get up and find a deep <u>snow.</u> The 110 Regt. Pa. V. left for Hancock. To-night there is heavy fireing heard in the direction of Hancock and there is various rumors afloat concerning it.

January 3, 1862

The pro-Confederate newspaper, the *Hagerstown Mail*, ran a weekly summary of local war news. The issue dated January 10, 1862 had an article entitled, "Military affairs around us," a portion of which dealt with the so-called "whiskey fight" among companies of the 110th Pennsylvania. It reads as follows:

> During the afternoon of Friday a number of Irishmen belonging to the regiment under the influence of a little too much of the 'oh! Be joyful' got into a melee on the turnpike near town which was conducted in the Hiberian style and resulted, as is usual in such cases, in a number of broken heads and bruised and scared faces. The Cavalry companies of Capt. Cole and Kurl were ordered from the Fair Ground to the scene of the disturbance but before they arrived the fight was suppresses by the officers of the regiment. Captain Welsh's company was also out during the night guarding the town."[91]

This account is similar to that of our diarist with the exception that John King stated that Captain Welsh's company "… was called out to quell the riot." The Captain Welsh mentioned and in several other diary entries is probably Charles A. Welsh, Captain of Company B of the Third Regiment, Potomac Home Brigade. Captain Welsh enlisted October 11, 1861 and was mustered out October 4, 1862. Captain Cole may be Henry A. Cole of Frederick, Maryland of "Cole's Cavalry" also known as the First Potomac Home Brigade Cavalry. This brigade was composed of four companies that originally enlisted from August 10 and November 27, 1861. Captain Kurl was Pearce K. Curll, in command of Company D, First Regiment, Potomac Home Brigade.[92]

The incident began with ten companies composing the 110th Pennsylvania Volunteers who came to Hagerstown early on the morning of January 3rd after a twenty-six mile forced march. These soldiers were new recruits and had not yet been issued their muskets. Four companies were Irish boys recruited from the City of Philadelphia while the other six companies were from the farms and small towns of rural Pennsylvania. To quench their extreme thirsts, they went into the bars and saloons and many became inebriated. The regimental officers, including Colonel William D. Lewis, had gone into the hotels for early morning breakfasts. Fist fighting started when one of the country soldiers attempted to take the regimental flag from the color guard of the men from Philadelphia. The officers soon restored order and marched the troops out of town. However, once there, some soldiers became picking up loose, large limestone rocks from the recently macadamized National Turnpike and starting throwing them at the other group. Soon, a major riot ensued with one side pelting the other with rocks for twenty minutes. The First Maryland Cavalry, also known the 1st Potomac Home Brigade or Cole's Cavalry, was called to stop the intra-regimental "rock battle." Casualties were three killed and more than forty severely wounded. The regiment was later marched to Romney, Virginia (now West Virginia) to face a Confederate force commanded by General Thomas E. "Stonewall Jackson,

January 4, 1862

John may have heard skirmishing fire coming from Bath, Virginia (now West Virginia) which is only 5.61 miles from Hancock, Maryland and 27 miles from Hagerstown. John may have been mistaken about the actual direction he heard firing. Although the sounds of battle traveled many miles, depending in part upon atmospheric conditions, ascertaining the directional source of the sound may have been difficult.

Sunday Jan. 5th 1862

This is without exception the coldest morning we have had this Winter. The Town is full of rumors this morning concerning the heavy fireing heard last night, the Qr. Master (Union Quartermaster) send 10,000 rounds of Cartridges up to Hancock last night at 10 O'clock with orders to reach there by day-light. The statement of the Mare driver to—Hancock, that the commander of the Rebels opposite that Town sent a flag of Truce for our forces to surrender, or give the Women and children 2 hours to leave, that he intended to shell the Town, is pretty generally credited, we wait the results.

January 6th 1862

There was a heavy fall of snow last night, and was kept buisy all morning cleaning off the snow. About 4 O'clock the Town was thrown into a state of excitement caused by the arrival of Gen. William's Brigade, there was four Regts, the 46th Pa, 5" Conn, 28th and 19th N.Y., they are on their way to Hancock, they quartered in the different Public buildings in Town, including the Female Seminary and M. E. Church.

January 4, 1862 continued

During the early morning hours of New Year's Day, Confederate General Stonewall Jackson left his headquarters at Winchester, Virginia on his Romney campaign or expedition. He led his troops in a northwesterly direction heading for Bath, Virginia (now West Virginia) via Pughtown and Unger's Store. By the evening of January 2, 1862, Jackson had been reinforced with militia and two cavalry companies so that his total body numbered approximately 8,500 soldiers. By the evening of January 3, Jacksons' lead units had reached Bath and camped on the outskirts that town. Bath was then occupied by Union troops. On the next day, January 4, after several hours of skirmishing, the Federals abandoned Bath and fled to Hancock. Jackson's Confederate force followed and camped on the other side of the Potomac River from Hancock. On January 5, Jackson demanded surrender of the garrison, but the Union commander refused and Jackson's artillery began shelling the town from Orrick's Hill in retaliation for a prior Federal shelling of the Confederate-friendly town of Shepherdstown, Virginia (now West Virginia). The following day, the Confederate artillery resumed the bombardment, but General Jackson decided to forfeit Hancock and began a march back towards Unger's Store. Jackson was not to reach Romney with the vanguard of his army until January 14, 1862. Leaving troops in various locations including Romney, Bath, Martinsburg and some in the South Branch Valley, General Jackson with his old Stone-wall Brigade returned to Winchester on January 24, 1862. Jackson felt that his objective of clearing the northwestern counties of Virginia, such as Hampshire, Berkeley, and Morgan, of Union troops had been met. He also repaid the North for the shelling of Shepherdstown and tore up some track of the Baltimore & Ohio Railroad. Some historians suggest that the outcome of the Romney Campaign was inconclusive.[93]

January 5, 1862

As it turns out, the statement of the driver was accurate. However, the name of the Confederate commander, General Stonewall Jackson, threatening the town of Hancock is never mentioned by the diarist. Apparently, the Federal forces were expecting a severe engagement to follow, as noted by the many troops and cartridges being rushed to the town. But Jackson did not choose to engage the defenders further because he was now outnumbered by the arrival of reinforcements, Jackson ceased fire and left the Hancock area the morning of January 7, 1862, and headed southward towards Unger's Store.[94]

January 7th 1862

This was one of the liviest morning I have ever seen in Hagerstown, Gen. Williams Brigade leaving for the seat of War; the sweet strains of the Regimental Bands, the sharp quick command of the Officer and the rumbling of Army Wagon, made old Hagerstown seem like a Broadway N.Y.

Wednesday Jan. 8th 1862

This is a beautiful morning like that of a morning in May. There is very good Sleighing which makes the Town look lively.

January 7, 1862

While General William's Brigade was entering Hagerstown, General Stonewall Jackson had already shelled Hancock January 5 and lobbed a few more the next day. The General Williams that John King spoke of was Brigadier General Alpheus S. Williams, who had been promoted to brigade command on May 17, 1861. He was now one of General Nathaniel Bank's brigade commanders of the Army of the Potomac and served in this capacity from October 8, 1861, taking charge of the Third Brigade until March of 1862. On March 13, he was further promoted to division commander in the V Corps of the Army of the Potomac. Our diarist has indicated that Brigadier General Williams led a brigade composed of the 46th Pennsylvania Regiment, the 5th Connecticut Regiment, the 28th New York Regiment and the 19th New York Regiment.

The 46th Pennsylvania Infantry was mustered into service September 4, 1861, under the command of Colonel Joseph F. Knipe. The author of the regimental history notes that,

> Soon after its organization, the 46th was ordered to General Banks command. Upon its arrival it was assigned to the First Brigade, of the Second Division, of his corps. Little of interest, save the usual drill and camp duty, and an occasional skirmish with the enemy, occurred until the opening of the spring campaign. Stonewall Jackson, with a well-appointed force of all arms, having for some time occupied the Shenandoah Valley, had pushed out as far west as Hancock where he was met and driven back by General Lander. Lander pursued but soon after died, and was succeeded in command by General Shields, who continued the pursuit to Winchester.[95]

During the period, late September 1861 to February, 1862, this regiment was stationed along the upper Potomac and did outpost and did guard duty in William's division.

The 5th Regiment of the Connecticut Infantry was organized at Hartford on July 26, 1861 and marched to Harper's Ferry, Virginia (now West Virginia) arriving July 30. The regiment remained there until August 16, 1861. The commanding colonel was Colonel O. S. Ferry. According to the regimental history of the 5th Connecticut Infantry, the troops received orders on the evening of January 5, 1862, to move at short notice. On January 6th, the men turned out at 4 and broke camp at 5 a.m., and marched out upon the road, the National Pike, three or four miles west of Frederick, and after some delay we moved forward. The soldiers had "marched all day in the snow and arrived at Hagerstown about 5 p.m."[96] The regimental historian adds that,

> The people opened the large buildings of the Female Seminary, at that time discontinued, for us, and we had a fine time, notwithstanding the disagreeable features of the day's march in a snow storm.[97]

The next day, the regiment marched on to Clear Spring and stayed in a meeting house for the night. On January 8, 1862, the 5th Connecticut left Clear Spring at 8 a.m. and entered Hancock about 5 p.m.

The 28th New York Infantry Regiment was organized at Albany and was mustered into service for two years beginning May 22, 1861. It was also known as the Niagara Rifles and the Scott Life Guard. Its commanding officers were Colonels Dudley Donnelly and Edwin F. Brown. During the period, December

5, 1861 until January 6, 1862, the unit was camped at Fredericksburg, Virginia. It was in Hancock by January 6, 1862 and stayed there until March 1, 1862. This account differs from what John King recorded in his diary. If the 28th New York did not arrive until 4 p.m. on January 6, it is difficult to imagine that it could have marched the same day to Hancock.

The 19th New York Infantry Regiment was mustered into service at Albany May 22, 1861. Also called the Cayuga County Regiment, the 19th was made up of nine companies from Cayuga County and one company from Seneca. Its commanders were Colonels John S. Clarke and James H. Ledlie. During the period, September 6 to the 25th of 1861, the regiment was camped at Darnestown. Then it was ordered to Muddy Branch and was assigned to General Williams' and thereafter marched to Hancock in December, where it remained until February 17, 1862. Another source adds the following:

> Although the rebels remained quiet on the upper Potomac, they were gathering there in large force. It was deemed expedient to strengthen the Federal lines there, and General Banks ordered the 3rd brigade to proceed to Hancock for this purpose. Preparing two days' rations, the brigade marched at 5 A.M. on January 6th, the 28th in advance with the 5th Connecticut, 46th Pennsylvania, and the 19th New York following in the order named, which was their regular order in the brigade. Camp was left standing by the 19th, for owing to the ice and snow tents could not be struck. Company F stayed to pack up and bring on the baggage. The sick were left under care of Dr. McClelllan, of the 5th Connecticut. The brigade, being temporarily under the command of Col. Donnelly, of the 28th New York, made a headlong march, through snow four inches deep, over mountain ranges and rough roads to Hagerstown. The 19th, nearly starved, without sufficient rations, was by Donnelly's orders, kept out in the open country that night, to bivouac and freeze in barns, while other regiments were housed and fed in the village(i.e., Hagerstown—Editor). The next day Gen. Williams overtook the command while plodding through the snow on another forced march of twenty-six miles, and at once halted it at Clear Spring, a good Union village, on the bank of the Potomac, after giving Donnelly a thorough talking to for his disgraceful treatment of the 19th.[98]

The 3rd Brigade did not enter Hancock until 3 p.m. on January 8, 1862, after the Confederates had left. After the Hancock siege, the 3rd Brigade went on to skirmish with Stonewall Jackson in the Shenandoah and to fight in the battles of First Kernstown, First Winchester, Cedar Mountain, Antietam, Chancellorsville, Gettysburg, Wauhatchie and Lookout Mountain. Another portion of the aforementioned article of January 10, 1862, from the *Hagerstown Mail* summarized the effects of Stonewall Jackson's Romney Campaign from a pro-Southern point of view:

> On Saturday the Confederates, to number of 6,000 to 8,000, drove the Federal troops across the Potomac to Hancock. Among the advance troops at Bath, six miles from the river, was Russell's cavalry, of this county, who lost their tents etc. Col. Light's Illinois regiment was also compelled to retire. In the meantime the Confederates destroyed the railroad, the bridges, the telegraph lines, this cutting off communication with Cumberland. Gen Lander arrived at Hancock on Sunday and took command of the Federal troops, to the number of about 3,000. On Sunday morning, the Confederates demanded the evacuation of the town by the Federal troops; but the demand was unheeded. The Confederates did not, as stated in the daily papers, then commence to shell the town. But a few shot, we believe, were thrown into the town, one of which passed through the hotel of Mr. Barton. It is said the Federals lost one man reaching the Maryland shore. On Monday the Confederates retired but reappeared in strong force. General? (Williams) of the 46th Penn, 19th and 28th York and 5th Conn. reached this town on Monday evening, having marched 26 miles upon snow, remained overnight and then left-the first named for Williamsport and the others for Hancock, where the latter arrived on Wednesday evening.[99]

Russell's Cavalry refers to Company I of the First Regiment Maryland Cavalry, of which Charles H. Russell was captain. Charles H. Russell entered service as a captain August 5, 1862, with the First Virginia Union Cavalry. On January 28, 1862, he was transferred to the First Maryland Cavalry and was later promoted to Major October 9, 1862. He was discharged on December 31, 1863.

The Hagerstown Female Seminary that John King mentions opened in 1853 and was operated by the Maryland Synod of the Evangelical Lutheran Church. In the summer of 1863, the buildings of the Female Seminary were used by the Confederates as a hospital.[100]

Thursday Jan. 9th 1862

This is a very disagreeable day the snow is melting and there was a little rain last night which froze and made walking very disagreeable.

Friday Jan 10th 1862

This is a day like yesterday, muddy and disagreeable walking. Last night there was a false alarm of fire, and Junior Engine was fooled out.

Saturday Jan. 11th 1862

It is cloudy this morning and looks very much like rain. Wm/" Armstrong and myself printed & wrote some Hose Co. notices for the Annual meeting for the election of Officers, as the Secretary was absent & the President neglected to do it. To-night was proud one for me, this Saturday night, Jan. 11" 1862. I J. Rigdon King was admitted as a member of the "First Hagerstown Hose Co.," the election was a spirited one, and each respective candidate worked hard, Ed. M. Mobley was beaten by Jno. Swartz, and Chas. Byers was elected first Vice President and Danl. K. Wantz was elected Recording Secretary. After the meeting the successful candidates treated at Capt. Heists.

January 11, 1862

John had worked fighting fires previously in town. Now he had the honor of being elected to the First Hagerstown Hose Company. He is obviously very proud of his accomplishment. John King shows considerable maturity and civil pride for a teenager of seventeen years. Ed. or Edward M. Mobley, a Republican, was president of the Hose Company beginning January 15, 1853 and was later elected Sheriff of Hagerstown in 1859.[101] He was born about 1824. Hence, at this time in 1862, he was about thirty-eight years of age, depending on whether his birthday was before or after June 20 in 1860. The home of the Sheriff was located next to the county jail on Jonathan Street and the 1860 U.S. Census was taken there. Living with Sheriff Mobley were his wife, Ellen C., born *c.* 1837, and seven sons, according to the census.[102] Also present in the jail were Henry Hoffman, the turnkey, Elizabeth Allenepa, servant, John Arehar, blacksmith, and Joseph Coxer, laborer. Edward M. Mobley later became better known as a soldier than as a sheriff. On August 8, 1862, Edward Mobley entered Union service as a Captain of Company A, Seventh Maryland Infantry. His regiment, combined with the 1st, 4th, 6th and 8th Regiments of Maryland Infantry with Alexander's Battery of Baltimore Light Artillery, under the command of Brigadier-General John R. Kenly, became known as the famous Maryland Brigade and served until the end of the war. Captain Mobley was promoted to Major January 21, 1864 and later to Brevet Lieutenant-Colonel April 4, 1865, for "gallant and meritorious services" during the campaign that resulted in General Lee's surrender at Appomattox Court House on April 9, 1865, where he was present. As we will learn later, our diarist will have a very important role to play in the regimental history of the Maryland Brigade.[103] After the Civil War, Captain Edward, nicknamed "Ned," Mobley worked in public service. A business directory for Hagerstown of 1875 shows E. M. Mobley as an assessor for the U.S. internal revenue, located at 4 Public Square.[104] Certainly, being an assessor was a much less glamorous and glorified job than that of an infantry commander. One of his ancestors, his great-grandson Charles "Jim" Mobley, cherishes the Colonels' old weapons of war, a cartridge box, a Savage revolver, and a sword as well as his dairies of his exploits in the Shenandoah Valley.[105]

Sunday Jan. 12th 1862

This morning the weather was cloudy, but about 10 O'clock it cleared up beautiful. I attended the M.E. Church this morning & heard an excellent sermon from the Rev. Harden of Chambersburg. I attended S. School in the afternoon and took charge of my class. I had five present. At night I went to the Lutheran Church, the first time for three or four years, and heard an ordinary sermon from their Pastor, Rev. Evens.

January 11, 1862 continued

However, in the Fire Hose Company election of January 11, 1862, Edward Mobley was not victorious. He was beaten in the voting for President by a tailor, John Swartz. On the 1860 U.S. Census, Mr. Swartz is shown as a tailor who was born in Hesse-Darmstadt in 1804.[106] In 1862, Mr. Swartz was approximately fifty-eight years old. Mr. Swartz' wife, Margaret and his oldest son, John D., were also born in Hesse-Darmstadt. His son, John D. was twenty-nine years old in 1860 and was also a tailor. On the census, two other sons were shown as were three daughters. The family was fairly well-off as shown by real estate of $5,000 owned by the father as well as $500 in personal property. Even the son, John D. is listed as owning personal property of $2,000. In any case, Mr. John Swartz won the election of January the 11th and had the honor of the next president of the Hagerstown Fire Hose Company.

The 1860 U. S. Census for Hagerstown shows that Byers family.[107] Listed in the household were the father, John, age forty-nine and his wife, Ann, age forty-eight. Charles was only sixteen years old. John Byers gave his occupation as a teacher. Charles was a very young First Vice President of the fire company.

The U.S. Census of 1860 taken June 6, shows that Daniel K. Wantz was also a young man when he was elected to the position of Recording Secretary of the First Hagerstown Hose Company on that Saturday evening of January 11th, 1862.[108] Daniel was also only sixteen years of age in 1860 and therefore only eighteen or nineteen at the time of the election. In 1860, he was living at home with him mother. Daniel gave his job as a clerk. Also present were a younger brother, an older sister and two other younger sisters. The family owned no real estate and estimated their personal property as being worth $175.

Hagerstown had no organized fire company before 1791[109] The citizens would have used the old "bucket brigade" system. In the early days of the town, buildings were constructed of wood and the roofs were also wooden. As there was no central heating, the households would have used open fireplaces for both cooking and heating. It must have been very easy for the sparks from a chimney to set a roof afire either on one's own home or store or that of a neighbor. Later, structures were built of more than two stories and the more wealthy owners requested brick construction.

Fire was a constant threat in these towns. Prior to 1790, Hagerstown residents used the services of "Dick" a young Negro boy who offered his services as a chimney sweep. Dick would travel the town every six weeks to clean the chimneys. The town imposed an ordinance which carried a "... fine of seven shillings and six pence for allowing chimneys to take fire and burn from the top."[110] The author added that, wood was the only fuel and most of the buildings and all of the roofs of the town were of wood and hence a chimney on fire was only to be prevented by the employment of a chimney sweep.[111] Finally, on New Year's Day of 1791, a public meeting was called "... for the purpose of organizing a regular fire company when all who choose to have their buckets insured please produce them in order that they may be inspected and registered."[112] At this meeting, the Union Fire Company was founded, but it was only to last until 1814. Early members were Jonathan Hager, founder of Hagerstown, Abraham King, Jacob King and eighty-nine other citizens. In 1815, the First Hagerstown Hose Company, also known as Engine 1, was organized. This company was incorporated by an act of the Maryland General Assembly in 1823. Therefore, by the time that John King had the honor of being elected to serve for it on January 11, 1862, at the young age of seventeen years, the company had been in operation for some time.

The First Hagerstown Fire Company is still in operation today and is one of five engine companies in the town.

Monday Jan. 13th 1862

This morning is windy and cold. While I am writing I hear the solemn peal of the Church Bell, which is enough to tell us that some Spirit has fled to peaceful rest. This morning Capt. Welsh brought his Co. in Town and Quartered in the County Hall.

Tuesday Jan. 14th 1862

This morning there is about 2 inches of snow on the ground and still snowing hard. To-night there was a grand Wedding in the Catholic Church a Miss Holm was married to a strange Gentleman.

Wednesday Jan. 15th 1862

This is a disagreeable morning hailing and raining, there was a little snow fell last night & had a job of cleaning the pavement. I took a little sleigh ride before breakfast with Davey Gumbert. After breakfast I went a sleighing with a friend went all around Town and then started for Funkstown. Got there is a short time warmed up and returned. I had a good deal of fun last night, Snow balling.

Thursday Jan 16th 1862

I was buisy all morning doing some sewing for myself and greasing shoes.

January 12, 1862

The pastor mentioned was Rev. J. Evans of St. John's Lutheran Church, who arrived in Hagerstown during December of 1860 and remained there until April of 1868, in answer to a call from the Lutheran Church.[113,114] Over these years, Rev. Evans officiated at numerous services and married many couples. In addition, he served on the Examining Committee of the Hagerstown Female Institute.[115]

January 13, 1862

Captain Welsh is Charles A. Welsh, captain of Company B, the Third Regiment, Potomac Home Brigade Infantry. Captain Welsh enlisted October 11, 1861 and was mustered out of service October 4, 1862.[116]

January 15, 1862

During the 19th and early 20th century, riding in a horse-drawn sleigh was a widespread recreational activity in the Eastern United States in the winter. People bundled up, covered themselves from the waist down with a heavy wool lap blanket and soared over the snowy countryside on wintry days. Some even carried boxes filled with hot embers as foot warmers. John and his unknown friend must have had a great time of it riding all the way to Funkstown and back, which was about five miles round-trip.

Davey Gumbert, one of Johns' best friends, was several years younger. David was born January 16, 1850, in Hagerstown. Hence, he was only twelve years old at the time of this diary entry.

Friday Jan. 17th 1862

This morning the weather is cold and cloudy. The Town is very dull to-day, and I have nothing of importance to note.

Saturday Jan. 18th 1862

This morning the weather is awful disagreeable. It is cold and raining very hard. Every thing is so dull as to leave me entirely without a note.

Sunday Jan. 19th 1862

This morning is very disagreeable raining hard. I went in company with Wm/" Armstrong to the Reformed Church and heard a very good sermon by their Pastor Rev. Wagnor, from the 10th chap. 14th verse of St. John. I attended S. School in the afternoon and had five scholars present. At night, I attended the Lutheran Church and heard a sermon by their Pastor Rev. Evens, from the 3rd Chap 4" verse of Paul's Epistle to the Romans.

Monday Jan 20th 1862

This morning it is raining very hard. I made application to-day for a situation in A. Levi's Store. I will get an answer this week. I received $2.50 to-day of G. House.

January 19, 1862

John Henry Bernard Wagner, Esq. and Samuel G. Wagner D.D. were two of Reverend Henry and Sarah Magdalene (Wiestling) Wagner's seven children. Both John and Samuel spent some time in Hagerstown during the Civil War. The pastor mentioned in this diary entry by John King was John Henry Bernard Wagner.

Zion Reformed Church was founded in 1770 and is the oldest building in Washington County, Maryland, that has been in continuous use as a church since it was built.[117] The church still stands at 201 North Potomac Street. During his tenure at Zion, Reverend Wagner performed at least twenty-two marriages from March 6, 1861 to June 15, 1864, according to the local newspapers of that era.[118,119]

The U.S. Census for 1860 shows a William Armstrong residing in Washington County, Maryland.[120] He was born in 1845 and was thus about seventeen years old in 1862. William was probably still in school in 1862. His father, sixty-two years old in 1860 was named Alex and his mother, aged fifty years was named Susan.[121] William Armstrong had two sisters and two brothers. The Armstrong's lived three doors down from the Gumbert's home and were wealthy. Mr. Armstrong's occupation was given as a "merchant."

January 20, 1862

An application "for a situation" is nineteenth-century vernacular for an application for employment. Abraham Levi ran a store in Hagerstown for a number of years. His first advertisement appeared in one of the local papers March 30, 1853.[122] Another advertisement mentioned dry goods, clothing, shoes and groceries for sale.[123]

Tuesday Jan 21st 1862

This morning I was hurried out of Bed by an alarm of Fire. I looked out of my window I seen a big blaze, I dressed in a hurry and ran up street & caught up with "F. H. H" Reel" and took ahold of the tongue & ran to the fire which was on Church St. it was a stable the property of Mr. Lookingland an old German I got very muddy.

Wednesday Jan 22th 1862

It is very muddy walking this morning. A detachment of the Michigan Cavelry stationed at Frederick brought 21 deserters through here on their way to Hancock. Capt. Harners(?) Cavelry left here this morning to guard the Telegraph from Fredk to Hancock.

January 20, 1862 continued

Still another advertisement spoke of coffee, spices and tobacco being available.[124] Levi's store was a basic mid-nineteenth century general store. It was located in a house across the street, i.e., South Potomac Street, from the Lutheran church and was thus on the same block as John's home. In an announcement placed February 24, 1864, Mr. Levi stated that he was "...intending to remove from Hagerstown" and apparently he did as his advertisements no longer appear in the newspapers.[125]

January 21, 1862

This is the first fire that John responded to since being elected to the town fire company, according to his diary. It is so close to home that he can see from his window. The "F. H. H." Reel that he refers to is the First Hagerstown Hose company and he apparently manned the reel carriage referred to earlier which held the hose. John does not mention the outcome of his company's firefighting efforts.

January 22, 1862

The only Michigan cavalry regiment stationed in the area was the First Michigan. The First Michigan Cavalry was organized at Detroit and was mustered into service September 13, 1861. The regiment was composed of twelve companies under the command of Colonel Thornton E. Broadhead. The First Michigan left Michigan for Washington, D.C. and then went to Frederick, Maryland, where it camped for several months. It was part of General Nathaniel Banks' command which had the task of guarding the Potomac line. In February of 1862, the regiment was stationed at Harper's Ferry and later relocated to the Shenandoah Valley to pursue Stonewall Jackson and his Confederate army as far south as Winchester, Virginia.[126]

Captain Horner is most certainly Captain John C. Harner of Company C, "Cole's Cavalry," First Regiment Potomac Home Brigade. John C. Horner was a wealthy farmer from Mounjoy, Adams County Pennsylvania. On the 1860 U.S. Census, he reported real estate valued at $7,350 and personal property at $6,500.[127] He organized Company C and was mustered into service August 27, 1861, along with his son, William, First Lieutenant and his nephew, Oliver A. Horner, 2nd Lieutenant. Captain Horner was fifty-nine years old at the time, an age hardly conducive for the arduous life of a cavalry commander. Cole's Cavalry, also called the First Regiment Potomac Home Brigade Cavalry, got its name from Captain Henry A. Cole, who was later promoted to Major, Lieutenant-Colonel and then Colonel.[128] Between August 10, 1861 and November 27, 1861, Companies A, C and D were organized at Frederick City while Company B was recruited at Cumberland, Maryland. Companies A, C and D picketed the fords and guarded telegraph lines along the left bank of the Potomac River from Frederick to Hancock during the winter of 1861-1862, as John King correctly notes in his diary.[129,130] Although other companies were added later, these four composed the heart of Cole's Cavalry. The regiment saw hard service scouting, raiding and skirmishing in Maryland, Virginia, West Virginia and Pennsylvania and may have rode as many as 7,000 miles during its four years of service. Captain Harner had to resign June 10, 1862 due to poor health and old age.[131]

Thursday Jan. 23rd 1862

To-day is a damp cloudy one and very dull with me. To-day the wife of Christian Mush was consigned to the silent Tombe, she was a young woman married only about 6 months.

Friday Jan. 24th 1862

This is an other damp and cloudy day. To-day A. Levi gave me an answer wither or not he would give me a situation, and it was in the affirmative, I go at five dollars pr. Month ($5"/)/ To-night I helped to wrap Kisses up at Geo. Bowmans, and we had plenty of fun.

Saturday Jan 25th 1862

This morning it is hailing, snowing and raining, and very disagreeable. I met with some Officers of the 1st/" Md/' Regt/", with whom I am acquainted.

Sunday Jan., 26th 1862

This morning is very cold and windy, otherwise a beautiful day. I attended M.E. Church and heard a splendid sermon from Rev. Norris of Waynesboro, from the 53d/" Chap. Isah 5" verse, "With His stripe are we healed" At night I went to the same place and heard a good sermon form Mr. Sears from (illegible) King's, 5" verse, there is a revival going on.

January 24, 1862

John King was continually working at one job or another and was frequently helping someone with a task. He must have been very energetic and quite capable. In this instance, he is helping a George Bowman "... to wrap Kisses." The Kisses mentioned are apparently a candy, perhaps not unlike the present day Hershey kisses. In any case, George W. Bowman, age sixty-nine, was a confectioner and baker in Hagerstown. His wife, Catharine, age fifty-nine, "kept house" and his son, George W., age nineteen, was a jeweler, per the 1860 U.S. Census taken June 2 at their residence.[132]

January 25, 1862

Unfortunately, John does not mention the names of the officers of the First Maryland Regiment. However, the First Maryland Infantry Regiment was the first to be recruited in Maryland and was commanded by Colonel John R. Kenly.[133] It was assigned to the defense of the Upper Potomac River and had been called to Hancock, Maryland, in response to General Stonewall Jackson's threat, earlier in January. It would remain on the upper Potomac until February 28, when it marched to Williamsport, Maryland. About this time, the First Maryland Regiment was brigaded with the 46th Pennsylvania Infantry, the 28th New York Infantry and 5th Connecticut Infantry to form a new brigade, the 3rd brigade of General Banks' Division commanded by General Alpheus S. Williams.[134] Under the reorganization of the Army, this brigade, would become the First Brigade, First Division, in the 5th Army Corps, until April of 1862.

Monday Jan 27th 1862

This morning I went into A. Levi's Store as clerk for $60-the first year, I got along tolerably well but it went mighty awkward with me. To-night I received a letter from Frank Darby, Balto., & I wrote one to Silas Hall of the 5" Regt. Conn. Vol., a member of the Band.

Tuesday Jan 28th 1862

This most an awful disagreeable day, it is raining and freezing. This is a tolerably busy day at the Store notwithstanding the disagreeableness. After 9 O'clock Dan Wantz and me went to church.

Wednesday Jan 29th 1862

This morning the Sun came out beautifully but about 10 O'clock clouded up and rained and then cleared up again, Pa & Bro. Mc/"

January 27, 1862

John R. King secured, what was possibly his first steady employment in the store of Abraham Levi and earned $5.00 a month. John mentions feeling awkward after his first day on a new job, but does not explain further. He probably just had first day jitters.

Abraham Levi was previously mentioned under the diary entry for January 20. Mr. Levi, born in Württemberg, Germany, about 1817, immigrated to the United States and arrived in Hagerstown by July 10, 1850, since he appears on the U.S. Census for that date.[135] At that time, he was single, gave his occupation as a merchant and resided with the Fred Sener family. According to a newspaper announcement of February 12, 1851, Abraham Levi married Pauline Arnold, also born in Württemberg, with the Reverend S. L. Levi presiding.[136] Abraham apparently rented a building for his store since the real estate records show no deeds in his name. By 1860, Abraham and his wife had six children, the oldest only eight years old.[137] Hence, none of the Levi children were old enough in January of 1862 to clerk in his store and that is possibly why he hired John King. Abraham Levi's last advertisement came November 18, 1863, and mentioned that he was "selling off at cost" his inventory of dry goods, clothing and shoes.[138] As stated earlier, in the February 24, 1864, edition of the town paper, Mr. Levi's advertisement stated that he "is intending to remove from Hagerstown."[139] Apparently unable to support a large family, Abraham Levi left town in 1864 and sought to ply his trade elsewhere. In the city directory of 1867 for Philadelphia, Pennsylvania, Abraham Levi is shown as having a clothing business at 514 South Street.[140] By 1870, Abraham was fifty-two years old and residing with his wife, Pauline, and their six children in Philadelphia.[141] He gave his occupation as a "retail clothier" and now owned real estate valued at $6,000 and personal goods worth $2,800. His oldest son, Mayer, age 18, also worked in the family business. Obviously, Abraham Levi's business fared much better in the big city of Philadelphia than it did during the eleven years it was open in Hagerstown. Perhaps, Mr. Levi was able to build a larger customer base with more expendable income in a heavily populated city.

Silas L. Hall is listed as a regimental musician in the official records of Fifth Regiment Connecticut Volunteers. He hailed from Westbrook and was mustered into the service July 23, 1861. Silas was mustered out August 16, 1862 and was residing in Wallingford, Connecticut after the war.[142]

January 28, 1862

This is the same Dan Wantz that had just been elected as Recording Secretary for the First Hagerstown Fire Company.

are busy getting ready to open a Store in Hancock, Pa goes up early in the morning in the Stage.

Thursday Jan 30th 1862

This is another very disagreeable day snowing & raining which has been the state of the weather for about four weeks. I was buisy a while this morning helping Bro. Mac/' to get ready to start for Hancock with things for the Store. Pa went early in the Stage. I went to church after 9 O'clock.

Friday Jan. 31st 1862

This is a beautiful day, and it being discount day at the Bank makes business brisk. At night after we shut up store I went to Church.

Saturday February 1st 62

This is the first day of February, and this morning we get up and find the ground covered with snow, but it does not last long the sun came out, and it soon disappeared. Buisiness was tolerable good to-day. It is reported that the 1st/' Md/" Regt., Capt. Russels Cavelry and Capt. Curls do. & Capt. Chas. Welsh's Co. was all going to Ft. Mc/"Henry, whether true or not I am not able to say.

January 29, 1862

This entry is the first time our diarist mentions his father, Samuel L. King. The brother "Mc/" or "Mac" that John refers to is actually his brother-in-law, Sam McLaughlin, who is married to his sister Addie. The distance from Hagerstown to Hancock, Maryland is 24.8 miles, which would have been a pretty good ride on horseback or by wagon.

January 30, 1862

Samuel King now opened a new retail business in the nearby town of Hancock, Maryland, the scene of Stonewall Jackson's recent bombardment.

January 31, 1862

Discount day is a particular day of the week when the bank discounts notes and bills.

February 1, 1862

Fort McHenry in Baltimore, Maryland, was employed by the Union as a military prison which housed not only Confederate soldiers but also many Maryland civilians who were thought to be Confederate sympathizers.

Sunday Feb. 2nd 1862

This is a beautiful day. I attended M. E. Church this morning and heard a good sermon from Mr. Sears, after which there was "Sacrament of the Lords Supper." I attended School & had five scholars present, I was also appointed one of a committee of three to investigate the condition of the Library. I went to Church at night and heard a powerful sermon from Mr. Sears, from the 4th Chap, 5" vers "John," there was four persons seeking religion.

Monday Feb. 3rd 62

This morning it commenced snowing and keeps up all day. I went to the Church at 5 O'clock & the committee appointed, investigated the condition of Library.

Tuesday Feb. 4th 62

This is very pleasant morning and sleighs are running. This was a mighty buisy day, the Store was crowded all day, the Town was lively. At night, I attended in infair (? an affair) of a Friends wedding Miss Cramer was married to John W. Crowley, of the 13" Mass. Regt/". I had a nice time I made the acquaintance of a good many members of that Regt/", I got home about Midnight.

February 2, 1862

John was chosen to check the condition of books in the church library. Perhaps the committee as a group would determine which books were in need of replacement.

This task is yet another example of the responsibilities that our diarist accepted. Whether of a civic, political or religious nature, John served in the community.

February 4, 1862

The marriage of Crawley (*sic*) Cramer appeared in the February 12th edition of the *Hagerstown Freedom and Torch Light* newspaper.[143] John W. Crowley enlisted as a private in Company K on July 16, 1861. He was born in East Boston, Massachusetts and was twenty-one years old at the time of enlistment.[144] His occupation was as a lastmaker. Private Crowley was dropped from the rolls August 16, 1863, the reason not given. Perhaps he had only enlisted for a two-year period.

The Thirteenth Massachusetts Regiment spent time during the fall and winter of 1861 guarding the fords and dams along the Potomac River. They went into camp, called Camp Jackson, near Williamsport, Maryland on October 13, 1861, and remained there until March 1, 1862, when the regiment crossed the Potomac and marched into Virginia. Only a few miles from Hagerstown, many soldiers made the brief journey to explore the sites and socialize with the citizens. The Glee Club of the regiment sang in Hagerstown on January 15, 1862, and was to sing again in a second concert at Lyceum Hall Tuesday evening, February 4.[145] Edwin E. Davis, Jr. wrote in his history of the regiment:

Wednesday Feb 5th 1862

This is a bitter cold morning. There was a right brisk buisinefs done to-day. I received a letter from Pa at Hancock, and he is doing right well, Mc/" is in Town.

Thursday Feby 6th 1862

This morning it is hailing and very disagreeable. Bro. Mc/" went to Hancock with a pretty good load. This evening one Co. of the Michigan Cavelry brought here a lot of deserters from Frederick, and are going to take them to Hancock. I received a letter from B. F. Darby & Co. this evening.

Friday Feby 7th 1862

This is a most delightful morning. This being discount day at the Banks, makes business brisk. Towards evening it clouded up and got cold. Bro. came down from Hancock to-day.

Saturday Feby. 8th 1862

This morning it is cloudy and cold, and looks as if we would have snow. This was a right buisy day in the Store. There was another grand victory in "Old Kintuck" the other day, which resulted in the taking of Ft. Henry on the Tennessee River, by our forces under Gen. Garnet, we took the Rebel Gen. Tilghman of Balto. & his staff, a large amount of Prisoners & ammunition ordnance etc. Last night Tom Hilliard, Dan Wantz, Walter Mobley & myself rode around in a buggy & had lots of fun. Report says that Gen Lander has taken Romney Va. and the Rebels left without fighting.

February 4, 1862

Hagerstown, the place where we first landed on our journey from home, was only six miles away, and was the shire town of Washington County. Many were the visits we paid that place, and many the acquaintances we made among the people. The provost marshal of the town was an officer detailed from the Thirteenth, and his administration of martial law was liberal as it was sensible, though when occasion required he could be as inexorable as circumstances needed. All but twelve members of Company B served in Hagerstown as part of the Provost Guard. Company D was also stationed there part of the time, therefore no lack of inducement existed to make it a pleasant place to visit.[146]

February 8, 1862

Tom Hilliard, one of John King's best friends, was mentioned earlier. Walter Mobley, another friend, was about seventeen years old in 1862. On the 1860 U.S. Census, his father, Ely, stated that he was a "master coach maker" and gave his real estate worth as $1,200 and personal property as $1,000.[147]

Sunday Feby 8th 1862

This is a very cold, clear day. I attended M. E. Church this morning and heard a very forcible sermon from Mr. Sears, Book of "Daniel 6th/" Chap. " verse. I attended S. School in the afternoon and had three (3) scholars present. After School the committee on the Library finished their work.

Monday Feby 10th 1862

This morning is bitter cold. About 10 O'clock Capt. Hampton's Artilery paraded the streets it consists of 6 10 pound Parrot Guns. Buisiness tolerably good in the store to-day. I received a letter from a Lady friend of Beaver Creek.

February 8, 1862 continued

An older sister, Lavenia, was in the household as well as an older brother, Peter, who said he was a "journeyman coach maker." Other employees of the father's business were also shown, John Eagle, an apprentice coach maker, and Isaac Peters, an apprentice blacksmith. John "Rig" King also mentions another friend, Dan Wantz. According to the 1860 Census for Hagerstown, Daniel Wantz was a sixteen year old clerk.[148] He resided with his mother, Eliza, age forty-four and an older brother, George, who was a painter, an older sister, Sarah, one younger brother, John P., and two younger sisters, Eliza and Rebecca. The Wantz family was not wealthy as evidenced by the lack of real estate ownership and only $75 worth of personal property.

Not surprisingly, Walter Mobley and Daniel Wantz joined the same Union regiment and company, probably as soon as they turned eighteen years of age. Mobley became a corporal in the 7th Maryland Infantry after enlisting August 18, 1862 and Dan Wantz was a private after being mustered in August 27, 1862.[149] Both survived the war and were mustered out during May of 1865. Five years after end of the Civil War, Walter was employed with his father as a coach maker and lived at home.[150] Dan worked in "land forestry" in 1870 and was residing in the household of Sarah Keller.[151]

February 9, 1862

John incorrectly gave both his Saturday and Sunday diary entries as February, but the second entry is actually Sunday, February 9.

February 10, 1862

A "Parrot Gun" was a type of cannon invented by Robert P. Parrott in 1860 at the West Point Foundry in Cold Spring, New York.[152] They were capable of firing 10, 20 and 30 pound elliptical-shaped rounds.

Captain Robert B. Hampton was born on November 14, 1814, at Rock Hill in Fauquier County, Virginia. Following the death of his parents at a young age, he was reared by his aunt, Miss Kittie Shacklett, at her farm known as Yew Hill near Warrenton, in Fauquier County.[153] Before the war, Captain Hampton was a merchant. He recruited and organized Battery F in Pittsburgh during August and September of 1861. His battery was mustered into Union service October 8, 1861, to serve for three years or for the war. The Battery had sixty-nine original members and was placed under the command of General Nathaniel Banks, General Williams' Division.[154] Captain Hampton and his men were ordered to Williamsport, Maryland, and encamped at Camp Lamon nearby October 11. Soon thereafter,

> Captain Hampton and a squad of men, crossed the Potomac River at Dam No. 5 and burned the old mill at that place, which the enemy had been using as a rendezvous, and returned with a lot of blankets, entrenching tools, etc. and found the dam but little damaged.[155]

Tuesday Feby 11th 1862

This is a beautiful morning but bitter cold. Buisiness was very brisk at the Store and I was kept very buisy, this morning Capt. Chas. Welsh's Infantry Co. left Town for Frederick where they will be attached to a Regt/". I recd/" a Telegraphic dispatch from Pa. to order some goods by Express from Balto.

Wednesday Feby 12th 1862

This is a very pretty morning, business tolerably. Today we got glorious news. A dispatcher came to the effect that Gen. Burnside with his Navel Expedition, had taken Roanoke Island, 1000 Rebels killed & 5 or 10 our prisoner, later news is that Norfolk is taken, I hope it may be true. Ex Gov. Wise is reported taken prisoner!

February 10, 1862 continued

On January 1, 1862, they were ordered to support General Lander at Hancock, Maryland, and had their first engagements with Confederate forces from January 4 through January 6. Next, as reported in their history,

> On January 27th, we broke camp at Williamsport, marched to Hagerstown, Maryland, on February 1st, 1862, we received our equipment-six ten-pound Parrot guns and one-hundred and ten horses, with battery wagon, forge, harness, etc.[156]

Of note is that our diarist got the number of cannons exactly right. Captain Hampton and his battery must have been very proud of the new guns that they paraded down the streets of Hagerstown. Their camp at Hagerstown was named Camp Bradford. However, they received new orders to move again and then marched to Boonsboro on February twelfth and arrived in Frederick, Maryland, February thirteenth.[157] Battery F saw action in many of the major battles of the Civil War, including Antietam, Second Bull Run, Gettysburg, Cedar Creek, Second Winchester, and Chancellorsville. Unfortunately, Captain Hampton did not survive the latter battle. As a part of Captain Best's large battery attempting to impede the charging Confederates on the fiercest day of fighting, Sunday, May 3, 1863,

> Captain Hampton, waiting to give the enemy a last round, was struck by a shell above the left knee, which severed the leg completely and cut his horse almost in two.[158]

The Confederates had captured one of Captain Best's batteries and turned the guns on the Federals. At the age of forty-seven, Captain Hampton was dead. However, his famous unit fought on throughout the rest of the war until mustered out of service on June 26, 1865. Battery F was also given the honor of leading the funeral procession in Washington D.C. that carried the body and coffin of President Lincoln from the White House to the train that took him home to Springfield, Illinois for interment.

February 12, 1862

Brigadier General Ambrose Burnside commanded the Union forces in an attack on Roanoke Island, North Carolina, in what became known as the Burnside Expedition. A Union infantry force of about 13,000 soldiers and naval supporting ships attacked a Confederate force of less than 3,000 under the initial command of the former Governor of West Virginia, Henry A. Wise. The battle took place on February 7 and 8, 1862. However, Brigadier General Wise was ill with pleurisy and was confined to bed in Nags Head, North Carolina.[159]

Thursday Feby 13th 1862

This is a beautiful morning, like that of one in June. This evening we got definite news from Roanoke Island, taken by Gen. Burnside; the fight last nearly three days, great slaughtering on both sides over one thousand killed and wounded on the Rebel side and six or eight hundred on the Union side, the Federal troops took over 3000 prisoners, the forces also attacked Elizabeth City N.C., and that was evacuated and set on fire. The Federal Troops are reported marching on Edenton, N.C. The Rebels at Norfolk are in great consternation, they fear an attack on that place, the place has been reinforced by 10,000 Troops. We can expect stirring from that direction soon.

Friday Feby 14th 1862

This is another disagreeable morning cold, damp and raining. Buisiness was tolerably brisk in the Store.

Saturday Feby 15th 1862

This morning it commenced to snow about 7 O'clock & snowed very hard. I went to Hancock with Bro. Mc/", and had a very hard time of it, the Horse I drove was not rough shod and going up a hill he was all the time slipping. We was stopped three times by the Pickets

---

February 12, 1862 continued

The Confederate second in command, Colonel Henry M. Shaw, was overwhelmed by the superior force challenging him and surrendered his troops on February 8, 1862. A total of 2,675 Confederate soldiers and 32 cannon were given up, but the casualties were only 264 Union soldiers and 143 Rebel troops.[160] Roanoke Island remained in Union hands for the remainder of the war. Thus, the news that our diarist received four days after the battle was generally correct, but the number of Confederate casualties and prisoners was exaggerated. Brigadier General Wise was not taken prisoner. One-thousand Confederates were not killed. In addition, the City of Norfolk would not be surrendered to Federal forces until May of 1982. However, the loss of Roanoke Island opened up the road to Norfolk and Norfolk was vital to shipbuilding.

February 13, 1862

The news of the Battle of Roanoke John received the next day was also erroneous. The battle did not last three days and there was no "great slaughtering." Once again, the newspaper reports apparently exaggerated the casualty figures. Like the capture of Roanoke Island, the Battle of Elizabeth City was a minor engagement as part of the "Burnside Expedition." It occurred on February 10, 1862, when the U.S. Navy's North Atlantic Blockading Squadron attacked and defeated the Confederate Navy's so-called Mosquito Fleet. The retreating Rebels set fires in Elizabeth City over an area of several blocks which were then extinguished by advancing Union forces.[161] The number of casualties on both sides was minimal with only two killed and seven wounded in the Union fleet and only four killed, six wounded and thirty-four captured among the Confederates.[162] The town of Edenton, North Carolina was taken February 12, 1862, by the Federals without any casualties.

of the 1st/" Md/" Regt/", we reached the Town about 12 O'clk. We unloaded our Wagons fed the Horses & unpacked the goods, and laid down about 4 O'clock in the morning & slept.

Sunday Feby. 16th 1862

This morning I feel mighty rocky, (?) not getting much sleep. This is a beautiful morning, the Sun shining in all his glory. Sam and I started for Home about 12 O'clock and I had a hard time of it, my Horse being bare-footed got very lame, and managed to get to Clearspring, so there here we got a Blacksmith to put shoes on him. We stopped at Mr. Newcommers and had a nice supper of hot Buckwheat Cakes and hot Coffee we got home at 9 O"clock.

February 15, 1862

John called his brother-in-law, Sam McLaughlin, his Bro. Also, Sam and John's father had recently opened a retail store in Hancock, Maryland, and John and Sam were restocking the merchandise. It seems they could not have picked a worse day to travel.

February 16, 1862

Hancock, Maryland to Clearspring, Maryland is 13.5 miles, a long way to go with a shoeless horse. The distance from Clearspring back home to Hagerstown was 11.3 miles, but John mentions that he and Sam stopped at "Mr. Newcommers" beforehand. John mentioned "Newcommers" often in his diary, beginning on October 23, 1861, when he went there to meet his sister, Addie McLaughlin, on a business trip to Hancock, Maryland. He said at that time that it was about four miles from Hagerstown, but never actually tells us what kind of establishment it was "Newcommers" was a tavern and a stage stop located 4.28 miles west of Hagerstown on what is now called US40. Newcomer Tavern Stand was a two story, well-made, large building made of fieldstone, as are many early Frederick and Washington county structures. Newcomer's tavern was located on the historic road and was a very busy establishment in its heyday. As Williams notes in his *History of Washington County,*

> After the making of the National Turnpike road the Hagerstown taverns became stopping places for the enormous travel between the East and the West, and their yards were crowded with teamsters, wagons, stage coaches, sheep and cattle on the way to the East or West.[163]

The tavern was on a tract called "Rocky Spring" and consisted of 1,124 and ¾ acres granted in a patent of April 30, 1800, to Martin Kershner.[164] Major Martin Kersher was a member of the Maryland legislature and a Justice of the Peace. His heirs sold the tract on which the tavern is located to Daniel H. Newcomer on April 11, 1843.[165] The date of construction was not recorded, but one prior owner suggested 1812.[166] The 1860 U.S. Census at the Newcomer home showed David to be fifty-two years old and his wife, Elizabeth, age thirty-one years.[167] There were no children present. The occupation of the head of the household was shown as "farmer." David Newcomer listed his real estate holdings as being $8,000 in value and his personal property as only worth $50. Newcomer had previously purchased other portions of Rocky Spring in 1844, 1854 and 1855.[168] The property was listed as for sale in 1865, but did not sell until years later. An advertisement dated September 6, 1865, was placed in the *Herald & Torch Light* newspaper of September 13, 1865,[169] and read:

Monday Feby 17th 162

This is a very disagreeable day, it is hailing & raining. There are rumors afloat that Ft. Donnelson on the Cumberland River is taken by the Federal Troops, great slaughtering is reported on both sides.

Tuesday Feby 18th 162

This is an ugly morning, very damp and cloudy. This is always considered a buisy day in the Store, but it was not so to-day owing to the bad state of the weather. I sold 1500 Cigars to Wm/" Wetrzenberger, at $6 pr. thousand.

Wednesday Feby 19th 162

This is another most awful disagreeable day, raining and snowing. We have definite news from Ft. Donelson, on the Cumberland River, it was attacked on Friday Feby 14", the attack was kept up until Sunday morning, when it was surrendered unconditionally to Gen. Grand of the Union Troops, there was desperate fighting on both sides, and great loss of life, Gen. A. S. Johnson & Gen,______ two other Gens. name I forgot & 15000 Prisoners.

February 16, 1862 continued

Tavern Stand
at
Public Sale

The undersigned will expose to Public Sale in front of the Court House in Hagerstown, On Tuesday, September 26th, 1865, that well known and valuable Tavern Stand situate 4 miles West of Hagerstown on the Western Turnpike, formerly kept by the late David Newcomer, deceased. There are **THIRTY-FOUR ACRES OF LAND,** (more or less,) belonging to the property, and is in a good state of cultivation The improvements consist of **Stable, Blacksmith Shop** and a comfortable **Brick Dwelling House** belonging to the Blacksmith Shop

The sale will take place at 10 o'clock on said day, when the terms will be made known

For particulars, call upon or address the undersigned, residing on the premises

David H. Newcomer

The tract of land known as "Rocky Spring" was finally sold by David H. Newcomer and his wife, Elizabeth, to Jacob Funk (of Jno.) for $1,868 March 23, 1868, and the deed was recorded May 20, 1868.[170] The old building was restored and now is a private residence.

February 19, 1862

The news that reached John by word of mouth or by newspaper was mostly correct this time. The Battle of Fort Donelson, fought from February 11 to February 16, 1862, was a major victory for Brigadier General Ulysses S. Grant and the North and a complete disaster for the Confederacy. Other Union Brigadier Generals present were John A. McClernand, Charles F. Smith and Lew Wallace.

Thursday Feby 20th 1862

This has been a delightful day over head, but very sloppy and muddy. We are buisy in the store, taking an inventory of the Stock and it is a pretty hard job. This evening about 7 O'clock, Capt. Matthews Battery of 6 pieces came into Town.

February 19, 1862 continued

Brigadier General John B. Floyd was the Confederate commander of the fort with Brigadier General Gideon J. Pillow second in command and Brigadier Simon Bolivar Buckner third in command. Troop strength was "… three divisions facing the Confederate two, eleven brigades investing seven, 27,500 troops in blue opposing 17,500 in gray."[171] In the end, many Confederates were captured, but many others, including Brigadier General Bushrod Johnson, simply escaped by walking away. In addition, Colonel Bedford Forrest with seven hundred of his cavalry and some infantry escaped on horseback.[172]

Brigadier General Buckner thought that he might get generous terms from Grant because they had previously known each other and because Buckner had lent Grant some money and other "… certain personal services …" earlier when Grant had returned to California in disgrace.[173] Such was not to be the case. In fact, Brigadier Grant gave no terms and demanded that the Confederates surrender "unconditionally." It is here that Ulysses S. Grant earned the sobriquet "Unconditional Surrender" Grant. Neither side ever provided the total number of prisoners taken at the battle, because a formal count was not taken and no one knew how many Confederates just walked away at the end. Brigadier General Buchrod Johnson was one of the Confederate soldiers who left the scene on foot.[174] One author suggests that 507 Union soldiers were killed, 1,976 wounded, and 208 were captured or missing and on the Confederate side, 327 killed, 1,127 wounded and 12,393 captured or missing.[175] Brigadier Generals Floyd and Pillow were soon reprimanded by President Jefferson Davis for their conduct on several counts and both were relieved of command.[175] Grant was promoted to Major General by President Lincoln for his achievement. Brigadier Simon Bolivar Buckner would later be elected Governor of Kentucky.

In summary, although a portion of what John heard or read was true, i.e., that the Union had secured a major victory at Fort Donelson with an unconditional surrender, some of the news was simply once again exaggerated by the press. One general was taken prisoner, Brigadier General Buckner, not four. The number of prisoners taken was really not known. Lastly, compared to many other battles during the Civil War, while there may have been "desperate fighting," there really was not "great loss of life" at Fort Donelson.

February 20, 1862

Captain Ezra W. Matthews was mustered into service July 8, 1861 for three years of service. He was commander of Battery F of the First Pennsylvania Light Artillery until April 11, 1863, when he was promoted to Major. As such, he served under Major General Abner Doubleday's Third Division of the First Army Corps.[177] Battery F was initially furnished by the State of Pennsylvania during August of 1861 with horses, equipment and only four smooth bore pieces and was soon transferred to the Reserve Corps at Tenallytown.[178] On October 8, 1861, two Parrott steel rifled, ten-pounder guns were added to the battery and it got orders to report to Williamsport, Maryland.[179] A portion of Battery F was sent during early January of 1862 to support General Lander in resisting and causing the retreat of General Stonewall Jackson at Hancock, Maryland. According to Battery F's regimental history:

> Until February, 1862, the guns were kept in motion singly and in sections between Edward's Ferry and Hancock, occasionally engaging detachments of the enemy. On the 20th, the sections were united in Hagerstown, where new equipments were received, and the guns furnished by the State were exchanged for six regulation, three-inch, rifled guns, together with new carriages and Sibley tents. The morning report of the first of March showed its effective strength to be 119 officers and men, with 105 horses. On the same day, the battery moved to Williamsport, where it crossed the river with Bank's advance, and moved on up the Shenandoah Valley.[180]

Matthews' battery had engagements at Bunker Hill, Virginia, and then against Ashby at Newton, Virginia, where they were routed. Colonel Turner Ashby was General Stonewall Jackson's cavalry commander.

Friday Feby 21st 1862

This (day?) the weather is cold and cloudy. This morning David Darby Esqr, of Baltimore, of the firm of Darby & Co. came to see me.

Saturday Feby 22nd 1862

This being the 22d/" of February, the birthday of the Father of our Country, Geo. Washington, the Town is pretty lively at 12 O'clock Capt. Matthews Battery fired a National salute, the farewell address of Washington was read by D. Weisel Esq. and a military parade.

February 20, 1862 continued

Next, at the Battle of Second Bull Run or Second Manassas from August 28 to August 30, 1862, Battery F suffered numerous losses and casualties. The battery was placed on the left of the Union line of battle, near the old Henry House, but the Confederates charged in mass and the section of the battery under Lieutenant Brockway had no means of escape since the enemy also held the Sudley Springs Road.[181] All of those guns were lost and only three of thirty-five of the men involved were left.[182] Then, another gun and caisson were lost as well as eight more men, leaving only one gun that was saved. Fortunately for Battery F, some guns and horses were available from an Indiana battery for a partial refitting.[183] Overall, during the series of engagements with General Pope's Virginia campaign, which included Second Bull Run of course, Captain Matthews' Battery F lost eight men killed, fifteen wounded and five captured for a total of twenty-eight. However, the battery did not cease to exist. Instead, it opened the Battle of Sharpsburg (the Confederate name) or Antietam (the Union name). And, once again, it suffered numerous losses, including four men killed, fifteen wounded, and the loss of most of its horses being killed or wounded.[184] Antietam was a one-day battle of immense casualties on both sides that was fought on September 17, 1862. Battery F ended up losing four of their six guns during the battle and on September 23, Captain Ezra W. Matthews relinquished command due to illness and would never resume command of this unit. Battery F of the First Pennsylvania Light Artillery received new recruits and was again refitted and went to fight at Chancellorsville, the Wilderness, Cold Harbor and at Petersburg. The history of Battery F illustrates the dangers of being an artillerist on either side during the Civil War. Casualties of men and animals were high. Either with or without infantry support, the enemy soon sighted the position of opposing batteries. If their charging infantry did not route you out of your position, there was always a good chance that the enemy batteries would sight your position and deliver a hot welcome of cannon balls or Parrott shells.

February 21, 1862

John finally tells the name of one of the Darbys from the Baltimore where he buys his cigars wholesale for resale in Hagerstown. However, he fails to mention why David Darby is in town.

February 22, 1862

Daniel Weisel was born January 25, 1803, at Williamsport, Maryland to Daniel W. Weisel (b. April 19, 1765) of Bucks County Pennsylvania and Margaret Startzman (b. Sept. 16, 1773).[185] Judge Weisel then graduated from Princeton University in 1824, read law and was admitted to the bar in 1826, and began the practice of law in Hagerstown and Williamsport.[186] In 1847, Lawyer Weisel was appointed associate judge of the judicial district made up of Frederick, Washington and Alleghany counties by Governor Pratt, due to the death of Thomas Buchanan.[187] However, this judgeship ended in 1852. Then, in an election of 1861, Judge Dan Weisel defeated the incumbent, Thomas Johns Perry, for the position of judge of the Fourth Judicial Circuit, which included both Washington and Alleghany counties. In total, the Honorable Daniel Weisel spent over fifty years both as a lawyer in private practice and as a judge in the service of his community.

Sunday Feby 23rd/62

To-day I was with two Friends of the 13th/" Mass. Rgt/" ER Marsh & Mr. Baunert, both good fellows. I attended S. School and had three scholars present, I attended the Lutheran Church at night and heard a poor sermon.

February 22, 1862 continued

A The 1860 presidential election returns for Washington County were surprising. Was the county primarily Democratic or Republican? It voted primarily Democratic, but that "... vote was divided and that lost the election."[188] John Bell of Tennessee and of the Constitutional Union party got 2,567 votes, Democrat John Breckinridge of Kentucky garnered 2,475, Democrat Stephen Douglas of Illinois received 283 and Republican Abraham Lincoln of Illinois got only 95 votes.[189] Lincoln was able to secure only twelve votes in Hagerstown.[190] Many Hagerstonians were upset with the election results and by January of 1861 were beginning to align themselves with political factions. However, the large number of votes cast for Breckinridge did not mean that one-half of Washington County favored succession if he was defeated.[191] Some of the leaders of Washington County urged moderation and restraint. One such person was Judge Weisel who served on several pro-Union committees to adopt resolutions stating their position. He was chairman of at least one such committee and also gave pro-Union and pro-Constitutional speeches including one on January 3, 1861, in Williamsport, Maryland, where a Union flag was raised with a motto that read, "Constitution and the Union."[192] Then, on January 15, the residents of the county assembled at the Court House in Hagerstown and according to historian Williams "...regardless of party and it was at this meeting that the first sign was made of that violent division of sentiment which afterwards drifted into rancorous hate."[193] On the following Saturday, January 19, 1861, a group of strong Unionists withdrew and organized an outdoor meeting in the Square of Hagerstown and Daniel Weisel gave a pro-Union speech reporting the moderate stance of his group. At that time, with snow falling, Judge Weisel said:

> As much as we deeply regret the election of men to the highest office of the Republic, nominated and sustained by a section, yet we do not regard their election as a cause for revolution; that their election should have been resisted at the ballot box, in the Union, by the united votes of those who were opposed to them, and failing in their duty, it does not now become us to revolutionize or overturn the government, because of their election, but it is the duty of all good citizens to submit to the Constitutional action of the people, and to judge of the incoming administration by its acts and measures, holding ourselves ready to resist by all Constitutional means any aggressions upon the rights of any portion of the Country; and never except when grievances become intolerable, and the necessity becomes absolute to resort to revolutionary action for relief or change.[194]

Daniel Weisel served as judge of the Circuit Court until November 8, 1863, when he was elected to the Court of Appeals of Maryland and continued in this position until 1867.[195] Overall, the Honorable Daniel Weisel spent over fifty years both as a lawyer in private practice and as a judge in the service of his community.

February 23, 1862

E. P. Marsh, age 24, born in Newfare, Vermont, was a clerk before the war. He was mustered into Company D of the 13th Massachusetts Regiment on July 16, 1861 and was mustered out as a commissary sergeant August 1, 1864 and then resided in Greenfield, Massachusetts.[196] Thus, this soldier friend of Johns was six years older than him. No listing was shown for a Mr. Baunert in the 13th Massachusetts. Apparently, John misspelled the name "Baunert" since no soldier with that name appears on the regimental roster of the 13th Mass. The Lutheran Church John refers to was St. John's Lutheran Church at 141 South Potomac Street in Hagerstown, across the street from the King residence. This church was established in 1770, was built in 1795 and still stands today.

Monday Feby 24th/62

To-day we commence to take Stock in earnest and we are very buisy. This evening windiest evenings I have experienced for a long while.

Tuesday Feby 25/62

This morning it is cold and clear. There are reports afloat that our forces at Williamsport crossed the River last night, some contradict it.

Wednesday Feby 26/62

To-day it is very cold and windy. We are very buisy in the Store taking Stock, which is a mighty ugly job.

Thursday Feby 27th/62

To-day it is again very cold and the wind is blowing a perfect hurricane. To-day we finished taking an Inventory of the Stock, and I am mighty glad of it. To-night I slept with Dan.Wantz up at the other Store.

Friday Feby 28" 1862

Today it is still very windy and cold. This always considered a buisy day at the Store, but it is very dull to-day.

Saturday March 1st 62

This a tolerably fine day buisinefs good. There are rumers current that the "U.S." Troops are crossing at Williamsport.

Sunday March 2d 1862

This morning I concluded to go to Williamsport to see the Troops cross the River, I got a seat in Geo. Middlekauffs Omnibus and went over, arrived about 11 ½ Oclock, went to the River, but seen them

---

February 24, 1862

John continues to work in Abraham Levi's store and is apparently taking an inventory of the stock in the store.

all on the other side, the Bands playing "Dixie," the Regts/' crossed were the 1st/" Maryland 12" Indiana 46 Pa 28" N.Y, 13 Mass and 5" Conn., under Brig. Gen. A. S. Williams of Michigan. Martinsburg was occupied in the evening without resistance.

Monday March 3rd 1862

This morning I left Abrm/" Levi's Store to learn the Photographic business with J. E. Norris, he is to learn me for $15.00/". I squared accts. with Levi and left. I bought a Sloutch Hat for $1.50/".

March 2, 1862

Our diarist, John, went on a Sunday drive riding on an omnibus to observe the crossing of Union troops over the Potomac River by ferry. Many of the citizens of both Hagerstown and Williamsport had become friends with the soldiers. They came out to say their farewells at the time of the crossing. In addition, people of the nineteenth century, much as we do today, enjoyed watching troops in movement whether watching a parade or observing them cross a river. Apparently, many citizens from Hagerstown and from Williamsport came out to watch the spectacle. George G. Middlekauff is shown on the 1860 U.S. Census, taken June 4, in Hagerstown as a twenty-six year old "livery man," meaning that he worked in a livery stable caring for horses.[197] It is not surprising that he would have an omnibus available, for rental. The household head and all of his children were born in Maryland. George told the census taker in 1860 that his personal property was worth $1,600 (no doubt his horses, saddles, and riding vehicles such as carriages) and that he owned no real estate. Living with him at that time were Mary Middlekauf, age 19 years, and Ella Middlekauf, age two months. While no wife is listed, there is also another woman in the home, Ellen Cunningham, with no occupation given. George also told the census taker that he owned no real estate.

An omnibus might be described as a cross between a carriage and a stagecoach. It is a horse-drawn, four-wheeled carriage with seats for multiple passengers. The word is defined as "carriage for all, common conveyance," from L. omnibus "for all" and was introduced by Laffitte in Paris in 1820.[198] The body is an enclosed rectangular box with walls and a top for protection from the elements and with windows for viewing. New York City used omnibuses from 1827 to 1907 which ran along established routes, much like a modern motorized bus. So John and probably some of his friends most likely contacted George at the livery stable and rented the omnibus for a Sunday afternoon excursion so that they could express their well wishes and, at the same time, view the spectacular crossing. There was no pontoon bridge at Williamsport for a quick and easy crossing. Instead, there was a swing ferry in place. A swing ferry was simply a ferryboat attached to a cable that made use of the river current.

John states in his diary that all six regiments of General Williams' brigade had already crossed the Potomac River by the time he got there Sunday morning at about 11:30 a.m. on March 2 and were on the Virginia side playing "Dixie."

March 3, 1862

Joseph E., J. E. or Joe Norris is a previously unknown Maryland photographer. He is not listed on any list of 19th century photographers in the United States nor is he shown in any Hagerstown business directory. However, the Joseph E. Norris that "Rig" makes reference to here is probably the same Joseph Norris who lived one door away from John's uncle, Charles G. Lane, on North Potomac St. Mr. Norris was born *c.* 1833 in Virginia, lived with his mother and sister and was employed as a printer. He may have had a secondary interest in ambrotype photography and thus taught it to John King. According to his obituary, Joseph E. Norris

> ... was well-known in this city, being for a number of years engaged in the newspaper business. In 1870, in company with Emmert Fechtig and William P. Gruber, he established the *Twice-A-Week*, afterward known as the *Yeoman's Guard and Democrat*, but which suspended in the year 1879. He was a forcible and entertaining writer, and after leaving Hagerstown was engaged by a historical publishing firm in Chicago and for several years was employed in compiling war records of various sections of the South and West.[199]

Tuesday March 4 1862

This morning I go to work with J. E. Norris to learn the Photographic Art; toward evening I began to take a picture. At night I attended the Theatre that is in Town at present, it was right good. Pa came from Hancock today.

Wednesday March 5 1862

Pa went (or tried to go) to Martinsburg to-day. I was at work to-day at my new profession, and getting along very well.

Thursday March 6 1862

This is a tolerably clear day. I am progressing finely with my new business. I took a very good picture of Ben. House (Col.)

Friday March 7th 1862

This morning I went down to Dr. Fahney, to consult him about Ma, who is very poorly, he said her case was evidently a bad one, one not very easily remedied, he gave me some medicine for her. I stopped at Mr. Henry Fishach's as I came back and got dinner there In enjoyed myself very much with the young Ladys.

March 4, 1862

An article appeared in the March 5, 1862 issue of the *Hagerstown Freedom & Torch Light* announcing a theatrical troupe performing at Lyceum Hall.[200]March 6, 1862

The 1860 Hagerstown U.S. Census lists a Benjamin House residing in a home with his parents, George and Harriet.[201] Benjamin was nineteen years old. Hence, as of this diary entry, he would have been either twenty or twenty- one, depending on whether his birthday was before or after the date the census was taken. In the record, George's "color" is shown as "B" for black and his employment was as a "Pedlar." No occupation is shown for Benjamin, but his "Color" was given as "M" for mulatto. This family did not list any real estate, but they had personal property valued at $200.00. Benjamin had three younger brothers and two younger sisters. All family members were born in Maryland. John King apparently used the abbreviation "Col." for Colored. It is not known if John R. King signed or marked any of the ambrotypes he took. The photo taken on this date of Benjamin House may or may not have survived, but would be difficult to identify since it did not have John King's name on it.

March 7, 1862

Dr. Daniel Fahrney is probably the doctor that saw John King's mother on this day in 1862. Although the mode of treatment he provided will never be known, it was unsuccessful as John King's mother, Eliza Lane King would die five months later. Dr. David Fahrney was born August 20, 1819, in Mapleville, Washington County Maryland. Dr. Fahrney married Amy Weltz on November 8, 1839 and (1820-1898) who bore him three children: Dr. Daniel Peter Fahrney (1841-1905), Amy Ann C. Fahrney (1846-1857) and Lewis Weltz Fahrney (1858-1906).[202] This Fahrney family lived in District 1 of Washington County.

Saturday March 8th 1862

This morning Pa went to Martinsburg. I was with Lieut. Bingham of the 28" N.Y. Regiment a while this morning when I left him & went to work at my new buisiness. I got along first rate to-day, learnt a good deal.

Sunday March 9th 1862

Yesterday the Remains of two Soldiers who gallantly rallied to the defence of their Government and their Country's Flag was silently and solemnly committed to the Tomb, they died at the Hospittle: may they receive their just rewards in Heaven. Pa & Mc/" went to Martinsburg this morn. I attended S. School this afternoon. Report is current that Winchester has been taken by our Troops without fireing a shot!

March 7, 1862 continnued

By 1850, Dr. Daniel Fahrney had already accumulated real estate valued at $7,000.[203] However, while still a young man of forty-seven years, the doctor died February 25, 1867 and was buried in the Fahrney family cemetery.

As the diary shows, John frequently visited the home of Henry Fishack to see his two daughters, Susan and Magdaline.

George A. Bingham, aged thirty-one years, enrolled May 12, 1861, at Niagara Falls, to serve two years and was mustered in as a second lieutenant, Company I, May 22, 1861.[204] However, according to New York State records, Lieutenant George A. Bingham was not an officer of the 28th New York Regiment as of this diary entry as he had resigned on January 30, 1862.[205] The reason for this officer's resignation as not provided. Perhaps, he had made his resignation retroactive or the date of his resignation is incorrect.

March 9, 1862

Our diarist had received some erroneous information, probably by word of mouth. Although the Union army was concentrating at Bunker Hill, Virginia, they had not yet entered Winchester. General Stonewall Jackson and his small army had spent the winter in Winchester, Virginia, and did not wish to give in to superior Union forces without a fight. On March 7, 1862, he sent a communique to General Joseph E. Johnston requesting reinforcements thereby enabling him "... to inflict a terrible wound and to effect a safe retreat in the event of having to fall back."[206] However, Jackson never received any additional troops. Without help, he knew that his army of 4,600 was no match for the approaching Union army of 38,000.[207] In a communication of March 9, 1862, Brigadier General R. B. Marcy, Chief of Staff, informed General Banks that he had heard from four sources that the Confederates "... either have or are about abandoning Manassas" and directs Bank to send reconnaissance to Winchester in force."[208] Hence, the Union army was now aware that General Joseph E. Johnston's army was now withdrawing and that Banks should be alert to Stonewall Jackson's next move in the Shenandoah Valley. As a result, also on March 9, 1862, General Banks communicated to General Williams that he should move two regiments towards Bunker Hill at daybreak and follow with his brigade.[209] Unfortunately for General Jackson, he learned too late that his brigade commanders had ordered his army to start moving south towards Strasburg during the morning of March 11.[210] Following a council of war, his officers had done this without his knowledge and Stonewall later said "That is the last council of war I will ever hold" and he never held one again.[211] On March 13, General Banks notified Chief of Staff Marcy that "General Hamilton occupied Winchester this morning at 7 o'clock" as the "rebel force left town at 5 o'clock yesterday" with the Confederate cavalry leaving "...but an hour in advance."[212]

Thus, the Union army entered the town of Winchester, Virginia, on March 13, not on March 9, 1862, as our diarist had stated.

Monday March 10th 1862

This morning it is raining very hard. I was up at Joe Norris' all day studying and practicing my new art.

Tuesday March 11th 1862

This is a beautiful day, the Sun is out beautiful. This was rather a cloudy day for taking pictures. There is a good many people in Town, and busisiness seems brisk.

Wednesday Mch 12th 1862

This morning Bro.Mc/" started for Martinsburg Va/", with stock for the Store. Today, I wrote to James Lett, Harrisburg, for my Stock of Ambrotype utensils &c.

March 10, 1862

John continues to learn his new profession as a photographer under the tutelage of Joe Norris.

March 12, 1862

James Lett was a thirty-four-year-old photographic goods merchant from Harrisburg, Pennsylvania, who provided John King with the necessary materials for the latter's photographic study. James Lett immigrated to the United States June 20, 1848 at the age of twenty-one years.[213] He arrived aboard the ship *Republic* from Liverpool, England and arrived in New York City. Born in Cheltenham, Gloucestershire, England on November 28, 1827, Mr. Lett initially engaged in import of silk velvets, but had to give up this trade due to "a throat infection."[214] By the time of the July 16, 1860 census, Mr. Lett was residing in Brooklyn Ward 2, District 1 in New York City with his wife, Teresa and one child, James A.[215] However, by 1863, he had already moved to Harrisburg, Pennsylvania, Ward 4. At this time, he first appears on the business tax lists, paying ten dollars for a class B license, and in the Harrisburg City Directory as a supplier of "photographic materials" at 23 North Second Street.[216,217] James was drafted for Union service in June of 1862 in the Fourth Ward of Harrisburg, but avoided duty due to being a conscientious objector.[218]

James Lett's photography business remained in the Lett family when "unfortunately, due to the economic climate of small business in relation to the Box Stores it was necessary to close shop in 2005 after 145 years of continuous business.[219] To this day, the James Lett Company holds the distinction of being the oldest photographic supply business in continuous operation in the history of the United States.

The 1st Regt/" P. H. B. is, of course, the Potomac Home Brigade, First Regiment. Captain "Yonts" was the Captain William H. H. Yontz, mentioned earlier in John King's diary when Company E was presented with a silk battle flag. Company E was also the one to which our diarist's brother, Harrison, joined. The regimental rolls show Henry C. Bohn as a private who was mustered into Union service September 14, 1861 and who was mustered out October 1, 1864.[220] William P. Maulsby was Colonel of the First Regiment, Potomac Home Brigade. He was mustered into service November 28, 1861 and resigned effective August 26, 1864.[221] Colonel Maulsby was a true son of Maryland. He was born in Bel Air, Maryland, July 10, 1815, the son of Israel David and Jane (Hall) Maulsby.[222] Before the Civil War, he was a lawyer and a politician in Frederick and Carroll counties. Attorney Maulsby was the first state senator from Carroll County from 1838 to 1843 and the first state's attorney in that county from 1844 to 1846.

Thursday Mch. 13th 1862

This is a beautiful day, a fine one to take Pictures quick, but not as nice as on a cloudy day. This morning Sargent H. C. Bohn of Co. E" Capt. Yonts 1st Regt/" P. H. B. Col. Maulsly, came to Town from Charlestown Va/" and is looking very well. Him and me went to see some Ladys in the evening.

Friday Mch. 14th 1862.

This is cloudy day, and threatens rain. To-day I was practicing on taking views, and got along very well.

Saturday Mch 15 1862

To-day it is raining all day, and we did not take many picture. My Stock came this evening

Sunday March 16th 1862

This is a beautiful morning Bro. Mc/' went down the country. I attended S. School this afternoon and all my scholars present. The Teachers were requested to remain a while after school for the purpose of electing an assistant Librarian. I nominated Mr. Oliver B. Ridenour for that position and he was unanimously chosen.

Monday Mch17 1862

This is a cold cloudy and windy day. Cousin Kate Lane was up here from Boonsboro. There was no important war news this evening, no more than the Rebels are evacuating a good many of their strong holds, Manassas, Columbus, Bowling Green &e.

March 13, 1862

Colonel Maulsby served admirably and bravely as regimental commander and received special commendations for his regiments role in the battle of Gettysburg.[223] After the war, the Colonel was a delegate from Frederick County to the 1867 Constitutional Convention of Maryland, was appointed chief judge of the Sixth Judicial Circuit Court in 1870 and was made judge of the Maryland Court of Appeals, from 1870 to 1871.[224]

March 16, 1862

John is again attended Episcopal Methodist Church in town. In his Sunday school class, he had a group of students. Oliver Ridenour, aged 20, is listed on the 1860 census as a clerk living with his father, Samuel, age 58, his mother, Elizabeth, age 48, Laura, age 32, and five other children.[225]

Tuesday Mch 18th 1862

This is a beautiful morning, very pleasant. I expect to go to Winchester to-morrow to tell Pa to come home. This evening I received a letter from Pa. stating that he had rented Seibert's new house which saves me the trouble of going to Winchester, I was all packed up ready to go in the morning. To-night some one set fire to a Fodder Stack & raised an alarm of fire. I was on hand with the "Hook & Ladder Truck" F. H. H. C.

Wednesday Mch 19th 1862

This has been a dull day with me, I had a picture taken of myself and gave it to a Lady.

Thursday Mch 20th 1862

To-day Mc/" came from Winchester and told me I had to go along with him back. I paid J. E. Norris Esq. $5 on account.

March 17, 1862

In a communique dated March 11, 1862, from Major General McClellan at Fairfax Court House (Virginia) to Secretary of War E. M. Stanton, the former stated that he had just returned from a forty-mile ride from Centreville, (near Manassas, Virginia) Blackburn's Ford, and other sites and determined that "The rebels have left all their positions... they have fallen back behind the Rapidan (i.e. River), holding Fredericksburg and Gordonsville."[226] On the same day, McClellan ordered Chief of Staff Marcy to,

> "Telegraph to General Banks that the troops have all left Manassas, and probably the whole or the greater part of the troops have left Winchester ... that he push forward to that place as soon as possible..."[227]

Not only were the Confederates pulling back from their camp at Manassas/Centreville, but also from their former positions in Tennessee and Kentucky. After defeats at Fort Henry (February 6) and Fort Donelson (February 12–16) in February, the Confederate high command sought to fall back and reorganize their armies in Tennessee and Kentucky. The Union was not going to allow Kentucky to succeed and become another Confederate state. During February 14-15, Bowling Green, Kentucky, was evacuated by the Confederates and occupied by Union forces.[228] Likewise, Nashville changed hands following the engagement of February 23-25, 1862. In addition, Columbus, Kentucky was evacuated by the Confederates and occupied by Union troops. Despite his source, when John King said that "... the Rebels are evacuating a good many of their strongholds..." he was right.

March 19, 1862

One wonders which of his "lady friends" received this ambrotype and what became of it. I

March 20, 1862

John R. King, for some reason, did not make a diary entry for Friday, March 21, 1862. As a result, he incorrectly calls March 22nd a Friday, when it was actually Saturday. He realizes his mistake on Wednesday, March 27 and crosses through the 27 and replaces it with 26. Thus, he has two March 26 entries, one for Tuesday and one for Wednesday. By doing so, he corrects the earlier omission of Friday, March 21.

Friday Mch 22

This morning we started for Winchester: when we got to Williamsport we had to wait at the Ferry for about one hour. We got as far as Martinsburg when we put up for the night. I looked around Martinsburg & seen the wanton ruin and destruction of property by the Rebels. We staid at Uncle John Kings all night.

Saturday Mch 23rd/62

This morning at 7 ½ O'clock we started for Winchester, we got along very well until we passed Bunker Hill when the road got miserable. I had to walk for about five miles, when the road got better; we arrived at Winchester about 1 O'clock. This evening the Rebel Col. Ashby appeared before this place, & drove inn our Pickets with expectation of getting into the Town, but a messenger soon brought about 5000 infantry & cavalry and drove them back. We lost one man killed and 3 or 4 wounded including Gen. Shields, the Rebels lost about 10- killed and as many wounded. There is a great stir amongst the Troops. I was out on a hill and could see the fighting.

March 22, 1862

This is actually Friday, March 21, 1862. Our diarist's uncle, John H. King, resided in Martinsburg, Virginia. On the 1860 U.S. Census, he was fifty-four years of age and his occupation was given as a "merchant"[229] In addition, his household consisted of his wife, Mary, aged fifty-two, a son, Oliver, age twenty-two, a son, George H., aged twenty-one, and another son, Arthur, aged nineteen. Two of the sons were employed. Oliver was listed as a machinist and George H. as a telegraph operator. Uncle John was a man of some means as he had real estate worth $3,800. By 1870, all of his children had left the house and only he and Mary remained.[230]

March 23, 1862

This is actually Saturday, March 22, 1862. It took John and Sam five-and one-half hours to travel from Martinsburg, Virginia to Winchester, Virginia, on the Valley Pike, a distance of about twenty-three miles. They had arrived in time to witness the beginning of a significant battle of the Civil War, i.e., General Stonewall Jackson's first major battle against the Union led by Brigadier General James Shields, divisional commander under Major General Bank's Fifth Corps, Army of the Potomac.

Colonel Turner Ashby of Markham, Virginia, in Fauquier County, was General Stonewall Jackson's cavalry commander. Along with J.E.B. Stuart, Ashby presented himself as a dashing, chivalrous knight of the Confederacy. With a long, black beard and ostrich plume in his hat, he rode a white steed with ease. As master horsemen, Colonel Ashby and his cavalry expertly covered Jackson's retreat from Winchester to Strasburg and later to Mt. Jackson, Virginia. Confederate General Joseph E. Johnston had told Jackson that he must make a demonstration against General Banks so that he would not send a portion of his force to assist McClellan in his movements.[231] On March 21, Ashby and his command of horseman reported that the Union troops had left Strasburg and told Jackson that he was "… harassing their rear as they fell back into Winchester."[232] On March 22, 1862, Jackson started his army on a forced march of twenty-two miles to Strasburg, while Ashby had completed driving the Federals into Winchester. Whether true or not, Brigadier General Shields told Secretary of War Stanton in his report of March 29 that he only feigned a retreat to Winchester to draw out Jackson and attack his army.[233]

Sunday Mch 24th 1862

This morning Gen. Jackson, (Rebel) appeared in force to show battle, it commenced about 10 O'clock, and about 5 O'clock the battle raged furiously, our Troops charged their Battery which they contested bravely but had to break at the superior bravery of the U.S. Troops, and fled precipitately throwing away their arms in their flight. Our loss is heavy many a poor soul falling while gallantly defending the Flag of his Country and the supremacy of his Government. They are bringing in the dead & wounded as fast as they can and putting them in the Hospitals.

Monday Mch. 25th 1862

To-day they are still bring in the dead and dying, there are a great many Rebels, they not taking half of their dead & wounded. Tuesday

---

March 23, 1862 continued

General Shields stated that at 5 o'clock on March 22nd, Ashby's cavalry "... attacked and drove in some of our pickets."[234] Another source agrees that the Confederate cavalry had, by 5 o'clock on March 22nd, driven the retreating Union troops into Winchester.[235] General Shields contends that he continued his ruse to trick Jackson into believing that he had only a small force in his front. Shields stated

> By order of General Banks I put my command under arms and pushed forward one brigade and two batteries of artillery to drive back the enemy, but to keep him deceived as to our strength only let him see two regiments of infantry, a small body of cavalry, and part of the artillery.[236]

The Confederate record does not admit to Shields' chicanery, but acknowledges that Ashby's force of two-hundred and fifty horseman and three guns of Chew's battery was greatly outnumbered by one of Shields' infantry brigades, two batteries of artillery and some cavalry. During the engagement General Shields was hit by a shell fragment "...which fractured my arm above the elbow, bruised my shoulder, and injured my side."[237] When the opposing forces met, a "spirited skirmish" ensued with Ashby eventually retiring at Kernstown, three miles from Winchester, for the rest of the night.[238] Neither side produced casualty figures for this very minor battle, but instead choose to include them in the overall numbers of killed, wounded and missing for the larger battle of Kernstown the following day.

March 24, 1862

As mentioned, John has the day of the week right, but not the date. The Battle of Kernstown was fought on Sunday, March 23, 1862.

General Stonewall Jackson was a devout Christian and frowned upon giving battle on the Sabbath. On the other hand, he saw an opportunity to inflict a convincing blow on the Union army once he learned from his cavalry commander, Colonel Turner Ashby, that only four regiments remained in Winchester. As Ashby stated in his official report, "Having followed the enemy in his hasty retreat from Strasburg on Saturday evening, I came upon the forces remaining in Winchester within a mile of that place and became satisfied that he had but four regiments, and learned that they had orders to march in the direction of Harper's Ferry." Ashby did not divulge the source of his intelligence.[239] General Williams' brigade of the First Division of Banks' corps had already left for Centreville, Virginia, as the Confederates had earlier abandoned that place. General Banks was in camp in Harper's Ferry. Brigadier James Shields commanded a division of the 5th Army Corps and remained in Winchester accompanied by the Michigan cavalry. Shields' Second Division, just created March 3, 1862, was composed of the First Brigade under Colonel Nathan Kimball, the Second under Colonel J. C. Sullivan and the Third led by Brigadier General Erasmus B. Tyler.[240] While General Shields later reported that he had somewhere between 7,000 and 8,000 soldiers with him, he probably had closer to 9,000 troops at his disposal.[241]

Stonewall Jackson started with about 4,600 men in his forced march up the Shenandoah Valley pike, but due to straggling by a great number, arrived at the battlefield with only 3,000 ragged Confederates.[242] As one historian noted,

> ...by two in the afternoon of a raw, cold day Garnett's Stonewall Brigade, leading the march, approached the hamlet of Kernstown, followed closely by the brigades of Colonels Fulkerson (one of Loring's men) and Burks, in all about 3,000 men.[243]

Jackson gave his Stonewall Brigade, commanded by Richard Garnett, the tough assignment of holding the center of the Confederate line. Jackson later noted in his official report that,

> After ascertaining that the troops, part of which had marched over fourteen miles since dawn, and Garnett's and Burk's brigades, which had made a forced march of near twenty-five miles the previous day, were in good spirits at the prospect of meeting the enemy, I determined to advance at once.[244]

While others estimate that General Shields had about 9,000 troops, the General himself stated in his official report that he had only between 7,000 and 8,000 men.[245] The details of the Battle of Kernstown can be_found elsewhere and will not be repeated here. Suffice it to say that Shields, though still commanding from his bed due to the recent shrapnel injury, ordered a full attack on the Confederate line. He sent in Colonel Tyler's brigade, the 5th Ohio, the 13th Indiana,, the 62nd Ohio, of Sullivan's brigade, and the 14th Indiana, the 84th Pennsylvania, seven companies of the 67th Ohio,_and three companies of the 8th Ohio of Kimball's brigade. As General Shields later_reported,

> "...this united force dashed upon the enemy with a cheer and yell that rose high above the roar of battle, and though the rebels fought desperately, as their piles_of dead attest, they were forced back through the woods by a fire as destructive as ever_fell upon a retreating foe."[246]

With some of his troops running out of ammunition and seeing that he would be overrun, General Garnett ordered a retreat and the Confederate left followed suit. The soldiers fled to the rear in good order and the field belonged to the Union army. Major General Stonewall Jackson had suffered defeat in his first major battle at the hands of a vastly superior in numbers Union division. Jackson had broken two of his cardinal rules: do not give battle on Sunday and fight only when you have a two to one numerical advantage. Jackson's army retreated up the Shenandoah Valley to the hamlet of Mt. Jackson some forty miles south of Winchester. Casualties for both sides were relatively light compared to other major battles during the Civil War. Official Confederate casualties were 80 officers and men killed, 375 wounded and 263 captured or missing for a total of 718 troops.[247] Official Union casualties were 112 officers and enlisted men killed, 423 wounded and 22 captured or missing, for a total of 590 soldiers.[248] In his official report dated April 9, 1862, Stonewall Jackson blamed both the faulty intelligence report of Colonel Ashby and the retreat ordered by Brigadier General Garnett, commander of the Stonewall Brigade. In fact, Jackson had Garnett arrested for "neglect of duty" for issuing an unauthorized order to retreat and relieved him of command on April 1, 1862.[249] General Robert E. Lee later suspended the charges and assigned Garnett as commander of George Pickett's Brigade, when the later became ill, in the First Corps of Lieutenant General James Longstreet's command. Jackson also tried to end his Kernstown report on a positive note by saying that,

> "Though Winchester was not recovered, yet the more important object for the present, that of calling back troops that were leaving the valley, and through preventing a junction of Banks' command with other forces, was accomplished."[250]

Jackson kept a large number of Union forces engaged in the Shenandoah Valley thereby making them unable to assist McClellan in his Peninsula campaign.

March 25, 1862

The date of this diary entry is actually Monday, March 24. John has not yet corrected his error. In his reports, General Shields mentioned that General Jackson was reported to have taken at least six wagonloads of the wounded and dead with him on his retreat up the Valley Pike to Woodstock and then to Mt. Jackson. Shields also noted many graves just a short distance from the road. General Stonewall Jackson stated is his official report of the battle that "Our wounded received that care and attention from the patriotic ladies of Winchester which they know so well how to give, and our killed were buried by the loyal citizens of that town" and added that "the hospitality of Baltimoreans relieved the wants of the captured."[251]

Mch.26th 1862

Our Troops have occupied the town of Strasburg without opposition, the Rebels having left.

Wednesday Mch 26th 1862

This morning buisiness is very dull the Soldiers having pretty near all gone. Pa came from Hagerstown to-day, with stock for Store. Busisiness towards evening got a little more brisk.

Thursday Mch 27th /62

This morning Mc/" went to Hagerstown. To-day Mr. Charles Graves of this place & myself took a Buggy ride which was very pleasant. Busisiness this afternoon is very dull.

Friday March 28th 1862

This morning Pa went to Strasburg and I am alone and keeps me pretty buisy. There is no news of any importance to-day. Pa got home about (number is crossed out—Editor) O'clock.

March 26, 1862

The date of this diary entry is actually that of Tuesday, March 25. The Confederate army did not linger near Kernstown for long. Jackson made his way south along the Valley Pike to set up camp near Mt. Jackson and New Market, Virginia.

March 26, 1862

John finally realizes his date error and now corrects it. Since his new livelihood is ambrotype portrait photography, he cannot make much money if he is not near the Union camps. Therefore, like the sutlers, he is dependent upon the movement of the army and has to go where the army goes.

March 27, 1862

"Mc" is a nickname for John's brother-in-law, Samuel McLaughlin.

Charles E. Graves would have been about twenty-one years of age at this time. He was married to Mary R. Graves and was working in Winchester as a jeweler.[252] His assets were shown as $1,200 in real estate and $7,000 in personal property, the later probably in his stock of jewelry, and his wife claimed $700 in real estate. John King apparently made friends with ease. However, he does not divulge if he knew Mr. Graves beforehand, perhaps in business dealings, or if he just met him for the first time.

Saturday Mch 29th 1862

This is a cloudy morning & indications of falling (failing) weather. I am again alone in the Store & buisiness is not very brisk. Pa did (not) get back from Strasburg until 10 O'clock at night.

Sunday Mch 30th 1862

This is mighty disagreeable day raining and hailing. I attended the Lutheran Church of this place (Winchester) and heard as I thought a very poor sermon.

Monday Mch 31st 1861

To-day Mc/" came from Maryland with a load. This evening I was taken sick with chills and fever. Mr. Chas. Graves took me to his house, and his better half made me a glass of composition Tea which warmed me up considerably.

Tuesday Apl. 1st 1862

Last night was one long to be remembered by me, I had a burning fever all night. I slept very little. I started for Hagerstown this morning, and I had a hard time, I was so sick I could not hold my head up, I got there about 9 O'clock.

March 29, 1862

Strasburg is only about eleven miles from Newtown, the latter which was later renamed Stephens City.

March 30, 1862

Most likely, John attended Grace Evangelical Church which is located at 26 West Boscawen Street in the heart of Winchester A new church was erected in 1842, was two stories high, and was the largest meeting place in the area. This church was used by both the Southern and the Northern soldiers during the Civil War, depending upon which side had control of the city.[253]

March 31, 1862

George W. Graves and Charles Edward Graves were well-known business owners in Winchester. Perhaps after 1861, Charles decided to go into business for himself. It seems a bit odd for John to have been invited to Charles' home if they had just met in Winchester. Perhaps, our diarist knew him through a business connection.

April 1, 1862

The distance from Winchester to Hagerstown is about fifty miles and would have taken John many hours of travel time by horse or by wagon.

Wednesday Apl 2d 1862

This morning I feel better bit I am sick on the stomach. I was kept buisy getting my load ready to start. I started about 12 O'clock for Martinsburg.

Thursday Apl. 3 d 1862

I started for Winchester this morning had a rough time, arrived there at 3 O'clock. This is a very pleasant day.

Friday Apl. 4th 1862

To-day Mc/" and me started for home, about ½ mile from Bunker Hill our old Horse fell, broke a shaft, and cut himself up bad. We tied the shaft up and started on our way; fed at Martinsburg and reached home about 7 O'clock.

Saturday Apl. 5 1862

This morning the weather is cloudy. To-day I bought a pound of Collodian from E. M. Recher paid $1.25oo/" for it.

Sunday Apl. 6th 1862

This is a very fine day. I attended church this morning & heard a good sermon this morning from Mr. Sears. I attended S. School in the afternoon.

April 2, 1862

John apparently came home to pick up another load of goods to return to his fathers' and brother-in-law's store in Winchester.

April 4, 1862

Bunker Hill is a small town located in Berkeley County, Virginia (now West Virginia) on the Winchester Pike (Route 11).

A wagon shaft is one of two wooden poles by which an animal is harnessed to a vehicle.[254]

April 5, 1862

Collodion is "the sticky transparent solution that holds light sensitive chemicals on glass and, as such, was the key ingredient for early photography.[255]

Like John R. King, Elias Marken Recher was a Hagerstown photographer. Mr. Recher was born in Wolfsville, Frederick County, Maryland, in 1828 and later set up shop in Hagerstown. While John was trained by J. E. Norris, B. W. T. Phreaner "learned his trade in Recher's employ."[256] Recher later became famous for his publication of battlefield views of Antietam in stereographic form and for his portraits of Civil War officers and soldiers

Monday April 7th 1862

This morning Mc/" and I started for Winchester, he with a two horse team and I with our own team. I only went as far as Martinsburg Mc/" went through. It is hailing and raining very hard.

Tuesday Apl. 8th 1862

This morning it is steal hailing and raining I started for Winchester about 8 O'clock and I got along very slow as our poor old horse is most wore out. I got at Winchester about 5 O'clock.

Wednesday Apl 9th 1862

To-day it is still hailing & raining. Mc/" came from Bunker Hill this morning, & started back to Hagerstown again with passengers about 2 O'clock.

Thursday Apl. 10th 1862

This morning who should walk into the store but Harrison E. King, and he looks very well. Pa started for Woodstock and I am left alone. This being pay day of the Regiment stationed here, I was kept very buisy. My net receipts was $106.66.

Friday Apl. 11th 1862

This morning feel miserably sore and stiff. H. E. King stayed with me last night also Benj. Harris & M. Swartz of Hagerstown. Buisiness very good to-day.

April 8, 1862

The distance between Martinsburg and Winchester, Virginia is twenty-three miles. It took John nine hours driving his wagon in adverse conditions.

April 10, 1862

Harrison was John's older brother who enlisted in Company D of the First Regiment of the Potomac Brigade Home Brigade. This regiment was part of Banks' Fifth Corps, Army of the Potomac.

The distance from the King's store in Winchester, Virginia to Woodstock, in Shenandoah County, Virginia is about thirty-two miles along the Valley Pike (Route 11 today). John does not tell us why his father was going to Woodstock, but Samuel King must have felt relatively safe probably knowing that Stonewall Jackson and his army were camped at Rude's Hill, just south of Mount Jackson. Jackson had set up his headquarters at the home of a Danish Lutheran, the Reverend A. R. Rude on April 2. Hence, Jackson was only about thirteen miles away. If Samuel King was carrying goods for sale, he still could have been attacked and robbed by Ashby's Confederate Cavalry or by local guerillas.

Saturday Apl. 12th 1862

Pa came home last night from Woodstock, also Mac. from Hagerstown. Buisiness very brisk to-night.

Sunday Apl. 13th 1862

Taking the advantage of the Day, set apart by, the Maker and Ruler of the Universe as a day of rest I laid on my Blanket (Soldierlike) until 10 O'clock A.M. When I got up, put on my good clothes and went to the M. E. Church (North) and heard a good sermon from their Pastor Mr. Brooke; they have an elegant Choir. In the afternoon I went to the Church again & heard a good sermon from the Chaplain of the 7" Va/" (Loyal) Regt/".

April 11, 1862

Also visiting and spending the night with John and his brother were two of his friends from Hagerstown. How they got through the Union lines is not known. William B. Harris is shown on both the 1850 and 1860 U.S. Census living with his large family in Hagerstown.[257,258] The letter "B" most likely denotes Benjamin, also the name of his father. William B., the son, was sixteen years old in 1860. Hence, as of this diary date, he would have been eighteen years old. Michael Swartz was also residing with his family in Hagerstown in 1850 and again in 1860 as revealed by the U.S. Census for those years.[259,260] Michael was about twenty-four years old at this time.

William Benjamin Harris was working in Hagerstown in 1860 as a "clerk" as stated earlier. He was residing with his father, the Benjamin Harris from whom John King had purchased a pair of boots, his mother, Eliza, and five siblings. At age nineteen, William B. Harris, like so many other young Hagerstown men, joined the Union Army and served from August 8, 1862 as a private until the end of the war when he was mustered out May 31, 1865.[261] Like many other Hagerstown boys, he enlisted in Hagerstown with Company A, 7th Regiment, Maryland Infantry.[262] He must have survived the war for, on the 1870 U.S. Census, there is a William Harris, aged twenty-six, living in Funkstown, Maryland, with his wife, Mary, and employed as a shoemaker.[263]

April 13, 1862

The "Pastor Mr. Brooke" mentioned by John King served in the Methodist Episcopal church on Market Street. He was remembered as quite a speaker by those who recall his sermons. As one later stated, "… it is doubtful if the old Tabernacle will ever see the old time crowds that assembled there in the long ago, and heard with rapturous delight Rev. Ben. Brooke, when at his zenith as an Orator."[264]

The chaplain of the 7th West Virginia Infantry (Union) from January 4, 1862 until February 21, 1863, was a pastor from Parkersburg named John W. Reger.[265] Pastor Reger is most likely the chaplain John King mentions in this diary note. At the age of twenty-two, John W. Reger was licensed to preach by the Methodist Episcopal Church.[266] Initially, Rev. Reger was commissioned to Company S, but on February 27, 1864, he was commissioned with the Hospital Chaplains Regiment of the U.S. Volunteers and was promoted to Full Chaplain, serving at Grafton Hospital, West Virginia.[267] After the war, John W. Reger became a trustee and one of the founders of Wesleyan College in West Virginia.[268]

Monday Apl. 14th 1862

This morning we got up early as Col. Maulsby's Regt/" left for Harpers Ferry, they left about Noon. Buisiness towards evening got very dull.

Tuesday Apl. 15th 1862

This morning is a very disagreeable one, raining very hard. I am making arrangement to go up to Woodstock to follow the Ambrotype buisiness in Co. with Charles E. Graves. We have a Portable House.

Wednesday Apl. 16 1862

The weather still continues bad, and consequently buisiness is dull. There is no news of importance. but rumers are numerous.

Thursday Apl. 17th 1862

To-day the weather is clear, and to-wards evening the weather get very warm. It is reported that one company of Ashbys Cavelry (Rebel) was taken prisoner, near Mt. Jackson.

Friday Apl. 18th 1862

To-day the weather is still very warm. About 2 O'clock a detachment of the 46" Pa. Regt/" brought in 67 of Ashby's Rebel Cavelry which was taken while at breakfast in a Church without fireing a shot,

---

April 14, 1862

John King's brother, Harrison, was in town briefly with his regiment under Colonel Maulsby after they had been ordered to march south to Winchester in the spring of 1862. However, they were soon required to march back north to guard the Baltimore & Ohio Railroad in Virginia and Maryland.[269] Later in May of 1862, the regiment would be sent to Harper's Ferry to prevent that village from being captured by the Confederates.

April 15, 1862

When John says he is "to go up" to Woodstock, he actually means that he is traveling south. This is because the Shenandoah River runs south to north. Charles E. Graves is shown on both the 1850 and the 1860 U.S. Census as a resident of Winchester.[270,271] His age is given as twenty years on the 1850 and he was thus born about 1830. Thus, as of April 15, 1862, Charles was either thirty-one or thirty-two years old. His occupation on the 1850 was shown as a "watchmaker" and as a "jeweler" on the 1860. His father, George B. Graves apprenticed under the noted surveyor's compass maker, Goldsmith Chandlee of Winchester.[272] From 1846 to 1861, the father, George, and two of his sons, George and Charles, had an instrument making and jewelry store business on Loudoun Street in Winchester.[273] The "Portable House" mentioned in this diary entry is not really a house, but a portable photography studio.

there one Capt. 2 Lieutenants and 64 privates & noncommissioned officers, they looked hard.

Saturday, Apl. 19th 1862

This morning, I was the recipient of a splendid Gold pen and holder, the gift of Capt. J. P. Emmons, of the 1st/" Michigan Cavelry, I record the proceeding of this day with the gift. It is raining again to-day. There is nothing new to note, Gen. Rozencratz's Division about 15000 strong are encamped about 3 miles from the city.

April 18, 1862

Addison Harper was Captain of Company H of the 7th Virginia (Confederate) Cavalry, also known as the Brock's Gap Sharpshooters. When the Civil War began, Mr. Harper was fifty-one years old, but still managed to recruit and organize a company of mounted soldiers from Rockingham County with himself as captain. In a report of February 21, 1862, General Stonewall Jackson praised Captain Harper and his company because of gallantry shown in a charge made on Union troops at Hancock, Maryland.[274]

John King mentioned the bad weather and hard rain in his diary entries of April 15th and 16th. Company H and some troopers from Captain Everett Shands' Company I were in the area of Columbia Furnace and decided to take cover in one of the local churches located at the "Cross Roads Church." Unfortunately, Captain Harper was not present and the officer in charge forgot to post any pickets. Then, as noted in the official "Record of Events" of the Army of the Shenandoah (Union),

> On the 15th instant this squadron [First Squadron Pennsylvania Cavalry], under command of the junior captain, Greenfield, assisted by detachments of infantry from the 14th Indiana, 5th Connecticut, 28th New York, and 46th Pennsylvania, made a dash upon a company of the enemy's cavalry quartered in a church near Columbia Furnace, and succeeded in capturing the entire force of three officers and about fifty men, with all their horses, arms, and baggage.[275]

The raid occurred at night in the early hours of the morning of April 16.[276] Some of the Confederates attempted to escape, but were soon captured. Amazingly, not a single shot was fired in this capture. When General Banks learned of this incident, at 7 p.m. on April 16th, he quickly wired Secretary of State Staunton of the good news. The prisoners were to be marched to Baltimore. In actuality, as mentioned above, the prisoners were not all from one company, but contained several members of Company I, also from Rockingham County.[277] This fact is also proven by a review of the service records of the prisoners. J. Horatio Loker and Archibald Loftis were both privates in Company I of the 7th Virginia Cavalry. According to the official Confederate service records, both were captured at the Cross Roads April 16, 1862, confined at Fort Delaware, and then exchanged as part of the ongoing Prisoner Exchange Program at Aiken's Landing on August 5, 1862.[278] Aiken's Landing is located on the James River in Virginia. Likewise, Andrew J. Holsinger, W. F. M. Houser, J. May and D.T. (J.) Showalter, all of Company H, all suffered exactly the same fate. These troopers were also taken prisoner at the Cross Roads on April 16th, were imprisoned at Fort Delaware, and then exchanged August 5, 1862, at Aiken's Landing.[279]

Overall, then, John's diary entry of April 18 was generally correct. Apparently, the transport of the prisoners took two days from the date of capture near Columbia Furnace in Shenandoah County to Winchester in Frederick County where our diarist saw them. However, no captain was taken prisoner and the group totaled closer to fifty then to sixty-seven men, as John said, unless he actually counted them and all other records are wrong. We shall never know for sure.

April 19, 1862

The Captain Emmons, who befriended John with the gift of a new ink pen, was Jed P. C. Emmons of Ypsilanti, Michigan. Jed Emmons, age 40, enlisted in Company K August 19, 1861, at Trenton for a period of three years.[280] The First Michigan Cavalry Regiment was organized at Detroit and was

Sunday Apl. 20th 1862

This is Easter, but a very dul one to me, it is raining very hard. I attended the M. E. Church this morning and heard a very good sermon from Rev. Mr. Brooke. I reced/" some nice desert to-day from a young Lady. (Miss Hoover of this Town.)

Monday, Apl. 21st 1862

This morning, it is raining very hard and buisiness is dull. I took Dinner to-day with Capt. J. P. Emmons, and enjoyed it very much.

Tuesday, Apl. 22th 1822

It is still raining this morning, buisiness though is brisk notwithstanding, oweing to the number of Troops stationed here.

Wednesday Apl. 23th 1862

This morning is a clear one but pretty cool. Mc/" came to-day with a load of goods. Very buisy in the store to-day.

April 19, 1862 continued

mustered into service September 13, 1861, with 1,144 officers and enlisted men.[281] On September 29, 1861, the regiment headed for Washington, D.C. and then to Frederick, Maryland, where it went into camp for several months. The First Michigan, with seven companies, comprised one regiment of ten that made up General Banks' Cavalry Command. In February of 1862, it was transferred to Harper's Ferry and then advanced to Winchester with other regiments. Thus, the First Michigan repeatedly opposed Jackson's Confederate cavalry under Colonel Turner Ashby. The regiment and its brigade clashed with their Confederate counterparts at Winchester March 23, 1862, at Middleton March 25, at Strasburg March 27, at Harrisonburg April 22 and at Winchester again May 24, 1862. Unfortunately for Captain Emmons, he was taken prisoner by Jacksons' forces either on May 24 when Jackson captured Banks' Front Royal garrison or on May 25, the date of the First Battle of Winchester. His name appears on a list of prisoners captured by Stonewall Jackson "in his recent brilliant victory over Banks (which) arrived in Petersburg Wednesday last on their way to Salisbury, North Carolina."[282] After obtaining his freedom in the prisoner exchange program, Captain Emmons resigned from the U.S. Army. Before the war, Captain Emmons had been a lawyer, practicing in Hamtramck, Wayne County, Michigan and then in Orion, Oakland County, Michigan.[283,284] After the war, he resided in Tallahassee and again listed his occupation as a lawyer.[285]

April 20, 1862

There were only two young ladies residing in Winchester at this time with the surname of Hoover. The lady John mentions was either Ann V., about eighteen years of age in 1862 or her sister, Lucinda, about sixteen years old.[451] However, since John did not provide her first name, it is not possible to know which one sent him the "nice" desert. The 1860 census showed the Hoover sisters living with their father, Philip, an innkeeper, and their mother, Lucinda, in Winchester City.[286] Once again, no matter where he travels, John King seems to easily make friends with either sex. The Hoover sisters lived in a large household with their father, Philip, an innkeeper, age forty-four, their mother, Lucinda, age forty-six, and two brothers, Jacob and Francis.

Thursday, Apl. 24th 1862

Mc/" started to Martinsburg this morning for a load of goods. Buisiness brisk. I bought a Portable House to-day of John Vilwig of this place, for Sixty-Five dollars $65oo/"

Friday Apl. 25th 1862

This morning it is again raining. Mc/' came about 2 O'clock with a load. I had my supper sent to this evening by a Young Lady.

Saturday. Apl. 26th 1862

This morning Pa started for Hagerstown Md. and will not be back before next Tuesday or Wednesday. This is a cloudy, ugly morning.

Sunday. Apl. 27th 1862

This is a beautiful morning, the Sun shining in all its glory. I took a walk this morning with two newly made acquaintances named W. Richardson & W. Dickonson. We walked to the Shawnee Spring, a spring of some Historical note, it is said that the Shawnee Tribe was encamped there and cut off Gen. Washington's water supply, and he was compelled to dig a well in the northern section of the

---

April 24, 1862

Our diarist would have been very much surprised if he had known that Mr. Vilwig also did business with Confederate General Stonewall Jackson. Apparently, John Vilwig was impartial in his business dealings during the war. John Samuel Apperson, hospital steward for the Stonewall Brigade, notes in his Civil War diary that Captain A. G. Pendleton, aid to Jackson, had Apperson pick up six camp chairs made by Mr. Vilwif at "an enormous price for them—4$ apiece."[287] Not only did the hospital steward complain of Vilwigs' high prices; he also questioned his loyalty to the Southern cause. In his diary, he notes that the cabinet maker

> "... professes to have been from the outset a firm upholder of the South... but not withstanding his assertions I should be very particular what sort of information I put into his hands though he may [be] all right," but then adds that Vilwig was "very solicituous to find out something from me."[288]

John Vilwig, who called himself a "master cabinet maker," was born in Bavaria about 1820. Along with his wife Barbara, who was also from Germany, he immigrated to the United States sometime after 1850 and opened a cabinet store in Winchester at 142–144 Loudoun Street.[289] With the help of another German cabinetmaker he hired, the Vilwig shop made a variety of furniture forms, from plain to elaborate, as well as railroad station desks, caskets, coffins and even church altars. In 1862, he purchased the "Fred Boyd house" at 215 N. Washington Street and owned it until 1898.[290] On the 1870 census, the census taker estimated the value of his real estate at $10,000 and his personal property at $4,000.[291] By 1870, he had three children, Mary E. aged thirteen, Catherine or "Katie" aged 10, and John E. or "Edward" aged 4, as well as a house servant. Unfortunately, Mr. Vilwig's store on Loudoun Street was destroyed by a fire of 1895.

Town. I attended M. E. Church and heard a good sermon from Mr. Brook. I attended S. School in the afternoon.

Monday Apl. 28th 1862

This is another fine day, but not quite as warm as yesterday. Buisinefs was tolerable brisk to-day, receipts over $60.00/". I attended the Funeral of the Major of the 39th/" Regt/" Garibaldi Guards N. Y. Vol. it was a grand spectical.

April 27, 1862

Once again, although John was a northerner, he had no qualms about introducing himself and making friends with the young men of a southern town. Webster Richardson and William Dickerson were both local boys who were probably sympathetic to the Confederate cause. Webster Richardson was a young man of seventeen years of age, who was residing with his mother and siblings in Winchester on the 1860 U. S Census.[292] All family members were born in New Jersey. No father was shown as having been in the household. No occupation was given for Webster on the 1860 census. By 1870, Webster became a druggist in Fauquier County, Virginia, married and had one son.[293]

William A. Dickinson was fifteen years old when he met John King. He resided with his parents, John and Emily Dickinson, and his siblings in Winchester. His father was a "coach trimmer." John's father was a coach maker so their fathers had something in common. William died at the age of forty-four years on July 26, 1889, and is buried in Mount Hebron Cemetery in Winchester.

April 28, 1862

In his journal, Colonel Eugene A. Kozlay, commander of the 54th New York Volunteers entered the following for April 29, 1862:

> I am sorry to record the death of my countryman, Major Wikey of these Garibaldis. I have no doubt that he was the best officer in that regiment and honest. I have no doubt that Repetti will not shed tears after him, because Wikey knew all the rascalities of Repetti and Utasy. I cannot forget his words, what he said at that famous meeting at Warrenton Junction. He said: Gentlemen! If you are as much against Utasy, why don't you bring forward your charges. I know something about him, as well as about others of our regiment; but I am not the proper person to bring it forward. You must know, however, that in our regiment (Garibaldi) everything was and is carried on, on the principle & *via divide et para*. Some funny stories are told about the decease of our friend. It was hinted to me yesterday that he was poisoned. This story appears to be absurd; because he was sick for many days. Yet, everything is possible to rascals and men of means.[294]

"Repetti" was Lieutenant Colonel Alexander Repetti of the 39th Regiment, Garibaldi Guards, New York Volunteers.

More than one-hundred and eighty thousand men of German origin fought in the Union army during the Civil War plus tens of thousands of Austrians, Poles, Hungarians and Czechs, as well as many other nationalities. Garibaldi's Guard was organized and recruited by Colonel Frederick George D'Utassy and was mustered into service for three years at Washington, D.C., June 6, 1861, to date from May 28, 1861.[295] The regiment was named after the renowned Italian general and politician, Giuseppe Garabaldi, who Lincoln tried unsuccessfully to recruit into the U.S. Army. The 39th New York has also been referred to as "Lincoln Foreign Legion," as the "First Foreign Rifles." and as "Garibaldi's Hungarian Legion." The 39th New York Infantry had three companies of Germans, three of Hungarians, one of Swiss, one of Italians, one of Frenchmen, and one of Spaniards and Portuguese.[296] From October 15, 1861, the regiment was in Stahel's Brigade of Blenker's Division, Army of the Potomac and then in the First Brigade, same division, of the Mountain Department, from April, 1862, until they became part of White's Brigade, Army of Virginia, at Winchester, from July, 1862. Unfortunately, the major John refers to in this entry would not see any further action. The major of the Garibaldi Guards who died in a Winchester hospital was Major Anthony Weekey, also spelled Vekey, of German descent. At the age of 28 years, he enrolled in the Union army at New York City to serve three years and was mustered in as first lieutenant of Company C.[297] Anthony was promoted to captain of Company F, July 15, 1861, and then to major, February 1, 1862, and died April 28, 1862.

Tuesday Apl. 29th 1862

This morning it is pouring down raining and a most disagreeable day. Buisiness very dull in Store.

Wednesday . Apl. 30 1862

This morning Mr. Jno. Burgess of this place, & me took a walk out to the Camp of the 1st/" Brigade, Rozencrantz Divis. Pa came from Bunker Hill this morning with a load.

Thursday AplXX. May 1st 1862

Mc/" left this morning with the team for Hagerstown. It is still raining, buisiness dull. A Four Horse team came this evening from Hagerstown loaded with goods for us.

Friday May 2d/" 1862

This morning the weather is clear and Sun shining beautiful. Buisiness brisk. Gen. Scott's Brigade, Rosencrantz Divis, left this morning for Wester Va/".

April 30, 1862

Born in October, 1844, John Burgess was also a young man, just a few months younger than John King, who was residing in Winchester. In 1850, his father, Abraham was shown on the census as a wealthy miller living in Frederick County, Virginia.[298] At that time, there was a total of seven children living in the household in addition four unrelated workers who worked in the family business, i.e., a clerk, a wagoner, a cooper and another miller. In 1860, John was working as a clerk and was living with his father, Abraham, a machinist, and his mother, Sarah, along with three siblings.[299]

In his diary, John King tells us that Rosecran's camp was only three miles distant, which was an easy walk for two young men. Rosecrans said in official correspondence that the division was encamped five miles from Winchester, a discrepancy of two miles. The First Brigade of Blenker's division was commanded by Brigadier General Julius H. Stahel and was composed of the previously mentioned 39th New York under Colonel D'Utassy, the 8th New York under Colonel Francis Wutschel, the 45th New York under Colonel George Von Amsberg and the 27th Pennsylvania under Colonel Adolph E. Buschbeck.[300] If John ventured out to visit the large camp for a reason other than simple curiosity, he did not mention it.

May 2, 1862

There was no General Scott in Rosecrans Division. John may have meant Brigadier Julius H. Stahel, commander of the First Brigade. In a communication from Rosecrans to Stanton on May 3 from Winchester, the former states that "Since my dispatch of yesterday morning the First Brigade, General Stahel commanding, having obtained shoes for the barefooted, started for Romney, with orders to stop there and get clothing."[301] Also, the journal of Colonel Kozlay confirms that the First Brigade finally left Winchester after a review and inspection on May 1st, but gave the date as April 30 and the time as 4 o'clock in the afternoon. Whatever the exact date they departed to join General Fremont, it took General Rosecrans almost three weeks to get them ready. John meant to write "Western Virginia" instead of "Wester Va."

Saturday May 3rd 1862

This is another beautiful day, but rather warm. I expected to go down to Camp with My House to operate but was disappointed in getting a Horse & Wagon.

Sunday May 4th 1862

This is a lovely morning again. I took a walk this morning with some of my Winchester Friends, Wm/" Dickinson, W. Richardson, Jas. Ginn, G. H. Harper, and Thos. Wall and we all went to Church and heard a good sermon from Rev. Raswel. In the afternoon the same party with two additional ones Wm/" Rusell John Burgess and had a nice time, we went to a Mr. Hollingsworth Farm, took a ride in a Rowe Boat, the dwelling House was one time Gen Washingtons HeadQuarters, and was built 1754, we came back and walked around to see some Lady. In the evening I went with Harper to see a Young Man that was wounded in the Battle of Winchester, he was in the Confederate service and is name is Daly.

May 3, 1862

Apparently, at this time, John did not have his own means of transport and had to rent both horses and a wagon to haul his portable photography studio, or "House" as he called it.

May 4, 1862

John King spent the day frolicking with his new Winchester friends. Webster Richardson and William Dickinson were mentioned under an earlier diary entry. These boys were all local teenagers of about the same age as John. All of them were too young to enlist in the army. Although John was a Northerner with decidedly Union proclivities and all of these new friends were Virginia Southerners, it did not matter. This group of boys was out to have fun that day regardless of the fighting everywhere around them. Most but not all of these boys were the sons of well-to-do Winchester fathers. James Ginn, aged seventeen, was the son of wealthy "founder" named George Ginn, age fifty-three. On the 1860 U.S. Census, George listed a large household of eight children and one domestic servant.[302] He also stated that he owned real estate valued at $23,000 and personal property worth $500. Coincidentally, the Ginn family lived just a few doors down from the home of Abraham Burgess, the father of John's new friend, John Burgess. Thomas T. Wall, another resident of Winchester, was about seventeen years old at this time, as he is shown on the 1860 U.S. Census as being sixteen, residing with his mother and four siblings.[303] At the time, he was employed as a "clerk in store" just as John King had been before he became a sutler and photographer. Thomas T. Wall died in 1917 and is buried in Mt. Hebron Cemetery in Winchester, as are most of these boys. William Greenway Russell was born October 28, 1842, and hence would have been nineteen-years-old in April of 1862. His father was a wealthy merchant in Winchester and his brother was a physician. William Sr. owned $10,000 in both real estate and in personal property.[304] Lastly, the G. H. Harper that John King cited in his diary was most likely George H. Harper of Loudoun County, Virginia, who was about twenty years old in April of 1862. The oddball in this group of teenage Winchester lads, George Harper had previously been employed as a laborer on the farm of Samuel and Elizabeth Baker.[305] It is not clear what he was doing in Winchester at this time. Perhaps, George was working for the father of one of the other boys. It is simply amazing that a Union supporter like John R. King could find and interact with seven, young "Winchester Friends" in the midst of a horrific Civil War going.

Monday May 5th 1862

This morning John Burgess & me went to work fixing up our House to try our Chemicals. We got fixed about 2 O'clock and took a few pictures and was satisfied they worked well.

Tuesday May 6 1862

Last night I slept in My House and slept very well. To-day the whole of Gen. Rosecrantz's Divis. moved away. My Buisisness is very dull, I was practicing some to-day. It is reported that Gen. Banks is falling back from Harrisonburg.

Wednesday May 7th 1862

Buisiness being very dull here I concluded to make arrangements for going to Strasburg.

Thursday May 8th 1862

This morning Burgess and me got up early & commenced taking the House to pieces and after much delay, we got off about 12 O'clock. I

May 4, 1862

John does not write a single antagonistic word about any of these young men nor does he discuss their probable Southern sentiments. Instead, he spoke of the adventures he had with these locals. Some of these Winchester youths probably had their wealthy fathers pay for a substitute for their required service to the Confederacy. Several may have joined the Confederate cause. In his papers, John King never mentioned any of them again.

There was only one farm in the Winchester area which was owned by the Hollingsworth family. It was built in the year 1754 and was named "Abram's Delight."[306] Also called the Hollingsworth House, it is the oldest surviving homestead in the Winchester area.

The only male Hollingsworth heir alive in 1862 was Jonah Isaac. Hence, Jonah Isaac was probably the gentleman who invited John King and his friends to his farm in the afternoon of May 4, 1862. Unfortunately for historical preservationists, later during the Civil War, the Hollingsworth "barn and outbuildings were burned by Union troops during the Civil War and the mansion house was rendered unfit for habitation."[307] The City of Winchester purchased the Hollingsworth House and grounds in 1943. The oldest home in Winchester was restored over a period of nine years by the Winchester–Frederick Historical Society and opened to the public as a museum in 1961.

May 7, 1862

John tells us once again that he was compelled to go where the troops were, for the sake of successfully operating his photography business.

May 8, 1862

The "Burgess" John refers to is the John Burgess mentioned earlier in the April 30, 1862, diary entry. As stated earlier, J. H. Lockwood of the 7th Virginia Regiment, later called the 7th West Virginia Regiment, was Provost Marshal of Winchester. While John may have had a pass from Major Lockwood to go through the lines, it was bogus. Also, he surely made up the above order allowing him "all means possible" to travel to Strasburg.

had some difficulty in getting a Pass but I got Major J. H. Lockwood of the 7" Va/" Regt/" to vouch for me. We got along very nicly until we reached Newtown when our Wheel broke & had to stop, we did'nt know what to do; passing off as a Government Official, I set about to press something, a wheel or Wagon. I went to a couple of Shops & could get nothing. I went to a Blacksmith Shop & seen a Cart & thought the Wheels of it would suit made a Darkey (very much against his) take it off & take it down but it was too large. I then waited awhile & started out on another hunt. I saw a Wagon, belonging to a Mr. Newcommer, I told him I must make Strasburg next day at noon & must have his wagon, as I had broke down. I had an order in my Pocket purporting to have come from Major Lockwood which I showed him, he read & was satisfied & lent us his wagon. The order read thus,

Newtown May 8th 1862

This is to certify that Jno R. King & Co. has orders to reach Strasburg as soon as possible, & employ all means in doing so.

By order of
J.H. Lockwood
Maj 7" Regt. Va/" Vol.

We transferred our load had the Horses put away & got permission to stay in the Toll Gate House, kept by Mrs. Niswanger, she has a couple Young Daughters & we passed the evening very pleasantly.

May 8, 1862 continued

By using guile and chicanery, John was able to secure a replacement wagon from poor Mr. Newcommer. Having gone only seven-and-one-half miles from Winchester, John still had another ten miles to go before he reached his final destination of Strasburg, Virginia.

The "Mr. Newcommer" that John mentions was probably Jacob Newcomer, an elderly farmer who, according to the 1860 census, resided in Stephensburg (now Stephens City) with his wife, two children and one domestic servant.[308] His real estate was valued at $2,000 while his personal property was listed as $2,480 on the 1860 U.S. Census. On the 1850 U. S Census for Frederick County, Mr. Newcomer stated that he and his son, William, were potters.[309] As such, they are previously undocumented potters of Frederick County, Virginia.

Mrs. Lucinda Nisewanger lived in and was in charge of the Newtown Toll House. Newtown is now called Stephens City. She had seven daughters and no sons. Their names were Margaret, Martha Ellen, Catharine, Amanda, Mary Ann, Virginia and Lucinda. Abraham Nisewanger.[310] the father of all these girls was a long-distance wagon driver, and as such, was frequently away from home.[311] By the time of John's visit, all but three of these women were married and residing elsewhere. Most likely, the two daughters that John met were Virginia, nicknamed Ginnie, and Lucinda, also called Lucie. The other single sibling, Catharine, would have been about twenty-seven at this time. Moreover, Ginnie and Lucie would have an important role to play in what would unfold in regard to the disposition of John's diary. The Nisewanger family will be discussed in length later in the next section.

Friday May 9th 1862

This morning we got up bright & early & started for Strasburg at Sun Rise reached there at 8 O'clock I there met Major Lockwood found there was no Soldier here I pushed on toward Woodstock got within 3 miles of that place, had heard such discouraging news that Gen. Banks was going to move back to Strasburg & concluded to go back, got to Strasburg about 1 O'clock, I rented a piece of ground in an Orchard & we put up our Shanty after hard work we got it fixed up.

Saturday May 10th 1862

This morning we got ready about 10 O'clock to operate & was kept buise all day & had right good luck. I don $16.00/" of work.

Sunday May 11th 1862

This morning we was wakened up by a Gentlemen who wanted his picture taken. I took him one and sent him on his way rejoiceing. On my way here I did not make notice of this beautiful Valley. Large and handsomely improved Farms greets you as far as the eye can reach. Wheat is looking splendid, Fruit Trees in full bloom, and every thing looks promising, but Alas there is one thing that casts a gloom over all this! that is this War, this war between Brothers, would to God that the day is not far distant when we shall again see our glorious Country in peace, prosperity & happiness.

May 9, 1862

It is surprising that Major Lockwood did not tell John that Banks' army was moving back to Strasburg. But, here again, John has to track the army and set up his "House," which he calls a "shanty" here, for his photography business.

May 10, 1862

This was quite a bit of money for one day's work. John does not tell us how many soldiers sat for their likenesses and the cost of an ambrotype varied according to size. The price of an ambrotype ranged from 25 cents to $2.50 in the United States depending upon size and if extras were purchased.[312] Available sizes were the Imperial or Mammoth Plate, larger than 6.5 by 8.5 inches, Whole Plate, 6.5 by 8.5 inches, Half Plate, 4.25 by 5.5, inches, Quarter Plate, 3.25 by 4.25 inches, Sixth Plate, 2.75 by 3.25 inches, Ninth Plate, 2 by 2.5 inches and the Sixteenth Plate, 1.5 by 1.75 inches.[313] The images were sold in cases or fancy frames and were covered with glass and brass mat for protection of the negative. Because of the expense for the larger sizes, Civil War soldiers would normally purchase the smaller sizes.
Officers might select the large sizes. While we do not know how many photographs John took on May 10th, if each one was the twenty-five cent variety, the number of sittings would have been sixty-four

Monday May 12th 1862

This was buisy day amongst the Troops, three Brigades came here to-day from Woodstock. Gen. Banks also arrived, and took up his Quarters in the Northern section of the Town.

Tuesday May 13th 1862

This morning I bought a Flag & paid $1.50/" for it & throwed it to the breeze from my shanty.

Wednesday May 14

This is very dreary day raining very hard. Uncle Jno. King was to see me this morning & is looking well. Buisiness with me is tolerable.

Thursday May 15th 1862

This is another rainy, disagreeable day. I received a nice Box of Edible from Pa (at Winchester) to-day & was very welcome. Buisiness very dull.

Friday May 16th 1862

This is another of those disagreeable day. My Buisiness was better to-day than yesterday. While we was at Tea this evening when were suddenly struck by Music we went to the door & found it was the 1st/" Michigan Cavely Mounted Band in front of our Shanty, serenading their Colonel, who has his HeadQuarters just opposite our Shanty: they played very well.

May 13, 1862

For some reason, John drops his use of the double underline of the date.

May 16, 1862

The First Michigan Cavalry regiment and the brigade to which they were attached to engaged the Confederates at Winchester, March 23, 1862; Middleton, Virginia, March 24, 1862; Strasburg, Virginia, March 27, 1862; Harrisonburg, Virginia, April 22, 1862; Winchester May 24, 1862 and Orange County Courthouse, July 16, 1862.[314] At this time, the leader of the First Michigan Cavalry Mounted Band was Livius Tenny, aged forty-three, who enlisted August 20, 1861, at Detroit for three years at the age of forty-five, and who was discharged September 4, 1862, at Ball's Cross Roads, Virginia.[315] Other musicians of the band included Julius Bates, age nineteen, Elbert Chandler, aged thirty-four, Joel S. Harrison, Rollin Jenny, aged twenty-four, George Leline, aged twenty-four, and Charles Sheldon, aged twenty-one.[316]

Saturday May 17th 1862

This is a lovely morning, the Sun is shining is all its glory, the air is scented with the sweet fragrant Flower & the Birds are singing sweetly, & the morning bears altogether a different aspect then that of yesterday. Buisiness is slow.

Sunday May 18th 1862

This is another beautiful morning but a very warm one. Regardless of the commandments of the Most High (Thou shall not work) I have done a little work to-day. The 1st/" Mich. Band again serenaded their Col. this evening.

May 16, 1862 continued

All of these enlisted men were mustered in at Detroit during September of 1861 for three years and all, for some reason, were discharged at Ball's Cross Roads September 4, 1862, well before their enlistment was up. Perhaps the War Department determined that a mounted cavalry band was impractical. Two of this group of musicians, Jenny and Sheldon reenlisted September 1, 1864, with the Second Brigade, Fourth Division, Twenty-Third Army Corps, and would remain until they were discharged June 15, 1865, at Knoxville, Tennessee. Elbert Chandler re-enlisted with Second Brigade, Third Division, Cavalry Corps, April 13, 1864, and stayed with that unit until discharged May 18, 1865, at Frederick, Maryland. George Leline re-enlisted with Company C of the 8th Cavalry, was promoted to sergeant, and died of wounds received in action December 5, 1864.

Colonel Thornton Fleming Brodhead was commander of the First Michigan Cavalry. He was born September 22, 1822 at South New Market, New Hampshire and studied law at Harvard.[317] He was elected to the Michigan Senate at the age of twenty-seven and later became the owner and editor of the *Democrat Free Press* and then purchased *Detroit Commercial Bulletin.*[318] In 1853, President Pierce appointed him Postmaster General of Detroit and Brodhead continued in this position until 1857. When the Civil War broke out, Brodhead received a commission to raise a regiment of cavalry with him as its colonel. In addition to the engagements cited earlier under the April 19 entry, the First Michigan would play an important in what was soon to take place at Winchester. Unfortunately, Colonel Brodhead would not survive the war. He was later mortally at the Battle of Second Manassas August 30, 1862.[319] When confronted and asked to surrender by Lewis Harman, Adjutant of the 12th Virginia Cavalry, the Colonel refused and was wounded, having been shot through both lungs.[320] His horse, pistol and sabre were then confiscated by his antagonist. He died a few days later on September 2, 1862, just twenty days before what would have been his fortieth birthday. In a letter to his wife on this deathbed, he soundly criticized General Pope and McDowell for losing the battle. Colonel Brodhead was later made Brevet Brigadier General as of August 30. During the early part of 1863, the First Michigan Cavalry would become part of the famous Michigan Cavalry Brigade, being composed of the 1st, 5th, 6th, and 7th regiments. The newly promoted George Armstrong Custer would assume command of this brigade.

At this time, Colonel Broadhead was ill and that is probably why the regimental band continued to serenade him. In his official report which was rendered later, the Colonel states, in addressing General Banks, "Your order of the evening of the 24th instant was received by me while prostrate with lung fever and hemorrhage, which for ten days has confined me to my quarters"[321]

Tuesday May 20th 1862

To-day it looks as if we would have rain. Buisiness has been very brisk to-day. I took a picture of Lieut. Col. Brown (Acting Col.) of the 28" N. Y. Regt/". Raining this evening.

Wednesday May 21st 62

This is a very pretty morning, but promises a very warm day. Buisisness is very slow to-day. I recd/" some stock of James Lelt, Harrisburg to-day.

Thursday May 22th 1862

This is a very warm day, & Buisiness has been the dullest I have experienced since I have opened.

Abruptly, here ends the diary of John Rigdon King—Editor

May 20, 1862

The 28th New York Regiment, part of General Williams Brigade was mentioned briefly under the diary entry of March 2 when Union troops crossed the Potomac into Virginia. The 28th was composed mainly of young men from Niagara, Orleans, Genesce, Ontario and Sullivan counties and was organized at Albany in response to President Lincoln's call for seventy-five thousand troops at the onset of the war. The regiment was mustered into U.S. Service May 22, 1861, with Dudley Donnelly as Colonel and Edwin F. Brown as Lieutenant Colonel.[322] Shortly after this diary entry, the regiment celebrated its one year "muster-in" anniversary at headquarters with speeches by the officers.[323] Edwin Franklin Brown was born near Medina, New York, on April 23, 1823. Hence, he had just turned thirty-nine years of age when John took his photograph. He was Acting Colonel of the 28th New York at this time because Colonel Donnelly was temporarily serving in General Williams role as acting brigade commander since the latter was away. In any case, Lieutenant Colonel Brown served admirably until he was wounded at the Battle of Cedar Mountain on August 9, 1862, and required amputation of his left arm.[324] He was left at Culpeper, Virginia, August 19, was taken prisoner and was later exchanged at Aikens Landing October 6, 1862. He rejoined his regiment February 9, 1863, was promoted to Colonel and was mustered out with them June 2, 1863. After the war, Colonel Brown continued to serve his troops. He accepted a position as Governor of the Central Branch of the National Home for Disabled Volunteers in 1868 and later became Inspector General for all National Homes in the United States.[325] Colonel Brown died of a heart disease January 10, 1903, at his apartment in the Westleigh, in the West 123rd Street.[326]

At this time, the First Brigade, commanded by Alpheus S. Williams was encamped at Round Hill, Virginia. The brigade consisted of the 46th Pennsylvania regiment, the 28th New York, the 5th Connecticut and Best's battery of the 4th U.S. Artillery.[327] The First Maryland Infantry Regiment was on detached service at Front Royal. Presumably, the First Michigan Cavalry shared this_camp with the infantry regiments. Lying within Shenandoah County, Round Hill is a three-hundred foot geological formation located 1.3 miles from Toms Brook, two miles southwest of Fisher's Hill and about four miles from Strasburg.[328] Apparently, John R. King and his friend, James Burgess, as well as several regiments had set up their quarters along the base of Round Hill.

III

The Battles of Front Royal and Winchester

Friday May 23, 1862

A rapidly moving body of Confederate infantry, cavalry and artillery sneaking north via the Luray Valley soon surprised unsuspecting Union army outposts and fortifications in and near Front Royal. None of the Union commanders was aware of what was about to transpire. General Stonewall Jackson probably had the best division in Lee's army with twelve regiments of infantry, eleven from Virginia and one from Maryland, as well as six batteries of artillery. General Richard Ewell, who was with General Jackson at this time, also had a formidable division, composed of six Virginia regiments, four Louisiana regiments and four from other Southern states. Moreover, his division included the famed, bellicose Special Batallion of former New Orleans dock workers known as the Louisiana Tiger Zoaves, commanded by Major Roberdeau (Rob) Wheat.[1] Jackson had, including the troops of General Ewell, a total army of 17,000 infantrymen and cavalry while Colonel John Reese Kenly, commanding the Maryland Brigade, had a garrison total of only about 1,000 soldiers. Realizing that he had to remove the Front Royal garrison to get at General Nathaniel Banks and his larger and widely scattered army of 9,000 in and around Winchester, Jackson was eager to get the job done. He knew that the quaint village of Front Royal was the key to the capture of Winchester and thus of the entire Shenandoah Valley.[2]

Numerous sutlers, like John King who was taking photographic portraits, had camped adjacent to the army in the hopes of profiting from the war and were now just about thirteen miles away in a Union camp at Round

Hill. John King's life, like those of the other sutlers, was soon be affected forever by what was about to transpire.

Lieutenant Henry Kyd Douglas, aide-de-camp to General Stonewall Jackson, riding in the vanguard of the column, reached a hill overlooking the village of Front Royal. He soon noticed a rider approaching and later described the event as follows:

> I observed, almost immediately, the figure of a woman, in white glide swiftly out of town on our right and, after making a little circuit, run rapidly up a ravine in our direction and then disappear from sight. She seemed, when I saw her, to heed neither weeds nor fences, but waved a bonnet as she came on, trying, it was evident, to keep the hill between herself and the village. I called General Jackson's attention to the singular movement…and…he sent me to meet her and ascertain what she wanted. That was just to my taste and it took only a few minutes for my horse to carry me to greet the romantic maiden whose tall, supple, and graceful figure struck me as soon as I came in sight of her. As I drew near, her speed slackened, and I was startled, momentarily, at hearing her call my name. But I was not much astonished when I saw that the visitor was the well-known Belle Boyd whom I had known from her earliest girlhood. She was just to dare to do this thing. Nearly exhausted, and with her hand pressed against her heart, she said in gasps, "I knew it must be Stonewall, when I heard the first gun. Go back and tell him that the Yankee force is very small-one regiment of Maryland infantry, several pieces of artillery and several companies of cavalry. Tell him I know, for I went through the camps and got it out of an officer. Tell him to charge right down and he will catch them all. I must hurry back. Good-by. My love to all the dear boys—and remember if you meet me in town you haven't seen me today. I raised my cap, kissed her hand and was gone. I delivered her message speedily, and while Jackson was asking me questions about her-for until then he had never heard of her—I saw the wave of her white bonnet as she entered the village and disappeared among its houses.[3]

Henry Kyd Douglas was a young lawyer from Shepherdstown, Virginia, before the war. He also had taught at the Hagerstown Academy and may have met student John King at some point. After the Civil War, Douglas and King would become well-acquainted with one another. Belle Boyd was a young lady from Martinsburg, Virginia, visiting friends in the small village of Front Royal, Virginia. She was born in the same year, 1844, as our diarist John King. Belle was born on May 4th, thus having just turned eighteen years old, while John

King would not reach his eighteenth birthday until June 24 of 1862. Henry was about six years older than both of them, as he was born September 29, 1838, in Ireland.[4] It is interesting to note that both Belle Boyd and John R. King were also of Irish descent. Belle and Henry had known each other since childhood. Before the war, Henry K. Douglas lived with his parents at Ferry Hill Plantation, located on the bluffs across the Potomac River from Shepherdstown, Virginia, in Washington County, Maryland. Belle Boyd and John King probably did not know each other before the war. While Henry's home and Belle's were very near (less than ten miles apart), Shepherdstown and Martinsburg, they were both some distance from Hagerstown, about eighteen miles and twenty-three miles respectively.[5] Belle Boyd would later describe her flight across the field from the village towards the head of the Confederate column a bit differently than Henry Douglas:

> At this moment, the Federal pickets, who were rapidly falling back, perceived me still running as fast as I was able, and immediately fired upon me. My escape was most providential; for, although I was not hit, the rifle-balls flew thick and fast around me, and more than one struck the ground so near my feet as to throw the dust in my eyes. Upon this occasion my life was spared by what seemed to me then, and seems still, little short of a miracle; for, besides the numerous bullets that whistled by my ears, several actually pierced different parts of my clothing, but not one reached my body. Besides all this, I was exposed to a cross-fire from the Federal and Confederate artillery, whose short and shell flew whistling and hissing over my head. At length a Federal shell struck the ground within twenty yards of my feet; and the explosion, of course, sent shell fragments flying in every direction around me. I had, however, just time to throw myself flat upon the ground before the deadly engine burst; and again Providence spared my life.[6]

Belle added:

> As I neared our line I waved my bonnet to our soldiers, to intimate that they should press forward, upon which one regiment, the First Maryland 'rebel infantry,' and Hay's Louisiana Brigade, gave me a loud cheer, and without waiting for further orders, dashed upon the town at a rapid pace.[7]

[Harry Hays was colonel of the 4th Louisiana Regiment.—Editor].
She then describes the encounter with her old acquaintance,

> I rose from my kneeling posture, and had proceeded but a short distance, when, to my unspeakable, indescribable joy, I caught site of the main body fast approaching; and soon an old friend and connection of mine, Major Harry Douglas, rode up, and recognizing me, cried out, while he seized my hand. 'Good God, Belle, you here! What is it' [8]

While both of these recollections are most likely overly dramatized, others have confirmed both the encounter and the importance of Belle's information for the outcome of the battle. Another memoir that mentions Belle Boyd's role in the Battle of Front Royal on May 23, 1862, is that of Brigadier General Richard "Dick" Taylor. Dick Taylor, the son of former President Zachary Taylor, was commanding the Louisiana Brigade under Major General Richard S. Ewell. Taylor's Louisiana Brigade was leading General Jackson's long column of rebels. In his post-war book, General Taylor described the event as follows:

> Past midday we reached a wood extending from the mountain to the river, when a mounted officer from the rear called Jackson's attention, who rode back with him. A moment later, there rushed out of the wood to meet us a young, rather well-looking woman, afterward known as Belle Boyd. Breathless with speed and agitation, some time elapsed before she found her voice. Then, with much volubility, she said we were near Front Royal, beyond the wood; that the town was filled with Federals, whose camp was on the west side of the river, where they had guns in position to cover the wagon bridge, but none bearing on the railroad bridge below the former; that they believed Jackson to be west of Massanutten, near Harrisonburg; that General Bank's, the Federal commander, was at Winchester, twenty miles northwest of Front Royal, where he was slowly concentrating his widely scattered forces to meet Jackson's advance, which was expected some days later. All this she told with the precision of a staff officer making a report, and it was true to the letter.[9]

Also in Jackson's attacking column was another person very well known to Belle Boyd, her father. Benjamin Reed Boyd, born February 23, 1816, was a well-to-do grocer and merchant in Martinsburg, Virginia, before the Civil War. Stonewall Jackson, after obtaining Belle Boyd's information, was quick to prepare his troops for battle. He ordered Johnson, Wheat and Taylor forward at about two o'clock in the afternoon of May 23, 1862. Perhaps because he knew he was facing Colonel Kenly's Maryland Brigade, Jackson called up his own Maryland regiment, Colonel Bradley

T. Johnson's First Maryland Volunteer Infantry and placed it in the center of his attacking formation. "The Confederate Marylanders moved up and were greatly cheered by the news that the 1st Maryland Infantry (U.S.) held Front Royal."[10]

This was the first time in the history of the United States that military units from the same state fought each other. Easily brushing aside the Federal pickets, the Confederates moved quickly towards the Union camp at Front Royal. Colonel Kenley soon realized that Front Royal was lost and retreated to the main camp located on the heights near the North Fork Bridge of the Shenandoah River.[11] Kenley immediately sent a rider to Winchester to inform General Banks that a large Confederate force was attacking him. The Union commander also learned that Confederate cavalry were attempting to get in his rear to close off any chance of retreat. Therefore, he fell back and with his men scampered across the North Fork Bridge and then set it afire and disappeared over a ridge.[12] Colonel Thomas Flournoy's cavalry, having just returned from their mission of cutting telegraph lines west of Front Royal, returned and were ordered to pursue the enemy across the bridge.[13] Some of Jackson's skirmishers had just put out the blaze. Flournoy's cavalry, four companies numbering about 250 riders, soon caught up the Colonel Kenly and his men. Colonel Kenly, aware that he was vastly outnumbered, retreated to set up a defensive line one and one-half miles away with his some infantry and artillery near the little town of Cedarville. Jackson's men pursued them with vigor, but they made a good fight. General Jackson himself raced along with the Confederate cavalry to chase the fleeing Federals. Finally, Jackson called upon his Cavalry Regiment to make a charge upon the Union line. Flournoy's mounted men made several charges, the Yankee line broke, reformed and broke again. The battle was soon over. The Confederates ran over the defensive line and soon routed the entire Union brigade. As the author Shelby Foote noted, "gleefully the rebel Marylanders beat the bushes, rounding up their late compatriots and neighbors."[14] Almost all of the Union Maryland Brigade were taken as prisoners, including Colonel Kenly who was wounded. Some of the Union Marylanders fraternized with their Confederate counterparts as many had previously known each other. However, not everyone was happy to see their former acquaintances. Overall, the Federals lost 904 men killed or captured while the Confederate casualties were less than 50 men killed and those were mostly cavalry shot from their horses during the charges.[15]

While John King and his acquaintance from Winchester, John Burgess, were encamped with the First Michigan Cavalry and the rest of General Williams Brigade at Round Hill, the Battle of Front Royal was raging during the afternoon of May 23, 1862. Whether these young men heard the roar of cannons and the clatter of musketry from nearby is not known with certainty, but they probably did. Camped just across the lane from the tent of Colonel Thornton F. Broadhead, commander of the First Michigan Cavalry, the two Johns must have previously felt very safe in the midst of such a large body of friendly Union soldiers. Their anxiety level must have begun to pique when they realized that a battle was looming just miles away. John King had just taken an ambrotype photograph of Lt. Colonel Edward F. Brown three days earlier on May 20. The two young men, boys really were now in a very dangerous, exposed position in a brigade camp just a few miles from Strasburg. General Banks now realized that Stonewall Jackson was no longer to his south in Harrisonburg. However, Banks really did not know exactly where Jackson was. At one point, Banks believed that Jackson's division was in his front at Strasburg and that Ewell's division was on his left flank. However, Banks had very poor intelligence, as evidenced by the sneak attack on Front Royal. Initially, the Union commander thought he would make a fight of it. He did not wish to be branded a coward. Hence, Banks ordered that reinforcements be sent to Front Royal, but then he soon countermanded that order at 3 o'clock, the morning of May 24. One of Banks' officers suggested that it would be wiser to retreat for Winchester and the safety of the Potomac River. Thus, General Banks issued an order to Colonel Dudley Donnelly, commander of the First Brigade, Williams' Brigade at Round Hill, which was received in the early morning of Saturday, May 24, 1862.[16] A portion of Colonel Donnelly's report to General Banks of May 29, 1862, reads as follows:

> General: In obedience to orders received from you, on the morning of the 24th of May instant, at 1 o'clock, the 1st Brigade, comprising the 46th Pennsylvania, 28th New York, and 5th Connecticut Volunteers (the 1st Maryland being at Front Royal on detached service), and Best's battery of the 4th U.S. Artillery, broke up their encampment at Round Hill and marched to Strasburg, at which place we halted for one hour. I was then directed by Major General to march to Middletown on the road to Winchester, a large portion of our train having preceded us in that direction.[17]

John King must have broken his camp at the same time the First Brigade began to move. He and his acquaintance, John Burgess, would have taken John's portable photographic studio apart, loaded it onto the wagon, hitched up their borrowed horse, and prepared to leave. It is doubtful that they would have been in the Union supply train. Most likely, they would have had to join the wagon train of the other sutlers that traveled with the Union army. As such, they would not have had the armed protection that the military wagon train had.

For his part, Stonewall Jackson was in his element. His men said that his bright blue eyes lit up when the army was preparing for battle. Jackson had easily taken the garrison at Front Royal with the loss of only a few men. Now, he had a bigger prize in mind. Jackson wanted to bag Banks' army of 9,000 soldiers at Strasburg and the huge supply depot at Winchester. His division, now united with General Ewell's division, numbered about 17,000. In addition, he was not at Strasburg as General Banks' had erroneously surmised. Instead, Jackson ordered Ewell to march northwest along the Middletown Road while he followed a parallel route towards the same objective: to catch Banks in motion along the Valley Pike at Middletown. The whole matter really came down to a question of which army would win the race there first. As Abraham Lincoln said, it was "a question of legs."[18] However, Banks had two distinct advantages over Jackson in this contest. First, the distance from Strasburg to Winchester along the Valley Pike was less than the distance from Front Royal to Winchester. As the crow flies, it is about nine miles from Front Royal to Middletown, but only about five miles from Strasburg to Middletown.[19] Secondly, it had rained and the roads for the Confederates were muddy making travel tougher. On the other hand, the Union Army was marching along the macadamized Valley Pike. Macadam is a "pavement of layers of compacted broken stone" and traveling on it would be much easier than on rain-soaked ground.[20]

Without a doubt, John King and John Burgess drove their loaded wagon along the Valley Pike behind the main Union Army as it slogged along the road to its northern destination. They would have ridden along with the other sutlers' wagons in the long train leaving Strasburg. It is not known for certainty if the sutlers were part of the "large portion of our train" that preceded Colonel Donnellys' soldiers, but evidence suggests that it was a part of that group of wagons. Most definitely, King and Burgess were not with Union Colonel Othneil DeForest of the 5th New York Cavalry. He took an immense band of infantrymen and cavalrymen on a safe route along the back roads west of Winchester and never actually went to Winchester. His group included "two hundred and fifty men of the First Vermont Cavalry, sixty-five members of General Banks' body guard, some of the 1st Maine, 1st Virginia, 1st Maryland, 1st Michigan, 8th New York Cavalry, 5th Connecticut and 10th Maine Infantry, four companies of the 5th New York Cavalry, some sutlers, telegraph operators, wagoners, one of the Signal Corps, and some of the 1st Maryland Artillery (more properly Battery F, Pennsylvania Light Artillery)."

[21] This massive group escaped without any injuries or captures and the loss of only three of its thirty-five wagons and ended up at Williamsport, Maryland, covering eighty-four miles in three days, Saturday, Sunday and Monday.[22] The rest of the Banks' command and the other sutlers would not be so lucky. When General Stonewall Jackson finally reached the Valley Pile just below Middletown, he caught the Union column in motion. In his official report, Jackson described the scene:

> I accompanied the movement of the main body of the army to Middletown. Upon arriving there we found the Valley turnpike crowded with the retreating Federal cavalry, upon which the batteries of Poague and Chew, with Taylor's infantry, promptly opened, and in a few moments the turnpike, which had just before teemed with life, presented a most appalling spectacle of carnage and destruction. The road was literally obstructed with the mingled and confused mass of struggling and dying horses and riders. Among the surviving cavalry in disorder in the wildest confusion ensued, and they scattered in disorder in various directions, leaving however, some 200 prisoners, with their equipments in our hands. A train of wagons was seen disappearing in the distance toward Winchester and Ashby, with his cavalry, some artillery, and a supporting infantry force from Taylor's brigade was sent in pursuit.

General Banks and most of his infantry had already passed this point on the Valley Pike and were streaking towards Winchester, thirteen miles distant. However, in his report official report under the heading of "A Stampede," Banks wrote the following:

> The column had passed Cedar Creek, about three miles from Strasburg, with the exception of the rear guard, still in front of Strasburg, when information was received from the front that the enemy had attacked the train and was in full possession of the road at Middletown. This report was confirmed by the return of fugitives, refugees, and wagons, which came tumbling to the rear in fearful confusion.[24]

In his report of the operations of May 24, Union Colonel Joseph F. Knipe, commanding the 46th Pennsylvania Infantry, part of Williams brigade that camped at Round Hill near John King's photography studio, described the first day as follows:

> In accordance with orders received at 3 o'clock a.m. Saturday, May 24, my command was immediately put in readiness to move, and, with the

> regiment train ahead, reached the turnpike leading to Strasburg at 4:30 o'clock a.m. Pushing at a rapid rate until we reached Strasburg ... when, with the whole train, numbering about 500 wagons, in front, we again took up the line of march for Winchester when with a short distance of Middletown an alarm in front caused a stampede of teamsters, sutlers, and civilians, who came rushing back upon us in the wildest confusion.[25]

In all probability, John King and John Burgess were among this throng of sutlers and civilians who were scurrying back to the rear to reach the safety of the Union force south of them on the Valley Pike. The Confederate army was in their front on the road and there was nothing they could do but flee. Most likely, John King's wagon veered off the pike here and went into the woods traveling in a westerly direction to avoid the Confederate onslaught. Of course, John King could have exited the Valley Pile at any point between Middletown and Winchester. The Valley Pike was riddled with the flotsam of battle for many miles as reported by Jackson's aide-de-camp, Henry Kyd Douglas:

> The next day General Jackson moved on toward Middletown. It was evident that Banks either was late in getting information of the result of Front Royal or did not appreciate its meaning. He hesitated, delayed, and seemed unwilling to leave Strasburg until convinced that he must do it. His column was struck and cut in two before it passed Middletown, although General Banks himself and the bulk of his infantry had gone. With the cavalry and the artillery left behind and some little infantry, all sorts of a mixed-up fight ensued....Colonel Oliver R. Funsten of Ashby's cavalry was sent to the right, accompanied by a section of W. T. Poague's battery, to intercept the retreating enemy in the direction of Newtown. The road was literally lined with wagons of all kinds, miles of them. Funsten's and Poague's attack soon created a stampede and the train of Quartermaster and commissary stores fell into our hands. With all possible promptness we moved on toward Winchester by the pike. The road was encumbered with evidence of the hurry of flight. Wagons broken down, overturned, some with their contents scattered, some sound and untouched, some with good teams, some horseless, sutlers' stores, officers' luggage, knapsacks, Bibles, cards, photographs, song books and cooking utensils-a general wreck of military matter.[26]

Here at Middletown, the Confederates began taking many prisoners and scattered those soldiers who managed to get away. While we do not know exactly where our protagonist, John King, laden with his "shanty" and expensive photographic materials, left the Valley Pike during Williams Brigade's retreat from Round Hill to Winchester, we do know that he never reached that town. Unbeknownst to him at the time, John King would embark on an adventure that would forever change his life.

General Banks developed a plan for his eventual retreat down the Shenandoah Valley in a northerly direction. After ordering Colonel Donnelly's Brigade, his advance guard, to return to Strasburg, Banks placed General Hatch in charge of "... the protection of the rear of the column and destruction of any stores for which transportation was not provided, with instructions to remain in front of town (Winchester—Ed.) as long as possible and hold the enemy in check..."[27] In his official report, General Banks added that "...soon after 9 o'clock the column was on the march, Colonel Donnelly in front, Colonel Gordon in center, and General Hatch in the rear, the whole under the directions of Brigadier General Williams, commanding division."[28]

In the meantime, on Saturday afternoon, May 24, once Stonewall Jackson had gained access to the Valley Pike at Middletown, he urged his infantry and cavalry onward in an attempt to reach Winchester before the Federals took two commanding hills south of town. However, two factors would impede the progress of Jackson's army as it pursued Banks along the pike. First, many of Ashby's cavalrymen and Taylor's infantrymen stopped to enjoy the spoils of victory. They pillaged amongst a vast array of goods and stores left by the retreating Union army. Some of Jackson's men, taking horses, even went to their nearby homes and farms, to drop them off. Jackson would later say, that some of his men "...deserted their colors, and abandoned themselves to pillage to such an extent as to make it necessary... to discontinue further pursuit."[29] Secondly, Jackson's men were extremely fatigued after the day's pursuit and fighting and some fell to sleep along the wayside. After midnight, Jackson, seemingly have no need to rest or sleep, pursued the Federals through Newtown, but finally listened to Colonel Sam Fulkerson and ordered his men to rest for a few hours.[30] Jackson knew that Banks would take the hills south of Winchester where Federals would place artillery that would wreak havoc upon his troops as they approached.

Observations of Colonel Knipe, commanding the 46th Pennsylvania Infantry, provide an example of what the Union troops faced during their retreat:

> ...we arrived at Winchester at 9 o'clock p.m., taking position on the Front Royal road about a mile from town and bivouacked; my men being entirely

> without blankets, overcoats, or food...At this juncture I received orders to support a section of Best's artillery on an eminence in our rear, and accordingly fell back midst a raking fire of shot and shell to the position assigned me, which we held securely until we received orders to retreat, when we moved through the town in perfect order, the civilians firing upon us from the houses in an inhuman manner....Seeing larger numbers of the enemy within a short distance of our rear I halted the regiment determined to drive them back, when the number of stragglers (soldiers and civilians) between us caused me to refrain...after a fatiguing march under fire of the enemy's artillery, who pressed us within three miles of Martinsburg ... we reached Williamsport at 10 o'clock p.m.[31]

Jackson used the 33rd Virginia Infantry, a regiment of his old Stonewall Brigade, and Taylor's men to clear the ridges below Winchester of Union artillery and supporting infantry. Confederates soon entered the town driving the Union army before it. Initially, the Union soldiers retreated through Winchester in good order, but soon after they cleared the town, "... Banks's men stumbled and jostled together in a large amorphous mass of humanity."[32] As Jackson entered Winchester, the townspeople came out in front of their homes and shops lining the street and cheered the advancing troops. During the Civil War, composed mostly of Southern sympathizers, Winchester changed hands over seventy times, highlighting its strategic importance.[33] General Jackson himself was given a special welcome by the citizens, who were thrilled to get rid of the occupying Union force. The Confederates chased the Federals as far as Martinsburg before giving up the fight. More prisoners were scooped up by Jackson's advancing army. Just as they had done after the Battle of Front Royal, the Confederates placed about 2800 Union enlisted men and officers, including those from the battle of Front Royal, within the confines of an iron fence that circled the Winchester courthouse. The Union prisoners remained in that temporary stockade until the morning of May thirty-first when Colonel Cunningham, commanding the 21st Virginia Regiment, left Winchester and moved up (south) the Valley toward Staunton.[34]

Officially, General Banks reported the following causalities: 2 officers and 60 enlisted men killed, 16 officers and 227 enlisted men wounded, and 51 officers and 1,663 enlisted men captured or missing for an aggregate of 2,019.[35] General Jackson put his losses at 68 killed, 329 wounded and only 3 missing in action, making a total loss of 400.[36] In addition, Stonewall captured much needed supplies. As he stated in his official report:

Commissary supplies, consisting of upward of 100 head of cattle, 34,000 pounds of bacon, flour, salt, sugar, coffee, hard bread, and cheese ... besides large amounts taken by the troops and not accounted for. Sutlers' stores valued at $25,185 were secured, besides an immense amount destroyed. Among the stores taken and removed in safety were 9,354 small arms and two pieces of artillery and their caissons.[37]

IV

The Capture

May 25, 1862

What happened to John King and John Burgess in the Shenandoah Valley? What became of John's two horses and his photography studio and equipment? Was Mr. Newcomer's wagon ever returned to him? In future years, John King never mentioned that he was a Civil War sutler photographer. Instead, he merely stated that he was "with General Banks at Winchester." Perhaps, once he became famous, he was embarrassed about telling his friends and the general public what really occurred in the Shenandoah Valley from May 23 to May 25, 1862. If not for the following article which appeared in the August 27, 1862 issue of the *Herald Freedom and Torch Light* newspaper of Hagerstown, the complete story might never have been known.

> Escaped Photographer Vows Revenge on Rebels
>
> RETURNED TO HIS HOME—P. Rigdon King [sic], son of Samuel L. King of this town, who has been in the hands of the rebels as a prisoner since Gen. Banks' retreat from Strasburg in May last, returned to his home recently. Mr. King was not connected with the army in a military capacity, but was engaged in the business of taking likenesses while it laid near Strasburg, and when the retreat commenced sought with the rest to make his escape, but after just wandering through the adjacent mountains for several days was captured and taken into Jackson's camp at Winchester. When Jackson's army retreated from Winchester, he was taken South with

> the other prisoners and like them received the most cruel and inhuman treatment from the rebels, having been furnished with scarcely enough food to keep body and soul together and that of the most revolting kind, and marched 25 and 30 miles a day. He gives a very deplorable account of the manner in which our prisoners are fed and lodged by the rebels, but we have not room to write it in detail. He managed to pass himself off as the 2nd Lieut. of a Wisconsin Company and as such was included in the recent exchange of prisoners.
>
> If he had not done this, he would probably have had to remain until the close of the war, as there seems to have been no arrangements made for the exchange or release of persons not connected with the army. William H. Protzman and J. H. Duffy, both citizens of this town, who were in the employ of Mr. Mong and who were taken at the same time that Mr. King was, are still at Richmond and as civic prisoners may have to remain a long time. Mr. King represents the Hagerstown boys in the rebel army, Cramer, Shirey and others, as heartily sick and tired of the war and anxious to desert as they can do so safely.
>
> Mr. King informs us that he has volunteered and plans to pay the Rebels another visit, in Lieut. Small's company, but not in the harmless character of an artist.[1]

King and Burgess were now in the hands of the Confederate army after being captured a few days after the Battle of First Winchester on May 25, 1862. While John King had previously been peripherally involved in the war, he was now directly involved in the conflict as a prisoner of war. He and John Burgess must have been terrified when Confederate soldiers seized them. In Hagerstown, John King had a ringside seat to all the gaiety and hoopla associated with the bands playing, intense political speeches against the Secessionists, and parades in the streets. His brother, Harrison, was a Union officer. In Hagerstown and in the field, John King befriended numerous Federal officers and enlisted men. He went to the Potomac River and watched the spectacle of an army crossing to the Virginia side. Going to Winchester later, he was a sutler who sold goods and photographs to eager Union troops. In that town, he also acted like a tourist traveling with local boys to Shawnee Springs, George Washington's headquarters and then spent the day at the Hollingsworth estate paddling a boat on its lake. This was all about to change when he got lost in the woods outside of Winchester as he attempted to flee north along with a train of other sutlers. To date, John King had not seen firsthand the other side of war. He had watched a skirmish from afar and then saw a captured group of

Ashby's cavalrymen whom he described as looking "hard." Now, the tables were turned and some of these "hard men" had him. He knew nothing of the suffering, horror and death of those caught up in the Civil War either as civilians or soldiers. He would soon see more of the horrid side of war than he ever thought possible.

Most likely, the troops that captured King and Burgess were Ashby's cavalry. Surely, after inspecting his wagon and seeing that he was a sutler and photographer, at least one Confederate officer interrogated the boys back at Jackson's headquarters in Winchester. Although both were dressed in civilian attire, once the Confederates viewed King's diary, they may have thought that at least one of them was a spy. Of course, as he did with Mr. Newcomer in Newtown, John would have tried to use his cunning and intellect to talk his way out of his predicament, but this time to no avail. John King was still only seventeen years old and would not turn eighteen until June 24. Burgess was also only seventeen and would not reach his eighteenth birthday until October. However, John King's civilian status and age apparently made no difference to the Confederates. Both the North and South were taking civilians as political prisoners, some for later exchange. To add insult to injury, his captors not only confiscated John King's portable photographic studio, his camera and chemicals, his two horses and Mr. Newcomer's wagon, but, more importantly, they also took his personal diary. John had been recording his observations and thoughts since October 22, 1861, and now it was apparently lost forever.

The newspaper article above does not mention John's assistant, John Burgess. Possibly, the Confederates released John Burgess after learning that he was a citizen of Winchester. The only John Burgess shown on the 1860 census for Winchester was John W. Burgess, son of Abraham S. and Sarah Burgess, who was nineteen years old in 1860.[2] Another source indicates that John Burgess was in school at the beginning of the Civil War and "… leaving school, he enlisted in the Confederate army."[3] It seems likely that this is the same young man who so easily left home and traveled with John King to the front lines to take photographs. However, this same source also relates that John Burgess enlisted in the Confederate Baltimore Light Artillery under Captain Brockenbrough of Lexington, Virginia, at Richmond, Virginia, in 1861. Additional research absolutely refutes this statement. Actual Confederate muster rolls show that John W. Burgess joined Company B of the 2nd Battery Maryland Artillery, also known as the Baltimore Light Artillery, as a private under Captain Brockenbrough on June 13, 1862, at Port Republic, Virginia, "for three years or the war."[4] June 13 was just over two weeks from the Battle of First Winchester on May 25, 1862. Did

Jackson or his men force John Burgess to join the army after being taken prisoner or did he join of his own accord? Had John Burgess avoided the draft following the enactment of the first American draft passed April 16, 1862? Technically, he could not be drafted until age eighteen. Did John Burgess later attempt to hide his capture by changing the circumstances of his enlistment? The answers to these questions will probably never be known. What is known is that John Burgess served with an artillery unit until the end of the war. He appears on a "list of Prisoners of War, belonging to the Army of the Confederate States, who have been this day surrendered by General Robert E. Lee, C.S.A., commanding said Army, to Lieut. Genl. U.S. Grant, commanding Armies of the United States."[5] This list was dated Lynchburg, Virginia, April 13, 1865, or four days after the surrender of Lee to Grant. John Burgess was paroled at Lynchburg on April 16, 1865 and returned home to Winchester. Six months later, he moved to Williamsport, Maryland, not far from where John King lived in Hagerstown.[6] By 1880, Mr. Burgess had gone to Hancock, Maryland, where he worked as a carpenter and was still single.[7] By 1900, he was still living in Hancock employed as a carpenter, but had married Mary Dallas Burgess and had one child, Mary M., age eighteen, who was born in January of 1882.[8] As of 1910, at age sixty-five, he was superintendent of the C & O Canal in Hancock, lived with his wife, daughter, son-in-law, two grandchildren and two domestic servants.[9] John West Burgess died in 1918 in Hancock, Maryland, and is buried in the Saint Thomas Episcopal Church Cemetery.[10] It is not known if he and John King ever spoke after John's capture and imprisonment by the Confederates in May of 1862. John King apparently never mentioned John Burgess in any letters, historical accounts or other writings.

According to the above newspaper article, William H. Protzman and James H. Duffy, both civilians and residents of Hagerstown who were in the employ of a Mr. Mong, also were captured and marched to prison. Protzman is shown on the 1860 U.S. Census as residing in his father's household in Hagerstown along with three siblings. At that time, his age was twenty-six and his occupation was shown as a "clerk."[11] In 1870, he was residing in Hagerstown, now with a wife, three children and a domestic servant.[12] He had real estate valued at $14,200 and personal property worth $2,000 and gave his occupation as a "clerk in a factory."[13] In contrast, there is no record of James H. Duffy living in Hagerstown in 1860 or 1870 although obviously he was residing there for some time in 1862. The Mr. Mong mentioned in the newspaper was probably Joseph P. Mong of Hagerstown, a local politician and businessman who sold groceries, liquor and bricks before the war. His listed occupation on the 1850 U.S. Census was as a "grocer."[14] Mong was probably using Protzman and Duffy as his agents for a business of selling goods to the Union Army, much like the King family. These two men and Mr. Mongs' wares were most likely snatched up by the attacking Confederates on the Valley Pike below Middletown as they also tried to escape north with the rest of Banks' fleeing army.

The *Herald Freedom and Torch Light*, a strictly pro-Union newspaper, also opined that John King told them that "...the Hagerstown boys in the rebel army, Cramer, Shirey and others, as heartily sick and tired of the war and anxious to desert as they can do so safely."[15] The Cramer mentioned may have been Jacob I. Cramer/Creamer, of Hagerstown, who enlisted in Company D, 1st Maryland Infantry.[16] The Shirey referred to was most likely Charles Shirey/Sherry, who joined Company F of the 1st Maryland (Confederate) Cavalry.[17] Although Maryland Confederate records are scanty, those available make no mention of either of these men as having been deserters. Likewise, for several Hagerstown young men that John King later referred to as his friends before the war, their service records also show no desertions. For this and several other reasons, the above newspaper article has to be taken with a grain of salt. While John may have been treated harshly and poorly fed on his forced march away from Winchester to prison in the South, other sources gave differing accounts of the actual prison conditions. Others gave similar reports. One soldier who was a prisoner at the same time as John King, Captain Shurtleff of the 7th Ohio Volunteer Infantry found the forced march through Virginia to Libby Prison, in Richmond, not to his liking. He mentioned that his "enlisted men were tied together with a rope like a gang of slaves" perhaps in an attempt to humble them.[18] We will probably never know exactly what John Kings' captors, the 21st Virginia Regiment, did to him on his march eastward. While the newspaper article does not specify where John was taken initially, other records show that the 2,300 Federal prisoners taken by Jackson in the Battles of Front Royal and Winchester and which were corralled within the iron gates of Winchester Court House, were forcibly marched up the Shenandoah Valley (actually south) toward Staunton beginning on the morning of May 31st.[19] As mentioned, these Union soldiers were guarded by the 21st Virginia Infantry under the command of Lt. Colonel Richard H Cunningham of Jackson's Second Brigade.[20] The distance between Winchester and Staunton is eighty-seven miles as the crow flies and ninety-five miles on todays' roads.[21] Hence, covering at least twenty-five to thirty miles per day, as stated in the newspaper article, it would have taken this group of prisoners four days to walk to Staunton, Virginia. The 21st Virginia Regiment may have loaded the Federals on board trains bound for Petersburg, Virginia. On June 13, 1862, the *Richmond Daily Dispatch* newspaper reported that this large group of Jacksons' prisoners arrived in Petersburg and published the names, ranks and regiments of the Union officers. The article read as follows:

> The Federal officers, named below, captured by Stonewall Jackson in his recent brilliant victory over Banks, arrived in Petersburg on Wednesday last, on their way to Salisbury N.C. The remainder of the prisoners has not reached Petersburg yesterday morning but were hourly expected.[22]

Since nearly one-thousand men from the Union Maryland Brigade were captured at the Battle of Front Royal, many of the men on this list were officers from that brigade. They included Lt. Colonel Nathan T. Dushane, Captain G. W. Kugler, and Captain B. H. Sibley of the 1st Maryland Volunteers, Lieutenants John Knoppel, Robert Neeley, James L. Fair, Josiah B. Coloney, Virgil T. Mercer, Maurice Abough, Daniel L. Stanton and William E. George of the 1st Maryland Volunteers as well as several other officers and many other non-commissioned officers.[23] Of course, since he was a civilian prisoner, John King's name was not on the officer's list. However, he was definitely in this group of prisoners heading to a southern prison. Still only seventeen years of age, John would be soon rolling along on a train through the Virginia and North Carolina countryside awaiting an uncertain destiny in a Confederate pen.

V

The Imprisonment June to August, 1862

Situated in western North Carolina, the prison to which John King and other Union soldiers were sent, was located near the city of Salisbury. Originally constructed twenty years earlier for use as a textile mill by Maxwell Chambers, it had been then used as a school but was vacated in early 1861 when the state of North Carolina purchased it.[1] Salisbury prison was noteworthy for two reasons. First, it was the first state prison established during the Civil War. Secondly, it housed the first prisoners of war taken during the conflict. Captured at the Battle of First Manassas on July 21, 1861, the first group of one hundred and twenty Union soldiers arrived December 9, followed by another one hundred and seventy-six on December 26, 1861.[2] Handling this group of almost three hundred would not be difficult as the prison was capable of housing between fifteen hundred and two thousand men.[3] However, Salisbury Prison was not reserved just for captured Union enlisted men and officers. Very soon, the soldiers would be joined with a ragtag bunch of "deserters from both armies, Confederate criminals, Southern unionists and other Southern dissenters" who would outnumber Union soldiers taken in battle until near the end of the war.[4]

The property consisted of a four-story brick building with an attic and a domed cupola, several wooden outbuildings and sixteen acres of land, four of which were set aside for recreational use by the inmates. The grounds were exceedingly spacious as compared to other Civil War prisons. However, another more important feature was that the prison was situated near a railroad line.[5] Once purchased from its owner, a high stockade fence with walkways was installed around the perimeter and a deadline was established. Any prisoner who crossed the deadline toward the fence was instantly shot by a guard.

The first commandant was Reverend Braxton Craven, president of nearby Trinity College, who formed a Confederate company from students, but then used those same students temporarily as guards in the prison.[6] After a few weeks, Craven was replaced by Captain A. C. Godwin of Richmond who "showed some compassion for the prisoners and became well-liked by them." [7] Later in the war when the South had a dwindling number of soldiers, old men and young boys guarded the prisoners.

In the early part of the war, conditions at Salisbury Prison while probably not very pleasant, were at least comfortable. Union officers got the best housing, had free use of the open space and were sometimes even given passes to visit the town.[8] Food, water, housing, and recreational areas and sanitation were all more than adequate. The imprisoned soldiers passed the time "performed in concerts and theatrical routines," played cards and chess, carved trinkets, and exercised in the large four-acre yard. [9] Colonel John S. Crocker, who arrived at the prison May 17, 1862, stated that it was "a flourishing place and beautifully situated." [10] Another inmate said that it was "more endurable than any other place in rebeldom."[11]

The favorite activity of the prisoners was playing baseball and this they did almost every day providing the weather was good. Teams were formed and the various rivalries were recorded by soldiers in their diaries.[12] Captain Giles Waldo Shurtleff, of the 7th Ohio Volunteer Infantry, who was an inmate from May to August of 1862, noted in his memoirs that "baseball had come into vogue..." and that "we formed an association and played every day."[13] Baseball was very popular during the Civil War in camps, near battlefields and in some prison camps. Contrary to popular opinion, the game of baseball was not invented by Abner Doubleday, a Union Major General in the Civil War, in 1839 in Cooperstown, New York. Its actual origins have never been determined. What is known is that the game was popular in New York and New England in the eighteen fifties and that soldiers from those regions brought it to other areas of the country.[14] Another captain, Otto Boetticher of the 68th New York Volunteer Infantry, who was a painter and lithographer before the war, was also imprisoned at Salisbury.[15] While there, he did a natural, scenic drawing of a baseball game taking place in the prison yard. This artwork later became famous one of the earliest known depictions of a baseball game in progress.[16]

A letter from an unnamed Union prisoner was posted in the *Richmond Times Dispatch* newspaper of June 28, 1862. It read as follows:

> There are nearly two hundred officers and privates, and one hundred and fifty citizens confined here. Privates Gould and Schwarts, of Philadelphia--,

> of Buffalo, and six citizens have died within the last fortnight. There are fifty patients in the hospital. Scurvy is the prevalent complaint. There has been very little sickness among the officers confined here, and that they are only joying good health. We have received this morning permission from Major Gordon, C.S.A. commanding the post, to celebrate the coming anniversary of our independence, with certain restrictions. The 4th of July committee consists of Col. Murphy, 29th Pennsylvania, Lieut. Colonel Neff, 2nd Kentucky; Dr. Gray, U.S. Army; Paymaster Stockwell, U.S. Army; Lieut. Watson, 3rd Connecticut; Capt. Fish, 32th New York; and Major Cassidy, 93th New York. Colonel Crocker, of the 39th New York, was selected to read the Declaration of Independence, and Lieut. Colonel Benedict, of the 75th New York to read Washington's Farewell Address. An original poem is to be recited by Capt. Drew of the 2nd Vermont. Vocal music, under the direction of Lieut. Lombard. Games and races by the privates in the afternoon, for which the officers have contributed prizes. Major Gordon displays a willingness to do all in his power for the comfort of the officers. We live in hopes of exchange.[17]

The Fourth of July of 1862 was a big day at Salisbury Prison. Captain Shurtleff later described the scene:

> As the Fourth of July approached we determined to have an old-fashioned celebration. In the afternoon, were read the Declaration of Independence, sang "My Country, Tis of Thee" and had some spirited patriotic addresses. The afternoon was given up to games, among which were the greased pig, the sack race, wheelbarrow race, and some burlesque games, ending with a match of baseball.[18]

John King was at Salisbury Prison at this time, but never mentioned the Fourth of July festivities in the *Herald Freedom and Torch Light* article regarding his imprisonment nor did he ever speak of it in later life. In fact, John only later mentioned one experience of his imprisonment, one occurring upon his arrival. After passing through Petersburg, Virginia, on June 4, 1862, John King traveled by rail to Salisbury Prison. Hence, he should have arrived at the prison by June 5th or June 6th. However, in a newspaper obituary of January 31, 1930, John stated that he came to the prison at dawn one day in May of 1862.[19] Perhaps because sixty-eight years had passed since he was at the prison, his memory of the arrival date had faded. Earlier, it was mentioned in General Stonewall Jackson's report that the prisoners taken at Front Royal and at Winchester did not leave the latter town until May

31, 1862. Thus, assuming that report was correct, John could not have possibly entered Salisbury Prison in May of 1962. In any case, the following conversation, contained in a newspaper obituary of General David Gordon, is the only known written record, aside from the previous *Herald Freedom and Torch Light* article, of John King's period of incarceration in Salisbury Prison. In his youth, John had last seen Gordon when the latter was employed in Armstrong's Dry Goods Store on Washington Street in Hagerstown. As King recalled:

> I saw and heard no more of Gordon until May, 1862, when a prisoner of war those who had preceded us were out to greet us. As we stood in the gray dawn, I observed carried with others to Salisbury, N. C. We arrived there just at dawn. Other prisoners, one of the reviewers eyeing me intently. Finally he approached me and asked "Are you from Maryland?" "I am." "Are you from Hagerstown/" "I am." "Are you a brother of Addie King?" "Why yes, who are you?" Just then he smiled. "This is Davy Gordon," I exclaimed, and Davy embraced me, saying, "This is little 'Rig' King." I'll never forget that coincidence.[20]

A few weeks after his arrival at the prison, John R. King became eighteen years old and thus was old enough to enlist in one of the military services had he not been in prison. Whether or not John celebrated his birthday in any meaningful way will never be known, but surely he must have been very displeased to have his birthday in prison. Another event that would certainly also have angered John was death of his mother, Mrs. Eliza King, on August 1, 1862. John had mentioned in his diary that his mother was ill and took her to see Dr. Fahrney. He would have desperately wanted to see his mother if she was ill and would also have wished to attend her funeral. Unfortunately, even if John had gotten word soon after her death, the commander of the prison, Major Gordon would not have allowed him to attend. It is no wonder that John spoke poorly of his captors and promised revenge for the treatment of his rebel captors when he was interviewed by the press after he returned home.

During the early years of the Civil War, paroles became commonplace. A parole was simply a sworn statement by the prisoner that he would not take up arms until a proper exchange had taken place. An exchange was the physical transfer of one soldier for another. Soldiers were well aware of the exchange program. Prisoners arriving at Salisbury early in the war did not expect a lengthy confinement.[21] In fact, about fourteen hundred men were exchanged at the end of May of 1862.[22] That is why the Union soldier who wrote the article that appeared in the *Richmond Times Dispatch* of June 28, 1862, reported that only about two hundred Federal officers and men were at the prison. During the early years of the Civil War, paroles and exchanges became commonplace. A problem, some Union soldiers came "... to realize that capture no longer meant months of confinement in a dreary Southern prison... that the likely result would be a lengthy furlough and a trip home until exchanged."[23] That "loophole" would soon be corrected, however, by the War Department on June 28, 1862, when General Orders No. 72 was issued. Instead of receiving a furlough upon exchange to recuperate, the Union soldier was sent to one of three parole camps built specifically for them.[24] Exchanged Union prisoners from the Eastern seaboard had to report to Camp Parole in Annapolis, Maryland.

On July 22, 1862, Union Major General John A. Dix met with Confederate Major General D. H. Hill at Haxall's Landing on the James River in Virginia to negotiate a formal agreement for the parole and exchange of prisoners.[25] The Dix-Hill Cartel, as it was known, specified that "prisoners to be exchanged man for man and officer for officer...but also that men and officers of lower grades may be exchanged for officers of a higher grade, and men and officers of different services may be exchanged according to the following scale of equivalents."[26] The scale stipulated ten different equivalent combinations. Most importantly for captured teamsters, sutlers and "all civilians in the actual service of either party" could be also exchanged, but only for other civilians.[27] This meant that John King, William H. Protzman and James H. Duffy, who were all from Hagerstown, could be exchanged now as long as they were traded for Southern civilians held in the North. Another important provision of the Dix-Hill Cartel was the naming of the actual locations for the exchanges. Aiken's Landing, part of the plantation of Mr. A. M. Aiken on the James River in the Varina District of Henrico County, would serve as the exchange point in the Eastern Theatre of War. Vicksburg, Mississippi, would be employed in the west for the transfer point. The Cartel appointed Brigadier General Lorenzo Thomas as the exchange agent for the Union while Robert Ould was appointed as the agent for the Confederacy. The men went to work immediately to plan large prisoner exchanges, including releasing hundreds of Federal soldiers being held in Salisbury Prison in North Carolina.

Several large transfers and exchanges of prisoners were planned for August and September of 1862. Once again, John R. King used his guile and ingenuity to plan for his release even though he was not a Union officer or enlisted man. Somehow, he knew that the soldiers would be exchanged before the civilian teamsters and sutlers. Therefore, as shown in the previously cited *Herald Freedom and Torch Light* newspaper of August 27, 1862, "he managed to pass himself off as the 2nd Lieut. of a Wisconsin Company and as such was included in the recent exchange of prisoners."[28] John may have impersonated either Lt. E. Gittings of the 3rd Wisconsin Regiment or Lt. M. C. Spencer of the same regiment. Both of these officers were among the lieutenants captured by Stonewall Jackson in the action of May 23 to May 25.[29] However, since John King's name does not appear on any official records, the identity he assumed will probably never be known. The *Richmond Times Dispatch* reported in the August 15, 1862, edition that "the Petersburg train arriving Saturday night brought largely over 300 Yankee prisoners being the last of those for some months past confined at Salisbury, N. C."[30] It seems likely that John R. King was exchanged at Aiken's Landing on August 17. A train would have transported the prisoners from Salisbury to Petersburg, Virginia, and then on to Richmond by rail and lastly by foot about thirteen miles to the exchange location on Mr. Aiken's wharf on the James River. According to official records, numerous officers including Lt. Colonel Nathan Dushane, Captains George W. Kugler, Benjamin H. Schley, and Joseph B. Coloney, George H. Bean and Lieutenants David L. Stanton and Virgil T. Mercer were all paroled and exchanged at Aiken's Landing on August 17, 1862. All of these men, except Captain Bean, were with the First Maryland Volunteer Infantry. In addition, all of these officers were captured by Jacksons' troops either at Front Royal, Middleton or Winchester during the campaign of May 23-May 25, 1862. A correspondent for *The New York Times* described the following scene based upon a conversation he had with a Union prisoner of war on Thursday, August 7, 1862:

> A gentleman who was at Aiken's Landing on Thursday, gives an interesting account of the exchange of prisoners at that point. Our vessels arrived there at one in the afternoon, and in the course of six hours delivered the 3,013 rebel prisoners to Commissioner Robert Ould. The United States prisoners walked thirteen miles, and were in an almost famished condition, their food having been two small biscuits each the entire day. They had suffered extremely for want of water, and it was only after the entreaty of Mr. Ould with the Colonel having charged of them, they were permitted in squads to quench their excessive thirst at a well. Capt. J. S. Stevenson, of the Marine Artillery, connected with our boats, distributed food, and otherwise relieved their necessities. They remained overnight at the landing, Mr. Aiken, the proprietor of the plantation, furnishing them straw on which to sleep. Early the next day they were taken on board

> our transports....The exchange has been completed so far as concerns private soldiers lately confined in Richmond and vicinity, and sometime this week the arrangement for the exchange of officers is expected to be consummated.[31]

Large transport ships took the former prisoners of war to one of the Northern ports, perhaps to Alexandria, Virginia. From there, the paroled and exchanged enlisted men and officers would not be able to simply return to their units immediately. Instead, under the conditions of General Orders No. 72 mentioned, they would all have to go to Camp Parole in Annapolis, Maryland, before rejoining their regiments. However, since John King was not actually a Union soldier but instead a civilian sutler, he would not have had to report to Camp Parole and he did not. Within a day or two after the exchange of August 17, he most likely traveled by train and was soon back in Hagerstown on or about August 19.

John King was now ready to begin to fulfill his vow to get revenge from the Confederates who mistreated and wrongly imprisoned him for about two and one-half months. John King was correct in thinking that he would be released from prison earlier posing as a Union officer rather than awaiting parole and exchange as a civilian. A brief article in the Maryland Free Press issue of October 31, 1862, confirmed that belief. It stated that "William H. Pretzman and James Duffy, who were captured by the Rebels in May when General Banks retreated from Strasburg, returned to their homes in this town on Monday evening last, (i. e., October 27-Ed.) having been released after an imprisonment of six months."[32] Pretzman and Duffy were the two civilians who were employees of a Mr. Mong, who had been captured about the same time as John during the Battle of Winchester. Both were incarcerated at Salisbury Prison with John R. King. If he had been released with them at the end of October of 1862, John R. King would never have been able to enlist in the Union Army in a company with his old friend, Rench Small, in August of 1862.

VI

The Enlistment August 26, 1862 to May 18, 1865

Many years after the Civil War was over, John R. King recalled an evening with his friends trying to decide which army to join. He described the gathering in a letter he wrote to Lenora Hamilton, daughter of Maryland Governor William T. Hamilton:

> I will never forget one moonlight night in Aug., 1862 when 'of us boys,' each 17 years of age, John Hager, Charlie Smith, Jim MacGill, and 'Rig' (himself) stood on Eichelberger's corner on S. Potomac Street, they trying to persuade me to go with them that night across the Potomac to join the Rebel army, and I trying to persuade them to go with me the other way. So, at midnight we parted, shook hands all around, pledging that whatever happened, we would be the same old friends. They went South, and with Rench Small, we raised a company for the 6th Maryland Regiment.[1]

Did John, Charlie and Jim cross the river that night and join the Confederacy? Unfortunately, First Maryland Confederate Cavalry service records do not include date of enlistments so it is not known when John Hager and Jim MacGill went over to the Confederate side. However, Charlie Smith enlisted August 18, 1862, according to his service records, but he, like John R. King, decided to join the United States Army.[2]

John also wrote the following in his letter to Lenora Hamilton:

> The Union sentiment largely predominated. Over 4,000-most of them were boys, the flower of the young manhood of Washington Co., enrolled

in the Union Army, as against 20 on the other side. And I knew them all. Dr. MacGill, and 4 sons, John Hager, Otho Hurley, Charlie Smith, Alf Merrick, Geiger Holliday, Harry Wat Hughes, Dave Protzman, Bill Herbert and Jim Breathed. [3]

While more information is provided in the Appendix, the following young men of Hagerstown, Maryland, named by John King joined the listed units:

1. John Hager enlisted in Company C of the First Maryland Cavalry as a private (Confederate), date unknown.[4]
2. Charles "Charlie" R. Smith enlisted as a private in Captain Anderson's Company of the 7th Regiment, Maryland Infantry (Union) August 18, 1862.[5]
3. James "Jim" MacGill enlisted as a private in Company C, First Maryland Cavalry (Confederate), date unknown, son of Charles MacGill.[6]
4. Davidge MacGill enlisted in Company C, First Maryland Cavalry (Confederate) date unknown, son of Dr. Charles MacGill.[7]
5. Dr. Charles G. W. MacGill joined the 2nd Virginia Regiment (Confederate) as a surgeon in 1863, son of Dr. Charles MacGill.[8]
6. William D. MacGill, also enlisted in Company C, 1st Maryland Cavalry (Confederate) date unknown, son of Dr. Charles MacGill.[9]
7. Otho J. Hurley enlisted as a private in Captain Gaither's Company K, 1st Virginia (Confederate) in Richmond, Virginia on June 1, 1863.[10]
8. Alfred "Alf" D. Merrick enlisted in the Rockbridge 1st Light Artillery Battery, at Winchester, Virginia (Confederate) as a private on December 30, 1861.[11]
9. Geiger Holliday/Hollyday enlisted in Company C, 1st Maryland Cavalry (Confederate) as a private, date unknown.
10. Harry Wat Hughes, no military information available
11. David "Dave" Protzman, enlisted in Company A, 1st Maryland Cavalry (Confederate), July 1, 1863, in Hagerstown, Maryland.[12]
12. William "Bill" H. Herbert, joined Company C January 1, 1862, as a private, 12th Virginia Cavalry (Confederate).[13]
13. James "Jim" Breathed, enlisted April 19, 1861, in Company B, 1st Virginia Cavalry (Confederate).[14]

All of the above soldiers were either friends or acquaintances of John King in Hagerstown before the war. All but one, i. e., Charlie Smith, took up arms for the Southern cause. John's statement that "over 4,000…enrolled in the Union Army as against 20 on the other side" was incorrect. The actual numbers of soldiers positively identified with either a Union or Confederate company and regiment and residing in Washington County, Maryland, before or after the war are 137 Rebels and 1,580 Federals. These numbers were obtained by adding up all soldiers listed as fighting for one side or the other and subtracting those men whose companies and regiments were either sketchy or unknown. Obviously, John grossly underestimated the number of citizens who joined the Confederacy and, overstated the number of citizens from Washington County who fought for the Union.

In a letter to President Abraham Lincoln dated June 28, 1862, the governors of the Northern States, including A. W. Bradford of Maryland, wrote the following:

> The undersigned, governors of the State of the Union... respectfully request...that you at once call upon the several States for such number of men as may be require to fill up all the military organizations now in the field, and add to the armies heretofore organized such additional number of men as may in your judgment, be necessary to garrison and hold all the numerous cities and military positions that have been captured by our armies, and to speedily crush the rebellion that still exists in several of the Southern States, thus practically restoring to the civilized world our great and good Government.[16]

Lincoln responded to the governors July 1, 1862 by writing:

> Fully concurring in the wisdom of the views expressed to me in so patriotic a manner by you in the communication of the 28th day of June, I have decided to call into service an additional force of 300,000 men. I suggest and recommend that the troops be chiefly of infantry. The quota of your state would be ______. I trust that they be enrolled without delay, so as to bring this unnecessary and injurious civil war to a speedy and satisfactory conclusion. An order fixing the quotas of the respective States will be issued by War Department tomorrow.[17]

The quota for the state of Maryland was four regiments. One of those four regiments was the 6th Volunteer Infantry. Maryland did not need a draft to fill its regiments and would complete the 6th with a call of volunteers from Washington County and the surrounding area. Although John King states above that "and with Rench Small, we raised company for the 6th Maryland

Regiment," he does not mention the names of the other men. They were most likely the officers recruited from the county, i. e., Adam Martin and James A. Robinson of Smithsburg, and James H. C. Brewer of Clear Spring. Since they were born and raised in Hagerstown and knew everyone, John R. King and his friend, Rench Small probably recruited heavily from there and nearby Franklin County, Pennsylvania. Adam Martin and James A. Robinson most likely gathered recruits from the Cavetown, Leitersburg and Smithsburg area since that is where they resided.

The 6th Maryland Volunteer Infantry Regiment was organized at Baltimore, Maryland, from August 12 to September 8, 1862, and was active for three years.[18] As stated, the regiment was meant to fulfill President Lincoln's call for more troops in his letter of July 2, 1862, and "was essentially a representative Maryland regiment.[19] The eight companies of the regiment were recruited in the following counties: Company A from Carroll; Company B from Cecil; Company C also from Carroll; Company D from Frederick; Companies E and G also from Cecil; Company H from Washington; Company K from Queen Anne; and the other two companies, F and I, were recruited from Baltimore City.[20]

The following men were the Commissioned Officers of Company H, 6th Maryland Volunteer Infantry.[21]

Adam D. Martin, Captain, from Smithsburg, Washington County, Maryland; mustered in September 5, 1862, as captain of the company.

William H. Abercrombie, Captain, from New York, entered the service as First Sergeant of Company B July 24, 1862; promoted 2nd Lieutenant, November 1, 1862; First Lieutenant of Company H, November 17, 1864 and then to Captain on January 28, 1865.

Melville Rench Small, First Lieutenant, of Hagerstown, Washington County, Maryland enlisted as 1st Lieutenant of Company H September 5, 1862; was promoted to Adjutant February 11, 1863.

James H. C. Brewer, 1st Lieutenant, of Clear Spring, Washington County, Maryland, entered the service as a 2nd Lieutenant September 5, 1862; promoted to 1st Lieutenant February 11, 1863 and then to Regimental Quartermaster November 17, 1864.

Alexander Leeds, 1st Lieutenant, of Michigan, enlisted as a private August 2, 1862; promoted 4th Sergeant November 1, 1862; 2nd Sergeant April 10, 1863 and then 1st Lieutenant, February 21, 1865.

James A. Robinson, 2nd Lieutenant, from Smithsburg, Washington County, Maryland, enlisted August 21, 1862, as 1st Sergeant of Company H; was later promoted to 2nd Lieutenant, February 11, 1863, but resigned his commission March 17, 1864 due to a non-combat physical impairment.

John R. King, 1st Lieutenant and Captain after the war, enlisted in Company H as a private on August 21, 1862; then promoted to 2nd Sergeant August 28, 1862; promoted to 1st Sergeant February 4, 1863; promoted to 1st Lieutenant of Company C, 6th Maryland Volunteer Infantry; received a post-war promotion to Captain. In Company H's Descriptive Book, John Rigdon King had the following physical characteristics at the time of his enlistment: 5 feet 6 inches high, fair complexion, blue eyes and brown hair. John further stated that he was 18 years of age and was born in Hagerstown, Maryland. He gave his occupation as an "artist." John "Rig" King's enlistment in the Union Army during August of 1862 was a defining moment in his life. Over the ensuing seventy years, his entire being would be affected by that decision. His patriotism, evident in his diary even before he joined the military, would serve and guide him well after the Civil War in his efforts to assist other veterans to rebuild their lives.

The ninety-two men who were recruited to fill Company H were largely second and third generation immigrants from either Ireland or Germany. They were the children of Irish or German farmers as shown on the 1860 U.S. Census. Some of the other surnames listed on that census were of English, Scottish or French origin. The name "King" is of both English and Scottish ancestry.[22] The ages of the recruits varied from fifteen years for the drummer boy to age fifty-three for the oldest man, as seen in Table I titled "Age at Enlistment." Nearly 30 percent of the men were either just eighteen or nineteen years old. Almost 60 percent of the men (59.78percent) were twenty-two years of age or younger. Table II, named the "Pre-war Residences of Company H, 6th Maryland Volunteer Infantry," shows that while over seventy (70.65 percent) percent of the men came from Washington County, only 8.7 percent were recruited from Hagerstown. In addition, almost thirty-five (34.78 percent) percent were from the northeast portion of Washington County. Three were from nearby Frederick County and one was recruited from the City of Baltimore. As might be expected, almost 87 percent (86.96 percent) of the recruits were from the state of Maryland. Five soldiers hailed from nearby Franklin County, Pennsylvania and three more were from other counties in Pennsylvania. Virginia provided two recruits, West Virginia one and the state of Michigan one. Table III is titled "Pre-war Occupations of Soldiers of Company H, 6th Regiment, Maryland Volunteer Infantry." These statistics were obtained from both the enlistment data provided by the recruit to the U.S. Army or from both the 1850 and 1860 U.S. Censuses for the place of residence of the soldier. Many of the occupations of these recruits were the same as their fathers because quite a few of these young men were living at home on a farm. In any case, twenty-one or 33.87 percent stated that they were "laborers" or "day laborers." Another fifteen recruits or 24.19 percent gave their livelihood as a "farm hand, farmer or farm laborer." Taken together, thirty-six of the men who joined Company H or 58 percent of the total enlisted for whom occupations were available (62 men) said that they were laborers, farm or otherwise. Of the other twenty-six soldiers, nearly all of the specialized trades of the mid-19th century were represented: cabinet maker, shoemaker, mechanic, blacksmith, cooper, miller, artist (John R. King), carpenter, teacher, merchant, tailor, gunsmith, millwright, and fence maker. Unfortunately, for thirty of the ninety-two total members of Company H or 32.6 percent, no occupation was listed on the 1850 or 1860 U.S. Census and no occupations were included in their military service records. Hence, in actuality, the figures and percentages given were based upon a total N (sample size) of sixty-two instead of ninety-two soldiers. In conclusion, based upon Tables I, II and III, the following trends can be observed. First, the lion's share of the recruits were of either Irish or German descent. Secondly, the majority of the men were young. Almost 60 percent were age 22 or younger. The ages of the other 40 percent were evenly divided from age twenty- three to fifty years of age. Lastly, these young men had no established trade. Most were laborers of one type or another. However, the older men had been employed for some years in a specialized trade. Hence, the recruits fell into one of two categories, either a young laborer, a farmer or an older tradesman.

Table I
Age at Enlistment of Co. H, 6th Regiment, Maryland Volunteer Infantry

Age	Number of Soldiers	Age	Number of Soldiers
15	1	29	1
16	0	30	1
17	1	31	2
18	13	33	2
19	14	35	1
20	4	36	1
21	13	37	2
22	9	38	2
23	4	41	1
24	6	42	1
25	3	45	1

26	1	46	1
27	2	53	1
28	1		N=92

Table II
Pre-War Residences of Soldiers of Company H, 6th Regiment Maryland Volunteer Infantry

	Residence	Number of Soldiers
1.	Cavetown, Washington County, Maryland	17
2.	Washington County, not further specified	13
3.	Smithsburg, Washington County, Maryland	10
4.	Hagerstown, Washington County, Maryland	8
5.	Clear Spring, Washington County, Maryland	5
6.	Sharpsburg, Washington County, Maryland	3
7.	Leitersburg, Washington County, Maryland	3
8.	Ringgold, Washington County, Maryland	2
9.	Williamsport, Washington County, Maryland	2
10.	Boonsboro, Washington County, Maryland	1
11.	Sandy Hook, Washington County, Maryland	1
	Subtotal Washington County, Maryland	65 or 70.65 percent
12.	Frederick County, Maryland	3
13.	Baltimore, Maryland	1
	Total Maryland	68-74 percent
14.	Franklin County, Pennsylvania	5
15.	Pennsylvania, Other	3
16.	Virginia	2
17.	West Virginia	1
18.	Michigan	1
19.	Ireland	1
20.	Unknown	10
		N=92

Table III
Pre-War Occupations of Soldiers of Co. H, 6th Regiment, Maryland Volunteer Infantry

Occupation		Number of Soldiers Listing That Occupation
1.	Laborer	17
2.	Farm hand	6
3.	Farmer	5
4.	Farm Laborer	4
5.	Day Laborer	4
6.	Cabinet Maker	3
7.	Shoemaker	3
8.	Clerk	3
9.	Mechanic	2
10.	Blacksmith	2
11.	Cooper	2
12.	Miller	2
13.	Artist (John R. King)	1
14.	Carpenter	1
15.	Teacher	1
16.	Merchant	1
17.	Tailor	1
18.	Gunsmith	1
19.	Millwright	1
20.	Fence Maker	1
21.	Wood Chopper	1
22.	On 1850 or 1860 U.S. Census, but no job listed	27
23.	Unknown—soldier could not be located	3
		N=92

On September 3, 1862, the following article, simply titled "Company H" appeared in the Hagerstown newspaper *Herald Freedom & Torch Light:*

> This company, recruited by Lieut. Small, and which left Hagerstown last week was mustered into service as Company H of the Sixth Regiment, Col Howard. Immediately after it was mustered in, a committee of gentlemen of this town, consisted of Messrs. Peter B. Small, Richard Sheckles, John G. Knode, W. D. Levy, F. Dorsey Herbert and Samuel L. King, on behalf of the patriotic citizens of this county, present to each officer a splendid sword and to each private one hundred dollars bounty, S. L. King, Esq.,

> the last named of the committee, delivering to each officer an appropriate address, as the swords were handed over to them. The members sent a large portion of their bounty money to their friends and relatives at home, of which we shall give a detailed account hereafter."[23]

The following is a list of the company as was shown in the newspaper article. Shown are sixteen officers and sixty-two privates. However, the total number of men that served in Company H during the war was ninety-four soldiers.

Captain,	Adam B. Martin
1st Lieut.	Melville R. Small
2nd "	James H. C. Brewer
1st Sergeant	James A. Robinson
2nd "	John R. King
3rd "	Adam Shank
4th "	Alexander Leeds
5th "	Thomas E. Koontz
1st	Corp'ral John C. Barkdoll
2nd "	Peter E. Kizer
3rd "	Wm. Crissinger
4th "	Charles Smith
5th "	Stephen H. Martin
6th "	Ferdinand H. Bikle
7th "	John H. Moore
8th "	Daniel B. Reynold

Privates

Jacob H. F. Adams	Daniel Jackson
John Adams	George B. Jennings
Lewis L. Bachtell	Patrick H. Jennings
Harrison Bridendolph	John J. B. Justice
Leonard Britweser	Patrick King
Andrew S. Bonebrake	William H. King
Salmon I. Brown	George Kough
James Clay	James M. Lowry
William Ditlow	Charles A. Lowry
John I. Flory	George Masters
Daniel W. Flory	Charles Miller

Benjamin Flory
Columbus Flory
Henry Fishack
Jeremiah Fishack
John Fleckenstine
Geo. W. Fogler
Luther Fogler
George W. Gans
Joseph H. Garrish
George F. Gossard
Elias Gouker
Joseph W. Gouker
Geo. W. Grim
Abraham Grove
James H. Harne
James Hanes
Freeland Hickman
Jacob Hovis
Samuel Houser
Hezakiah Irvin
Levi Miller
William W. Moore
Jacob Newcomer
Jos. G. Norfoard
John Penner
George P. Pickett
Amos Reynold
David Rife
John D. Sweitzer
George C. Siccore
Andrew J. Sites
Abraham Sidenstriker
Abraham Stoner
Jacob C. Studenwalk
Samuel B. Sterline
John H. Shields
Michael Thomas
Daniel Watson
George A. Weagley
Henry Young

Peter B. Small, a shoe dealer in Hagerstown, was the father of Melville Rench Small while Samuel L. King, a coach maker before the war, was John R. King's father.[24] The union army provided an enlistment bounty of $100, paid when a soldier was mustered out of the service. However, this additional $100 was paid upfront by the locality and was a real incentive to enlist as $100 was quite a bit of money in 1862. Annual incomes only averaged from $300 to $1,000.[25]

In his memoirs, John King reminisced about his enlistment in Company H. John mentions that his father,

> had made arrangements for me to go to Baltimore to (see) his old friend James Young, job printer, to finish my trade where I remained until the Civil broke out. I caught the war fever and went back to Hagerstown. Captain A. B. Martin and Rench Small my boyhood chums were recruiting a company for the 6th Maryland Regiment, the quota was soon filled and one bright day in August of 1862 we assembled in the square; after addresses were made by Thomas Boultt, Richard Sheckels and others, we took up the line of march out South Potomac street on our way to Frederick and Baltimore, as we passed my home a pale face (unreadable) through the bowd...[26]

On January 7, 1915, John R. King read a paper entitled, "A Brief History of the Sixth Regiment, Maryland Infantry Volunteers, Second Brigade, Third Division, Sixth Army Corps" before the Commandery of the State of Maryland, Military Order of the Loyal Legion, at the Hotel Belvedere in Baltimore, Maryland.[27] This speech is presented her in its entirety thanks to the generosity the Harper's Ferry Rare Book Collection of the National Park Service who provided a copy to the author. John's paper and speech was partly based upon Wilmer, Jarnett and Vernon's *History and Roster of Maryland Volunteers, War of 1861-66* published in Baltimore, Maryland, by the State Commission in 1898. Of course, such historical accounts by both sides were fraught with overstatements of accomplishments and understatements of losses. John, among many others, certainly succumbed to such embellishments.

At the top of John's paper is the latin phrase "Laudemus Viros Gloriosos," which translates to, "Let Us Praise Famous Men." John R. King's version is as follows, excluding the first four paragraphs:

> After a brief period of drill and discipline the regiment left Baltimore on September 20, 1862, to join the Army of the Potomac, then in Western Maryland. The Regiment was assigned to the Maryland Brigade (1st, 4th, 6th, 7th and 8th Regiments) under the command of General John R. Kenly.

This is the same John R. Kenly who was Colonel of the First Maryland Regiment (Union) and who was wounded and captured with most of his command by General Stonewall Jackson at the Battle of Front Royal on May 23, 1862. Many of these prisoners were with John King at Salisbury Prison. Colonel Kenly and his men were paroled and exchanged. He was promoted to Brigadier General because of his defiant stand against overwhelming odds at the Battle of Front Royal. In fact, his efforts at Front Royal were largely responsible for the safe escape and retreat of General Banks.

Second Battle of Winchester, June 13 to June 15, 1864

> The 6th Regiment remained with the Maryland Brigade on the upper Potomac until December, 1862, when it marched to Harper's Ferry and encamped on Bolivar Heights, remaining there until March, 1863, when it was detached from the Brigade and ordered to Berryville, Va., and assigned to the 3rd Brigade, 2nd Division, 8th army corps. On June 13th Rodes' divisions of the Army of Northern Virginia attacked the brigade

with superior numbers and after a brief resistance our commander, General McReynolds, ordered a retirement towards Winchester. The 6th regiment and Alexander's Baltimore battery covered the retreat and during the retiring movement we were constantly harassed by the Confederate cavalry. At the ford of the Opequon Creek a charge in force was made on us which was handsomely repulsed with severe loss to the enemy, our loss being slight. This attempt of the enemy to impede our march seemed to satisfy them, as we had no further trouble from that source before reaching Winchester where we joined the Command of General R. H. Milroy, there furiously engaged with Lee's Army. Our regiment was assigned to a small isolated breastwork some distance north of the Star Fort, holding that position until the enemy posted on Round Mountain opened a terrific artillery fire on us; we were then drawn into the Fort where the regiment gallantly assisted Alexander's Battery in its defense. At 2 A. M. on the morning of the 15th we were ordered to retire with the Division, as Milroy's whole command was surrounded by Lee's Army, and surrender seemed inevitable. When surrender was suggested to Colonel Horn, then in command of our regiment, he replied, "No, Sir, the Sixth Maryland Regiment will never surrender as long as there is a chance to fight," and proceeded to cut his way through the enemy's lines, engaging them on the Martinsburg Pike and by a skillful maneuver passed around his flank and escaped almost intact, arriving at Harper's Ferry at a late hour, having marched forty miles. Some years ago, in a conversation with the late General Snowden R. Andrews, who commanded a Confederate battery in that section, I referred to the escape of our regiment and he said: 'That regiment should never have been allowed to escape; I saw the regiment getting away and sent a few shells after it.' He did not know until I told him that it was the Sixth Maryland, and his concluding remark was. 'It was a d---d slick trick."

The Second Battle of Winchester was fought from June 13 to June 15, 1863. General Lee was moving his Army of Northern Virginia into southern Pennsylvania when General Ewell's Corps as vanguard engaged Major General Robert H. Milroy's command holding Winchester. Milroy was not aware of the size of the force facing him and should have retreated immediately. Instead, he decided to fight. Richard Snowden Andrews was an architect in Baltimore, Maryland, before the war. He became commander of the First Maryland Artillery (CSA) also known as Andrews Batallion and oversaw the employment of several guns at the Battle of Second Winchester on June 15th. Lt. Colonel Andrews described the scene as follows:

> During the night Milroy cut down his guns and attempted a precipitate retreat to Harper's Ferry. A small part of his command had passed, when Johnson, (Confederate division commander Edward Johnson) who had been delayed getting into position, arrived about daylight at the Martinsville road, and at once attacked the passing column. General Ewell then said that the enemy made repeated and desperate attempts to cut their way through. Here was the hardest fighting which took place during the attack, the odds being greatly in favour of the enemy, who were successfully repulsed and scattered by the gallantry of General Johnson and his brave command. In a few minutes, the greater part of them surrendered, twenty-three to twenty-five hundred men. The rest scattered through the woods and fields, but most of them were subsequently captured by our cavalry. General Milroy, with two hundred fifty or three hundred cavalry, made his way to Harper's Ferry.[28]

The battle was a complete disaster for the Federals and General Milroy was later arrested for incompetence. Out of a total command of 6,900, 144 Union officers and 3,856 enlisted men were listed as captured or missing. Seven officers and 88 enlisted men were killed in action and twelve officers and 336 enlisted men were wounded in action.[29] The Sixth Maryland Regiment had six enlisted men wounded, three officers and 164 enlisted men captured or missing. Hence, while most of the Sixth Maryland Regiment escaped the Second Battle of Winchester, about twenty percent of its men were either missing in action or captured.

John's speech continued:

> At Harper's Ferry the regiment was assigned to the Second Brigade, Third Division, Third Army Corps, under command of Major General Wm. H. French, a Marylander and a regular army officer. With that organization we participated in the battles incident to the movements of the Army of the Potomac under General George G. Meade in the autumn and winter of 1863-4.

Unfortunately, First Sergeant John R. King was one of the six wounded infantrymen. He received a slight wound of this right knee. His injury was probably minor because his service record shows no hospitalization for it and also shows no break in his service. Also unlucky were the twenty-one infantrymen of Company H who were captured June 15, 1863, and sent to one of the Confederate prisons in Richmond: Sergeants Adam Shank and Charles Smith and Privates Ferdinand Bikle, Andrew Bonebrake, Leonard Breitnesser, Amos Davis, William H. Didlow, Henry F. Fishach, Jeremiah Fishach, Luther Fogler, Elias Gouker, George W.Grim, D. Clinton Henneberger, Jacob Hovis, Daniel Jackson, William H. King, James M. Lowry, Joseph G. Norford, George W. Secore, and drummer boy Charles Robinson.[30] Most of these soldiers were paroled in just over a month at City Point in Virginia. For example, Jacob Hovis was paroled June 23, Sergeant Charles Smith July 14, and Leonard Breitnesser on July 23, 1863.[31] Other men of Company H, however, were confined in Richmond much longer. For instance, Henry F. Fishach, who was initially incarcerated in Richmond June 18, 1863, was not paroled at City Point until March 15, 1864. Once paroled and released by the Confederate government, the men were transported to Camp Parole in Annapolis, Maryland. As mentioned earlier, established in June of 1862, Camp Parole was a holding or processing facility for Union soldiers before they were sent home or returned to their regiment. The released Union prisoners remained at Camp Parole in a non-combat role until exchanged for a Confederate prisoner. Thousands of Union prisoners were held in this state of limbo. Although they were allowed to freely leave and go to town for whatever purpose, Camp Parole was a far less than ideal place to recuperate. In fact, several of the twenty-one men of Company H who had been sent to Camp Parole simply deserted. These included William H. Didlow and Daniel Jackson.[32]

John's speech continued:

> The regiment joined in the pursuit of Lee's Army, which crossed the Potomac July 13, 1863. (Lee had retreated over the Potomac River and south through Virginia to safety after his devastating defeat at Gettysburg July 1-3.—Editor). Keeping along the east side of the Blue Ridge, we caught up with the rear of the enemy near Manassas and Thoroughfare Gaps, where sharp skirmishing took place. Lee's army took position behind the Rapidan River, covering Raccoon and other fords. Our brigade went into camp on August 6th, near Fox's Ford on the Rappanhannock River and on the 15th we crossed the Rappahannock and went into camp near Culpeper, where we remained until the 10th of October. From this point the Army of the Potomac fell back to Centreville Heights, the movement being a rapid and most trying one, thoroughly testing the endurance of the men of that army. It marched day and night and lost much sleep, and every man was supposed to have eight days rations on his person. I shall relate an amusing incident which occurred on the occasion of a

> Division inspection. As the inspecting officer was going down the rear of the line examining cartridge boxes and haversacks, he stopped and tapped a haversack of one of the men and said to him, "Soldier, what have you in there?" "Sposens," was the reply. "Sposens, what do you mean by Sposens?" the officer sharply asked. "Sposed to have eight days' rations, but d---d I have the half of them," was the reply.
>
> Advancing again on the evening of the 7th of October, our brigade crossed the Rappahannock and marched toward Brandy Station, the Sixth Maryland in advance. About two miles from the station the enemy was encountered in considerable forces, principally cavalry and artillery, occupying a hill near the home of John Miner Botts.[33] A spirited charge was made and the hill was carried with but slight loss and the enemy was pursued to a point beyond Brandy Station.

Born in Dumfries, Virginia, September 16, 1802, John Minor Botts was a Virginia lawyer, politician, Whig and ardent Unionist who served three terms in the U.S. House of Representatives. The four columned two-story portico of his 2,000 plus acre plantation called "Auburn" was the site of General Lee's grand review of General J. E. B. Stuarts' cavalrymen on June 8, 1863. Stuart later placed Botts under arrest for catering to Union troops. In fact, a well-known photograph of Botts and his family taken in October, 1863, on the front porch of the Greek Revival style home, includes several Union soldiers. On April 29, 1864, General Grant and his officers dined with Botts at Auburn.[34] The house and 422 acres, on the National Register of Historic Places, was recently offered for sale at $3.25 million.

Battle of Mine Run or Payne's Farm, November 27, 1863 to December 2, 1863

John's speech continued:

> On the 26th of November, 1863, a turning movement was started by General Meade, having for its objective the envelopement of Lee's right flank. A force of 25,000 men, consisting of details from the 1st, 2nd, 3rd and 5th corps, under the command of General Warren, was used in the movement. Crossing to the south side of the Rapidan, at Jacob's Ford, we bivouacked for the night on the road leading to Orange Court House. Marching was resumed early the next morning. About noon brisk firing commenced in our front and, marching 'left in front' as we were, we soon

> received the command, 'Right flank forward.' The enemy was swiftly driven from its position in the dense woods of the Wilderness by our plunge, but taking a new position at about 500 yards in our front he made two desperate assaults, which we repulsed with great loss to the enemy.

The Army of the Potomac crossed the Rapidan on November 26th with Meade hoping to reach Robertson's tavern on the Orange Turnpike the same day, but muddy roads slowed the advance...at sunset the Union Army halted far short of their destination.[35] The opportunity for a surprise attack was missed and the Confederates became aware of the large troop movement and prepared for an encounter.

John's speech continued:

> General J. Warren Keifer, our gallant Brigade Commander, in his report says: "The 6th Maryland Regiment was under heavy fire from the commencement of the action until near its close and maintained its ground gallantly and remained in its position until the battle was about ended. It was relieved about 6 P. M. Its supply of ammunition was also exhausted."[36]

John King cited portions of Col. J. Warren Keifer's report dated December 3, 1863, to Lieut. J. Johnson, Acting Assistant Adjutant-General.

John's speech continued:

> As we were retiring, General Morris, commanding the First Brigade rode up to Colonel Horn and asked him to remain a while longer to protect his right. Col. Horn replied, "I cannot do it, sir, my men have been out of ammunition for a half hour, but if you say the word I will join you in a charge on the enemy." This offer was declined. This action, in which our regiment suffered severe loss, is designated as the battle of Locust Grove in the Wilderness, and was brought about by General French taking the wrong road. To this unfortunate error is attributed the failure of General Meade's splendidly conceived plan of the Mine Run Campaign, as it puts General Lee wise to Meade's plans and enabled him to rush reinforcements to his right flank so that on the morning of the 29th we were confronted by Lee's army in a strongly fortified position behind Mine Run. Our troops were formed in three lines (the 6th Maryland in front line) preparing for a charge, but at 2 P.M. General Meade arrived at the front and seeing the strong opposition of the enemy concluded, after using some pretty

> severe adjectives, it would be useless to attempt an assault with the men at hand. In this battle of Locust Grove, or Payne's Farm, I witnessed an exhibition of superb courage. After we had repulsed two charges of the enemy they fell back to a piece of woods to form, as we supposed, for another charge. Suddenly a Confederate ran out from behind a stack of corn or hay, carrying a flag. Well out to the front and entirely alone, he stopped, planted his flag in the ground, remained there for some little while, then got up and cooly hunted cover. Hundreds of shots were fired at him-we could see the ground cut all around him-but none apparently touched him. I could hear men all around me cry out "shoot the man with the flag." I heard a Sergeant near me say that I called to him and said, "don't shoot that man, he is too brave to kill." Why the man did such a rash thing and why none of his comrades followed him still remains a mystery. I have since learned it was a man named Barclay, of the Fourth Virginia Regiment. Such an act of heroic courage would have rewarded in our army with a Medal of Honor.

On the written copy of his regimental history, John King added the following:

> NOTE:-Referring to the incident of the Confederate Color Bearer at the battle of Locust Grove, I have learned since the above paper, through the Hon. William A. Anderson, who was an officer in the 4th Virginia Regiment, and from my friend Wm. Taylor Thom, that Alexander T. Barclay, is still living in Lexington, Va.

Born into an old Rockbridge, Virginia family on May 16, 1844, Alexander Tedford "Ted" Barclay, Jr. was the eldest child of Col. Alexander T. Barclay and Mary Eleanor Paxton Barclay of Lexington.[38] Alexander Sr. was a farmer and served as an Emeritus Trustee of Washington College from 1835 until his early death at age fifty-one in 1848.[39] Ted or A. T. became a student of Washington College at the age of fifteen and joined Company I of the Liberty Hall Volunteers, 4th Virginia Infantry, Stonewall Brigade, on June 2, 1861, along with many other students and some professors.[40] Ted was promoted to Sergeant and then to Lieutenant on April 20, 1864. Like most of the Stonewall Brigade, he was captured at the Muleshoe at the Battle of Spotsylvania Court House May 12, 1864, and spent the remainder of the war as a prisoner. After the war, Ted Barclay returned to his home town of Lexington and married Virginia B. Moore on May 17, 1876, and raised a family of seven children. Ted became a prosperous farmer and, like his father, gave many years of service as a Trustee of Washington College, now renamed Washington and Lee University. He died in 1915.

John R. King was among those wounded in the above action. He received a flesh wound of the right leg.

Wilderness Campaign, May 4 to June 24, 1864

John's speech continued:

> Returning to Brandy Station, our forces established winter quarters and remained there until the following May. In the meantime the Army of the Potomac was reorganized. The old Third Corps was broken up and our Division was attached to the Sixth Corps, and thenceforth our regiment was to follow the fortunes of that General J. B. Ricketts (Pap Ricketts), was assigned to the command of the Division, with the late Adam E. King as Assistant Adjutant General.
>
> At daylight on the 4th of May, 1864, we broke camp, crossed the Rapidan at Germania Ford, and the ever memorable Wilderness campaign was on. To give in detail the wonderful events of the succeeding 30 days of marching and fighting by day and by night all along that bloody trail from the Wilderness to Spotsylvania (where old General Sedgwick was killed near the Sixth Maryland Regiment), across the Ny to the North Anna, to the Pomonky and to the Tolopotomy would mean a recital of the harrowing details and the superb exhibition of human courage incident to the loss in killed and wounded of forty thousand young men in the full bloom of manhood. In this campaign I met with a serious personal loss in the death, May 6th, of Captain Adam M. Martin, Company H, who was mortally wounded at my side. He was a courageous, Christian soldier. By order of Colonel Horn, I assumed command of the Company. Crossing the Tolopotomy at midnight on the 31st, the march to Cold Harbor was commenced, arriving there on the morning of the June 1st. At noon our Division was formed in four lines preparatory to a charge, the Sixth Maryland regiment, as usual in the front line. Late in the evening a general assault was made on the enemy's works in our front, which were handsomely carried and several hundred prisoners taken. Repeated efforts were made during the night to retake the works, but each was repulsed with heavy loss."

Captain Adam B. Martin was wounded twice in action on the evening of May 5, 1864 and died during surgery the next day in a field hospital.[41,42] May 5, 1864, was the same day that John R. King suffered a severe gunshot wound of his right leg. Thus, John's command of Company H must have been somewhat short-lived since he was probably taken soon from the field. He would never return to duty due to his injury although he probably did not know it at the time.

Stephen Martin, Adam Benjamin Martin's father, arrived in the Leitersburg area as a young man and purchased 220 acres of land from his father-in-law, Christian Good and resided there until his death in 1839. Stephen's grandfather, Hana Stephan Martin, immigrated from Germany and arrived in Lancaster County, Pennsylvania in 1751. Stephen's father, Adam Martin, had served as a lieutenant in the American Revolution.[43,44] Two of Stephen Martin's ten children were Adam B. and Stephen G. Following the family's military tradition, Adam B. enlisted in U.S. Army to fight in the Mexican War on April 26, 1847, married Susan Oswald April 4, 1849 and began to raise a family of seven children in Smithsburg.[45] Although Adam was working as a merchant in 1850 and as a clerk in 1860, he owned no real estate.[46] Adam B. Martin was mustered in Company H as a private in the 6th Maryland Regiment August 21, 1862, and was soon promoted to captain September 5, 1862. His older brother, Stephen G., was mustered in Company H on the same day and was promoted to 2nd corporal and then to sergeant on April 1, 1863.[47] On March 9, 1863, Captain Martin wrote a letter to Lieut. Col. W. D. Whipple, Assistant Adjutant General, 8th Army Corps, requesting his first furlough to go home and "...to secure the proper legal title for the same (a house and lot), and make arrangements to have the property repaired, and place it in a condition for the removal of my family there."[48] Thus far, Captain had never gone home even though his encampments were frequently very close to his home. While he had been renting a home for his family for years, he now found it important to provide them with a permanent residence. While he was waiting on his request to be honored, he was wounded in the right leg during the Battle of Locust Grove November 27, 1863, but refused to leave his company.[49] On February 16, 1864, just three months before he was killed in action, Col. John W. Horn approved a ten-day furlough so that Captain Martin could purchase a home and a surrounding lot. On May 5th, 1864, he was shot twice, once in the face and once in a limb, leading a charge in the Battle of the Wilderness.[50] He was taken to a field hospital where his limb was amputated, but Captain Martin died the next day, May 6th.[51] Remarkably, Sergeant Stephen G. Martin, Adam's brother, survived the war completely unscathed. Mrs. Martin had the home her husband purchased and received pensions for herself and her children.

Casualty estimates (KIA, WIA and missing/captured) for the Wilderness are quite variable depending upon the source. They range from 14,000-18,400 for the North and from 7,500-11,400 for the South.[52]

John's speech continued:

The following highly commendatory order was issued (129): 'By telegraph from Headquarters, A. P. Dated June 1, 1864

'To Major General Wright:
'Please give my thanks to Brigadier General Ricketts and his gallant command for the very handsome manner in which they have conducted themselves today. The success attained by them is of great importance, and if followed up, will materially advance our operations.

Respectfully yours,
(Signed) 'George G. Meade,
'Major General Commanding.'

'General:
'Major General Wright directs me to say that he transmits the within to you with great pleasure.'

'Your obd't servant,
(Signed) "R. F. Halstead, A. A. Gen'l.'

'Brigadier General Ricketts,
'Headquarters, 3rd Div., 6th a. c.
'Official:

(Signed) 'Adam E. King,
'Captain and A. A. General.'

This commendation by General Meade can also be found in the Official Records.[53]

Battle of the Monocacy, July 9, 1864; Battle of the Opequon or Third Winchester, September 19, 1864 and Battle of Fisher's Hill, September 21 to September 22, 1864

John's speech continued:

On the 3rd of June Colonel John W. Horn (6th Md.) was placed in command of the brigade and in the fierce conflict of that day many valiant officers and men were killed and wounded, some ten thousand in all.

Of this engagement, Gen'l Grant in his Memoirs says:

'I have always regretted that the last assault at Cold Harbor was made, no advantage whatever was gained to compensate for the heavy loss we sustained.'

On the 12th the 6th corps moved across the Chicahominy River, thence to the James, thence by transports to Bermuda Hundred, arriving in front of Petersburg on the 21st. Here for the first time since May 4th the troops took a rest.

On July 6th our Division took transports at City Point bound for Baltimore, where it arrived on the 8th, and immediately entrained, via B & O.R.R., for scene of the battle of the Monocacy, in which it took a major part.

After the battle of the Monocacy the division rejoined the other two divisions of the 6th corps and participated in the pursuit of Early's army.

On the 19th of September the regiment took part in the battle of the Opequon in which it suffered severe loss. Lieutenant Burns, of Co. A was killed; Col. Horn severely wounded, supposed at the time to be mortally; Captains Hawkins and Rouzer and Lieut. Smith wounded; and a large number of enlisted men killed and wounded.

Sept. 21st the battle of Fisher's Hill was fought, the 6th Md. and 126th Ohio playing the most conspicuous part. These two regiments, in a gallant charge, carried the heights, took many prisoners, and gained an important position upon which they bivouacked for the night. On the 22nd our regiment being on the skirmish line was constantly engaged with the enemy's skirmishes. About noon on that day our brigade moved to the right, attacked and drove the enemy from two hills which they held in considerable force, and so rapid was their flight that they abandoned shelter, tents, blankets and much infantry ammunition. Our line pushed on over the crest of the hill within range of the enemy's works in which were mounted heavy guns. Skirmishing continued until about 4 P. M. when a general advance was ordered.

The 6th corps, with the 8th in support, charged with a wild shout and carried the works, capturing many prisoners and guns and leaving neither a regiment nor a company in anything like order. The pursuit was followed as far as Harrisonburg. Thus ended the glorious victory at Fisher's Hill, the boasted "haven of security" of the enemy. During the engagement three different color bearers of the 6th regiment were shot down, but "the old flag never touched the ground." One of the men who took the colors, George Picket, of Co. H, soon to be shot himself, wrote to me from the hospital asking if he should not be appointed a corporal in reward for his gallantry. General Keifer, who displayed his accustomed gallantry in this battle, made special mention of the 6th in his report and gave our brigade loss as 4 officers and 54 men killed and 25 officers and 314 men wounded.

The Battle of Fisher's Hill, near Strasburg, Virginia, very close to where John King camped with the Union Army at Round Hill during May of 1862, was fought from September 19-22, 1864. On the 20th of September, the 6th Maryland along with the 126th Ohio took an important hill while on the 21st, they seized two eminences while the 8th corps attacked the Confederate left flank.[54] The battle was a complete victory for Major General Philip H. Sheridan. Colonel J. Warren Keifer, commanding the 2nd Brigade, composed of the 6th Maryland, 110th, 122nd, and 126th Ohio Regiments as well as the 67th and 138th Pennsylvania, reported only 10 enlisted men killed, one officer and 51 enlisted men wounded and only enlisted man captured or missing.[55] Captain Clifton K. Prentiss, a staff officer of the 6th Maryland, and Captain John J. Bradshaw, of Company I, 6th Maryland, were cited by Colonel Keifer for "great bravery."[56]

Battle of Cedar Creek, October 19, 1864

Colonel Keifer later reported that "a charge was ordered and the guns were retaken" and that "the regiments principally engaged in this charge were the 10th Vermont and the 6th Maryland, commanded by Capt. C. K. Prentiss."[57] He added that "great gallantry was displayed in this charge by the officers and men."[58] Adjutant Small did the majority of the recruiting of Company H. Like John King, he was born and raised in Hagerstown, Maryland. Rench, as he preferred to be called, was the third son of Peter B. and Sarah Small. He was commissioned as a 2nd Lieutenant July 24, 1862 under General Order No. 75.[59] According to a recruiting notice which appeared in the August 13, 1862, issue of the *Herald Freedom & Torch Light* newspaper in Hagerstown, Lieut. M. R. Small was commissioned by Governor Bradford and was assigned as recruiting officer of the 6th Maryland Regiment.[60] Rench Small was later promoted from 1st Lieutenant to Adjutant of the regiment February 4, 1863 when vice J.B. Ash resigned.[61] Oddly, at one point in the war, when his whereabouts were unknown and he was deemed AWOL, Adjutant Small was cited in a letter of August 6, 1863, by Colonel J. Warren Keifer as having been found of desertion as of June 20 in a court martial at Harper's Ferry. The Union Army did not realize that he had been taken prisoner at Harper's Ferry July 26, 1863, by the Confederates and was incarcerated in Libby Prison in Richmond.[62] On February 9, 1864, the largest prison break in American history took place when 109 Union officers, led by Colonel Thomas Rose of the 77th Pennsylvania, tunneled out of Libby Prison.[63] While over one-half of the escapees reached the Union lines, Adjutant Small was not one of them. Recaptured, he was not paroled until April 30, 1864 at City Point and reported to Camp Parole May 2, 1864.[64] Adjutant Small was released from Camp Parole and was returned to his regiment June 7, 1864.[65] He had been gone from his unit nearly a year. Unfortunately, Rench received a gunshot wound to his left leg during the Battle of Cedar Creek on October 19, 1864 and was given thirty days of leave because of the severity of the injury. Colonel John W. Horn, commander of the 6th Maryland Regiment wrote the following letter when he learned of Adjutant Small's injury.

> Dear Adjutant: I received the paper sadly informing me of your misfortune you have met with in the loss of your leg, and feel by that, I have lost a valuable officer and a true friend one, (although young) I could depend on in all circumstances, both in camp and march, in action or out of action, you have proved yourself a gallant soldier, and a high-toned gentleman, and I shall always hold you in high remembrance. I hope that you may be so far recovered as to be out of danger, and that you will soon be able to move about again. My own wounds are healing up fast, and I am slowly gaining strength again and hope soon to be at the head of my regiment again, and would to God you might be there with me, as I know you have reflected credit upon yourself and the command. With that best wishes for your speedy recovery and future welfare.
>
> I am truly your friend. J. W. Horn[66]

Rench Small was recovering from his wound, but pyemia, a form of septicemia, developed and terminated his life on November 17, 1864. The *Herald & Torch Light* said in his obituary said that "his talents, his native gentility and manly address, his integrity, commanded esteem and love from all. "… and that Adjutant Small shared the dangers of many battlefields, was nine months a prisoner in Libby Prison, and was no less distinguished for his endurance than for his performance."[67] At the time of his death, Adjutant Small was only 19 years, 11 months and 7 days of age.

The Siege of Petersburg, June 9, 1864 to March 25, 1865

John's speech continued:

On December 3rd, we broke camp, entrained at Stevenson Depot and proceeded to Washington, thence by transport to City Point, arriving in front of Petersburg on the 7th, relieving a portion of the 5th corps, and occupied the comfortable quarters kindly prepared for us by our old comrades of the Maryland brigade. One regiment of our brigade (138th Pa.) garrisoned Fort Dushane, the other regiments occupying the line from Fort Fisher to Fort Gregg.

On the 25th of March, 1865, the brigade, under the personal leadership of General Keifer, made a brilliant assault on the enemy's strongly entrenched picket lines immediately in our front, capturing them with many prisoners. This movement was necessary prelude of the more serious action to follow a few days later. General Meade had planned to make the final assault on the defenses of Petersburg on April 2nd. The orders for the 6th corps, to which was assigned the major part of the movement, were to form in line at 3 A. M. on the morning of the 2nd of April, and at the sound of the signal gun from Fort Fisher to move forward. To show the esprit du corps prevailing among the men of the sixth corps General Wright, our Corps Commander, at 11 P. M., April 1st, telegraphed General Meade's Chief of Staff (Webb) as follows:

'The corps will go in solid and I am sure will make the fur fly. All orders thoroughly understood. If the corps does half as well as I expect, we will have broken through the rebel lines 15 minutes from the word Go.'

Accordingly, at 3 a.m. of the 2nd of our brigade, which was destined to carry off the honors of the day, formed in line for the final assault on the seemingly impregnable works in front of Petersburg, the right resting on an almost impassable swamp and a ravine separating it from the left of the Second Division of our corps. In consequence of the darkness and the deep swamp much difficulty was experienced in perfecting the formation, a number of men being killed and wounded during the process. The Sixth Maryland and 110th Ohio regiments formed the front line.

The signal gun for the assault was fired at 4 A. M. and immediately the front line moved rapidly upon the outer works, which were held by a strong line of pickets. These works were captured, and without halting or discharging a piece, although receiving a heavy fire, we moved upon the main works. Not even a temporary check was experienced in passing through and over the double line of abattis, ditch and strong earthworks, and a hand to hand fight ensued within the main works in which many gallant officers and men fell, killed and wounded. The enemy in our front

> were soon killed, wounded, captured, or put to flight, all of their artillery falling into our hands. Our brigade captured ten pieces of artillery, a large number of prisoners, three battle flags, and the headquarters flag of Major General Heath's division.
>
> The Confederate, General A. P. Hill, was killed in this engagement by either Sergeant Monk or Daniel Woolford, of the 138th Pa. regiment of our brigade.[68] They were charged upon by two mounted men with drawn pistols and their surrender demanded. Refusing to surrender, they opened fire on the mounted men, killing one of them, the other escaping. It was subsequently learned that the man killed was General Hill.

General Hill was killed by Corporal John W. Mauck of the 138th Pennsylvania Infantry Regiment.[68]

John's speech continued:

> In the assault, the colors of the 6th Maryland were first along the 6th corps line to be placed on the enemy's works, three Sergeants of the Color Guard, John E. Buffington, Daniel Tatum and Robert Spence displaying the most distinguished gallantry in gaining this honor for the regiment. Major C. K. Prentiss was the first commissioned officer of the sixth corps to enter the enemy's works.
>
> General Keifer in his report says:
>
> 'Major Prentiss with a large portion of the 6th Maryland regiment was the first to penetrate the enemy's works here, after a most bloody struggle, he fell mortally wounded very soon after entering the fortification. Too much praise cannot be given the officers and men of this regiment.'

John Ezra Buffington was born in Maryland to David and Susanna Angel Buffington on July 3, 1841.[69] He was mustered in August 21, 1862 with Company C of the 6th Maryland Volunteer Infantry and was mustered out June 20, 1865.[70] He married his wife, Agnes, in 1867 and remained married for over forty-three years. Having worked as a farmer in Carroll County his entire life, he and Agnes raised one son and five daughters. For his gallantry and meritorious service on April 2, 1865, at the assault on the Confederate line at Petersburg, Sergeant, now Lieutenant, Buffington was awarded the Congressional Medal of Honor just after the end of the war. He also received a portion of a cash reward of $400 offered by General U.S. Grant. However, due to modesty, he never made application for the actual metal. When John R. King learned of this lapse, he along with Congressman John A. Goulden, of New York, persuaded Lieutenant Buffington to obtain the award.[71,72] Consequently, on March 28, 1908, a ceremony was held at Reindollar's Opera House in Taneytown, Maryland, during which John R. King made the following address:

> General Grant had placed in his hands the sum of $400 as a reward of gallantry for the man who should first raise our flag over Richmond. As Richmond was not taken by assault, he deemed the donor's wishes would best be carried out by dividing the sum among three men, one to be selected by General Wright of the Sixth Corps, as most conspicuous for gallantry in carrying the lines at Petersburg, one to be selected by General Gibbons for gallantry in the assault on the fort south of Petersburg and one by Sheridan for gallantry at the battle of Five Forks. When General Grant addressed General Wright to designate the man of the Sixth Corps he referred the order to the commander of the Third Division of the Sixth Corps and General Ricketts in turn referred the order to the commander of the Second Brigade of the Third Division of the Sixth Corps, and here is the endorsement and recommendation:
>
> Sergeant John E. Buffington, Company C, 6th Maryland (Second Brigade) is believed to have been the first enlisted man of the Third Division who mounted the parapet of the enemy's lines at Petersburg, April 2, 1865.
>
> Signed T. Seymour, Brigadier General
>
> And now it will be surmised, why was not Comrade Buffington honored with the medal long ago? For my part I did not know until a few months ago that he was not in possession of a medal. It was the general belief among his comrades that he had one. You got the money, didn't you, Comrade Buffington, and how much of it have you left; enough to pay the expenses of this occasion? When I heard from Comrade Buffington himself that he did not have the medal I at once enlisted the interest of Comrade Goulden, and that was easily obtained, and it is due entirely to his unceasing efforts that we are enabled to present this medal today.
>
> Now in closing, Comrade let me say how much pleasure I have in witnessing the fruition of a long delayed bestowal of this medal of honor. Your comrades of the Sixth Maryland are proud of you. Your life in this community, where you were born and raised, has been that of an upright and honorable citizen as this large gathering of your neighbors and friends attest.[73]

David Tatum was born in April of 1842 in Maryland.[74] He was mustered into the 6th Maryland Regiment on August 4, 1862 and became a Color Sergeant for Company I. In his report of April 16, 1865, Lieutenant Colonel Joseph C. Hill of the 6th Maryland gave him special recognition for "planting the first colors on the enemy's works.[75] Sergeant Tatum was mustered out of service on June 20, 1865. After the Civil War, he lived in the City of Baltimore, was employed as a carpenter for the railroad and married Mary. Together, they had ten children; nine lived to adulthood. David was very active in the Grand Army of the Republic, a patriotic and charitable organization for Union veterans. In 1905, he was Donor of the National Flag for Lansdowne Christian Church in Maryland and Chairman of the Memorial Window Committee.[76] A large stained glass window with the G. A. R. emblem was installed in the church, the only church in the nation dedicated to that organization.

Robert D. Spence was born in 1836 in Cecil County Maryland.[77] He enlisted with Company B of the 6th Maryland August 9, 1862, was wounded March 25, 1863 and reached the rank of Color Sergeant.[78] Lt. Colonel Hill cited him for gallant and meritorious service during an assault on the Confederate lines of Petersburg, in his official report of April 16, 1865, for "being the first man in the works, and planted our starry banner thereon, shortly after which he was wounded in the neck by a bullet.... and is a fair way to recover."[79] Sergeant Spence, a farmer in 1870, married Catharine M. Holt and they had at least one child, a son named George G. "Robert D. Spence."[80] Perhaps due to his war injuries, Sergeant Spence died at the age of thirty-seven in 1873 in Cecil County, Maryland.

John King's speech continued:

> Major Clifton K. Prentiss, a Baltimorean and our Major, was a man of exceptional bravery, a veritable cavalier. On this morning he fell mortally wounded as, with waving sword, he urged forward his men to be the first to mount the enemy's works. After the field had been cleared of the enemy the wants of wounded were cared for, without regard for the uniform they wore. Some of the men of our regiment came upon a wounded confederate to whom they gave water. He asked them if the 6th Md. Regiment was nearby, to which they replied that they belonged to that regiment and wanted to know why he asked. The wounded man replied that his brother, Captain Prentiss, was in that regiment. He was gently raised and carried to the side of our Major and the mutual recognition was pathetic. They were both carried back in the same ambulance and both died in the same hospital. I doubt if

there was a similar instance during the whole war. Many brave men that day fell on that field of Glory and there was great Glory.

Battle of Sailor's Creek, April 6, 1865

John's speech continued:

On the morning of the 3rd of April our division and corps commenced the pursuit of the enemy by the Appomattox River road, in the direction of Burkville Junction. After dark, on the 5th, our brigade went into position on the left of the corps, in two lines, facing Amelia Court House, near Jettersville, connecting on the left with the 5th corps. Early in the morning of the 6th the brigade advanced towards Amelia Court House, in the vicinity of which it was known that the army of Northern Virginia had been concentrated. After moving forward some three or four miles, information was obtained that Lee had withdrawn his army and was then moving around our left flank in the direction of Burkville Junction. About 3 P. M. we came up with Sheridan's cavalry, and our, brigade was quickly formed in two lines of battle and pushed forward. The 6th Maryland and the 67th and 138th Pennsylvania regiments were deployed across the main road upon which the enemy was moving and at once commenced pursuit. The enemy being cut off from retreat by Custer's cavalry was forced to give battle, and for that purpose formed his line behind Sailor's Creek. The divisions of Generals Pickett, Custis Lee, and the marine brigade, under command of Commodore Tucker, the whole under the command of Lieutenant General R. S. Ewell, are known to have participated in the sanguinary battle that ensued. The weather was intensely hot. Under cover of artillery fire our line advanced through and across swampy ground and charged up the steep hills on which the enemy were posted. As the opposing lines grew closer the conflict became fiercer, many men on both sides receiving the bayonet. The enemy was soon routed at all points. Some general officers and thousands of prisoners threw down their arms and surrendered. Among those captured were Lieutenant-General Ewell, Major-Generals Kershaw, Custis Lee, Pickett, and Brigadier-Generals Barton, Corse and Lewis. I have always felt that this battle should never have been fought, and resulted in a useless and inexcusable loss of life.

General Ewell, in a conversation with Dr. Smith (a relative), said: 'After the crossing of the James River their cause was lost, and for every man killed after that somebody would be responsible, and it would be little

> better than murder. He could not tell what General Lee would do, but he hoped he would at once surrender his army.'

The story goes that General Ewell said these words in anger around a campfire after he was taken prisoner and that a relative, Dr. Smith, a Union surgeon, heard them. The following day, Dr. Smith reported them to General Grant. Apparently, Ewells' words, along with a positive report from General Sheridan, prompted Grant to send a proposal April 7 for the surrender of Lee's Army of Northern Virginia.[81]

Appomattox Court House, April 9, 1865

John's speech continued:

> An interesting incident of this battle was the capture of our colonel, Joseph C. Hill. He was taken back to the woods in our front, disarmed and his horse taken from him. Very soon the bullets began whistling all around, and the colonel was not long in persuading the Confederates to surrender to him and, mounted on his own horse and carrying his restored sword, he led his captors into our lines where brave old Colonel Hill received a hearty welcome.
>
> The enemy was closely followed on the 8th and 9th of April until noon on the 9th, when information of Lee's surrender was received, which occasioned the wildest enthusiasm. Captain James H. C. Brewer, quartermaster of the 6th Maryland regiment, was detailed to issue rations to the prisoners and was privileged to hear General Lee's last words to his army. Captain Brewer is now the last survivor of our field and staff officers.

At the age of twenty-four years, James Henry Clay Brewer enlisted as a private in the 6th Maryland Regiment on September 5, 1862.[82] On the same day, he was promoted to 2nd Lieutenant and then on February 11, 1863, to 1st Lieutenant. Lastly, he attained the rank of captain as Regimental Quartermaster for the regiment on November 17, 1864. Captain Brewer was mustered out of the service on June 20, 1865, and later moved to Kansas. Born July 11, 1838, Captain Brewer was older than John King. On December 15, 1927, he died at the age of eighty-nine years.[83]

John King's speech continued:

On the morning of the 11th of April the 6th corps commenced the march to Burkville Junction, where they arrived on the 13th and remained until the 23rd, when, under orders, the corps commenced a forced march towards Danville for the purpose of assisting in the capture of the Confederate Army under General Joseph E. Johnston. Arriving at Danville on the 27th, news was received of the surrender of Johnston's army to General William T. Sherman.

The 6th corps remained at Danville until May 16th, at which time it moved by rail to Richmond, thence overland to Washington, arriving at Balls Cross Roads on June 3rd. The corps marched in review through the streets of Washington on June 8th, and was reviewed by the President, Generals Grant and Sherman and other high officers and officials of the Government. After this the 6th regiment entrained for Baltimore, when it was mustered out of service on June 20, 1865, having served two years and nine months.

The long association of the 6th regiment with the other regiments of this brigade generated among us a spirit of comradery not surpassed by any organization in the Army of the Potomac. The regimental officers were men of high courage and efficiency, and greatly loved and respected by the men. Colonel John W. Horn, later brevet brigadier general, and Colonel Joseph C. Hill, affectionately called "Uncle Joe," were especially dear to the men and their courage was of a superb character. Taken, man for man, this regiment was composed of men equal in courage, equal in social scale, and, as representative sons of Maryland, equal to any men who fought in that great war, whatever their uniform they wore. The one passion of its men was to win victories and uphold the honor and glory of the Flag of their Fathers. It never failed to receive honorable mention for gallantry in every engagement in which it took part.

In addition to many skirmishes and minor engagements the regiment took part in the following major engagements: Winchester, Mine Run, Locust Grove, Wilderness, Spotsylvania, Brandy Station, Bristow Station, Petersburg, Hatchers Run, Cold Harbor, Opequon, Fisher's Hill, Cedar Creek, Wopping Heights, Monocacy, Sailers Creek and Appomattox.

The late Colonel Wm. F. Fox, recognized as the greatest statistician of the Civil War, in his wonderful book, Losses in the Civil War, selects from the more than two thousand regiments of the Union Army, three hundred regiments as being most conspicuous for gallantry. Included in this number are the 1st and 6th Maryland regiments. Of the regiment Col. Fox states:

'The Battle of Locust Grove devolved almost wholly on Carr's division, and largely on the 6th Maryland regiment.'

Referring to the Battle of the Wilderness and Cold Harbor, he says:

'The 6th Maryland fought with signal gallantry, its losses being unusually large.

The regiment did good fighting in the valley and in the final battles of the war.'

The total enrollment of this regiment, first to last, was 1,110 men, and its casualties were: Killed, 72; wounded, 431; missing, 214; total, 717; about 65 per cent.

Thus ends the story of a Maryland regiment, covered with imperishable glory,

'Whose deeds are known
In words that kindle glory from the stone.'

With impetuous, unyielding valor in the thickest of the fight they faced not only the peril of battle and the risk of life, but they endured hardships that may well make the stoutest heart quake.

Few, very few, survivors of that splendid organization remain. Father Time, with relentless fury, is doing His work, conscious of duty well performed.

JNO. R. KING

John R. King borrowed the above quote from Johann Christoph Friedrich von Schiller, a German poet, historian, philosopher and playwright (b. November 10, 1759, d. May 9, 1805). "And fame was yours and conquest/-yet alone/Fame-and not life returned: your deeds are known/In words that Kindle glory from the stone."[84]

John R. King then quoted a poem by Thomas Wentworth Higginson, which will appear in the Epilogue.

Following a gunshot wound to his lower, right leg during the Battle of Locust Grove in the Battle of the Wilderness on May 5, 1864, John R. King was transported to the U.S. General Hospital in Hagerstown. For further care, he was later taken to the U.S. General Hospital in Frederick, Maryland. Although he had suffered two prior battlefield injuries from which he had recovered, this one was far more serious. According to the Certificate of Disability for Discharge completed by his surgeon, the most recent injury was a "gunshot fracture of right fibula" which necessitated a "resection of 3 ½ inches of fibula" and which caused "the resultant contraction of extensor muscles impeding the use of limb and rendering him unable to walk without a cane."[85] His surgeon, Dr. Thomas H. Helsby rated John with a one-fourth disability. Prior to discharge from the U.S. Army, John R. King was promoted from First Sergeant to First Lieutenant of Company C of the 6th Maryland Volunteer Infantry on April 26, 1865. On May 18, 1865, according to the certificate, John was medically discharged from the U.S. Army. Finally, by Special Order No. 205, in an extract dated September 1, 1884, from the Headquarters of the Army, signed by Chauncey McKeever, Acting Adjutant General, by command of Lieutenant General Sheridan:

> By direction of the Secretary of War, under the act approved June 3, 1884, and to complete his record, the discharge of Sergeant John R. King, Company H, 6th Maryland Volunteers, May 16, 1865, is amended to take effect April 25, 1865. He is mustered into service as 1st lieutenant, Company C, same regiment, to date April 26, 1865; honorably discharged as 1st lieutenant on account of physical disability from wounds received in action to date May 16,1865; and he is mustered for pay in said grade during the period embraced between the foresaid dates.[86]

In effect, the act of June 3, 1884, increased the pension of Civil War veterans.

Overall, 8 officers and 120 enlisted men from the 6th Maryland Regiment were killed in action during the Civil War; 1 officer and 127 men died from disease for a total of 236 men and 233 were wounded in battle.[87]

Table IV is a summary table, taken from the service records of Company H, which illustrates the heavy toll on the men during two years and ten months of hard service. Surprisingly, considering the numerous skirmishes and battles in which they engaged, just seven soldiers were either killed outright in battle or died from wounds inflicted. Death in combat was thus 7.6 percent of the ninety-two men in the company. Two soldiers from Company H, Sergeant John C. Barkdall and Corporal Jacob H. T. Adams, perished in prison at Andersonville, Georgia. Private Joseph G. Norford, sent to Charleston, South Carolina, was also believed to have died in prison, but his body was never found. Table IV shows a total of only four soldiers or 3.26 percent who died from disease during the war. Sgt. Thomas E. Koontz and Private George A. Weagley both passed away from typhoid fever. Sergeant Daniel B. Reynolds died from "rheumatism of the heart" and Private Freeland Hickman got stricken with consumption, otherwise known as tuberculosis, and lost his life. Only twenty-four years old, William Moore died in camp from the accidental discharge of his musket. Overall, during the entire term of service for Company H, basically from the end of August of 1862 until the muster out of June 20, 1865, fifteen men or 16.3 percent loss their lives.

Here is a list of the heroes of Company H that gave their lives for their regiment and for their country:[88]

Captain Adam B. Martin, from wounds received in battle
Adjutant Melville R. Small, from wounds received in battle
Sergeant John C. Barkdall, in prison
Sergeant Thomas E. Koontz, from disease
Sergeant Daniel B. Reynolds, from wounds received in battle
Corporal Jacob J. T. Adams, in prison
Private John Fleckenstine, in battle
Private George W. Fogler, from wounds received in battle
Private Luther Fogler, from wounds received in battle
Private Freeland Hickman, from disease
Private William Moore, accidentally
Private Jacob Newcomer, in battle
Private Joseph G. Norford, in prison
Private Daniel Watson, in battle
Private George A. Weagley, from disease

Table IV also shows that sixteen men or 17.4 percent of Company H were wounded, but did not perish from their injuries. Some of these soldiers were able to return to duty, but others would be disabled for life. John R. King was one such man who would have to live the remainder of his life with a disability. Another soldier, Corporal John Henry Shields lost his arm by amputation after receiving a gunshot injury. Likewise, Corporal Ferdinand Bikle became ill after being wounded and had to leave Company H permanently.

In addition, Table IV shows that 23 soldiers or 25 percent of Company H were taken as prisoners. The majority of these men, 21, were captured at the Union disaster known as the Second Battle of Winchester on June 15, 1863. All twenty three men were eventually paroled and sent to Camp Parole in Annapolis, Maryland.

Table IV
Summary of Casualties, Prisoners, Desertions, Court Martials, etc. of Soldiers of
Co. H, 6th Maryland Volunteer Infantry

Killed in Action	3	3.26
Died Due to Wounds	4	5.43
Died in Prison	3	3.26

Died Due to Disease	4	5.43
Died Accidentally	1	1.09
Total Died	15	16.3
Wounded in Action	16	17.4
Taken Prisoner	23	25.0
Desertions	23	25.0
Desertions & Court Martial*	20	21.74
Discharged for Disability	12	13.0
Officers Who Resigned	1	1.09
Transferred to 1st Md. Inf.	4	4.35
Served Full Term Without Injury or AWOL	17	18.48

Note: A Soldier Could Be In One or More Categories
*The erroneous court martial of Melville R. Small is not included in this total.

As early as November 29, 1862, Colonel W. Hoffman, Commissary-General of Prisoners, sent a letter to Lieutenant Colonel George Sangster, commander of Camp Parole, informing him of complaints received by the War Department "of great disorders at your camp-drunkenness, gambling, fighting and even murders."[89] A few of those enlisted men released by the Confederate government never made it to Camp Parole and were soon listed as deserters.

Only one officer resigned from Company H, Lieutenant James A. Robinson. Lieutenant Robinson was honorably discharged on March 19, 1864, for "phthisis pulmonalis, which has been progressing for several months and which produced its usual effects of emaciation, loss of strength, and disordered respiration," according Doctor C. G. Simpers, surgeon of the 6th Maryland Volunteers.[90] Phthisis pulmonalis is tuberculosis and was not readily treatable in the nineteenth century. A total of 12 soldiers or 13 percent of the company were honorably discharged for disability of one kind or another.[91] All of these veterans would receive U.S. Army pensions. Their names are:

Lieutenant John R. King-wounded in battle with a fracture of the leg
Lieutenant James A. Robinson-tuberculosis
Corporal John H. Shields-wounded in battle
Corporal Ferninand Bikle-wounded in battle
Private John Adams-not specified
Private James G. Gouker-deformity of knees and ankles

Private Peter Keizer-chronic rheumatism and chronic bronchitis
Private David A. Rife-chronic hepatization of right lung and pneumonia
Corporal Abraham A. Seidenstricker-spinal injury
Sergeant Adam Shank-wounded in battle
Corporal John Henry Shields-wounded in battle
Private John J. Sweitzer-loss of vision in right eye and partial loss of teeth

By far, the largest two categories of Table IV are the number of desertions without a court martial, 23 instances, or 25 percent, and the number of desertions with a court martial, 20, or 21.74 percent. Thus, the total number of soldiers who took an unauthorized leave of absence at least one time was 43 or almost half (46.8 percent) of the total Company H strength of 92 men. At first glance, such a high number of desertions may be shocking. However, it is estimated that when Major General Joseph Hooker took over as commander of the Army of the Potomac, there were over 85,000 soldiers classified as "absent without leave" or AWOL. In both the Union and Confederate armies, the penalty for desertion was death by firing squad or hanging. However, the total executed by both sides during the conflict was only about five hundred men.[92] Soldiers left their regiments for a variety of reasons. Some men did not like the army discipline. Others did not care for the hard life of a soldier with its strenuous marching and sleeping out in the cold. Many left their posts or camp and returned home because of fear for the well-being of their wives and children. Some were simply homesick. Other men were upset that could not obtain a furlough. Indeed, the Union army imposed severe restrictions in this regard. For example, Major General Hooker had a policy which allowed just 2 percent of a regiment to be gone at one time.[93] In addition, if a soldier desired a furlough or leave, he could not go until those already on leave returned. If the previously furloughed man deserted, then no one else could leave. In effect, this action "bottlenecked official absentees and skyrocketed desertions." A review of all the services records of Company H shows that furloughs were rarely given and the desertion rate was very high. Another reason for the increasing number of desertions was the passage of Lincoln's Emancipation Proclamation and its release January 1, 1863.[94] Lastly, the Army of the Potomac had not been paid for six months and the men were rightfully upset.[94] Due to the above reasons, men were deserting from the Army of the Potomac at the rate of eighty per day according to the testimony of Major General Hooker.[95] President Lincoln had to do something to stem this tide or he was going to lose a considerable portion of his army. Therefore, on March 10, 1863, President Lincoln made the following Proclamation to recall soldiers to their regiments:

> In pursuance of the 26th section of the act of Congress entitled "An act for enrolling and calling the national forces, and for other purposes," approved on the 3rd day of March, 1863, I, Abraham Lincoln, President and Commander in Chief of the Army and Navy of the United States, do hereby order and command that all soldiers enlisted or drafted in the service of United States now absent from their regiments without leave shall forthwith return to their respective regiments.
>
> And I do hereby declare and proclaim that all soldiers now absent from their respective regiments without leave who shall, on or before the 1st day of April, 1863, report themselves at any rendezvous designated by the general orders of the War Department No. 58, hereto annexed may be restored to their regiments without punishment, except the forfeiture of pay and allowances during their absence; and all who do not return within the time above specified shall be arrested as deserters and punished as the law allows.[96] (italics added by author).

Basically, all would be forgiven with exception of pay and allowances (clothing, transportation, etc.) for the period of absence. Overall, Lincoln offered a very fair resolution of the problem. Although Lincoln was certainly cognizant of the possible reasons for a soldier's desertion stated above, he did not publicly blame the soldier. Instead, he accused "evil-disposed and disloyal persons at sundry places have enticed and procured soldiers to desert and absent themselves from their regiments."[97]

Company H of the 6th Maryland Regiment had its share of deserters, but probably no more than other companies. A review of desertions in Company D shows similar numbers of soldiers who left camp without authorized leave. Company H had ten men who went AWOL in 1862.

Captain Adam B. Martin's brother, Stephen G. Martin, entered the service as a corporal, but for some reason, was absent from camp at the original muster. He was found guilty at a court martial and fined five dollars. When returned to his regiment, he was promoted to corporal and then to Sergeant on April 1, 1863. On September 2, 1862, just twelve days after they were mustered in, Privates Patrick King and John Penner left Camp Maffit in Baltimore. Neither ever returned to his regiment, nor were they court martialed because they could not be located. The reason for their absence will always remain a mystery. During October of 1862, Privates Thomas Ingram, John Sweitzer, and Michael Thomas all took unauthorized leave. At this time, the regimental camp was at Williamsport, Maryland, in Washington County, a stone's throw from Hagerstown. Private Ingram went AWOL again July 29, 1864, but was never arrested or court martialed. In fact, he served the brigade admirably as a sharpshooter and was mustered out of the service June 20, 1865, with most of the other members of Company H. Private Thomas left camp October 30 and was arrested November 25, but was not court martialed. However, he deserted again January 12, 1865, was arrested by the Provost Marshal, and had ten dollars deducted from his pay monthly until his fines were paid off. He also completed his entire term of service and was discharged honorably June 20, 1865. The previously mentioned Private Sweitzer left camp October 21, but returned April 1, 1863 under Lincoln's Proclamation until he was discharged due to a disability. All of the soldiers mentioned thus far cooperated fully with the U.S. Army after returning to their units and fulfilled their commitments.[98]

While the regiment was still at Williamsport, 3rd Sergeant Shank deserted December 13, but was only reduced in rank. As John King stated in his regimental history, the 6th Maryland moved their camp to Harper's Ferry during December of 1862. From this encampment, a pair of men, Corporal Bikle and Private Gans, from Company H deserted just before Christmas on December 22.[99] Both had very brief periods of absence and were soon back with their units without much punishment. Corporal Bikle was demoted back to a private. Perhaps these men simply wanted to see their families over the holidays.

During the cold winter month of January of 1863, five men left the encampment at Harper's Ferry. Private Ferdinand Bonebrake was listed as absent without leave, but returned to his regiment. He was court martialed and had six dollars monthly taken from his pay. On November 12, 1864, he deserted from Company H's camp at Martinsburg, Virginia. To his credit, Private Bonebrake returned both times and completed his term of enlistment. Likewise, Private Daniel Watson went AWOL January 16, 1863, from the Harper's Ferry camp, but soon returned and said he was "homesick." His service records show no punishment administered. Lastly, on January 18, 1863, a trio of men apparently left camp together. Privates Lewis Flory, George F. Gossard and Abraham Stoner all went AWOL. Private Flory moved to Ohio where he joined their National Guard unit May 2, 1864 and served until September 4, 1864, when the Guard was mustered out of the service. Years later, Private Flory applied for and received a pension with the assistance of an attorney. Privates Gossard and Stoner were never located by the Provost Marshal. Neither of them would receive would a veterans pension. Private Gossard relocated to Pennsylvania according to the 1880 and 1900 U.S. Censuses while Private Stoner took refuge in Wyoming per that states' 1880 and 1900 U.S. Censuses. Three more enlisted men would take leave without approval from the camp in Harper's Ferry during

February of 1863. On February 7, Corporal Columbus Flory and Private James H. Harne deserted. Corporal Flory voluntarily returned to his unit more than a year later on March 28, 1864, and was court martialed April 21, 1864. His punishment consisted of thirteen months added to his term of service and a transfer to the 1st Maryland Infantry. Likewise, Private Harne returned March 28, was court martialed and found guilty of desertion. His enlistment extended thirteen months, and he was transferred to the 1st Maryland. However, for some reason not clearly explained in his service records, Private Harne's charge of desertion was expunged from his record on March 27, 1888. While Corporal Flory was approved for a military pension March 17, 1891, with the help of attorney O. A. Cheney, Private Harne never even filed for benefits. Lastly, Private George C. Reynolds left his regiment at Harper's Ferry due to sickness February 16, 1863, and again March 25, 1863, due to being "homesick." Once again, he "left the wagon train at Boonsboro" July 12, 1863 and this time he was court martialed.[100] His is only punishment was a fine of twenty-six dollars to be deducted from his pay, probably to cover his apprehension fee and court costs. Private Reynolds then did diligent service until the 6th Maryland was mustered out June 20, 1865. Private Reynolds died December 25, 1888, and never received a veteran's pension.[101] However, on January 31, 1890, his widow was approved for a pension.

Doing the administrative work connected with attendance, desertions and court martials took up a great deal of the time of the officers, both commissioned and non-commissioned. For example, on March 4, 1863, the following advertisement ran in *The Herald of Freedom & Torch Light* newspaper of Hagerstown regarding some of the aforementioned enlisted men:

> Capt. A. B. Martin of Co. H, 6th MD Regiment Volunteers submitted a list of 7 deserters from the regiment at Harper's Ferry. A reward of $5 is offered for each. The deserters are: John Sweitzer (near Clear Spring), Frank Gossard, James H. Harne, Columbus Flory, Lewis Flory, Abm. Stoner (the above five from near Smithsburg) and Michael Bower (near Cavetown).[102]

In addition to seeking deserters, the commanding officer was required to write a document called "Charges and Specifications" for each man who either returned voluntarily or was captured and who now had to appear before a court martial hearing. Captain Martin was required to author several such documents and used both Lieutenant James A. Robinson and First Sergeant John R. King as witnesses. Efforts to locate missing men were time consuming both for the company officers and for the Provost Marshal. Even worse, desertion greatly decreased the fighting strength of the entire regiment. At one time, an officer of Company H noted that down from the original number of ninety-two men, there were only fifty-four present at roll call.[103]

In March of 1863, the 6th Maryland was detached from the Maryland Brigade and was ordered to Berryville, Virginia and was now assigned to the 3rd Brigade, 2nd Division, 8th Army Corps.[104] Oddly enough, not one soldier left camp without leave during April of 1863. However, in May, the enlisted men began in depart again from camp. On May 10, 1863, Private George Kough left his camp at Berryville and was never heard from or seen again. He had earlier been arrested in Williamsport November 20, 1862, for some reason. There is no record of any other arrest, confinement or court martial. Surprisingly, Private Kough completed the 1890-C U.S. Census for veterans while residing in Pennsylvania and stated that his discharge papers were lost in the Johnstown flood. According to U.S. Censuses, he lived in Logan, Blair County, Pennsylvania in 1870, moved to Altoona in 1880 and ended up in Johnstown, Cambria County in 1900.[105] He had been working as a laborer. Neither Private Kough nor his wife, Catharine Annie, ever applied for or received a veteran's pension.[106]

Another man who deserted Company H was Sergeant Major and Lieutenant John M. Martin. He was not related to Captain Martin. Lieutenant Martin's unusual military history began September 21, 1861, when he was mustered into Company E, First Potomac Home Brigade. Coincidentally, this was the same company and regiment to which John King's brother, Lieutenant Harrison King, belonged. John M. Martin resigned as a 2nd Lieutenant April 30, 1862, because of health problems. He then joined Company H as a sergeant major August 21, 1862. On February 19, 1863, Sgt. Major Martin wrote a letter to Lt. Colonel W. H. Cheesebrough, A. A. General, at Harper's Ferry, stating that "I have received news from home that my wife and child are dangerously ill, and should my wife be taken away it will leave my family in a helpless condition, as none of my children have arrived at the age of maturity."[107] His request for a ten-day furlough was granted by the army. Sgt. Major Martin returned from leave, but on May 20, 1863, he deserted the Berryville camp, probably to again care for his family. He was never arrested, confined or court martialed for this unauthorized leave of absence. His service record provides no further information as to his status or whereabouts. However, on his 1871 pension application, Sgt. Major wrote that he had lost his discharge papers. Furthermore, he indicated that he had been using an alias, John M.

McAninch, and that he had served in Company H, 6th Maryland Infantry. In addition, he mentioned also serving in the First Potomac Home Brigade and the 205th Pennsylvania Infantry. Oddly, the roster of the 205th does not list him as a member. Apparently, when he left Company H, Sgt. Major Martin returned to the state where he was born. In fact, the 1890-C U.S. Veterans Census shows him using the last name McNinch and residing in Metal Township, Franklin County, Pennsylvania. Despite his earlier desertion from Company H, John M. Martin, also known as John M. McAnich received a veteran's pension.[108]

On June 12, 1863, the day before the Second Battle of Winchester began, four enlisted men of Company left their encampment at Berryville, Virginia. Private Frisby T. Fisher went AWOL, but returned to his regiment October 8 and awaited his court martial. However, his missing time was simply changed to "absent without leave."[109] In fact, he was later promoted to Corporal April 3, 1865. Private Hezekiah Irvin deserted his post three times during the Civil War: December 5, 1862, June 12, 1863 and May 1, 1865. After the second time, he was arrested at his home in Washington County, was found guilty and sentenced to forfeit five months pay and allowances and was fined $11.25 for his apprehension and would "forfeit one-half of his pay and allowances during the remainder of his term of service by G. O. (General Order-ed).[110] However, in an act of charity and compassion, Captain Martin, Lieutenants Brewer and Robinson and First Sergeant John R. King later wrote letters in support of a lesser sentence for Private Irvin. Dated June 27, 1864, Lieutenant James H. C. Robinson's letter to Captain A. E. King, A. A. A. General, 3rd Division, 6th Army Corps, said that "he (Pvt. Irvin) has proven himself to be one the best men I have in my company always ready and willing to perform duty....i would also state that he is the only support of an aged and infirm mother."[111] In addition, Colonel John W. Horn, commander of the 6th Maryland, wrote that "this man has performed his duty, during the entire campaign and application is worthy of consideration. The U.S. Army agreed with the regimental officers and dispensed with the deduction of one-half of Private Irvin's pay. Unfortunately, Private Irvin deserted again while absent on furlough May 1, 1865.[112] This time, however, he returned to duty without a trial or loss of pay and was mustered out with the regiment June 20, 1865. On May 9, 1879, he was granted a veteran's pension and subsequent to his death in Illinois September 16, 1887, his widow received benefits. The third man to leave Camp Berryville just before the battle was Private George F. Pickett. He returned August 10 after an absence of two months, was arrested and court martialed. His sentence was a fine of $31.28 to be deducted from his pay. Private Pickett soon became ill and was transferred to the Invalid Corps. In May of 1864, he returned to Company H. However, he was wounded in battle in September, 1864, and spent a considerable amount of time hospitalized. Like the other two soldiers mentioned above, he was discharged with the regiment on June 20, 1865, and later received a military pension.[113] The last man to go AWOL on June 12, 1863, was Private Henry Young. The Provost Marshal arrested him at his home in Washington County, September 22, 1863, and his court marital took place December 11, 1863 in camp at Brandy Station, Virginia. Like the others, Private Young lost his pay and allowances for the period he was absent, five months in his case. In addition, he was fined $11.25 as an apprehension fee and, similar to Private Irvin's sentence, one-half of his pay and allowances for the remainder of his term of service would also be deducted.[114] Private Young was transferred to the Veterans Reserve Corps April 15, 1864, and is listed on the regimental muster out roll dated June 20, 1865. Probably related to the same illness or injury which necessitated a transfer to the V. R. C., Private Young died June 16, 1866 at the age of fifty-four years. Although he was married and had five children, his widow never filed an application for benefits.

Only one other enlisted man deserted Company H during June of 1863 and he did not simply leave camp without authorization. Private Jacob Hovis was one of twenty one soldiers of Company H who were taken prisoner at the Second Battle of Winchester June 15. He was very fortunate and got an early parole on June 23 at City Point, Virginia, and was sent to Camp Parole in Annapolis, as were all released Union prisoners of war in the East. However, Private Hovis got into trouble when he did not arrive at Camp Parole until August 2. As a result, Private Hovis was court martialed for desertion and had $6.00 deducted from his pay. Like the majority of men who went AWOL from Company H, Private Hovis served the full term of his service, was mustered out June 20, 1865, and received a veteran's pension. After the war, he became a basketmaker.[115]

As John King mentions in his regimental history, the 6th Maryland retreated to the safety of Harper's Ferry on June 15, 1863, following the Second Battle of Winchester, after a march of forty miles. At Harper's Ferry, they were assigned to the Second Brigade, Third Division, Third Corps, commanded by Major General William H. French.[116] Just before joining the pursuit of General Lee's Army on July 13, 1863, following the Battle of Gettysburg, Corporal John H. Shields left his unit without leave on July 7 "near Frederick Junction."[117] He was arrested and court martialed and fined $10 for apprehension and $15 for the court martial. Again, like many others who deserted temporarily, Corporal Shields was soon back with his regiment. The Union Army simply did not severely punish those who deserted with long confinement or displays of public humiliation. President Lincoln and the army needed these men to fight. Like many other men of the 6th Maryland who were wounded or killed in Grant's 1864 campaign to seize Richmond, Corporal Shields was later severely wounded in battle near Spotsylvania Court House May 9, 1864. His injury was so severe that he had to have his left arm amputated. On February 3, 1865, Major General Christopher C. Auger discharged him "by reason of wounds." Corporal Shields is shown on the prior list of those discharged for disability.[117]

During August of 1863, two enlisted men who had been captured June 15, 1863, on the retreat from Winchester, and who had been exchanged and paroled left Camp Parole without leave. Private Elias Gouker deserted from Camp Parole about August 1. He was arrested in Smithsburg, Maryland, probably at this home, on October 5, 1863, and was court martialed. His apprehender received a reward of $10 and $.83 for boarding. As punishment, Private Gouker had $6.00 deducted from his pay. Having rejoined his company, the private was "wounded by an explosive ball in the assault on the Rebel picket line near Petersburg."[118] Likewise, Private George W. Grim was captured June 15, 1863, paroled and sent to Camp Parole. Perhaps because he did not enjoy his temporary confinement, Private Grim also departed without authorization. He "gave himself up" November 19, 1863 in Frederick, Maryland.[119] Unlike Gouker, Private was not court martialed. Instead, he was considered a straggler and later served as the regimental butcher. Why one man was court martialed as a deserter and the other only deemed a straggler for seemingly the same offence is not known. Both men later received pensions.

As John King mentions in his regimental history speech, the 6th Maryland crossed the Rappahannock River August 15, 1863, and went into camp near Culpeper until October 10. Another prisoner taken June 15, 1863, at Winchester, was Private James M. Lowry. Like the above enlisted men, he too was paroled, exchanged, and sent to Camp Parole July 24, but did not return to duty until October 5, because he had deserted. He was court martialed and fined $18.75 for both his apprehension fee and sentence. By November, Private Lowry was in the Pioneer Corps until he became ill and was admitted to Columbia U.S. Army General Hospital April 1, 1865 and then was admitted to Mt. Pleasant Hospital in Washington, D. C. for "chronic diarrhea" June 10, 1865.[120] Finally, he was mustered out of the service June 26, 1865. He was later approved for a veteran's pension.

Another enlisted man who was apparently displeased with the U.S. Army and Camp Parole was Private Daniel L. Jackson. He also had been taken prisoner at the Second Battle of Winchester, was confined in Richmond briefly, was paroled at City Point July 23 and was sent to Camp Parole July 24. Private Jackson deserted from Camp Parole November 16, 1863, was never arrested, confined or court martialed.[121] The Provost Marshal was unable to find him. On February 10, 1892, he applied for a military pension and after his death, his wife also filed for a widow's pension on September 29, 1896. Neither was approved.

On November 24, 1863, just two days before Union General Meade began his turning movement to get behind General Robert E. Lee's Army of Northern Virginia, 2nd Sergeant Daniel B. Reynolds left the camp of the 6th Maryland at Brandy Station without permission from his commanding officer. According to the "Specifications of Court Martial" prepared by Captain Adam B. Martin and signed by 2nd Lieutenant Robinson and 1st Sergeant King, Private Reynolds " remained absent until January 3, 1864, and returned to his company and regiment voluntarily at Brandy Station."[122] The reason for his absence was not shown in his service records; perhaps he simply wished to see his wife during the holidays. Still, Sergeant Reynolds was reduced in rank, forfeited forty days pay and allowance and also forfeited four months pay proper.[123] These fines were in accordance with President Lincoln's policy of amnesty for deserters. Unfortunately, Private Reynolds was severely wounded in action at Cold Harbor June 1, 1864, and spent seven months in the Confederate "hell hole" called Andersonville. After being released, he died January 29, 1865, in the post hospital in Hagerstown from "rheumatism of the heart" at the age of twenty-nine years.[124] His widow, Lydia A. Reynolds, filed for a pension October 21, 1865, and her claim was approved.

For unknown reasons, not one soldier from Company H deserted during the period November 25, 1863 until July 9, 1864. During this time period, the 6th Maryland remained in their encampment at Brandy Station except for the brief Battle of Locust Grove or Payne's Farm. Beginning with the crossing of the Rapidan River on May 4, the regiment was heavily immersed in the Wilderness Campaign. Grant constantly tried to get between Lee's Army and Richmond, but the former continually sidled further south.

John King's regimental history speech states that the 6th Maryland left City Point, Virginia, on transport ships on July 6, 1864, bound for Baltimore.[125] The Union Army had to rush troops into Frederick County, Maryland, to block Confederate General Jubal Early's advance on Washington, D. C. The ship arrived on July 8 and the regiment was immediately put on railroad cars to travel to Frederick. The Battle of the Monocacy was fought around the river of the same name on July 9, 1864. On that same day, the drummer boy for Company H, Charles Robinson, left his unit, never to return.[126] Only fourteen years old, perhaps he simply went home to be with his family.

Company H had several enlisted men detailed in various duties during the almost two and one years of its existence. Already depleted because of desertions, the company faced further reductions in strength because of these special assignments. Men were variously deployed as a teamster, butcher, or Provost Guard member. Since November of 1863, Private Jeremiah Fishach was detailed to the Provost Marshall. According to Charges and Specifications filed against him, Private Fishach,

> serving as a member of the Provost Guards on or about July 28, 1864 at Jefferson, Frederick County, went AWOL without permission from said Guard and did go to his home in Smithsburg, Washington County and did remain so AWOL until September 2, 1864.[127]

By command of Brigadier Ricketts, Private Fishach forfeited thirty-two dollars of his pay and returned to his unit. On January 1, 1865, he was promoted to 5th Corporal, but was soon "reduced to ranks from Corporal April 3, 1865, for some unspecified transgression. Well after the war, Private Fishach applied for and received a pension as did his widow upon his death on October 15, 1888, at the age of fifty years.[128]

As cited earlier, a short leave or straggling did not usually constitute desertion in the Union Army and should certainly not have been considered as such. In the Company Descriptive Book, Private Thomas Ingram was listed as a sharpshooter for the 3rd Division, 6th Army Corps, who "knew no fear and was daring to recklessness." However, he erred twice during his service. For some reason, he was shown as "absent from camp at the original muster" and then appeared on a "Returns" list as AWOL during October of 1862. Later, he shows up on a List of Deserters dated August 8, 1864, for being absent July 29, 1864, "from Rendevous of Distribution, near Alexandria, Virginia.[129] Rendevous of Distribution was the name of a place near Alexandria where Amy Morris Bradly published the popular "The Soldier's Journal," to offer military news to Union soldiers.[130] The site was established in 1864 as a hospital camp "restructured as Camp Distribution, a station for soldiers awaiting their deployment orders.[131] Despite these transgressions, Private Ingram's service records show that he was never arrested or court martialed. Instead, although only eighteen years old, Private Ingram served admirably as one of the brigade sharpshooters. After the war, his July 26, 1890 application for a veteran's pension was approved.

Towards the end of the Civil War, the number of desertions from Company H had steadily decreased. Perhaps those who were to go had already gone. In the late summer and fall of 1864, after the Battle of Monocacy and before the Battle of Opequon, the 6th Maryland was encamped near the Martinsburg-Charlestown area of Virginia (now West Virginia). Private George W. Secore, who had earlier been a prisoner of war after being taken at the Second Battle of Winchester June 15, 1863, deserted from camp August 15, 1864.[132] Never apprehended by the Provost Marshall, Private Secore would eventually make his way to Luzerne, Pennsylvania, never to return to the state of Maryland. In his later years, he would not even apply for a military pension. Private Secore would add his name to a group of ten deserters from Company who dishonored themselves by deserting and never made any reparations whatsoever.

About three weeks after the 6th Maryland fought at the Battle of Cedar Creek on October 6, 1864, two more enlisted men, 2nd Corporal Charles Miller and 3rd Corporal Samuel Sterling left camp at Martinsburg without authorized leave on November 11.[133] Corporal Miller had been previously hospitalized at Fairfax Seminary near Alexandria for a fever and was later wounded in the Battle of the Wilderness. He would also join a group of ten Company H deserters, as there is no record of arrest in his file. Private Miller seems to have been completely lost to the U.S. Army. The circumstances surrounding his disappearance will never be known. However, on November 4, 1885, he applied for a military pension.[134] Neither his nor his wife's applications were approved. On that same day in November, Corporal Sterling departed camp, perhaps with Corporal Miller. In this example of desertion, the reason for doing so is understandable in lieu of the following letter from Dr. H. F. Perry of Clear Spring, Maryland (Corporal Sterling's hometown) dated May 2, 1865 to H. Clay Naill, Captain and Provost, 4th Military District:

> Samuel Sterling is a son of the late Samuel Sterling who died Dec. 23rd 1864. The family now consists of a widowed mother and eight children-five sons and three daughters. Four sons of which Samuel B. Sterling is one-are now in the federal army. One son nearly twelve years of age and three daughters remain at home on the property belonging to the family cannot, I think, exceed in value eight hundred dollars. The family, since the death of the father, has been supported mainly by contributions from the sons now in the army, aided by the liberality and charity of the landlord—The daughters and son remaining at home are not old enough to contribute much to their support. They greatly need the assistance of one of the older brothers to exercise a general supervision over the interests of the family.

> I believe the application that been made to the Secretary of War for the discharge of Samuel B. Sterling from military service is just and that his assistance at home would contribute largely to the interest and welfare of his mother, Sisters and Brothers.[135]

Unfortunately for Samuel B. Sterling and his family, neither Captain Nail nor the U.S. Army were moved enough by Dr. Perry's letter to release him from his duty. It did not help his plea that he had also deserted and was court martialed in 1863.[136] However, Corporal Sterling was able to return to the army May 4, 1865 under President Lincoln's Proclamation of March 11, 1865. As he did in the issuance of his first Amnesty Proclamation of March 10, 1863, Lincoln again called for the return of Union soldiers and sailors to their regiments and naval units. In part, the March 11, 1865, Proclamation read (italics added):

> Now, therefore, be it known that I, Abraham Lincoln, President of the United States, do issue this my proclamation, as required by said act, ordering and requiring all deserters to return to their proper posts; and I do hereby notify them that all deserters who shall, within sixty days from the date of this proclamation, viz, on or before the 10th day of May, 1865, return to service or report themselves to a provost-marshall shall be pardoned, on condition that they return to their regiments and companies or to such other organizations as they may be assigned to and serve the remainder of their original terms of enlistment and in addition thereto a period equal to the time lost by desertion.[137]

Hence, while Lincoln would not inflict any punishment with his pardon, he did not excuse the time that the soldier or sailor missed. He wanted that time added on to the soldier's term of enlistment. Thus, Corporal Sterling returned under the terms of Lincoln's newest Proclamation on May 4, 1865, just before Lincoln's deadline. Apparently, he was able to spend some time at home helping his mother and three sisters. However, Corporal Sterling would not return to Company H. As were other soldiers in the 6th Maryland who had deserted, Corporal Sterling was transferred to the 1st Maryland Infantry Regiment. With Company A of that unit, he would serve out his now lengthened term of service. With the assistance of Attorney W. Chrissinger, Corporal Sterling made application for a military pension May 4, 1892, and his case was approved.[138]

The last man to desert from Company H was Private Michael Thomas. Earlier, on October 27, 1862, he left the regiment's encampment at

Williamsport, was arrested there and was removed to Harper's Ferry.[139] His service record is not clear as to the outcome of this occurrence of being absent without leave. Next, at the Battle of Spotsylvania Court House on May 12, 1864, Private Thomas was wounded and was sent to a U.S. General Hospital near Soldiers Rest in Alexandria, Virginia.[140] The sequence of events that followed is an instance of a summary written by the Adjutant General's Office, War Department, Washington, August 30th, 1887:

> Entered Emory G. H. (General Hospital-Ed.) Washington, D. C. May 17th 1864 from field with G. S. wound (gunshot-Ed.) right index finger received at Spotsylvania May 12, 64 and returned to duty July 12. 64. Entered Auguar G. H. Alexandria Va. August 9, 1864 with Inflammation of face, was furloughed Oct. 12th 1864 to Oct. 31, 64 and Nov. 2 to 13, 64, and returned to duty Jan'y 12th 1865. Received at Camp Distribution Alex'a Jany 12, 65 and sent to Regiment Jan'y 12 1865, again received Jany 28th 1865 and sent to Regiment Feby 11, 1865, again received Feby 12th 1865. and sent to Regiment Feby 18, 1865. He was received at Soldiers Rest Alex'a Va. March 12th 1865 as of 1st Md. H. G. Deserted March 20, 1865, Near Soldier's Rest. Washington D.C. and was apprehended about March 23, 1865. The charge of desertion of Jany 12th 1865 on roll of Co. for Jany and Feby 1865 is removed. He was tried by a Genl Court Martial for the desertion of March 20, 1865, found not guilty, but guilty of absence without leave. He was absent without leave from March 20, 1865, to March 23, 1865. Sentenced to forfeit ten (10) dollars per month of his monthly pay for two Months per G. O. (General Order-Ed.) 207, Hd. Qrs. Military Governor of Alex. Va.
>
> April 12, 1865.[141]

This is an example of how the War Department kept records of a soldiers' injuries, furloughs, authorized absences, charges and results of military hearings on those charges. Camp Distribution in Alexandria, Virginia, was "a station for (Union) soldiers awaiting their deployment orders."[142] Soldier's Rest, located near the Orange and Alexandria Rail Road Depot, was initially used as a "Rest" for men in trains, but was later employed as a hospital.[143] Both were situated near Alexandria, Virginia. Apparently, Private Thomas felt that he was not ready to return to his 6th Maryland Regiment and lingered longer than he should have. Nevertheless, he was the only man who was cleared of desertion charges during a court martial. He was later admitted into the National Home for Disabled Volunteer

Soldiers in Elizabeth City, Virginia, on November 2, 1887.[144] In addition, his claim for a military pension was filed on November 10, 1888, and was approved.[145] Private Miller never married. His closest relative was William Thomas, a cousin from Sharpsburg, Maryland. In 1911, Private Miller died and was interred in Cedar Grove Cemetery in Chambersburg, Pennsylvania.

Overall, of the forty-three enlisted men of Company H who deserted, only twenty were court martialed. Ten of those forty-three who deserted were never caught by the Provost Marshall. Some members of this group of ten applied for a veteran's pension, but were not approved because the old service records were still available to the War Department. Two of these ten deserters used an alias in the state where they were residing. Only one of them returned to Washington County, Maryland. The others who could be located in later years had moved to other states, apparently in an effort to elude the U.S. Army. Of the twenty men who were court martialed, only one soldier was sent to prison and was publicly humiliated. Private Harrison Bridendolph of Clear Spring, Washington County, Maryland, enlisted in Company H in Hagerstown August 14, 1862, and then was sent to camp near Baltimore with the rest of the regiment. As mentioned earlier, every man of Company H received a second bounty (the fee granted for enlistment) of one hundred dollars from Washington County itself before he left for Baltimore the last week of August of 1862. In addition, the U.S. Army would pay another one-hundred dollar bounty, but only at the end of the soldier's service. Private Bridendolph went AWOL September 12, 1862, from Camp Howard in Franklinville, Maryland, just after the enlistment bonus was paid, just four weeks after he had enlisted.[146] However, he was soon arrested on November 27, 1862, at Williamsport, Maryland. On April 10, 1863, a Special Court Martial was held and Private Bridendolph was sentenced to confinement in Fort McHenry for two and one-half years, forfeited all pay and allowance and was to be "drummed out of the U.S. Service."[147] During that two and one-half years, he was "to wear an iron ball weighing twenty pounds attached to his right leg by an iron chain four feet in length" and when his sentence was completed he was "to have one-half of his head shaved the buttons cut off his coat and a board on his back with the word 'Deserter' marked thereon" and his drumming out of the service would be to the tune of 'The Poor Old Soldier.'[148] At some point, he was transferred to Company A of the 1st Maryland Infantry and dishonorably discharged.[149] Thus, early on, the U. S Army wanted to make an example of Private Bridendolph. Although several other soldiers who received the one hundred dollar bounty from Washington County also later deserted, (for example, Lewis Flory, Charles Miller, and Charles Robinson) they were never apprehended. None of the twenty men who were arrested and court martialed were subjected to the harsh punishment that Private Bridendolph received. One of the reasons for this were the two proclamations from Lincoln ensuring amnesty and pardons for those who had deserted their companies.

With the Union military forces, both Army and Navy, depleted by as many as 600,000 men, including about 200,000 missing from the Army of the Potomac, President Lincoln had to excuse their behavior in some fashion and bring them back to their units. Like many of the other enlisted soldiers and sailors who took unauthorized leave, most of the deserters from Company H were good men. Their character and reputations should not be besmirched for taking unauthorized leave for several reasons. First, with the exception of the ten soldiers who dishonored the oath they took when they enlisted by deserting, the majority did due diligence and honored their commitment. The forty-three enlisted men of Company H, except for these ten, totally fulfilled their obligations when they returned to duty. Some were wounded and some were killed. But, they all otherwise completed their terms of service with dignity. As a result, those who survived the war and who deserved a pension received one. Secondly, the system in place set by the U.S. Army was flawed in that it actually encouraged desertion. Failure to pay the soldiers for six months led to poor morale and more desertion. Most of these men had families who needed a portion of that pay to survive. The policy of not allowing a soldier a furlough until another soldier who was already on furlough returned to his company was also short-sighted. As their service records testify to, many of these men who deserted had families who were in dire straits. Some could not simply wait for the furloughed soldier to return. Thirdly, a review of the ninety-two service records of Company H shows that approved furloughs were very rare occurrences. Captain Martin obtained one to go home and purchase a home for his family, but the records do not show any other furloughs allowed to see families. Occasionally, an enlisted man got a furlough if he was ill or had just been paroled and exchanged after imprisonment in the South. As a company that was engaged frequently in some of the most hard-fought battles of the Civil War, the men of Company H should be proud of their gallantry and courage. It should also be mentioned that Company H never received a single replacement soldier for those wounded, killed, or missing due to temporary or permanent desertion. Simply put, despite the unauthorized or "French furloughs" they occasionally took, Company H and their comrades in the 6th Maryland Infantry helped win the war.

Private Bridendolph was the only soldier imprisoned from Company H and also the only man dishonorably discharged from Company H. Surprisingly, after the war, he returned to live amongst his former comrades in Washington County, Maryland. He married Franey Forsyth on October 15, 1864.[150] By1870, he was residing in Indian Springs, had four young children and was employed as a farm laborer.[151] By 1880, Harrison Bridendolph was a farmer, still living in Indian Springs west of Hagerstown, and had now had seven children. Of course, he never received a veteran's pension. On January 26, 1894, he died in Washington County.

It would be interesting to see what happened to the other men in Company H after the Civil War. Where did they live? Did they simply return to Washington County and pick up where they left off or did they move to another part of the United States seeking to improve their fortunes? Did they seek higher education and better jobs or simply return to their former employment? Table V, entitled "Post-War Residences of Company H" shows that nearly 40 percent (39.74) percent of the veterans remained in Washington County and 51.28 percent stayed in the State of Maryland. John R. King was one of those veterans who elected to remain in the state of Maryland. These figures compare to Pre-War percentages of 70.65 percent who were living in Washington County and nearly 87 percent (86.96 percent) who were from the State of Maryland. Many of the former soldiers wished to make their mark in another state. After the war, ten men lived in Pennsylvania, four went to Illinois to farm, five moved to Kansas to pursue farming, two lived in West Virginia, and one each in Wyoming, South Dakota, Iowa and New York City. Only three soldiers could not be located. As previously cited, before the Civil War, twenty-one men or 33.87 percent stated that they were either laborers or day laborers while another fifteen said that they were either a farm hand, farmer or farm laborer. Taken together, 58 percent of the men for whom occupations were available stated that they were laborers, farm or otherwise. Table VI is titled "Post-War Occupations of Company H." For those for whom occupations were available, the percentage was almost exactly as it had been years earlier. For a total of sixty-six veterans, 57.58 percent listed their occupations as farmer (19), farm laborer (12), laborer (4), or farm hand (3). Occupations for eleven veterans could not be found. Such a result would not be surprising considering that Washington County was primarily agricultural and that the veterans who moved to Illinois, Kansas, Wyoming, South Dakota and Iowa went those states to buy land and to farm. Prior to joining the U.S. Army and aside from the 58 percent who were either laborers, farm hands or farmers, the other occupations cut across a wide range of blue collar trades. (See Table III, "Pre-War Occupations of Company H). As shown in Table VI, many of the veterans continued in these trades. For example, some of the occupations were carpenter, shoemaker, blacksmith, stone mason, etc. However, what really changed with age and advanced education were the number of professional and managerial jobs obtained by these former soldiers of Company H. The occupations of these men were as listed in Table VI: physician, dentist, railroad supervisor, pension agent (John R. King), merchant, U.S. Marshal, railroad stationary engineer, insurance agent, surveyor, and C & O canal supervisor. Some of the soldiers who had been labeled as deserters earlier and many who had never left their camp without permission, proved their worth in later years in the positions they obtained and by the families they raised. One such man, who had never taken any recorded leave while 1st Sergeant in Company H was our diarist, John R. King. One of his post-war jobs was as a Pension Agent for the United States, a position he was selected to fill by Presidential appointment and by Senate confirmation.

(See the Appendix for a brief summary of each soldier in Company H: age, physical description if known, age, pre-war occupation and place of residence, post-war occupation and place of residence, name of wife and children, date of death, cemetery of interment and military service record.-Ed.)

Table V

Post-War Residences of Co. H, 6th Regiment, Maryland Volunteer Infantry

	Residence	Number of Soldiers
1.	Cavetown, Washington County, Maryland	9
2.	Ringgold, Washington County, Maryland	5
3.	Hagerstown, Washington County, Maryland	4
4.	Clear Spring, Washington County, Maryland	3
5.	Smithsburg, Washington County, Maryland	3
6.	Beaver Creek, Washington County, Maryland	2
7.	Rohrersville, Washington County, Maryland	1
8.	Indian Spring, Washington County, Maryland	1
9.	Hancock, Washington County, Maryland	1
10.	Pleasant Valley, Washington County, Maryland	1

11.	Washington County, Maryland, not further specified	1
	Subtotal Washington County=31 or 34percent	
12.	Frederick County, Maryland	3
13.	Baltimore City, Maryland	3
14.	Carroll County, Maryland	2
15.	Alleghany County, Maryland	1
	Total State of Maryland=40 or 51.28percent	
16.	Franklin County, Pennsylvania	6
17.	Pennsylvania, not further specified	4
18.	Illinois	4
19.	Kansas	5
20.	West Virginia	2
21.	Wyoming	1
22.	South Dakota	1
23.	Iowa	1
24.	New York City, New York	1
25.	Soldiers Not Located	3
26.	Soldiers Killed or Died of Disease	14
		N=92

Table VI
Post-War Occupations of Co. H, 6th Regiment, Maryland Volunteer Infantry

Occupation	Number of Soldiers Listing That Occupation
1. Farmer	19
2. Farm Laborer	12
3. Laborer	4
4. Farm Hand	3
5. Carpenter	2
6. Confectioner	2
7. Shoemaker	2
8. Physician	1
9. Dentist	1
10. Railroad Supervisor	1
11. Pension Agent- John R. King	1
12. Blacksmith	1
13. Basket Maker	1

14.	Printer	1
15.	Cabinet Maker	1
16.	Mail Carrier	1
17.	Merchant	1
18.	U.S. Marshal	1
19.	Stone Mason	1
20.	Railroad Stationary Engineer	1
21.	Boatsman	1
22.	Watchman	1
23.	Foundry Laborer	1
24.	Insurance Agent	1
25.	Surveyor	1
26.	C & O Canal Supervisor	1
27.	Gunsmith	1
28.	Wood Chopper	1
29.	Disabled and unable to work	1
30.	Soldiers Not Located	11
31.	Soldiers Killed or Died of Disease	14
		N=92

VII

The Lost Diary and Nisewanger/Hillyard Families

The discovery of John R. King's Civil War diary raised several important questions. First, what did the Confederate cavalrymen who captured both John and his traveling companion, John Burgess, do with the diary? Secondly, if they gave it to one of their officers at Stonewall Jackson's camp, what did that officer do with it? Thirdly, who gave diary to the Nisewanger family in Newtown, Virginia? Lastly, who moved the diary from the Nisewangers in Frederick County, Virginia, to Broadway, Virginia, in Rockingham County where it was found?

John R. King had his diary, Mr. Newcommer's borrowed wagon and horse, his ambrotype camera and all of his photographic chemicals and materials with him at the time when he was taken prisoner sometime after his last diary entry on May 22, 1862. The Confederate cavalrymen who took the boys were probably men of Ashby's cavalry. The two teenagers were found wandering around in the mountains west of the Valley Pike (current Route 11). The two Johns became entangled in the rout made by General Stonewall Jackson when he attacked General Nathaniel Banks' Union troops at Battle of First Winchester. Most likely, whoever went through the boys' belongings noticed the diary written in beautiful script. One of the cavalrymen would have next taken the diary to an officer to determine if the diary was of any military importance or had any intelligence value. When the Confederate officers realized that the book was simply a young man's diary, it was probably discarded by someone on Jackson's staff. A staff officer may have spotted the Nisewanger surname or another soldier who had the opportunity to skim the diary saw the name. One of them most likely noticed the diary entry of May 8th, 1862:

> We transferred our load had the horses put away & got permission to stay in the Toll House, kept by Mrs. Niswanger, she has a couple Young Daughters & we passed the evening very pleasantly.

Perhaps one of the Confederates was curious about the "Young Daughters" mentioned in the May 8, 1862, diary entry. Certainly, some of Jackson's men had heard of the Nisewanger since the family was well-known in the Shenandoah Valley and many of Jacksons' troops were from the Valley. One might surmise that John's diary was obtained by James "Jimmy" D. Hillyard in Winchester since he was a Confederate soldier and the diary was found at the home of his granddaughter. However, such was not the case. Jimmy Hillyard was not mustered into Confederate service until April 3, 1864, when he joined Company A, 3rd Battalion Virginia Reserves, so he was nowhere near Winchester in 1862. In fact, Jimmy Hillyard was not even a soldier at that time. Jimmy was only eighteen years old when he enlisted. Instead, one of Stonewall Jackson's men must have taken the diary to the Nisewanger home which was also known as the "Toll House." The Nisewangers lived Newtown (now Stephens City), a small village in Frederick County, Virginia. One of the soldiers may have offered it as a gift to the family since their names appeared in it. In addition, the soldier may have wished to ask some questions about the prior owner, John R. King. The Nisewangers were probably told by the Confederate soldiers that John had been taken as a civilian prisoner of war or as a possible spy for the Union. They may also have known that John R. King's diary as well as the items for his photography business, his two horses and Mr. Newcomer's wagon were all taken as spoils of war by Stonewall Jacksons' Confederate troops.

What is known with certainty is that John's diary came to be in the possession of the two youngest Nisewanger daughters, Lucinda and Emma Virginia, at some point during the Civil War. The two teenagers wrote their names, using nicknames, "Lucie Nisewanger" and "Ginnie Nisewanger" numerous times in the blank pages of the diary as if they were practicing writing their signatures. At the time of John's visit to the Toll House in 1862, Lucinda was only fourteen years of age while Emma Virginia was just sixteen. These two girls were just two daughters of the large Nisewanger family of seven daughters that was raised in the Toll House. Abraham and Lucinda Nisewanger had no sons. At the time of John's and John Burgess' stay at the Toll House, only the daughters Lucinda (nicknamed Lucie), Emma (nicknamed Ginnie or Virginia), their older sister Sarah Catherine and Mrs. Lucinda Nisewanger, their mother, were present. The other four daughters had already married and left home. Their father, Abraham was probably away from home at his job as a long distance wagoner.

In the following pages, a brief biography of each of the seven Nisewanger daughters, beginning with the oldest, will be presented. Then, a brief Hillyard family history will be given because the two families intermarried. The marriage of one of the Nisewanger daughters to James "Jimmy" Hillyard is the key to the mystery of *The Lost Diary of John Rigdon King*.

The Nisewanger Family of Newtown and Rockingham County, Virginia

Of German origin, the Neuschwanger/Niswanger/Nisewanger family was among the earliest settlers of Frederick County, Virginia, in the late 18th century. Abraham Nisewanger, son of George, married Lucinda Kipps in Shenandoah, Virginia, on August 13,1823.[2] The bride was only nineteen years of age (born 1805) and the groom was twenty-seven. Abraham was apparently a veteran of the War of 1812 as an application was later made by Lucinda for his pension. It stated that Abraham was a member of Captain John Pittman's Company of Virginia militia.[3] Apparently, Abraham did not apply for bounty land to which he may have been entitled. His application index card at the National Archives says there was "no claim for bounty land found after thorough search."[4] In addition, Abraham's name does not appear on a list of Virginia War of 1812 pensioners. After his marriage to Lucinda, the couple settled in Newtown in Frederick County, Virginia. On the 1850 U.S. Census, Abraham's occupation is given as a "waggoner," a job he probably held for the majority of his life.[5] Unfortunately for his family, his teamster job required long distance delivery of goods to the South.[6] Like modern day semi-truck driving, this employment kept Abraham away from his family for long periods of time. However, his wife, Lucinda, seemed to do exceedingly well on her own, not only by working, but also by raising seven daughters largely by herself.

Lucinda Nisewanger tended the toll gate on the Valley Pike (now Route 11) at Newtown for much of her life. She collected toll money from travelers and then raised the toll bar so that they might pass and continue their trip southward. The old Toll House was located on the western side at the south end of town, just a stone's throw from the bridge that crosses Stephens Run. Previously called Stephensburg after its founder, Peter Stephens, the town today is called Stephens City. Local lore says that the Toll House burned to the ground during the Civil War.[7] Today, the land upon which the Toll House once stood is a pasture for a working dairy. Fortunately, a pastel drawing of the log cabin and garden was accomplished about 1858 by Corporal Frances "Frank" Staling, who had lived there before the Civil War.

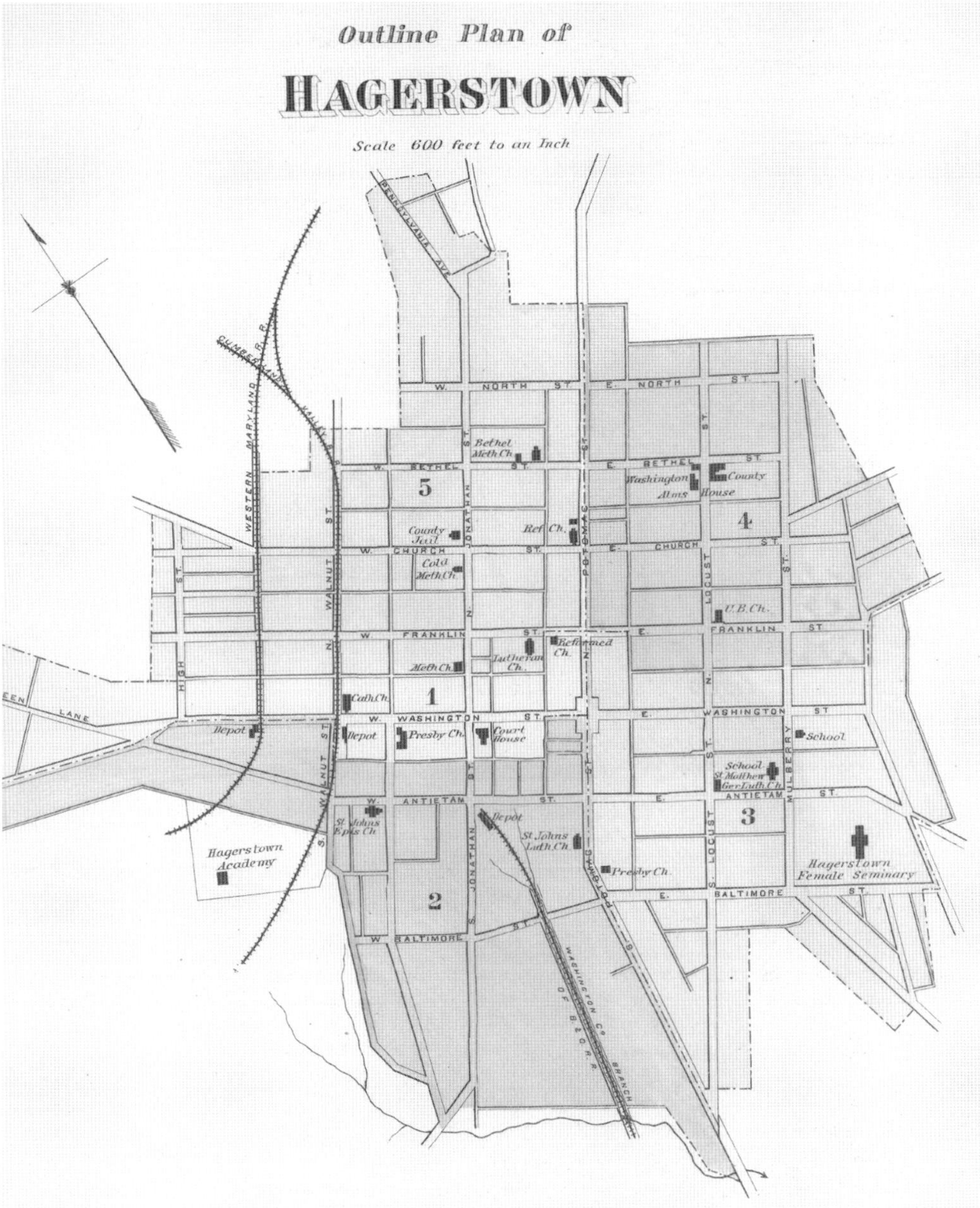

This is a district map of Hagerstown taken from Page's 1877 Atlas. The King home was directly across the street from St. John's Lutheran Church in District 3. As can be seen from the map, John had an easy walk to the Public Square downtown and to the Hagerstown Academy, which he attended for some years. (*Western Maryland Historical Library*)

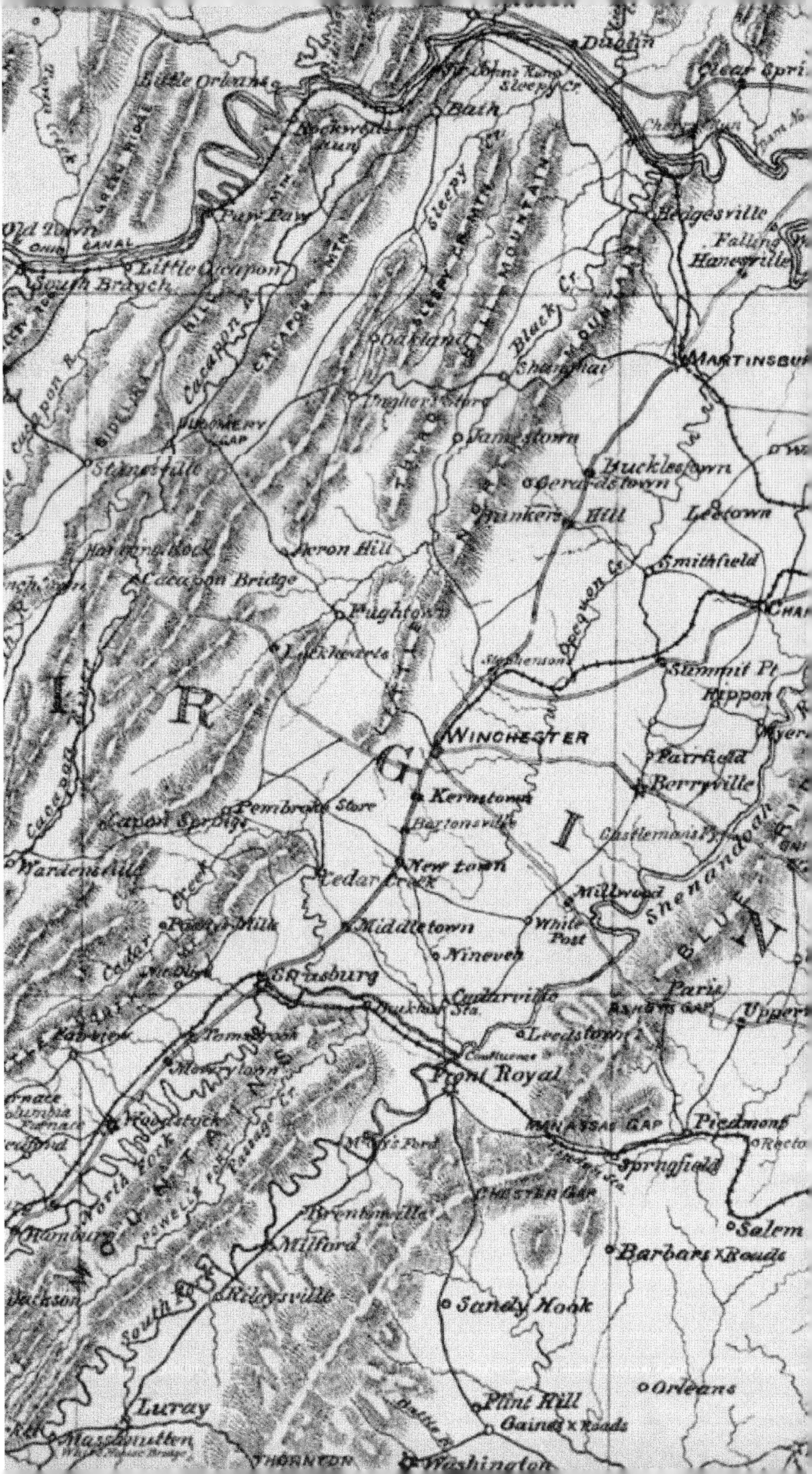
Little Orleans
Bath
Sleepy Cr.
Hedgesville
Falling
Hainesville
Old Town
CANAL
Paw Paw
Little Cacapon
South Branch
Cacapon R.
Oakland
Black Cr.
MARTINSBURG
Jamestown
Bucklestown
Gerardstown
Bunkers Hill
Leetown
Smithfield
Cacapon Bridge
Pughtown
Opequon Cr.
Summit Pt.
I
R
G
I
N
WINCHESTER
Fairfield
Berryville
Kernstown
Bartonsville
New town
Cedar Creek
Millwood
Middletown
White Post
Shenandoah
BLUE
Nineveh
Paris
Leedstown
Front Royal
Woodstock
MANASSAS GAP
Piedmont
Springfield
CHESTER GAP
Brentsville
Milford
Salem
Barbars X Roads
Sandy Hook
Orleans
Luray
Flint Hill
Gaines X Roads
Washington
THORNTON

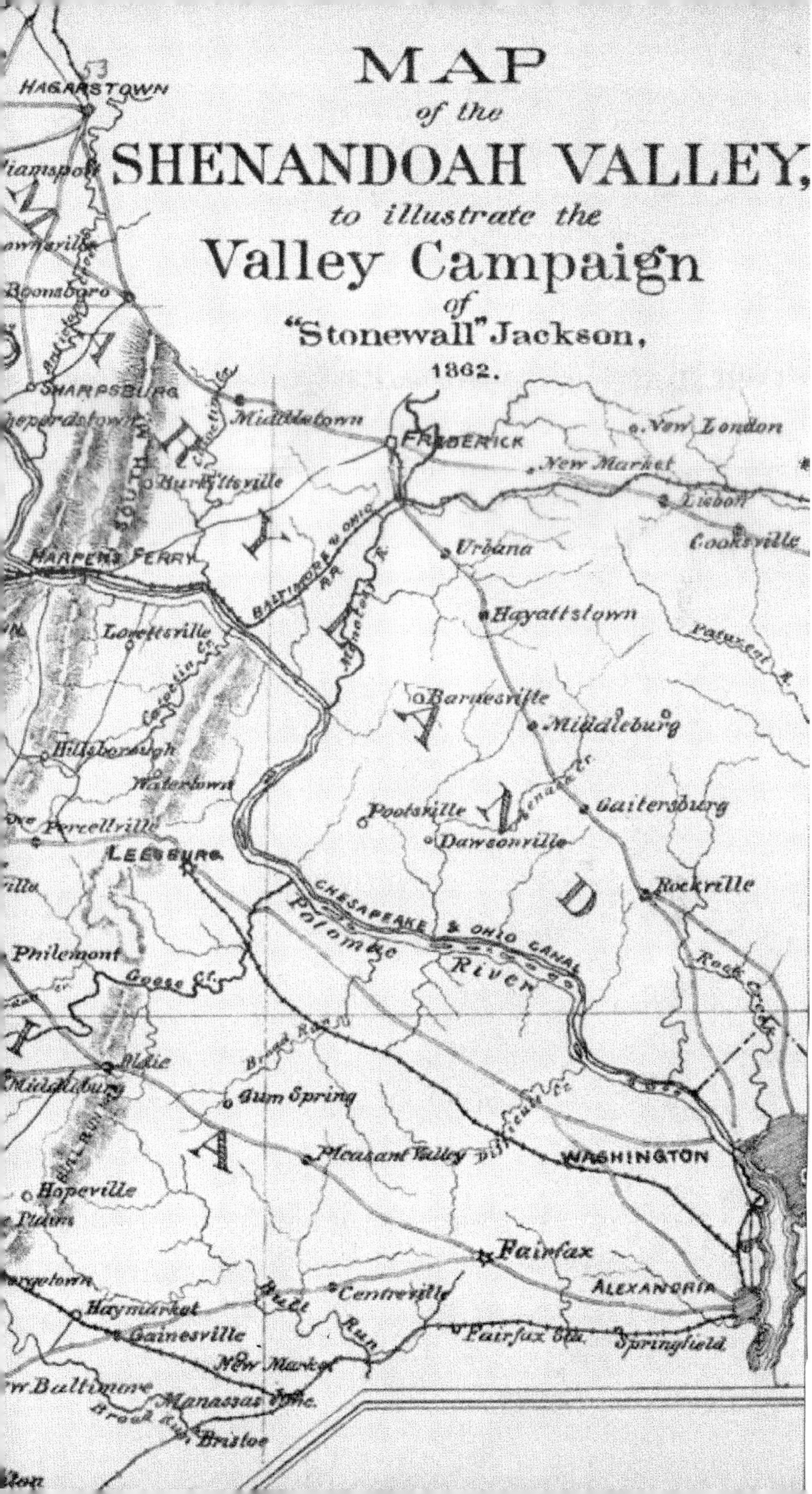
MAP
of the
SHENANDOAH VALLEY,
to illustrate the
Valley Campaign
of
"Stonewall" Jackson,
1862.
HAGARSTOWN
Boonsboro
SHARPSBURG
Middletown
FREDERICK
New London
New Market
Lisbon
Cooksville
Urbana
Hyattstown
Patuxent R.
HARPERS FERRY
SOUTH MT.
BALTIMORE & OHIO RR
Lovettsville
Hillsborough
Waterford
Purcellville
LEESBURG
Barnesville
Middleburg
Poolsville
Dawsonville
Gaitersburg
Rockville
CHESAPEAKE & OHIO CANAL
Potomac River
Rock Creek
Philemont
Goose Cr.
Aldie
Middleburg
Gum Spring
Broad Run
Pleasant Valley
WASHINGTON
Hopeville
Fairfax
Centreville
ALEXANDRIA
Haymarket
Gainesville
Bull Run
New Market
Fairfax Ctr.
Springfield
Manassas Junc.
Broad Run
Bristoe
New Baltimore

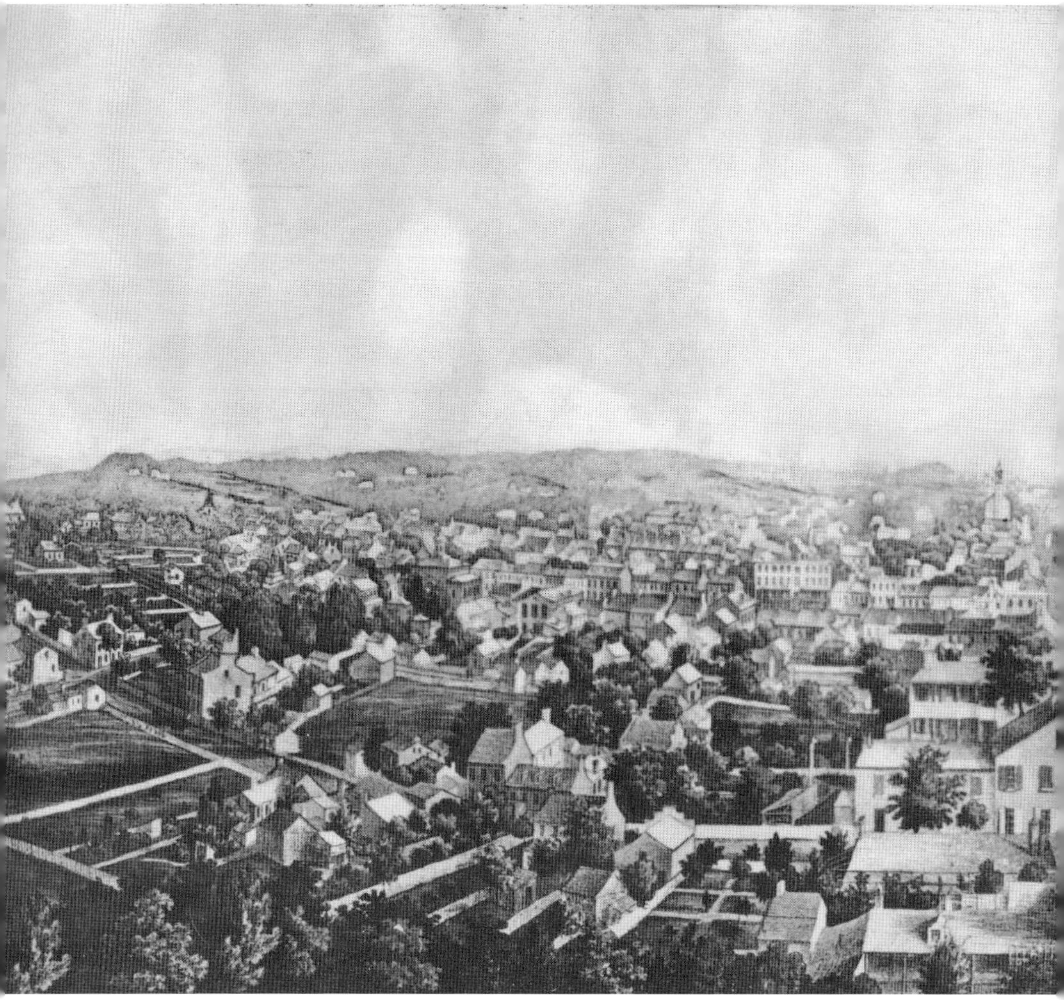

Previous page: This is a portion of a larger map prepared by Jedediah Hotchkiss to illustrate the Valley Campaign of Stonewall Jackson of 1862. Hotchkiss was a well-known cartographer and topographer who prepared maps for General Stonewall Jackson during the Civil War. This map shows some of the towns and cities mentioned in John King's diary such as Hagerstown, Clear Spring, Williamsport, and Martinsburg in West Virginia and Winchester, Newtown, Front Royal and Strasburg in Virginia. (*Library of Congress*)

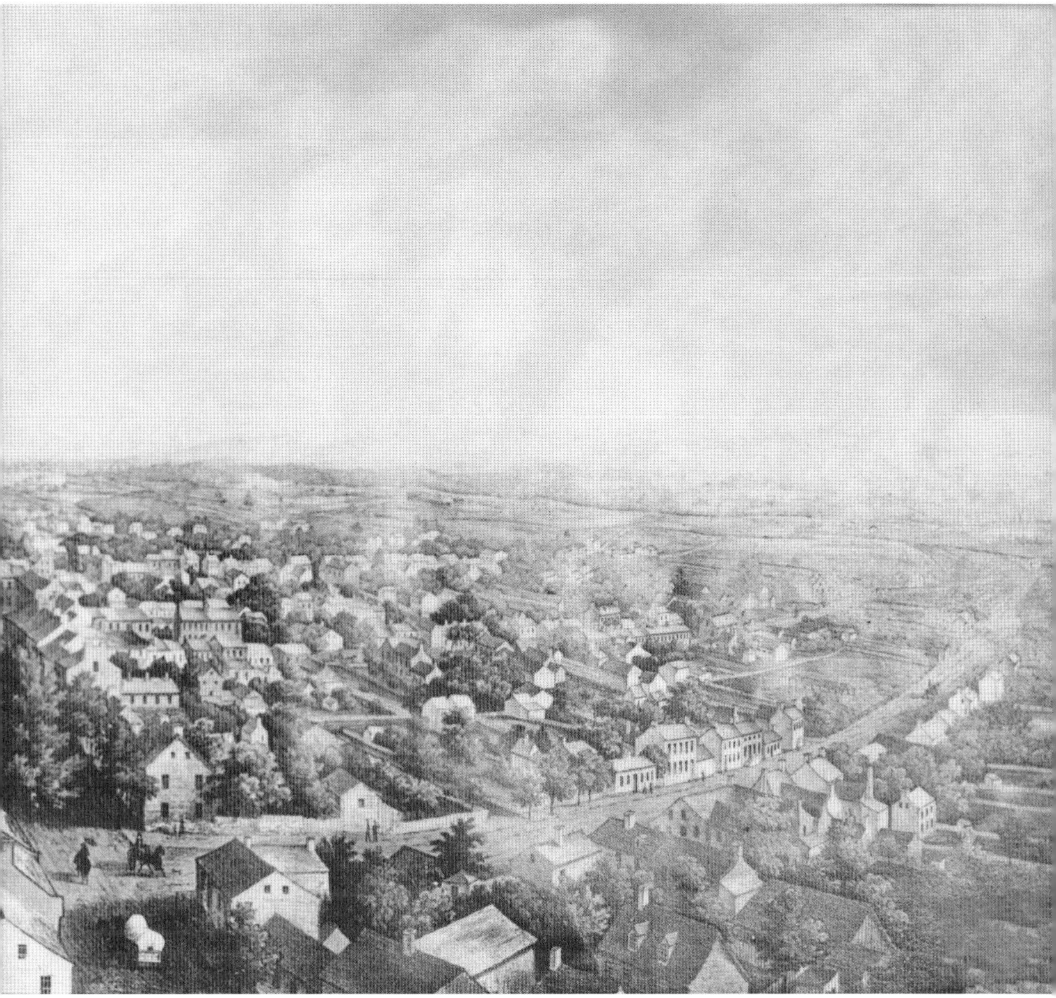

Pictured above is an artist's aerial rendition of Hagerstown viewed from the steeple of St. John's Lutheran Church looking north along Potomac Street towards Public Square. Note the lone horseman, a buggy and a conestoga wagon in the foreground. John's home is not shown, but would have been located in the right, lower corner across from St. John's. (*Washington County Historical Society Archives Collection*)

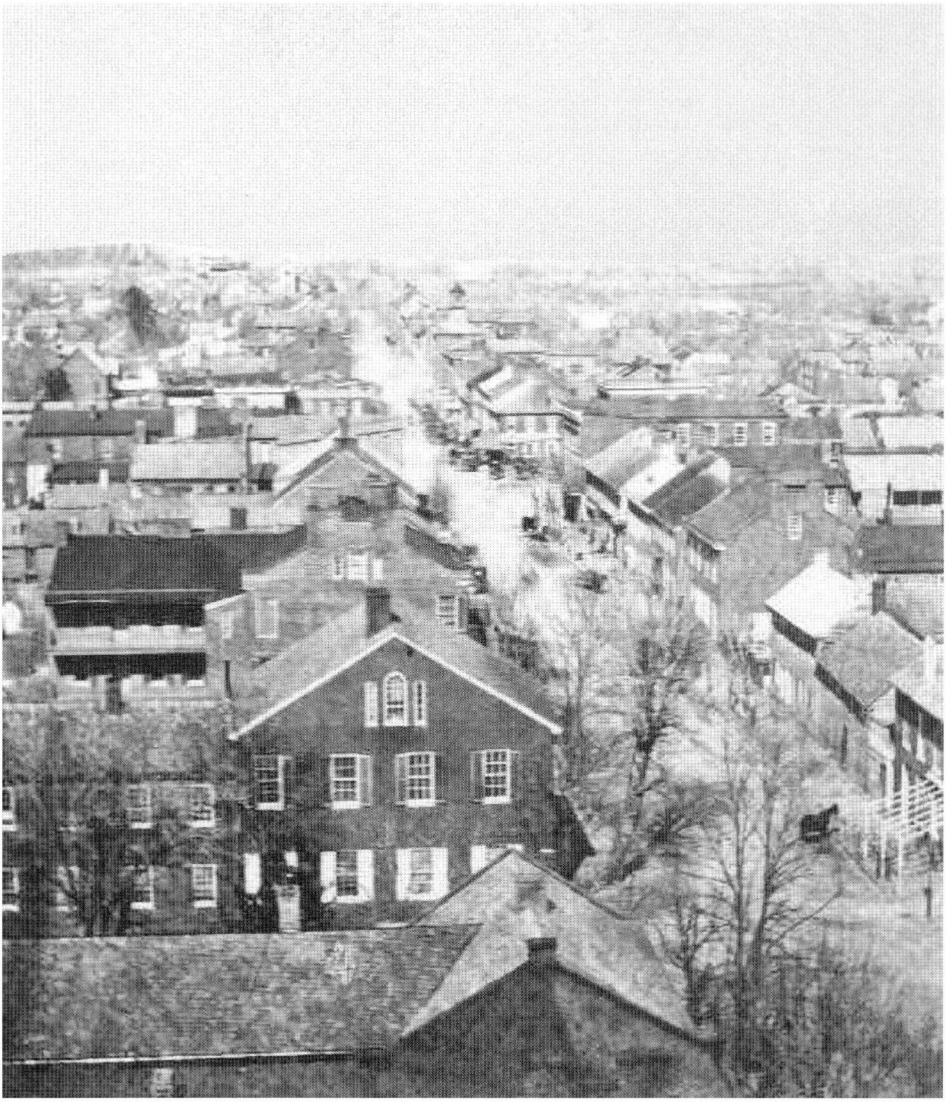

Here is another view of Hagerstown taken by a camera from atop St. John's Lutheran Church looking north along South Potomac Street. The King home was in the right near corner of the photo and is not visible. It probably would have been similar to the houses shown in that corner. (*Washington County Historical Society Archives Collection*)

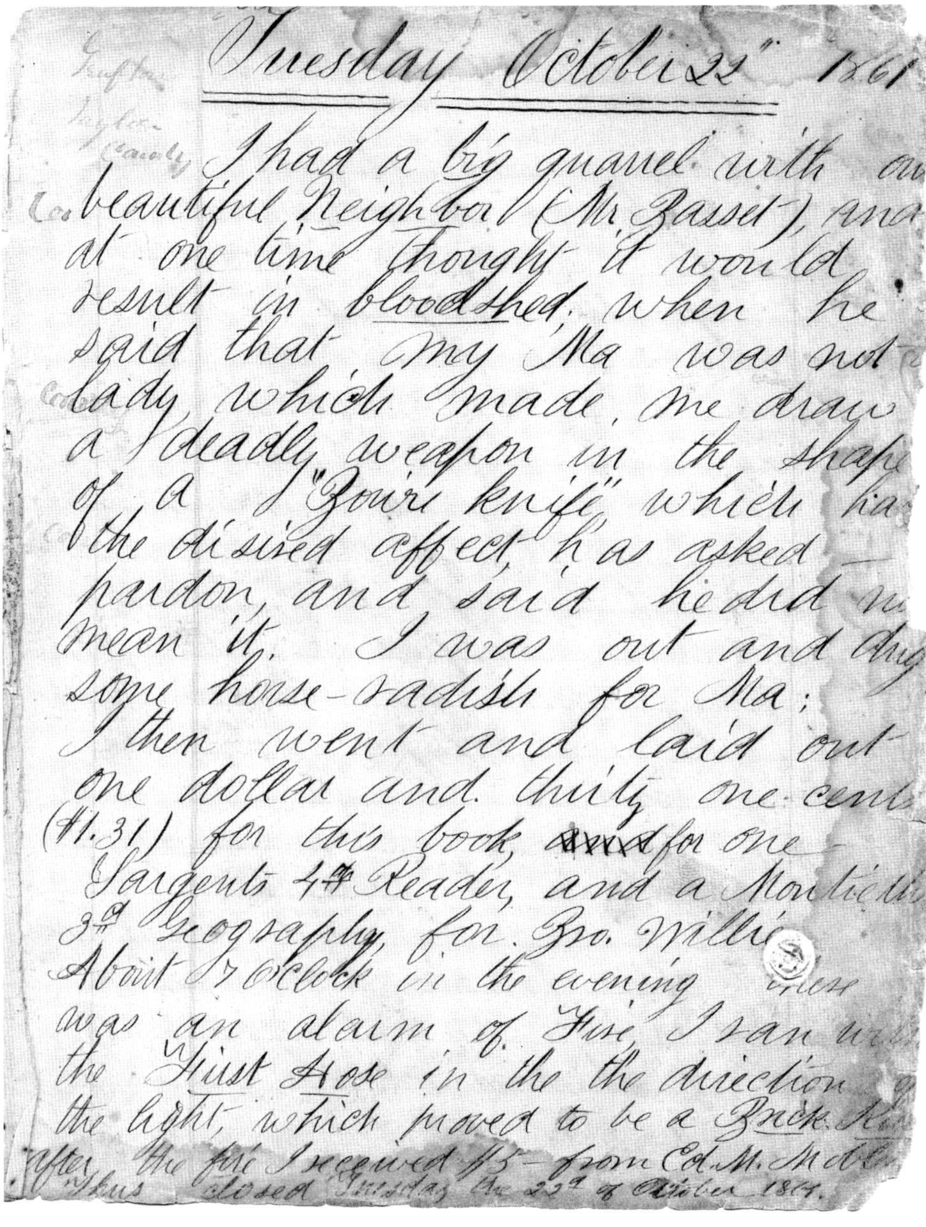
Tuesday October 22nd 1861
I had a big quarrel with ou[r] beautiful Neighbor (Mr. Russet), and at one time thought it would result in bloodshed; when he said that my Ma was not a lady which made me draw a deadly weapon in the shape of a "Bowie knife" which ha[d] the disired affect, he asked pardon, and said he did n[ot] mean it. I was out and dug some horse-radish for Ma; I then went and laid out one dollar and thirty one cent[s] ($1.31) for this book, xxxx for one Sargents 4th Reader, and a Monteith's 3rd Geography for Bro. Willie. About 7 O'clock in the evening there was an alarm of Fire, I ran with the First Hose in the the direction of the light, which proved to be a Brick Ki[ln]
After the fire I received $5 from Col. M. McK[illegible]
Thus closed Tuesday the 22nd of October 1861.

This is the first page of the diary of John R. King dated Tuesday, October 22, 1861. The notebook with a black-and-white marbleized cover and lined paper that John bought is very similar to those school composition books that are still used by students today. Each page of the diary measures 6 by 7½ inches. The entire diary was written in beautiful Spencerian script that John probably had learned while a pupil at the Hagerstown Academy. The diary plus two school books for his youngest brother, Willie, cost John only $1.31. On October 22, John had a busy first day beginning with a "big quarrel" with a neighbor, Mr. Russett. Then, at seven in the evening, John was called upon to fight a fire in town because he was a member of the Hagerstown First Hose Company. He was paid $5.00 for his firefighting efforts. (*Diary of John Rigdon King*)

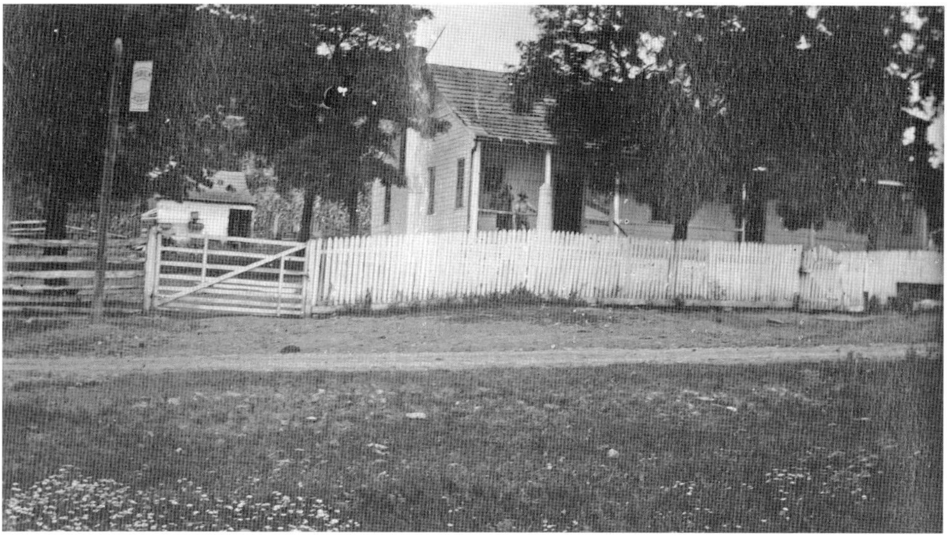

This rare photograph of Fair View House was taken by the Biscoe brothers after the Civil War. John King often stopped at Fair View House, which sat atop Fairview Mountain at 1,690 feet, for drink and a meal when traveling. Fairview Mountain is just west of Clear Spring, Maryland, just off the National Pike. Dwight Biscoe is shown on the porch with an opera glass along with an unidentified boy. Walter S. Biscoe took the photograph. The building is no longer standing. (*DeGolyer Library, Southern Methodist University, Civil War Photographs, Manuscripts, and Imprints*)

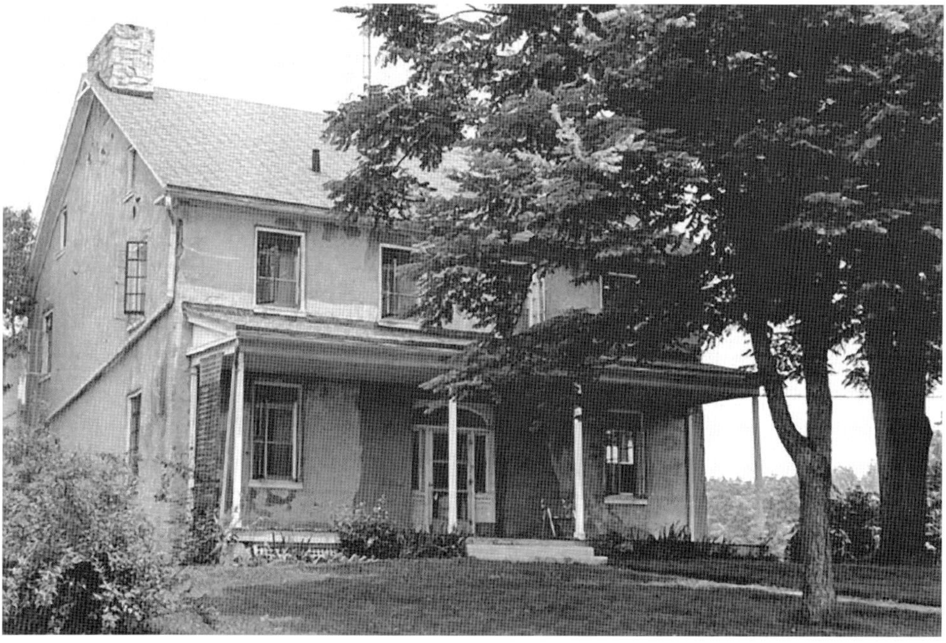

Newcomer's Tavern Stand, was built *c.* 1812 and was located four miles west of Hagerstown. It was a very busy tavern and stagecoach stop during the nineteenth century. John King frequented the tavern when traveling on business for his father. The structure (pictured) was restored after the above photo was taken in 1975 and is now a private residence. (*Maryland Historic Trust Library and Paula Stoner Dickey*)

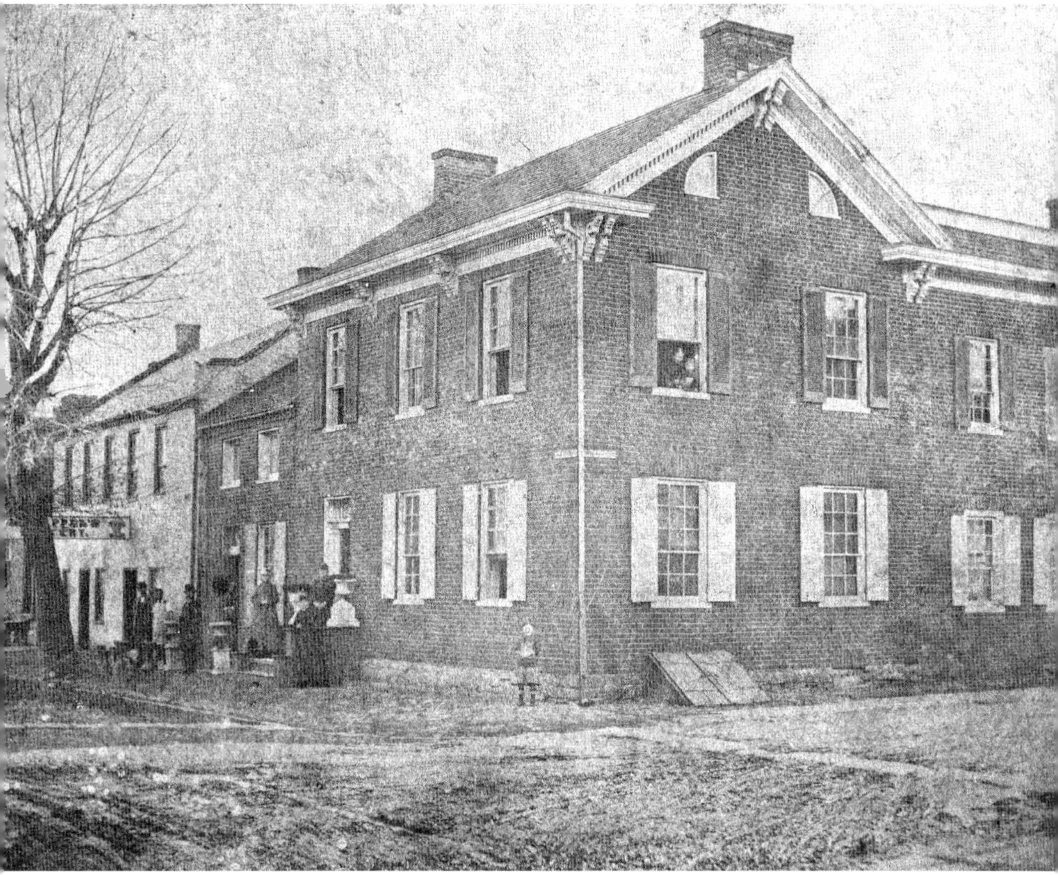

A very rare, previously unpublished, nineteenth-century photograph of the front of Martin Happel's earthenware pottery shop at 75 East Washington Street. The cross street is Locust. A variety of finished pottery items offered for sale are shown displayed in front of the store. Also note the large advertising sign overhead which seems to depict a flowerpot. Pottery kilns were eventually banned from towns and cities because of the danger of their sparks causing a fire. Hagerstown and Washington County had a number of potters plying their trade during the nineteenth century. (*Author's collection*)

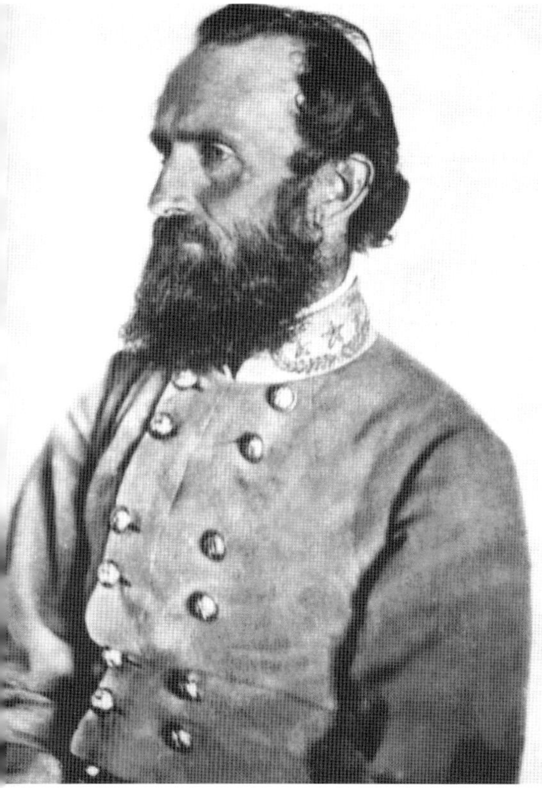

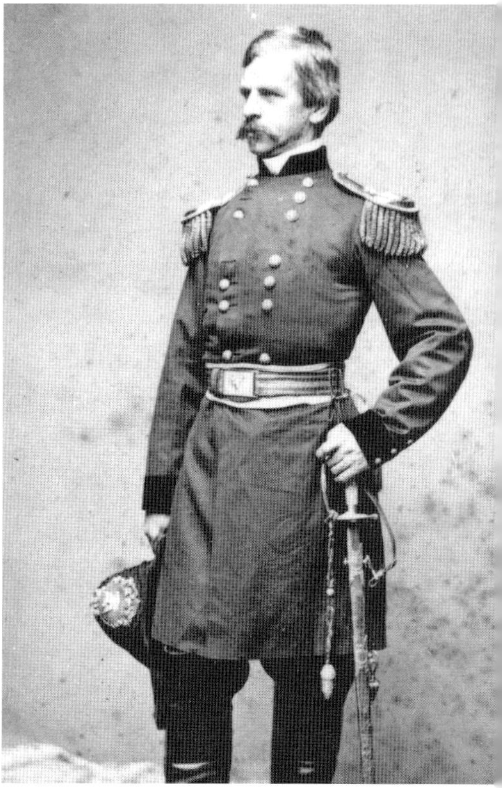

Above left: Lt-General Thomas J. "Stonewall" Jackson began his famous 1862 Shenandoah Valley campaign with a loss at Kernstown on March 23 and ended it with victories at Cross Keys and Port Republic on June 8 and June 9. Between those dates, he routed Union Colonel John R. Kenly on May 23, 1862, in a surprise attack at Front Royal and then put Major General Nathaniel P. Banks in flight at the battle of First Winchester May 25. On May 9, 1862, John R. King and his companion, John Burgess, were camped with the First Michigan Cavalry at Round Hill near Strasburg. The two teenage boys were busy taking photographs of Union soldiers and officers when they learned that Banks' army was retreating north due to Jackson's onslaught. When a massive stampede began, John R. King "sought with the rest to make his escape, but after wandering through the adjacent woods for several days was captured and taken into Jackson's camp at Winchester." Jackson's men must have enjoyed leafing through John's confiscated diary until one of them probably gave it to the Nisewanger family. (*National Archives*)

Above right: Although he had no military experience, Nathaniel P. Banks was appointed by President Lincoln to the rank of major general. From April 4, 1862, until June 26, 1862, Banks commanded the Department of the Shenandoah. His job was to contain Stonewall Jackson in the Shenandoah Valley so that Jackson would be unable to assist Lee in the defense of Richmond during the Peninsula Campaign. Instead, Banks was soundly defeated by Jackson on May 25, 1862, at the battle of First Winchester. Stonewall Jackson later joined General Robert E. Lee to help drive the Union army off the peninsula and saved Richmond from capture. Banks would again meet Jackson on August 9, 1862, at the battle of Cedar Mountain. After the Civil War, when someone asked Captain John R. King what he was doing in Winchester in the spring of 1862, John merely said that "I was with General Banks." John was apparently reluctant to tell others that he was selling goods to the Union soldiers in Winchester and that he also "engaged in the business of taking likenesses" with his camera. (*Library of Congress*)

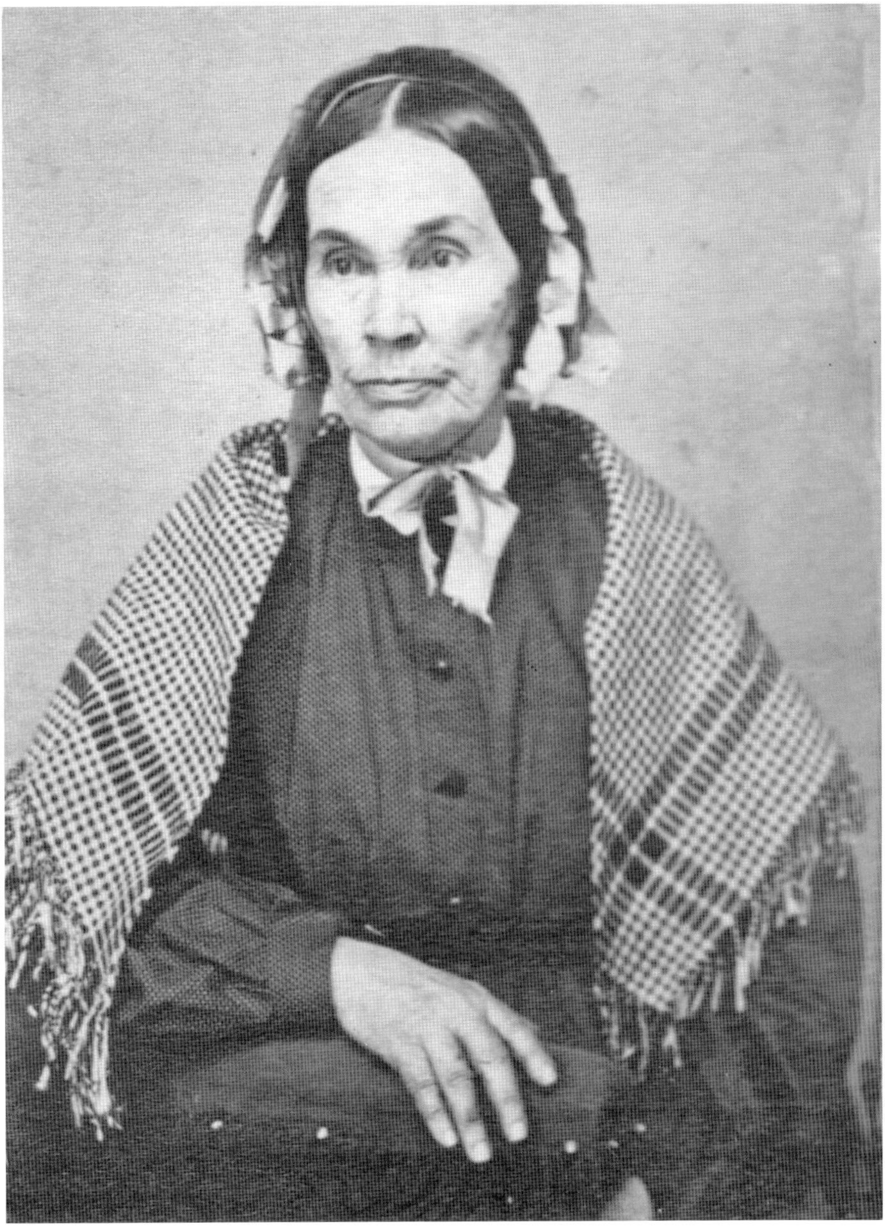

The above is a photograph of Mrs. Lucinda Evelina Nicewanger (Nisewanger), *c.* 1870. Lucinda Evilina Kipps was born in 1805 and married Abraham Nisewanger in Shenandoah County, Virginia, on August 13, 1823. A truly remarkable woman, she raised her seven daughters in Newtown largely by herself since her husband, a wagoner, was frequently absent from the home driving his wagon long distances hauling freight. Mrs. Nisewanger lived in the old Tollgate House on Route 11 in Newtown and operated the toll gate for much of her life. She also made extra money by renting out rooms. On Thursday, May 8, 1862, Mrs. Nisewanger rented a room to John R. King and his friend, John Burgess for the night. In his diary for that date, John King said, "she has a couple of young daughters and we passed the evening very pleasantly." At this time, unmarried daughters Sarah Catharine, Emma Virginia (Ginnie) and Lucinda (Lucie or Lucy) E. were all living at home with their mother. (*Private collection*)

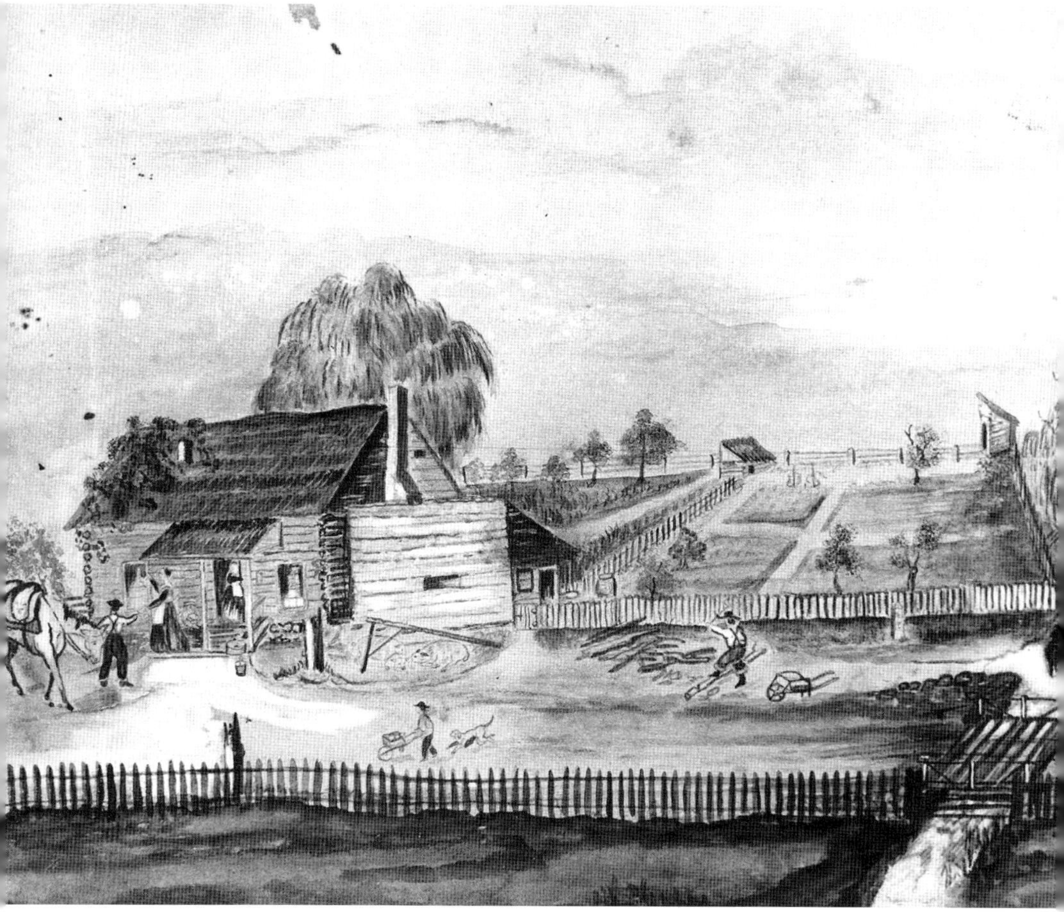

A drawing of the Old Toll House by Frank Staling was done *c.* 1857. This log cabin was also called the Nisewanger house because Mrs. Lucinda Nisewanger lived there most of her life, operated the toll gate and rented rooms. Frank Staling married Amanda Nisewanger on January 29, 1857. Frank later enlisted in the Confederate Army and earned the rank of sergeant. After the war, Frank did the drawing from his memories of the farm. John King and John Burgess stayed at the Toll House the night of May 8, 1862 and recorded the visit in his diary. John King's diary was confiscated when he was captured by Stonewall Jacksons' troops May 23. Someone, probably a Confederate soldier, then gave the King diary to the Nisewanger family while Mrs. Nisewanger and her daughters resided in the Tollgate House. (*Mildred Lee Grove Collection, Stewart Bell Jr. Archives, Handley Regional Library, Winchester, Virginia*)

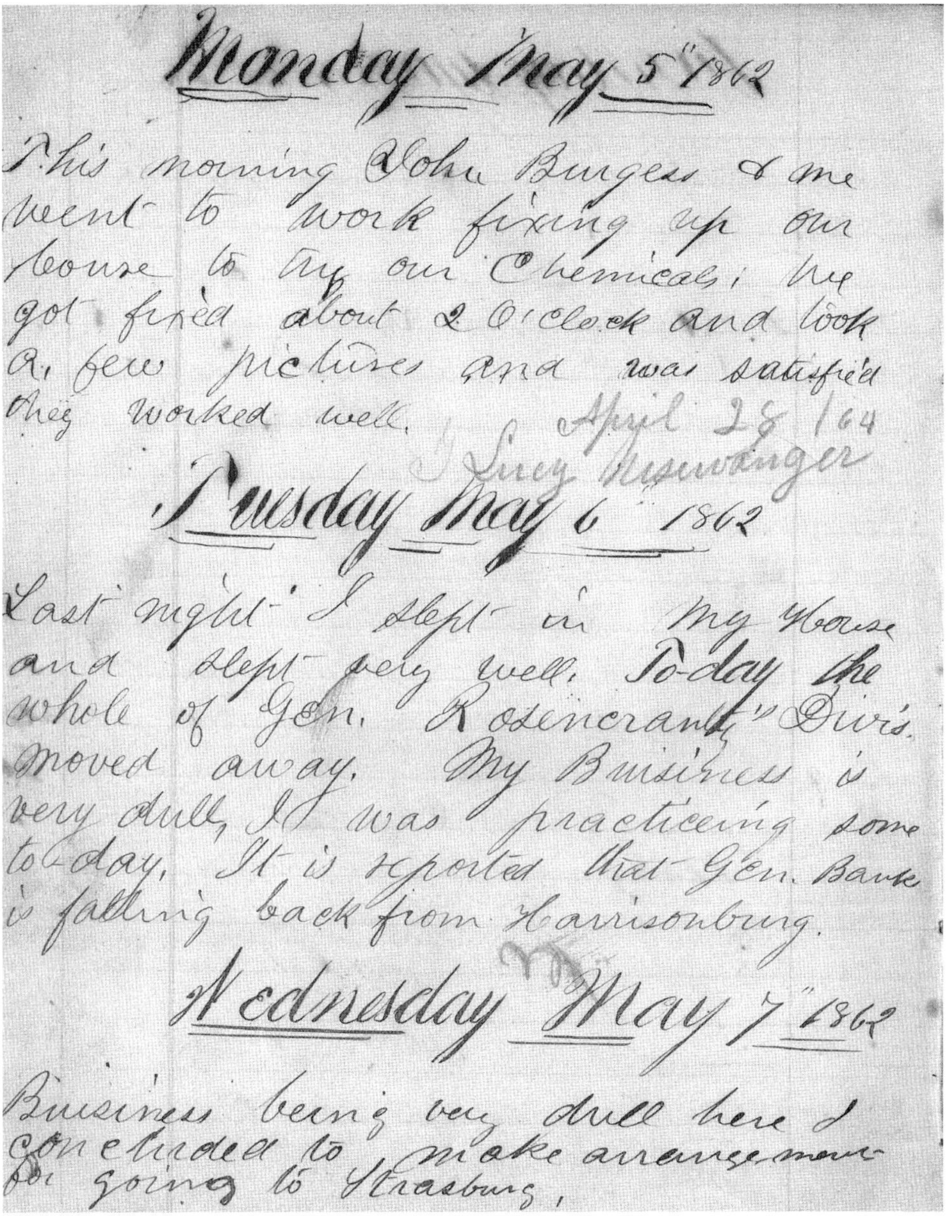

Monday May 5th 1862

This morning John Burgess & me went to work fixing up our house to try our Chemicals; we got fixed about 2 O'clock and took a few pictures and was satisfied they worked well.

April 28 / 64
Lucy Nisewanger

Tuesday May 6th 1862

Last night I slept in my House and slept very well. To-day the whole of Gen. Rosencrantz's Divis. moved away. My Business is very dull, I was practiceing some to-day. It is reported that Gen. Bank is falling back from Harrisonburg.

Wednesday May 7th 1862

Business being very dull here I concluded to make arrangements for going to Strasburg.

This page of John R. King diary includes Monday, May 5, 1862, through Wednesday, May 7, 1862. At this time, the teenage boys were in Winchester and were testing their photographic chemicals and completing the assembly of a portable studio John had bought from John Vilwig on April 24. They were successful taking a few ambrotype photographs. John reported that General Rosecrans had left with his troops and that General Banks was withdrawing from Harrisonburg. John said that since business was "very dull here, I concluded to make arrangements for going to Strasburg." For some reason, Lucy Nisewanger signed her name in pencil under the diary entry of May 5 and dated it April 28/64. The significance of that date for her is not known. (*Diary of John R. King*)

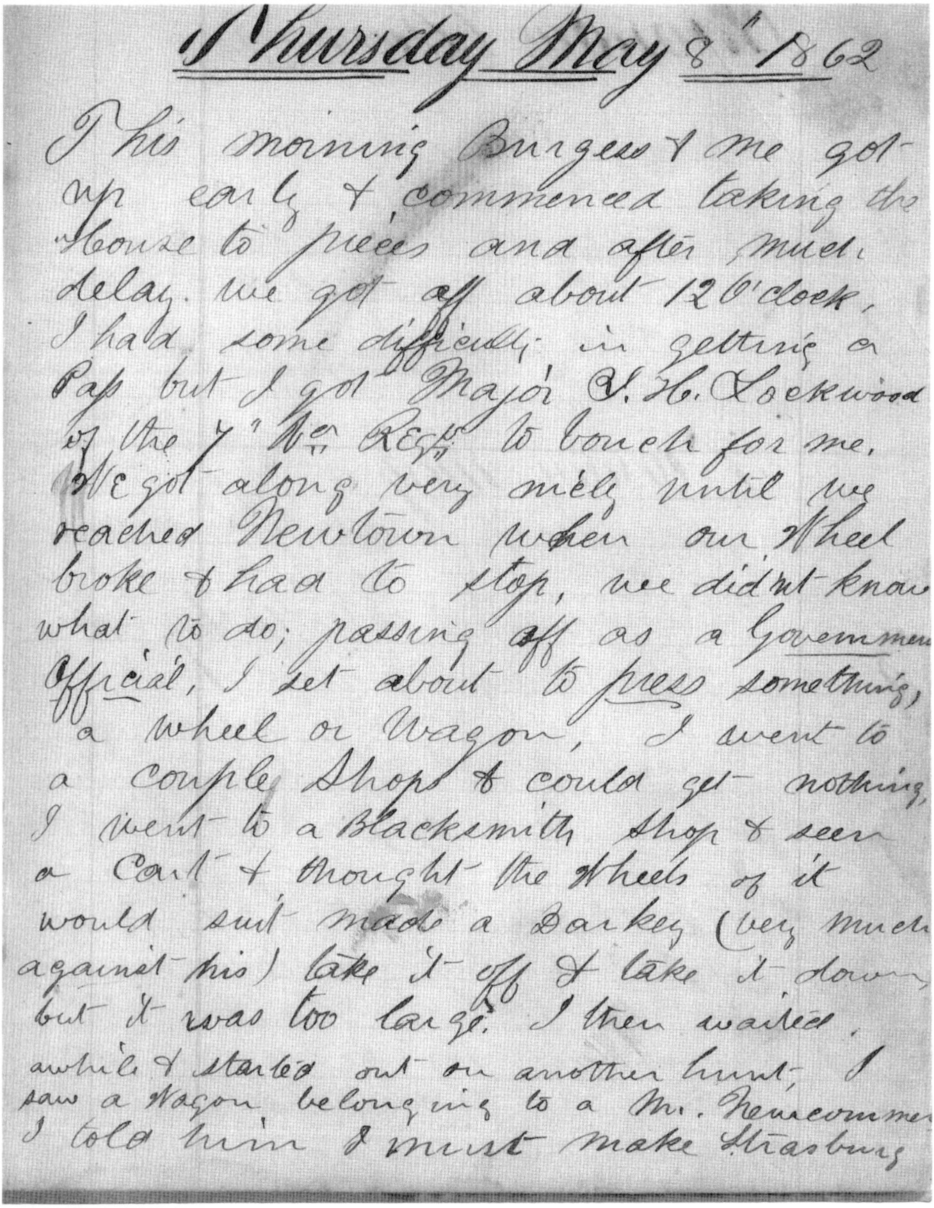

Thursday May 8th 1862

This morning Burgess & me got up early & commenced taking the House to pieces and after much delay. we got off about 12 O'clock. I had some difficulty in getting a Pass but I got Major J. H. Lockwood of the 7th Va Regt to vouch for me. We got along very nicely until we reached Newtown when our Wheel broke & had to stop, we didn't know what to do; passing off as a Government Official, I set about to press something, a wheel or Wagon, I went to a couple Shops & could get nothing, I went to a Blacksmith Shop & seen a Cart & thought the Wheels of it would suit made a Darkey (very much against his) take it off & take it down, but it was too large. I then waited awhile & started out on another hunt, I saw a Wagon belonging to a Mr. Newcommer I told him I must make Strasburg

On May 7, John R. King along his traveling companion left Winchester for Strasburg in the hope of getting more business taking photographs. On the first page of John's diary for Thursday, May 8, 1862, he states that Major Lockwood "vouched" for him in getting through the Union lines. Then, a wagon wheel broke and John sought help in Newtown, Virginia. However, the new wheel did not fit and John resorted to chicanery to obtain another wagon. On the second page for Thursday, May 8, John said that he wrote a fake pass to confiscate anything he needed and included a facsimile in his diary. John told Mr. Newcomer that he "must make Strasburg the next day at noon and must have his wagon." Mr. Newcomer fell for the trick and lent the boys his wagon. The teenagers also needed lodging for the evening. John wrote that we "got permission to stay in the Tollgate House, kept by Mrs. Nisewanger, she has a couple young daughters & we passed the evening very pleasantly." (*Diary of John R. King*)

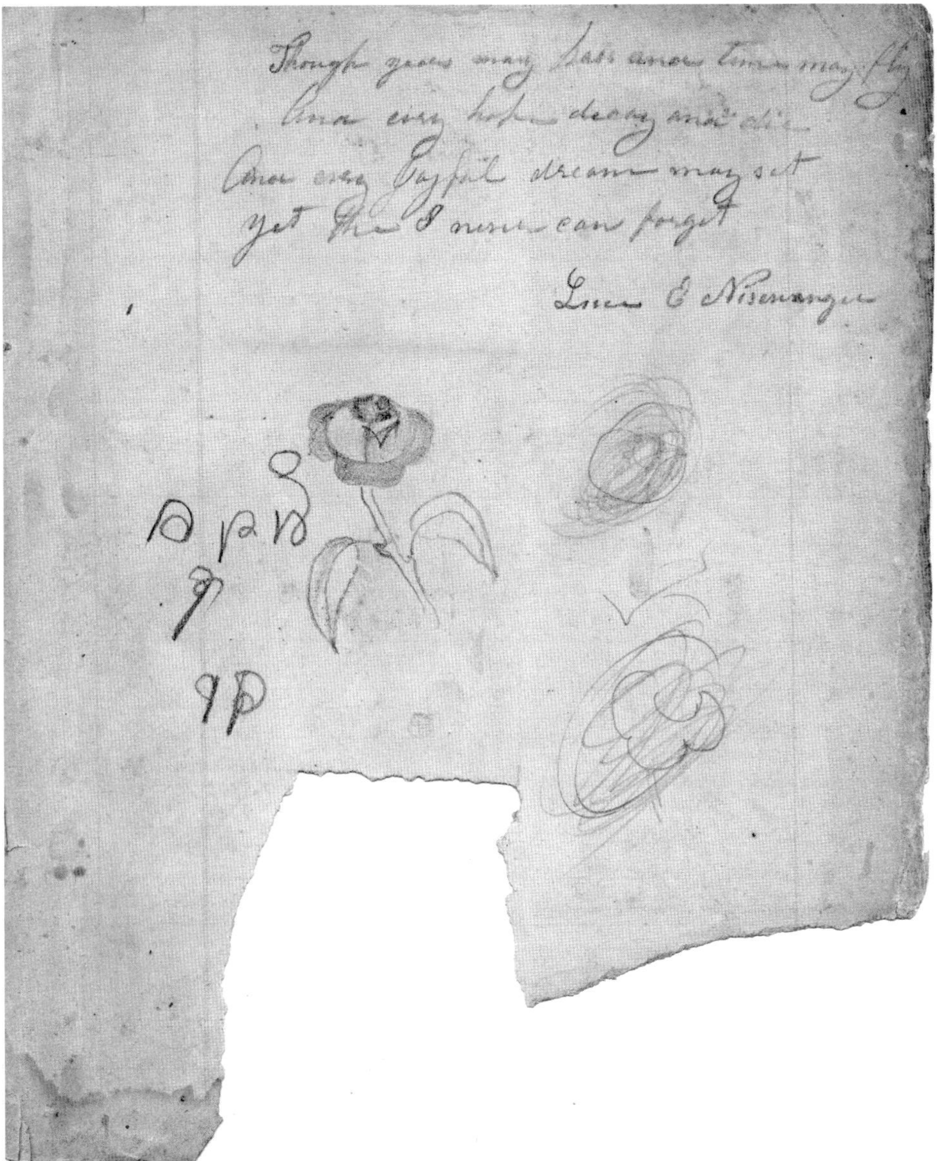

When the Nisewanger daughters obtained John R. King's diary during the Civil War, they used the few blank pages remaining for their personal use. This image shown above is of the front end paper of John R. King's diary. A short poem written in pencil was signed by Lucie E. Nisewanger. However, Lucie was not the author of this poem. She probably copied it from a very old pledge that "I'll remember you" that was frequently found in "friendship albums" which school girls kept during the nineteenth century. Lucie most likely also did the doodle work below the poem. Lucinda signed her name four times in the diary, three times as Lucie and once as Lucy. She never used Lucinda. Virginia signed her name four times as Ginnie, once on her list of friends and three times on the rear end board. She never used the name Virginia in the diary. This is the only torn page in the entire diary. (*The Diary of John Rigdon King*)

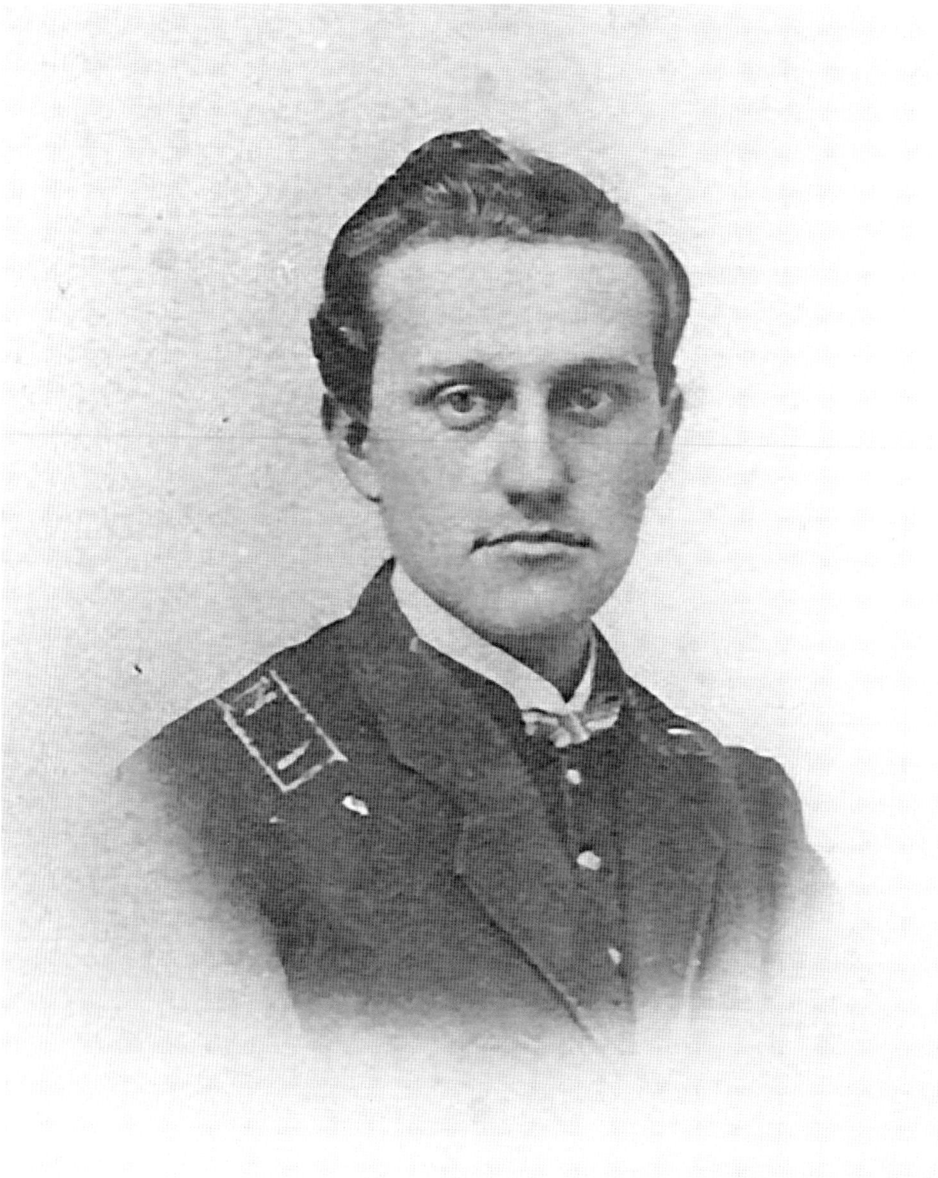

John R. King, known to his friends as "Rig," was enlisted by his friend, Lt. Rench Small, into Company H of the 6th Maryland Volunteers in Hagerstown on August 21, 1862. John had only recently returned from his ordeal as a civilian prisoner of war. Rig was soon promoted to First Sergeant and served his regiment admirably until he was wounded for a third time on May 5, 1864, in the Wilderness. On April 25, 1864, John was promoted to First Lieutenant of Company C of the 6th Maryland Infantry. The above photograph of John in his officer's uniform was probably taken just after that promotion. The photograph is from a *carte de visite* that is in the King family album. John was later promoted to the rank of captain. (*Courtesy of Elizabeth Foster*)

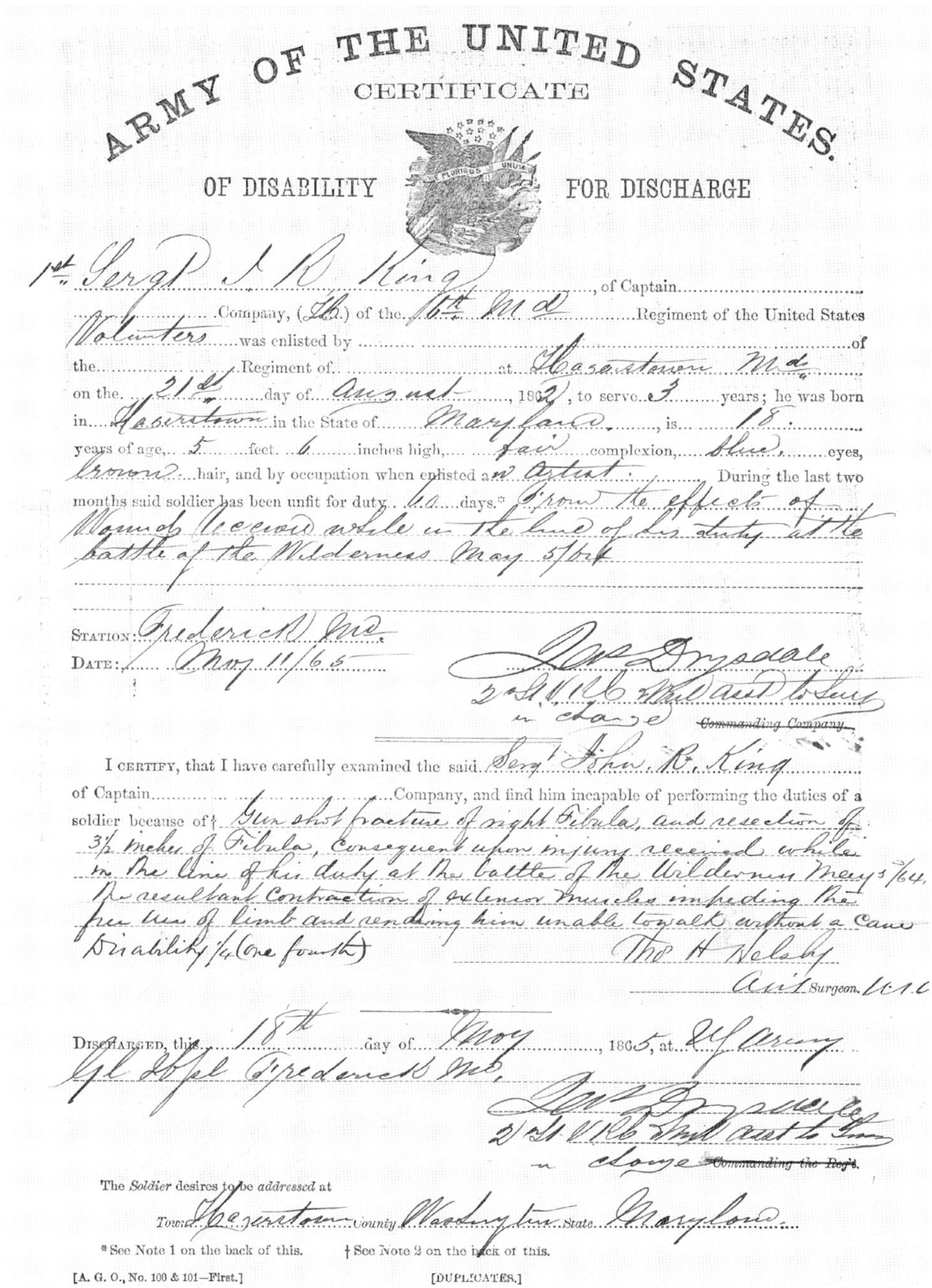
ARMY OF THE UNITED STATES.

CERTIFICATE

OF DISABILITY FOR DISCHARGE

1st Sergt J. R. King, of Captain .... Company, (Sth.) of the 6th Md Regiment of the United States Volunteers was enlisted by .... of the .... Regiment of .... at Hagerstown Md on the 21st day of August, 1862, to serve 3 years; he was born in Hagerstown in the State of Maryland, is 18 years of age, 5 feet 6 inches high, fair complexion, blue eyes, brown hair, and by occupation when enlisted an Artist. During the last two months said soldier has been unfit for duty 60 days.* From the effects of Wounds received while in the line of his duty at the battle of the Wilderness May 5/64

STATION: Frederick Md.

DATE: May 11/65

Wm Drysdale
2d Lt V R C & Mil Asst to Surg in charge
~~Commanding Company.~~

I CERTIFY, that I have carefully examined the said Sergt John R. King of Captain .... Company, and find him incapable of performing the duties of a soldier because of † Gun shot fracture of right Fibula, and resection of 3½ inches of Fibula, consequent upon injury received while in the line of his duty at the battle of the Wilderness May 5/64. The resultant Contraction of Extensor muscles impeding the free use of limb and rendering him unable to walk without a Cane Disability ¼ (one fourth)

Thos H Helsby
Ass't Surgeon. U.S.A.

DISCHARGED, this 18th day of May, 1865, at U S Army Gl Hospl Frederick Md.

Wm Drysdale
2d Lt V R C & Mil Asst to Surg in charge
~~Commanding the Reg't.~~

The *Soldier* desires to be *addressed* at

Town Hagerstown *County* Washington *State* Maryland.

*See Note 1 on the back of this. † See Note 2 on the back of this.

[A. G. O., No. 100 & 101—First.] [DUPLICATES.]

John R. King was discharged from the U.S. Army on May 11, 1865. Since he was found unfit for further military service due to a permanent condition, the Union doctor and officer completed the above Certificate of Disability for Discharge instead of a pension application. John would never walk normally again due to a leg injury received in battle. On the form, he is described as being five foot six inches tall with blue eyes, a fair complexion and brown hair. Due to a gunshot fracture of his right tibia received in battle on May 5, 1864, John was found to be partially disabled. He would require the use of a cane for ambulation for the rest of his life. He had already been hospitalized for a year and needed several more months of recuperation when he returned to his home in Hagerstown. (*National Archives*)

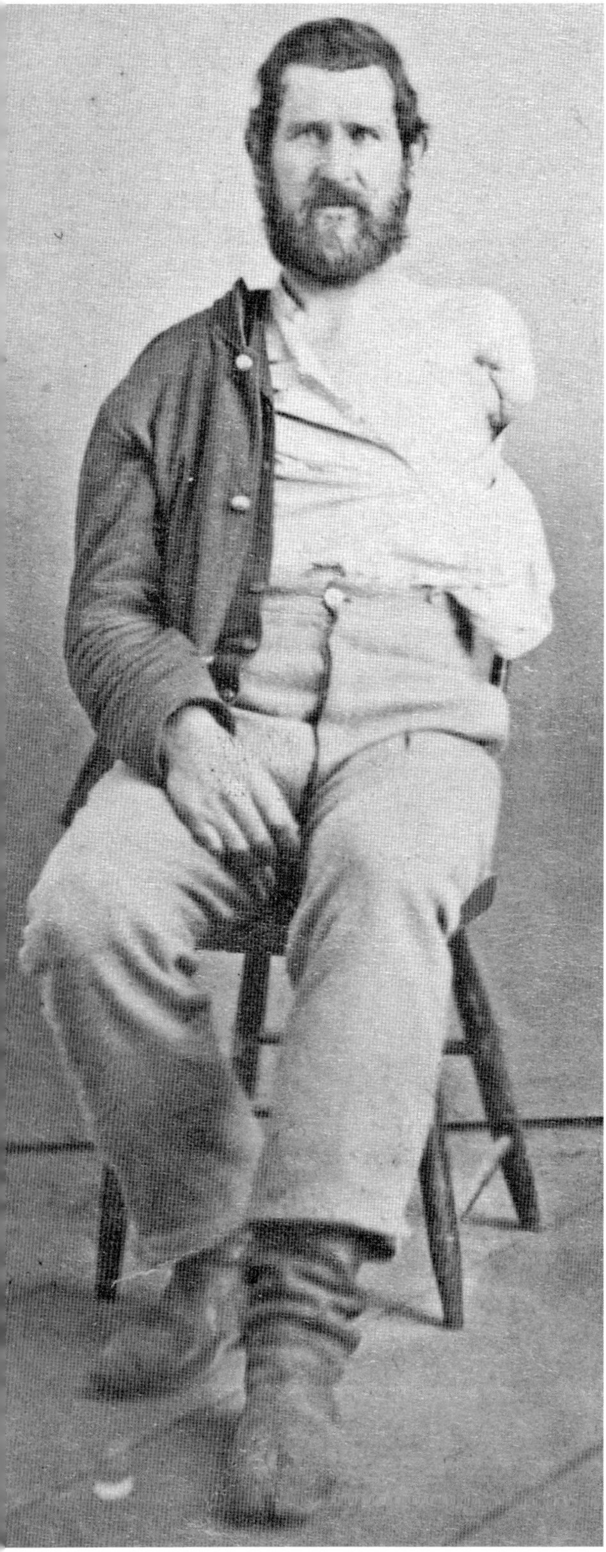

Civil War photographs of the enlisted men of Company H of the 6th Maryland Volunteer Infantry are very scarce. The above image of Private John H. Shields was found attached to his Certificate of Disability for Discharge in the National Archives. John was described five foot eleven inches in height, with hazel eyes and auburn hair. He was promoted to Second Corporal April 10, 1863, but later took "French leave" and left his regiment July 7, 1863 near Frederick Junction. Like many other soldiers, he probably deserted to visit his family. He was soon apprehended and was returned to his unit. On May 9, 1864, John suffered a gunshot fracture of his left arm at Spotsylvania Court House which required amputation at the shoulder. He was found disabled for further military service and was discharged February 3, 1865, on a full pension. After the war, Private Shields worked as both as a surveyor and as a farmer in Emmitsburg, Maryland. (*National Archives*)

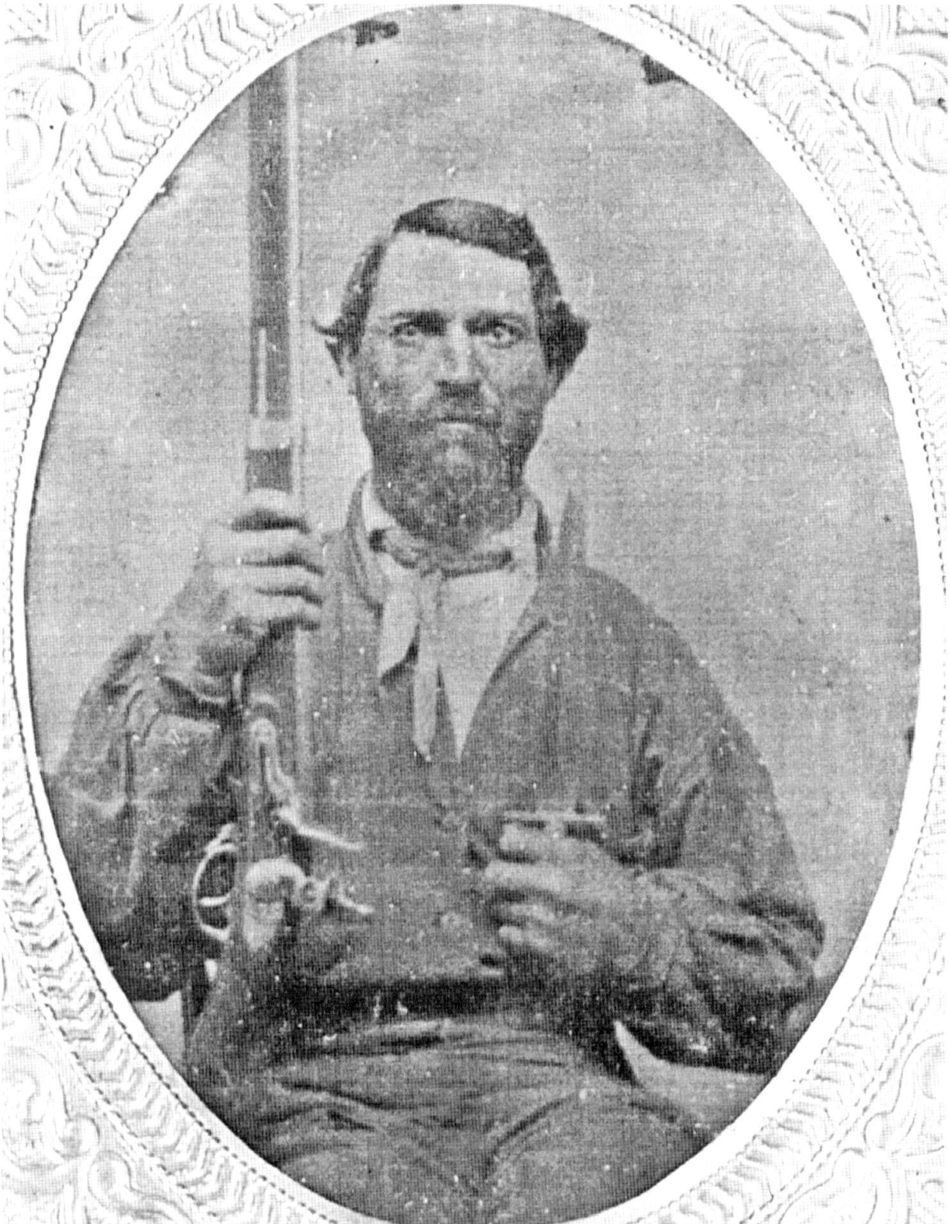

The above photograph is a previously unpublished ambrotype of Confederate Private James "Jimmy" A. Hillyard of Rockingham County, Virginia, holding a Bowie knife in his left hand and a flintlock in his right. This image was probably taken in Harrisonburg, Virginia, soon after he was mustered into Confederate service on April 3, 1863. Jimmy was only eighteen years old when he joined Chrisman's Boy Company, officially known as Company A, 3rd Battalion, Virginia Mounted Reserves. Also called the White Horse Cavalry, the Boy Company served under the command Brigadier General John D. Imboden. John R. King's diary was found in Helen Hillyard's home in Broadway, Virginia home along with this photograph of her ancestor. Was Private Hillyard the Confederate soldier who came across John King's diary? Did he give it to the Nisewanger family? (*Author's collection*)

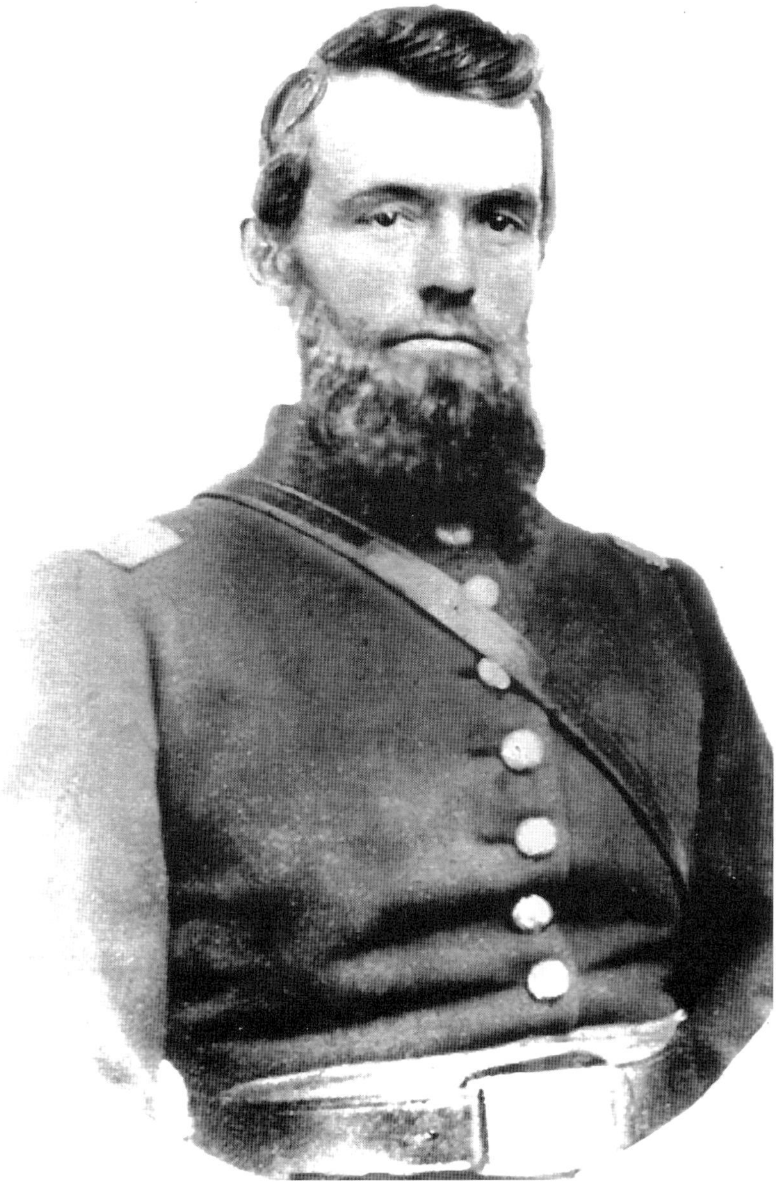

Captain Adam B. Martin, commander of Company H, 6th Maryland Volunteer Infantry, is shown above in his uniform. The grandson of a Revolutionary War soldier, Adam carried on the family tradition of military service by enlisting April 26, 1847, in the U. S. Army to fight in the war with Mexico. He later enlisted again on September 5, 1862, with the Union Army and was made Captain of Company H. Initially wounded November 27, 1863, during the Mine Run campaign, Captain Martin made a good recovery and returned to this post. On May 5, 1864, at the Battle of the Wilderness, Captain Martin was again injured, but this time mortally. Shot in the face and in the arm while standing beside First Sergeant John King in battle, Captain Martin died May 6 during amputation surgery. With the fall of Captain Martin, John King assumed command of Company H by order of Colonel Horn until he took was seriously wounded days later. Fortunately for the Martin family, three months previously, Captain took leave to purchase a home for wife and children in case he was killed in battle. (*Private collection*)

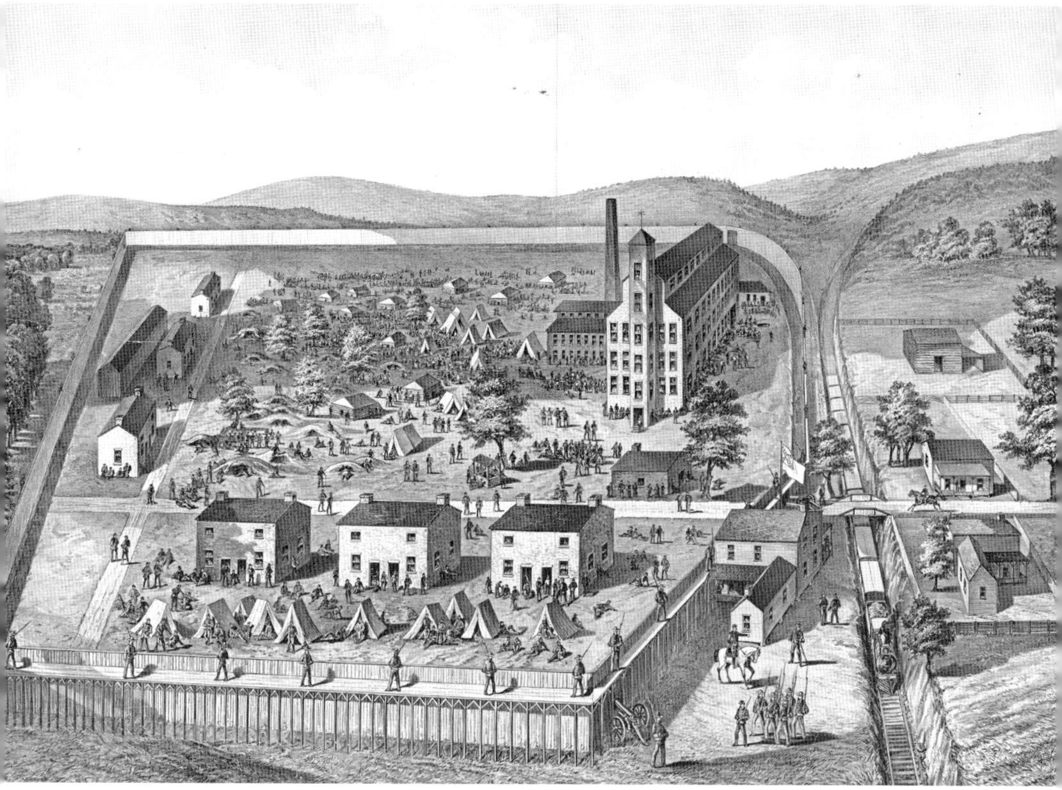

Pictured above is a bird's eye view of the Confederate prison pen at Salisbury, N.C., taken in 1864 and printed in 1886. Before overcrowding, Salisbury Prison was one of the better Confederate prisons. Prison authorities allowed baseball games to be played by inmates. A print by former inmate Otto Boeticher depicting a July 4, 1862, game was published in 1863. John King, a civilian, spent nearly three months in this prison and was erroneously exchanged when he impersonated a Wisconsin lieutenant in August of 1863. John did not have fond memories of his months of imprisonment. Instead, he later gave a "very deplorable account of the manner in which our prisoners are fed and lodged by the rebels." Other former Union inmates spoke more highly of the facility. (*Courtesy of C. A. Kraus and Wikipedia*)

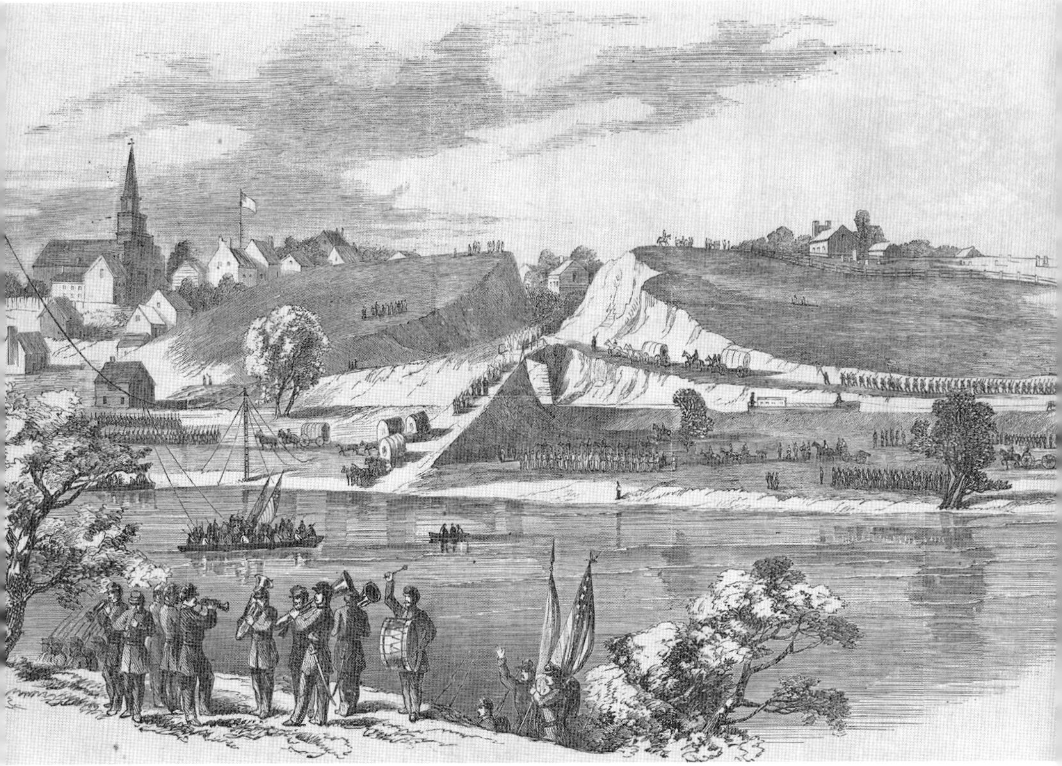

The above illustration is a drawing from *Frank Leslie's Illustrated Newspaper* of Union General Banks' Union troops crossing the Potomac River from Williamsport, Maryland to pursue Stonewall Jackson into Virginia. The band of the 46th Pennsylvania is playing in the foreground. Such displays of large scale military activities attracted local spectators. John King took a group of spectators from Hagerstown on an omnibus to view this scene on a Sunday afternoon. (*Author's collection*)

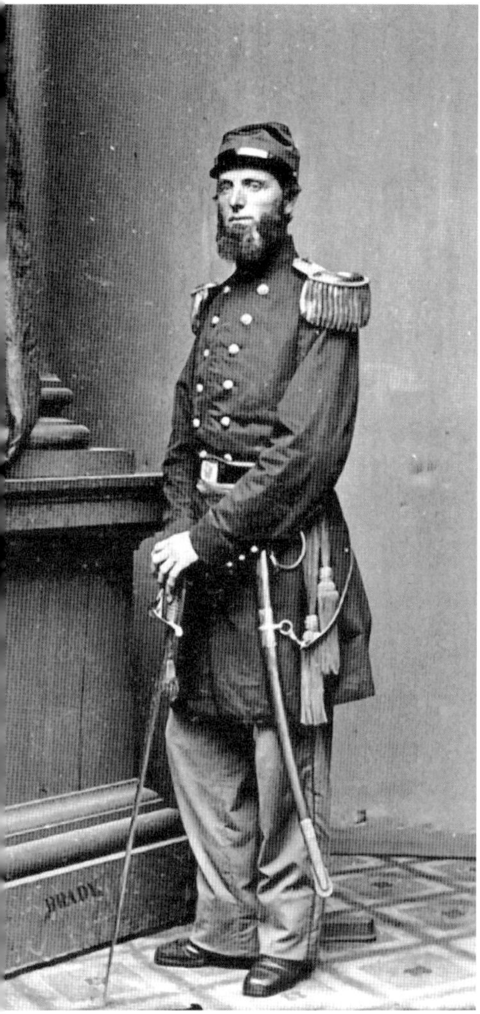

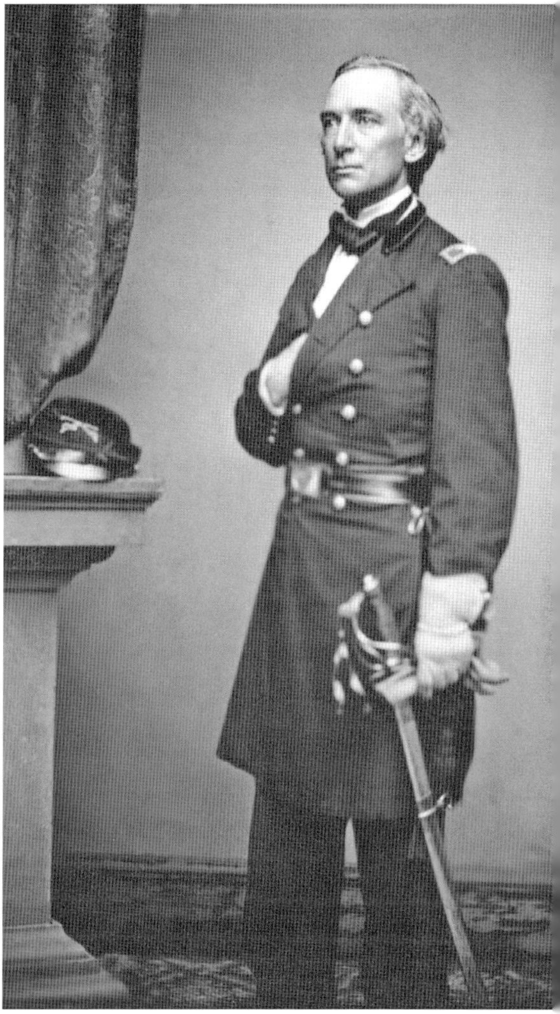

Above left: Union Colonel Edwin Franklin Brown, 28th New York Infantry, had the above image taken by Matthew Brady. John King also took an ambrotype of Colonel Brown on May 20, 1862, just before the Battle of Winchester. Apparently, John did not mark any of his ambrotypes with his name making it virtually impossible to locate any portraits done by him. Just a few months later on August 9, 1862, Colonel Brown so seriously wounded at the Battle of Cedar Mountain that his left arm needed amputation. After the war, like John King, Colonel Brown continued to serve veterans as a civilian by becoming Governor of the Central Branch of the National Home for Disabled Volunteers in 1868. He then became Inspector General for all National Homes in the United States. (*The Medford Historical Society and Museum Civil War collection*)

Above right: Union Colonel Thornton Fleming Brodhead, First Michigan Cavalry, was camped at Round Hill, Virginia, just before the First Battle of Winchester. John King set up his shanty across from the colonel's tent and heard the serenading by the regimental band on May 16, 1862. Unfortunately, Colonel Brodhead did not survive the war. He was mortally wounded at the Battle of Second Manassas on August 30, 1862. (*Author's collection*)

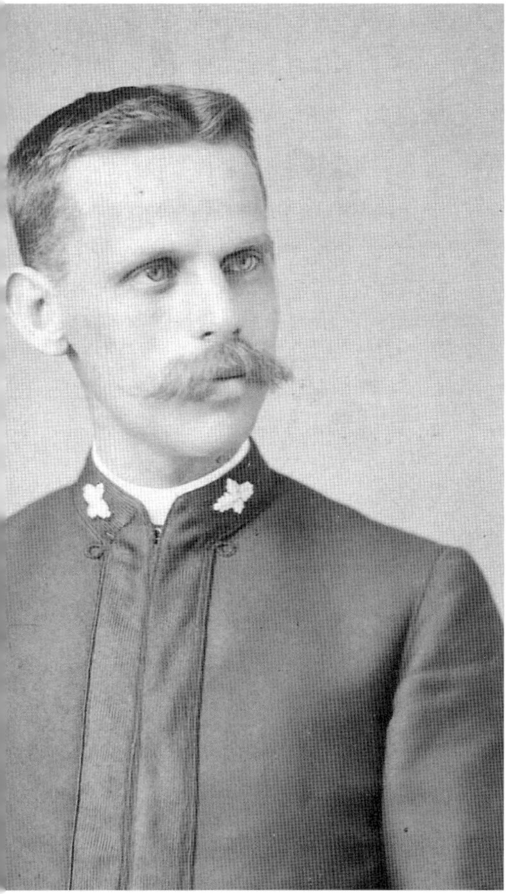

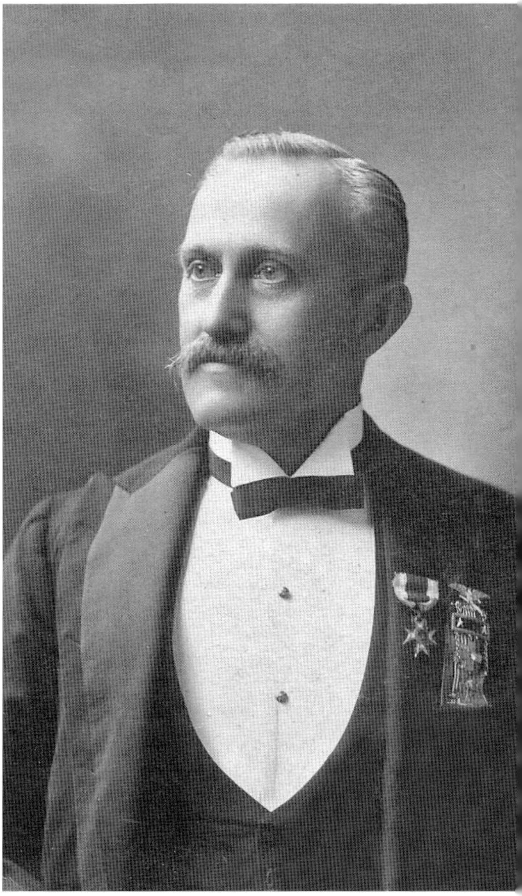

Above left: Lieutenant William Richard King is shown above in his U.S. Navy tunic. He received an appointment to the U.S. Naval Academy beginning October 1, 1872. In 1875, he graduated as an assistant engineer and was given a two-year tour of duty in the Far East aboard the U.S.S. *Swatara*, a screw sloop. In April of 1881, William returned to the United States and continued to serve in the Navy until he retired on March 18, 1891. (*Courtesy of Elizabeth Foster*)

Above right: Captain John R. King in his civilian dress with his Grand Army of the Republic metals, *c.* 1900. Probably as a political favor from President Grant, John received his first Federal appointment as an assistant appraiser with the Baltimore Custom House. He then attained the position of Chief Marine Clerk at the Custom House. In 1902, Captain King was appointed by President Theodore Roosevelt to the position of Regional Pension Agent. The U.S. Senate soon confirmed his nomination. John was now responsible for payment of Union soldier, widow and orphan pension benefits in all of the Middle Atlantic states and in all foreign countries. He would go on to serve three four-year terms as such under President Roosevelt and then under President Taft. (*Courtesy of Elizabeth Foster*)

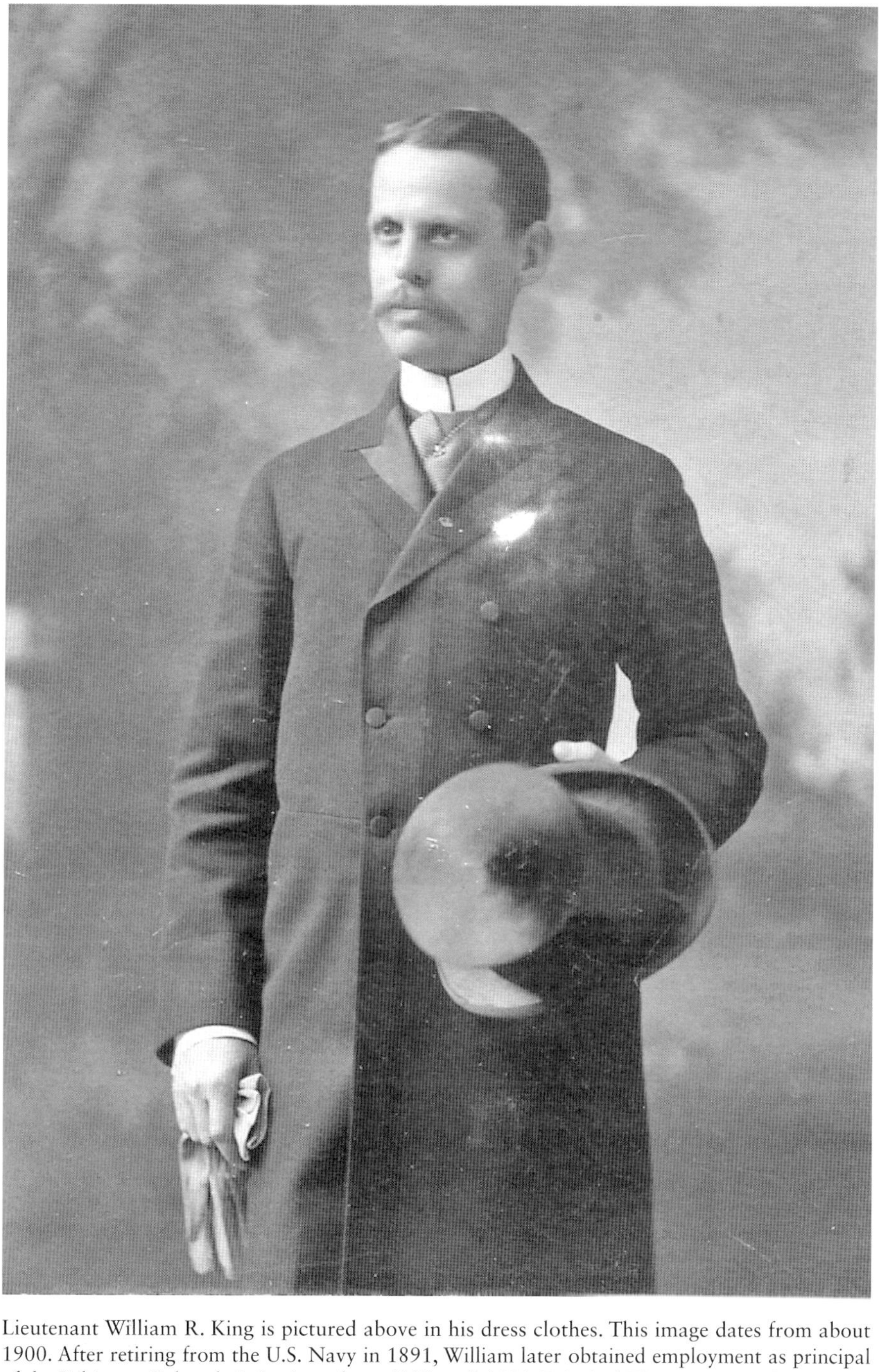

Lieutenant William R. King is pictured above in his dress clothes. This image dates from about 1900. After retiring from the U.S. Navy in 1891, William later obtained employment as principal of the Baltimore Polytechnic Institute from 1899 until 1921. Principal King was more than just an administrator. He also taught several advanced engineering courses. When he could not get proper textbooks, he wrote his own. Both of these textbooks are still in use today. In addition, numerous changes he made to the curriculum of the school were of great benefit to students seeking engineering careers. (*Courtesy of Elizabeth Foster*)

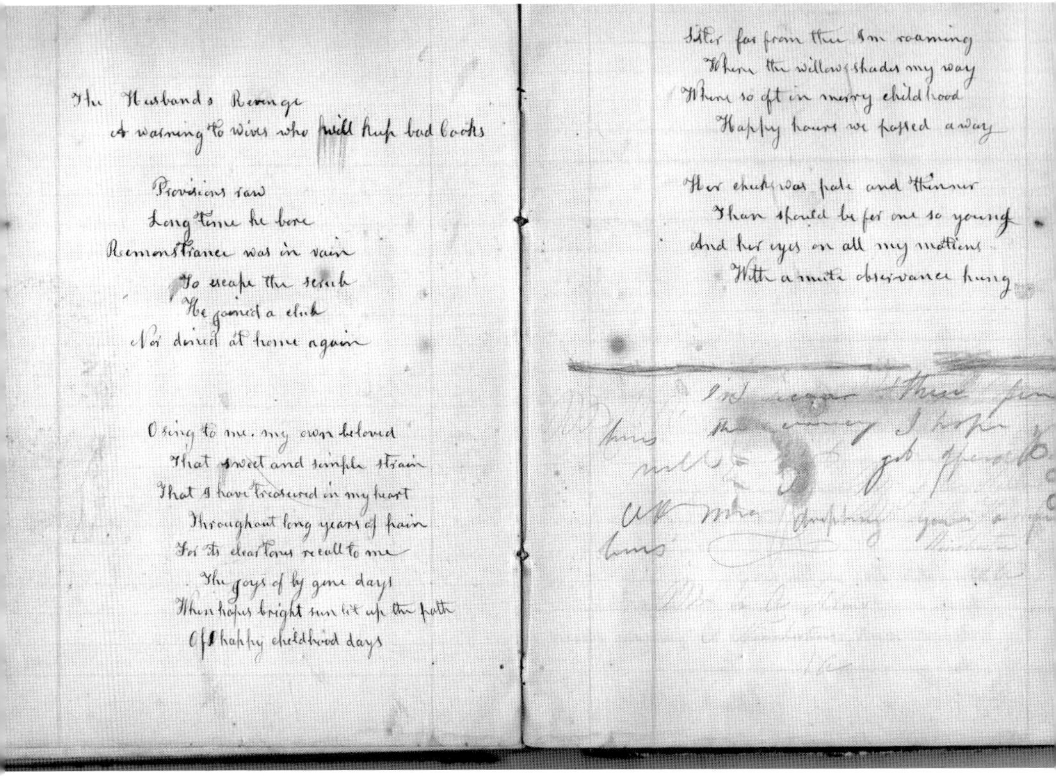

The Husband's Revenge
A warning to Wives who will keep bad cooks

Provisions raw
Long time he bore
Remonstrance was in vain
To escape the scrub
He joined a club
Nor dined at home again

O sing to me, my own beloved
That sweet and simple strain
That I have treasured in my heart
Throughout long years of pain
For its dear tones recall to me
The joys of by gone days
When hopes bright sun lit up the path
Of happy childhood days

Sister far from thee I'm roaming
Where the willows shade my way
Where so oft in merry childhood
Happy hours we passed away

Her cheek was pale and thinner
Than should be for one so young
And her eyes on all my motions
With a mute observance hung

Two end pages from the diary of John King are shown above. Once they received John King's diary, Ginnie and Lucie Nisewanger used all of the blank pages for practice writing their signatures and for writing and pasting poems. A poem named "Husband's Revenge" begins on the left page and continues on the right. These two pages are from blank pages at the rear of the diary. A pencil drawing of a spider web and some illegible words were written over a faint rendition of a man's profile on the right page. This is most certainly a self-portrait of Jacob A. Helms as he signed it twice in pencil as "Mr. J. A. Helms" of "Winchester Va." Obviously, Private Helms had visited the Nisewanger daughters at the Tollgate House. Was Private Helms the Confederate soldier who gave John King's diary to the Nisewanger family? (*Diary of John Rigdon King*)

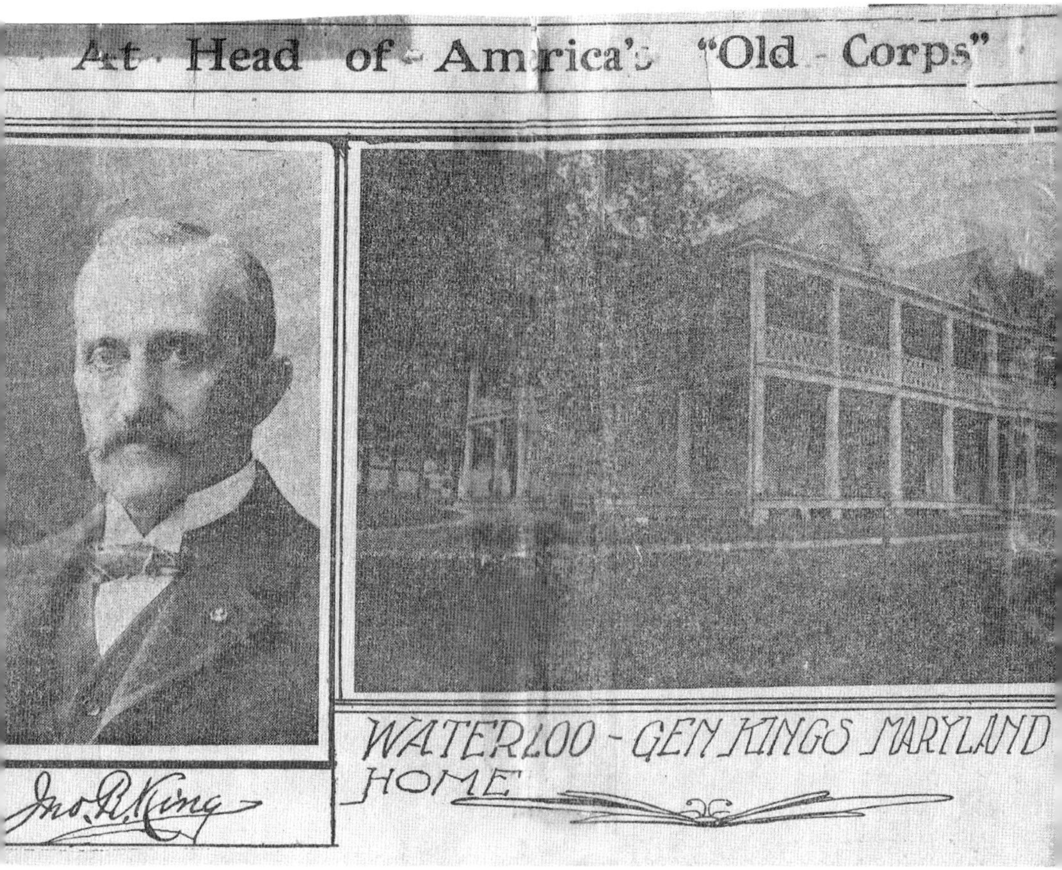

A rare photograph of John and Annie King's home in Jessup, Maryland, *c.* 1900 is shown in this undated newspaper clipping from the King family album. The home and accompanying acreage was called "Waterloo" and was part of Annie King's inheritance. John King thus became a gentleman farmer after his wife was bequeathed Waterloo. One day, John saw his old friend, Governor William T. Hamilton of Maryland, and asked him to pay a visit to Waterloo to see his crop of peas. The Governor obliged. John King was a gentleman farmer until he and Annie decided to purchase a home in Baltimore. As he aged, perhaps the time required to operate a farm, to work full-time and to attend GAR functions became too much for John King and Annie. (*Courtesy of Elizabeth Foster*)

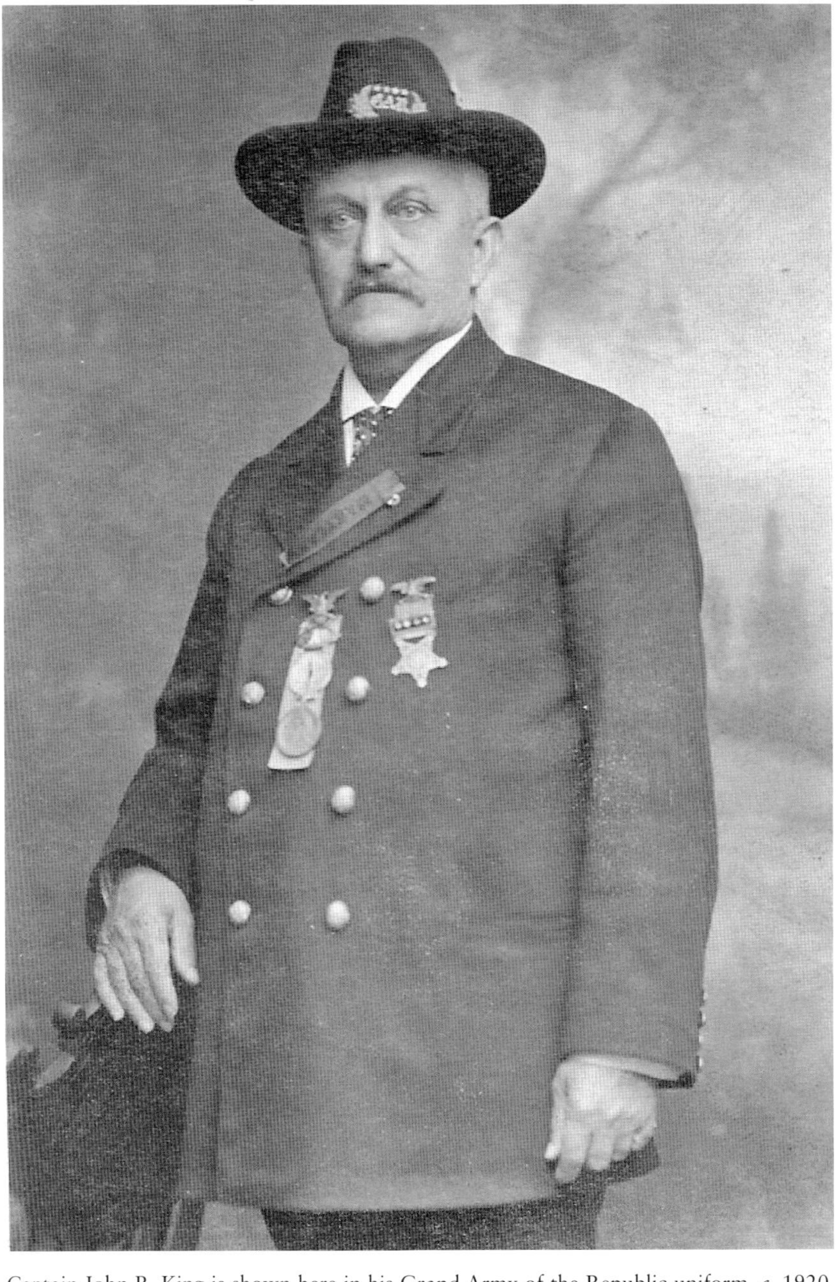

Captain John R. King is shown here in his Grand Army of the Republic uniform, *c.* 1920. The GAR was a fraternal organization that advocated for government benefits for Union veterans, their widows and children. It was formed April 6, 1866, in Decatur, Illinois with only twelve members or "comrades" as they called each other. They dressed in quasi-military uniforms and wore metals. John R. King was a life-long member of Post 1 in Baltimore. When he became Commander-in-Chief of the GAR in 1905, John had 232,455 comrades under his command. These men addressed him now as "General" rather than as Captain King. Meetings and encampments were held locally, statewide and nationally. Confederate veterans had a similar organization called the United Confederate Veterans. The Grand Army of the Republic ceased to exist as of August 2, 1956. (*Courtesy of Elizabeth Foster*)

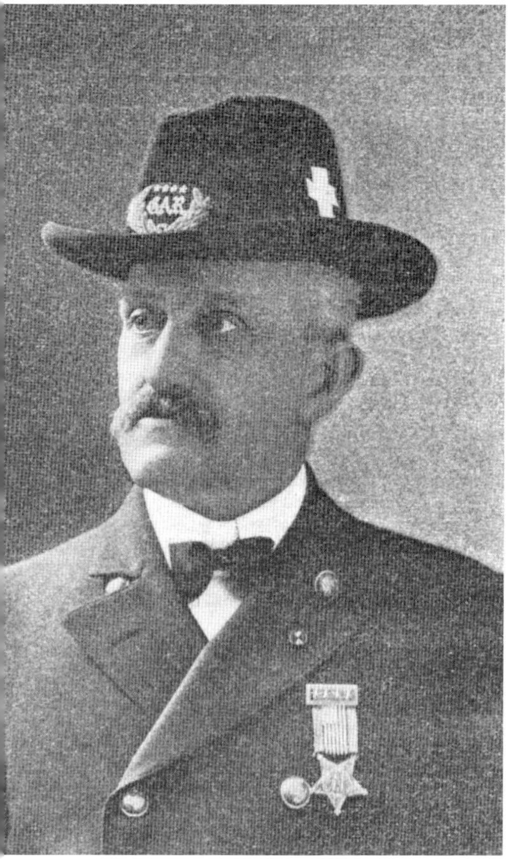

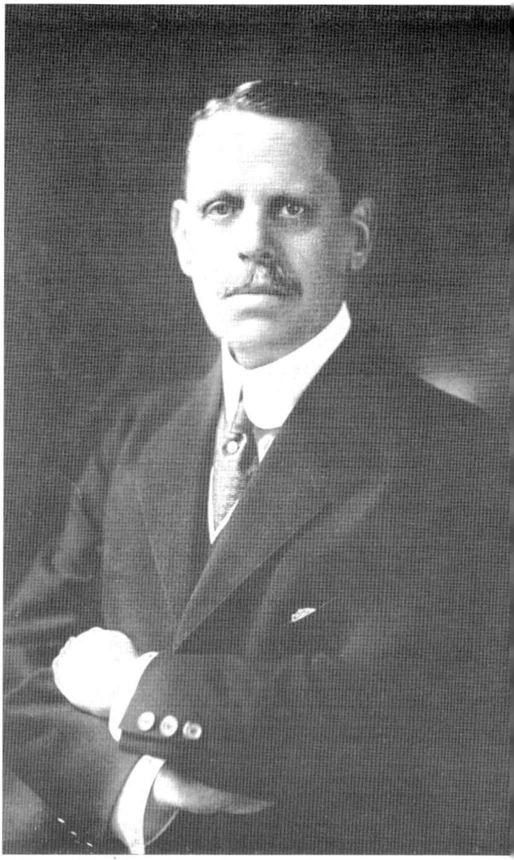

Above left: This is another image of Captain John R. King in his GAR uniform is pictured above. Notice the cross, the symbol of the 6th Corps, Army of the Potomac, on the left side of his hat. Different colors of the cross were used for the three divisions of the corps. The 6th Maryland Infantry was in the 3rd Division. John signed his portrait "sincerely yours in F. C. & L" which meant in "Faith, Charity and Loyalty," the three virtues of the GAR. (*The Harper's Ferry Center Rare Book Collection*)

Above right: Lieutenant William R. King, shown above, later became Dean of Institution of the Baltimore Polytechnic Institute in 1921 and served as such until his death on January 13, 1923. Recently, a new wing of the school was named after him. (*Courtesy of the Baltimore Polytechnic Institute*)

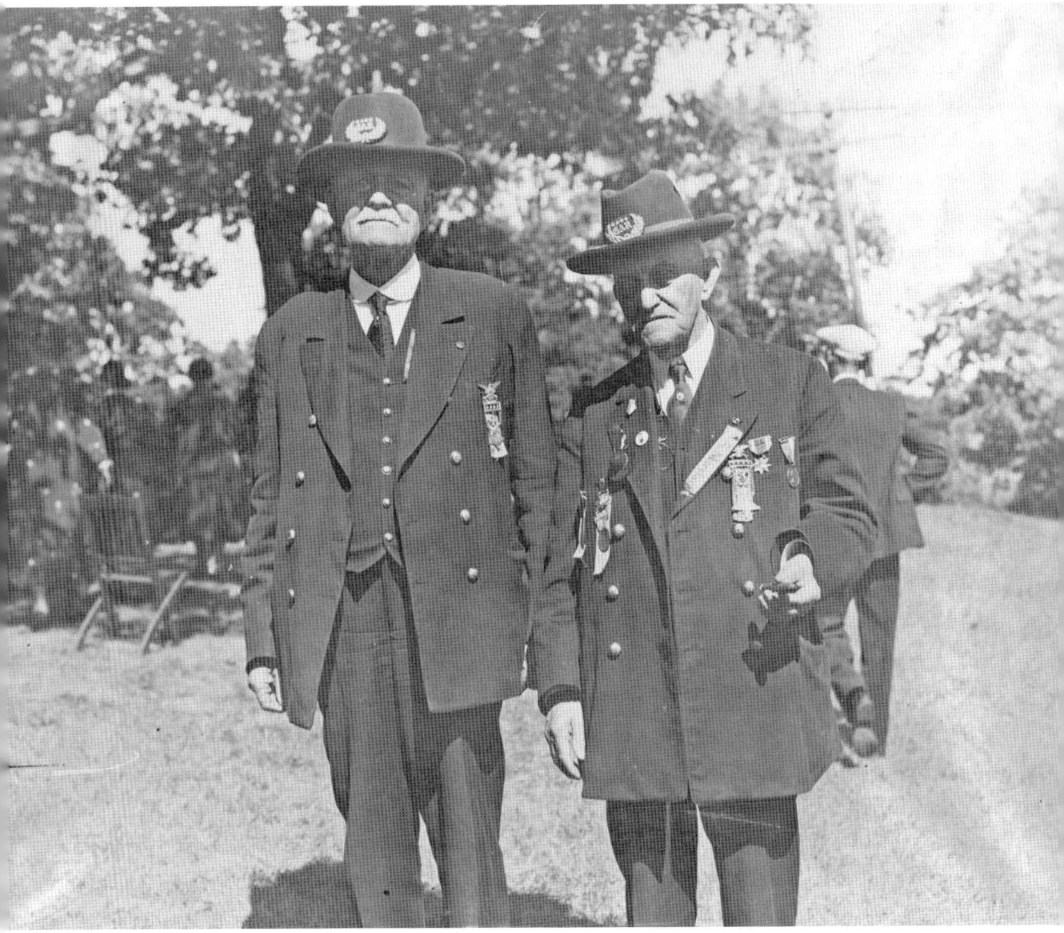

The above photograph was taken at the National Encampment of September 18–24, 1932. It shows John R. King, left, standing beside the current Grand Army of the Republic Commander-in-Chief, James Jewell of Colorado. John had earlier served as Commander-in-Chief in 1905, but had chosen not to continue in that role because he wanted to spend more time in his position as Regional Pension Agent. About eighteen months after the above picture was taken, John R. King suffered a heart attack while working at the U.S. Capitol. He returned home to his apartment in Baltimore and died there three days later on March 3, 1934. (*Lincoln Presidential Library*)

Corporal Staling was a housepainter, originally from Frankfurt, Germany, who painted the Toll House from memory after he moved to Baltimore. Although not proportionately correct, the drawing shows a considerable amount to detail including a fenced garden, horses, a weeping willow tree, outbuildings and even an outhouse. Also, the actual tollgate may be seen close to the Toll House. Mrs. Lucinda Nisewanger collected the road tolls and then turned the funds over to the toll road company which would have been responsible for maintaining the thoroughfare. To supplement her income, she also took in overnight boarders such as John King and John Burgess. According to an obituary that appeared in the *Shenandoah Herald* in 1894:

> Mrs. Lucinda Nisewarner died at her home in Tenth Legion, on Sunday evening, in the 90th year of her age. She was well and favorably known throughout the Valley, having lived for many years at Stephens City, where she kept toll-gate up to and during the war. In 1867 she removed to Tenth Legion where she also continued to keep toll-gate to the date of her death. Her remains were taken to Stephens City ... where they will be interred by those of her husband, who proceeded her to the grave many years ago. Her husband died about 12 years ago leaving her a widow with seven children, all girls, who survive her.[8]

After the Civil War, Mrs. Lucinda Nisewanger moved to Tenth Legion with her unmarried daughters, Sarah Catharine, Emma Virginia and Lucinda E. and resided in another Toll House, which was located on the eastern side of the Valley Pike. Tenth Legion is a small unincorporated community in Rockingham County, Virginia. It lies just six miles by road from Broadway, a rural town just off the Valley Pike (Route 11). However, Lucinda Nisewanger did much more than just operate the tollgate in Tenth Legion. Beginning in 1868, she was U.S. Postmaster of Tenth Legion. But, Lucinda Nisewanger's greatest achievement in life was not as a toll operator or as a postmaster, but as a mother who raised seven daughters almost singlehandedly. Today, the Toll House still stands in Tenth Legion as a private residence. It has had considerable alterations since the Nisewangers lived there in the 19th century.

The Nisewangers first child was Mary A., born July 23, 1824, just eleven months after they married. About 1847, Mary A. married a local blacksmith named James Lemley, born August 14, 1821. The couple had seven children over the ensuing years: Lucy E., William, Mary S., Ida J., Hall, Emma and Robert M.[9]

On June 13, 1861, James Lemley enlisted in Company B of the 51st Virginia Militia by Captain Samuel M. Marks. Both James and Marks signed up at Newtown on the same day.[10] His company and regiment would make good use of the skills James acquired employed as a blacksmith. Just six weeks after enlistment, he was sent "at or near" Newtown "on government work "to obtain" a harness for Artillery and clothing."[11] In fact, because James did so much blacksmith work during the Civil War, he now has a thirteen-page Confederate Citizen File of vouchers in the National Archives. Employed as a citizen, he was paid for this work. Here is a compilation of his civilian services performed for the army: After shoeing four horses at fifty cents apiece and setting thirty mule shoes at fifty cents apiece, James was paid $17.00 on July 18, 1863. On July 23, 1863, James was paid $6.00 for shoeing twelve horses In Newtown. His captain apparently allowed his charge to return home to complete these tasks in his blacksmith shop in Newtown. For his work repairing a wagon, cutting and welding, and shoeing six horses, James Lemley was paid $5.00, $5.00 and &1.50 respectively, or $11.50 total on October 23, 1862. Lastly, on September 16, 1864, he was paid $5.00 for welding a wagon.[12] Hence, James not only served the Confederacy as a soldier in a militia unit, he also used his occupational skills as a private contractor. James survived the war without any injuries. After the war, he returned to his profession and his large, thriving family. James Lemley died before his wife on February 1, 1899. Mary A. (Nisewanger) Lemley died on March 3, 1903 and both are buried in Green Hill Cemetery in Stephens City.[13]

Abraham and Lucinda's second daughter, Martha Ellen., was born April 20, 1828.[14] At about the age of nineteen years, Martha married James H. Redd on March 26, 1849 in Frederick County, Virginia.[15] On the 1850 U.S. Census taken November 20 for Stephens City, the newly married couple are shown, but without occupations. James was thirty-one years old while Martha was only nineteen.[16] No children were recorded. Unfortunately, Martha became a young widow in the spring of 1851 when James died.[17] In1855, Martha remarried.[18] Her second husband, Joseph S. Redd, was probably James' brother. The 1870 U.S. Census shows Joseph and Martha living in the village of Aldie, in the Southern District of Loudoun County, Virginia, with their two children, Josephine "Josie" A., age twelve, and Emma A., age ten years.[19] Joseph's occupation was given as a farmer. Andrew J. Redd, Joseph's older brother, was also in the household and was working as a farmer. The Redd family financial status must have improved because ten years later, Joseph had two servants in his home and gave his occupation as a "merchant." [20] Martha gave her occupation as "keeping house." Tragedy again soon struck the Redd family. On November 18, 1885, Martha's younger child, Emma A., died at the age of twenty-two years.[21] By 1900,

Joseph had also died and Martha was once again a widow. On the 1900 U.S. Census, Martha, now age seventy years, is shown as residing in the Mercer District of Loudoun County with her daughter, Josephine, who had married a local farmer, William Moore.[22] William and Josephine had five children: Eddie R., Matilda D., Martha E., Joseph W. and Mildred A. Moore. Martha E. Redd died July 8, 1925 and is buried at the Sharon Cemetery, Middleburg, Virginia.[23]

The third daughter, Margaret W. Nisewanger, was born circa 1831. Margaret married a local carpenter by the name of Alfred J. Watson about 1846.[24] He was born January 6, 1818. From this union, the couple had a daughter which they named Altha W., born January 3, 1847. Unfortunately, Alfred was hit by lighting and killed on July 19, 1847, when Altha was only six months old.[25] He was buried at the Stephens City United Methodist Church Cemetery.

Before the Civil War began, Margaret and Altha moved in with her parents at the Toll House log cabin at the south end of Newtown and stayed there awhile. Then she met and married another local man, David William Rosenberger, a plasterer. He took Margaret and Altha to Hannibal, Missouri. However, the couple returned to Newtown before the beginning of the Civil War. David Rosenberger was a tall man, six foot four inches in height, with a dark complexion and dark hair according to his Civil War service records.[26] At Newtown on May 10, 1861, he enlisted at the age of thirty-one with Company A of the 1st Virginia Cavalry under the overall command of the famous Major General J.E.B. Stuart, who was then only a Colonel. Captain James H. Drake, who had previously joined Company A on April 19, 1861, in Newtown, enlisted David W. Rosenberger. The 1st Virginia Cavalry completed its organization at Winchester, Virginia, and on May 10, 1861, reported to Colonel Stonewall Jackson in Harper's Ferry. As Driver notes in his book "First Virginia Cavalry," all six companies that went were pre-war militia cavalry and Company A, which was called the Newtown Troop. The Newtown Troop was organized in 1858 at Middletown, Frederick County, and was the first company to arrive in Harper's Ferry.[27] Company A's first major conflict was at the Battle of First Manassas, but it would be engaged in over two-hundred skirmishes and battles during the Civil War. Rosenberger entered the service as a sergeant, but on January 5, 1862, was "reduced to the rank…by order of Colonel W. E. Jones, probably for some minor infraction. Colonel "Grumble" Jones, a former West Pointer, had a reputation for being quarrelsome and thus earned the sobriquet "Grumble." Fortunately for Private Rosenberger, the Confederate government changed its policy of electing officers. Officers were to be elected by the enlisted men now. As a result, David W. Rosenberger was elected second lieutenant of Company A on April 22, 1862, and later was promoted to first lieutenant.[28] Although his pay was often late, Lt. Rosenberger earned $90.00 monthly during the war as an officer.[29] He served with distinction during the war and never was seriously injured. Lt. Rosenberger appears on a list of prisoners of war who were paroled April 18, 1865, in Winchester, Virginia.[30] After the war, much like his neighbor James Lemley, David returned to his family and profession as a plaster. He and Margaret had one child, a son named Williams, who was born about 1861. In 1870, they were living next door to Margaret's sister, Mary, and the Lemley family.[31] Margaret's occupation on this census was "keeping house." However, tragedy struck the Rosenberger family just three years later. David William Rosenberger died at the early age of just forty-three years on May 1, 1873, and was buried in the Old Lutheran Church Cemetery in Stephens City.[32]

Like several of her aunts, Altha, Margaret's daughter by Alfred J. Watson, also married a Confederate veteran. On March 22, 1870, she wed Milton Boyd Steele.[33] Before they were married, both were active participants in the Civil War. The Newtown History Center notes that Altha, when only seventeen years old, took oyster soup to the wounded soldiers at the local Lutheran church following the Battle of Cedar Creek fought October 19, 1864.[34] As a result, Altha "was so horrified at the sights that she saw there, that she was never able to smell or eat oyster stew again without remembering that terrible scene of carnage."[35]

For his part, Milton Boyd Steele began serving Virginia and the Confederacy when he was just fifteen years old.[36] He drove a wagon for Company A of the 1st Virginia Cavalry before enlisting and was present at the Battle of Gettysburg in July of 1863.[37] Although he had turned eighteen years of age by this time, Milton had not yet officially enlisted. Then, on September 1, 1863, he was enlisted by Captain John M. Lock at Newtown into Company A for the duration of the war.[38] Fortunately, Milton suffered no severe injuries during his period of service. Like his superior, Lieutenant Rosenberger, Milton is listed as a prisoner of war and was paroled in Winchester April 18, 1865. He was described as being nineteen years old, six feet in height with dark hair and hazel eyes.[39] Upon returning home in 1865, he ran a successful dry goods business called Steele & Bro. with his older brother, Mager William Steele, in Newtown.[40] Milton and Altha had three children: Elmer M., Cara A. and Julian. A bout of meningitis caused the premature death of Private Milton Boyd Steele, on February 3, 1884.[41] The 1900 U.S. Census shows Altha Steele as a widow residing with her three children and a son-in-law, Samuel B. Grovz, husband of Cara.[42] Altha did not remarry and yet lived a long life. She did not die until September 12, 1938. She and Milton are both buried in the Green Hill Cemetery in Stephens City.

Abraham and Lucinda's fourth daughter was named Sarah Catherine, born October 1, 1834. Unlike her sisters, Sarah never married. Instead, she lived with her mother her entire life, helping with the Toll House duties in Newtown and later at Tenth Legion. When Lucinda and her two remaining unmarried daughters, Emma Virginia also known as "Ginnie" and Lucinda "Lucy" E., moved to Rockingham County in 1867 to work the toll at Tenth Legion, Sarah went with them. When her mother was no longer able to perform the duties of Postmaster for Tenth Legion, Sarah took over that position on June 5, 1886 and continued as such until, at least, July 1, 1897.[43] Sarah Catharine Nisewanger died December 23, 1916, and is buried in the Trinity Evangelical Lutheran Church Cemetery in Stephens City.[44]

The Nisewanger's fifth daughter, Amanda, was born September 6, 1837.[45] At age twenty, she married Frances Staling, a former citizen of Kirchasel Kurnessen, Germany, who sought to avoid compulsory military service by immigrating to the United States. Frances also went by his German name, G. Franz Stehling, which is given along with his anglicized name, Staling, on his tombstone.[46] His parents were Franz and Elizabeth C. Staling. Amanda and Frances were married January 29, 1857, at Stephensburg (also called Newtown and later Stephens City).[47] Born on September 6, 1829, Frances was twenty-eight years old at the time of his marriage. The Staling family is shown on the 1860 U.S. Census for Stephensburg. Frances gave his profession as a "master painter" while his wife, Amanda, was said to be involved in "housewivery."[48] Although Frances painted the pleasing, folk art rendition of the Nisewanger Toll House shown on the cover of this book, he was really a house painter. Frances must have done well at his job since by the 1860 census, he already had real estate valued at two-thousand dollars and personal property worth over three-hundred dollars.[49] He was also able to afford a female African-American domestic servant named Peggy to help with household tasks.

However, while he may have avoided military service in his homeland of Germany, the Confederate government also required compulsory service for all able-bodied men of Virginia who were eighteen to forty-five years old. But, Frances did not wait to be drafted into the Confederate army. Instead, on June 13, 1861, he enlisted at Newtown with Company B of the 51st Virginia Militia.[50] His enlistment was conducted by Captain Samuel M. Marks, the same officer who enlisted James Lemley, the blacksmith of Newtown. In fact, as James Lemley had done earlier, Company B also detailed Frances on August 12, 1861, "on government work" to obtain an "artillery harness and clothing, at or near Newtown."[51] During the Civil War, Frances reached the rank of sergeant and survived without serious injury.

After the war, Frances returned home to his growing family and his profession. He and Amanda had six children: three sons named Frances E., George L., and John C. and three daughters, Cora V., Lena A. and Kate L. Like the Nisewanger family, the Stalings moved to Rockingham County after the Civil War. By 1870, the parents and three children are shown as residing in Harrisonburg Township.[52] Frances' real estate was valued at twenty-five hundred dollars as of September 8, 1870, when the census was taken at the Staling home. The 1880 U. S Census shows all six children living with their parents. Frances continued to be employed as a painter.[53] However, on December 26, 1897, Frances Staling died and the family lost its main source of income. To accommodate, his widow, Amanda, began taking in boarders. As of 1900, she had ten boarders ranging in age from twenty to eighty-seven years of age.[54] The three sons of the family were also helping financially by being employed. Frank and George were continuing their father's business of house painting, while John was a druggist.[55] On September 11, 1919, their mother, Amanda, died at the age of eighty-three years. The last Staling sibling, Katie L., did not pass away until September 26, 1957. Frances and Amanda along with all six of the Staling children are buried in Woodbine Cemetery in Harrisonburg, Virginia.[56]

Not only did the community of Newtown provide the Confederacy with some of its finest soldiers, but its citizens also supported the South with material resources. Although some of these transactions were never officially recorded, others remain part of the official archives of the Confederacy. One source of these documents is the Confederate Citizens File previously mentioned which contains receipts for sales to the Confederate government, many signed by Assistant Quarter-masters. Three instances will be presented for supplies rendered by residents of Newtown, Virginia. A September 19, 1861 receipt notes that James Lemley, who was not yet old enough to enlist in the army, furnished the 9th Regiment of Georgia Volunteers two and one-half cords of firewood at $2.00 per cord at Stephensburg on June 29th 1861.[57] He was paid $5.00 total for his wood.

On March 22, 1862, Mrs. Mary Nisewanger, wife of local innkeeper John Nisewanger, provided the 7th Virginia Cavalry with a large supply of fodder for their horses. From her stable, she furnished twenty-six bushels of corn at $1.50 per bushel or $39.00 dollars, one ton of hay for $22.00, and 2 ½ bushels of oats at $1.00 a bushel or $2.50, for an overall total due of $63.50.[58] The transaction document stated further in the portion signed by Notary Steele:

> Frederick County State of Virginia. Personally appeared before me Mr. Mager Steele Notary Public for the County aforesaid Mary Nisewanger and made oath that the above account is just and Correct that Hay and Grain was furnished by the order of Col. Ashby for the use of his Cavalry Horses. Witness my hand this 6th day of Nov. 1862.[59]

The next part of the document was penned by Lt. Colonel Oliver R. Funsten of the 17th Battalion Cavalry:

> I certify that a number of horses belonging to companies of the 7th Regiment of Virginia Cavalry were fed at the stable of Mrs. Nisewanger on the day above named but I do not know by whose orders it was done.[60]

It is unclear why Lt. Colonel stated that he did not know by whose orders it was done when the paragraph above stated that it was by order of Colonel Ashby. Mrs. Nisewanger appears to have waited almost six months before she received payment for her feed. Mager Steele was one of three Steele brothers of Newtown served in the Confederate army. In fact, although he performed as Notary Public in the above document, he was already a member of the army. On June 13, 1861, Mager enlisted as a private in Company B of the Virginia Militia.

The last document found concerning assistance from citizens of Newtown refers to Mrs. Lucinda Nisewanger, matriarch of the family of seven daughters, many who married or would marry a Confederate veteran. Although she had no sons in the army, she was an ardent supporter of the South. On July 26, 1864, she too furnished fodder for the Confederacy's horses. At Newtown, she sold twenty-five pounds of grain, at fifty cents a pound, or for a total $12.50 to Captain C. G. Merritt, Assistant Quartermaster of the 25th Virginia Regiment of Gordon's Division.[61]

Despite poor economic conditions in the village of Newtown during the Civil War, its citizens continued to support Confederate military efforts. The three citizens mentioned were most likely paid in Confederate script. Each of them probably could have made much more money by offering their resources to the Union army and would have been paid in U.S. dollars. However, they elected not to do so.

Abraham and Lucinda's two youngest children, the sixth and seventh daughters, were Lucinda E., born in September of 1847 and Emma Virginia, who was born September 15, 1845. Lucinda, to help distinguish her from her mother, was nicknamed "Lucy" or "Lucie." Emma Virginia's nickname was "Ginnie." When John King boarded at the Nisewanger Toll House on the evening of May 8, 1862, these two daughters, ages fourteen and sixteen at the time, were living in the log house along with Sarah Catharine and Mrs. Lucinda Nisewanger. John King's diary later came into the possession of Lucie and Ginnie. As mentioned above, the name of the Confederate soldier who gave the diary to the Nisewanger family remains unknown. Whoever he was, the soldier probably presented it to Mrs. Nisewanger, since she was cited by name in the diary and since she was widely known in the Shenandoah Valley. Mrs. Nisewanger may have read the diary herself and then passed it on to her two teenage daughters. The names and regiments of two Confederate soldiers, possibly by the hand of Lucie, are written in the diary, but there is no way to be certain that one of these soldiers obtained the diary from the Confederate staff in Winchester and later presented the diary to the Nisewanger family in Newtown. As shown at the bottom of the rear endpapers of the diary, their names appear written in very fine, cursive script:

Mr. John N. Calwallader
Carpenters Battery
Andrews Batallion
Johnsons Division

Mr. John W. Blaker
Valley Brass Band
48th Volunteers
2nd Brigade
Ewells Corps

Of course, these men could also have simply been visitors at the Nisewanger Toll House and had nothing at all to do with the diary.

Private Cadwallader was a local man, only twenty-two years old in 1862. He may have been a suitor of one of the Nisewanger daughters. Did he try to win favor with the unmarried Nisewanger daughters by presenting them with John King's diary as a gift? When the war started, he enlisted on April 19, 1861, into the Newtown Artillery, for one year's service. John Cadwallader's enlistment officer was Captain George A. Groves.[62] His unit was called Grove's Battery of Light Artillery. Regimental returns dated November 30, 1861, show that the volunteer company known as the Newtown Artillery, under Captain Groves, disbanded.[63]

As a member of the Newtown Artillery, John Cadwallader would have known both James Lemley and Francis Staling before he enlisted in another unit. In fact, twenty-one men re-enlisted in Company B of the 51st Virginia Militia from Groves Battery of Virginia Artillery, known also as the Newtown Artillery. John Cadwallader, James Lemley and Francis Staling were three of those men. Private Cadwallader then enlisted with Captain Wilfred E. Cutshaw's Company of Virginia Light Artillery on March 10, 1862.[64] Since Francis Staling was already married to one of the Nisewanger daughters, Amanda, he may have been the one who introduced John Cadwallader to his three unmarried sister-in-laws who resided at the Toll House. Private Cadwallader survived the war without any significant injury. By 1870, he was working on his father Ezra's land as a farmer in Newtown.[65] John did not marry one of the Nisewanger daughters. Instead, on December 1, 1870, he married Ella Carter. Unfortunately, after just less than six years of marriage, John Newton Cadwallader died on September 8, 1876, and was buried in Green Hill Cemetery.[66]

John W. Blaker was a pre-war resident of Newtown in King and Queen County. He was married with children before the war and was thus not a likely suitor at the Nisewanger home. John was not a fighting soldier per se. Instead, he served with the F & S (Field and Staff) as a musician with the Valley Brass Band of the 48th Virginia Infantry.[67] He had enlisted August 1, 1862, at Gordonsville in Orange County, just a couple of months after John King lost his diary May 22, 1862. Private Blaker was a musician in the same F & S unit with the previously mentioned Mager William Steele, an older brother of Milton Boyd Steele. Apparently Mager Steele's service with Company B of the Virginia Militia was over for he had enlisted in the 48th Virginia Infantry on November 1, 1862, in Berryville, Clark County, as a Field and Staff member and served as a musician.[68] Hence, Private Blaker was most likely in Newtown to visit with fellow musician, Mager Steele, when his name was recorded in the diary. Why Private Blaker visited the Nisewanger household and had his name and unit information written in the diary remains a mystery. Did both Privates John Blaker and Mager Steele visit the Nisewangers at the Toll House to give Mrs. Nisewanger the diary? Or did Private Blaker somehow obtain the diary from a Confederate staff member and present it himself? Perhaps neither one had any part in placing John King's diary in the hands of the Nisewangers, but simply visited the Toll House one day. Privates John Blaker and Mager Steele both were present throughout the rest of the war with the 48th Virginia Infantry. Also, both were paroled at Appomattox Court House, the site of General Robert E. Lee's surrender, on April 9, 1865.[69] From 1870 until his retirement in 1916, Private Blaker worked as a merchant in Hampshire, Preston and Tucker Counties in West Virginia and even traveled to Texas.[70] After a brief illness, he died in Tucker County, West Virginia on April 17, 1923.

However the Nisewanger teenagers obtained the diary, they made good use of it. Much like a modern, lined school composition book with a black marbleized cover, John King's diary was six by eight inches in size and about the same number of pages. In the 19th century, paper was expensive. As may be recalled from John King's first entry on October 22, 1861, he paid $1.31 for "this book" and two school books for his brother, Willie.

In 2017 dollars, that translates to $36.30 .[71] John, when beginning his diary, left one blank endpaper in the front of the book. Because he was never able to complete the diary, there were also six pages in the rear which were blank. Hence, there were a total of seven blank pages left by John King. Taking the unused pages as their own, Ginnie and Lucie Nisewanger used every inch of space. For explanatory purposes those pages will be referred to by a numbering system from one to fourteen. Hence, each page will have an odd and even number referencing front and back, odd representing the front of a page and even standing for the back of that page. The handwritten poems by the sisters are shown just as they appeared in the diary including spelling and grammatical errors. The front of the first endpaper or page one shows a one verse poem written handwritten in pencil and signed by Lucie E. Nisewanger:

Though years may pass, and times may fly,
And every hope decay and die
And every joyful dream may set
Yet then I never can forget

Lucie does not mention the name of the poet, the name of the poem or the source from which she borrowed the poem. While it is not possible to determine her actual source, the poem appeared as early as 1820 in a volume called "The Pocket Magazine of classic and polite literature" which was printed and published by John Arliss in London. It was taken from E. H. Hays' novel "Principle" and was called "Stanza." Perhaps due to lack of space on the page, Lucie did not transcribe the entire poem. The original first and second stanza originally appeared in 1820 as follows:

Yes, time may pass and the year fly,
And every hope may withering die:
But, oh! I never can forget

Mine was not love that every breath
Could so scorch to fire, or cool to death.
Mine was that love which nought could severe.
It burned—it burns—and will forever,
Though faithless thou—yet still my heart,
From hope and thee can ne'er depart;
I'll bless the time when we first met,
For oh! I can never forget.[72]

Lucie apparently copied it from a very old pledge that "I'll remember you" that often appeared in "friendship albums," kept mostly by school-age young women beginning in the 1820's. Cassandra Good notes that "friendship albums became popular...as the blossoming culture of sentimentalism made its mark on personal relationships, especially those of young women."[73] The young ladies did not write original poems, but instead copied them from magazines or books and put them in albums that resembled scrapbooks. Infrequently, they also completed drawings. The subject matter of such poems was usually about "friendship, religion, or womanhood and many referenced separation of friends or even death."[74] Hence, Ginnie and Lucie Nisewanger's additions to the empty pages of John King's diary are reminiscent of the earlier concept of a friendship album. Although Ginnie and Lucie included a list of friends or schoolmates in their mini-album, it appears that none of these friends wrote in John King's diary. The two Nisewanger teenage girls also cut out quite a few poems from magazines and newspapers and pasted them onto the blank pages. They wrote many poems, some that exhibit their calligraphic skills. Some poems had authors' names and the titles of the poems while others did not. Ginnie and Lucie also practiced writing and rewriting their names. The types of poems selected by the teenagers clearly show a fascination with the fashionable sentimentalism. Friendship, romance, womanhood, marital relations and even death were common topics.

Although there are no signatures of friends in the Ginnie and Lucie Nisewanger album, there is a list of either schoolmates and/or friends. Because the list is in the fine hand of a calligraphic style, it is probably the work of the older of the two girls, Ginnie. Also, her name comes first. Ginnie was two years older than her sister Lucie. This list was written on the sixth page:

Ginnie Nisewanger
Nelie Rosenburger
Dol (?) Schenck
Manda Gibson
Rink (?) Schenck
Molly Ash
Harriet Chrisman
Ginnie Chrisman

Apparently, most if not all of these friends lived in Newtown (also called Stephensburg). All of them were most likely the same age as the Nisewanger teenagers. Nelie Rosenburger was probably related to them through their uncle, David Rosenberger. Amanda or "Manda" Gibson is shown on the 1860 U.S. Census for Stephensburg with her father, master wagonmaker, Hamilton Gibson and her mother, Rebecca Gibson.[75] Likewise, Harriet A. Chrisman and her sister, Lucy V. (probably Virginia or Ginnie) are also listed on the 1860 U.S. Census for Stephensburg living with their father, a farmer named John H. Chrisman, and mother, Lucinda.[76] Harriet was twenty-one years of age while Lucy V. was sixteen years of age in 1860. In addition, there was only one family of Shenks, also spelled Schenck, living in Stephensburg in 1850 and 1860 as shown by the U.S. Censuses. The daughters' names were Octavia and Caroline. Octavia was seventeen in 1860 while Caroline was sixteen, according to the census.[77] Perhaps the names "Dol" and "Rink" were nicknames for the two Schenck daughters, Octavia and Caroline.

The poems recorded in the album by the Nisewanger girls are of two types, printed and handwritten. The first two printed poems were glued onto the rear of the front endpaper, or on page two. Thirteen verses of the poem "The New Ballad of Lord Lovell" (From the Philadelphia Evening Bulletin) were put in first, but no author was given. The second poem was:
Song of the Southern Loyalist

Up with the Old Flag; fling out its folds
Stand by to witness it wave once more;
Crowd round it readily, lift it up steadily
Braver it looks than ever before

Not a Star varnished,—each one is there
Not a Stripe faded, no where a stain;
Welcome it merrily, speak of it cheerily
God bless the day for the Old Flag again!
Sad was the season when it was struck;
Darker, still darker, day languished on;
Guard it now forcefully, touch it remorsefully,
Love it more for all said and done.

Up with the Old Flag; long may it float;
Never a pleiad lost from its plain;
Lift it up lovingly, shout all approvingly--
God bless the day for the Old Flag again!

The only mention of an author of this poem was the letter "A." Research showed that this poem was written by J. H. Alexander, L.L.D., and appeared in a collection of prose and verse called "Our Country, in its Relations to the Past, Present and Future: A National Book" edited by Mrs. Lincoln Phelps and title"Under the Sanction of the State Fair Association of the Women in Maryland, for Benefit of the U.S. Christian and Sanitary Commission."[78] It was published in Baltimore by John D. Troy in 1864. This poem was no doubt in circulation prior to it being published in book form in 1864 and one of the Nisewanger sisters probably cut it out and pasted it into the diary sometime between May, 1862 and 1864. However, it seems odd that a pro-Southern family like the Nisewangers would have any interest in such a pro-Union poem. The editor, Mrs. Phelps, stated that one of her intentions in publishing the "National Book" was to "soften that asperity of feeling which would condemn every attempt to win back our erring brethren of the South to their allegiance."[79]

Other printed poems pasted by Ginnie and Lucie into the diary were, in order of appearance: "Absent Friends—To J.V.H.E." (no author shown), "The Valley Lilie" by Maud Irvin, "I Am Thine" by James S. Watkins, "The Beggar Women" by Augustine D., "Thou Art Not Mine" (no author shown), 'Give Me One Glance" by C. S. Baron, "Evening" written for the Waverly Magazine by Leon C. Weld, "The Sunfish" by James Ristine, "A Waif" by W.P. T., "Work and Wait" by Andrew Downing, "Good-Night" By George G. Small. The source of only one of these poems is given, i.e., The Waverly Magazine. Down at the bottom of the first page of printed poems, Ginnie or Lucie also pasted the following, probably cut out of a magazine:

..........Women are called the "softer sex,"
because they are so easily humbugged. Out of
one hundred girls, ninety-five would prefer ostentation
to happiness----a dandy husband to a mechanic.
........."That's very singular sir," said a young lady to a gentleman,
who had just kissed her.
"O, well, my dear Miss, I will soon make it plural."

The sisters also selected some humorous items out of the newspapers and magazines. Attached to the bottom of the printed poem "Good-Night" was the following:

.................A countryman went into one of our fashionable refreshment rooms, and was

surprised at seeing nothing on the table but the cloth, knives, and forks, and glasses.

"What will you have?" asked the waiter. Giles stared like a stuck pig, and said "I dun

know." "Would you like a bill of fare, sir?" "Thank you, I don't care if I do take a small piece."

Although the Nisewangers cited no source for this funny anecdote, it was published as early as 1860 in the British volume, "Jokes, Conundrums, Sentiments and Aphorisms" and probably could have been found in numerous other books, papers or magazines.[80]

All of the above printed poems were glued onto blank pages eight, ten and eleven in the rear section of the book. Although the authors of all of these poems are not known, they undoubtedly were the work of popular mid-nineteenth century poets who often published in newspapers and ladies' books and magazines of the day. Andrew Downing (b. March 11, 1838 d. December 26, 1917) had his poems published in newspapers and in 1897 published a volume of poems called "The Trumpeters and Other Poems." James Ristine was probably better known to the public because he published his works in the national *Godey's Lady's Book and Magazine*. In one volume for January to June, 1877, he published three poems: "The Dawn of Spring," The Mystic Change" and "Marigold."[81] Most of the pages that the Nisewanger teenagers used in John King's diary were not taken up with printed poems but with poems that they wrote by hand. Perhaps they enjoyed the process of writing them and, at the same time, had an opportunity to practice their penmanship skills.

Perhaps of more significance to the sisters than the printed works were the several poems that they took the time to copy in to their album by hand. Although there appear to be at least three styles of handwriting, the majority of the poems were probably transcribed by Ginnie Nisewanger. Lucie may have done a few and another person may have completed one or more of the handwritten poems The name of the third, single sister, Sarah Catherine, is not cited once in the album. It is unlikely that she had any part in composing the mini-album.

The only printed narrative that the Nisewanger daughters glued into the album was one called "A Midnight Reverie." The author's name does not appear. This poem appears on page thirteen of the album. The same work had appeared earlier in *The Weekly Courier* of February 25, 1860, a newspaper from Fayetteville, North Carolina.[82] Unfortunately, again, the author was not cited. However, the poem as it appeared in *The Weekly*

Courier is in exactly the same format as printed poem in the album and may well have come from this Fayetteville newspaper.

The second handwritten poem was done in pencil, using letters that slanted to the left and was probably accomplished by a friend. There are no other poems in the album that exhibit this left-slanting cursive script. The transcriber did not provide either the name of the author or the name of the poem. It appears on page three in the rear of the album, directly after John King's last diary entry on May 22, 1862, and reads as shown below:

Torn from the stem that fed they rosy breath
In vain the sunbeam seek
To warm that faded cheek
The dews of heav'n that once like balm fell over thee
Now are but tears, to weep they early death
So droops the maid whose lover hath forsaken her
Thrown from his arms, as lone and lost as thou
In vain the smiles of all
Like sunbeams round her fall
The only smile that could from death awaken her
That smile. alas! is gone to others now

Those love no more will silent weep
O'er joys which have departed.
But all be present fair and sweet
And healed the broken-hearted
There mourn no more o'er broken ties.
For death no more will sever;
There love and life all 'round us lies
We live and bloom forever.

Somehow, the transcriber omitted the first line of the poem:
Poor broken flow'r! what art can now recover thee?

The name of the poem is "Poor Broken Flower." It was written by the famous Irish poet, singer and songwriter, Thomas Moore. Moore was born in Ireland May 28, 1779 and died in England on February 25, 1852. A ten volume set of his collected poems was called *The Poetical Works of Thomas Moore* and was published in London in 1841.[83] Hence, the person who entered this poem into the Nisewanger album could have obtained it anywhere, but probably found it in a magazine or newspaper.

The next short handwritten poem was probably transcribed by Ginnie Nisewanger. It was done in a calligraphic style using black ink and begins on the reverse page of the poem "Poor Broken Flowers" or on page four. The name of the poem was given by the transcriber. It reads as follows in the format used by the transcriber:

The Husbands Revenge

A warning to wives who will keep bad Cooks
Provisions raw
Long time he bore
Remonstrance was in vain
To escape the scrab
He joined a club
Nor dined at home again

"The Husband's Revenge" was published in March of 1856 in *Punch*, also known as "The London Charivari," a British weekly magazine of humor and satire established by Henry Mayhew and engraver Ebenezer Landells in 1841.[84] The magazine was well-known for the comical illustrations by Landells. It was "most influential in the eighteen forties and eighteen fifties when it helped to coin the term 'cartoon' in its modern sense."[85] Whether the Nisewanger teens transcribed the poem from *Punch*, the magazine or from another source is not known.

Just below "The Husband's Revenge" the transcriber wrote another verse and continued with two more verses on the next blank page. All three verses were done in the same accomplished hand as the "The Husband's Revenge," probably that of Ginnie Nisewanger. Initially, it appears that these three verses are part of the same poem when in fact they are verses taken from three different ones. Verses one and two reminisce about fond memories of childhood. The first verse is as follows:

O sing to me, my own beloved
That sweet and simple strain
That I have treasured in my heart
Throughout long years of pain
For its clear tones recall to me
The joys of by gone days
When hopes bright sun lit up the path
Of happy childhood days

This poem appeared on the front page of the *Reading Times* newspaper of Reading, Pennsylvania, dated Thursday, August 11, 1859.[86] The author was Finley Johnson. Finley Johnson was a Victorian age poet who also penned "There's Rest For All in Heaven" and "A Song for the New Year." Some of his works were set to music. The Nisewanger transcriber did not include all of "O Sing to me." The second verse written by either Ginnie or Lucie Nisewanger is on page five and reads:

Sister far from thee I'm roaming
Where the willows shades my way
Where so oft in merry childhood
Happy hours we passed away

This verse is the first of eleven taken from a poem called "Sister Mary" that appeared in Volume 52 of *Godey's Lady's Book and Magazine* for January to June of 1856.[87]

The third verse in the so-called "three-verse" poem, on page five just below the above verse, was as follows:

Her cheekbones pale and thinner
Than should be for one so young
And her eyes in all my motions
With a mute observance hung

This verse was written by Lord Alfred Tennyson, the most noted English poet of the Victorian age.[88] It is the eleventh verse of the well-known poem "Locksley Hall." The Nisewanger girls could have obtained this verse from any one of a number magazines and newspapers that published it in the mid-Victorian period.

The next handwritten poem was also probably copied by Ginnie Nisewanger. She gave the name of the poem, but not its author or her source. This poem is found on page six of the album. It was also done in fine calligraphic cursive script:

For M

This calm, this gentle eve
I fain would pen a few sweet thoughts for thee
Not cold and formal words, but fancies warm
And glowing-pure and true
I think of thee

This poem was written by Clarence May and appeared in the August, 1859, issue of the "Peterson Magazine."[89]

Next on page six was the list of names already given. Below that list, the young lady who transcribed the first portion of "For M-," wrote the poem a second time. This rendition shows much better cursive writing with strong, bold strokes using much darker ink. Clearly, she was practicing her penmanship.

One half of the next page, seven, has been crossed out. Apparently, the transcriber was not satisfied with her work. The verse of the poem "Teddy Ragan" was written, then was crossed out in heavy ink. The bottom half of that page was lost due to an apparent spill of liquid or was simply wiped clean of ink. Traces of ink and letters were all that remained on page seven. The few letters that were left were indecipherable. Perhaps one of the ladies was not pleased with her work.

On page eight, the poem "Good Night" was written in average cursive script. This transcription was also most likely done by Ginnie Nisewanger.

Good night! Aye breath it gently
With accents soft and low
And whisper once thy blessing
As from thy sight I go
Remember earth seems dearer
And moon and stars more bright
While they dear voice is breathing
In gentle Tones, good night

And when my soul is passing
From this vain world away
And borne by angels upward
To realms of endlys day
Still be our accents fondly
Ere I reach that home of light
A soft and gentle whisper
A long and last good night

The poem "Good Night" was written by Mrs. Eleanor Clair, who was a frequent contributor to *The Peterson Magazine.* "Good Night" appeared in the August, 1859 issue of the magazine, just two pages after the above poem, "For M-."[90] In the February, 1859, issue of *The Peterson Magazine,*

Mrs. Clair had three of her other poems published: "Dream," "Charlotte Bronte," and "A Child's Thoughts."

The next penned poem is a lengthy one and begins on page eleven with two verses and, for some reason, the last verse was written on the top of page fourteen. It was also most likely copied by Ginnie Nisewanger. Although the author and title are not provided, the poem is "Teddy Ragan" and was done by White Ghost, an obvious pseudonym. "Teddy Ragan" was set to music and appeared in volume 28 of Henry DeMarsa's "New Comic and Sentimental Singer's Journal," which was published in 1868.[91] A single issue of the journal could be purchased for two cents. The transcriber did not copy the verses in which they were originally presented nor did she copy all the stanzas. There were a total of seven stanzas, but Ginnie only wrote three. The order presented was stanza five, stanza six, and lastly stanza seven . As done in the album, the poem reads:

My curse attend you, Teddy Ragan
And the hour when we were wed
I thought that I had suffered plenty
From the aching of my head
Says the Doctor to the mother
Give her some tea that's in the pot
No: we will make her some gruel
For to keep her body hot

Chorus: Fal de ral de val de raddy, & c.

They began to prepare the babys linen
Every thing along that way
Tea and coffee and the best of spirits
For the long expected day
Why are you so idling standing
Don't you hear the Doctor bawl
Faith I do says Bridget Murphy
And the baby began to squal

When the hurry it was over
Winnie she lay snug in her bed
It's then she was in her clover
She began to think of Tedd
Then says Winnie to her mother

Make us a strong cup of Tea
And give some to poor Teddy
For I'll want Ted another day

Ginnie did not include the chorus, "Fal de ral de val de raddy & c" in her transcription.

The last handwritten poem appears on page twelve of the album surrounded by printed poems that were pasted onto the paper. Again, the style of handwriting seems to be that of Ginnie Nisewanger. No title or author was provided by the copyist. It appears as follows:

Speak gently; Love doth whisper low
The vows that true hearts bind
And gently Friendships accents flow
Affection's voice is kind

Speak gently; Tis a little thing
Dropped in the hearts deep well
The good, the joy which it may bring
Eternity should test.

These are verses two and nine of the highly praised poem "Speak Gently" by David Bates. The original work was nine verses. David Bates, a Philadelphia merchant, was born March 6, 1809 and died January 27, 1870. In 1870, his son, Stockton Bates, published his fathers' collected works in the volume titled "The Poetical Works of David Bates."[92] By this time, he had already achieved worldwide recognition for his most famous poems, "Speak Gently" and "Childhood." "Speak Gently" was set to music by William Vincent. Because "Speak Gently" appeared in so many publications, it is not possible to determine where Ginnie may have found a copy.

Overall, thirteen printed poems, nine transcribed poems, several humorous comments and one short narrative were posted in the album or scrapbook by Ginnie and Lucie Nisewanger. The poems selected by the Nisewanger sisters were typical of the popular Victorian sentimentality of the day. It is unlikely that the teenagers obtained many poems, if any, from books such as the collected works of the poets. In fact, several of these were published after the time the poems were entered into the scrapbook. It is much more likely that the girls found the poems in magazines and newspapers than in any collected volumes of poetry. In fact, the inexpensive paper on which the printed poems were done seems to have come from magazines or newspapers. In addition, in consideration of the dates of the cited periodicals from which many of the poems were taken, it is clear that the Nisewanger daughters had saved old magazines and newspapers. *The Weekly Courier* from which one poem was probably copied was dated February 25, 1859. One poem was most likely borrowed from the *Reading Times* issued August 11, 1859. Two poems were apparently transcribed from the August, 1859, issue of *The Peterson Magazine* while another was copied from the August 11, 1859, issue of *Godey's Lady's Book and Magazine.* It appears that one was taken from an 1856 issue of the British satirical magazine *Punch* while yet another came from the January-June, 1856, issue of *The Peterson Magazine.* Filled with color fashion plates of the latest styles, women's and children's clothing designs, embroidery designs, health tips, stories and poems, *Godey's* and its major competitor, *Peterson's*, were both especially appealing to young women. Since all of these periodicals had pre-Civil War dates, it is probable that the Nisewanger teens obtained them from either civilian travelers going up and down the Valley Pike and possibly from boarders who stayed at the Nisewanger Toll House. The travelers most likely simply gave the magazines to the girls or left them at the Toll House for others to read. Once Ginnie and Lucie received the diary with its fourteen blank pages sometime after May 22 of 1862 when John King had it taken from him, they started to go through their collection of periodicals and began pasting poems into the diary. Ginnie and Lucie would have certainly treasured the album after all of their efforts to make it.

Private Jacob A. Helms

In addition to the poems, there were also a few drawings. Two were simple, pencil renditions of a flower and of a spider's web. However, the third was much more interesting since it was not done by the Nisewangers. Instead, it is a small, pencil profile of a man's face. It is a self-portrait signed three times by "Mr. J. A. Helms/Winchester Va." The sketch is not dated. Was Mr. Helms the person or Confederate soldier who gave the Nisewangers John King's diary? Why did he place a portrait of himself in their book? Was he a suitor?

Jacob A. Helms was the son of Andrew and Elizabeth Helms of Rockingham County, Virginia. Jacob was born about 1841 and was only twenty years old when the Civil War began.[93] He has a very interesting and checkered Confederate service record. On July 25, 1861, he enlisted in the 4th Regiment, 7th Brigade of the Virginia Militia at Harrisonburg.[94] Captain Abraham Shoemaker signed his enlistment papers. Jacob A. Helms was soon promoted to 2nd Sergeant in his regiment. When his period of service expired, Jacob next enlisted in Company I of the 33rd Virginia Regiment, part of the infamous Stonewall Brigade, on April 20, 1862, at Swift Run Gap.[95] He was enlisted "for the war" by First Lieutenant George Huston. Private Helms was present with Company I until he deserted July 24, 1862.[96] However, he returned to camp on September 25, 1862, and was then scheduled for a court martial under General Orders No. 33 written by General Robert E. Lee's Headquarters, Army of Northern Virginia.[97] A court martial was held, but Private Helms was "freed on a technicality" and was released back to his regiment.[98] All went well For Private Helms until the Battle of Gettysburg which raged from July 1 to July 3, 1863. Commanded by Brigadier General James A., "Stonewall Jim" Walker, the Stonewall Brigade was ordered to march at three a.m., on the morning of July 3 "into the presence of strongly entrenched Federals" on Culp's Hill.[99] Three times the Stonewall Brigade attempted to scale the slopes of Culp's Hill and three times, they were ordered by Brigadier General Walker to withdraw. The 33rd Virginia suffered the most casualties of the five regiments of the brigade with eleven killed and thirty-seven wounded. Several Confederate soldiers, near the top of the eminence, simply threw up white flags and surrendered to the Union forces atop the hill. Private Jacob A. Helms was wounded with a "contusion of the leg" and was taken as a prisoner of war. He was then taken to DeCamp General Hospital on David's Island in New York Harbor. In his diary entry of August 10, 1863, John B. Sheets, another member of Company I recorded that he "heard from J. A. Helms by letter from him from NY."[100] Although the exact date is unknown, sometime after this diary entry, Privates Helms was paroled after taking the Oath of Allegiance to the United States. His service record makes no mention of him ever returning to Company I of the 33rd Virginia. On August 16, 1864, Jacob was "arrested by U. S forces near Newtown, Va."[101] According to official documents, he was charged with "having been in the rebel service Company I, 33rd Va. Infy."[102] Also, the Union documents state that "the prisoner admits charges, was forcibly taken from this home and is a deserter."[103] Instead of being taken to New York as before, Private Helms was transferred to Camp Chase, Ohio, and was received there September 2, 1864.[104] While at Camp Chase, something very unusual happened. A number of citizens of Meigs County, Ohio, upon learning that Private Helms had been forcibly removed from his home in Virginia petitioned the Union Army for his release. A committee met and recommended his release on two conditions, i.e., that he take the Oath of Allegiance to the United States and that he "remain north and west of the Ohio River." Hence, on March 23, 1865, the following release was written at Camp Chase:

> By virtue of an Order from The President dated at Washington City, DC March 10th 1865 Jacob A. Helms Pri 33/Va. Inf. resident of Rockingham Cty, and State of Va Prisoner of this Post; after having complied with the requirements of, and subscribed the following oath & Declaration, is hereby released from confinement.[105]

The standard Oath of Allegiance at the bottom of the letter was signed by "J. A . Helms" and was "subscribed and sworn to before me, this 23rd day of March AD 1865 by W.P. Richardson, Bvt Brigadier General Comd't of Post."[106] The sworn oath also contained a clause whereby Jacob pledged "... to remain north of the Ohio River until permitted to go elsewhere by Order of the Secretary of War."[107] Included on the oath was also a description of the prisoner as twenty-three years old with a florid complexion, five foot seven inches in height, and with dark hair and grey eyes.

The signature by Jacob A. Helms on his prison release letter is an exact match with the signature written three times in the Nisewanger album. This Jacob Helms is the same person who visited the Toll House in Newtown and sketched a self-portrait. Also of note is that the entry of August 10, 1863, in John B. Sheets diary referred to him as "J. A. Helms" not as Jacob Helms, further confirming that he went by the name J. A. Helms.

Jacob A. Holmes was probably the Confederate soldier who gave John R. King's diary to the Nisewanger family. His unit, Company I of the 33rd Regiment of the Stonewall Brigade, was present when General Stonewall Jackson fought and won the First Battle of Winchester on May 25, 1862. Word of the confiscation of a diary that mentioned the Nisewanger family probably circulated through Stonewall Jackson's army. Private Helms may have heard of this story and may have volunteered to carry the King diary to the Nisewangers. Private Helms did not desert until July 24, 1862 so he was most definitely with his regiment in the battle and probably obtained John King's diary prior to deserting. Unfortunately, since Jacob did not date his signature and self-portrait, the day he completed the drawing remains unknown. However, his Confederate service records prove that Private Helms was in Newtown on August 16, 1864, because that is that date that he was arrested there by Union forces. He was not with the 33rd Virginia at the time of his arrest. Perhaps, he was in Newtown simply to visit the Nisewanger daughters. Most likely, he gave the King diary to the Nisewanger family before August 16, 1864. Hence, although Helms did not date his signature in the King diary, his Confederate service records prove that he was present in Winchester when the diary was lost and he was also later present in Newtown where the Nisewanger girls lived. Thirdly, Jacob must have visited before 1867 because that is when the Nisewangers moved to Tenth Legion in Rockingham County.

On December 24, 1867, Jacob A. Helms married Anna Hohn in Winchester.[108] By the time of the 1870 U.S. Census, Jacob and Anna or "Annie" as she was sometimes called, had moved to Franklin Township of Rockingham County, and had one child, Ernest E. Helms.[109] After years of employment as a carpenter, on the 1900 U.S. Census, Jacob stated that his occupation was a "commercial traveler."[110] At the age of seventy-two years, Jacob A. Helms died at his home in Mt. Crawford suddenly on March 6, 1913.[111] He was buried at Mt. Crawford Cemetery in Rockingham County, Virginia. There is no record of Jacob Helms having any association with the Nisewanger family after he was married.

As stated earlier, Abraham and Lucinda along with three of their unmarried daughters packed their belongings and moved to Tenth Legion in Rockingham County in 1867. Ginnie and Lucie took John King's diary with them to their new home. Mrs. Nisewanger not only now operated the toll in Tenth Legion on a more southern portion of the Valley Pike, but also became Postmaster of Tenth Legion in 1868. Two of her daughters, Emma Virginia, also known as Ginnie and Lucinda E., also known as Lucie got married in Rockingham County just two days apart. Emma Virginia married James D. Hillyard on March 20, 1870 and Lucinda E. married Jacob Pickering on March 22, 1870.[112] Both James and Emma Virginia were twenty-four years old. Jacob Pickering was twenty-one years old and Lucinda was twenty-two years of age at the time of their wedding. On the 1870 U. S Census, taken July 29, Mrs. Nisewanger, age sixty-five, Sarah Kate, Lucie and her new husband, Jacob Pickering, were shown as residing together in Tenth Legion.[113]Although no occupation was shown for Sarah Kate, now twenty-eight years old, the Pickerings were both listed as farm workers. While living in Rockingham County, Lucinda and Jacob Pickering had three children: Arthur M. born in March of 1871, Pearl Estelle born October 16, 1878, Cornelia born in 1879, and Walter born February 1, 1881.[114] By 1900, the Pickerings had moved to Cohocton in Steuben County, southwestern New York, and purchased a farm.[115] Three of their children, Arthur, Pearle, and Walter, continued to reside with them with the sons working the farm with their father. Two years later, after almost thirty-two years of marriage, Lucie E. (Nisewanger) Pickering died on March 9, 1902 and was buried in Clearview Cemetery, North Cohocton, Steuben County, New York.[116] Jacob Pickering remained in Cohocton until his death on May 24, 1925, and is buried next to his wife.[117]

The Hillyards of Rockingham County, Virginia

Perhaps because she had transcribed most of the poems in the King diary/Nisewanger album, Ginnie kept it and took it along with her other personal belongings to the home of her new husband, James D. Hillyard, also of Tenth Legion, Virginia. There is no question that Emma Virginia or Ginnie Nisewanger had possession of the John King diary and took it with her to Rockingham County when her family moved to Rockingham County, Virginia, in 1867.

James, known to his family and friends as "Jimmy," was the third child and oldest son of Frederick and Emeline Hillyard. His siblings included Mary, Elizabeth, Frederick, Martha, Emily and Julia.[118] James' parents owned considerable real estate and personal property in Rockingham County. The 1860 U.S. Census listed a value of $7,000 for their home and property and $1,500 for their personal belongings.[119] In 2017 dollars, those amounts translate to $193,988 and $41,568 .[120] James Hillyard was born September 2, 1845. Hence, by the time the Civil War began in April of 1861, James was only fifteen years old and much too young to serve. He worked on his family's farm until he reached the age of eighteen.

The Confederacy was always short of men. Its population was much smaller than that of the North. The simple fact remained that the North had a seemingly endless supply of recruits. Men just entering Northern ports were enlisted at the docks. Others were drafted. Grant knew that he could win the war by attrition. Southern units had no ready replacements for those wounded and killed in action. Over the course of the war, Confederate companies and regiments continually shrank. Some just disappeared or were consolidated with other units. Initially, the age limits for conscripting soldiers was between the age of eighteen and forty-five. The Confederate Congress wanted those already fighting to remain. Hence, they forced those who had enlisted for one year to extend their term of service to last as long as the war lasted or "for the war." In February of 1864, in anticipation of a new spring Union offensive, the Confederate Congress once again changed the age limits. Although the State of Virginia already had a reserve system, composed of boys and old men, most people believed that they would never see combat. As Jefferson Davis said earlier, "we ought not to destroy the seed corn," referring to boys.[121] However, a third Conscription Act stated that all males between seventeen and fifty years of age would be subject to military service. The belief that in Virginia the reserves, seventeen-year old boys and men over the age of forty-five, would remain in a safe haven was squelched. On April 26, 1864, a newspaper, *The Staunton Spectator*, published Orders 95 and 97 written by Brigadier John

D. Imboden, commander of the Valley District.[122] Imbodens' orders called out "the reserves of the Valley of Virginia from Shenandoah County in the north to Craig County in the south." Imboden further declared that "he would call the boys between 17 and 18 into the service immediately" but that the men over age 45 would not be called up until "times of greatest need." [123] *The Staunton Spectator*, in a May 8, 1864, article about the boys, stated that "it would seem that the 'seed corn' of this section is to be sent immediately to the mill to be ground up"...and that "the stress of circumstances which will justify the grinding of 'seed corn' must be great."[124]

However, even before Imboden issued his orders, Rockingham County had already begun to organize its reserve troops. The boy soldiers of Company A, which was probably organized from companies of the 5th and 7th Battalions of Virginia Reserves, had already been mustered into service on April 3, 1864.[125] Company A was deemed a cavalry unit, not an infantry company. These young soldiers, composed mostly of seventeen year olds with a few sixteen and eighteen years old, came from the hamlets, small towns and countryside of Rockingham County. Many, like James D. Hillyard, were the sons of farmers. Aside from its captain, George Chrisman, who was from west-central Rockingham County, and its first lieutenant, William McCue, all of Company A's officers were only seventeen years of age.[126] The boys brought whatever weapons they could get from home including outdated flintlocks and old shotguns. Although these boys had been raised learning how to ride and hunt, they were lacking in military drilling and procedures. Company A was known as the Boy Company. Because so many of the young men reported for service riding white horses, the company also was known as the "White Horse Cavalry." The Confederacy did not provide horses for its cavalry. Hence, each trooper had to bring his own mount from home. No doubt, some of those mounts were farm horses.

The name, James Hillyard, along with those of Captain George Chrisman, three lieutenants, five sergeants, four corporals and seventy-three privates, appears of the rolls of Colonel D. H. Lee Martz, for Company A, 3rd Battalion Virginia Reserves.[127] James or "Jimmy" as he liked to be called, was a bit older than most of the boys, but he was still just eighteen years old when he was mustered in April 3, 1863. Jimmy had an ambrotype portrait taken probably soon after he entered Confederate service. With a solemn expression on his face and a bandanna around his neck, Jimmy seems ready for action. He is holding an old flintlock rifle in his right hand and a large Bowie knife in his left. The boys later replaced their out-of-date flintlocks and shotguns with issued .69 caliber Mississippi muskets and captured Union weapons, including the revolvers that were needed for mounted close quarter fighting.[128]

After minimal training by Captain Chrisman, Brigadier General John Imboden ordered the Boy Company to report to him at his camp on the Grassy Dale plantation of Peter Roller south of Mount Crawford, Virginia, on the Valley Pike (present day Route 11).[129] The White Horse Cavalry was added to Imboden's cavalry command , which consisted of the 18th Virginia Cavalry under his brother, Colonel George Imboden, the Partisan Rangers, commanded by Captain Hanse McNeill, the 41st Battalion of Virginia Cavalry under Colonel Robert White, the 62nd Virginia Mounted Infantry led by Colonel George H. Smith, and Captain John McClanahan's Battery of Horse Artillery. By May 2, 1864, Imboden also had Major Harry Gilmor's Battalion of Maryland Cavalry and Major Sturgis Davis' Battalion of Maryland Cavalry and Captain J. H. Bartlett's Valley District Signal Corps. Captain Chrisman's Boy Company was placed under the direct command of Major Davis. Altogether, including about one-thousand militiamen and the reserve units of boys and old men, General Imboden had approximately three-thousand effectives. He had good reason calling up and adding Chrisman's Boy Company and Harnsberger's Old Man Company to his command. With a vastly smaller force than his enemy, Imboden's job was to check Union Army advances up the Shenandoah Valley. In May of 1864, his immediate assignment was to unite with Confederate General Breckenridge who had been ordered to march from southwest Virginia and join Imboden's force as its commander. The combined Confederate force would greet Union General Franz Sigel who with a force of 9,000, consisting mostly of the 1st Infantry and 1st Cavalry Divisions and five artillery batteries, was down the Valley Turnpike and threatened to take Staunton and Charlottesville and to destroy their railroad depots and supply storehouses.[130] Every Confederate soldier available was needed to meet this home front crisis.

While camped just north of New Market near Rude's Hill, General Imboden learned of his adversary's ploy to send some three hundred 1st New York Union cavalrymen under Colonel Boyd south down the Luray Valley and then through the New Market/Luray Gap.[131] In response, Imboden set a trap to snare them by sending out the 18th and 23rd Virginia Cavalry and Chrisman's Boy Company. While part of the Confederate force met them head on and held them, the other portion of troopers got around behind the Union cavalry and prevented their retreat. The fight at New Market Gap was a total Confederate rout.

The editor of the Harrisonburg newspaper, *The Rockingham Register*, rode with the Confederates to view the action firsthand at and near New Market, Virginia. The engagement of May 13, culminating in the Battle of New Market on May 15, was a Confederate victory. The editor, John Wartmann, later wrote about the part played by Chrisman's Boy Company:

> Some decided success had attended our arms in the movements of cavalry on Friday [May 13, 1864] evening and Saturday morning, Gen. Imboden outgeneraling and entrapping the Yankees, and taking a number of prisoners, with their horses, trappings, &c., Capt. Chrisman's Company of "Rockingham Reserves" themselves flashing their maiden swords in the capture of some 17 or more Federal prisoners.[131]

Company A and their comrades had met the veterans of Union cavalry in the skirmish at New Market Gap and did well. This engagement was the Boy Company's initiation to combat or "baptism by fire" and they performed bravely. The fight at New Market was not only their first taste of battle; it was also their first taste of victory. One Union cavalry later related that the fight at New Market Gap cost the Union dearly and that "about one hundred men of the First New York, nearly half the number engaged, were either killed or captured."[132] After the skirmish of May 13, Chrisman's Boy Company was ordered to the rear to camp on and near the site of the Bethlehem Stone Church on the western side of the Valley Pike in Tenth Legion, about six miles southwest of New Market. About three miles below them on the Valley Pike, a Confederate force commanded by General John Breckenridge with about 4,200 infantry, including the V.M.I. cadets picked up in Lexington, had arrived in Lacey Springs on May 14. From their campsite on the grounds of the church, in the early morning of May 15, the boys of Company A watched the V.M.I. cadets march past them northward on the Valley Pike. Apparently unscathed by the fight at the New Market Gap, Private Jimmy Hillyard watched them go by and made some comments:

> One of the soldiers camped on the church grounds, Private James D. Hillyard of Capt. George Chrisman's Boy Company, Co. A, 3rd Battalion, Virginia Mounted Reserves, recalled how he and his fellow soldiers teased the young cadets of the Virginia Military Institute as they marched past Bethlehem Church. Hillyard and his companions shouted "Where did you leave your mother?" and other remarks at the passing cadets. The boys never returned a word, Hillyard recalled but stepped along in silence toward their fate in the battle of New Market.[133]

It is ironic that Jimmy Hillyard, still only eighteen years old himself, would taut the V.M.I. cadets, some of whom just a bit younger than himself. Maybe Jimmy felt himself to be superior because his band of boys had already been baptized by fire.

With a charge by the two-hundred and sixty-one cadets of V.M.I. and the eclectic band of soldiers assembled by Imboden and Breckenridge and hard fighting by all, the relatively small Confederate force defeated the Union army of General Franz Sigel at the Battle of New Market on May 15, 1864, and sent them surrying back down, i.e., north, the Valley Pike beyond Cedar Creek.

Although the skirmish with the 21st New York Cavalry was James Hillyard's and his comrades first fight, it would not be long before they would comfront their enemy again. Chrismans' boys, along with Captain Henry Harnsberger's Old Man Company, had been assigned to Captain Thomas Sturgis Davis's command of some fifty Baltimoreans.[134] All of these units were led by General Imboden who was now seeking help from Brigadier General William E. "Grumble" Jones to meet the advance of a new Union general, David Hunter. Hunter was marching south with a large army to once again attempt to take Staunton. Once again, Imboden wanted to slow the Union advance and awaited General Jones's arrival. The Confederates set up "a cheerless camp a mile south of Mount Meridian on the hill of Samuel Crawford's Bonnie Doon estate."[135] On the morning of June 5, 1864, a strong Union cavalry force attacked General Imboden, who was leading the 18th Virginia Cavalry, and became trapped in the fenced lane that led up to Bonnie Doon. Some of the Confederate troopers, along with General Imboden, rode horses that were jumpers. These Confederates escaped the Union onslaught by bounding over a board fence in the rear of the estate. General Imboden came very close to being captured. However, the Confederate cavalrymen whose horses could not make the jump were momentarily trapped in a cross fire. The 1st New York Cavalry Lincoln and 21st New York Cavalry were both threatening the startled Confederates. The Union cavalry "would have destroyed the regiment (18th Virginia) entirely had it not been for the timely arrival of reinforcements" from the Davis's Maryland Battalion, which included Captain Harnbergers and Chrisman's companies.[136] By this time, the 23rd Virginia Cavalry had also mounted up and rode towards the sounds of battle. The Old Man and the Boy Companies charged headlong into the 21st New York down the East Road perpendicular to Crawford's lane and sent them reeling. The 23rd Virginia supported them and the 18th Virginia got out of its trapped position with fire coming from three sides and reformed. The tough fight at Bonnie Doon was soon over and was a decidedly Confederate victory. For its part, "the quick and decisive action of the Boy Company and the Old Man Company was crucial in the fighting of the morning."[137] The Boy Company had now won two significant cavalry skirmishes. Unfortunately, they took a number of casualties. Even worse, the next day, June 5, Generals Imboden and Jones were soundly defeated at the Battle of Piedmont by an overwhelming force. In addition to those killed in action and wounded, the Confederates also had 1,500 men taken as prisoners. In the action, Brigadier General "Grumble" Jones was killed leading his men. General Hunter took Lynchburg and would soon take Staunton.

Although no official records of the casualties incurred by the Boy Company in the fights at New Market Gap and Bonnie Doon were given at the time, years later Captain George Chrisman provided information in 1908 to the Harrisonburg newspaper, *The Daily News*. He recalled that he had only forty-five men under his command when the action took place at Bonnie Doon on June 3, 1864.[138] This figure implies that twenty-nine enlisted men were lost in the prior skirmish at New Market for one reason or another. Those reasons would include men wounded and killed in action, men who became ill and had to return home, men who lost their horses in battle, men who deserted and men who may have been detailed to another unit.[139] Chrisman also said that his company lost an additional thirty troopers, either killed or wounded, along the East Road at Bonnie Doon. In other words, he had only fifteen boys who left the field at Bonnie Doon uninjured. After the fight, Chrisman stated that "the valor of the boys spread through the Valley."[140]

Although we know with certainty that James "Jimmy" Hilliard fought with his comrades at New Market Gap and at Bonnie Doon, it is not known if he was among those wounded at Bonnie Doon. Like many other Virginia cavalry companies and regiments, muster rolls were simply not kept. If Jimmy Hilliard was among those wounded at Bonnie Doon, the injury must have been minor because records show that he was with Company A later in 1864.

Chrisman's Boy Company continued skirmishing with Union cavalry in the Shenandoah Valley. On June 20, there was a bitter encounter at Buford's Gap again with the 21st New York Cavalry and with the 34th Mounted Ohio Infantry. Private George Sellers of Chrisman's Boy Company later recalled that "the fight at Buford's Gap was the hardest combat he took part in during the war."[141] They eventfully joined General Jubal Early briefly as he charged north up the Valley on his way to threaten Maryland and Washington, D.C. However, instead of going with him, the boys of Chrisman's Company were given a thirty-day furlough to go to their homes in Rockingham County and recuperate after their arduous fighting up and down the Shenandoah Valley. The Boy Company "...had ridden over four-hundred and fifty miles" in six weeks and "... had an unreported number of casualties due to combat and fatigue."[142]

In August of 1864, probably the worst order that cavalrymen could possibly receive was given to them. The boys who remained healthy enough to render further service were ordered to Camp Lee in Richmond. Those who were over eighteen years of age and who still had mounts, could join other cavalry units. Four joined either Mosby's Rangers or McNeill's Partisan Rangers while fourteen enlisted with the 6th, 7th, 10th, 11th or 12th Virginia cavalry regiments. Those who were without horses or could not get into a cavalry regiment were stuck and forced to go east away from their homes in the Valley. Jimmy Hilliard, who would turn age nineteen on September, was one of those young men who went to Richmond. Initially, James Hilliard and his fellow soldiers were assigned as guards at Libby Prison in Richmond. In the fall of 1864, members of the Boy Company "along with older reserves from the Shenandoah Valley, began to strengthen breastworks and guarded artillery batteries along one of the most volatile sections of forts and trenchworks around the Confederate capitol."[143] The Boy Company was one of five companies that made up the 3rd Battalion Virginia Reserves, and a part of a brigade under Brigadier General Seth M. Barton. Captain D. C. Stith inspected the trenches of Barton's Brigade on December 24, 1864, for strength and for weaponry, clothing, number of tents and amount of cooking kettles and mess cans.[144] The 3rd Battalion had the highest number of men AWOL and their clothing and equipment was deficient. Perhaps, as a result of this inspection, Private Jimmy Hilliard was issued additional clothing in December of 1864. By January of 1865, what remained of the Boy Company was stationed at Battery Fields and Fort Johnson.[145] The trenches that stretched from Richmond to Petersburg were a horrible place to live. Living conditions were deplorable. Food and water were strictly rationed. Disease and illness was rampant. The number of desertions increased every day. According to his Virginia Confederate pension application, James Hilliard left the trenches during January of 1865 due to "typhoid fever" and presumably returned home to Rockingham County to recover.[146] He never returned to his unit.

The siege of Petersburg and Richmond would, of course, continue until Union forces broke through the Confederate lines on April 2, 1865. As Heatwole notes, "when Richmond fell the remaining members of the Boy Company who were still in the lines either scattered, or were captured by Union forces."[147] In fact, only two members of the original Boy Company were present at Lee's surrender, Joseph Altaffer and John W. Meyerhoeffer. Both of these troopers had enlisted with the 12th Virginia Cavalry prior to the order which sent the others to Richmond in August of 1864.[148]

After the Civil War, James returned to work on his parent's farm in Tenth Legion. He was still very young, only nineteen years old. About five years later, he married Emma Virginia Nisewanger, also of Tenth Legion, on March 20, 1870. Emma, also called Virginia or Ginnie, was the young lady who took ownership of the John King diary. As it were, the couple would not remain in Virginia long after their marriage. By the time the 1870 U.S. Census was taken in Illinois on their farm July 12, Jimmy and Emma Virginia were residing in the small township of Mount Hope in McLean County.[149] Perhaps Jimmy no longer wished to work on his father's farm and wanted one of his own. In any case, their first child, a son named Earnest A. Hillyard, was born in Bloomington, McLean County, Illinois, on Christmas Eve, 1870. The Hillyards spent four years living in the state of Illinois. Seemingly dissatisfied with their lives there and perhaps homesick, the Hillyards returned home to Rockingham County. Their second son, Elmer E. Hillyard, was born at Long Meadows in Rockingham County on January 16, 1873.[150] Jimmy Hillyard went back into farming and bought his own farm in the Plains District of Rockingham County. By 1910, he reported to the census taker that he owned a farm free of any mortgage.[151] In addition to farming, he learned the carpentry trade. Perhaps following the example of his mother-in-law, Mrs. Lucinda Nisewanger, and his sister-in-law, Sarah Nisewanger, who both served as postmasters in Tenth Legion, Jimmy Hilliard obtained the position of postmaster as well. From his official appointment date of January 13, 1891, until Solomon B. Spitzer took over on May 21, 1895, Jimmy was postmaster of Mayland, Virginia.[152]

After the Civil War, he returned to the church where he and some of his comrades had badgered V.M.I. cadets marching to battle during May of 1864, and became a deacon of Bethlehem Stone Church in Tenth Legion.[153] Built in 1844 by Jacob Martz, the old church suffered quite of bit of damage during the Civil War on September 24, 1864, when Union General Sheridan's artillery shells hit the roof and destroyed the rear gable as well as shattering the doors and interior.[154] Although numerous repairs were done over the years since the war, a major restoration effort was initiated in 2008. Today, the Bethlehem Stone Church sits in a rural countryside in pristine condition and is available for public use.

On April 14, 1920, at the age of seventy-four years, Mrs. James D. Hillyard, also known as Emma Virginia (Nisewanger) Hillyard preceded her husband in death. She was buried in the Linville Creek Church of the Brethren Cemetery in Broadway, Virginia. She had obtained John King's diary during the Civil War and had kept it all those years since. "Ginnie" as she called herself and her sister, Lucinda, used the remaining blank pages to transcribe their favorite poems and to record the names of two Confederate soldiers, Privates John Cadwallader and John W. Blake. In addition, the sisters allowed a third Confederate soldier, Jacob A. Helms, to sketch a self-portrait in King's diary. To Ginnie, once it was altered, the book became her album or scrapbook and she probably kept it more as a keepsake than for its historical value as a Civil War diary. At some point, Ginnie probably showed the diary to her husband, Jimmy. Perhaps he even read it. In any case, at her death, the King diary/Nisewanger scrapbook was in the possession of Ginnie's husband, Jimmy Hillyard.

In the Circuit Court of Rockingham County, on February 10, 1927, Jimmy filed an application for a Confederate pension from the state of Virginia and gave his address as Broadway, Virginia, R.F.D. 1. At that time, Jimmy was eighty-one years old and reported an annual income of $200 and real estate valued at $835.[155] He alleged partial disability due to "age and chronic bronchitis." It is not known why he waited so long to file for a Civil War pension. To qualify for a Virginia Confederate pension, the veteran had to provide statements from two fellow soldiers who served with him. Jimmy Hilliard chose Jacob B. Sellers and W. H. Neff, each of whom provided the necessary documents. Jimmy's pension was approved. However, compared to Union Federal pensions and other Southern pensions, the state of Virginia paid very little. Initial Virginia pension amounts were from $10 to $60 annually depending upon the nature of a veteran's disability, but the average was only $23.30 per year.[156] In contrast, pension payments for Union soldiers averaged $100 annually while those of other Southern states averaged $47.24 per annum.[158]

Because Jimmy Hillyard was now a widow, by 1930, he had moved in with his son, Elmer E., his daughter-in-law, Katie, and his granddaughter, Hazel R. Hillyard. His personal belongings, including photographs and John King's diary, no doubt went with him. Jimmy was now eighty-four years old and was no longer able to farm or to work as a carpenter. However, he was able to attend various Confederate reunions in the area. In John Heatwole's book, "Chrisman's Boy Company," Jimmy is shown in a photograph taken at the 1933 Memorial Day Reunion held in Harrisonburg, Virginia.[159] Nine veterans attended the reunion, but of those nine, only two were veterans of the Boy Company. Sadly, just five years later on October 21, 1938, James "Jimmy" D. Hillard died at the age of ninety-three years of atherosclerosis. As were many members of the Hillyard family, he was buried at the Linville Creek Church of the Brethren Cemetery. An inscription on his tombstone reads:

> Their foils are past, their work is done
> They fought the fight-the victory won.[160]

Jimmy Hilliard's oldest son, Ernest, married Martha "Mattie" Ellen Lohr on October 31, 1895, in Rockingham County, Virginia. Mattie was born August 11, 1870, just about four months before her husband. As shown on the 1910 U.S. Census, Ernest and Mattie has a son, Carroll M., and a daughter, Charlotte V., and lived in the Mayland area of Rockingham County.[161] Earnest not only owned a farm free of a mortgage, but he also owned a local grocery store where his son, Carroll, worked for some time as a salesman. This Hillyard family must have done well financially since they were later able to hire a servant, Kittie Galiday.[162] Carroll Hillyard married Grace Mabel Kline and by 1940 was working as a poultry dealer in Rockingham County.[163] Carroll' s sister, Charlotte, completed three of college and obtained her teaching certificate. She was employed as a teacher in the public schools. Apparently, neither Carroll nor Charlotte had any children.

Mattie Hillyard preceded Earnest in death on April 7, 1932. Earnest died on November 22, 1942 of a cardiac condition, and both are buried in the Linville Creek Cemetery.[164] Earnest and Mattie's only son, Carroll, also from Mayland, died in 1957 and his wife, the former Grace Mabel Kline, did not die until 1996. Both are buried in the Bethel Church of the Brethren Cemetery in Mayland, Virginia.[165]

Following the family tradition set by his grandfather and father, Elmer Elsworth Hillyard, Jimmy's other son, spent his entire life farming in the Plains District of Rockingham County. A descendant of the Hillyard family mentioned to the author that Elmer was given the middle name "Elsworth" as a token of respect paid to the memory of Union Colonel Elmer E. Elsworth, a friend of Abraham Lincoln and the first Federal officer killed in the Civil War on May 24, 1861.[166] In any case, Elmer E. Hillyard married Catherine "Katie" Zigler on October 22, 1902, in Rockingham County, Virginia.[167] The couple set up housekeeping in Broadway, Virginia. Elmer had only a seventh-grade education, but he knew how to operate a successful farming business. Elmer and Katie had two sons and a daughter. Elmer lived until the age of seventy-seven years when he died of heart failure. He is also buried at Linville Creek Church.

Elmer and Catherine's first child, James Frank Hillyard was born April 16, 1904, and married Reba I. Miller. They apparently had no children. James Frank Hillyard, known better as J. Frank taught school all his life and later became a school principle. J. Frank died April 13, 1977 of gastrointestinal problems and is also buried at Linville Creek Church. The J. Frank Hillyard Middle School in Broadway was named in his honor.

The second son of Elmer and Katie Hillyard, Isaac A. Hillyard was born April 25, 1908 at Broadway. Isaac married Bonnie Virginia Neff from Ohio

joke" in the newspaper which had a circulation of almost one-thousand readers.[26] Principal King was outraged and took immediate action, action that may have been too harsh. He "ordered the publication of the Polytechnic Bulletin indefinitely suspended."[27] While they all denied any hand in the matter, the entire editorial staff, treasurer and secretary found themselves out of work. Apparently, the guilty party was never discovered.

World War I does not seem to have had a significant impact on the operations of the Baltimore Polytechnic Institute. However, Principal King was away from the school on military duty for some time. William H. Hall served as Acting Principal during this time. However, Lieutenant William R. King, U.S.N., was "present by virtue of special leave of absence from a Northern Federal rendezvous to give parting advice to 'his boys' at the graduation ceremony the evening of June 13, 1917."[28] *The Sun* newspaper reported that "… with fourteen of its 128 members in the uniforms of United States military service, the graduating class of the Polytechnic Institute last night received its diplomas from Mayor Preston at the thirty-first annual commencement of the institute, held at the Lyric."[29] The main speaker for the graduation was Alfred S. Loizeaux, electrical engineer for the Consolidated Gas Electric Light and Power Company. Mr. Loizeaux gave an encouraging and gracious speech to the graduates and offered high praise for other BPI graduates who have been employed with his company. He said that "those boys have a made a remarkable showing and compare favorably with graduates of other institutions and even with college graduates in their understanding of the fundamentals of engineering."[30] Later, Acting Principal Hall "read his report, in which was shown that of the 128 graduates 28 have signified their intention of entering universities, principally Johns Hopkins, Lehigh and Cornell; that 20 were scheduled for employment in local public service corporations, that three had been selected for the training school of the Westinghouse Electric and Manufacturing Company at Pittsburgh, and that 14 had enlisted in the services of their country."[31] Overall, this was a very special graduating class of young men.

Principal King had accomplished a great deal in strengthening the curriculum, increasing the number of pupils in the various grades and perhaps, most importantly, in preparing the students for their careers, whether they went directly to employment or went on to enter a college or university. There were only thirteen boys in the ninth grade who graduated in 1900. In 1908, the number of graduates rose to fifty-four young men. Amazingly, under the guidance of William R. King, that number would more than double to one-hundred and twenty-eight graduates in 1917.

While some may have called him a stern disciplinarian, Principal King led the school in the early days of the twentieth-century to become a very professional technical school in the City of Baltimore.

The only major change that Principal King did not accomplish in his tenure of twenty-two years was the inability to convert the Baltimore Polytechnic Institute into a four-year, degree conferring technical college. As early as 1908, he stated that "to have an advanced school such as would be competent to teach all the higher technical branches and confer degrees which would carry weight it would not be necessary to build and maintain a separate institution-all that would be needed would be to add two years to the present curriculum."[32] King argued that, according to his calculations, not only would doing so reduce the cost for the students from $475 annually, but "if the courses mentioned were added to the present Polytechnic, 70 percent of those who leave our school to work would continue until they were fully trained as engineers and master mechanics."[33]

Due to health issues, William R. King resigned his position as Principal of Baltimore Polytechnic Institute after twenty-two years of service.[34] His resignation was accepted by the School Board June 17, 1921, to be effective July 1. Mr. W. A. Dehuff was named as his replacement. When a reporter asked if he rued his decision, King said that "he regretted it more than he could say, but that he realized the time had come when the great responsibility of running the school would have to be placed upon younger shoulders."[35] However, in the letter of resignation to Henry S. West, Superintendent of Schools, Lieutenant King asked if there was another way thereby he could be "relieved of the burden of principalship," but which "will nevertheless permit me to contribute further to the development of the school."[36] Although he would take a pay cut from $4,000 annually to $2,000, William R. King was appointed to a newly created position, Dean of Institution.[37] When William was promoted from principal to dean, Dr. David E. Weglein paid tribute to "Billy" King's work at the school and summarized his records by saying that "the present Baltimore Polytechnic Institute is a monument to the work of Lieutenant King, who has devoted himself exclusively to the development of this school, and his accomplishment along this line constitutes the crowning achievement of his active career."[38] Unfortunately, Dean King would only spend about eighteen months at this new post. Dean William R. King died January 13, 1923. A portion of his long obituary that appeared in *The Sun* newspaper of Baltimore read as follows:

> The funeral of Lieut. William R. King, U.S. N., retired, former dean of the Polytechnic Institute, who died yesterday morning at Franklin Square

Hospital, will take place at 3 o'clock Tuesday afternoon at Old St. Paul's Protestant Episcopal Church. The rector, the Rev. Arthur B. Kinsolving, will officiate. Burial will be in Loudon Park Cemetery. Lieutenant King had been at Franklin Square Hospital about two weeks, but he had been in ill health before resigned from the Polytechnic Institute in 1921. His death was due to a complication of diseases. He was 70 years old.

He developed the Polytechnic from a small school on Courtland street to the point at which it overflowed its walls so completely that it was necessary to house it in the present structure on North Avenue, with an average enrollment of 2,021 students.

"My boys" was the way he referred to the students who attended his school, and this term of affection found its answer in the universal esteem of thousands of men, including some of the most prominent in the community. Hundreds of messages of sympathy were sent yesterday to his home at the Anneslie Apartments.

Members of the School Board were particularly distressed yesterday when they learned of his death. Isaac S. Field, president of the School Board, said: I am deeply shocked. Lieutenant King was an extraordinary man and enjoyed the confidence of the board to the fullest extent. He was an outstanding figure as an educator and had a wonderful personality.

It must be a great comfort today to the people of the Polytechnic to remember that they did not wait until Lieutenant King's death to tell him what they thought of him. When he retired from his active work there they presented him with a portrait of himself and told him how much they loved him. He never lost interest in the institution, however, and retained active contact with it until a few days ago. The community has lost a great man.

Lieutenant King is survived by a widow, Mrs. Margaret King; a sister, Miss Florence C. King, of Hagerstown, and two brothers, John R. King, connected with the United States Custom Service in this city, and Samuel L. King, of Pittsburgh.[39]

Today, the Baltimore Polytechnic Institute remains a thriving high school of 1,647 students and is located on Falls Road and West Spring Lane in Baltimore, Maryland. The school became co-educational in 1974 and continues to specialize in preparing students for careers in math and engineering. A new wing was dedicated last year. The front hall of the school's main building is called "King Memorial Hall."[40]

X

Achievement, Loss and Fame October, 1902 to March 4, 1934

With the first Union casualty of the Civil War came the beginning of a new pension system. When the first married Union soldier died in combat, he left a wife and possibly children who needed financial assistance. When the first Union fighting man was wounded so badly that he would be unable to perform manual labor, he was due some measure of financial assistance. In fact, at the time of the Civil War, there were already veterans and widows on the pension rolls from the two other wars that the United States fought with Great Britain, namely the Revolutionary War and the War of 1812. However, the number of these ex-soldiers and widows was very small, 25,000 and 20,000 respectively, compared to the numbers that would later appear on the rolls for the Union Civil War veterans, widows and dependents.[1] The rate at which the numbers on the Civil War pension list increased was astronomical. Just one year after the end of the war in 1866, there were just a bit more than 100,000 beneficiaries.[2] By 1885, the number on the pension rolls had increased to 325,000 veterans, widows and other dependents.[3] By June 30, 1902, the number of Civil War pensioners reached its maximum. At that time, there were just under one million people on the rolls, i.e., 999,446.[4] These increases occurred because the United States, under pressure from a number of stakeholders, passed numerous acts between 1862 and 1912 to aid the veterans and their families.

On July 22, 1861, when Congress approved President Lincoln's call for a half million volunteers to fight against the Southern Confederacy, it planted the seed for a more elaborate system of army pensions. Each volunteer would receive one-hundred dollars in the event he got "wounded or disabled in the service of his country.[5] If he was killed, the money would go to his widow or to another family member. Even with this apparently simple program, claim processing was a lengthy procedure. For instance, "out of 1,651 pension applications filed before July 1862, fewer than half—721—were approved before July 1865; another 126 were approved during 1866-1875; and another 204 were approved during 1876-1885," the remaining 600 were denied, abandoned or remained pending.[6] Although this measure was not really a pension program *per se*, it heralded the beginning of a much more complex system of rules and regulations.

The first true Union army pension program came into existence on July 14, 1862, when Congress passed the an act which became known as the General Law pension system.[7] The law was well-summarized by Costa in her book entitled *Union Army Pensions and Civil War Records*:

> It provided for pensions for soldiers who had incurred permanent bodily injury or disability while in the service of the Union army after 4 March 1861 and provided for the dependents of soldiers who had died from causes that could be traced directly to injuries received or diseases contracted while in Union army service.
>
> The dollar amount that was received depended on the degree of disability, where total disability meant 'a total disability for the performance of manual labor requiring severe and continuous exertion' and provided enlisted men with a pension of $8.00 per month, an amount equivalent to 30 percent of the earnings of a skilled laborer. If the claimant had lesser disabilities, he received an amount proportionate to the degree of disabilities.[8]

A key portion of the Act stated that it applied to soldiers "who died from causes that could be traced *directly* to injuries received or diseases contracted *while in the Union army service*." Hence, if the veteran died or was disabled by injury or disease after he had been discharged, he was not eligible for this benefit. This exception later changed as the pension program became more and more complex with the enactment of new laws. However, even the July 14, 1862, Act vastly altered the Pension Bureau, which was in charge of administration of the program. Many more office clerks, designated pension agents, namely those who actually made payment to the veterans, and a large number of examining surgeons were hired to process the increasing number of claims. In addition, there developed a cottage industry of attorney representatives and claimant intermediaries who, for a fee, would assist a veteran. Some persons believed that the 1862 Act involved too much complexity. In 1862, the Commissioner of the Pension Bureau, Joseph H.

Barrett stated that "a simpler system is urgently demanded."[9] A simpler system never materialized. In fact, the pension program became more complex and more expensive. By November 15, 1862, the Pension Bureau had received 4,411 applications just from wounded veterans, under the Act of July, 1862.[10] Also, whereas the anticipated cost of Civil War soldier and sailor pensions was $7 million, the actual cost turned out to be over $8.5 million by 1865.[11] The definition of manual labor was liberalized and in 1866, Congress increased the monthly amount for total disability for *any manual labor* from $8.00 to $20.00.[12]

The pension program for Union Civil War veterans became a massive entitlement program and was difficult to manage. A number of stakeholders facilitated the growth of the numbers of pensioners and added to the cost of the system. Some of these stakeholders included veteran groups such the Grand Army of the Republic, private interests such as claimant attorneys and claimant intermediaries, policy makers including U.S. Presidents, numerous congressmen, congressional committees and the government bureaucracies who served veterans. All of these persons and groups attempted to influence the major bills regarding Civil War pensions that were introduced in Congress over the next forty-five years.

After the Act of 1862, the next bill of importance that received both Congressional and Presidential approval was the Consolidation Act of 1873. With this Act, the commissioner of pensions was given the power to establish rates for disabilities not specified by the prior law.[13] For example, instead of receiving the $24.00 monthly payment a totally disabled veteran received, a man with the loss of sight in one eye would get a lesser amount of $12.00. The next important and costly bill that passed was known as the Arrears Act of 1879 which "held that those Civil War veterans or their survivors who never filed for a service or disability pension were still entitled to do so, with a retroactive date at the time of the soldier's discharge."[14] President Rutherford B. Hayes, a Republican and former Brevet Brigadier General, signed the bill into law on January 25, 1879. The passage of this legislation resulted in an enormous increase in the number of applications and a corresponding jump in expenditures. The next significant pension legislation that came before Congress in 1887 would grant disability to all Union veterans whether or not that disability was service connected or not. However, when the bill came to President Grover Cleveland's desk for signature, the first Democratic President elected after the Civil War, he vetoed it on February 11. President Cleveland said that it was too expensive and too difficult to implement. The Grand Army of the Republic was enraged and vowed to make veterans' pensions a major issue in the next presidential election when Cleveland attempted to secure a second term. The Republican Party, with the support of the G.A.R., ran Benjamin Harrison of Indiana, another former Civil War Brevet Brigadier General, against Cleveland in the election of 1888. Although Cleveland won the popular vote, Harrison won the crucial swing states of Indiana and New York by a margin of only 2,300 and 13,000 votes, respectively, and won the election. These two states also had 38,000 and 45,000 Union veterans on the pension rolls.[15] Thus, the Republican Party and the Grand Army of the Republic were victorious. On June 27, 1890, the most comprehensive, most liberal, and most expensive pension reform act in the history of the United States was written and signed into law by President Harrison. The Dependent and Disability Act of 1890 "marked the beginning of a universal disability and old age pension program." The new provision included a new definition of disability read as follows:

> That all persons who served ninety days or more in the military or naval service of the United States during the late war of Rebellion and who have been honorably discharged therefrom, and who are now or who may hereafter be suffering from a mental or physical disability of a permanent character, not the result of their own habits, which incapacitates them from the performance of manual labor (U.S. Statutes at Large, 1890, 182).[16]

Just meeting this very liberal provision qualified the veteran for a pension of $6.00 to $12.00 monthly. If the veteran died from any cause, his dependents also met the requirement for a pension. The Act of 1890 was far different from any one that had preceded it because it did not necessitate that the disability be related to military service. However, veterans who could trace their disability to their wartime service received far more for the same disability than those who could not.[17] Applications and Federal spending soared after passage of the 1890 Act. The number of veterans receiving Civil War pensions "almost doubled between 1889 and 1892.[18] Federal government spending on the pension program mushroomed to a shocking 41.5 percent of the budget by 1893.[19] However, the Dependent and Disability Act of 1890 did not signify the end of the government's generosity to Union veterans.

The hero of San Juan Hill in the Spanish-American War, a former lieutenant colonel and a Republican, Theodore Roosevelt was elected as President and served from 1901 to 1909. Roosevelt was also a strong advocate of veterans' pensions and especially for the growing number of aged ex-soldiers and sailors. Thus, in 1904, he issued Executive Order 78, "which authorized the

Pension Bureau to grant pensions on the basis of age."[20] This order was more fully developed when Congress passed a bill on February 6, 1907, called the Service and Age Pension. This bill was signed into law by Roosevelt and increased the amount the veteran received based upon his age.

The U.S. Pension Bureau had to hire more employees to handle the above mentioned changes to the pension program. A large government bureaucracy developed for the administration of program benefits. By the end of the 1881 fiscal year, there were only 784 pension office employees.[21] That number would soon increase to 1,500 workers. In addition, the Pension Bureau required a bigger building to house the growing number of employees. The building, called the "Old Kirkwood House" at 12th Street, NW and Pennsylvania Avenue, was soon outgrown and a new building was desperately needed. Between November 2, 1882, when construction began and September 3, 1887, when it was complete, the new Pension Bureau building which covered the entire block bounded by 4th and 5th Streets, NW, and F and G Streets, and which cost $886 million, was finished.[22] Composed of fifteen million bricks at the time it was constructed, it was "the largest brick building in the world."[23] Today, the old Pension Building at 401 F Street NW, Washington D.C., houses the National Building Museum.

In addition to the pension clerks hired to actually process the applications and physicians to conduct examinations, the Federal government hired fifty-eight designated pension agents by 1871 to make actual payments to individuals. The Pension Bureau also hired a number of Special Pension Agents to administer the large regional expenditures to states. The Special Pension Agent positions, like the pension program itself, were influenced by political preference. Veterans were given preference in the hiring of clerks for the Pension Bureau in Washington, D.C. and also for appointments to the position of regional pension agents. The President of the United States, of course, selected both the Commissioner of the Pension Bureau and the Special Pension Agents. He was under pressure from a number of Congressmen to pick a representative from the Congressman's home state. Theodore Roosevelt, who took office in 1901, chose E. F. Ware as his Pension Commissioner. Under the domain of the Department of the Interior, Commissioner Ware's bureau was variously referred to as the United States Pension Office, the Pension Bureau or the Bureau of Pensions. The President, however, selected the Special Pension Agents and with the death of S. L. Willson, there was an opening for one of the special agent positions.

In a special dispatch sent to Baltimore's newspaper, *The Sun,* from Washington, D.C., the evening of October 3, 1902, the White House reported the following:

> President Roosevelt today announced the appointment of Capt. John R. King, of Baltimore, as special pensions agent. The President believes that the appointment will be satisfactory. The President did not care to wait any longer in considering the appointment, it is understood, in view of possible complications, and so he acted promptly.[24]

The article went on to mention that "the appointment is regarded as a great personal triumph for Senator McComas, who, it is said, antagonized the Senators from New York and West Virginia, all of them having candidates" and that "Corporal Tanner was also a strong aspirant, with backing from all over the country."[25] Louis Emory McComas was a Republican U.S. Senator from Maryland (b. 1846 d. 1907) who served in the 56th, 57th and 58th Congress from 1899 to 1904.[26] In addition to Senator McComas, Captain King had the endorsement of William T. Dixon, John B. Ramsay, Captain R. M. Spedden, Reverend John Timothy Stone and the Grand Army of the Republic.[27] All of these endorsers were from Baltimore and knew John R. King very well. William T. Dixon was a trustee of Johns Hopkins Hospital and University. John B. Ramsay was a leading financier in Baltimore. Captain R. M. Spedden was the owner of a shipbuilding company located in the Fells Point neighborhood at 1707 Thames Street.[28] Reverend John Timothy Stone was pastor of the church John attended, Brown Presbyterian. John King's boss at the U.S. Custom House in Baltimore was pleased with his promotion, but said that "he regretted very much to lose his services."[29]

The following day, October 5, 1902, *The Sun* ran another article which highly praised Captain King and included a nice photograph of him in formal civilian attire. The fairly brief second article read as follows:

> Capt. John R. King head of the marine department in the Baltimore Custom House, who has been appointed special pension agent for the district embracing Maryland, the District of Columbia, Virginia, West Virginia, Tennessee and Kentucky, at a salary of $4,000 a year, was the recipient of numerous congratulations and the opinion found general expression that the President had made an excellent selection. Captain King not only stands high in Grand Army circles, but is held to have made a commendable record at the custom house. He is considered a most capable official and has an enviable reputation for personal integrity. Those who know him best are most positive in the assertion that the promotion is well merited, and that Captain King will bring to the discharge of his new duties conspicuous ability and earnest zeal.[30]

Although the article does not mention it, Captain King was also responsible for pension payments to all of the Union veterans residing in foreign countries.

In his appointments of Special Pension Agents, President Roosevelt was interested in men who were veterans, who had worked in a noteworthy post-war civilian position and who belonged to the Grand Army of the Republic. In a later letter to Senator Henry E. Burnham of New Hampshire regarding the possible nomination of Osmon Baker Warren for Pension Agent in the Northeast states, the President said "I understand he is now Deputy Department Commander...and that his services in the war and his record in civil life since would make it peculiarly appropriate to give him this position."[31] By the time of his appointment, John R. King had not only a proven military record as First Sergeant, then First Lieutenant in the 6th Maryland Infantry, but he also had served as G.A.R. Department Commander for Maryland. In addition, he was a disabled hero of the war, having been wounded three times in battle. President Roosevelt found him an ideal candidate for the position of Special Pension Agent in the Bureau of Pensions. The U. S. Senate confirmed John's nomination by President Roosevelt.

The Pension Bureau assigned John to both the Mid-Atlantic States region and to foreign countries. John's responsibility was to insure that all Union veterans, widows and orphans received their proper benefits. His job was to manage and to distribute an enormous amount of Federal funds. Annual disbursements just in the Baltimore area amounted to $1.5 million in 1902.[32] In terms of his new annual salary, his promotion was substantial. Previously, he had earned $1,200 a year at the Custom House; now he would make $4,000 annually. In 2017 dollars, his annual salary jumped from $34,486 to $119,554.[33] However, John's transportation and housing costs would increase since he was now stationed at the Pension Building on F Street in Washington, D. C. instead of working at the Baltimore Custom House. Even at the turn of the century, the Nation's Capital was an expensive place to live. The King farm, named "Waterloo," was about twenty-six miles from Washington, D. C. John King took the train to Washington, D.C. from railroad station at Jessup, Maryland. Perhaps because of the commuting distance and due to Johns' new responsibilities at the Pension Bureau, Annie decided to sell the forty-one acre farm she had inherited from her maternal grandfather, David Hays. In any case, just one day before President Theodore Roosevelt announced his selection of John King, Annie L. King signed a deed that sold her estate "Waterloo" to Estelle B. Storm and Rosalie A. Storm for $4,000 on October 2, 1902.[34] Annie also had to pay a five-percent brokerage fee so she netted $3,800. The Kings saved this money for a few years while they rented a home at 25 West Mt. Royal Avenue in the City of Baltimore.[35] Then just less than two months after President Roosevelt announced John's reappointment, on November 28, 1908, they bought the modest house they had rented at 25 West Mt. Royal Avenue for $5,000.[36] The front of their row house measured only just under fifteen feet, but the land was very deep, measuring ninety feet in depth. Situated in the north part of Baltimore City just east of N. Howard Street, the Kings had an excellent location. The King home in Baltimore was demolished years ago. The site now is part of the University of Baltimore Student Center.

President Theodore Roosevelt had issued a dispatch reappointing Captain John R. King as Special Pension Agent and the news appeared in the October 6, 1906, issue of the *Baltimore Sun*.[37] Although his current term would not expire for several more weeks, the President wished to inform the public that Captain King would serve another four-year term. About one year later, John decided that "it would facilitate business and simplify matters to have a single depository (in Baltimore instead of Washington, D.C. and New York) and he deposited the whole of his funds in Baltimore."[38] Of course, this maneuver was financially favorable for the City of Baltimore. After this change was made by Special Pension Agent King, "Baltimore has had deposits, and his disbursements amounting to $10 million annually" made from that city.[39] In 1907, John was serving 55,000 veterans, widows and orphans in his region which included the five states mentioned plus the District of Columbia as well as 5,000 other pensioners living overseas.[40] In the bank in Baltimore, he had $2.5 million on deposit.[41]

In April of 1908, a new law went into effect which increased the monthly pension amounts for widows and children. "All widows and children would now receive $12 monthly up from $8, and if they were not required to complete a new application, they should be paid the new amount on June 4, 1908."[42] In 2017 dollars, the increase was from $221.57 to $332.35 per month, a substantial difference.[43] In 1909, William Howard Taft, a Republican, began his presidential term. Like his predecessor, he nominated Captain John R. King for the position of U.S. Special Pension Agent for the same region he served previously. On February 1, 1911, the *Baltimore American* newspaper reported that John King had been confirmed by the U.S. Senate on January 31 as pension agent at Washington, his third term.[44] John would serve in this capacity until his four year term expired in 1915. At that time, the position of Special Pension Agent was abolished.

Just about the time John King had settled into his new assignment during his first term as pension agent, tragedy struck the King household in 1903, then again nine months later. On October 11, 1903, Mary Elizabeth (King) Adams, John's eldest daughter, and wife of Alvin Phillips Adams, died at her home at 107 Hawthorne Road, North Baltimore City.[45] She was only twenty-eight years, five months and fifteen days old. Mary died of what was once termed "consumption" and is now called pulmonary tuberculosis or TB. TB is an illness which is defined as a slow-growing bacterial infection. In the early part of the twentieth-century, tuberculosis killed one out of seven people in the United States and Europe. It was not until the 1940s that American researchers began to develop a viable treatment plan based upon new medications for this hard-to-control disease.[46] Mary Elizabeth King Adams was interred in Loudon Park Cemetery, Baltimore. After her death, Mary's husband, Alvin P. Adams, married Marie Cowell.[47] Alvin and Marie were residing at 6 E. Read Street, Baltimore, where, by 1917, he was employed as chief executive officer for Fairmont & Baltimore Coal & Coke Company.[48] They had no children. Alvin lived until 1949.

On July 14, 1904, the King's youngest daughter, Anna L., who had remained single and was living at home and who had asthma perished due to a four-day episode of pulmonary tuberculosis.[49] She was only twenty-two years, two months and eight days old. It must have been overwhelming to John and Annie to have lost one daughter, but the loss of their other daughter less than twelve months later must have been almost too much to bear. They must have had strong convictions in their Presbyterian faith in order to continue with their lives. John was now sixty years old and his wife, Annie, was fifty-three in 1904. They had no more children. As mentioned in Chapter VII, John R. King was elected as Department Commander for Maryland at the 24th Annual Encampment of the Grand Army of the Republic. Perhaps, both his further immersion into the G.A.R. and into his new position as Special Pension Agent helped to lessen the impact of the death of his two children. How he managed to maintain and even increase his activity level will never be known, but John continued to serve well in both the G.A.R. and in the Pension Bureau.

The 38th National Encampment of the G.A.R. opened Monday, August 15, 1904, in Boston. Both the Maryland G.A.R. and the Maryland Women's Relief Corps made arrangements to attend. The W.R.C. had been an auxiliary to the G.A.R. since 1883. John's wife, Annie, was a member. The *Boston Globe* newspaper, reported that "the department has a candidate for Senior Vice-Commander-in-Chief in Past Department Commander, John R. King, and will use every legitimate means to elect him."[50] The reporter went on to describe John as "one of the best-known members of the order in Maryland, ever ready to lend a helping hand."[51] In its August 19, 1904 issue, the *Baltimore Sun* ran the headline, "Blackmar Elected. Boston Man New Commander. John R. King Next in Line."[52] Thus, Wilmon W. Blackmar of

Massachusetts was chosen to lead the Grand Army of the Republic while John R. King would serve as his second-in-command. In the newspaper biography of John, it was mentioned that he "had been for many years been prominently identified with the G.A.R.," had an extensive knowledge of navigation laws due to his employment at the Custom House, "served on the Chickamauga Battlefield Commission, and on one to preserve Maryland battleflags."[53] Unfortunately, this National Encampment chose to shelve a proposal to have a reunion of both Union and Confederate Army veterans to be held in Washington, D. C.[54] The next national encampment, the 39th, would be held in Denver, Colorado, in September of 1905.

As part of this duties as Senior Vice-Commander of the G.A.R., John King traveled extensively. During June of 1905, he visited the annual encampment of the New Jersey Department which met June 23 and June 24 in Trenton. One of the newspapers covering the encampment reported the following:

> The people of Trenton have made elaborate preparations to give the veterans a big time. Tomorrow (i.e., June 23) afternoon there will be a parade, in which the local battalion of the National Guard and about 1,500 Grand Army men will participate.[55]

Scheduled to speak at the campfire held at the Taylor Opera House on the evening of the 23rd were Past Commander-in-Chief Thomas J. Stewart, of Pennsylvania; Senior Vice Commander-in-Chief John R. King; Governor Edward C. Stokes and Mayor Frank S. Katzenback, both from Trenton.[56] Friday, June 24, was apparently reserved for business meetings. It is apparent that the citizens of the Northern states took great pride in welcoming G.A.R. veterans to their cities and honoring their sacrifices.

On July 15, 1905, based upon his extensive travels to other states, Senior Vice Commander-in-Chief King wrote the following report from Washington, D.C. to Adjutant-General John E. Gilman.[57] The report is shown in its entirety.

> Comrade: In making my report as Senior Vice-Commander-in-Chief, I desire at the onset to make grateful acknowledge of the high honor conferred upon me by the comrades of the Thirty-eighth Annual Encampment. I promised then to give my best efforts to advance the interests of the order in the limited opportunities that might be presented. The exceptional honor conferred by the encampment of 1904, in selecting two of the highest officers from among the comrades living south of the Mason and Dixon's line, was a graceful compliment to the men of 1861-65, who for

many long years have held aloft the banner of our order throughout that country and in many communities where public sentiment is anything but cordial. However, that action has had the result of quickening the spirit and awaking renewed interest in comrades who were growing indifferent to their obligations of membership.

The time is passing when we can hope for a material increase in our membership, yet there are many, very many survivors of the Union armies of the Civil War who still hold aloof and fail to avail themselves of the eligibility to join the Grand Army of the Republic.

In view of the great benefit the influence of our order has been to them in the way of influencing legislation among the line of pension enactments, it is surprisingly astounding why there are so many who are willing to reap the benefits of our organized efforts, and yet remain outside of our ranks, leaving to a relatively few the burden of fighting for the rights of the old soldiers. It was not so in 1861-65. Then they were willing to get into line and take the touch of elbow and move forward in one common cause. Then it was a fight for the preservation of the best government ever devised among men. Then it was a common cause for country. Why should we not now get together and make common cause for ourselves?

It has been my pleasure to visit officially the Departments of Delaware, Maryland, the Potomac, Tennessee, and New Jersey, the first three in company with the Commander-in-Chief; and on each occasion I received the most cordial welcome from our old comrades. The encampment at Cleveland, Tenn., was an inspiration. In that sturdy section of West Tennessee I met men who, like those of my own State of Maryland in the dark days of '61, were confronted by a divided sentiment, father against son, brother against brother, kindred against kindred, but thought it best and wisest to cast their lot with those who elected to stand by Old Glory and defend the Union established by their fathers. These men of Tennessee, still true and loyal to the cause they knew was right, were enthusiastic in keeping alive the spirit of comradeship and maintaining the principles of our great order. The encampment was largely attended, the occasion being a public holiday in that beautiful mountain town. The procedures were harmonious, and good and true men were elected as officers of the ensuing year, whom it was my pleasure to install. I also met there Comrade George W. Patten, Junior Vice-Commander-in-Chief, always a favorite with his comrades of Tennessee, then as ever enthusiastic for the upbuilding of the Grand Army. By invitation I visited the convention of the Woman's Relief Corps, then in session; and the pleasant occasion and cordial reception accorded me with remain a "joy forever."

The noble women of this Department have a pleasuring custom of presenting to the high school of the town or city in which they meet a flag. Cleveland was not an exception, and the ceremony was inspiring. At the appointed time a line was formed, consisting of the women of the Relief Corps, the Grand Army of the Republic, and citizens, and headed by a splendid band of music, marched to the high school, where the presentation was made, the good women imposing upon me the pleasing duty of acting as their spokesman. The flag was received by the president of the school board in words full of patriotism; and, as Old Glory was broken from the staff, the whole assembly sang "The Star-spangled Banner." This custom of the loyal women of Tennessee, in the line of patriotic education in our public schools, is worthy of emulation by the women of other Departments.

On my return from Cleveland I paid a visit to the new National Soldiers Home at Johnson City, Tenn.; and I was pleased beyond expression with the magnificent buildings that have been erected for the care and comfort of our comrades, who, broken in health or incapacitated by reason of old age, may there pass in peace and comfort their remaining days, until the "sunset gun shall sound for them, and their colors come down."

My visit to the Department of New Jersey at Trenton, on the occasion of their Thirty-eighth Annual Encampment, was no less pleasing. This beautiful city was in holiday attire, and the decorations reminded one of the sights which greet us at National Encampments. The attendance of old soldiers was very large. Posts from all over the State came in a body. The parade on the afternoon of June 22 was an event long to be remembered, and the campfire in the Opera House at night was an inspiring occasion.

I had the pleasure of meeting at Trenton Past Commanders-in-Chief Robert B. Beath and Thomas J. Stewart, who, it seems, are never happy unless they are in the midst of their comrades of the Grand Army. Comrade James M. Schoonmaker, Chief of Staff of the Grand Army, was also there, and he was also at the encampment in Baltimore in April.

I cannot close my report without reference to the unselfish and generous act of Comrade Charles W. Hull, of Post 3, Department of Maryland. Comrade Hull is an enthusiastic Grand Army man; and, having prospered in worldly affairs, he felt that it was his duty to leave behind him a memorial of some kind that would mark his esteem of comrades of the Grand Army. After much thought he decided that a church erected to the glory of the God who "covered our heads in the day of battle," and in memory of the Grand Army of the Republic would be the most appropriate, so in the little village of Lansdowne, five miles south of Baltimore, on the line of the Baltimore & Ohio Railroad, he erected a beautiful edifice;

and in the deed of gift, in which his good wife joined him, it is stipulated that, "as long as this church stands, the second Lord's Day in May shall be observed as a memorial to the Grand Army of the Republic and in honor of the men who fought to save the Union," and over this church at every service Old Glory waves.

During the present year the Department of Maryland will place a memorial window in the east front, over the chancel, the design being a large representation of the Grand Army badge. Post No. 2, of which Comrade Hull is a member will also follow with a memorial window, as this privilege is extended to any Department or Post in the order. I trust many will avail themselves of it. Correspondence may be addressed to General R. N. Bowerman, Commander Department of Maryland, Baltimore.

This, I fancy, is the only Grand Army church in the world; and for his generous forethought and disinterested comradeship I recommend that Comrade Hull receive the thanks of the Thirty-ninth Encampment of the Grand Army of the Republic, and that a picture of this Grand Army church appear in the published journal of proceedings at that encampment.

In closing my report I wish to make acknowledgement of the very kind and partial consideration shown me by our dear Commander-in-Chief, who will go down in our history as one of the most strenuous and enthusiastic men among the great men who have been chosen to lead the hosts of the Grand Army of the Republic; and at your hands, Comrade Gilman, I have always received the most cordial consideration, for which you have my thanks.

Respectfully submitted in F., C, and L., (Fraternity, Charity and Loyalty)

John R. King
Senior Vice Commander-in-Chief to July 16, 1905.

Vice Commander-in-Chief King was displeased with the number of veterans who chose for one reason or another not to join the ranks of the Grand Army. The G.A.R. had established a special committee to study the pension program in the hope of getting more favorable laws passed. In addition, the G.A.R. lobbied Presidents and Congress tirelessly to bestow additional benefits upon all Union Civil War veterans, their widows and their orphan children. Yet, many veterans gladly accepted the higher rates paid by the government based upon more generous laws without contributing either time or money to the G.A.R. President Theodore Roosevelt had just issued Executive Order 78 in 1904 which allowed the Pension Bureau to

grant Civil War soldiers' and sailors' pensions based solely on the basis of age. By so doing, the number of beneficiaries had increased substantially from 151,211 certificates issued in 1904 to 182,207 issued in 1905, but G.A.R. membership had dropped by 13,806 comrades from 1904 to 1905, i.e., from 246,261 to 232,455.[58] Although John did not specifically address the loss of G.A.R. comrades due to death at old age, he certainly was aware of it. He did note that the "time is passing when we can hope for a matter increase in our membership." A soldier or sailor who had been eighteen years at the time of his muster into service was sixty-one years old in 1904. Between 1899 and 1900, the G.A.R. lost 11,306 comrades. The losses for the periods, 1900 to 1901, 1901 to 1902, 1902 to 1903, and 1903 to 1904 were 7,105, 5,762, 7,235 and 9,170 respectively.[59] Even if some new members were added by stronger recruiting efforts, the losses due to the death of aging comrades could not be overcome.

The church which Comrade Charles Hull built in 1903, called the Hull Memorial Christian Church or the Lansdowne Christian Church, still stands today. It was listed on the Register of Historic Places in 1977 and is the only church in the United States dedicated to the Grand Army of the Republic. Beautiful stained glass windows were donated by the Grand Army in 1905. Under the purview of a denomination called the Disciples of Christ, the church remains open on Sundays and on special occasions. It is located at 101 Clyde Avenue, Baltimore County, Maryland.

At the beginning of the Civil War, Wilmon W. Blackmar joined the 15th Pennsylvania Cavalry as a private and was eventually promoted to orderly sergeant.[60] He was later given a lieutenancy and was transferred to the veteran cavalry regiment, the 1st West Virginia (Union) under Brigadier General George Custer. Because of gallantry shown in battle, he was promoted to a captain on the field at Five Forks.[61] Captain Blackmar survived the war uninjured, serving as adjutant general of the brigade and then as provost marshal until Lee's surrender at Appomattox. After the war, Blackmar graduated from Harvard Law School and then served as Judge Advocate of Massachusetts under three different administrations.[62]

On July 17, 1905, John King received the following telegram from Adjutant General John E. Gilman from Boston. Probably in order to avoid the hot and humid District of Columbia summer, John and his wife, Annie, were spending the summer at the Mt. Holly Inn, an historical resort in the Gap of the South Mountains in Cumberland County, Pennsylvania.

> John R. King, Commander-in-Chief Grand Army of the Republic, Washington, D.C.

> General Blackmar died Sunday afternoon in Boise, Idaho. You succeed him. I await your orders; funeral details later. Shall you issue general order?

New Commander King issued a general order, but before he did so, he sent a reply:

> Gilman:
>
> Your sad announcement is received. I ask you to continue as adjutant general. Please prepare and publish full, worthy and proper statement to comrades and public as to General Blackmar for me and in my name. Take all necessary measures for funeral. Advise me what you do. Later I will prepare and send you formal general order assuming command.

Then, Commander-in-Chief King received the following telegram from Past Commander-in-Chief Torrance at Minneapolis:

> May you have divine wisdom to discharge the great duties so unexpectedly committed to your keeping.[63]

The former Commander-in-Chief of the G.A.R., General Blackmar had a history of nephritis that he may not have mentioned to his comrades. To the surprise of many veterans, Commander Blackmar died less than one year after taking office, on July 17, 1905. He was on an inspection tour of the G.A.R. posts of the northwest. While in Boise, Idaho, the GAR Commander fell ill and soon died of intestinal nephritis, a disease that can lead to kidney failure.[64] It is puzzling that W. W. Blackmar accepted the nomination as Commander if he knew that he had a chronic illness. Under the rules of the G.A.R., General Blackmar was succeeded by the Vice Commander-in Chief, John R. King.

On July 18, 1905, the *Baltimore American* had as its headline, "Capt. John R. King Head of Grand Army of Republic. Baltimorean Becomes Commander-in-Chief." The article stated that:

> Captain King will serve as Commander-in-Chief until the meeting of the National Encampment in Denver, Colo., during the first week in September next, and throughout that encampment until the election and installation of a new Commander-in-Chief, which generally takes place during the last day's meeting of the encampment.[65]

Being the responsible person that he was and in spite of the fame and glory associated with being Commander-in-Chief, John declined to seek the position for the 1905-1906 term. He was a realist and knew that he would be unable to perform his job as a Special Pension Agent at his best, if he was also Commander-in-Chief of the GAR. However, he was still Commander-in-Chief for the time being and had to issue his first order.

On July 19, 1905, Captain John Rigdon King issued his first general order as he assumed command of the Grand Army of the Republic. Most comrades would thereafter refer to him as "General" King, not Captain King. As reported by the *Baltimore American:*

> The order pays tribute to the recently deceased commander-in-chief of the organization, Wilmon W. Blackmar, and directs that the colors be draped for 10 days at every headquarters and every post of the G.A.R. A committee is appointed to draft suitable resolutions for the action of the organization at next annual encampment at Denver. This committee consists of the adjutant general, the inspector general, the judge advocate general and E. B. Stillings, of Boston. The order announces that because of his urgent request, Comrade Schoomaker is relieved as chief of staff and Comrade McCardy, past department commander of the department of Minnesota is appointed to that office. Announcement is made that the adjutant general is to continue in his duties until his successor is chosen at the annual encampment. All the other officers of the staff are requested to remain on duty in accordance with their appointments.[66]

On July 22, 1905, Commander King and many fellow comrades arrived in Boston to attend the funeral of Past Commander Blackmar. At that time, John R. King also announced that the national headquarters of the Grand Army would stay in that city and that he would make no changes to the plans that Blackmar had laid out.[67] Most of the other general orders he issued dealt with the 39th Annual Encampment to be held at Denver, Colorado, on September 7 and 8, 1905.

The 39th Annual Encampment of the Grand Army of the Republic convened on Thursday morning at 10 o'clock at the Broadway Theatre, Denver, Colorado, Commander-in-Chief King presiding. George W. Patten of Chattanooga, Tennessee, was serving as Senior Vice Commander-in-Chief and Joseph J. McCardy of Minnesota was acting as Chief of Staff. President Theodore Roosevelt wrote a note to Commander King expressing his regrets for not being to attend and John made an appropriate reply. The encampment began with state and city officials offering a welcome to the old soldiers. Commander King and others responded in kind, but the minutes of the rest of the meeting were kept secret, at least for the time being.[68] After a divine blessing by the Chaplain-in-Chief, J. H. Bradford, a Report of the Committee on Credentials. a lengthy roll call, etc., Commander King addressed the assembly with a glowing tribute to Past Commander, Wilmon W. Blackmar. In part, he said:

> From the very beginning of his term Commander-in-Chief Blackmar's purpose was to do all that man could do to encourage the several departments, particularly those that were weakest or most remote, and so far as lay in his power, infuse new life and energy and zeal into their ranks, and give to them added inspiration to continue bravely and manfully in the great work they were carrying on for God and country and humanity.[69]

Commander King then went through the issues and topics his predecessor had previously supported. He began with the Committee on Pensions, citing statistics and noting that "the work this year had been mainly devoted to urging the passage of a Service Pension bill," which did not get approved by Congress.[70] In his speech, John also reported the rapid spike in new, approved pensions from 1904 to 1905 of more than 30,000, following President Roosevelt's Order No. 78 of 1904. John had previously mentioned this increase in his July 15, 1905, report to Commander Blackmar. In reference to that spike, John went on to report the following:

> The large number was due to operation of order No. 78, the bureau granting 12,438 original pensions and 34,540 increased pensions, under the order. Since the order was issued, April 13, 1904, the total number of allowances under it was 65,612, most of them, however, having been for increase. The pension roll now contains the names of 684,608 survivors of the Civil War, as against 690,792 at the close of 1904. The deaths in 1905 of survivors of the Civil War were 30,324.[71]

Hence, by 1905, although the number of Union Civil War pension holders was 684,608, only about one-third (33.95 percent), 232,455, were G.A.R. members. Oddly, the reports of the 39th National Encampment made no mention of efforts to recruit new members. Perhaps, the G.A.R. decline in membership was a foregone conclusion.

The next topic addressed by Commander King involved the Committee of Legislation to Veterans in Public Service. John R. King was a member of this committee and at the same time, he was a public servant at the Pension Bureau. The question of a conflict of interest apparently did not arise. The issue that concerned the G.A.R. was the mandatory retirement age of public servants.

This G.A.R. committee, through the efforts of Chairman I. G. Kimball, John R. King and five others helped to defeat a bill that called for forced retirement of those employees over the age of seventy years.[72] In his speech, Commander King said that "vigilance must not be relaxed, however, as similar measures are liable at any time to be introduced in Congress, and upon this most important committee must devolve the duty of preventing our office-holding comrades from being deprived of their well-earned means of livelihood."[73] Of course, John knew that he eventually might be affected by such legislation, as he was a public servant who would be seventy-years old in just nine years.

Other items discussed by Commander King in his speech before the 39th National Encampment of the Grand Army were highly important patriotic issues. Many involved the placement of the Stars and Stripes and the funding, construction and dedication of Civil War monuments and battlefields. Also, the G.A.R. sought to build and to maintain hospitals for disabled and elderly veterans. Some projects honored not only the living and deceased Civil War veterans but also U.S. veterans of other wars as well. Commander King mentioned the Stars and Stripes as being the "keystone of the arch upon which the Grand Army has been built" and praised the Flag Committee for having secured flag legislation in thirty-two states during the past seven years including Idaho, Kansas and Wyoming during the past twelve months.[74] Next, John addressed the progress of funding for the Stephenson Memorial. In 1909, a monument to the founder of the Grand Army of the Republic, Dr. Benjamin F. Stephenson was dedicated. It is located on Indiana Plaza, Washington, D.C. Next on the Commander's speaking agenda was an appeal for Congress to establish a Fredericksburg Battlefield Park. As John said, the ground was "remarkably historical" because "one-hundred thousand men lost their lives within a triangular piece of ground measuring thirty miles on each side."[75] Congress, of course, would later approve funds for such a battlefield and it would later be named the Fredericksburg and Spotsylvania National Park. John also announced the need for a national monument to President Abraham Lincoln, the need for a new amphitheater in Arlington Cemetery, the need for iron tablets with Lincoln's Gettysburg Address written on them to be placed in National Cemeteries and the establishment of a National Soldiers Home in Yountville, California. While not all of these projects were financed by the Grand Army, many of the ideas were formulated by them and came to fruition through the efforts of the U.S. Congress. The Lincoln Memorial in the District of Columbia was built and was dedicated on May 30, 1922, with hundreds of Civil War veterans and Robert Todd Lincoln, the president's only surviving son, in attendance. Also, the tablets were installed and, as recently as 2009, a new series of black and silver tablets with Lincoln's Gettysburg Address were constructed to both replace old ones and to provide tablets to some cemeteries that never had them initially.

Probably the most important issue that Commander King discussed was Memorial Day. The Grand Army of the Republic was largely responsible for the establishment of this National Holiday to honor and salute veterans of all wars. John King described the revered day:

> That sweetly solemn day, so dear to the heart of every patriotic citizen, and so doubly dear to the valiant men whose loyal service of more than twoscore years ago led to its inception, has now become an institution of the land as firmly rooted and as immovable as Independence Day itself. And well it should be, for in the world's whole history no more sentiment is more generally and appropriately expressed is this fidelity of the loyal living to the memory of the dead. The observance of the exercises of Memorial Day has become so widespread at the present time scarcely a city, town or village can be found in this great Republic that does not in some manner pay tribute to the nation's honored dead. And what a graceful form this tribute takes![76]

Commander King, In his address of September 7, 1905, also praised his Staff Officers, the Sons and Daughters of Veterans associations, the Army Nurses, the Women's Relief Corps, an axillary group to the G.A.R., and the Ladies of the Grand Army of the Repubic, composed of "our wives, sisters, daughters, and alas! only in some cases, our mothers." According to one newspaper account, at this point in his speech, the minutes noted that:

> When he came to that part referring to the Daughters of Veterans, memory of his loss of his daughters, who were members of the above association, overcame him, and he sat down, the tears streaming down his cheeks. The paragraph was read by Past Commander-in-Chief Walker.[77]

Both of Johns' daughters served many years in the Daughters of Veterans organization. John's wife, Annie, participated in the Women's Relief Corps until her death.

The Report of the Staff Officers of this encampment praised the efforts of John R. King as he performed the duties of Senior Vice Commander-in-Chief:

> The Commander-in-Chief was singularly fortunate for his associates and counselors men who had both the will and the ability to labor wisely for

> the upbuilding and upholding of our order, and there was never a day of his incumbency of the office that he did not accord them their full meed of praise for their unselfish devotion to their duties. The report of Senior Vice Commander-in-Chief, who served in that capacity up to July 15, 1905, is worthy of a careful perusal, especially his account of the only Grand Army Church in the country. On account of his daily presence in the national capitol he was often drafted into service by the Commander-in-Chief, and his response was always will and effective.[78]

For his exemplary work with the Grand Army of the Republic, John R. King was given an ornate G.A.R. badge decorated with diamonds. Before John got a salute and the unexpected gift, the presenter, Comrade McCardy said:

> As one of that vast army that stood by the flag, I am proud of that record. Away off on the flanks, the crack of our carbines was sweet music to our rifleman, as he lay in the trenches and dashed over the earth-works in front, and the joy of a nip from our canteens, whether it was mountain dew or moonshine, gave new life to his tired soul. One of those Southern boys, a Marylander by birth, and a member of the Sixth Maryland of the Sixth Army Corps who stood by the flag is now Commander-in-Chief of this great organization. He is a battle-scarred veteran, a true comrade, a cultured gentleman, a boy in blue now grown gray. Following a happy custom, his official staff have presented this testimonial in the high regard they bear towards him; and I am requested, in their behalf, to present to you, Commander-in-Chief, this badge. It is with great pleasure that I perform this duty. My comrade, wear it over a heart so loyal, so patriotic, so vigilant and so brave it will be an incentive to others to the most unselfish patriotism. and to yourself a guard against everything that disgrace the past that you have helped to make honorable, and our dead have made sacred.[79]

Ever gracious and humble, John's response, in part, was the following:

> I do not deserve this testimonial, because my services have been brief. I feel that it belongs to the dead. Since you and your associates have been so kind, I accept it … I thank you again and again and through you the members of the staff for this beautiful souvenir.[80]

John King concluded his speech by making another tribute to Past Commander-in-Chief Wilmon W. Blackmar and by revisiting the steps he went through following word of the latter's death. In part, John said:

> The foregoing is a record of the administration of our late Commander-in-Chief, Wilmon W. Blackmar, whose service during eleven months of the term for which he was elected embraced all that part of the year when the presence of the Commander-in-Chief was required by the different Departments.[81]

He went on to recite the contents of his entire General Order No. 9 when he assumed command of the Grand Army.

The next day, September 8, 1905, following the refusal of John R. King to serve further as Commander-in-Chief for the 1905-1906 term, the gathering in Denver chose Corporal James Tanner as its new Commander-in-Chief. Corporal Tanner, born April 4, 1844, served with the 87th New York Volunteer Infantry during the Civil War. At the Battle of Second Manassas, fought from August 29 to August 30, 1862, Corporal Tanner lost both legs. He was later fitted with a double prosthesis. As mentioned earlier, Corporal Tanner had been seriously considered for the position of Special Pension Agent by President Theodore Roosevelt in 1902 but did not receive it. Roosevelt selected John R. King instead.

It is evident from the list of proposed in-the-works projects of the 39th National Encampment that the Grand Army was strictly guided by their three principles: fraternity, charity and loyalty. Fraternity was clearly shown by the thousands of veterans who attended the two-day encampment. Charity was illustrated by the works of the Association of Army Nurses, the Women's Relief Corps, the Ladies of the G.A.R. and by the number of old soldiers' homes that were paid for by the Grand Army. The opening of the California Soldiers' Home in Yountville was only one of many made possible by the generosity of the Grand Army. Just because the G.A.R. was a patriotic association for honorably discharged Union veterans did not mean they did not also address the needs of ex-Confederate soldiers. In fact, the Grand Army had also established Confederate homes in the states of Kentucky, Louisiana, Mississippi, Tennessee and Missouri. Across the United States, in 1905, there were thirty-eight states with old soldiers' homes as well as those National Military Homes erected by the Federal government. Of course, the charity principle was also exemplified by the continuous work by the Grand Army in attempting to expand pension benefits to Union Civil War veterans, their widows and children and to orphans.

Once John R. King became Commander-in-Chief of the G.A.R., he became the best known Union veteran in the state of Maryland. There was a newspaper story, usually with a photograph of him in his G.A.R. uniform, for any and everything he did. While the Baltimore newspapers ran about five articles about his promotion to Special Pension Agent, after he became head of the GAR over one-hundred stories appeared between 1905 and his death. These included not just articles from the local papers, the *Baltimore American* and the *Baltimore Sun,* but from national newspapers such as the *Washington Post,* the *New York Times,* the *Chicago Tribune and* the *Atlanta Constitution.* He was so popular in the state of Maryland that he could have entered politics and probably could have eventually won a governorship. Instead, John, after he forfeited his office of G.A.R. Commander-in-Chief, chose to serve his organization in other ways. In addition, he would also continue to work as a Special Pension Agent for the Pension Bureau in Washington, D.C. for three, four-year terms until his position was abolished in 1914.

Just as the 39th National Encampment upheld their core principles in their projects, John King devoted his life to these same tenets. As of 1905, he had already spent thirty-eight years of his avocational life as an active G.A.R. member. Several examples of his efforts will highlight some of the projects and activities in which he continued his G.A.R. involvement. On May 28, 1906, Thursday, the Grand Army met in Baltimore on what, at that time, was called Decoration Day. On May 5, 1868, one of the early Commanders of the Grand Army, General John A. Logan, "established a day to decorate the graves of those fallen during the Civil War."[82] After the end of World War I, Americans began to honor all those fallen soldiers killed in war and the name of that day was eventfully changed to Memorial Day. Today, that day is the last Monday in the month of May. On this particular Decoration Day of May 28, 1906, a colorful parade and then lengthy ceremony was held. John King, a featured speaker, read Lincoln's Gettysburg Address. This event actually illustrated two of the principles or ideals of the Grand Army, fraternity and loyalty. Fraternity was the uniting of comrades on Decoration Day and loyalty that meant maintaining "true allegiance to the United States of America based upon a paramount respect for, and fidelity to, its constitution and laws."[83]

Loyalty, to the Grand Army, was exemplified in several manners. Some of these included soliciting funds to construct statutes of Union soldiers, monuments, memorials, tablets and the mounting of cannons. The G.A.R. also wished to preserve historical battlefields, battle flags and Civil War documents. Just two days after Decoration Day ceremony, on May 30, 1906, it was announced that Captain John R. King, Admiral Yates Stirling, and Captain H. F. Dorton were elected to the Maryland Union Memorial Commission "to select a site and erect a monument to the Union Soldiers and sailors in the Civil War, for which purpose $23,000 was appropriated by the Legislature."[84] The committee of three had met at the Union League Club in Baltimore the previous evening. However, before further action could be taken, the group first had to wait for the cooperation of the Municipal Art Commission to offer their choice of a site and of a design.[85] The proposed memorial would be called the Union Soldiers and Sailors Monument. John King served on the Monument Commission from 1906 to 1909. Other Baltimoreans who served after the initial committee of three was formed were Colonel George W. F. Vernon, General R. N. Bowerman, and Captain William Stahl.[86] A rancorous debate erupted in the press well before John was even elected to the Commission. It seems that many people were opposed to it, but for entirely different reasons. In March of 1906, one Union veteran and his friends in patriotic orders protested because they wanted a monument to "commemorate the courage and patriotism of those Marylanders who responded to the call to arms for the preservation of the Union, not one dedicated to all the "soldiers and sailors for all the wars in which the Republic has been engaged."[87] In April, a former Maryland Confederate veteran, H. H. Matthews, who was residing in a Confederate home, was upset because he felt that since the United Daughters of the Confederacy had financed and constructed a monument to the Confederate fallen, without using public funds, that the Grand Army should do the same. Mr. Matthews said the following in a letter to the Editor published in the *Sun*:

> It seems to me that is their patriotism is of such a high type, and that they deem it absolutely necessary to perpetuate the records of their State comrades by building this monument, why, in the name of Heaven, did they not build it and not go before the Legislature of their State to try and coerce these gentlemen into their way of thinking, and virtually in the name of patriotism compel them to erect this piece of stone. Is it not a matter of fact that every soldier who served in the Federal armies during the struggle for even so short a time as 90 days or a fraction part thereof receives of the money of the United States Treasury a pension of the money of the realm to sooth his aches and also as an inducement to vote for those who upheld the old flag and appropriation?[88]

Mr. Matthews statements hit a raw nerve in John King and he responded angrily in defense of utilizing public funds for the monument and of Marylanders who fought on the Union side. In another letter to the Editor John said:

> In response to a Mr. H. H. Matthews who was opposed to the expense of a Union monument. I am not sure Mr. Matthews is a Marylander to the manor born: be that as it may, however, it seems that a reasonable degree of modesty would prompt one who is living off the bounty of the taxpayers of Maryland, a tax eater and not a taxpayer to refrain from criticizing our lawmakers or offering them suggestions as to the disposition of the revenues of the State. His gratuitous slur on those who answered the call of the State to fill her quota of troops for the Union army, I am happy to say, is not shared by the brave Marylanders of German and Irish descent who were residents of our State during that unhappy period, many of whom were important factors in our commercial and industrial development and who felt it their duty and privilege to take up arms in support of the best government ever devised by men. I pass without comment further than to say that there were many such among the 62,000 Union soldiers who volunteered from Maryland and who were good and true men.... The loudest talkers now—were not the men who were in every engagement and saw everything that transpired—were not the men who followed Murray, Herbert, Torsch, Elzy and others. They were not like my boyhood friends, the MacGills (father and four sons), Jim Breathed, John Hager and other brave Washington county boys, who quit fighting at Appomattox leaving the latter-day fighting to be done by those who were 'invisible in war and invisible in peace.' I am also proud of the distinguished Maryland men who reached high rank in the Confederate Army, but I am more so of Kenly, Sykes, Emory, Orr, Denison, Rogers, Schley, Stirling, Fleusser and others who reached high and honorable rank in the Union Army and Navy.[89]

Dr. Charles J. MacGill, Dr. Charles G. W. MacGill, William D. MacGill, Davidge MacGill, James MacGill, James Breathed, and John Hager were all Hagerstonians who joined the Confederate Army. They were all friends and neighbors of John King before the war.

The Union Soldiers and Sailors Monument in Baltimore was built using public funds and was dedicated November 6, 1909. Originally located in Druid Hill Park, it had to be moved to Wyman Park in 1959 because of the construction of the Jones Fall Expressway.

As reported by the *Baltimore Sun* on January 14, 2016, a seven-member commission appointed by Baltimore Mayor Stephanie Rawlings-Blake recommended that two of the four Confederate era monuments be removed from the cities' public parks.[90] The two selected included monuments to Roger B. Taney, author of the U.S. Supreme Court Dred Scott decision, and that of Robert E. Lee and Thomas J. "Stonewall" Jackson. The final decision was to be made by the mayor. The Lee-Jackson monument might be offered to the U.S. Park Service in Chancellorsville, Virginia. The commission voted to retain the Confederate Soldiers and Sailors Monument on Mount Royal Avenue and the Confederate Women's Monument on West University Parkway. Some people said that Baltimore had too many monuments to the Confederacy considering that the city had only one monument to Union soldiers and sailors though more than twice as many Marylanders fought for the Union than for the Confederacy. Later, other voices and issues arose concerning the inappropriateness of all four Baltimore Confederate monuments. Mayor Catherine Pugh and the Baltimore City Council decided to remove all of them. In the dead of night on August 15-16, 2017, the Confederate Soldiers and Sailors Monument, the Confederate Women's Monument, the Lee and Jackson Monument and the Roger B. Taney Monument were all moved to city-owned property. The Mayor of Baltimore stated that requests to obtain the statues would be considered by the city.

In addition to his public service work as part of the Union Soldiers and Sailors Monument, John served on a number of other noteworthy commissions. For instance, from 1902 to 1904, he was part of the Chickamauga-Chattanooga Battlefield Commission. Other Baltimoreans who participated were Thomas J. Cannon, William L. Ritter, J. Leonard Hoffman, William Stahl, Charles Hull and Benjamin Taylor.[91] This was a bipartisan commission composed of both former Union and Confederate soldiers. Hence, there was little debate in the state. The State of Maryland appropriated $7,000 "for the erection of suitable monuments and markers to commemorate the 3rd Maryland Infantry, Federal army, and Latrobe's Maryland Battery, Confederate Army."[92] Appointed by Governor John Walter Smith, Captain John R. King also served on the Battle Flag Commission of Maryland from 1900 until 1908. Governor Smith selected "four, two of whom shall be Union soldiers and two Confederate soldiers, whose duty is to provide a suitable place at the State Capitol for the preservation and display of the battle-flags of the State."[93] John King and George W. Johnson were chosen to represent the Union troops while James R. Wheeler and Spencer C. Jones were selected to represent the Confederate soldiers. However, "as the appropriation of $1,500 by the General Assembly was inadequate to purchase the kind of cases required by the Act, Governor Warfield contributed $1,000 from his contingent fund for this purpose; and in addition the sum of $285.00 to pay for a case for the flags carried by Maryland troops in the War of Independence and during the War of 1812."[94] In 1903, another Hagerstonian also served on the Flag Commission. John's old nemesis, Stonewall Jackson's aide-de-camp, Henry Kyd Douglas was chosen. Colonel Douglas was not only a teacher at the Hagerstown Academy which John attended, he was with General Jackson at the Battles of Front Royal and Winchester. When John King was taken prisoner by Jacksons' forces on May 23, 1862, he may have been interviewed by Douglas. They certainly knew each other. After the Civil War, Colonel Douglas practiced law in Hagerstown. In any case, the Flag Commission of Maryland completed its work by the end of Governor Edwin Warfield's term, that is, by January 8, 1908.

In addition to the commissions cited, John R. King was also appointed as chairman of the Gettysburg Commission in 1912, a group dedicated to reuniting old foes for a fiftieth anniversary in Gettysburg, Pennsylvania. By June of 1913, arrangements for a large reunion to be held July 1 had been completed. However, instead of having just a small number complete the application to attend, "the encampment at the Blue and Gray at Gettysburg far exceeded expectation and we have been compelled to notify many applicants that we will be unable to take care of them officially" said King.[95] Chairman King's quota of five-hundred Maryland Union veterans was easily met. Since so many men wanted to go, the Maryland contingent could not get special rates. They would have to make their own travel and lodging arrangements and then later meet as a unit. Lastly, Captain King, who was frequently called General by his G.A.R. comrades, not only served as a Trustee for the Grand Army, but he was also on the Board of Trustees of St. Mary's Industrial School for Boys from 1914 to 1920. In 1918, "a notion was brought up during a Maryland Assembly House Judiciary Committee hearing that would prohibit state aid to private institutions such as Western Maryland College, the Maryland School for Boys, John Hopkins University and the Jewish Hospital for Consumptives, as well as many Catholic institutions."[96] In a letter to the editor at the *Sun* newspaper, John King, as a Presbyterian, Republican and Civil War veteran, vehemently denounced a bill to end state subsidies.[97]

Besides his public service work on these commissions and in addition to his long years with the Grand Army, John King also was a member of an important subgroup of the G.A.R., called the Military Order of the Loyal Legion. The group's acronym was MOLLUS. Also referred to as simply the Loyal Legion, this patriotic association was "the first society formed by officers honorably discharged from the services."[98] MOLLUS began to be organized just after the assassination of President Lincoln in May of 1865. Similar to the organization of the Grand Army, it "provided for District (local) Commanderies, Grand (State) Commanderies, and a Commandery-in-Chief."[99] John King probably joined the Maryland local and state commanderies about the same time that he joined the Grand Army, in 1867. The Maryland Commandery of the Loyal Legion held their annual meetings and banquets in the evening during the first week in January. Such events were considered newsworthy as they were reported frequently in the *Baltimore Sun*. John King was often a featured speaker as he excelled in discussing specific Civil War battles. On January 3 of 1908, the Loyal Legion banquet was held at the ritzy Hotel Altamont in Baltimore. At that venue, Captain King "told of the retreat of the Union troops from Berryville, Va. to Winchester, Va. in 1863" and "described the falling back of the Union troops vividly, and was warmly applauded."[100] Also present at the event were Eric Bergland, G. W. F. Vernon, E. H. Sterling, Dr. George R. Graham, Henry P. Goddard and General Peter Leary, Jr.[101] On Friday, January 7, 1915, the Loyal Legion met at the Belvedere Hotel in Baltimore and "Gen. John R. King read a stirring 'History of a Maryland Regiment."[102] This is the speech cited in full earlier and will not repeated here. In addition, as the United States was already in the midst of World War I, the former military officers of MOLLUS urged Congress "to prepare for the defense of the nation and called on all patriotic societies to take similar action."[103] Lastly, on Friday evening, January 7, 1920, the Loyal Legion got together again at the Belvedere for their annual meeting. Elections were held at the annual meetings and the following were selected for the upcoming year; Lieutenant John A. Thompson, Jr., commander; E. Edmunds Foster, senior vice commander, Colonel Clarence Reems, junior vice commander, Lieutenant Joseph J. Janney, recorder, C. Warner Stork, registrar, Edwin C. Ireland, treasurer, and Frederick T. Dorton, chancellor.[104] The executive council consisted of Captain John R. King, Colonel G. W. F. Vernon, Honorable P. L. Goldesborough, Dr. John R. Oliver, and A. De R. Sappington.[105] At this event, Captain King read another paper about a Civil War battle. He spoke of the Battle of Cold Harbor of May 31 to June 12, 1864, as one of the worst Union defeats of the Civil War. Although John summarized the battle in this speech, he had not participated in it. Earlier in May of 1863, he had been wounded for a third time and was hospitalized at the time of the Battle of Cold Harbor. In his brief memoirs written in 1925, John King mentions that he was serving his fourth term as Commander of the Maryland Commandery and that he also was a member of the Council of the Commandery-in-Chief of the Order.[106]

The U.S. Census for Baltimore City, taken April 20, 1910, showed the Kings residing in Ward 11.[107] Their address was 25 West Mt. Royal Avenue. John's youngest brother, William, and his wife, Margaret, lived just one house away at 29 West Mt. Royal Avenue. Of course, John was still working in

Washington D. C. at the time and listed his occupation as simply "pension agent." He gave his age as sixty-five years old. John King had no intention of retiring any time soon although he would turn sixty-six years old on June 24. His wife, Annie Maria, was shown as being fifty-eight years of age. Also residing in the household were Annie's sister, Ruth P. Ould, age fifty and widowed. In addition to the family, Margaret Holmes, twenty-four, was shown as an African-American cook and Louisa Spence, a twenty year-old, African-American housemaid.

Living in the City of Baltimore during his later years, John and his brother, William, probably saw alot of each other and would have remained very close. Hopefully, William provided some emotional support to John after the loss of both his daughters. However, their older brother, Harrison or Harry as he was nicknamed, did not see much of either brother. Not only was he not in Baltimore, Harry did not even reside in the state of Maryland. Instead, over the years, he moved from one state to another.

Harrison Eader King was born July 25, 1840, four years before John. At age twenty-one, Harrison enlisted for duty in Company E of the First Potomac Home Brigade (Union) September 30, 1861, and was mustered in October 1, 1861, in Frederick, Maryland.[108] At the time, William, nicknamed "Willie," had not yet turned nine years old and John was only seventeen. In December of 1861, Harrison King was detached from his regiment as a baker. He was then promoted to corporal and later to sergeant. Then, in Harpers Ferry on February 23, 1864, he was "discharged by reason of re-enlistment as Veterans Volunteers under G.O. (General Order) 191."[109] At age twenty-four, after serving three and one-half years, Harrison received a promotion to First Lieutenant of Company E of the 13th Maryland Infantry on March 1, 1865. On May 29, 1865, Lieutenant Harrison King was mustered out in Baltimore and returned home to live with his father in Hagerstown. The U.S. Census taken June 5, 1880, in Hagerstown, shows Harrison as single, working as a "confectioner," and still living with his father. A confectioner is a person who makes or sells confections, such as chocolates or candies.[110] Harry's temporary job in the army as a baker undoubtedly gave his some experience with which to enter the confectionary industry.

On November 15, 1880, Harrison E. King purchased a large lot on the east side of North Potomac Street in Hagerstown for $600 from James I. and Sophia A. Hurley.[111] There was no building on the land at the time of purchase. Apparently, Harry bought it as an investment since he did not improve the property and sold it four years later. At the time he purchased the lot in Hagerstown, Harrison had already left the state of Maryland and was residing in Pittsburg, Pennsylvania. For some reason, Harry was erroneously listed on the 1880 U.S. Census twice. When counted on the Hagerstown census with his father, either his father incorrectly added him or he was merely visiting. Because, on the 1880 U.S. Census taken just ten days later, on June 15, Harrison was shown living in the household of his uncle, James King, James' wife Eliza and their four children in Pittsburgh.[112] His uncle was employed a "R.R. painter" and two of his daughters, Lizzie and Jennie, were music teachers. Harry was still single, thirty-nine years old and was working as a "confectioner." He did not stay much longer in Pennsylvania because a note in a land record book showed that he was residing in Newark, Ohio as of August, 1882.[113] By 1884, Harrison had again moved and was now living in Cleveland, Ohio. On July 18, 1884, Harrison sold his lot in Hagerstown for a nice profit to Samuel M. Bloom for $1,500.[114] In 1894, Clara Tice acquired the land and had a beautiful, two-story Victorian home constructed on the site. Located at 434 North Potomac Street, it is now called the Historic Clara Tice House and stands in an elegant section of Hagerstown. In March of 2014, the Clara Tice House sold for $227,000.

The 1900 U.S. Census shows that Harrison E. King was still residing in Cleveland, Cuyahoga County, Ohio.[115] Harry was now fifty-nine years old, single and was still employed as a confectioner. However, he was no longer staying with any relatives. Instead, he was living with the Daniel P. Miller family as a roomer. Mr. Miller told the census taker that he was a "stationary engineer," an individual who operates industrial machinery and equipment. Also residing in the household were Daniel's wife, Anna, two Miller children and another roomer. Still not free of his nomadic tendencies, Harry moved again. By 1910, he was living in Precinct 4, Osceola County, Florida.[116] South of Orlando, the county seat of Osceola County is Kissimmee. Although Harrison had been receiving an "Army Invalid" pension since February 24, 1899, he did not go to Florida for retirement.[117]Like his brother, John, he had a strong work ethic and would not retire until forced to do so. However, Harry was no longer employed as a confectioner. Now, at the age of sixty-nine years, he was a postmaster in Florida. It is not known how long he remained in Florida. At some point, Harrison returned to his hometown of Hagerstown and later died there October 3, 1919. Surviving him were his two brothers, Captain John King, of Baltimore, with the U.S. Custom House and Lieutenant William R. King, of Baltimore Polytechnic Institute, a half-brother, Samuel L. King, of Pittsburgh; and a half-sister, Miss Laura King, a school teacher in Hagerstown.[118] Harrison Eader King is buried in the Rose Hill Cemetery in Hagerstown. He remained a bachelor his entire life.

Unlike her younger brothers, Mary Adelaide King, Samuel L. King's oldest child, remained in Hagerstown her entire life. On October 10, 1861, Mary, nicknamed "Addie," married Samuel Z. McLaughlin at the Methodist Parsonage in Mercersburg, Pennsylvania.[119] Samuel was the son of an Irish immigrant and a resident of Hagerstown. Addie was twenty-three years old and Samuel was twenty-five. It was the marriage of a young Irish lass to a young Irish lad. The ceremony was performed by Reverend James Curns. As recorded by John R. King in his diary, Samuel entered business with his father-in-law, Samuel L. King, during the Civil War. They became sutlers selling goods and supplies to the Union army in western Maryland and in the Shenandoah Valley. Before the end of the war, Samuel Z. and Samuel L. had opened stores in rented buildings in Hancock, Maryland and in Winchester, Virginia. John's father and his son-in-law probably purchased an assortment of items wholesale in Baltimore and had them shipped by rail to Hagerstown. In addition to their thriving business selling to the Union army, the two men also opened and operated a livery stable in the heart of Hagerstown. An interesting story about two of their horses appeared in the *Herald & Torch Light* on August 31, 1864:

> On Monday night of last week, the Livery Stable of Messsrs. King and McLaughlin of that place, was entered and two horses stolen therefrom. The thieves had a key to fit the lock, and after taking the horses from the stable, again locked the door. As soon as the robbery was known, Mr. King started in the direction of Hancock. Mr. McLaughlin to Chambersburg and Mr. Robert Shuster toward Sharpsburg. Mr. Shuster hearing of the horses on his route, traced them to a Cavalry camp, where he succeeded in getting them, they having been taken by dismounted Cavalrymen.[120]

While her husband was traveling and otherwise occupied by his businesses, Addie began to raise a family. Her first child, Mary Emma, was born in July of 1863, followed by Harry Dixon in 1865, Clara Lulu in July of 1866 and Clyde Rigdon on March 4, 1870. Addie King McLaughlin was the only child of Samuel L. King that had any surviving children. Harrison never married, William had no children and John lost both of his daughters to disease. Although their father, Samuel L. King, remarried and had children after his first wife died August 2 1862, those children were only half nieces and half nephews. Their names were Samuel L. King, Jr. and Laura Cornelia King. John King treated his nieces and nephews very kindly, almost as if they were his own children. This adoration is reflected in his will. On the other hand, John did not treat his half nephews and half nieces as well, leaving them nothing in his will. Addies' descendants were the distant relatives who provided photographic and written materials for this publication.

According to the 1870 U.S. Census, Samuel Z. McLaughlin was now thirty-two years old while Addie was thirty.[121] Samuel was working as a "Livery man" in the business that he owned jointly with his father-in-law, Samuel L. King. All four children were residing in the home, the oldest was Mary Emma, age seven. At the time of the 1880, U.S. Census all four children were still present, the oldest was now seventeen years old.[122] In 1891, Samuel and Addie purchased a fine home in the heart of Hagerstown. For the amount of $1,000, they bought a house and lot No. 118 on East Washington Street from Julia C. McComas.[123] Their property measured forty-one feet on East Washington and extended back two-hundred and forty feet.

By the time of the 1900 U.S. Census, the household composition had changed appreciably. Mary Adelaide "Addie" (King) McLaughlin died in 1898. Samuel Z. McLaughlin, now age sixty-four, was a widowed, household head.[124] Mary Emma had married Charles E. Clapp, a railroad office clerk and both were also in the residence. Also, Clara Lulu had married Harry B. Irvin, a glove salesman and they too were in the home. Both Harry Dixon and Clyde Rigdon McLaughlin had left home to go their own way. Then, in 1905, Samuel Z. McLaughlin died. Both Samuel and Addie are buried in Rose Hill Cemetery in Hagerstown.

Samuel L. King, father of Addie, Harrison, John and William, and two other children who did not survive to adulthood (Virginia and Lellie) married a second time. His new wife was thirty-four year old Ann Rebecca Clay Herbert. On March 29, 1866, they married in St. Paul's Methodist Episcopal Church in Hagerstown.[125] The couple soon had their first child, Laura Cornelia, Jr., born November 28, 1867. Laura was not christened until November 22, 1874, at St. Paul's Methodist Episcopal Church.[126] On the 1870 U.S. Census for Hagerstown, Samuel, age fifty-eight, gave his occupation as a "coach maker."[127] The family did not own any real estate, but had personal property valued at $1,500. Also living in the household were Ann R., age thirty-eight, William, age seventeen, who was employed as a tinner apprentice and William's half-sister, age two. Just forty-seven days after the census taker visited, the King's second child, Samuel L. King, Jr. was born August 3, 1870 and was christened on same day as his sister.[128]

After the Civil War, it is unlikely that Samuel L. King continued with his retail stores in Winchester and Hancock. Although he did not place any ads in the Hagerstown newspapers after the Civil War for his coach making business, according to the 1870 census, he did continue to make and to sell coaches. In addition to that, he and Samuel McLaughlin continued to operate their livery stable business. "Boyd's Business Directory" of 1875 listed "King and McLaughlin Livery" in the center of Hagerstown in the rear of Washington House.[129] Samuel King would have assuredly made the carriages and coaches rented out to the public at this livery business.

On December 12, 1872, Samuel L. King purchased a home for his new family. The deed stated that he bought "a half lot with a framed dwelling."[130] Samuel and his wife, Ann Rebecca, spent the rest of their days in this home. On June 5, 1880 the U.S. Census taker came by the Samuel King household. Samuel was now sixty-eight years old while his wife was only forty-eight years old.[131] He gave his occupation as "proprietor of livery" although he may have also been building coaches and selling retail goods. The census taker listed Samuel's son, William R., as also being in the household although he was "In the Navy." Lastly, Samuel's two children by Ann Rebecca were shown, Laura, age twelve, and Samuel L. Jr., age nine.

As he was before the Civil War, Samuel L. King was not only a businessman but he also was a community leader. He belonged to a number of business and civil organizations. For example, he was a member of the Hagerstown Business Association. For the 50th anniversary of the International Order of the Odd Fellows on April 26, 1869, Potomac Lodge No. 31, Samuel served on the Committee of Arrangements.[132] He was also the presiding Grand Worthy Chief of the Grand Lodge of the Maryland Independent Order of the Good Templars on Wednesday evening, November 22, 1871.[133] The Templars met at the Temperance Temple in Baltimore. A year later, in the 5th annual Maryland meeting of the Grand Lodge meeting of the Good Templars held in Port Deposit on November 20, Samuel L. King was elected as G. W. Treasurer.[134]

Like his son, John, Samuel King was a lifelong Republican. On Wednesday, April 8, 1874, he presided over a meeting of local Republicans.[135] This group sought to nominate candidates for upcoming municipal elections. Samuel was also a lifelong member of St. Paul's Methodist Church where he served as a deacon. In addition, Samuel served on a standing committee called Conference Stewards at the Baltimore Conference of the Methodist Episcopal Church in March of 1873.[136] On Friday, May 14, 1875, Samuel was nominated and elected as Vice President of the Temperance Alliance.[137] Delegates from different churches and Sabbath Schools met in the Y.M.C.A. room to organize a local branch of the Temperance Alliance. Considering the number of organizations of which he was a member, it is a wonder he had time for his family and job.

Samuel Liles King Sr., father of Mary Adelaide, Harrison E., John R., William R., Samuel L. Jr., and Laura C. King, died at the age of eighty-two years, seven days on November 7, 1893. Samuel had been a lieutenant in the Maryland militia and all three of his sons were also military men. John R. reached the rank of captain while Harrison and William were lieutenants in the army and navy, respectively. Samuel Sr. was the husband of Eliza Lane King and later of Ann Rebecca King. The pastor of that church wrote in his obituary,

> Mr. Samuel L. King, Sr., an old and highly regarded citizen who died recently, was the oldest member living (of this church) ... he was a devoted and true Christian, commanding the admiration of all members of the church.[138]

Samuel Sr. was buried in Rose Hill Cemetery, Hagerstown. His second wife, Ann Rebecca (Herbert) King died at the age of seventy years, on February 16, 1902. She is buried next to Samuel Sr. at the Rose Hill Cemetery.

Samuel King's oldest child by his second wife, Laura Cornelia King, never married and thus left no descendants. Beginning in 1935, she resided as a boarder in the Dogman Hotel in Hagerstown. On April 8, 1940, when the U.S. census taker came to the hotel, she was still there.[139] She was seventy-two years old at the time. Laura died four years later in September of 1944. She is buried in Rose Hill Cemetery in Hagerstown.

Samuel's other child by Ann Rebecca King, Samuel L. Jr., graduated from high school in Washington County. He then began employment as a clerk with the United States Express Company in the Hagerstown office.[140] On October 24, 1893, Samuel Jr. married Carrie Estella Show at Saint Paul's Methodist Episcopal Church in Hagerstown.[141] Carrie, the daughter of George W. and Henrietta (Orndorff) Show, was born and raised in Shepherdstown, West Virginia.[142] When operations ceased with U.S. Express, Samuel was obligated to move out-of-state to find work. After the death of his father, Samuel Jr. moved to Ward 2 in Trenton, New Jersey. He was now twenty-six years old and gave the census taker his occupation as "express agent."[143] Also In the household were his wife, Carrie Estella, age twenty-eight, and their newborn child, William Liles King, only one month old. By 1920, Samuel L. Jr. and his wife had moved to Ward 11 in Pittsburgh, Pennsylvania. Oddly, the Samuel L. King family does not appear on the U.S. Census for 1910. Perhaps the census taker missed their house. By 1920, their son, William L., had apparently died as no further public record of him has been found. However, his parents were still living in Pittsburgh. Samuel L. Jr. was now forty-nine years old and Carrie was forty-seven. Samuel was now employed as a "traffic manager" for a department store.[144] When the 1930 U.S. Census was taken, the Kings were renting at the Margasetta Apartments in Pittsburgh and were paying fifty dollars monthly in rent. Samuel Jr. King was working as a "special Insurance agent" according to the census. In fact, he was a general agent for the Equitable Life Assurance Society in Pittsburgh.[145] His wife, Carrie, was not employed and apparently never worked. However, perhaps to earn some extra money, the Kings took in a couple of lodgers, Emily M. and Elsie V. Coulson.[146] Samuel, Jr. retired from the insurance industry on August 20, 1934, and returned to Hagerstown. During World War II, he was chairman of the Board for the Truck Gasoline Panel office of the Price Administration and also served as the chief clerk of the Price Administration. During his fourteen years of retirement in the town of his birth, Samuel served in many positions in St. Paul's Methodist Church including steward, trustee, and treasurer. On December 28, 1945, Carrie E. King died suddenly of complications at the age of seventy-three. Less than three years later, Samuel L. King, Jr. died of complications from a major operation while in Deaconess Hospital, Boston, Massachusetts.[147] He wa seventy-seven years old. Both Carrie and Samuel, Jr., are buried in Rose Hill Cemetery, Hagerstown.

By 1914, John King's three four-year terms as a United States pension agent had expired. At that time, the government decided to eradicate all such positions. John had no desire to retire from the Federal government even though he was now seventy years old. Instead, that same year, 1914, he returned to the U.S. Customs House in Baltimore, not in his former position as Chief Marine Clerk, but as one of four storekeepers.[148] Perhaps the Custom House officials considered him too old for his former position. It was the responsibility of the storekeepers to oversee the safety of goods confiscated and to hold them until they were cleared by customs. A book titled, "The Warehouse Manual and General Custom House Guide" describes the duties of a U.S. Custom House storekeeper:

> All bonded stores as well as stores occupied by the appraisers are placed by the collector in the custody of officers designated of the purpose who are known as storekeepers and assistant storekeepers. The storekeeper is required to keep the keys of the store in his own possession and personally superintend the opening closing of the doors and windows. Both the storekeeper and the assistant ... are required to be in constant attendance at the stores from 7 o'clock a.m. til sunset from April 1 to October 1, and for the residue of year from 8 o'clock a.m. to sunset.[149]

As reported in the *Baltimore American* on February 20, 1920, John R. King might be made Chief Clerk to the Harbor Board once again.[150] The prior Chief Clerk, James H. Irvin, had been fired by the Harbor Engineer Banecroft Hill. The Mayor of Baltimore, William F. Broening, "announced he would offer the place to John R. King, former pension agent and one of the most widely known Maryland veterans of the Civil War."[151] However, for reasons not specified in the press, John did not accept the position. He apparently decided to remain in the position of storekeeper. Perhaps his continuing work for the Grand Army was more important than regaining his old Chief Marine Clerk job.

While he was still employed at the Custom House, on December 10, 1915, Captain John King and his wife, Annie, sold their property in Baltimore City at 25 Mt. Royal Avenue "in consideration of the sum of five dollars and other valuable considerations."[152] The "other valuable considerations" were not specified in the deed. The couple then moved to the Preston Apartments in the city. The Kings may have sold their townhouse because they wanted to downsize to a smaller residence. John was now seventy-one years and Annie was sixty-four years old. The Kings could not have known at the time that, for health reasons, they should have stayed in their house on Mt. Royal Avenue.

The Preston Apartments were located next to the tracks of the Pennsylvania Railroad. Smokey fumes and the noise from the trains crept into the King's apartment. They could have kept the windows closed during part of the year, but air conditioning would not be invented until 1932. About a year and a half after the move to the new apartment, Annie Maria King died at the age of sixty-five years, nine months and four days. Her obituary appeared in both the *Baltimore Post* and the *Baltimore American* and read as follows:

> Mrs. John R. King died at the Preston Apartments early yesterday morning after an illness of seven weeks. She had not been in good health for more than a year and suffered from anemia. She is survived by four sisters, (Mrs. William A. Dickey, Mrs. Hannah W. Flush, Mrs. Ruth Ould and Mrs. J. J. Snyder.) Mrs. King was born in this city and has resided here all her life. She was the daughter of the later John J. Snyder, a prominent lawyer of this city. She was a member of Brown Memorial Church the past twenty-eight years and was also associated with the Federated Charities & Sailors' Anchorage. The funeral will take place Sunday at 2:30. Dr. John McDowell, pastor of Brown Memorial Church will officiate and burial will be in Loudon Park.[153]

Annie King's death certificate stated that she died of a "cerebral embolism," a condition which can cause a stroke.[154] At the time, John King had no idea of what was responsible for Annie's death. He blamed the poor air from the railroad as having a deleterious effect upon his wife's health. It certainly may have been a factor in her poor health. Just a day after Annie died, John addressed his concerns to the Mayor of Baltimore. The *Baltimore Sun* stated that "he had been fighting for the abolition of the smoke and noise from trains in Baltimore for twelve years."[155] John was quoted in the same article as saying the following:

> Mr. Mayor, I buried my wife yesterday. I have an apartment at the Preston, on the Guilford avenue side, and during the last week of my wife's illness I was obliged to sit at her bedside and listen to the noise made by the shifting of freights and watch the black smoke pouring in our windows until it seemed to me that I should go mad. Sleep for her was impossible and at times I almost considered getting a gun and going out to shoot one of those engineers. How far the Pennsylvania Railroad hastened the death of my wife, no one can say.[156]

John may have wished that they had never left their quiet Mt. Royal Avenue home.

In addition to accompanying her husband to many Grand Army banquets and meetings, Anna played a prominent part in the Women's Relief Corps, an auxiliary branch of the GAR. She also had spent time working with The Sailor's Anchorage charity and Federated Charities.

John not only remained in Baltimore, but continued to reside at the Preston Apartments despite his environmental concerns. He again openly complained about the air where he lived in a "Letter to the Editor" titled "Line Up Against the Smoke."[157] John spoke of the "intolerable smoke and coal gas which us mortals suffer within 40 blocks of the Pennsylvania Railroad," and challenged them "to visit me at the Preston and I will give them a seat facing the railroad where they can get a good mouthful ... and they will agree that something should be done at once."[158] Apparently, nothing would be done for some time to come.

His youngest brother, William, who still lived in Baltimore died just six years after Annie King's death, on January 13, 1923. John's oldest brother, Harrison, had already died on October 3, 1919 in Hagerstown. Also, John's sister, Addie, and her husband, Samuel Z. McLaughlin, died in 1898 and 1905, respectively. Thus, John R. King was the last remaining child of the six children of Samuel L. King and Eliza Lane King. Although John had some nieces and cousins still residing in Hagerstown, he had no relatives left in Baltimore. Even though he was born and raised in Hagerstown, John absolutely loved Baltimore despite problems with pollution. As he traveled to other areas in Maryland and to other states as part of his work for the Grand Army, John often praised Baltimore. As he said "when away from home and asked where I live my invariable answer is 'The best place on the map-Baltimore.'[159] John went on to explain:

> Coming from my home in Western Maryland in '59, my love for this good city has grown from year to year until it has become a passion. When President Taft once said to Admiral Stirling, General Leary and myself, when we invited him to dinner; "Baltimore? Why, everything that is good to eat, from the heavens above, the earth beneath or the water under the earth, you can get in Baltimore ... If you can't get it there, you can get it on the Eastern Sho'![160]

As with the passage cited, in his advanced years, John enjoyed citing the occasions where he met distinguished people. In 1930, he recalled a reception given for Cardinal Gibbons. Born in Baltimore in 1834, James Cardinal Gibbons was Baltimore's most distinguished churchman and served as the first Chancellor of The Catholic University of America in 1887. He died in 1921. In another "Letter to the Editor," titled "Things He Prizes," John wrote:

> On the occasion of the great reception to his eminence the late Cardinal Gibbons, in the 5th Regiment Armory, I was seated near his eminence, he turned to me and, when President Taft arrived, after greeting his eminence, he turned to me and, calling me by name, gave a handshake. Following him, came ex-President Roosevelt, who, following the greeting of the guest of the evening, turned to me and calling me by name, gave me one of those terrific handshakes for which he was famous. On the walls of my apartment are hand commissions-two signed by Roosevelt and one by Taft—which I prize highly. There also hangs a large photograph of Roosevelt, on which in my presence he inscribed: "To Comrade John R. King with regards of Theodore Roosevelt.[161]

His three commissions were signed by these two Presidents for the three terms John served as Special Pension Agent for the United States Pension Bureau.

In his later years, John was nostalgic for the old days of Hagerstown with its town picnics, Knights of the Roundtable celebrations and holidays like the Fourth of July. He fondly remembered his boyhood friends and the families that lived along the street of his boyhood home, South Potomac. In 1921, he reminisced:

> I would like to mention the names of the boys whom I knew so well, many of them have preceded me to that other and better land-the Blakes, Charley Smith, the Harrises, the Smalls, my cousin John C. Lane, dear Tom Hilliard, one of the last to go and his going has made a large hole in my life, Will and Alex. Armstrong, John and Sam Martin, S. Martin Bloom, Jake Late, Carver Mobley, John Weler, Charley Byers yet survive and served their country so well in the Civil War. I must not forget Col. E. M. Mobley the gallant Commander of the 7th Maryland Regiment-Pete Mayberry, the Radcliffs, but I must stop calling the roll it saddens me.[162]

The names of those friends and families that resided on South Potomac cited earlier included Armstrong, Chrissinger, Gumbert, Melheny Rouskulp, Miss Liza Snively, Biershing, Seibert, Small, Bouts, Benter, Frieze, Schner, Hershey, Blake, Harris, Z. B. Clark, Squire Handy, Billy Clark, Marmaduke Boyd and the Gelwicks.[163] In 1921, John King also recalled the surnames of families that lived in Washington County, but not in Hagerstown. As he stated:

> I could speak of old friends in different parts of the county, of the Landis, Adams, Baers, McCanley and others of Beaver Creek; the Gehrs, dear Hattie, who recently passed away, the Hitchews, Eakies, Leidys and others of Smithsburg; the Steffys, Grabers, Culbertsons, Cushwas and my cousin Mary Eliza Long who did so much to beautify the cemetery at Williamsport, but I have written too much I fear.[164]

In 1925, in a Letter to the Editor of the *Baltimore Sun,* John fondly recalled the fun of old-fashioned Fourth of July celebrations with "all of its attendant possibilities of personal injuries and fires," and added a political comment:

> The 'safe-and-sane' idea of celebrating the Fourth is an outgrowth of this miserable pacifist propaganda that is running all over the country, blunting the patriotic Instinct of young and old. Way back when I was a boy we had a real Fourth of July celebration in Hagerstown. The whole community would turn out and assemble in Fireoy' Woods, where the Young Americans...would have the time of their lives Patriotic songs and patriotic speeches ruled the day; the British lion's tail was twisted to beat the band, the tighter the twist the more uproarious the applause. I fought for the flag and learned to love it better than life...Let the small boy have an old-fashioned time. What if they do burn their fingers? It goes with the game What matters if a house or two is set fire. What's the Fire Department for?[165]

While the last part of his letter may have been said tongue-in-cheek, parents today would be aghast with such talk. Today, for safety's sake, only fireworks of the mildest variety are allowed. John might be in a state of shock if he saw the way we now celebrate the birth of our nation.

After the turn of the century and when he had completed his tenure as Commander-in-Chief of the Grand Army, John King had mixed sentiments about his former adversaries, the Confederate soldiers and their post-war activities. While he honored them for their valor in battle and believed that these veterans, like Union men, should be able to honor their fallen, he was opposed to some of their practices. For example, a large ceremony was held in Green Mount Cemetery in Baltimore, Maryland, on Memorial Day in 1906 to commemorate all Civil War veterans. The elaborate gathering was planned by "a handful of survivors belonging to Veteran Post 46, Department of Maryland, Grand Army of the Republic, assisted by the Women's Relief Corps, No. 6, and Camp No 11, Patriotic Sons of America."[166] Captain John R. King was one of the guest speakers. A portion of his speech was as follows:

> Once more we have come to this beautiful city of the dead soldiers of the republic. We come in the beautiful springtime, when the glad earth is rejoicing and putting on its mantle of green and Nature furnishes us her choicest floral gems to cast them as our heart offerings upon the last resting place of our fallen comrades. The men who we honor today made the greatest sacrifice due from a citizen to his country-that of their lives. It is right that a grateful people should honor its soldier dead.[167]

After the speeches, the veteran group then walked over to the grave of Confederate General Joseph E. Johnson and placed flowers as a tribute saying that "we are here to commemorate the lives of brave men and although General Johnston's views did not coincide with ours over the issues then at stake, our recognition of his heroism is highly appropriate to this occasion."[168] Thus, John and his comrades were conciliatory when it came to honoring the memories of fallen Confederate soldiers. Another instance of John's amiability was evidenced by his tribute to the late Colonel James W. Owens. Colonel Owens had served in the First Maryland Confederate Battery of Artillery during the war and was later a notable member of the United Confederate Veterans as Adjutant of the George H. Stewart Camp in Annapolis. John King said the following in the September 28, 1928 issue of the *Baltimore Sun*:

> In the passing of the late Colonel James W. Owens the State has lost one of its most unique and valuable citizens. It was my privilege to claim close friendship with him for many years. Although during the '61–'65 we fought on opposite sides, yet it made no difference in Jim Owens' choice of friends-and what a friend he was. He never failed to appreciate my interest in having the old Pikesville Armory set aside for a Confederate home.[169]

In fact, the Pikesville Confederate Home was largely made possible by John King's frequent lobbying trips to Annapolis when the bill was pending and through his friendship with two other Union veterans in the Maryland legislature, i. e., Captain William D. Burchnell in the Senate and Captain Bill Thompson in the House.[170] The bill was passed by a majority of Republican legislators.

Although John had many ex-Confederate soldier friends and acquaintances, he and his comrades in the Grand Army stood firm in their resolve to oppose some practices of both the United Daughters of the Confederacy and the United Confederate Veterans. Although there were many disagreements between these groups, only three issues will be presented.

In 1906, the United Daughters of the Confederacy sought to erect a statue of Captain Heinrich Hartmann Wirz, also known as Captain Henry Wirz. Captain Wirz was a Swiss-born Confederate soldier, commander of the infamous Fort Sumter, the "hell hole" prisoner-of-war camp which was located near Andersonville, Georgia. After the Civil War, Wirz was tried and executed for murder and conspiracy for his mistreatment of Union soldiers. Despite this, many Southerners viewed Wirz as a hero, not as a criminal. During the 40th National Encampment of the Grand Army in Minneapolis in August of 1906, comrades debated the issue of the proposed statue. One group, led by Past Commander-in-Chief E. Torrance, believed that "the Grand Army should not…take official cognizance of the question at this time."[171] However, Corporal James Tanner, current Commander-in-Chief and William A. Ketcham spoke in favor of taking action against the monument. On August 17, 1906, "…after an acrimonious debate", it was decided to write a letter of protest against the erection of a statue. A position statement was sent to General S. D. Lee, Commander-in-Chief of the United Confederate Veterans. Apparently, the letter of protest sent by the Grand Army fell on deaf ears. The United Daughters of the Confederacy erected a shaft statue as a tribute to Captain Wirz in the center of the community of Andersonville, but outside of the park. The monument was dedicated May 12, 1909 and remains standing today. During the same 40th encampment, John R. King was presented with a mahogany chest filled with a fine set of silver flatware in honor of his service to the Grand Army of the Republic.[172]

Another instance of enmity between the former Union and Confederate appeared during the Grand Army's 63th National Encampment which was held during September of 1929. President Herbert Hoover and thirty-one governors had endorsed a plan for a blue-gray reunion, but after another heated debate, the Grand Army disapproved the proposed reunion. One comrade, Frank O. Cole of New Jersey who spoke out against it said:

> They were wrong back in 1861 and when they admit they were wrong, and not until then will we join them. Let them fold up their battle flags, the flag we fought against and carried Old Glory against to victory. When they put those in museums then we will believe they want reunion.[173]

During the 63th National Encampment, John R. King of Baltimore was made a trustee of the permanent Grand Army Fund.[174] By the time this encampment was held, there had been only one Blue-Gray reunion in the 20th century held September 27, 1911 in Memphis, Tennessee. Only one more would be held. From June 29 to July 6, 1938, a large reunion was held in Gettysburg, Pennsylvania. Only about twenty-five veterans of the battle were there, but about two-thousand other Union and Confederate veterans made the trip.

The appropriateness of flying the Confederate battle flags and displaying Confederate monuments remain issues of contention to this day, almost two hundred years later. Some see it as a hated symbol of slavery while others view the flag as part of their Southern heritage. Many Confederate battle flags and monuments have already been removed by local and state governments and many more may suffer the same fate.

In 1931, another incident involving the Confederate battle flag arose in Baltimore on Flag Day when a Boy Scout carried it at the head of a column in a parade in the city. The Stars and Stripes and the flag of Maryland followed. At that time, "the Union veterans broke ranks, stepped aside and returned to their homes."[175] Apparently, John King heard of the plan to put the Confederate flag first although he was not even present. However, he strongly voiced his opinion on the matter:

> That flag represents the attempted destruction of the Stars and Stripes. It had no place in line. I told Capt. George T. Leech, commander of the Maryland encampment that I would not attend. What action he took, I do not know. But another protest of mine was that the Women's Relief Corps and the Daughters of Union Veterans were not among the organizations represented and they are two of the oldest organizations growing out of the Civil War.[176]

John's deceased wife was a member of the WRC and both of his deceased daughters were members of the Daughters of Union Veterans. John later added that "it's the Daughters of the Confederacy who are always scratching open the wound."[177]

Another area of contention in the early 20th century, in John King's Baltimore, revolved around issues associated with Memorial Day. John and his comrades in the Grand Army held Memorial Day as sacrosanct. It was a solemn occasion initiated originally in 1868 by the Grand Army to place flowers on the graves of fallen Union soldiers and sailors and was originally called Decoration Day. By the early twentieth-century, the opposing Union and Confederate celebrations of their dead with ceremonies held on different days merged into one day, now called Memorial Day. Memorial Day would also morph into a day for honoring all soldiers of the United States who died in any war, not just in the Civil War. Along with the placing of flowers on the soldiers' graves were parades honoring the fallen men. In April of 1919 in Baltimore, a proposal was made to include a parade of protest of the Eighteenth Amendment, also referred to as the Prohibition Amendment, on Memorial Day. John King had the following to say about the proposed, so-called "Wet Parade":

> ... a monster parade is being arranged for a protest against a certain amendment to the Constitution of the United States, known as the Prohibition Amendment should not be held. Resolved by the 45th encampment of the Grand Army of the Republic, That solemn protest is hereby made against such contemplated parade, which would mar the sanctity of Memorial Day, making it a day of ribald and hilarious desecration of what is held and intended to be day of holy patriotic sacrifice. We call upon the churches and patriotic societies, the Spanish War Veterans, the Veterans of Foreign Wars, the fathers and mothers whose sons, many of whom have made the supreme sacrifice and who sleep on "Flanders Field," the Argonne and Montfaucon to join with us in protesting to the Mayor of Baltimore city against granting a permit for the afore mentioned parade.[178]

The Mayor of Baltimore City later came out against the proposed parade.[179] Hence, the parade to protest the Prohibition Amendment was postponed to June 2, but John King's battle over keeping Decoration or Memorial Day sacred was not over yet.[180] Next came an attempt to include a reception on Thursday, May 30, for the soldiers of the 29th Infantry Division in the scheduled Memorial Day festivities. World War I was over and the City of Baltimore wanted to honor its returning heroes. Once again, John King spoke up:

> I trust that this will not be done. Arrangements have already been made for the proper observance of that day. Memorial Day has added significance this year; new griefs have come to many homes in America, new graves have been opened in our cemeteries where lie the flower of our young manhood. These graves are to be visited and services will be held in all of the cemeteries in and around the city. These services will be seriously interfered with if this proposed reception should be held on that day … the members of the Grand Army of the Republic and veterans of later wars are anxious to join in welcoming home the returning soldiers of the world war, but they consider it their bounden duty to do honor to their dead comrades.[181]

Once again, John King, the Grand Army and the Mayor of Baltimore got what they wanted. A homecoming, including a parade and celebration for the returning 29th Infantry Division, was held beginning at 11 a.m. on Saturday, May 26, instead of on Memorial Day, May 31. Many homes were open to the returning soldiers on May 31 as a gesture of good will.[182] Despite high temperatures on Memorial Day, services with decoration of the fallen heroes' graves were held in all of Baltimore's cemeteries. As the *Baltimore Sun* noted, "soldiers of the Big War join "Boys of '61' and '98 in celebration of Memorial Day.[183] Four months later, Captain John King was still angry about the attempts to change the original intent of Memorial Day. He slammed Peoples Court Associate James F. Klecka who was responsible for such ill-fated maneuvering. Johns' comments were summarized in an article that appeared in the September 8, 1919, issue of the *Baltimore Sun:*

> King criticizes Director-General Klecka for his attempt to desecrate Memorial Day by having a wet parade and 'who characterized the Grand Army as of no account, and despite its protest he assured the public that the parade would be held. Not until the splendid 100 per cent, mothers of Maryland's fighting boys rose in righteous indignation in protest did Mr. Klecka call off his parade.'[184]

In all of these "battles," whether they were with the United Confederate Veterans, United Daughters of the Confederacy, or local politicians who wanted to change Memorial Day, John R. King and the Grand Army held fast to their patriotic principles. John never hesitated to voice his concerns during national GAR encampments, in newspaper articles or via "Letters to the Editor" of local papers.

His 6th Maryland Regiment in the Civil War was attacked in a letter to the Editor , by a former Confederate soldier in April of 1918, for being cowards who ran during the Battle of Winchester on July 10, 1864. This same former Confederate soldier, O. C. Shipley, also spoke harshly of John's war record. A Union veteran responded by saying that "the 6th Maryland is recognized in history as one of the fighting regiments of the Civil War" and that "the men who Shipley says he saw running were probably some of a regiment of 100-day men, sent there for emergency duty. [185] John responded in the *Baltimore Sun* April 22 by saying:

> Shipley refers to my war record. That is easily obtained by reference to the records of the Adjutant-Generals office in Washington. I can only say that to the gentleman, however, that my three wounds are all in front. Shipley refers to July 10, 1864. I was not there; neither was my regiment.[186]

Someone in the War Department must have thought highly of John King's war record. At the age of eighty-eight years, Captain John R. King received the Purple Heart from Secretary of War, Patrick J. Hurley, on September, 12, 1932. The *Baltimore Sun* noted that the Purple Heart "was established by George Washington as a mark of distinction for valiant services in battle" and was given to John "on account of wounds received in action while serving in the Sixth Maryland Regiment in the Civil War."[187] John's last injury at the Battle of the Wilderness caused him to be hospitalized for over a year and resulted in a permanent disability which would forever require the use of a cane. At the time of this award, John King was the only Union soldier from Maryland so honored. He was also the last surviving officer of the 6th Maryland. John added:

> This about completes the honors that can come to me growing out of my military service. No other Marylander has received the honors that have come to me.[188]

John had been commander of Wilson Post, Department of Maryland, Grand Army of the Republic; national commander-in-chief of GAR; commander of the Military Order of the Loyal Legion and junior commander-in-chief of the Loyal Legion.

Since the death of his wife, Annie, in 1917, John continued to be active with his involvement in the Grand Army and also retained his strong work ethic.

He filled various officer positions in local Wilson Post No. 1 at 329 North Gay Street in Baltimore, attended Maryland state gatherings and went to forty-one National Encampments of GAR since joining in 1867. The sad part was that John was outliving everyone. Fewer and fewer comrades attended the meeting and encampments because death was taking its toll. If that was not bad enough, all of his close relatives, including his parents, sister and two brothers, had died.

Fortunately for John King, his lower limb disability and limp did not totally keep him from working. In 1912, John returned to work at the United States Custom House in Baltimore. Although he chose not to take his former position as Chief Marine Clerk, he was able to work as a storekeeper at Brown's Wharf in Baltimore until 1924. At that time, he was forced to retire because he had reached the seventy-year age limit for retirement of the Federal Government. In addition, according to the 1920 and the 1930 U.S. Censuses, John King also was employed with the Western Maryland Railroad.[189] He must have done this work on a part-time basis since he was employed full-time with the Custom House. In addition, forever the workaholic, John King worked in public relations for the U.S. House of Representatives beginning in 1928. No doubt, he used this position to attempt to influence Congressmen towards passing favorable bills for the veterans, widows and orphans. Then, one day while walking down a corridor of the Capitol, John King was stricken with a heart attack. On Wednesday, February, 1934, he was taken to his home at the Preston Apartments where he died three days later on Saturday, March 3. He was eighty-nine years, eight months and seven days old.[190] Apparently, he had no desire to be taken to a hospital. The death certificate confirmed a coronary thrombosis.[191] Funeral services were held at 11 a.m. at the Preston Apartments with Reverend T. Guthrie Speers from Brown Memorial Presbyterian Church officiating. He was interred at Loudon Park Cemetery next to his wife, Annie Maria King. The following obituary appeared March 4, 1934 in the *New York Times*:

> John Rigdon King, veteran of the Civil War and a past national commander of the Grand Army of the Republic, died today in this ninetieth year from a heart attack suffered in Washington on Wednesday.
>
> Mr. King was born in Hagerstown, Md., on June 24, 1844. He enlisted in August, 1862, in Company H, Sixth Maryland Volunteer Infantry, serving two years and ten months. He participated in several battles, including Spotsylvania, Cold Harbor, Petersburg and the Battle of the Wilderness, and was wounded three times. He is said to have organized and commanded the first company of the Boys in Blue, predecessor of the Grand Army of the Republic.

> Mr. King served in the Third and Sixth Army Corps, Army of the Potomac, and was a prisoner of war for six months in Salisbury (N. C.) prison and Libby prison. In the Grand Army of the Republic, he held every office. He was elected national senior vice president in 1904 and commander-in-chief the next year.
>
> Mr. King was employed in the Baltimore Custom House for thirty years and was United States pension agent at Washington until 1913. At his death he was president of the Grand Army Club of Maryland and the Maryland Union Soldiers and Sailors Commission. He was a member of the Loyal Legion and the Maryland World War Memorial Commission.[192]

In his will, John King dispersed his possessions as follows: he gave two antique heirlooms, a table in his library and a china pitcher on his buffet, to Mary Elizabeth Frush.[193] The jeweled Grand Army Badge, which was presented to him in 1905 by his official staff at Denver, Colorado, for his term as Commander-in-Chief of the Grand Army, was bequeathed to the City of Pittsburgh to be placed in their War Memorial Building. His great-grandniece, Jane Bikle, received the mahogany case of flat silver which was presented to him in Minneapolis in 1906 by the Grand Army. The remainder of his property, real and personal, was given to his nieces, Mary Emma Clapp and Clara Luella Irvin, both residents of Hagerstown.

At the conclusion of his speech at the Hotel Belvedere in Baltimore on January 7, 1915, to members of the Military Order of the Loyal Legion, John King read this poem written by Thomas Wentworth Higginson in 1888 called *Waiting for the Bugle*:

We wait for the bugle; the night dews are cold,
The limbs of the soldiers feel jaded and old,
The field of the bivouac is windy and bare,
There is lead in our joints, there is frost in our hair,
The future is veiled and its fortunes unknown,
As we lie with hushed breath till the bugle is blown.

At the sound of that bugle each comrade shall spring
Like an arrow released from the strain of the string;
The courage, the impulse of youth shall come back
To banish the chill of the drear bivouac,
And sorrows and losses and care fade away,
When that life-giving signal proclaims the new day.

Though the bivouac of age may put ice in our veins,
And no fiver of steel in our sinews remains;
Though the comrades of yesterday's march are not here,
And the sunlight seems pale and the branches are sere;
Though the sound of our cheering dies down to a moan
We shall find our last youth when the bugle is blown.[194]

Epilogue

Aside from brief stints employed as a sutler/photographer and as a clerk in Abraham Levi's store during the Civil War and two years of employment with the railroad just after the war, John R. King devoted his vocational pursuits to the U. S Army and the Federal government. He served with distinction with the 6th Maryland Volunteer Infantry from August 26, 1862, until he was discharged on disability on May 18, 1865. In his professional life, he never sought any position that allowed him to accumulate wealth. Thus, he was never a man of means. John was more interested in working for the public good. John was employed with the U. S Government first, by Presidential appointment, as a regional Pension Bureau agent. Later he served as Chief Marine Clerk and then during his senior years, as a storekeeper. He was a workaholic who was forced by the Federal government to retire from his position at the Baltimore Customs House. Even then, John found a way to keep working. He secured a job with the U.S. House of Representatives in public relations, greeting people as they entered the halls of Congress. Undoubtedly, John used this opportunity to speak with members of Congress to garner support for pending G.A.R. bills.

John R. King's contributions to his family and country were multifaceted. There are many types of legacies. Among them are items bequeathed in a will, oral traditions, written traditions or memoirs and the lasting effects of actions taken by the deceased individual. John King's legacies include all of these types.

One dictionary definition of legacy is as a gift by will especially of money or other personal property or as something transmitted by or received from an ancestor or predecessor. In his will, John King left two antique heirlooms to Mary Elizabeth Flush. His jeweled GAR badge was bequeathed to the City of Pittsburgh. The grand set of silver housed in a mahogany case which was also presented to him by the G.A.R. was passed on to Jane Bikle, John's great-grandniece. All other real and personal property was divided up and bequeathed to his nieces, Mary Emma Clapp and Clara Luella Irvin, both of Hagerstown. John's will did not specify what other real or personal property he owned. One of his descendants mentioned that she has his Civil War officer's sword. However, a legacy is much more than simply the passing of ones' material goods to ones' descendants. It can also be the actions taken and stories written that result in lasting benefits to others and for the sake of posterity.

The same descendant who has John's sword also has in her possession John King's personal scrapbook and his brief memoirs. The scrapbook contains family photos as well as copies various newspaper articles about important events related to his employment or to the GAR. In addition to those items bequeathed in his will and perhaps more importantly, John R. King left a brief memoir about his family's genealogy, his regiment's military history and his accomplishments in the GAR. There is also a large body of GAR papers that were donated to the Library of Congress sometime after that organization ceased to exist in 1956. The papers are available to anyone who wishes to research the various terms of office of its Commanders-in-Chief or the volumes of records that were retained by the GAR for posterity's sake. They would, of course, include the papers related to John R. Kings' terms as Commander-in-Chief and as Vice Commander. This body of John Kings' written material is part and parcel of his multi-faceted legacy.

John's avocational passion was the Grand Army of the Republic. During his lifetime, John held virtually every position in the GAR hierarchy. He was an active member for sixty-eight years, from 1867 when he first joined in Baltimore to 1934 when he died in Baltimore. He was an advocate for Union Civil War veterans, widows and orphans his entire life. Much of his legacy includes this advocacy and other work with the G.A.R. First, his legacy includes his work to help plan and build the first and only church dedicated to the Grand Army of the Republic in the United States, the Lansdowne Christian Church. This church in Lansdowne, Maryland, is known for its beautiful stained glass windows. Secondly, in part due to his leadership and lifetime commitment, the Grand Army of the Republic operated until 1956. Based upon that earlier model, the Sons of the Union Veterans continue today as the legal successor to the GAR. Their members continue to decorate the graves of veterans and to hold activities that preserve and commemorate military service. Thirdly, John King and his comrades established the holiday now known as Memorial Day, a day of remembrance of those who their lives in battle for their country. Fourth, John King served on two Maryland commissions after the Civil War. One established a permanent monument to Maryland Union soldiers at the National Chickamauga and Chattanooga Battlefield Park. The other, the Maryland Flag Commission preserved Union Maryland battle flags for posterity. Lastly, he dedicated his life both in terms of his job in the U.S. Pension Bureau and his lifetime involvement in the Grand Army of the Republic to the betterment and enrichment of the lives of tens of thousands of Union veterans, their widows and their orphan children.

Many of their descendants today owe John and his comrades a great deal of thanks for providing financial support during the post-Civil War era to their ancestors. Many of them would not be living today were it not for the success of the G.A.R. in helping to enact favorable pension laws. For many years following the Civil War, based in large part upon the influence and lobbying efforts of the GAR, the U.S. Pension Bureau bestowed much needed financial benefits to Union veterans, their widows and their orphan children. John King's work at the U.S. Pension Bureau and with the G.A.R. had enormous economic consequences for Civil War veterans, their wives, and their children and eventually for their descendants. In fact, the last Civil War widow and pensioner, Irene Triplett, who is eighty-six years young, still lives and receives a monthly check as the child of a veteran. Mrs. Tripletts' benefits are now administered by the Department of Veterans Affairs, the bureau which eventually replaced the Pension Bureau. Current disabled veterans and their survivors also receive financial assistance from that Federal agency.

In addition to the King memoir papers and his Pension Bureau and G.A.R. accomplishments and records, another important component of the King legacy is the diary upon which this book is based. It offers a rare opportunity to view the Civil War from the point of view of a teenage boy who was caught up in the conflict by accident. It is probably the only diary in existence that was written by a teenager who was both a sutler and a photographer. Perhaps by fate, his diary was found so that John's complete life story could be told. His diary will forever remain an integral part of Civil War history. It has already outlived John King by eighty-four years. One hundred and fifty-six years have passed since it was written and no one has seen it. Taken together, all of these written records and John's work with the pension programs are John R. King's most significant legacy. They tell a story of a man with great courage, character and charity. They are of much more consequence than any gift of money, personal property or real estate. These records including the transcription of his diary are now available for all to read.

After some effort, when the author and one descendant of a distantly-related family corresponded with one another, she was excited that the diary John kept as a soldier had finally been found. When informed that the newly discovered diary had been written by John when he was teenager, the family member was surprised. She was not aware that John had also kept a civilian diary. Of course, the family was still anxious to read John's first diary. Hence, a second "Lost Diary" is still out there somewhere. John R. King probably started it when he enlisted in the U. S. Army August 21, 1862. Perhaps this second diary will also be discovered one day at a farm auction.

At the end of his abbreviated autobiography, John wrote the following:

> And now as shadows lengthen, the day is not distant when the Sunset gun will sound for me, when I can almost hear the beating of waves on yonder Shore. I wait in calm resignation on the blessed hope of meeting my Comrades who have gone before, on Fames Eternal Camping Ground.

Union Soldiers of Company H, 6th Maryland Volunteer Infantry

Soldier	ABERCROMBIE, Captain William H. (surname is of Scottish origin)
Date of Birth	January, 1837
Age Given at Enlistment	25 years
Description at Enlistment	Not given
Place of Birth	New York
Pre-War Residence	Unknown
Pre-War Occupation	Unknown
Post-War Residence	814 E. 12th St. and then 56 Kent Ave., New York City, New York
Post-War Occupation	Printer
Names of Parents	George and Anna Abercrombie (tentative)
Names of Children	None
Name of Wife	Sarah Abercrombie and then married Mary Abercrombie in 1899
Date Soldier Filed Pension	August 22, 1890 in New York, disability "wounded left knee"
Date Widow Filed Pension	September 15, 1916
Date of Death	1907 (tentative)
Cemetery	Evergreen, El Paso County, Colorado (tentative)
Remarks	Enrolled June 9, 1862 at Elkton, Va.; 1st Sgt. Co. B Aug. 20, 1862; 2nd Lt. Nov. 1, 1862; 1st Lt. Co. H Nov. 17, 1864; Capt. January 23, 1865 to replace Capt. Martin; many leave requests for sick wife and dying child.

Soldier	ADAMS, Corporal Jacob H. T.
Date of Birth	About 1845
Age Given at Enlistment	18 years
Description at Enlistment	Unknown
Place of Birth	Maryland
Pre-War Residence	Smithsburg, Washington County, Maryland
Pre-War Occupation	None known.
Post-War Residence	N/A
Post-War Occupation	N/A
Names of Parents	William and Ann Adams
Names of Children	N/A
Name of Wife	N/A
Date Soldier Filed Pension	Not married
Date Widow Filed Pension	October 4, 1880
Date of Death	June 14, 1864 while a prisoner of war at the age of almost 20 years
Cemetery	Andersonville (Georgia) National Cemetery, gravesite 1928
Remarks	The soldier's father was a shoemaker. The Adams family lived two doors from the residence of Captain Adam D. Martin.

Soldier	ADAMS, Private John
Date of Birth	*c.* 1839
Age Given at Enlistment	23 years
Description at Enlistment	5' 8" in height, fair complexion, grey eyes, and black hair

Place of Birth	Born in Ireland
Pre-War Residence	Probably Washington County, Maryland
Pre-War Occupation	laborer
Post-War Residence	Hancock, Maryland (tentative)
Post-War Occupation	confectioner
Names of Parents	Unknown
Names of Children	James, Effie, James, Pleasant, Anna, Mary
Name of Wife	Christiana
Date Soldier Filed Pension	September 1, 1864 and approved
Date Widow Filed Pension	None filed
Date of Death	Unknown
Cemetery	Unknown
Remarks	Private Adams suffered the "loss of two fingers and loss of use of remaining fingers of right hand from a gunshot wound received at the Battle of Mine Run." He was found three-quarters disabled, unfit for duty in the V.R.C. and was discharged May 2, 1864.

Soldier	BACHTELL, Corporal Lewis L.
Date of Birth	April, 1841
Age Given at Enlistment	21 years
Description at Enlistment	Not given
Place of Birth	Unknown
Pre-War Residence	Washington County, Maryland
Pre-War Occupation	Unknown
Post-War Residence	Ringgold, Washington County, Maryland
Post-War Occupation	Laborer
Names of Parents	Unknown
Names of Children	Addie M., Jennie and Harry L.
Name of Wife	Elizabeth also known as "Lizzie"
Date Soldier Filed Pension	June 2, 1880 and approved
Date Widow Filed Pension	August 2, 1910 and approved
Date of Death	July 26, 1900 at 59 years of age
Cemetery	Smithsburg Cemetery, Smithsburg, Washington County, Maryland
Remarks	Soldier suffered a flesh wound of the abdominal parietes November 27, 1863, at the Battle of Mine Run and was transferred to the V.R.C. On the 1890 Veterans Census, he stated that he received a "gunshot wound in the right side, ball is still imbedded."

Soldier	BARKDALL, Sergeant John C. (surname sometimes written as Barkdoll)
Date of Birth	*c.* 1840
Age Given at Enlistment	22 years
Description at Enlistment	Not given.
Place of Birth	Maryland
Pre-War Residence	Cavetown, Washington County, Maryland
Pre-War Occupation	Helper on his father's farm.
Post-War Residence	N/A
Post-War Occupation	N/A

Names of Parents	John and Susan Barkdall
Names of Children	None. His siblings were Samuel, Daniel, and Elizabeth Barkdall
Name of Wife	Never married.
Date Soldier Filed Pension	None filed
Date Widow Filed Pension	
Date of Death	June 15, 1864 at the age of 24 years
Cemetery	Andersonville Memorial Cemetery (tentative)
Remarks	John was promoted to 4th Sergeant. He was captured in Loudon County, Virginia July 20, 1863 by Mosby's men, was confined in Richmond, Virginia, and was then sent to Andersonville Prison in Georgia on March 23, 1864, where he later died.

Soldier	BIKLE, Private Ferdinand H. (surname sometimes written as Bickle)
Date of Birth	September 27, 1842
Age Given at Enlistment	20 years
Description at Enlistment	5' 9 ½" dark complexion, gray eyes, and light hair
Place of Birth	Maryland
Pre-War Residence	Smithsburg, Washington County, Maryland
Pre-War Occupation	Cabinetmaker
Post-War Residence	Cavetown, Washington County, Md., & Hagerstown, Md. in 1922
Post-War Occupation	Cabinet maker and Farrier
Names of Parents	Christian and Barbara Bikle, both born in Germany.
Names of Children	Sorena and Philip
Name of Wife	Anna B., married for 43 years
Date Soldier Filed Pension	November 22, 1887 and approved. Listed "heart disease" 1890 Census
Date Widow Filed Pension	September 22, 1923 and approved
Date of Death	August 6, 1923 at age 80
Cemetery	Smithsburg Cemetery, Smithsburg, Washington County, Maryland
Remarks	Corporal Bikle was AWOL December 22. 1862 and was demoted to private. He was taken prisoner at Winchester, Va. June 15, 1863 and was exchanged. He then became ill and was discharged June 3, 1865.

Soldier	BONEBRAKE, Private Andrew Snively
Date of Birth	January 22, 1848
Age Given at Enlistment	18 years but he was only 14 1/2 years of age at the time
Description at Enlistment	5' 6" tall, fair complexion, brown eyes, light hair
Place of Birth	Franklin County, Pennsylvania
Pre-War Residence	Franklin County, Pennsylvania
Pre-War Occupation	clerk
Post-War Residence	Waynesboro, Pa. and later 1508 Eutaw Place, Baltimore, Maryland
Post-War Occupation	Druggist, U.S. Postmaster in Waynesboro from April 11, 1890 to May 2, 1894 and Physician in Baltimore, Md from at least 1901 to 1911
Names of Parents	Daniel and Margaret Stoner Bonebrake
Names of Children	Bertha H., Adela E., G. Mary and Benjamin S.
Name of Wife	Susan Catharine Price Bonebrake, married 39 years as of 1910

Date Soldier Filed Pension	March 11, 1910 and approved
Date Widow Filed Pension	May 12, 1913 and approved
Date of Death	April 24, 1913 at the age of 65
Cemetery	Green Hill Cemetery, Waynesboro, Pennsylvania
Remarks	Private Bonebrake was AWOL in February, 1863 and deserted November 12, 1864 but returned and completed his enlistment. He was also taken as a prisoner of war June 15, 1863, at Winchester, Va., was confined at Richmond, Va., and was exchanged at City Point, Va., reported to Camp Parole in Annapolis, Md. and returned to his regiment October 5, 1863.

Soldier	BOWARD, Corporal Michael K. (also known as Bowers)
Date of Birth	Unknown
Age Given at Enlistment	29 years
Description at Enlistment	5' 9" in height, dark complexion, grey eyes, black hair
Place of Birth	Born in Germany
Pre-War Residence	Unknown
Pre-War Occupation	Laborer
Name of Wife	Unknown
Date Soldier Filed Pension	None filed by him
Date Widow Filed Pension	February 5, 1931 but not approved
Date of Death	Before February 5, 1931
Remarks	Private Boward deserted November 20, 1862 from Williamsport, Md. He was never arrested or court martialed. However, in a statement from the War Dept. July 15, 1931, written by Major C. H. Bridges, Adju-tant General that read, "It has this day been determined ...that the above-named man (Michael Boward) was not in the military service...as a member of Co. H, 6th Regt. Vol. Infantry." The general provided no explanation of his statement.

Soldier	BRANDENBERG, Sergeant Amos (AKA Brautenberg, Brandenburg) The surname is of German origin.
Date of Birth	March 12, 1845
Age Given at Enlistment	18 years, but was only 17 years of age
Description at Enlistment	5' 9" tall, fair complexion, blue eyes, light hair
Place of Birth	Maryland
Pre-War Residence	Petersville. Frederick Co., then Pleasant Valley, Washington Co., Md.
Pre-War Occupation	None shown on census
Post-War Residence	Burkittsville, Frederick County, Maryland
Post-War Occupation	Mail carrier
Names of Parents	Peter and Hannah Brandenberg
Names of Children	Charles P., Harry L., and Hannah B.
Name of Wife	Alice S. Bradenberg
Date Soldier Filed Pension	August 3, 1865 and approved
Date Widow Filed Pension	February 8, 1898 and approved
Date of Death	January 22, 1898 at 52 years of age
Cemetery	Burkittsville Union Cemetery, Frederick County, Maryland
Remarks	On April 1, 1865, Private Brandenberg in a charge at the battle of Fort Fisher, of the Petersburg line, was struck by grapeshot in his right leg He developed gangrene and the leg was amputation below the knee.

Soldier	BRIDENDOLPH, Private Harrison
Date of Birth	*c.* 1830
Age Given at Enlistment	32 years
Description at Enlistment	Not provided
Place of Birth	Maryland
Pre-War Residence	Clear Spring, Washington County, Maryland
Pre-War Occupation	Day laborer
Post-War Residence	Indian Spring, Washington County, Maryland
Post-War Occupation	Farmer
Names of Parents	William and Martha Bridendolph. father b. Md., mother b. Germany
Names of Children	David, William H., Martha A., Samuel T., Peter, Edward and Gilbert
Name of Wife	Frannie Bridendolph
Date Soldier Filed Pension	None filed
Date Widow Filed Pension	None filed
Date of Death	January 26, 1894 at age 64 years
Cemetery	Unknown
Remarks	Soldier placed under arrest for desertion from Williamsport, Md., was confined in Fort McHenry with ball and chain for 2 ½ years by general court martial and was to be "drummed out of the service."

Soldier	BREITNESSER, Private Leonard (aka Breitweser and Brightwiser)
Date of Birth	*c.* 1843, emigrated with parents in 1846.
Age Given at Enlistment	19 years
Description at Enlistment	5' 10" fair complexion, blue eyes, brown hair
Place of Birth	Born in Germany
Pre-War Residence	Cavetown, Washington County, Maryland
Pre-War Occupation	Laborer
Post-War Residence	Maryland, Ogle County, IL., then Clay Center, Clay County, Kansas
Post-War Occupation	Farmer and Carpenter
Names of Parents	Samuel and Catharine Breitnesser
Names of Children	Charles, Nora, Lola, Daisey and William L.
Name of Wife	Amelia, married for 40 years as of 1910 and by 1930 a widower
Date Soldier Filed Pension	February 9, 1889 and approved
Date Widow Filed Pension	None filed.
Date of Death	April 29, 1935 at 92 years of age
Cemetery	Greenwood Cemetery, Clay Center, Clay County, Kansas
Remarks	Captured June 15, 1863 in Winchester, Va., confined in Richmond and exchanged at City Point. Wounded in action at Wilderness May 5, 1864

Soldier	BREWER, Quartermaster James Henry Clay
Date of Birth	July 11, 1838
Age Given at Enlistment	24 years
Description at Enlistment	Not given
Place of Birth	Maryland
Pre-War Residence	District 2, Washington County, Maryland
Pre-War Occupation	Unknown

Post-War Residence	Clear Spring, Md. in 1870 then Peabody Township, Marion, KS 1880+
Post-War Occupation	Merchant
Names of Parents	Daniel and Mary Margaret Heller Brewer
Names of Children	Carrie, Exlelie W., Nellie F. and William Ed
Name of Wife	Mary Loose Brewer
Date Soldier Filed Pension	March 17, 1896 and approved
Date Widow Filed Pension	None filed
Date of Death	December 15, 1927 at age 89
Cemetery	Prairie Lawn Cemetery, Peabody, Marion County, Kansas
Remarks	Enlisted as a Private, to 2nd Lieutenant September 5, 1862, to 1st Lieutenant February 11, 1863 and to Regiment QM November 17, 1864

Soldier	CRISSSINGER, Private William (aka Chrissinger)
Date of Birth	July, 1843
Age Given at Enlistment	19 years
Description at Enlistment	5' 6" tall, complexion fair, grey eyes, brown hair
Place of Birth	Hagerstown, Maryland
Pre-War Residence	Hagerstown, Maryland
Pre-War Occupation	Mechanic
Post-War Residence	Hagerstown, Maryland
Post-War Occupation	Clerk in store in 1870 and Deputy U.S. Marshall in 1910 and thereafter
Names of Parents	Samuel and Susan Crissinger
Names of Children	None known
Name of Wife	Sarah Shirley (tentative)
Date Soldier Filed Pension	May 27, 1880
Date Widow Filed Pension	None filed
Date of Death	July 18, 1925 at age 81 years
Cemetery	Rose Hill Cemetery, Hagerstown, Maryland
Remarks	Ill for two years in hospital. Provost Marshall found him in Martinsburg dressed in the uniform of an assistant surgical volunteer. Returned to Regt. March 15, 1865 and wounded on Petersburg line April 4, 1865.

Soldier	DAVIS, Corporal Amos C.
Date of Birth	January 5, 1843
Age Given at Enlistment	19 years
Description at Enlistment	None provided
Place of Birth	Maryland
Pre-War Residence	Unknown
Pre-War Occupation	Unknown
Post-War Residence	Beaver Creek, Washington County, Maryland
Post-War Occupation	Shoemaker
Names of Parents	Nathan C. and Mary E. Wood Davis
Names of Children	Viola V., William E., Maggie M., and Charles S. W.
Name of Wife	Sarah E. Davis, born in Hesse-Darmstadt

Date Soldier Filed Pension	March 12, 1878 and approved, with Charles E. Henson as guardian
Date Widow Filed Pension	None filed as his wife preceded him in death.
Date of Death	March 15, 1905 at 62 years of age
Cemetery	Rose Hill Cemetery, Hagerstown, Maryland
Remarks	Captured June 15, 1863 at Winchester, Va., paroled at City Point, Va., and sent to Regiment October 5, 1863. Promoted to Corp. Nov. 2, 1864

Soldier	DIDLOW, Private William H. (aka Ditlow and Dilton)
Date of Birth	January, 1841
Age Given at Enlistment	22 years
Actual Age at Enlistment	Not provided
Place of Birth	Pennsylvania
Pre-War Residence	South Middleton, Cumberland County, Pennsylvania (tentative)
Pre-War Occupation	Unknown
Post-War Residence	Williamsport, Washington County, Maryland
Post-War Occupation	Farm laborer and fence maker
Names of Parents	Henry and Susan Didlow
Names of Children	Milton C. and Susan C.
Name of Wife	Mary Ellen North Didlow
Date Soldier Filed Pension	January 22, 1891 but not approved
Date Widow Filed Pension	None filed
Date of Death	February 29, 1910 at 69 years of age
Cemetery	River View Cemetery, Williamsport, Maryland
Remarks	Captured at Winchester June 15, 1863, confined in Richmond until June 23, paroled June 23, but deserted from Camp Parole, Maryland.

Soldier	EAKLE, Private John C.
Date of Birth	March 31, 1837
Age Given at Enlistment	24 years
Description at Enlistment	Not given
Place of Birth	Maryland
Pre-War Residence	Unknown
Pre-War Occupation	Unknown
Post-War Residence	Smithsburg, Washington County, Maryland
Post-War Occupation	Farm hand
Names of Parents	Unknown
Names of Children	Gertrude, Charles, Clara, Nanny A., John S. and Percy C.
Name of Wife	Joanna Eakle
Date Soldier Filed Pension	May 26, 1879 having served 2 years, 9 months and 24 days
Date Widow Filed Pension	November 29, 1880
Date of Death	September 20, 1880 at 43 years of age
Cemetery	Smithsburg Cemetery, Smithsburg, Washington County, Maryland
Remarks	Served with distinction as Regimental Teamster, then Brigade Teamster. Shown as being present at every roll call.

Soldier	FISHACH, Private Henry F. (aka Fishack)
Date of Birth	March 15, 1842
Age Given at Enlistment	19 years
Description at Enlistment	Not provided
Place of Birth	Maryland
Pre-War Residence	Cavetown, Washington County, Maryland
Pre-War Occupation	None known
Post-War Residence	Ringgold, Washington County, Maryland
Post-War Occupation	Farm hand and fruit grower
Names of Parents	George and Mary Ann Reynolds Fishach
Names of Children	Mary, William, Carrie, Harry and John
Name of Wife	Mary E. Fishach and married for 28 years as of 1900
Date Soldier Filed Pension	May 26, 1893 and approved
Date Widow Filed Pension	January 23, 1902 and approved. Said that he had "piles rheumatism"
Date of Death	January 5, 1902 at 60 years of age
Cemetery	Saint Paul's Lutheran Cemetery, Leitersburg, Washington County, Md.
Remarks	Taken prisoner at Winchester June15, 1863, confined in Libby Prison and Belle Isle, paroled at City Point, Va. March 15, 1864 and reported to Camp Parole, Annapolis, Md., March 19, 1864.

Soldier	FISHACH, Private Jeremiah (Brother to Henry F. Fishach)
Date of Birth	September 5, 1843
Age Given at Enlistment	18 years of age
Description at Enlistment	None provided
Place of Birth	Maryland
Pre-War Residence	Ringgold, Washington County, Maryland
Pre-War Occupation	Unknown, if any
Post-War Residence	Ringgold, Washington County, Maryland
Post-War Occupation	Stone mason
Names of Parents	George and Mary A. Fishach
Names of Children	None known
Name of Wife	Annie Rebecca Willar Fishach
Date Soldier Filed Pension	March 13, 1891 and approved
Date Widow Filed Pension	December 6, 1898 and approved
Date of Death	October 15, 1898 at 55 years of age
Cemetery	Cavetown, Washington County, Maryland
Remarks	Captured June 15, 1863 at Winchester and paroled. Promoted Corporal Jan. 1, 1865 and assigned Provost Guard detail, but went home from about 7/28/64 to9/2/64 without leave and was court martialed.

Soldier	FISHER, Corporal Frisby Tillman
Date of Birth	June 15, 1845
Age Given at Enlistment	17 years of age
Description at Enlistment	5' 5" flush complexion, blue eyes, and light hair
Place of Birth	Washington County, Maryland
Pre-War Residence	Sharpsburg, Washington County, Maryland

Pre-War Occupation	Laborer
Post-War Residence	1900 Argill St., Fremont, Iowa, 1910 Luna, N.M., 1920 Spokane, Wash.
Post-War Occupation	1900 Stationary engineer,1910 RR wells pumper and 1920 laborer
Names of Parents	Thomas and Rebecca
Names of Children	Clarence, Nellie M. (Andres) and Earl
Name of Wife	Flora C. Swiggart Fisher
Date Soldier Filed Pension	September 15, 1890 in Iowa and approved
Date Widow Filed Pension	February 1, 1923 in Iowa
Date of Death	December 21, 1922 at 77 years of age
Cemetery	Hamburg Cemetery, Hamburg Township, Fremont, Iowa
Remarks	Absent without leave from camp in Berryville, Va. June 12, 1863 until October 8, 1863, but not court martialed. Promoted 7th Corp April 3, 65

Soldier	FLECKENSTINE, Private John (aka Fleckenstein) a German surname
Date of Birth	*c.* 1844
Age Given at Enlistment	18 years
Description at Enlistment	Not given
Place of Birth	Unknown
Pre-War Residence	Unknown
Pre-War Occupation	Unknown
Post-War Residence	Unknown
Post-War Occupation	Unknown
Names of Parents	Unknown
Names of Children	None
Name of Wife	None
Date Soldier Filed Pension	None filed
Date Widow Filed Pension	None
Date of Death	Killed in action at Opequon, Va., September 19, 1864 at age 20
Cemetery	Unknown
Remarks	He "was killed…in Sheridan's fight at Winchester, Virginia having eleven bullets shot through him"

Soldier	FLORY, Private Benjamin
Date of Birth	*c.* 1838
Age Given at Enlistment	21 years
Description at Enlistment	Not given
Place of Birth	Maryland
Pre-War Residence	Cavetown, Washington County, Maryland
Pre-War Occupation	Day laborer
Post-War Residence	Cavetown, Washington County, Maryland
Post-War Occupation	Laborer
Names of Parents	John and Catharine Flory
Names of Children	David G., George W., and Martha J.
Name of Wife	Elizabeth Flory
Date Soldier Filed Pension	July 17, 1890 with E. K. Buchman as lawyer

Date Widow Filed Pension	None filed
Date of Death	April, 1913 at 75 years of age
Cemetery	Unknown
Remarks	Exemplary soldier. No record of any absences without leave. Present at every roll call during his enlistment.

Soldier	FLORY, Corporal Columbus (aka Flora)
Date of Birth	February 25, 1837
Age Given at Enlistment	25 years
Description at Enlistment	Not given
State of Birth	Maryland
Pre-War Residence	Ringgold, Washington County, Maryland
Pre-War Occupation	Farm laborer
Post-War Residence	Linn, KS in 1870, Bourbon, KS in 1885, & Jackson, Douglas, MO in 1910
Post-War Occupation	Farmer and later a tree farm owner
Names of Parents	John and Nancy Flory
Names of Children	Charles, Myrtle, Franklin B, Bertie, and Carrie
Name of Wife	Emma Flory
Date Soldier Filed Pension	March 17, 1891 and approved with O. A. Cheney as attorney
Date Widow Filed Pension	None filed
Date of Death	September 26, 1921 at 84 years of age
Cemetery	Vanzant Cemetery, Vanzant, Douglas County, Missouri
Remarks	Deserted February 7, 1863 at Harper's Ferry, voluntarily returned to unit March 28, 1864, Court Martial April 21 which resulted in 13 months added, & transferred to First Maryland Infantry to comply.

Soldier	FLORY, Corporal Daniel Webster (Brother of Sgt. John J. Flory)
Date of Birth	January 26, 1844
Age Given at Enlistment	19 years
Description at Enlistment	Not provided
Place of Birth	Maryland
Pre-War Residence	Cavetown, Washington County, Maryland
Pre-War Occupation	None shown on census
Post-War Residence	Greenwich, Huron, Ohio in 1869 and then Fairview, Russell County, Kansas in 1880
Post-War Occupation	Farmer, owning 160 acres of land in Kansas and two horses as of 1879
Names of Parents	John Calvin and Rebecca Bachtell Flory
Names of Children	Walter F., Mabel E., Charles M., Geneva U., Clifton, Leroy, Alice, Berlin
Name of Wife	Jane Elizabeth Hopkins Flory
Date Soldier Filed Pension	December 19, 1885 and approved
Date Widow Filed Pension	February 8, 1892 in Ohio and for minor September 21, 1903, approved
Date of Death	November 16, 1891 at 47 years of age
Cemetery	Ninevah Cemetery, Greenwich, Huron, Ohio
Remarks	Promoted to 8th Corporal May 17, 1865. Served full term of his enlistment with no illnesses, wounds or absences without leave.

Soldier	FLORY, Sergeant John Jacob (Brother of Corp. Daniel W. Flory)
Date of Birth	December 26, 1842
Age Given at Enlistment	19 years
Description at Enlistment	5' 10" complexion dark, eyes brown, hair brown
Place of Birth	Washington County, Maryland
Pre-War Residence	Cavetown, Washington County, Maryland
Pre-War Occupation	None shown on census
Post-War Residence	Fairview, Russell County, KS & then Franklin, Jackson County, Kansas
Post-War Occupation	Farmer, owning 160 acres and two horses as of 1879 Farm Schedule
Names of Parents	John Calvin and Rebecca Bachtell Flory
Names of Children	Ella S., John C., George H., Portia M., James, Sr., William and Flossie F.
Name of Wife	Ella Sarah Brown Flory
Date Soldier Filed Pension	July 26, 1887 and approved, had chronic nephritis and myocarditis
Date Widow Filed Pension	None filed
Date of Death	September 4, 1919 at National Home for Disabled Soldiers at age 77
Cemetery	Leavenworth National Cemetery, Leavenworth, Kansas
Remarks	Two periods of being AWOL, but no arrest, confinement, or court martial. Promoted Corporal May 5, 1864 and Sergeant May, 1965, replacing Sergeant John R. King when he was mustered out.

Soldier	FLORY, Private Lewis L. (aka Louis) (used alias of Willard S. Johnson)
Date of Birth	1839
Age Given at Enlistment	22 years
Description at Enlistment	Not given
Place of Birth	Maryland
Pre-War Residence	Smithsburg, Washington County, Maryland
Pre-War Occupation	Day laborer
Post-War Residence	Geneva, Kane County, Illinois 1870, then Shannon, Caroll County, Illinois in 1880 and lastly Highland, Lincoln County, South Dakota
Post-War Occupation	Cooper and farmer
Names of Parents	Mother was Mary A. Flory
Names of Children	Hattie and Vallietta Flory
Name of Wife	Catharine, married for 44 years as of 1920
Date Soldier Filed Pension	May 12, 1891 with L. Heininger as attorney and approved
Date Widow Filed Pension	None filed
Date of Death	1921 at 82 years of age
Cemetery	Forest Hill Cemetery, Lincoln City, South Dakota
Remarks	Deserted January 18, 1863 at Harper's Ferry and never returned to his regiment. Enlisted in Company E, 169th Ohio National Guard May 2, 1864 and served until September 4, 1864 when it mustered out.

Soldier	FOGLER, Private George W.
Date of Birth	*c.* 1839
Age Given at Enlistment	23 years
Description at Enlistment	Not provided
Place of Birth	Maryland
Pre-War Residence	Cavetown, Washington County, Maryland
Pre-War Occupation	Son of a farmer
Post-War Residence	N/A
Post-War Occupation	N/A
Names of Parents	George and Hannah Fogler
Names of Children	N/A
Name of Wife	N/A
Date Soldier Filed Pension	None filed
Date Widow Filed Pension	N/A
Date of Death	May 24, 1864 at 25 years of age
Cemetery	Unknown
Remarks	Fined $3.00 to be deducted from pay for sick AWOL. Wounded May 5, 1864 at the Battle of the Wilderness and died from wounds May 24.

Soldier	FOGLER, Private Luther
Date of Birth	*c.* 1826
Age Given at Enlistment	36 years
Description at Enlistment	5' 10" dark complexion, blue eyes, black hair
Place of Birth	Maryland
Pre-War Residence	Smithsburg, Cavetown District, Washington County, Maryland
Pre-War Occupation	Blacksmith
Post-War Residence	N/A
Post-War Occupation	N/A
Names of Parents	Unknown
Names of Children	Elizabeth, Emma and George
Name of Wife	Margaret Fogler
Date Soldier Filed Pension	None filed
Date Widow Filed Pension	June 16, 1865 approved & August 30, 1871 for minor with guardian
Date of Death	April 21, 1865 at 39 years of age
Cemetery	Trinity Lutheran Church, Smithsburg, Washington County, Maryland
Remarks	Captured at Winchester June 15, 1863 and exchanged. Wounded at Fisher's Hill September 21, 1864 and recovered. Wounded April 2, 1865 during the assault on the Rebel line at Petersburg and later died.

Soldier	GANS, Private George W.
Date of Birth	April 2, 1841
Age Given at Enlistment	21 years
Description at Enlistment	Not given
Place of Birth	Maryland

Pre-War Residence	Smithsburg, Washington County, Maryland
Pre-War Occupation	None given, but the son of a house carpenter
Post-War Residence	Altoona, Blair County, Pa., 1880 then Washington, Franklin County, Pa.
Post-War Occupation	Carpenter and market master
Names of Parents	Jacob and Hannah Gans
Names of Children	Nina O., Wilson P., Annie S., Lidie M and Carl
Name of Wife	Jennie Gans, married for 43 years as of 1910 census
Date Soldier Filed Pension	October 5, 1882 and approved
Date Widow Filed Pension	Wife preceded him in death
Date of Death	February 1, 1924 at 82 years of age
Cemetery	Burns Hill Cemetery, Waynesboro, Franklin County, Pennsylvania
Remarks	Several illnesses requiring hospitalizations in Alexandria, Baltimore and Philadelphia. One brief AWOL starting Dec. 22, 1862.

Soldier	GARRISH, Private Joseph Henry
Date of Birth	February 14, 1844
Age Given at Enlistment	18 years
Description at Enlistment	5' 6" fair complexion, blue eyes, and light hair
Place of Birth	Williamsport, Maryland
Pre-War Residence	Williamsport, Maryland
Pre-War Occupation	Shoemaker
Post-War Residence	Williamsport, Maryland
Post-War Occupation	Boatsman as of 1870, RR repairer as of 1880, dray man as of 1900
Names of Parents	Joseph and Catharine Garrish, father was a cooper as of 1850
Names of Children	Sprig, George, Isaac, Bruce, Lewis, Frank, Isabell, Osman, Thomas, Joseph, Luite, Jack, Ellen, Florence and Clara
Name of Wife	Georgetta, married in 1873 and married 37 years as of 1910
Date Soldier Filed Pension	September 14, 1888 and approved, said throat infection 1890 Census
Date Widow Filed Pension	October 30, 1922 and approved
Date of Death	September 28, 1922 at 78 years of age
Cemetery	Riverview Cemetery, Williamsport, Maryland
Remarks	Illness with hospitalization in 1864. Served all of his enlistment.

Soldier	GOSSARD, Private George F.
Date of Birth	January 18, 1839
Age Given at Enlistment	23 years
Description at Enlistment	Not given
Place of Birth	Maryland
Pre-War Residence	Antrim, Franklin County, Pennsylvania
Pre-War Occupation	Unknown
Post-War Residence	Antrim, Pennsylvania in 1880 and Newton, Cumberland, Pa., in 1900
Post-War Occupation	Laborer
Names of Parents	John G. Gossard and Catherine Fales Gossard
Names of Children	Catherine, Mary, George, Daniel W., Frank, William H. and Samuel S.
Name of Wife	Sarah A. Reynolds Gossard, married 1861 for thirty-nine years

Date Soldier Filed Pension	None filed
Date Widow Filed Pension	None filed
Date of Death	March 28, 1908 at 69 years of age due to heart disease and failure
Cemetery	Centerville Memorial Park, Centerville, Pennsylvania
Remarks	After five months of service, he deserted January 18, 1863 and never returned. No record of any arrest, confinement or court martial.

Soldier	GOUKER, Private Elias (surname is German, also Jaeger, Jager) (On census, 1910 census shows name as Gaughes, 1920 as Goughler)
Date of Birth	November, 1843
Age Given at Enlistment	19 years
Description at Enlistment	5' 4" fair complexion, blue eyes, light hair
Place of Birth	Maryland
Pre-War Residence	Cavetown, Washington County, Maryland
Pre-War Occupation	None shown
Post-War Residence	Waynesboro, Franklin County, Pennsylvania
Post-War Occupation	Foundry laborer
Names of Parents	Daniel and Sophia Gouker
Names of Children	Lillie H., Mintie M., Maggie A. and Bessie B.
Name of Wife	Emma B. Gouker and married thirty-one years
Date Soldier Filed Pension	September 15, 1886 and approved
Date Widow Filed Pension	February 9, 1923 and approved
Date of Death	Before February 9, 1923
Cemetery	Unknown
Remarks	Captured at Winchester June 15, 1863, exchanged and paroled, but left Camp Parole about August 1 and arrested at Smithsburg October 5, 1863. Court martialed. Wounded by ball March 25, 1865 Petersburg.

Soldier	GOUKER, Private Joseph W.
Date of Birth	September 29, 1839
Age Given at Enlistment	22 years
Description at Enlistment	5' 9" dark complexion, gray eyes, and light hair
Place of Birth	Cavetown, Washington County, Maryland
Pre-War Residence	Cavetown, Washington County, Maryland
Pre-War Occupation	Farmer
Post-War Residence	Pinecreek, Ogle County, IL. 1880, Byron, Ogle County,IL. 1920, 1930
Post-War Occupation	Farmer
Names of Parents	Joseph and Julien Vionen Gouker
Names of Children	Daniel and Allancious with Mary as mother and then George, Elizabeth, Arthur, Ella, Edward, Mandie and two other children with Charlotte.
Name of Wife	Mary Gouker and then Charlotte Rice Gouker
Date Soldier Filed Pension	1890 and approved
Date Widow Filed Pension	None filed as both wives preceded him in death
Date of Death	October 2, 1931 in Hines Hospital in Maywood, Illinois at age 92 years

Cemetery	Byron Cemetery, Bryon, Illinois
Remarks	Teamster for Kenly's Maryland Brigade, then Division Teamster for General Milroy, 8th Corps, Discharged November 10, 1863 for disability due to deformity of knees and ankles. Unfit for the Invalid Corps.

Soldier	GRIM, Private George W. (aka Grimm)
Date of Birth	*c.* 1842
Age Given at Enlistment	21 years
Descriptin at Enlistment	5' 7" dark complexion, blue eyes, and light hair
Place of Birth	Washington County, Maryland
Pre-War Residence	Pleasant Valley District, Washington County, Maryland
Pre-War Occupation	Laborer
Post-War Residence	Leaf River, Ogle County, IL 1880, Freeport, Stephenson County, IL 1900
Post-War Occupation	Farmer 1880, laborer 1900 and then laborer at engine works in 1910
Names of Parents	Abraham and Susan Grim
Names of Children	Annie B., Ella M., Mary and Abram
Name of Wife	Vandalia Grim, married 42 years as of 1910
Date Soldier Filed Pension	March 14, 1877 and approved
Date Widow Filed Pension	November 15, 1918 and approved
Date of Death	Before November 15, 1918 at about 76 years of age
Cemetery	Unknown
Remarks	Captured June 15, 1863 at Winchester, paroled and exchanged, but left Camp Parole August, 1863 and gave himself up November 19, 1863 at Frederick, Maryland and considered a straggler. Regimental butcher.

Soldier	GROVE, Private Abraham
Date of Birth	January 23, 1789
Age Given at Enlistment	53 years
Actual Age at Enlistment	73 years
Place of Birth	Pennsylvania
Pre-War Residence	Lurgan, Franklin County, Pennsylvania
Pre-War Occupation	Farmer
Post-War Residence	Southhampton, Franklin Co., Pa. and then Orrstown, Franklin Co., Pa.
Post-War Occupation	Farmer
Names of Parents	Unknown
Names of Children	Isacc, Susanna, Samuel, Catharine, Mary "Elizabeth, Jacob, and Mary
Name of Wife	Catharine Grove
Date Soldier Filed Pension	December 19, 1879 under name Abraham Gove and approved
Date Widow Filed Pension	No record of filing
Date of Death	September 24, 1882 at 93 years old, at Orrstown, Franklin County, Pa.
Cemetery	Pleasant Hall Cemetery, Pleasant Hall, Franklin County, Pa.
Remarks	Perfect attendance. Transfer to Veteran Reserve Corps April 25, 1864.

Soldier	HANES, Private James
Date of Birth	1814
Age Given at Enlistment	45 years
Description at Enlistment	Not given
Place of Birth	Maryland
Pre-War Residence	Subdivision 2, Washington County, Maryland
Pre-War Occupation	Laborer
Post-War Residence	Sandy Hook, Washington County, Maryland
Post-War Occupation	Farmer
Names of Parents	Joseph and Delilah Hanes
Names of Children	Mary, Eliza, Susan, Joseph, and James
Name of Wife	Susan Hanes
Date Soldier Filed Pension	June 1, 1880 and approved
Date Widow Filed Pension	October 29, 1887
Date of Death	September 30, 1887
Cemetery	Samples Manor Cemetery, Harper's Ferry, West Virginia
Remarks	Periods of illness. Second Brigade teamster and detailed to the Pioneer Corps, 3rd Division, 3rd Army Corps late 1863 and early 1864.

Soldier	HARNE, Private James H. (aka Horne and Harn)
Date of Birth	*c.* 1834
Age Given at Enlistment	28 years
Description at Enlistment	Not given
Place of Birth	Maryland
Pre-War Residence	Unknown
Pre-War Occupation	Unknown
Post-War Residence	Aetna, Logan County, Illinois
Post-War Occupation	Farm hand
Names of Parents	Horatio Nelson and Anna Maria Harne
Names of Children	Horation Nelson, Desdemonia, and Inace
Name of Wife	Emma K. Harne
Date Soldier Filed Pension	None filed
Date Widow Filed Pension	None filed
Date of Death	Unknown
Cemetery	Unknown
Remarks	Deserted February 7, 1863 and returned March 28, 1864, was found guilty of desertion and his enlistment was extended for 13 months. Transferred to 1st Maryland Infantry when the 6th Md. was mustered out. However, on March 27, 1888, the desertion charge was expunged.

Soldier	HENNEBERGER, Private D. Clinton
Date of Birth	June 21, 1829
Age Given at Enlistment	33 years
Date of Enlistment	Enrolled at Baltimore, Md. Sept. 5, 1862 and mustered in Feb. 20, 1863
Place of Birth	Hagerstown, Maryland

Pre-War Residence	Leitersburg, Washington County, Maryland
Pre-War Occupation	Cabinet maker
Post-War Residence	Waynesboro, Franklin County, Pennsylvania
Post-War Occupation	Cabinet maker
Names of Parents	Unknown
Names of Children	William, Selah Cole, Dewitt C., Mary Olivia, Clinton and Harry E.
Name of Wife	Margaret Henneberger
Date Soldier Filed Pension	November 11, 1879 and approved
Date Widow Filed Pension	November 6, 1902
Date of Death	October 25, 1902
Cemetery	Burns Hill Cemetery, Waynesboro, Franklin County, Pennsylvania
Remarks	Captured on retreat from Winchester June 15, 1863, paroled and exchanged. Detailed as hospital cook 1864-1865, 3rd Division, 6th Corps.

Soldier	HICKMAN, Private Freeland H. (aka Freeling)
Date of Birth	*c.* 1844
Age Given at Enlistment	19 years
Description at Enlistment	5' 7" tall, fair complexion, black eyes, and brown hair
Place of Birth	Maryland
Pre-War Residence	Sharpsburg, Washington County, Maryland
Pre-War Occupation	Cooper
Post-War Residence	N/A
Post-War Occupation	N/A
Names of Parents	William T. and Sarah Hickman
Names of Children	N/A
Name of Wife	N/A
Date Soldier Filed Pension	N/A
Date Widow Filed Pension	Father and mother filed June 6, 1887 and approved
Date of Death	April 8, 1863
Cemetery	Unknown
Remarks	Sick and admitted to Regimental Hospital in Harper's Ferry, Virginia. Died of consumption or phthisis pulmonalis, aka tuberculosis.

Soldier	HOUSER, Corporal Samuel
Date of Birth	November 24, 1831
Age Given at Enlistment	31 years
Description at Enlistment	Not given
Place of Birth	Cavetown, Washington County, Maryland
Pre-War Residence	Cavetown, Washington County, Maryland
Pre-War Occupation	Day laborer
Post-War Residence	Cavetown, Washington County, Maryland
Post-War Occupation	Farm laborer
Names of Parents	John Leiter Houser and Rebecca Yeakle Houser
Names of Children	Emma K., George and John B.
Name of Wife	Caroline Catharine Burkhart Houser, married May 21, 1857, for 43 yrs.
Date Soldier Filed Pension	May 10, 1880 and approved

Date Widow Filed Pension	November 18, 1901 and approved
Date of Death	November 2, 1901 at 69 years of age
Cemetery	Smithsburg Cemetery, Smithsburg, Washington County, Maryland
Remarks	Had $5 taken from pay per sentence of Court Martial, but completed full term of enlistment; promoted to Corporal Jan. 1, 1865

Soldier	HOVIS, Private Jacob
Date of Birth	April 15, 1830
Age Given at Enlistment	32 years
Description at Enlistment	Not given
Place of Birth	Pennsylvania
Pre-War Residence	Lower Dickinson, Cumberland County, Pennsylvania
Pre-War Occupation	Miller
Post-War Residence	Leitersburg, Washington County, Maryland in 1870
Post-War Occupation	Basket maker
Names of Parents	John and Elizabeth Hovis (John was also a basket maker)
Names of Children	Phebe E., John H., Rebecca, Ben F., Emma M. and Mary
Name of Wife	Henrietta Hovis
Date Soldier Filed Pension	August 24, 1877 and approved
Date Widow Filed Pension	Not filed
Date of Death	November 25, 1883 at 53 years of age
Cemetery	Jacobs Lutheran Cemetery, Leitersburg, Washington County, Maryland
Remarks	Captured at Winchester June 15, 1863, paroled at City Point, Virginia June 23 but did not report to Camp Parole until August 2. Had $6 deducted from pay by sentence of Court Martial. Completed term.

Soldier	INGRAM, Private Thomas
Date of Birth	*c.* 1844
Age Given at Enlistment	18 years
Description at Enlistment	5' 7" tall, fair complexion, blue eyes and light hair
Place of Birth	Loudoun County, Virginia
Pre-War Residence	Loudoun County, Virginia
Pre-War Occupation	Laborer
Post-War Residence	Buckeystown, Frederick County, Maryland, 1880 and 1910 censuses
Post-War Occupation	Laborer 1870, canal worker 1880 and farmer 1910
Names of Parents	Unknown
Names of Children	Calvin, Charles, Frank, Bennetta, Carrie and Lula
Name of Wife	Annie Ingram
Date Soldier Filed Pension	July 26, 1890 and approved, served 2 years, 11 months per 1890-C
Date Widow Filed Pension	None filed as she preceded him in death
Date of Death	Unknown
Cemetery	Unknown
Remarks	AWOL October, 1862 and July 29, 1864, but no arrest or court martial. Served as Brigade Sharp Shooter, 3rd Division, 6th Army Corps.

Soldier	Irvin, Private Hezekiah (aka Irwin)
Date of Birth	*c.* 1828
Age Given at Enlistment	33 years
Description at Enlistment	Not given
Place of Birth	Maryland
Pre-War Residence	District 1, Washington County, Maryland
Pre-War Occupation	Farm laborer
Post-War Residence	Pine Creek, Ogle County, Illinois
Post-War Occupation	Laborer
Names of Parents	Sarah Irvin, father's name unknown
Names of Children	Hezekiah
Name of Wife	Martha Kline Irvin, married April 18, 1868 in Washington County, Md.
Date Soldier Filed Pension	May 9, 1879 but no certificate number shown
Date Widow Filed Pension	July 31, 1890 and approved
Date of Death	September 16, 1887 at about 59 years of age
Cemetery	German Baptist Cemetery, Pine Creek, Illinois
Remarks	AWOL three times; court martial with five months loss of pay, one-half of future pay & $11.25 for cost of arrest. Capt. Martin, Lts. Brewer & Robinson, & Sgt. King wrote letters requesting remittal of forfeiture of one-half pay due to "an aged and infirm mother" and the army agreed.

Soldier	JACKSON, Private Daniel L.
Date of Birth	*c.* 1840
Age Given at Enlistment	22 years
Description at Enlistment	Not given
Place of Birth	Maryland
Pre-War Residence	Clear Spring, Washington County, Maryland
Pre-War Occupation	Wood chopper
Post-War Residence	Unknown
Post-War Occupation	Unknown
Names of Parents	Unknown
Names of Children	Unknown
Name of Wife	Unknown
Date Soldier Filed Pension	February 10, 1892, but not approved
Date Widow Filed Pension	September 29, 1896, but not approved
Date of Death	Before September 29, 1896
Cemetery	Unknown
Remarks	Captured at Winchester June 15, 1863, confined at Richmond & paroled July 23, 1863 & reported to Camp Parole July 24, but deserted November 16, 1863 and never returned to duty. Army never found him

Soldier	JENNINGS, Sergeant George B. (brother of Patrick H. H. Jennings)
Date of Birth	March 19, 1841
Age Given at Enlistment	21 years
Description at Enlistment	5' 5" complexion dark, eyes blue, and hair light

Place of Birth	Washington County, Maryland
Pre-War Residence	Washington County, Maryland
Pre-War Occupation	Laborer
Post-War Residence	Pleasant Valley, Md. 1880 then Rohersville, Md., 1900-1926
Post-War Occupation	Farm laborer 1870 & 1880, RR supervisor 1910 and farmer 1920
Names of Parents	William and Sarah Norris Jennings
Names of Children	Cora S., Annie E. and Hannah Mary by first wife
Name of Wife	Hannah F. Jennings, first wife and Laura O. Jennings, second wife
Date Soldier Filed Pension	September 4, 1890 and approved with G. E. Liemon as attorney
Date Widow Filed Pension	None filed
Date of Death	February 18, 1926 at 84 years old from "heart trouble"
Cemetery	Old Brownsville Church of the Brethren, Washington County, Md.
Remarks	Excellent service record. Promoted to 8th Corporal August 18, 1862 & First Sgt. January 1, 1865 "vice King reduced to 2nd Sergt." In November of 1864, he was on extra daily duty in the Color Guard.

Soldier	JENNINGS, Sergeant Patrick H. H. (brother of Sgt. George B. Jennings)
Date of Birth	January 6, 1843
Age Given at Enlistment	21 years
Description at Enlistment	Not given
Place of Birth	Washington County, Maryland
Pre-War Residence	Washington County, Maryland
Pre-War Occupation	Carpenter
Post-War Residence	Brownsville, Maryland 1880 & Rohrersville, Maryland 1900
Post-War Occupation	Farmer in 1880, farm machinist in 1910 and railroad foreman
Names of Parents	William and Sarah Norris Jennings
Names of Children	William E. and Mary E.
Name of Wife	Anna M. Jennings
Date Soldier Filed Pension	January 30, 1879 and approved
Date Widow Filed Pension	None filed as Anna preceded him in death
Date of Death	March 26, 1912 at 69 year of age due to a heart attack
Cemetery	Old Brownsville Church of the Brethren Cemetery, Washington Co. Md.
Remarks	Excellent service record. Promoted from Cpl. to 4th Sgt.; severely wounded in the hip at Battle of Sailor's Creek April 6, 1965, admitted to White Hall Hospital and mustered out June 21, 1865.

Soldier	JONES, Private William
Date of Birth	November 17, 1820
Age Given at Enlistment	41 years
Description Age at Enlistment	5' 10 1/2 " dark complexion, dark eyes, and dark hair
Place of Birth	Maryland
Pre-War Residence	Cavetown, Washington County, Maryland
Pre-War Occupation	Blacksmith
Post-War Residence	Cavetown, Washington County, Maryland
Post-War Occupation	Blacksmith
Names of Parents	Unknown

Names of Children	Artesia, John, David, Ellen, Curtis, Mary, Marietta, Willamina, Emma J.
Name of Wife	Henrietta Jones
Date Soldier Filed Pension	March 3, 1866 and approved
Date Widow Filed Pension	None filed
Date of Death	November 25, 1900 at 80 years of age
Cemetery	Christ Church United Church of Christ Cemetery, Cavetown, Maryland
Remarks	Wounded at skirmish at Williamsport, Md. November, 1862, causing "a very large oblique inguinal hernia." Discharged as disabled on Dec. 26, 1863 by order of General Martindale. Degree of disability one-half.

Soldier	JUSTICE, Corporal John J. B.
Date of Birth	*c.* 1834
Age Given at Enlistment	27 years
Description at Enlistment	Not given
Place of Birth	Washington County, Maryland
Pre-War Residence	Smithsburg, Washington County, Maryland
Pre-War Occupation	Day laborer
Post-War Residence	Mt. Pleasant, Md. 1880 then Beaver Creek, Washington County, Md.
Post-War Occupation	Farm laborer
Names of Parents	Unknown
Names of Children	Frances, John, Claudius, Edward, Catharine, Elizabeth and Martin L.
Name of Wife	Lucretia Justice, married ten years as of 1900
Date Soldier Filed Pension	March 6, 1882 and approved
Date Widow Filed Pension	None filed
Date of Death	Unknown
Cemetery	Unknown
Remarks	Promoted to 8th Corporal; on detached duty as an ambulance driver from 1863 to the end of the war, 3rd Division, 6th Army Corps.

Soldier	KEIZER, Private Peter E. (aka Kizer)
Date of Birth	*c.* 1820
Age Given at Enlistment	42 years
Description at Enlistment	5' 11" tall, dark complexion, blue eyes, and dark hair
Place of Birth	Washington County, Maryland
Pre-War Residence	Martinsburg, West Virginia 1850 & Hagerstown, Maryland in 1860
Pre-War Occupation	Cooper
Post-War Residence	Smithsburg, Washington County, Maryland
Post-War Occupation	Unknown
Names of Parents	Unknown
Names of Children	John W., John D., Amanda, Theodore and Alice A.
Name of Wife	Elizabeth Keizer
Date Soldier Filed Pension	None filed
Date Widow Filed Pension	July 10, 1877 and approved

Date of Death	September 15, 1866 in Hagerstown, Maryland at about 46 years of age
Cemetery	unknown
Remarks	Sick in hospital when captured and then paroled June 15, 1863 in Berryville, Va. Discharged April 20, 1864 for chronic rheumatism and chronic bronchitis by General Auger. Unfit for Veteran Reserve Corps.

Soldier	KING, Lieutenant John Rigdon
Date of Birth	June 24, 1844
Age Given at Enlistment	18 years
Description at Enlistment	5' 6" high, fair complexion, blue eyes, and brown hair
Place of Birth	Hagerstown, Washington County, Maryland
Pre-War Residence	Baltimore, Maryland and Hagerstown, Maryland
Pre-War Occupation	Artist and sutler
Post-War Residence	District 6, Howard Co. 1880, 1900; Ward 11, Balt. Md., 1910-1934
Post-War Occupation	Railroad clerk, pension agent, customs house clerk and greeter
Names of Parents	Samuel L. and Eliza Lane King
Names of Children	Annie L. King and Mary Elizabeth (King) Adams
Name of Wife	Annie Maria King
Date Soldier Filed Pension	July 26, 1865 and approved
Date Widow Filed Pension	None filed as Annie M. preceded John in death, d. May 4, 1917
Date of Death	March 4, 1934 at 89 years of age
Cemetery	Loudon Park Cemetery, Baltimore, Maryland
Remarks	Promoted Cpl., Sgt., 1st Sgt. Feb. 14, 1863; WIA June 15, 1863 Winchester, Nov. 27, 1863 Mine Run & May 5, 1864 Wilderness; in Gen. Hosp. Frederick; promoted to 1st Lieutenant, Co. C April 25, 1865 and discharged on disability May 18, 1865. Wounded three times.

Soldier	KING, Private Patrick
Date of Birth	March, 1845
Age Given at Enlistment	19 years
Description at Enlistment	Not given
Place of Birth	Ireland, immigrated to the United States in 1860
Pre-War Residence	Ireland
Pre-War Occupation	Unknown
Post-War Residence	Rawlings, Alleghany Co., Md. 1880, Cumberland, Alleghany Co., 1900
Post-War Occupation	Watchman in 1900 and self-employed in 1900
Names of Parents	Unknown
Names of Children	Mary, Margaret, Stephen, James, Rose, John, Patrick, Stephen, William
Name of Wife	Margaret, also born in Ireland, and married 37 as of 1900
Date Soldier Filed Pension	None filed
Date Widow Filed Pension	None filed
Date of Death	Unknown
Cemetery	Unknown
Remarks	Deserted September 2, 1862 from Camp Maffit, Baltimore, Md. and never returned to his unit. No record of arrest or court martial.

Soldier	KING, Private William H.
Date of Birth	*c.* 1841
Age Given at Enlistment	21 years
Description at Enlistment	5' 9" tall, fair complexion, gray eyes, and black hair
Place of Birth	Washington County, Maryland
Pre-War Residence	Buckeystown, Frederick County, Maryland
Pre-War Occupation	Laborer
Post-War Residence	Clear Spring, Washington Co., Md. 1870, then Hagerstown, Md. 1900
Post-War Occupation	Farm laborer in 1870, then day laborer in 1900
Names of Parents	Singleton and Mary A. King
Names of Children	William H., Minerva, and George L. and nine others, names unknown
Name of Wife	Mary E. King, had twelve children, but only five living as of 1900
Date Soldier Filed Pension	June 1, 1889 and approved
Date Widow Filed Pension	October 9, 1919 and approved
Date of Death	Before October 9, 1919
Cemetery	Unknown
Remarks	Captured June 15, 1863 at Winchester, paroled and exchanged. Left Camp Parole Aug., '63 AWOL, but turned himself in Nov. 19, 1863. Considered a straggler. On 1890-C, said he was "shot in the foot."

Soldier	KOUGH, Private George
Date of Birth	*c.* 1840
Age Given at Enlistment	24 years
Description at Enlistment	Not given
Place of Birth	Pennsylvania
Pre-War Residence	Unknown
Pre-War Occupation	Unknown
Post-War Residence	Logan, Blair County, Pa. in 1870, then Altoona, Blair County in 1880, then Johnstown, Cambria County, Pa. in 1900
Post-War Occupation	Laborer
Names of Parents	Unknown
Names of Children	Mary E., Henrietta, Lucy A., Ella. George F., Grace A., Myrtle & Etha
Name of Wife	Catharine Annie Kough
Date Soldier Filed Pension	None filed. On 1890-C, said "discharge lost in Johnstown flood"
Date Widow Filed Pension	None filed
Date of Death	January 18, 1902 at about 62 years of age
Cemetery	Sandy Dale Cemetery, Johnstown, Cambria County, Pennsylvania
Remarks	Placed under arrest November 20, 1862 at Williamsport, Md., reason not given. Deserted May 10, 1863 at Berryville, Va. and never returned to duty with his regiment. No record of confinement or court martial.

Soldier	KOONTZ, Sergeant Thomas E.
Date of Birth	*c.* 1841
Age Given at Enlistment	21 years

Description at Enlistment	5' 8" in height, complexion fair, eyes blue, and hair light
Place of Birth	Maryland
Pre-War Residence	Petersville, Frederick County, Md. and Brownsville, Wash. County, Md.
Pre-War Occupation	Farmer
Post-War Residence	N/A
Post-War Occupation	N/A
Names of Parents	John and Sarah Koontz
Names of Children	N/A
Name of Wife	Catharine E. Koontz, married October 10, 1862
Date Soldier Filed Pension	N/A
Date Widow Filed Pension	March 11, 1863 and approved
Date of Death	November 20, 1862 at age 21 years
Cemetery	Unknown
Remarks	Entered the army as 5th Sergeant. Contracted typhoid fever and died at his home in Brownsville.

Soldier	LEEDS, Lieutenant Alexander (aka Alex)
Date of Birth	*c.* 1843
Age Given at Enlistment	19 years
Description at Enlistment	Not given
Place of Birth	New York
Pre-War Residence	Oronoko township, Berrien County, Michigan
Pre-War Occupation	Unknown
Post-War Residence	Waynesboro, Pa. 1870, Baltimore, Md. 1880, Grafton, West Va., 1900
Post-War Occupation	Jeweller in 1870 and dentist 1880 and thereafter
Names of Parents	Alexander and Lodowick C. Leeds
Names of Children	Mary C. Leeds, who became a music teacher
Name of Wife	Maria E. Leeds
Date Soldier Filed Pension	April 5, 1871 and approved
Date Widow Filed Pension	February 19, 1912 and approved
Date of Death	February 4, 1912 at about 69 years of age
Cemetery	Grafton National Cemetery, Grafton, Taylor County, West Virginia
Remarks	Served as Regimental General Guide in 1863; wounded in back in 1864; promoted from Sgt. to First Lieut. January 23, 1865, since Abercrombie promoted to Capt., and then Leeds commanded H company.

Soldier	LOWRY, Private Charles Andrew (Brother of James Madison Lowry)
Date of Birth	November 26, 1842
Age Given at Enlistment	19 years
Description at Enlistment	Not given
Place of Birth	Pennsylvania
Pre-War Residence	Williamsport, Washington County, Maryland
Pre-War Occupation	Unknown
Post War Residence	Sharpsburg, Washington County, Maryland
Post-War Occupation	Farmer 1870 and day laborer 1900

Names of Parents	George M and Anna Matilda Rich Lowry
Names of Children	John H. and Mary
Name of Wife	Susan Lowry, married in 1867 and married 33 years as of 1900
Date Soldier Filed Pension	July 9, 1890 and approved
Date Widow Filed Pension	None filed
Date of Death	March 28, 1918 at 75 years of age
Cemetery	Rose Hill Cemetery, Hagerstown, Washington County, Maryland
Remarks	Present at all roll calls. An exemplary service record.

Soldier	LOWRY, Private James Madison (Brother of Charles Andrew Lowry)
Date of Birth	May 13, 1832
Age Given at Enlistment	30 years
Description at Enlistment	Not given
Place of Birth	Pennsylvania
Pre-War Residence	Franklin County, Pennsylvania
Pre-War Occupation	Unknown
Post-War Residence	Benevola, Md. 1870, Boonsboro, Washington County, Md. 1880 on
Post-War Occupation	Farm laborer
Names of Parents	George M. and Anna Matilda Ruch Lowry
Names of Children	George J., Mary C., Martha Jane and Barbara Ellen
Name of Wife	Mary Catherine Hoover Lowry
Date Soldier Filed Pension	February 23, 1890 and approved
Date Widow Filed Pension	Not filed as his wife preceded him in death
Date of Death	March 6, 1908 at 75 years of age
Cemetery	Mount Zion Mennonite Church Cemetery
Remarks	Captured Winchester June 15, 1863, paroled, exchanged and sent to his unit October 5, 1863. Had $18.75 taken out of pay per sentence of court martial. In Pioneer Corps from end of 1863 to April 1, '65 when he got sick. Discharged June 29, 1865, Mount Pleasant Hospital, D. C.

Soldier	MARTIN, Captain Adam Benjamin (brother of Sgt. Stephen G. Martin)
Date of Birth	September 5, 1827 (Surname is of German origin)
Age Given at Enlistment	35 years
Description at Enlistment	Not given
Place of Birth	Maryland
Pre-War Residence	Smithsburg, Washington County, Maryland
Pre-War Occupation	Clerk
Post-War Residence	N/A
Post-War Occupation	N/A
Names of Parents	Stephen and Barbara Good Martin
Names of Children	Scott T., Clara B., Sarah T., Mary C., Ann E., Melinda B. and Lily
Name of Wife	Susan A. Oswald, married in 1849, nine children, seven living 1900
Date Soldier Filed Pension	Not filed
Date Widow Filed Pension	October 4, 1964 and approved, minor children included
Date of Death	May 6, 1864 at 36 years of age

Cemetery	Smithsburg Cemetery, Smithsburg, Washington County, Maryland
Remarks	Commanding officer of Co. H; wounded at Mine Run November 27, 1863 and again May 5, 1864 at Wilderness and died the next day.

Soldier	MARTIN, Lieutenant and Sergeant Major John M.
Date of Birth	*c.* 1831
Age Given at Enlistment	31 years
Description at Enlistment	Not given
Place of Birth	Pennsylvania
Pre-War Residence	Hagerstown, Washington County, Maryland
Pre-War Occupation	Teacher
Post-War Residence	Metal township, Franklin County, Pa. using alias John M. McNinch
Post-War Occupation	Unknown
Names of Parents	Unknown
Names of Children	Eliza J. and Margaret V.
Name of Wife	Caroline Martin
Date Soldier Filed Pension	May 29, 1871 and approved
Date Widow Filed Pension	Unknown
Date of Death	Unknown
Cemetery	Unknown
Remarks	Mustered in Co. E. 1st Potomac Home Brigade Sept. 21, 1861, but resigned as 2nd Lt. April 30, 1862. Joined Co. H as Sgt. Major August 21, 1862, but deserted May 20, 1863, perhaps due to family illness and never returned to regiment. May also have joined 205th Pa. Inf.

Soldier	MARTIN, Sergeant Stephen G. (brother of Captain Adam B. Martin)
Date of Birth	January 19, 1825 (Surname is of German origin)
Age Given at Enlistment	37 years
Description at Enlistment	Not given
Place of Birth	Leitersburg, Washington County, Maryland
Pre-War Residence	Leitersburg, Washington County, Maryland
Pre-War Occupation	Merchant
Post-War Residence	Ringgold, Washington County, Maryland
Post-War Occupation	Laborer 1870, clerk in store 1880, retired farmer 1900
Names of Parents	Stephen and Barbara Good Martin
Names of Children	Cora, Sarah, Anna, Alice, Laura, Mary and Frank
Name of Wife	Anna Funk Martin, m. 1848, seven children with six alive as of 1900
Date Soldier Filed Pension	August 8, 1890, approved; list chronic diarrhea as disability on 1890-C
Date Widow Filed Pension	February 27, 1901
Date of Death	January 24, 1901 at 76 years of age
Cemetery	Green Hill Cemetery, Waynesboro, Pennsylvania
Remarks	Absent from original muster; $5.00 deducted for regimental court martial. Entered service as a Cpl.; promoted to Sergeant April 1, 1863

Soldier	MASTERS, Private George P. (brother of Private William Masters_
Date of Birth	November 27, 1840
Age Given at Enlistment	21 years
Description at Enlistment	Not given
Place of Birth	Germany. The entire family immigrated to the United States in 1850.
Pre-War Residence	Cavetown, Washington County, Maryland
Pre-War Occupation	Unknown
Post-War Residence	Ringgold, Washington County, Maryland
Post-War Occupation	Farmer and laborer
Names of Parents	Johann (Martin) Masters and Elisabeth Schmidt Masters. The original family name of Meisters was anglicized to Masters.
Names of Children	John F., Joseph C., Margaret E., Anna M., Mary E. and Lucinda Pearl
Name of Wife	First was Catharine Fulton Masters, second was Sarah Maggie Masters
Date Soldier Filed Pension	September 24, 1881 and approved
Date Widow Filed Pension	May 15, 1919 by Sarah Maggie Masters and approved
Date of Death	March 6, 1919 at 78 years of age
Cemetery	Smithsburg Cemetery, Smithsburg, Washington County, Maryland
Remarks	On 1890-C, he said disability due to "erysipelas (a skin infection) and rheumatism." Private Masters served his full term of enlistment.

Soldier	MASTERS, Private William (brother of George P. Masters)
Date of Birth	January 5, 1844
Age Given at Enlistment	18 years
Description at Enlistment	5' 4" tall, dark complexion, brown eyes, and dark hair
Place of Birth	Wurttemberg, a region and former kingdom of southwest Germany
Pre-War Residence	Cavetown, Washington County, Maryland
Pre-War Occupation	Farmer
Post-War Residence	Cavetown 1870, Hanvers, Frederick Co., Md. 1880, Washington, Franklin County, Pennsylvania 1900
Post-War Occupation	Farmer 1870, laborer 1880 and liveryman 1900
Names of Parents	Johann (Martin) Masters and Elisabeth Schmidt Masters
Names of Children	James Martin, Elizabeth A., Ida Myrtle, Minnie and Bertha May
Name of Wife	Elizabeth Ann Matilda Gladhill Masters; married thirty-three years and had seven children with four still living as of 1900
Date Soldier Filed Pension	April 23, 1883 and approved
Date Widow Filed Pension	September 18, 1900 and approved
Date of Death	August 25, 1900 at 56 years of age
Cemetery	Saint John's UCC Cemetery, Sabillasville, Frederick County, Maryland
Remarks	Captured May 7, 1864 at the Battle of the Wilderness, paroled at Wilmington, N.C. February 25, 1865, and sent to Camp Parole where he became sick and was mustered out June 8, 1865.

Soldier	MCKENNA, Private James P.
Date of Birth	May 29, 1841
Age Given at Enlistment	21 years

Description at Enlistment	5' 9" in height, eyes blue, complexion dark, hair black
Place of Birth	Washington County, Maryland
Pre-War Residence	Clear Spring, Washington County, Maryland
Pre-War Occupation	Laborer
Post-War Residence	Indian Spring District, Md. 1880, Ward 3, Hagerstown, Md. 1900-1924
Post-War Occupation	Farmer 1880,laborer 1900 and 1910, furnace laborer 1920
Names of Parents	Hugh and Mary McKenna, both born in Ireland
Names of Children	Mary E., Susan L., Charles, Bertha A., and Alta M.
Name of Wife	Mary Ellen Mckenna, married 1872, five children, five living as of 1900
Date Soldier Filed Pension	July 21, 1897 and approved
Date Widow Filed Pension	None filed as wife preceded him in death
Date of Death	January 10, 1924 at 80 years of age
Cemetery	Saint Paul's Lutheran Church Cemetery, Clear Spring, Maryland
Remarks	Served as both Regimental and Brigade teamster from late 1862 until May, 1865. Excellent service record with no roll call absences, illnesses or unauthorized leave.

Soldier	MILLER, Corporal Charles H.
Date of Birth	*c.* 1840
Age Given at Enlistment	22 years
Description at Enlistment	Not given
Place of Birth	Maryland
Pre-War Residence	Unknown
Pre-War Occupation	Unknown
Post-War Residence	Unknown
Post-War Occupation	Unknown
Names of Parents	Unknown
Names of Children	Unknown
Name of Wife	Mary Miller
Date Soldier Filed Pension	Nov. 4, 1885, but not approved
Date Widow Filed Pension	Unknown but not approved
Date of Death	August 5, 1913 (tentative)
Cemetery	Pleasant Valley United Methodist, Smithsburg, Maryland (tentative)
Remarks	Promoted to 5th Cpl. December 1, 1862, then 4th and 2nd. Deserted at Martinsburg, Va. Nov. 12, 1864 and never returned to duty. No arrest.

Soldier	MILLER, Corporal Levi
Date of Birth	September 27, 1840
Age Given at Enlistment	21 years
Description at Enlistment	Not given
Place of Birth	Maryland
Pre-War Residence	District 1, Washington County, Maryland
Pre-War Occupation	Unknown
Post-War Residence	Cavetown, Md. 1870, then Ringgold, Maryland, 1880 and 1900
Post-War Occupation	Farm laborer
Names of Parents	Samuel and Elizabeth Miller
Names of Children	Aquilla, Mary, Relman, Samuel, Mahlon, and Chancey

Name of Wife	Sarah Miller, married 34 years as of 1900
Date Soldier Filed Pension	May 17, 1889 and approved
Date Widow Filed Pension	April 24, 1914 and approved
Date of Death	March 27, 1914 at 73 years of age
Cemetery	Welty Church of the Brethren Cemetery, Smithsburg, Maryland
Remarks	On 1890-C, reported "typhoid fever and rheumatism" and 2 yrs., nine months, 29 days of service. Sick with leave 1862 and early 1863. Attended 6th Regiment Reunion, the 4th, 1885, Mechanicstown, Md.

Soldier	MOORE, Corporal John Henry
Date of Birth	July 31, 1844
Age Given at Enlistment	18 years
Description at Enlistment	5' 5" tall, dark complexion, brown eyes, and brown hair
Place of Birth	Loudon County, Virginia
Pre-War Residence	Loudon County, Virginia
Pre-War Occupation	Unknown
Post-War Residence	Green Spring, Md. in 1870, Clear Spring, Md. in 1880, Hagerstown, Md. in 1900 and Antrim Township, Franklin County, Pa. in 1920
Post-War Occupation	Farm laborer
Names of Parents	John Moore (1811-1899) and Catharine Moore (1818-1872)
Names of Children	Lydia V., Joseph R., Charles A., Amanda L., Anna M., and Tamsin A.
Name of Wife	Martha Susan Myers Moore (1845-1924) married 1866 for 58 years
Date Soldier Filed Pension	December 24, 1881 and approved
Date Widow Filed Pension	None filed as she preceded him in death
Date of Death	July 15, 1927 at 82 years of age
Cemetery	Rose Hill Cemetery, Hagerstown, Maryland
Remarks	Per 1890-C, served 2 yrs., nine mos. & 4 days; sick in hospital Harper's Ferry April 10, 1863 to June, 1863; promoted to Corporal Jan. 1, 1865.

Soldier	MOORE, Private William W.
Date of Birth	September 30, 1838
Age Given at Enlistment	24 years
Description at Enlistment	5' 5" in height, dark complexion, grey eyes, and brown hair
Place of Birth	Chester County, Pennsylvania
Pre-War Residence	Clear Spring, Washington County, Maryland
Pre-War Occupation	Laborer
Post-War Residence	N/A
Post-War Occupation	N/A
Names of Parents	John Moore (1811-1899) and Catharine Moore (1818-1872)
Names of Children	None
Name of Wife	None
Date Soldier Filed Pension	None filed
Date Widow Filed Pension	N/A
Date of Death	November 13, 1862 at 24 years of age
Cemetery	Clear Spring Methodist Episcopal Cemetery, Clear Spring, Maryland
Remarks	Private Moore was accidentally shot by the premature discharge of a musket and died immediately

Soldier	NEWCOMER, Private Jacob E.
Date of Birth	December 5, 1843
Age Given at Enlistment	18 years
Description at Enlistment	5' 8" tall, dark complexion, grey eyes, and brown hair
Place of Birth	Unknown
Pre-War Residence	Tilmington District, Washington County, Maryland
Pre-War Occupation	Miller
Post-War Residence	N/A
Post-War Occupation	N/A
Names of Parents	John and Elizabeth Newcomer
Names of Children	N/A
Name of Wife	Not married
Date Soldier Filed Pension	None filed
Date Widow Filed Pension	N/A
Date of Death	May 27, 1864 at 20 years of age
Cemetery	Beaver Creek Church of the Brethren Cemetery, Beaver Creek, Md.
Remarks	Wounded May 5, 1864 (Wilderness), "a gunshot wound of flesh, lower extremity, left thigh, complicated with remittent fever (typhoid character) and died at U.S.A Gen. Hospital, Fairfax Seminary, Alex, Va.

Soldier	NORFORD, Private Joseph Gabby
Date of Birth	January 10, 1828
Age Given at Enlistment	32 years
Description at Enlistment	Not given
Place of Birth	Hagerstown, Washington County, Maryland
Pre-War Residence	Smithsburg, Washington County, Maryland
Pre-War Occupation	Tailor
Post-War Residence	N/A
Post-War Occupation	N/A
Names of Parents	James Monroe Norford (1793-1879) and Elizabeth Norford (1801-1875)
Names of Children	Flora B., Frank, Henry, George S. and S. Norford
Name of Wife	Caroline Norford
Date Soldier Filed Pension	N/A
Date Widow Filed Pension	June 12, 1866 and approved
Date of Death	December, 1864, possible but his body was never recovered.
Cemetery	Unknown
Remarks	Captured June 15, 1863 at Winchester, paroled and exchanged; taken prisoner at Wilderness May 6, 1864; delivered on parole at Charleston, S.C. Dec. 11, 1864, but alleged to have died in prison of starvation.

Soldier	PENNER, Private John
Date of Birth	*c.* 1839
Age Given at Enlistment	23 years
Description at Enlistment	None given
Place of Birth	Adams County, Pennsylvania
Pre-War Residence	Cavetown, Washington County, Maryland
Pre-War Occupation	Laborer

Post-War Residence	Cavetown, Washington County, Maryland
Post-War Occupation	Wood chopper
Names of Parents	Unknown
Names of Children	None
Name of Wife	Isabella (1837-1915, m. Nov. 16, 1859 at Gettysburg Theological Sem.
Date Soldier Filed Pension	None filed for Co. H
Date Widow Filed Pension	None filed for Co. H
Date of Death	Unknown
Cemetery	Unknown, but Isabella is buried at Smithsburg Cemetery, Md.
Remarks	Mustered in at Baltimore, Md., but deserted from Camp Maffitt in Baltimore Sept. 2, 1862; never located or court martialed.

Soldier	PICKETT, Private George F.
Date of Birth	December 15, 1845
Age Given at Enlistment	18 years
Description at Enlistment	5’ 8” in height, dark complexion, brown eyes and brown hair
Place of Birth	Washington County, Maryland
Pre-War Residence	Cavetown, Washington County, Maryland
Pre-War Occupation	Laborer
Post-War Residence	Carroll County, Maryland
Post-War Occupation	Carpenter
Names of Parents	John and Susanna Pickett
Names of Children	Teressa, Sarah E., Nicholas G., Harry B., Sewell, Edward S. & George R.
Name of Wife	Mary D. Pickett
Date Soldier Filed Pension	September 24, 1869 and approved
Date Widow Filed Pension	Not shown, but approved
Date of Death	Unknown
Cemetery	Unknown
Remarks	AWOL since June 12, 1863, left camp at Berryville, Va. & returned Aug. 10, 1863; $31.28 deducted from pay per court martial; transferred to Invalid Corps Nov. 6, 1863, then returned to Co. H; WIA in 1864.

Soldier	REYNOLD, Corporal Amos
Date of Birth	September 26, 1841
Age Given at Enlistment	22 years
Description at Enlistment	Not given
Place of Birth	Maryland
Pre-War Residence	Cavetown, Washington County, Maryland, next door to Levi Miller
Pre-War Occupation	Farm hand
Post-War Residence	Cavetown, Md. 1870, Carthage, Hancock County, IL. 1880
Post-War Occupation	Farm hand
Names of Parents	Peter and Susan Reynold
Names of Children	Unknown
Name of Wife	Cordelia Reynold (1842-1906)
Date Soldier Filed Pension	February 17, 1890 from Illinois and approved
Date Widow Filed Pension	April 14, 1890 from Illinois and approved

Date of Death	March 28, 1890 at 48 years of age
Cemetery	Shannon Brethren Cemetery, Shannon, Carroll County, Illinois
Remarks	Detailed as regimental and brigade teamster, 2nd Brigade., 3rd Division., 6th Corps., for his entire service; promoted Cpl. April 2, 1865 when Bradenburg was promoted to Sergeant.

Soldier	REYNOLDS, Sergeant Daniel B.
Date of Birth	December 9, 1835
Age Given at Enlistment	27 years
Description at Enlistment	5' 10" tall, fair complexion, brown eyes and light hair
Place of Birth	Washington County, Maryland
Pre-War Residence	Washington County, Maryland
Pre-War Occupation	Fence maker
Post-War Residence	Mrs. Reynolds resided in Ringgold, Maryland per 1890-C
Post-War Occupation	N/A
Names of Parents	Unknown
Names of Children	None
Name of Wife	Lydia Ann Reynolds (b. March 19, 1840 d. July 4, 1918)
Date Soldier Filed Pension	N/A
Date Widow Filed Pension	October 21, 1865 and approved
Date of Death	January 29, 1865 at 29 years of age
Cemetery	Smithsburg Cemetery, Smithsburg, Washington County, Maryland
Remarks	$4 deducted from pay per court martial for AWOL, with rank reduced from 2nd Sgt.; deserted Nov. 24, 1863, but returned voluntarily; Lincoln's desertion amnesty applied. Severely wounded June 1, 1864 and died in the Post Hospital at Hagerstown of "rheumatism of heart."

Soldier	REYNOLDS, Private George C.
Date of Birth	November 8, 1841
Age Given at Enlistment	20 years
Description at Enlistment	5' 5" tall, complexion dark, eyes brown, and hair dark
Place of Birth	Maryland
Pre-War Residence	Sandy Hook, Washington County, Maryland
Pre-War Occupation	Shoemaker
Post-War Residence	Cavetown, Washington County, Maryland
Post-War Occupation	Farm laborer
Names of Parents	Jacob and Sarah A. Reynolds
Names of Children	Effie May Reynolds Masters, Franklin and Aaron S.
Name of Wife	Lydia A. Reynolds b. March 19, 1840 d. July 4, 1918
Date Soldier Filed Pension	Not filed
Date Widow Filed Pension	January 31, 1890 and approved
Date of Death	December 25, 1888 at 47 years of age
Cemetery	Welty Church of the Brethren Cemetery, Smithsburg, Maryland
Remarks	AWOL Sick Feb. 16, 18 & March 25, 1863, $26 deducted by sentence of court martial; captured at Wilderness May 7, 1864; paroled at Charleston, S.C. Dec. 16, and reported to Camp Parole Dec. 24, 1864; furloughed 30 days Dec. 30, but did not return until March 30, 1865.

Soldier	RIFE, Private David A.
Date of Birth	November 27, 1840
Age Given at Enlistment	21 years
Description at Enlistment	5' 8" in height, fair complexion, brown eyes and brown hair
Place of Birth	Pennsylvania
Pre-War Residence	Hagerstown, Washington County, Maryland
Pre-War Occupation	Shoemaker
Post-War Residence	Hagerstown, Washington County, Maryland
Post-War Occupation	Shoemaker
Names of Parents	Unknown
Names of Children	None known
Name of Wife	Martha Rife
Date Soldier Filed Pension	Not filed
Date Widow Filed Pension	December 20, 1879 and approved
Date of Death	August 30, 1873 at 32 years of age
Cemetery	Rose Hill Cemetery, Hagerstown, Washington County, Maryland
Remarks	Sick in Harper's Ferry General Hospital April, 1863; transferred to Baltimore General Hospital; discharged on disability by Major General Robert C. Schenck July 3, 1863 for "chronic hepatization of right lung" & severe cough & nights sweats associated with pneumonia.

Soldier	ROBINSON, Charles (Drummer for Company H)
Date of Birth	*c.* 1853
Age Given at Enlistment	15 years
Description at Enlistment	Not given
Place of Birth	Maryland
Pre-War Residence	Hagerstown, Washington County, Maryland
Pre-War Occupation	None
Post-War Residence	Unknown
Post-War Occupation	Unknown
Names of Parents	T. G. and Charlotte Robinson
Names of Children	Unknown
Name of Wife	Unknown
Date Soldier Filed Pension	None filed
Date Widow Filed Pension	None filed
Date of Death	Unknown
Cemetery	Unknown
Remarks	Mustered in at Harper's Ferry Feb. 20, 1863; Captured at Winchester June 15, 1863, confined in Richmond, paroled at City Point and reported at Camp Parole July 24, 1863; deserted July 9, 1864 from Buttmon, Md., did not return, but never arrested or court martialed.

Soldier	ROBINSON, Lieutenant James A.
Date of Birth	March 31, 1839
Age Given at Enlistment	24 years
Description at Enlistment	Not given
Place of Birth	Pennsylvania
Pre-War Residence	Smithsburg, Washington County, Maryland

Pre-War Occupation	Cabinet maker
Post-War Residence	Waynesboro, Pa. in 1870 and Cheltenham, Pa. in 1900
Post-War Occupation	Agent for separator in 1870 and insurance agent in 1900
Names of Parents	Thomas and Catharine Robinson
Names of Children	Annie May, Addie F., Frances H. and Pauline B.
Name of Wife	Hannah C. Thompson Robinson, married February 17, 1862
Date Soldier Filed Pension	April 25, 1874 and approved
Date Widow Filed Pension	December 17, 1906
Date of Death	December 6, 1906 at 67 years of age
Cemetery	Richlandtown Union Cemetery, Richlandtown, Bucks County, Pa.
Remarks	Mustered in as 4th Sgt.; promoted 2nd Lt. when Lt. Brown promoted; resigned and honorably discharged March 17, 1864 due to "phthisis pulmonalis" (tuberculosis) with "emaciation ... loss of strength."

Soldier	SECORE, Private George W. (surname is of French origin)
Date of Birth	*c.* 1825
Age Given at Enlistment	37 years
Description at Enlistment	5' 10" tall, dark complexion, blue eyes, and brown hair
Place of Birth	Frederick, Maryland
Pre-War Residence	Unknown
Pre-War Occupation	Laborer
Post-War Residence	Madison, Luzerne, Pennsylvania in 1870
Post-War Occupation	Farm laborer
Names of Parents	Theoons and Esther Secore
Names of Children	Unknown
Name of Wife	Unknown
Date Soldier Filed Pension	None filed
Date Widow Filed Pension	None filed
Date of Death	Unknown
Cemetery	Unknown
Remarks	Captured at Winchester June 15, 1863, confined at Richmond, paroled at City Point July 23, reported at Camp Parole July 24 and sent to Co. H Oct. 29, 1863. Deserted Charlestown, Va. Aug. 12, 1864, didn't return.

Soldier	SEIDENSTRICKER, Corporal Abraham
Date of Birth	May 25, 1842
Age Given at Enlistment	20 years
Description at Enlistment	5' 6" in height, light complexion, blue eyes and light hair
Place of Birth	Maryland
Pre-War Residence	Boonsboro, Washington County, Maryland
Pre-War Occupation	Farm laborer
Post-War Residence	1001 Cathedral Street, Baltimore, Maryland
Post-War Occupation	Confectioner with his brother, Capt. William H. of Co. E, 13th Md. Inf.
Names of Parents	Solomon and Sarah Seidenstricker
Names of Children	None
Name of Wife	Mary McCardell Seidenstricker, m. November 10, 1884

Date Soldier Filed Pension	December 12, 1879 and approved
Date Widow Filed Pension	December 9, 1903 and approved
Date of Death	November 24, 1903 at 61 years of age of Bright's disease
Cemetery	Rose Hill Cemetery, Hagerstown, Maryland
Remarks	Promoted to Cpl.; suffered a spinal injury (contusion) in a fall of June 10, 1863 and discharged by Major General Auger, April 29, 1864

Soldier	SHANK, Sergeant Adam
Date of Birth	*c.* 1826
Age Given at Enlistment	38 years
Description at Enlistment	Not given
Place of Birth	Maryland
Pre-War Residence	Smithsburg, Washington County, Maryland
Pre-War Occupation	Farm hand
Post-War Residence	Smithsburg, Washington County, Maryland
Post-War Occupation	None-disabled
Names of Parents	Adam and M. Barbara Weagley Waltermyer Shank
Names of Children	Anna S., Jane A., Jiddy, Alice G., Charlie, Clarence E. and Robert F.
Name of Wife	Anne Sophia McGuire Shank (1825-1910) m. 1846
Date Soldier Filed Pension	September 10, 1866 and approved
Date Widow Filed Pension	September 3, 1867 and approved
Date of Death	September 3, 1867 at about 41 years of age
Cemetery	Unknown
Remarks	Elected 3rd Sgt.; AWOL Dec. 13, 1862 from Williamsport & reduced in rank temporarily; captured at Winchester, paroled and exchanged; wounded left side May 5, 1864 at Wilderness with severe injuries; discharged from Frederick Hosp. May 25 & mustered out May 26, 1865

Soldier	SHEILDS, Corporal John Henry
Date of Birth	August 8, 1824
Age Given at Enlistment	38 years
Description at Enlistment	5' 11" tall; fair complexion, hazel eyes and auburn hair
Place of Birth	Maryland
Pre-War Residence	Hamiltonban Township, Adams County, Pennsylvania
Pre-War Occupation	Millwright
Post-War Residence	Emmitsburg, Frederick County, Maryland
Post-War Occupation	Surveyor
Names of Parents	Margaret Morrison Shields, mother
Names of Children	Elmyra, David B., Lewis O., John S., Ellen A., U.S. Grant and William S.
Name of Wife	Eve Ann Benchoff Shields
Date Soldier Filed Pension	February 14, 1865 and approved
Date Widow Filed Pension	None filed
Date of Death	October 9, 1904 at 80 years of age
Cemetery	Elias Evangelical Lutheran Church Cemetery, Emmitsburg, Maryland
Remarks	Promoted Cpl.; AWOL July 7, 1863 at Frederick Junction; $15 deducted from pay for apprehension per court martial; WIA May 9, 1864 near Spots. C. H.; discharged by order Major Gen. Christopher Auger Feb. 2 1865 due to "loss of left arm near the shoulder by amputation."

Soldier	SITES, Private Andrew Jefferson
Date of Birth	April,1838
Age Given at Enlistment	24 years
Description at Enlistment	Not given
Place of Birth	Adams County, Pennsylvania
Pre-War Residence	Liberty, Adams County, Pennsylvania
Pre-War Occupation	Unknown
Post-War Residence	Fairfield, Ohio 1870, 1880; Blue Mound, Kansas 1900; Kansas City, Missouri 1910; National Military Home, Leavenworth, Kansas 1920
Post-War Occupation	Farmer
Names of Parents	Jeremiah B. and Louisa Sites
Names of Children	Jeremiah, William, John, George, Louisa, Frank, Charlotte and James
Name of Wife	Ida Pauline Lindig Sites, b. Germany, m. 1868, m. 32 years as of 1900
Date Soldier Filed Pension	October 5, 1864 and approved
Date Widow Filed Pension	None as wife preceded Private Sites in death
Date of Death	October 14, 1927 at Leavenworth, Kansas at 89 years of age
Cemetery	Leavenworth National Cemetery, 1694 4101 4th St., Leavenworth, KS
Remarks	In 1863, $7 deducted from pay per court martial; WIA at Mine Run, Va. in shoulder and hand; died of "myocardia and chronic cystitis in 1927.

Soldier	SMALL, Adjutant and Lieutenant Melville Rench
Date of Birth	October 19, 1845
Age Given at Enlistment	19 years
Description at Enlistment	Not given
Place of Birth	Maryland
Pre-War Residence	Hagerstown, Washington County, Maryland
Pre-War Occupation	None shown
Post-War Residence	N/A
Post-War Occupation	N/A
Names of Parents	Peter B. and Sarah Small
Names of Children	None
Name of Wife	None
Date Soldier Filed Pension	Not filed
Date Widow Filed Pension	N/A
Date of Death	November 17, 1864 at 19 years of age
Cemetery	Rose Hill Cemetery, Hagerstown, Maryland
Remarks	Commissioned 2nd Lt. July 24, 1862; promoted 1st Lt. Sept. 5, 1862; promoted to Adjutant Feb. 4, 1863, captured at Harper's Ferry July 19, 1863, confined in Libby Prison, escaped & recaptured, paroled at City Point, to Camp Parole April 30, 1864; suffered gunshot wound left leg Oct. 19, 1864, at Cedar Creek and later died in the General Hospital.

Soldier	SMITH, Sergeant Charles
Date of Birth	*c.* 1836
Age Given at Enlistment	26 years
Description at Enlistment	Not given

Place of Birth	Maryland
Pre-War Residence	Hagerstown, Washington County, Maryland
Pre-War Occupation	Clerk in drug store
Post-War Residence	4th District, Howard Co., Md. 1880; Mt. Airy, Carroll Co., Md., 1910
Post-War Occupation	Farmer in 1880 and self-employed in 1910
Names of Parents	Unknown
Names of Children	Ida E., Gertrude E., Ernest C. and Melisha
Name of Wife	Sarah A. Smith, married 48 years as of 1910
Date Soldier Filed Pension	May 18, 1880 and approved
Date Widow Filed Pension	Approved, but date not given
Date of Death	Unknown
Cemetery	Unknown
Remarks	Promoted to 5th Sgt. Dec. 1, 1862, then 4th, 3rd and 2nd Feb. 1, 1865 but reduced to ranks April 2, 1865; captured at Winchester June 15, 1863, paroled and exchanged; desertion charge later removed from record.

Soldier	STERLING, Corporal Samuel B. Sterling
Date of Birth	September 13, 1842
Age Given at Enlistment	20 years
Description at Enlistment	Not given
Place of Birth	Maryland
Pre-War Residence	Clear Spring, Washington County, Maryland
Pre-War Occupation	Unknown
Post-War Residence	Indian Spring, Washington Co. 1870-1910; Hagerstown, Maryland 1920
Post-War Occupation	Boatman 1870, Carpenter 1880, foreman, C & O Canal in 1910
Names of Parents	Samuel Sterling, d. December 23, 1864; mother unknown
Names of Children	Catharine W., Ellene, Samuel, Gracie, Harry, Bessie W. and Jennette J.
Name of Wife	Mary E. Sterling
Date Soldier Filed Pension	May 4, 1892 and approved. The attorney was W. Crissinger.
Date Widow Filed Pension	None filed
Date of Death	March 30, 1926 at 84 years of age
Cemetery	Saint Paul's Lutheran Church Cemetery, Clear Spring, Maryland
Remarks	Promoted Cpl. Dec. 4, 1862; July-Aug. 1863, $8 deducted for court martial; deserted Nov. 12, 1864 at Martinsburg, Va.; reported for duty May 5, 1865 under Lincoln's Proclamation; transferred to 1st Md. Inf. June 20, 1865; mustered out July 2, 1865 at Arlington Heights, Va.

Soldier	STONER, Private Abraham
Date of Birth	October 14, 1843
Age Given at Enlistment	19 years
Description at Enlistment	Not given
Place of Birth	Maryland
Pre-War Residence	Leitersburg, Washington County, Maryland
Pre-War Occupation	Farm laborer
Post-War Residence	Sublet Creek, Unita, WY in 1880; Cokeville, Unita, WY 1900
Post-War Occupation	Farmer in 1880 and ranch laborer in 1900
Names of Parents	John (1806-1882) and Mary A. Stoner (1805-1889)

Names of Children	Clarence A. and Grace P.
Name of Wife	Ella M. Whitney Stoner, m. 1882
Date Soldier Filed Pension	None filed
Date Widow Filed Pension	None filed
Date of Death	Prior to 1910
Cemetery	Unknown
Remarks	Deserted from Camp Harper's Ferry January 18, 1863; was never arrested, confined or court martialed and never returned to his unit.

Soldier	STUDENWALT, Private Jacob C.
Date of Birth	*c.* 1837
Age Given at Enlistment	25 years
Description at Enlistment	Not given
Place of Birth	West Virginia
Pre-War Residence	Hedgesville, Berkeley Va., now West Virginia
Pre-War Occupation	Laborer
Post-War Residence	Hedgesville, Berkeley, West Virginia
Post-War Occupation	Mechanic and farmer
Names of Parents	Unknown
Names of Children	John, Wesley, Dora, Charles, Bertie and Nanny
Name of Wife	Mary J. Studenwalt
Date Soldier Filed Pension	September 9, 1879 and approved
Date Widow Filed Pension	October 14, 1897 and approved
Date of Death	September 24, 1897 at Berkeley Springs, West Va. at 60 years of age
Cemetery	Unknown
Remarks	Appointed sharpshooter for 2nd Brigade, 3rd Division, 6th Corps; has an excellent service record with no absences or court martial.

Soldier	SWEITZER, Private John J.
Date of Birth	April 3, 1844
Age Given at Enlistment	19 years
Description at Enlistment	5' 11" tall, complexion dark, eyes dark, and hair dark
Place of Birth	Pennsylvania
Pre-War Residence	Unknown
Pre-War Occupation	Farm hand
Post-War Residence	Welsh Run, Franklin Co. 1880; Clear Spring, Maryland 1900 to 1910
Post-War Occupation	Farm laborer 1880
Names of Parents	Unknown
Names of Children	None
Name of Wife	Catharine C. Sweitzer, married 42 years as of 1910
Date Soldier Filed Pension	July 3, 1894, but not approved even though honorably discharged
Date Widow Filed Pension	October 2, 1916, but not approved
Date of Death	July 3, 1910 at 66 years of age
Cemetery	Clear Spring Mennonite Cemetery, Clear Spring, Maryland
Remarks	Deserted Camp Williamsport Oct. 21, 1862, but returned April 1, 1863 under President's Proclamation; served as teamster; deserted Oct. 30, 1863, while on march from Centreville to Catletts; discharged at Forrest Hall Prison, Georgetown, D.C. for "total loss of vision of right eye and partial loss of teeth" March 8, 1864, per order General Auger.

Soldier	THOMAS, Private Michael
Date of Birth	1843
Age Given at Enlistment	18 years
Description at Enlistment	Not given
Place of Birth	Maryland
Pre-War Residence	Sharpsburg, Washington County, Maryland
Pre-War Occupation	Farm hand
Post-War Residence	Admitted to National Home for Disabled Vol. Soldiers in Elizabeth City, Va. Nov. 2, 1887 until Jan. 10, 1897 for "hernia, gunshot wound right hand & pharyngitis"; then Chambersburg Ward 4, Pa. as of 1910.
Post-War Occupation	None known
Names of Parents	Peter and Mary Thomas
Names of Children	None
Name of Wife	None
Date Soldier Filed Pension	November 10, 1888 and approved
Date Widow Filed Pension	N/A
Date of Death	1911
Cemetery	Cedar Grove Cemetery, Chambersburg, Franklin County, Pa.
Remarks	Deserted Camp Williamsport Oct. 27, 1862, arrested Nov. 25 and removed to Harper's Ferry; captured at Winchester, paroled and exchanged; WIA Spots. C. H. May 12, 1864; deserted Jan. 12, 1865, arrested by Provost Marshall & $10 taken mthly per court martial.

Soldier	WATSON, Private Daniel W. (the surname is of Scottish origin)
Date of Birth	*c.* 1840
Age Given at Enlistment	22 years
Description at Enlistment	5' 9" height, dark complexion, blue eyes and light hair
Place of Birth	Maryland
Pre-War Residence	Tilmington, Washington County, Maryland
Pre-War Occupation	Farmer
Post-War Residence	N/A
Post-War Occupation	N/A
Names of Parents	Rachel Watson, mother
Names of Children	Unknown
Name of Wife	Mary A. (Smith) Watson
Date Soldier Filed Pension	N/A
Date Widow Filed Pension	February 26, 1864 and for minor, both approved
Date of Death	November 27, 1863 at age 23 years
Cemetery	Unknown
Remarks	bsent sick without leave, left Camp Harper's Ferry January 16, 1863, but returned to regiment; killed in action Battle of Locust Grove, Va.

Soldier	WEAGLEY, Private George A.
Date of Birth	September 9, 1840
Age Given at Enlistment	21 years of age
Description at Enlistment	5' 8" tall, fair complexion, blue eyes, and light hair
Place of Birth	Maryland
Pre-War Residence	Cavetown District, Smithsburg P. O., Washington County, Maryland

Pre-War Occupation	Laborer
Post-War Residence	N/A
Post-War Occupation	N/A
Names of Parents	Samuel C. Weagley (1816-1861) and Elizabeth Weagley (1831-1884)
Names of Children	None
Name of Wife	None
Date Soldier Filed Pension	Not filed
Date Widow Filed Pension	N/A
Date of Death	February 28, 1863 at 22 years of age
Cemetery	Welt Church of the Brethren Cemetery, Smithsburg, Maryland
Remarks	Mustered in at Baltimore, Md. August 21, 1862; died in the Harper's Ferry Hospital, February 28, 1863, of typhoid fever.

Soldier	WOODWARD, Private James F.
Date of Birth	December 13, 1841
Age Given at Enlistment	22 years
Description at Enlistment	5' 9 ¾" in height, complexion fair, eyes grey and hair black
Place of Birth	England, immigrated to Baltimore, Maryland in 1849
Pre-War Residence	Baltimore Ward 16, Baltimore, Maryland
Pre-War Occupation	Apprentice gunsmith
Post-War Residence	Gettysburg Ward 2, Adams County, Pa. at least from 1870
Post-War Occupation	Gunsmith 1870 and 1880 and day laborer 1900
Names of Parents	Edward and Ellen Woodward
Names of Children	James H., Mary E., John H., George W., Susanna, Daisy, Elsworth, Frederick, and Arthur
Name of Wife	Frances Mary Ana Marshall Woodward, married *c.* 1865
Date Soldier Filed Pension	July 9, 1867 and approved
Date Widow Filed Pension	None filed as Frances preceded her husband in death
Date of Death	January 3, 1909 at 67 years of age
Cemetery	Gettysburg National Cemetery, Gettysburg, Adams County, Pa.
Remarks	Drafted in 1863 into 1st Maryland Cavalry, but "discharged disability"; drafted again, in error, June 24, 1864 into 6th Md., Inf., but transferred to 1st Md. Inf. June 20, 1865 & mustered out July 2, 1865.

Soldier	YOUNG, Private Henry
Date of Birth	October 11, 1811
Age Given at Enlistment	46 years
Description at Enlistment	Not given
Place of Birth	Maryland
Pre-War Residence	Middletown Election District, Frederick County, Maryland
Pre-War Occupation	Laborer
Post-War Residence	Washington County, Maryland
Post-War Occupation	Unknown
Names of Parents	Unknown
Names of Children	Mary, Elizabeth, Charlotte, Abraham and Sarah
Name of Wife	Elizabeth Michael Young (1820-1854) m. March 28, 1836

Date Soldier Filed Pension	None filed
Date Widow Filed Pension	None filed
Date of Death	June 16, 1866 at 54 years of age
Cemetery	Beaver Creek Christian Church Disciples of Christ, Beaver Creek, Md.
Remarks	AWOL, left Berryville, Va. camp June 12, 1863; arrested at home Sept. 22, 1863 by Provost Marshall; Court Martial Dec. 11, 1863, $11.25 due government for apprehension, to forfeit 5 mos. pay & ½ of regular pay & allowance for rest of term; transferred to V. R. C. April 15, 1864.

Endnotes

Confederate Service Records	CSR
National Archives, Washington DC	NA
Union Service Records	USR

Chapter I

1 King, "Memoirs of September 15, 1925"; courtesy of Elizabeth Foster.
2 *Ibid.*
3 King, "Reminiscences of Washington County", February 10, 1921; courtesy of Elizabeth Foster.
4 "Washington County Marriages", *archiver.rootsweb.ancestry.com*, May 6, 2015.
5 "Coach Making", *Torch Light*, p. 1, (Hagerstown: November 7, 1833).
6 "Annual Meeting of First Hagerstown Hose Co.", *Torch Light*, pp. 2-3, (Hagerstown: January 21, 1836).
7 *Ibid.*
8 "Military Elections, Officers Received by Various Volunteer and Militia Companies", *Torch Light*, p. 2C, (Hagerstown: August 27, 1846).
9 "Election of Washington County Public School Trustees", *Herald Freedom & Torch Light*, p. 2D, (Hagerstown: January 3, 1855).
10 "Anniversary", *Herald Freedom & Torch Light*, p. 3A, (Hagerstown: April 14, 1852).
11 Land Records of Washington County, Maryland, Archives of Maryland Online, *mdlandrec.net*, Bill of Sale, Book SS, p. 538, August 2, 2015.
12 *Ibid.*, Bill of Sale, Book SS, p. 544.
13 *Ibid.*, Bill of Sale, Book SS, p. 548.
14 *Ibid.*, Bill of Sale, Book RR, p. 732.
15 "Official", *Herald Freedom*, p. 3C, (Hagerstown: February 12, 1845).
16 Land Records of Washington County, Maryland. Deed, Book IN4, p. 304, *mdlandrec.net*, August 2, 2015.
17 Bosse, Beverly L. "Redburn Family History: descendants of Henry Redburn of Maryland", *familysearch.org*, May 29, 2015.
18 *Ibid.*, Mortgage, Book IN4, p. 305.
19 *Ibid.*, Bill of Sale, Book IN4, p. 613.
20 "Public Sale", *Herald Freedom*, p. 3D, (Hagerstown: May 15, 1850).
21 Land Records of Washington County, Maryland. Mortgage, Book IN6, p. 318, *mdlandrec.net*, August 2, 2015.
22 *Ibid.*, Book IN6, p. 411, August 2, 2015.
23 "To The Public", *Herald Freedom & Torch Light*, p. 2G, (Hagerstown: February 25, 1852).
24 Land Records of Washington County, Maryland. Book IN8, p. 409. *mdlandrec.net*, August 2, 2015.
25 "For Sheriff in 1855", *Weekly Chronicle*, p. 6F, (Hagerstown: June 12, 1855)
26 Land Records of Washington County, Maryland. Book IN13, pp. 678-679. *mdlandrec.net*, August 2, 2015

27 "Public Sale", *Herald Freedom & Torch Light*, p. 2G, (Hagerstown: February 29, 1860).
28 1860 U.S. census for Hagerstown, Maryland, p. 10, NA.
29 *Ibid.*
30 *Ibid.*
31 *Ibid.*
32 1860 U.S. census for Baltimore City, Maryland, p. 187, NA.
33 King, "Letter to Lenore Hamilton", Undated; courtesy of Elizabeth Foster.
34 *Ibid.*
35 Irvin-Craig, Linda, "Washington County Historical Society founders had rich history in County", *Herald Mail*, *(*Hagerstown: September 23, 2011).
36 *Ibid.*
37 "Peter Waltz", The Official roster of the soldiers of the American Revolution buried in Pennsylvania, *interactive.ancestry.com*, April 29, 2014.
38 *Ibid.*
39 *Ibid.*
40 "Porter and Bowers and Everyone In Between", *wc.rootsweb.ancestry.com*, May 3, 2004.
41 "Colonel George Adam Woltz", *www.findagrave.com*, July 3, 2014.
42 "Porter and Bowers and Everyone In Between", *wc.rootsweb.ancestry.com*, May 3, 2014.
43 "Charles G. Lane", *findagrave.com*, February 5, 2014.
44 *Ibid.*
45 King, "Reminiscences of Washington County", February 10, 1921; courtesy of Elizabeth Foster.
46 Scharf, *The History of Western Maryland*, (Philadelphia: Louis H. Everts, 1882), vol. 2, p. 1158.
47 *Ibid.*
48 King, "Reminiscences of Washington County", February 10, 1921; courtesy of Elizabeth Foster.
49 *Ibid.*
50 1860 U.S. census for Hagerstown, Washington County, Maryland, p. 10, NA.
51 King, "Letter to Lenore Hamilton", Undated; courtesy of Elizabeth Foster.
52 Ernest, Ora Ann. "Briar-Covered Foundation The Only Remains of Old Academy", *The Daily Mail*, p. 6, (Hagerstown: March 23, 1974).
53 Williams, *The History of Washington County, Maryland*, *(*Chambersburg: Runk & Titsworth, 1906), p. 230.
54 Scharf, *op. cit.*, p. 1158.
55 Ernest, Ora Ann, "Briar-Covered Foundation The Only Remains of Old Academy", *The Daily Mail*, p. 6, (Hagerstown: March 23, 1974).
56 *Ibid.*
57 *Ibid.*
58 *Ibid.*
59 "Col. Buchanan Schley, Sr.", p. 4, (Frederick: *The Daily News*, October 12, 1916).
60 *Ibid.*
61 "Col Buchanan Schely, Sr", *findagrave.com*, May 19, 2015.
62 *Ibid.*
63 King, "Letter to Lenore Hamilton", Undated; courtesy of Elizabeth Foster.
64 King, "Reminiscences of Washington Co.", February 10, 1921; courtesy of Elizabeth Foster.
65 "Gen. David Gordon, Oldest Officer In The Army Dies; Former Resident Of City", *Morning Herald*, p. 16, (Hagerstown: January 31, 1930).
66 *Ibid.*
67 King, "Reminiscences of Washington Co.", February 10, 1921; courtesy of Elizabeth Foster.
68 1860 U.S. census for Hagerstown, Maryland, NA. pp. 10-15, 28, 29, 35, & 37.
69 King, "Reminiscences of Washington Co.", February 10, 1921; courtesy of Elizabeth Foster.
70 Woods, *Woods' Baltimore City Directory*, *(*Baltimore: James W. Woods, 1860), p. 424.
71 "Gen. John R. King III", *Baltimore Sun*, p. 14, (Baltimore: February 15, 1913).
72 1860 U.S. census for Baltimore, Maryland, p. 187, NA.
73 King, "Reminiscences of Washington Co.", February 10, 1921; courtesy of Elizabeth Foster.
74 "The South Succeeds", *ushistory.org*, June 3, 2015.
75 Williams, *op. cit.*, p. 308.
76 *Ibid.*, p, 308.
77 *Ibid.*, p. 300.
78 *Ibid.*, p. 307, p. 310.
79 *Ibid.*, p. 310.

80 *Ibid.*, p. 311.
81 *Ibid.*, p. 311.
82 *Ibid.*, p. 311.
83 *Ibid.*, p. 311.
84 *Ibid.*, p. 310.
85 "Married, McLaughlin–King", *Herald Freedom & Torch Light*, p. 2F, (Hagerstown: October 23, 1861).

Chapter II

1 1860 U.S. census for the City of Baltimore, Maryland, p. 187, NA.
2 1870 U.S. census for Hagerstown, Maryland, p. 131B, NA.
3 1900 U.S. census for Hagerstown, Maryland, p. 1B, NA.
4 Land Records of Washington County, Maryland, Book McK1, p. 170. *mdlandrec.net*, August 2, 2015.
5 Land Records of Washington County, Maryland, Book 73, p. 614, *mdlandrec.net*, August 2, 2015.
6 1860 U.S. census for Martinsburg, Virginia, p. 161, NA.
7 "Notes on Clear Spring & Fairview Mountain, (aka North Mountain)", *www.press.jhu.edu*, March 19, 2014.
8 *Official Records*, vol. 19, part II, p. 31.
9 *Ibid.*
10 *Ibid.*
11 1860 U.S. census for Hagerstown, Maryland, p. 26, NA.
12 "Proceedings of the Laymen's Association and Lay Electoral Conference, Fifty-Second Session", *Minutes of the Central Pennsylvania Annual Conference of the Methodist Episcopal Church*. vol. 52, part 4, 1920, p. 144.
13 Ayres, George B., "Complete Report of the Burning and Destruction of Chambersburg by the Rebels", *Herald and Torch Light*, July 30, 1864. *washcolibrary.org*, April 1, 2014.
14 Seilhamer, *Biographical Annals of Franklin County, Pennsylvania*, vol. II, (Chicago: Genealogical Pub. Co., 1905), p. 606.
15 "Boyd's Business Directory for Maryland, 1875", p. 316, *whilbr.org*, January 15, 2014.
16 1860 U.S. census for Hagerstown, Maryland, p. 12, NA.
17 Clark, *The History of the 39th Regiment Illinois Volunteer Veteran Infantry in the War of Rebellion, 1861–1865*, (Chicago: Veterans Assoc., 1889), p. 368.
18 Andreas, *The History of Chicago: From 1857 until the fire of 1871*, (Chicago: A. T. Andrea, 1885), vol. II, p. 204.
19 Clark, *op. cit.*, pp. 13-14.
20 Lamon, *Recollections of Abraham Lincoln, 1847–1865*, (Lincoln: University of Nebraska: 1994), p. xxxvii.
21 "A Brigade of Virginians", *nytimes.com*, February 28, 2014.
22 Clark, *op. cit.*, p. 18.
23 *Ibid.*
24 Clark, *op. cit.*, p. 51.
25 Current, *Lincoln's Loyalists: Union Soldiers in the Confederacy*, (Lawrenceville: Princeton University, 1992), p. 14.
26 Matchett, *Matchett's Baltimore Directory*, (Baltimore: Matchett, 1849), p. 142.
27 *Ibid.*, p. 99.
28 Woods, *Woods' Baltimore City Directory*, (Baltimore, Woods, 1860), p. 140.
29 Shepherd, *History of Baltimore, Maryland from its Founding as a Town to the Current*, (S. B. Nelson: Baltimore, 1898), p. 49.
30 "History and Roster of Maryland Volunteers, War of 1861–66", vol. I, *Archives of Maryland Online*, February 28, 2014.
31 "Temperance—A Good Movement", *Herald & Torch Light*, p. 2C, (Hagerstown: January 29, 1862).
32 "History and Roster of Maryland Volunteers, War of 1861–66", *op. cit.*, p. 483.
33 *Ibid.*, p. 483.
34 Newcomer, *Cole's Cavalry or Three Years in the Saddle*, (Baltimore: Cushing & Co., 1895), p. 70.
35 *Ibid.*, p. 71.
36 Woods, *Woods' Baltimore City Directory*, (Baltimore: Woods, 1865), p. 151.
37 Wilmer, Jarnett and Vernon, *History and Roster of Maryland Volunteers, War of 1861–5 vol. I*, (Baltimore: Guggenheim, Weil & Co., 1898), p. 443.
38 *Ibid.*, p. 505.
39 *Ibid.*, p. 483.
40 1860 U.S. census for Hagerstown, Maryland, p. 28, NA.
41 Wilmer, Jarnett and Vernon, *op. cit.*, p. 279.

42 Keller, *Roster of Civil War Soldiers from Washington County*, (Baltimore: Clearfield, 2008), p. 93.
43 "Peter Negley", *Herald & Torch Light*, p. 12, (Hagerstown: June 12, 1884).
44 "A Large Number of Union Men", *Herald & Torch Light*, p. 3A, (Hagerstown: September 27, 1865).
45 "We Are Requested", *Herald & Torch Light*, p. 3A, (Hagerstown: October 25, 1865).
46 *Ibid.*
47 "Peter Negley", *Herald & Torch Light and Hagerstown Odd Fellow*, p. 3, (Hagerstown: June 12, 1884).
48 "Death of a Maryland Patriot", *nytimes.com*, January 28, 2014.
49 Clark, *op. cit.*, p. 382.
50 *Ibid.*, pp. 382-383.
51 *Ibid.*, p. 383.
52 1860 U.S. census for Boonsboro District, Washington County, Maryland. p. 1500, NA.
53 *Ibid.*
54 Woods, *Baltimore City Directory*, (Baltimore: Woods, 1860), p. 96 and p. 212.
55 1860 U.S. census for Boonsboro District, Washington County, Maryland, p. 142, NA.
56 Keller, *op. cit.*, p. 90.
57 "New York Civil War Units Nicknames and Synonyms", *dmna.ny.gov*, February 17, 2014.
58 1850 U.S. census for Washington County, Maryland, p. 2, NA.
59 1870 U.S. census for Montgomery County, Maryland, p. 70, NA.
60 1880 U.S. census for Hagerstown, Maryland, p. 92A, NA.
61 1900 U.S. census for Columbus, Ohio, p. 6, NA.
62 1860 U.S. census for Boonsboro District, Maryland, p. 160, NA.
63 Comstock, *The Pottery of the Shenandoah Valley Region*, (Chapel Hill: University of North Carolina, 1994), pp. 465-466.
64 "39th Illinois Infantry Regiment", *illinoisgenweb.org*, January 8, 2014.
65 Clark, *op. cit.*, p. 530.
66 *Ibid.*
67 1860 U.S. census for Washington County, Maryland, p. 6, NA.
68 Wilmer, Jarrett and Vernon, *op. cit.*, p. 181.
69 Keller, *op. cit.*, p. 181.
70 Scharf, J. Thomas, *op. cit.*, p. 226.
71 Keller, *op. cit.*, p. 181.
72 1870 U.S. census for the District of Columbia, p. 24, NA.
73 1860 U.S. census for Washington County, Maryland, p. 215, NA.
74 Vandiver, *Mighty Stonewall*, (New York: McGraw Hill, 1957), pp. 182-183.
75 "Dam No. 5", *Herald of Freedom & Torch Light*, pp. 1, (Hagerstown: June 12, 1861).
76 1860 U.S. census for Boonsboro, Maryland, p. 205, NA.
77 "39th Illinois Infantry Regiment", *Illinoisgenweb.org*, January 8, 2014.
78 Clark, *op. cit.*, p. 14 and p. 18.
79 *Ibid.*, p. 18.
80 1860 U.S. census for Funkstown, Maryland, p. 5, NA.
81 1860 U.S. census for Hagerstown, Maryland, p. 311, NA.
82 "Rose Hill Cemetery", *findagrave.com*, April 2, 2014.
83 Untitled, *Herald & Torch*, p. 2, (Hagerstown: June 15, 1870).
84 Untitled, *Herald & Torch*, p. 2, (Hagerstown: January 17, 1872).
85 Untitled, *Herald & Torch*, p. 2, (Hagerstown: April 16, 1873).
86 "Boyd's Business Directory for Maryland, 1875", p. 316. *whilbr.org*, April 5, 2014.
87 "Lewis Heist", *findagrave.com*, April 5, 2014.
88 1870 U.S. census for Hagerstown, Maryland, pp. 105-106, NA.
89 1860 U.S. census for Hagerstown, Maryland, p. 44, NA.
90 1870 U.S. census for Hagerstown, Maryland, p. 39, NA.
91 "Military Affairs Around Us", *Hagerstown Mail*, p. 2C, (Hagerstown: January 10, 1862).
92 Wilmer, Jarnette and Vernon, *op. cit.*, p. 677.
93 Vandiver, *op. cit.*, pp. 186-190.
94 Henderson, *Stonewall Jackson and the American Civil War*, (New York: Konecky & Konecky, 1898), pp. 191-192.
95 Bates, *History of the Pennsylvania Volunteers, 1861–1865*, (Harrisburg: B. Singerly, 1869–1871), p. 1111.
96 Marvin, *The 5th Regiment Connecticut Volunteers: A History Compiled from Diaries & Official Reports*, (Hartford: Wiley, Waterman & Eaton, 1889), p. 54.
97 *Ibid.*, p. 54.

98 Hall and Hall, *Cayuga in the Field. A Record of the 19th N. Y. Volunteers*, (Auburn: Truair Smith, 1873), p. 86.
99 "The Civil War", *Hagerstown Mail*, p. 1F, (Hagerstown: January 10, 1862).
100 "A People at War: Hagerstown, Maryland, June 15–August 31, 1863", *Maryland Historical Magazine*, vol. 40, Issue 4, p. 257, (Baltimore: Maryland Historical Society, December, 1945).
101 Scarf, *op. cit.*, vol. II, p. 1185.
102 1860 U.S. census for Hagerstown, Maryland, p. 61, NA.
103 Wilmer, Jarnette and Vernon, *op. cit.*, p. 277.
104 Boyd, *Boyd's Business Directory of Maryland, 1875*, (Washington, D. C.: Wm H. Boyd, 1875), p. 317.
105 McMillion, Dave, "Hagerstown Man Preserves Great-Grandfather's Civil War Diaries" *antietam.com*, January 28, 2014.
106 1860 U.S. census for Hagerstown, Maryland, p. 18, NA.
107 *Ibid.,* p. 33.
108 *Ibid.,* p. 13.
109 Mayhue, *Firefighting in Hagerstown*, (Charleston: Arcadia Publishing, 2004). p. 2.
110 Williams, *op. cit.*, p. 115.
111 *Ibid.*
112 *Ibid.*
113 "A Pastoral Call", *Herald of Freedom & Torch Light*, p. 2C, (Hagerstown: October 23, 1860).
114 Untitled, *Herald & Torch*, p. 2, (Hagerstown: April 22, 1868).
115 "Hagerstown Female Institute, "*Herald & Torch Light*, p. 3D, (Hagerstown: June 21, 1865).
116 Wilmer, Jarnette and Vernon, *op. cit.*, p. 575.
117 "About Zion Reformed UCC", *zionhagerstown.org*, March 21, 2014.
118 "Married", *Herald of Freedom & Torch Light*, p. 2F, (Hagerstown: March 6, 1861).
119 *Ibid.,* p. 3B, (Hagerstown: June 15, 1864).
120 1860 U.S. census for Washington County, Maryland, p. 28, NA.
121 *Ibid.*
122 "Ad for Abraham Levi", *Herald of Freedom & Torch Light*, p. 3D, (Hagerstown: March 30, 1853).
123 *Ibid.,* p. 3A, (Hagerstown: April 18, 1860).
124 *Ibid.,* p. 3D, (Hagerstown: October 11, 1854).
125 "Public Sale", *Herald & Torch Light*, p. 2G, (Hagerstown: February 24, 1864).
126 Turner, *Record of Service of the Michigan Volunteers in the Civil War*, (Kalamazoo: Ihling Bros. & Everard, 1905), p. 1.
127 1860 U.S. census for Mountjoy, Adams County, Pennsylvania, p. 51, NA.
128 Wilmer, Jarnette and Vernon, *op. cit.*, p. 655.
129 Scarf, *op. cit.*, p. 323.
130 "The Elusive Major Horner", *emittsburg.net/archive*. February 21, 2014.
131 *Ibid.*
132 1860 U.S. census for Hagerstown, Maryland, p. 31.
133 Wilmer, Jarnette and Vernon, *op. cit.*, p. 367.
134 *Ibid.,* p. 368.
135 1850 U.S. census for Hagerstown, Maryland, p. 124A, NA.
136 "Married", *Herald & Freedom*, p. 2G, (Hagerstown: February 12, 1851).
137 1860 U.S. census for Hagerstown, Maryland, p. 62, NA.
138 "Selling Off At Cost", *Herald of Freedom & Torch Light*, p. 2E, (Hagerstown: November 18, 1863).
139 "Intending to Remove From Hagerstown", *Herald & Torch Light*, p. 2G, (Hagerstown: February 24, 1864).
140 McElroy, *Philadelphia Directory for 1867*, (Philadelphia: C. Sherman & Co., 1867), p. 533.
141 1870 U.S. census for Philadelphia, Pennsylvania, p. 195A, NA.
142 Marvin, *op. cit.*, p. 419.
143 "Married", *Hagerstown Freedom & Torch Light*, p. 2G, (Hagerstown: February 12, 1862).
144 Davis, *Three Years in the Army, the Story of the Thirteenth Massachusetts Volunteers from July 16, 1861 to August 1, 1864*, (Boston: Estes & Lauriat, 1894), p. 409.
145 Forbush, Bradley M., "13th Massachusetts Volunteers", 2009. *13thmass.org*, June 28, 2012.
146 Davis, *op. cit.*, p. 18.
147 1860 U.S. census for Hagerstown, Maryland, p. 36, NA.
148 *Ibid.,* p. 13.
149 Wilmer, Jarnette and Vernon, *op. cit.*, pp. 279-280.
150 1870 U.S. census for Hagerstown, Maryland, p. 98, NA.
151 *Ibid.,* p. 89.

152 Garrison and Garrison, *The Encyclopedia of Civil War Usage*, (New York: Castle Books, 2009), pp. 186-187.
153 Clark, *History of Hampton Battery F, Independent Pennsylvania Light Artillery* (Pittsburgh: Werner Co., 1909), p. 129.
154 *Ibid.*, p. 11.
155 *Ibid.*, p. 13.
156 *Ibid.*, p. 13
157 *Ibid.*, p. 13.
158 *Ibid.*, p. 41.
159 Foote, *op. cit.*, p. 229.
160 *Ibid.*, p. 230.
161 U.S. War Department, *War of the Rebellion: A compilation of the official records of the Union and Confederate armies*, Series 1, vol. 9, (Washington: Government Printing Office, 1886–1901), pp. 191-193.
162 U.S. Navy Department, *Official records of the Union and Confederate Navies in the War of the Rebellion*, Series 1, vol. 6, (Washington: Government Printing Office, 1894–1922), p. 621.
163 Williams, *op. cit.*, p. 91.
164 Land Patents of Washington County, Maryland. *mdlandrec.net*, Book 2, folio 288. *mdlandrec.net*, August 2, 2015.
165 Land Records of Washington County, Maryland. Book ZZ, folio 870. *mdlandrec.net*, August 2, 2015.
166 Dickey, Paula Stoner, "Nomination Form for the National Register of Historic Places", *msa.maryland.gov*, April 17, 2012.
167 1860 U.S. census for Washington County, Maryland, p. 37, NA.
168 Land Records of Washington County, Maryland. Book OHW2, folio 260, Book IN8, folio 577, and Book IN9, folio 699. *mdlandrec.net*, August 2, 2015.
169 "Tavern Stand at Public Sale", *Herald & Torch Light*, p. 3, (Hagerstown: September 13, 1865).
170 Land Records of Washington County, Maryland. Book LBN2, folio 662. *mdlandrec.net*, August 2, 2015.
171 *Official Records*, *op. cit.*, Series 1, vol. 7, p. 131.
172 Foote, *op. cit.*, p. 201.
173 *Ibid.*, p. 210.
174 *Ibid.*, p. 212.
175 Gott, *Where the South Lost the War: An Analysis of the Fort Henry–Fort Donelson Campaign, February, 1862*, (Mechanicsburg: Stackpole Books, 2003), pp. 284-285 and p. 288.
176 *Official Records*, *op. cit.*, p. 301.
177 *Official Records*, Series 1, vol. 25, part 1, p. 158.
178 Bates, Samuel P., *op. cit.*, vol. 1, p. 958.
179 *Ibid.*
180 *Ibid.*, pp. 958-959.
181 *Ibid.*, p. 960.
182 *Ibid.*, p. 960.
183 *Ibid.*, p. 961.
184 *Ibid.*
185 Branter, Lauren, "(George), Michael Weisel of Bucks County, PA 1732", *rootsweb.com*, May 30, 2012.
186 Scharf, *op. cit.*, p. 1125.
187 *Ibid.*, p. 1126.
188 Williams, *op. cit.*, p. 304.
189 *Ibid.*
190 *Ibid.*, p. 305.
191 Scharf, *op. cit.*, p. 196.
192 Williams, *op. cit.*, pp. 304-305.
193 *Ibid.*, p. 305.
194 *Ibid.*, p. 325.
195 "A History of the Maryland Court of Appeals", *msa.maryland.gov*, vol. 368, p. 202, May 30, 2012.
196 Davis, *op. cit.*, p. 437.
197 1860 U.S. census for Hagerstown, Maryland, p. 542, NA.
198 "Omnibus", Online Etymology Dictionary, *etymonline.com*, March 28, 2012.
199 "Died—Joseph E. Norris", *Herald & Torch Light*, p. 6, (Hagerstown: February 9, 1893).
200 "Theatre at Lyceum Hall", *Hagerstown Freedom & Torch Light*, p. 2D, (Hagerstown: March 5, 1862).
201 1860 U.S. census for Hagerstown, Maryland, p. 24, NA.
202 "Duncan Family Tree", *ancestry.com*, April 7, 2014.

203 1850 U.S. census for Washington County, Maryland, p. 215B, NA.
204 "Rosters of the New York Infantry Regiments during the Civil War", *dmna.ny.gov*, August 16, 2012.
205 *Ibid.*
206 *Official Records*, *op. cit.*, p. 1095.
207 Vandiver, *op. cit.*, p. 197.
208 *Official Records*, *op. cit.*, p. 739.
209 *Ibid.*, p. 740.
210 Vandiver, *op. cit.*, p. 200.
211 *Ibid.*, p. 201.
212 *Official Records*, *op. cit.*, p. 746.
213 "New York Passenger and Immigration Lists, 1820–1850", *ancestry.com*, May 8, 2014.
214 "Reynolds Family Tree", *ancestry.com*, May 8, 2014.
215 1860 U.S. census for Brooklyn, New York, p. 294, NA.
216 "IRS Tax Assessment Lists, 1862–1918 for Collection District", *ancestry.com*, May 8, 2014.
217 *Gopsill's Harrisburg Directory*, (Jersey City: John H. Lyon, 1863), p. 180.
218 "United States, Civil War Draft Registration Records, 1863–1865", *ancestry.com*, May 8, 2014.
219 "Bill Morrow on the James Lett Company", *linkedin.com*, May 8, 2014.
220 Wilmer, Jarnette and Vernon, *op. cit.*, p. 506.
221 *Ibid.*, p.485.
222 "William Maulsby", Archives of Maryland Biographical Series. *msa.maryland.gov*, August 18, 2012.
223 "Report of Brig. Gen. Henry H. Lockwood", *civilwarathome*, August 18, 2012.
224 "William Maulsby", *msa.maryland.gov*, August 18, 2012.
225 1860 U.S. census for Hagerstown, Maryland, p. 62, NA.
226 *Official Records*, *op. cit.*, p. 742.
227 *Ibid.*
228 *Official Records*, vol. 7, chapter 17, p. 2.
229 1860 U.S. census for Martinsburg, Virginia, p. 161, NA.
230 1870 U.S. census for Martinsburg, West Virginia, p. 12, NA.
231 McDonald, William N., *A History of the Laurel Brigade*, (Baltimore: Sun Job Printing, 1907), p. 39.
232 *Ibid.*
233 *Official Records*, vol. 12, chapter 24, pp. 338-339.
234 *Ibid.*
235 McDonald, *op. cit.*, p. 39.
236 *Official Records*, *op. cit.*, p. 339.
237 *Ibid.*
238 McDonald, *op. cit.*, p. 40.
239 *Official Records*, *op. cit.*, p. 385.
240 *Ibid.*, p. 334.
241 *Ibid.*, p. 336.
242 Foote, *op. cit.*, p. 270.
243 Vandiver, *op. cit.*, p. 204.
244 *Official Records*, *op. cit.*, p. 381.
245 *Ibid.*, p. 336.
246 *Ibid.*, p. 378.
247 *Ibid.*, p. 384.
248 *Ibid.*, p. 347.
249 Vandiver, *op. cit.*, p. 210.
250 *Official Records*, *op. cit.*, p. 383.
251 *Ibid.*
252 1860 U.S. census for Winchester, Virginia, p. 79, NA.
253 "History of Grace Evangelical Lütheran Church", *gracewin.org*, September 13, 2012.
254 "Shaft", *thefreedictionary.com*, September 17, 2012.
255 Kelbaugh, *op. cit.*, p. 48.
256 "Elias Marken Recher", *findagrave.com*, September 17, 2012.
257 1860 U.S. census for Hagerstown, Maryland, p. 292 NA.
258 1850 U.S. census for Hagerstown, Maryland, p. 243, NA.
259 1850 U.S. census for Hagerstown, Maryland, p. 255, NA.
260 1860 U.S. census for Hagerstown, Maryland, p. 37, NA.
261 Wilmer, Jarnette, Vernon, *op. cit.*, p. 279.

262 *Ibid.*

263 1870 U.S. census for Washington County, Maryland, p. 336A, NA.

264 Cartmell, *Shenandoah Pioneers and their Descendants*, (Winchester: Eddy Press Group, 1909), p. 202.

265 *Annual Report of the Adjutant General of the State of West Virginia for the year ending December 31, 1865*, (Wheeling: John Frew, 1866), p. 40.

266 Plummer, *A History of West Virginia Wesleyan College*, (Nashville: Parthenon Press, 1965), pp. 18-19.

267 Becker, Sharon, "Rev. Alfred Alphaeus Reger", Ringgold County IAGenWeb Project, p. 3, *iagenweb.org*, October 6, 2012.

268 Plummer, *op. cit.*, pp. 16-19.

269 Wilmer, Jarnette and Vernon, *op. cit.*, p. 483.

270 1850 U.S. census for Frederick County, Virginia, p. 152, NA.

271 1860 U.S. census for Frederick County, Virginia, p. 79, NA.

272 Elgin, Richard and Robin Elgin. "Goldsmith Chandlee", *surveyhistory.org*, September 29, 2012.

273 "Graves & Company Records", Handley Regional Library, *youseemore.com/handley*, September 29, 2012.

274 *Official Records*, vol. 5, chapter 24, p. 391.

275 *Official Records*, vol. 12, chapter 24, p. 427.

276 *Ibid.*, p. 426.

277 Armstrong, *7th Virginia Cavalry*, (Lynchburg: Howard Publishing Co., 1992), p. 25.

278 *Ibid.*, p. 184.

279 *Ibid.*, pgs. 165, 167, 192, 225.

280 Turner, *op. cit.*, vol. 31, p. 67.

281 *Ibid.*

282 "Federal Officers Captured by Jackson", *Richmond Times Dispatch*, June 13, 1862, *perseus.tufts.edu*, October 6, 2012.

283 1850 U.S. census for Wayne County, Michigan, p. 496, NA.

284 1860 U.S. census for Oakland County, Michigan, p. 167, NA.

285 1870 U.S. census for Tallahassee, Florida, p. 50, NA.

286 1860 U.S. census for Winchester, Virginia, p. 76, NA.

287 Roper, *Repairing the March to Mars: The Civil War Diaries of John Samuel Apperson*, (Macon: Mercer University Press, 2001), p. 308.

288 *Ibid.*

289 1850 U.S. census for Winchester, Virginia, p., NA.

290 "Past Perfect Online", *youseemore.com/handley & winchesterhistory.org*, November 4, 2012.

291 1870 U.S. census for Winchester, Virginia, p. 1, NA.

292 1860 U.S. census for Winchester, Virginia, p. 8A, NA.

293 1870 U.S. census for Fauquier County, Virginia, p. 114, NA.

294 Kozlay, Janet, "Regimental Journal of Colonel Eugene A. Kozlay Commanding 54th Regiment New York Volunteers", *dmna.ny.com*, November 16, 2012.

295 Phisterer, *From New York in the War of the Rebellion*, (Albany: J. B. Lyon Co., 1912), vol. 3, p. 2188.

296 *Ibid.*

297 *Annual Report of the Adjutant General of the State of New York for the Year 1900: Registers of the 39th, 40th, 41st, 42nd and 43rd Regiments*, (Albany: James B. Lyon, 1901), p. 296.

298 1850 U.S. census for Winchester, Virginia, p. 350, NA.

299 1860 U.S. census for Winchester, Virginia, p. 123, NA.

300 "Blenker's Division", *civilwarintheeast.com*, October 20, 2012.

301 *Official Records*, p. 129.

302 1860 U.S. census for Winchester, Virginia, p. 123, NA.

303 1860 U.S. census for Winchester, Virginia, p. 99, NA.

304 1860 U.S. census for Winchester, Virginia, p. 83 NA.

305 1860 U.S. census for Loudoun County, Virginia, p. 104, NA.

306 "Abrams Delight", *winchesterhistory.org*, December 20, 2012.

307 Cartmell, T. K., *op. cit.*, p. 421.

308 1860 U.S. census for Frederick County, Virginia, p. 161, NA.

309 1850 U.S. census for Frederick County, Virginia, p. 296, NA.

310 Smith, personal communication of October 30, 2012.

311 Smith, personal communication of October 21, 2012.

312 "Liljenquist Family Collection of Civil War Photographs", Library of Congress Prints and Photographs Online, *loc.gov/pictures*, January 7, 2013.

313 *Ibid.*

314 Turner, *op. cit.*, p. 5.
315 *Ibid.*, p. 182.
316 *Ibid.*, pp. 17-165.
317 "Thornton Fleming Brodhead", *elmwoodhistoriccemetery.org*, January 11, 2013.
318 *Ibid.*
319 Wittenburg, Eric J., "The Cavalry Fight at the Lewis Ford", *civilwarwili.net*, January 11, 2013.
320 *Ibid.*
321 *Official Records*, chapter 24, p. 579.
322 Boyce, *op. cit.*, 11.
323 *Ibid.*, p. 28.
324 *Ibid.*, p. 113.
325 *Ibid.*
326 "Obituary—Edwin F. Brown", *nytimes.com*, (New York: January 11, 1903).
327 *Official Records*, *op. cit.*, p. 605.
328 Magin, *Shenandoah County Gazetteer & Historical Geography*, (Stephens City Commercial Press, 1991), p. 87.

Chapter III

1 Foote, p. 430.
2 Schreckengost, Gary. "America's Civil War: Front Royal Was The Key to the Shenandoah Valley", *historynet.com*, June 12, 2006; October 22, 2014.
3 Douglas, *I Rode with Stonewall*, (Chapel Hill: University of North Carolina Press, 1940), pp. 51-52.
4 "Henry Kyd Douglas", *civilwartrust*, May 3, 2013.
5 "Distance Between Cities", *distancebetweencities*, May 3, 2013.
6 Boyd, *Belle Boyd in Camp and Prison*, (New York: Blelock & Co., 1866), pp. 124-125.
7 *Ibid.*, p. 126 .
8 *Ibid.*, p. 127 .
9 Taylor, *Destruction and Reconstruction: Personal Experiences of the Late War*, (New York: D. Appleton & Co., 1879), p. 30.
10 Ruffner, *Maryland's Blue and Gray*, (Baton Rouge: Louisiana State University Press. 1997), p. 105.
11 *Ibid.*
12 Foote, *op. cit.*, p. 431.
13 Vandiver, *op. cit.*, p. 243.
14 Foote, p. 431.
15 *Ibid.*
16 *Official Records*, *op. cit.*, vol.12, chapter 24, part I, p. 546.
17 *Ibid.*, p. 605.
18 Basler, "Lincoln to McClellan, Washington, May 24, 1862, 4 P.M.", vol. V, *Collected Works of Abraham Lincoln*, (New Brunswick: Abraham Lincoln Assoc., 1953–55), p. 232.
19 "Distance World Map", *distancecalculator.globefeed.com*, October 25, 2014.
20 *The American Heritage Dictionary*, (Boston: Houghton Mifflin Co., 1982), p. 751.
21 *Official Records*, *op. cit.*, vol. 12, chapter 24, p. 584.
22 *Ibid.*, p. 584.
23 *Ibid.*, vol. 12, chapter 24, p. 703.
24 *Ibid.*, vol. 12, chapter 24, p. 547.
25 *Ibid.*, vol. 12, chapter 24, pp. 612-613.
26 Douglas, *op. cit.*, pp. 53-54.
27 *Official Records*, *op. cit.*, p. 547.
28 *Official Records*, *op. cit.*, p. 547.
29 Vandiver, *op. cit.*, p. 248.
30 *Ibid.*, p. 250.
31 *Official Records*, *op. cit.*, p. 613.
32 Vandiver, p. 253.
33 Berkey, J. M. "Winchester During the Civil War", *encyclopediavirginia.org*, Virginia Foundation for the Humanities, January 31, 2012. November 23, 2014.
34 *Official Records*, *op. cit.*, p. 704.
35 *Ibid.*, p. 553.
36 *Official Records*, p. 701

37 *Ibid.*, p. 708.

Chapter IV

1 "Escaped Photographer Vows Revenge own Rebels", *Herald Freedom & Torch Light*, p. 2E, (Hagerstown 27 Aug 1862).
2 1860 U.S. census for Winchester and Frederick, Virginia, p. 433, NA.
3 CSR, John Burgess, *fold3.com,* August 11, 2014.
4 *Ibid.*
5 Williams, *op. cit.*, vol. 2, part 1, p. 976.
6 1880 U.S. census for Hancock, Washington County, Md., p. 148D, NA.
7 1900 U.S. census for Hancock, Washington County, Md., p. 2B, NA.
8 1910 U.S. census for Hancock, Washington County, Md., p. 4A, NA.
9 "John West Burgess", *findagrave.com*, December 27, 2014.
10 1860 U.S. census for Hagerstown, Washington County, Md. p. 567, NA.
11 1870 U.S. census for Hagerstown, Washington County, Md., p. 115B, NA.
12 *Ibid.*, p. 115B.
13 1850 U.S. census for Hagerstown, Washington County, Md., p. 144A, NA.
14 Untitled, *Herald Freedom and Torch Light*, p. 2E, (Hagerstown: August 27, 1862).
15 Goldsborough, *The Maryland Line in the Confederate Army.* Baltimore: Guggenheimer & Co., 1900), p. 76.
16 *Ibid.*, p. 236
17 Mercer, John. "Giles Waldo Shurtleff: Leadership in the Cause of Freedom", *oberlin.edu*, January 9, 2004.
18 *Official Records*, *op. cit.*, p. 708.
19 *Ibid.*, p. 708.
20 "Distance between cities calculator", *distance-cities.com*, January 2, 2015.
21 "Richmond Daily Dispatch: June 13, 1862", *dlxs.richmond.edu,* November 28, 2014.
22 *Ibid.*

Chapter V

1 Brown, Louis A., "A Confederate Prison, (Salisbury)", *ncpedia.org*, November 28, 2014.
2 *Ibid.*
3 Speer, *Portals to Hell: Military Prisons of the Civil War*, (Lincoln: University of Nebraska Press,1997), p. 31.
4 *Ibid.*, p. 31.
5 Cherry, Kevin, "The Salisbury Confederate Prison", *Tar Heel Junior Historian.* 40:1, (fall 2000), *ncmuseumofhistory.org*, November 28, 2014.
6 *Ibid.*
7 Speer, op .cit., p. 32.
8 *Ibid.*
9 "Salisbury Prison", *learnnc.org*, December 27, 2014.
10 "Civil War Era NC: Prisoner Views", *historyncus.edu,* November 29, 2014.
11 "Salisbury Prison", *learnnc.org*, December 27, 2014.
12 "Union Soldiers at Salisbury, N.C.", *reynoldhouse.* November 28, 2014.
13 Voorhees, *The Colors of Dignity: The Memoirs of Civil War Brigadier General Giles Waldo Shurtleff,* (Bloomington: Author House, 2013), p. 72.
14 *Ibid.*
15 *Ibid.*
16 "Letter from a Union prisoner, June 28, 1862, Richmond Times Dispatch", *dlxs.richmond.edu,* November 28, 2014.
17 Voorhees, *op. cit.*, p. 73.
18 "Gen. David Gordon, Oldest Officer in the Army Dies; Former Resident of the City", *MorningHerald. interactive.ancestry*, January 31, 1930. December 17, 2013.
19 *Ibid.*
20 Cherry, *op. cit.*, November 28, 2014.
21 Brown, *op. cit.*, November 28, 2014.
22 Pickenpaugh, Roger. "Prisoner Exchange and Parole", *civilwar.vt.edu,* November 28, 2014.
23 *Ibid.*
24 Brown, Louis. "The Salisbury Prison: A Case Study of Confederate Military Prisons 1861–1865. *history. ncsu.edu,* January 14, 2015.

25 *Ibid.*
26 *Ibid.*
27 "Escaped Photographer Vows Revenge on Rebels", *Herald Freedom and Torch Light.* p. 2E, (Hagerstown: August 27, 1862).
28 "Federal Officers captured by Jackson, June 13, 1862", *Richmond Daily Dispatch. dlxs.richmond.edu,* November 28, 2014.
29 "Last of the Mohicans, August 18, 1862", *Richmond Daily Dispatch. dlxs.richmond.edu,* November 28, 2014.
30 "The Exchange of Prisoners, August 11, 1863", *The New York Times. www.nytimes.com*, December 7, 2014.
31 "Release", *Maryland Free Press*, p. 1, (Hagerstown: October 31, 1862).

Chapter VI

1 King, Letter to Lenora Hamilton, undated, Courtesy of Elizabeth Foster.
2 USR, *fold3.com,* December 2, 2014.
3 King, Letter to Lenora Hamilton, undated, Courtesy of Elizabeth Foster.
4 CSR of John Hager. *fold3*.com, December 2, 2014.
5 USR of Charles Smith. *fold3.com* . December 2, 2014.
6 CSR of James McGill, *fold3.com*, December 2, 2014.
7 CSR of Davidge McGill, *fold3.com*, December 2, 2014.
8 Keller, *op. cit.*, pp. 138-139.
9 CSR of William D. McGill. *fold3.com,* December 2, 2014.
10 CSR of Otho J. Hurley. *fold3.com,* December 2, 2014.
11 CSR of Alfred D. Merrick. *fold3.com*, December 2, 2014.
12 CSR of David Protzman. *folds.com*, December 2, 2014.
13 Keller, *op. cit.*, p. 101-102.
14 CSR of James Breathed. *fold3.com,* December 2, 2014.
15 Keller, *op. cit.*, pp. 1-283.
16 "Lincoln's call for troops, 1861, 1862", *civilwartalk.com*, August 26, 2014.
17 "Northern Draft of 1862", *etymoline.com*, January 20, 2015.
18 Wilmer, Jarrett & Vernon, *op. cit.*, p. 222.
19 *Ibid.*, p. 222.
20 *Ibid.*, p. 222.
21 USR, *fold3.com*, May 27, 2014.
22 "King Family History", *ancestry.com*, February 13, 2015.
23 "Company H", *Herald Freedom &Torch Light.* p. 2D, (Hagerstown September 3, 1862).
24 1860 U.S. census for Hagerstown, Maryland, p. 293 & p. 26, NA.
25 Moffat, William C. Jr., "Soldiers Pay in the Civil War", *cincinnaticwrt.org*, January 1965, February 13, 2015.
26 King, John, "Memoirs"; courtesy of Elizabeth Foster.
27 King, "A Brief History of the Sixth Maryland Regiment, Maryland Infantry Volunteers, Third Division, Sixth Army Corps, 1915", *Military Order of the Loyal Legion of the United States.*
28 Smith, *Richard Snowden Andrews Lieutenant-Colonel Commanding the First Maryland Artillery, Confederate States Army Memoir*, (Baltimore: Sun Job Printing Co., 1910), p. 94.
29 *Official Records*, chapter 27, part II, p. 53.
30 USR, *fold3.com*, February 15, 2015.
31 *Ibid.*
32 *Ibid.*
33 "Botts, John Minor", *bioguide.congress.gov*, February 16, 2015.
34 Samuels, Joseph T. Jr., "Auburn Plantation", *jtsamuels.com*, February 17, 2015.
35 "Battle of Mine Run",*nps.gov*, February 13, 2015.
36 *Official Records*, vol. 29, chapter 41, part I, pp. 780-783.
37 *Ibid.*, p. 779.
38 "A. T. Barclay, Jr", *ancestry.com*, February 18, 2015.
39 "Emeritus Trustees of Washington-Lee University", *wlu.edu,* February 18, 2015.
40 "Alexander Tedford Barclay", *ancestry.com*, 2015, February 15, 2015.
41 USR " *fold3.com*, March 2, 2014.
42 "Captain Adam B. Martin", *findagrave.com*, July 28, 2014.
43 Bell, *History of Leitersburg District–Washington County, Maryland*, (Bell: Leitersburg, 1898), p. 277-278.
44 "Capt Adam Benjamin Martin", *6thmarylandinfantry.org*, April 7, 2011, July 28, 2014.
45 "Married Martin–Oswald", *Herald Freedom*, p. 3B, (Hagerstown. April 1, 1012).

46 1850 and 1860 U.S. census, Washington County, Maryland, p. 279A and p. 912, NA.
47 USR, *fold3.com*, July 28, 2014.
48 *Ibid.*
49 "Company H Descriptive Book", *6thmarylandinfantry.org*, March 12, 2011, February 21, 2015.
50 *Ibid.*
51 "Captain Martin", *geocoaching.com*, August 25, 2014.
52 "Battle of the Wilderness", *wikipedia.org*, January 21, 2015; February 21, 2015.
53 *Official Records*, part I, vol. 36, chapter 48, p. 726.
54 *Official Records*, part I, vol. 43, chapter 55, pp. 248-249.
55 *Ibid.*, p. 121.
56 *Ibid.*, p. 249.
57 *Ibid.*, p. 225.
58 *Ibid.*, p. 225.
59 USR, *fold3.com*, August 4, 2014.
60 "Recruiting in This Town", *Herald Freedom & Torch Light*, p. 2D, (Hagerstown 13 Aug 1862).
61 USR, *fold3.com*, June 19, 2014.
62 *Ibid.*
63 "HR0090", *ilga.gov*, February 25, 2015.
64 *Ibid.*
65 *Ibid.*
66 "Death of Lieut. Small", *Herald & Torch Light*, p. 3B, (Hagerstown November 23, 1864).
67 *Ibid.*
68 "Confederate Lt. General A. P. Hill", *richmondregister.com*, October 1, 2013, March 1, 2015.
69 "John E. Buffington", *ancestry.com*, March 1, 2015.
70 Wilmer, Jarrett and Vernon, *op. cit.*, p. 230.
71 Graybeal, Jay. "John E. Buffington's Medal of Honor", *Carol County Times*, *hscc.carr.org*, August 10, 1997, March 1, 2015.
72 Untitled, *American Sentinel*, (Westminster, Maryland April 3, 1908).
73 *Ibid.*
74 1900 U.S. census for Baltimore Ward 21, p. 15A, NA.
75 "Report of Lt. Colonel Joseph C. Hill", *ehistory.osu.edu*, Ohio State University, February 28, 2015.
76 *Proceeding of the 30th Annual Encampment of the Department of Maryland*, (Baltimore: N. C. Killam, 1906), p. 11.
77 "Robert D. Spence", *ancestry.com*, February 28, 2015.
78 "Robert Spence", *mdarchives.state.md.us*. July 24, 2009, February 28, 2015.
79 "Number 128. Siege of Petersburg Report of Lieutenant Colonel Joseph C. Hill, Sixth Maryland Infantry, of Operations March 25. " *beyondthecrater.com*, March 4, 2015.
80 "Robert D. Spence", *ancestry.com*, March 4, 2015.
81 Pfanz, *Richard S. Ewell: A Soldier's Life*, (Chapel Hill: University of North Carolina Press, 1998), p. 442.
82 "James H. C. Brewer", *mdarchives.state.md.us*, July 24, 2009; March 5, 2015).
83 "James H. C. Brewer", *findagrave.com*, May 30, 2014.
84 Schillers, *Schillers's Complete Works*, (New York: P. F. Collier & Son, 1902), vol. 1, p. 126.
85 USR of John R. King, *fold3.com*, July 8, 2014.
86 USR of John R. King, NA.
87 Wilmer, Jarrett and Vernon, *op. cit.*, p. 223.
88 USR of Company H, *fold3.com*, April 30, 2014.
89 *Official Records*, vol. IV, 1899, p. 771.
90 USR of James A. Robinson, *fold3.com*, n.p., 2014, August 2, 2014.
91 USR of Company H, *fold3.com*, August 2, 2014.
92 Cutrer, Thomas W. "Military Executions During the Civil War", *encyclopediavirginia.org*, Virginia Foundation for the Humanities, March 11, 2015.
93 "Lincoln Grants Temporary Amnesty to Deserters", *civilwardailygazette.com*, August 5, 2014
94 *Ibid.*
95 *Ibid.*
96 "Proclamation—Recalling Soldiers to Their Regiments", *presidency.ucsb.edu*, The American Presidency Project, March 7, 2015.
97 *Ibid.*
98 USR of Company H, *fold3.com*, May 26, 2014
99 *Ibid.*

100 USR of Company H, *fold3.com*, May 26, 2014.
101 "George C. Reynolds", *findagrave.com*, February 19, 2011, May 27, 2014.
102 "Deserters, Maryland and the Border in the Civil War", *crossroadsofwar.org* May 15, 2014.
103 USR of Company H, *fold3.com*, May 26, 2014.
104 King, John R., *op. cit.*, p. 1.
105 USR of George Kough, *fold3.com*, July 4, 2013.
106 "George Kough", *ancestry.com*, May 22, 2014.
107 USR of John M. Martin, *fold3.com*, May 23, 2014.
108 "John Martin", *ancestry.com*, May 23, 2014.
109 USR of John M. Martin, *fold3.com*, May 23, 2014.
110 USR of Hezekiah Irvin, *fold3.com*, May 21, 2014.
111 *Ibid.*
112 *Ibid.*
113 *Ibid.*
114 USR of Henry Young, *fold3.com*, July 3, 2014.
115 USR of Jacob Hovis, *fold3.com*, May 20, 2014.
116 King, John R., *op. cit.*, p. 2.
117 USR of John H. Shields, *fold3.com*, May 27, 2014.
118 USR of Elias Gouker, *fold3.com*, July 4, 2014.
119 USR of George W. Grim, *fold3.com*, July 10, 2014.
120 USR of James M. Lowry, *fold3.com*, July 28, 2014.
121 USR of Daniel L. Jackson, *fold3.com*, July 2, 2014.
122 USR of Daniel B. Reynolds, *fold3.com*, August 1, 2014.
123 *Ibid.*
124 *Ibid.*
125 King, *op. cit.*
126 USR of Charles Robinson, *fold3.com*, June 30, 2014.
127 USR of Jeremiah Fishach, *fold3.com*, July 15, 2014.
128 *Ibid.*
129 USR of Thomas Ingram, *fold3.com*, July 22, 2014.
130 "About The Soldiers' Journal, (Rendezvous of Distribution, Va.), 1864–1865", Library of Congress. *chroniclingamerica.loc./lccn.* April 18, 2015.
131 *Ibid.*
132 USR of George W. Secore, *fold3.com*, June 30, 2014.
133 USR of Charles Miller, *fold3.com*, June 30, 2014.
134 *Ibid.*
135 USR of Samuel B. Sterling, *fold3.com*, June 30, 2014.
136 *Ibid.*
137 Peters, Gerhard and John T. Woolley. "Proclamation 124—Offering Pardon to Deserters", The American Presidency Project. *presidency.ucsb.edu,* August 5, 2014.
138 USR of Samuel B. Sterling, *fold3.com*, June 30, 2014.
139 USR of Michael Thomas, *fold3.com*, June 30, 2014.
140 *Ibid.*
141 *Ibid.*
142 "About The Soldiers journal. Rendezvous of Distribution", *chroniclingamerica.olc.gov*, *lccn,* Library of Congress, April 18, 2015.
143 *Ibid.*
144 USR of Michael Thomas, *fold3.com*, August 5, 2014.
145 *Ibid.*
146 USR of Harrison Bridendolph, *fold3.com*, July 6, 2014.
147 *Ibid.*
148 *Ibid.*
149 Wilmer, Jarrett and Vernon, *op. cit.*, vol. 367. p. 20.
150 "Harrison Bridendolph", *ancestry.com*, June 4, 2014.
151 *Ibid.*

Chapter VII

1 1860 U.S. census of Stephensburg, Virginia p. 160, NA

2 "Virginia Marriages, 1785–1940", *family search.org*, December 5, 2014.
3 "United States War of 1812 Index to Pension Application Files, 1812–1910", *familysearch.org*, December 6, 2014.
4 *Ibid.*
5 1850 U.S. census for District 16, Frederick County, Virginia, p. 296, NA.
6 Smith, Bryon C., Personal Interview at Newtown History Center, October 21, 2012.
7 *Ibid.*
8 "Lucinda Nisewanger Obituary", *Shenandoah Herald*, (Woodstock, Virginia: 23 March 1894.
9 1870 and 1880 U.S. census for NewTown, Opequon Township, Frederick County, Virginia. p. 4 and p. 66, NA.
10 CSR of James Lemley and Samuel M. Marks, *fold3.com,* July 11, 2016.
11 CSR of James Lemley, *fold3.com,* July 11, 2016.
12 *Ibid.*
13 "Mary A. and James Lemley", *findagrave.com*, July 11, 2016.
14 "Martha E. Redd", *findagrave.com*, July 15, 2016.
15 "Martha Ellen Nicewanger", *ancestry.com*, July 15, 2016.
16 1850 U.S. census for Stephens City, Frederick County, Virginia. p. 689, NA.
17 Smith, Bryon C. "The Nisewanger Family", Email message to the author, October 30, 2012.
18 *Ibid.*
19 1870 U.S. census for Aldie, Loudoun County, Virginia, p.199, NA.
20 1880 U.S. census for Aldie, Loudoun County, Virginia, p. 3, NA.
21 "Virginia Deaths and Burials, 1853–1912", *familysearch.org*, December 5, 2014.
22 1900 U.S. census for Mercer District, Loudoun, Virginia. p. 170A, NA.
23 "Martha E. Redd", *findagrave.com*, July 15, 2016.
24 "The Nisewanger Family", *frenchfamilyassoc.com*, July 4, 2016.
25 "Alfred J. Watson", *findagrave.com*, July 10, 2016.
26 CSR of David William Rosenberger, *fold3.com*, July 10, 2016.
27 Driver, *First Virginia Cavalry*, (Lynchburg: H. E. Howard, 1991), p. 1.
28 CSR of Davis William Rosenberger, *fold3.com*, July 10, 2016.
29 *Ibid.*
30 *Ibid.*
31 1870 U.S. census for Newtown, Opequon Township, Frederick County, Virginia, p. 4, NA.
32 Driver, *op. cit.*, p. 222.
33 "Milton Boyd Steele", *newtownhistorycenter.org*, July 10, 2016.
34 "Altha Watson", *newtownhistorycenter.org*, July 10, 2016.
35 *Ibid.*
36 Driver, *op. cit.*, p. 230.
37 CSR of Milton B. Steele, *fold3.com*, July 20, 2016.
38 *Ibid.*
39 *Ibid.*
40 "Milton Boyd Steele", *newtownhistorycenter.org*, July 24, 2016.
41 *Ibid.*
42 1880 U.S. census for Opequon District, Frederick County, Virginia, p. 291, NA.
43 "Sarah C. Nisewanger", U.S. Register of Civil, Military and Naval Service. 1863–1959., Rockingham, Virginia. *ancestry.com*, July 15, 2016.
44 "Sarah Catharine Nicewanger", *findagrave.com*, July 4, 2016.
45 "Amanda Staling", Virginia Death Records. *ancestry.com*, July 15, 2016.
46 "G. Franz Staling", Harrisonburg–Rockingham Historical Society. Woodbine Cemetery, *heritagecenter.com*, July 25, 2016.
47 "Frances Staling and Amanda Nisewanger", Virginia Marriages. *ancestry.com*, July 15, 2016.
48 1860 U.S. census for Stephensburg, Virginia. *fold3.com*, July 20, 2016.
49 *Ibid.*
50 CSR of Frances Staling, *fold3.com*, July 20, 2016.
51 *Ibid.*
52 1870 U.S. census for Harrisonburg Township, Rockingham County, Virginia, p. 31, NA.
53 1880 U.S. census for Harrisonburg, Rockingham County, Virginia, p. 2, NA.
54 1900 U.S. census for Central Rockingham, Rockingham County, Virginia, p. 29, NA.
55 *Ibid.*
56 "The Staling Family", Harrisonburg–Rockingham Historical Society. Woodbine Cemetery. *heritagecenter.com*, July 15, 2016.

57 "James Lemley", Confederate Civilian File. *fold3.com,* July 20, 2016.
58 "Mary Nisewanger", Confederate Civilian File. *fold3.com,* July 20, 2016.
59 *Ibid.*
60 *Ibid.*
61 "Lucinda Nisewanger", Confederate Civilian File. *fold3.com,* July 20, 2016.
62 CSR of John N. Cadwallader, *fold3.com*, July 20, 2016.
63 CSR of John N Cadwallader, James Lemley and Francis Staling. *fold3.com*, August 7, 2016.
64 *Ibid.*
65 1870 U.S. census for Newtown, Opequon Township, Frederick County, Virginia, p. 69, NA.
66 "John Newton Cadwallader", *findagrave.com*, July 28, 2016.
67 Chapla, *Forty-Eighth Virginia Infantry*, (Lynchburg: H. E. Howard, 1989), p. 109.
68 *Ibid.*, p. 155.
69 *Ibid.*, p. 109 and p. 155.
70 *Ibid.*, p. 109.
71 Friedman, Morgan. "Inflation Calculator", *westegg.com*, August 1, 2016.
72 Hays, "Stanza" *The Pocket Magazine of classic and polite literature*, vol. VI, p. 51, (London: John Arliss, 1820).
73 Good, Cassandra. "How Early-19th-Century Students Cemented Their Bonds Through Friendship Albums", August 1, 2016.
74 *Ibid.*
75 1860 U.S. census for Stephensburg, Frederick County, Virginia, p. 152, NA.
76 *Ibid.*, p. 197.
77 *Ibid.*, p. 157.
78 Alexander, "Southern Loyalist", *Our Country, in its Relations to the Past, Present and Future"* p. 44, Edited by Almira Lincoln Phelps, (Baltimore: John D. Toy, 1864).
79 Phelps, *Our County, in its Relations to the Past, Present and Future*, (Baltimore: John D. Troy, 1864), p. viii.
80 Wit., *Wit and Wisdom: Jokes, Conundrums, Sentiments and Aphorisms*, (London: Ward & Lock, 1860), p. 227.
81 Ristine, *Godey's Lady's Book and Magazine*, vol. 94, p. 136, p. 271, p. 271 & p. 502, (Philadelphia: Louis A. Godey, 1877).
82 "Midnight Reverie", *The Weekly Courier*, p. 4, (Fayetteville: February 25, 1860)
83 Moore, *The Poetical Works of Thomas Moore*, (London: Longman, Orme, Brown, Green and Longmans, 1841), p. 398.
84 Mayhew and Lemon, "The Husband's Revenge", *Punch*, p. 89, (London: Bradbury Evans, March 1, 1856).
85 *Punch*, *wikipedia.com*, August 17, 2016.
86 Johnson, Findley. "O Sing to me", *Reading Times*, p. 1, (Reading, Pennsylvania: August 11, 1859).
87 Francis, "Sister Mary", *Godey's Lady's Book and Magazine*, p. 1, (Philadelphia: Louis A. Godey, August 11, 1859).
88 Tennyson, Alfred Lord. "Locksley Hall", *poetryfoundation.org*, August 12, 2016.
89 Johnson, "For M" p. 96, *The Peterson Magazine*, p. 96, (Philadelphia: C. J. Peterson, August, 1859).
90 Clair, "Good Night", p. 98, *The Peterson Magazine*, p. 98, (Philadelphia: C. J. Peterson, August, 1859).
91 Ghost, "Teddy Ragan", *Henry DeMarsan's New Comic and Sentimental Singer's Journal*, p. 186, (New York: Henry DeMarsan, 1868).
92 Bates, "The Poetical Works of David Bates" (Philadelphia: Claxton, Remsen Haffelfinger, 1870), p. 18.
93 "Jacob A. Helms", *findagrave.com*, August 6, 2012.
94 "Confederate Service Record of Jacob A. Helms, *fold3.com,* August 6, 2016.
95 *Ibid.*
96 *Ibid.*
97 *Ibid.*
98 Reidenbaugh, *33rd Virginia Infantry*, (Lynchburg: H. E. Howard, 1987), p. 124.
99 *Ibid.*, p. 70.
100 "Diary of John B. Sheets", Harrisonburg–Rockingham Historical Society Newsletter, vol. 31. No. 3. *heritagecenter.com*, Fall 2009, August 21, 2016.
101 "Confederate Service Record of Jacob A. Helms, *fold3.com,* August 6, 2016.
102 *Ibid.*
103 *Ibid.*
104 *Ibid.*
105 *Ibid.*
106 *Ibid.*
107 *Ibid.*
108 "Virginia Marriages, 1785–1940", *familysearch.org*, August 6, 2016.

109 1870 U.S. census for Franklin Township, Rockingham County, Virginia, p. 62, NA.
110 1900 U.S. census for Ashby District, Rockingham County, Virginia, p. 3, NA.
111 "Jacob A. Helms", *findagrave,* August 6, 2016.
112 "Virginia Marriages, 1785–1940", *familysearch.org*, August 6, 2016.
113 1870 U.S. census for Rockingham County, Virginia, p. 20, NA.
114 "Virginia Births and Christenings, 1853–1917", *familysearch.org*, August 6, 2016.
115 1900 U.S. census for Cohocton Township, Steuben County, New York, p. 238A, NA.
116 "Lucy Pickering", *findagrave.com*, July 16, 2016.
117 "Jacob Pickering", *findagrave.com*, July 16, 2016.
118 1860 U.S. census for District 1, Rockingham County, Virginia, p. 438, NA.
119 *Ibid.*
120 Friedman, Morgan. "The Inflation Calculator", *westegg.com*, January 12, 2018.
121 Davis, *Stand in the Day of Battle: The Imperiled Union, 1861–1865*, (New York: Doubleday, 1983), pp. 260-261.
122 Withers, John by Order of Brigadier-General J. D. Imboden. "Organization of the Reserves", p. 2, *The Staunton Spectator*, (Staunton, Virginia: April 26, 1864).
123 *Ibid.*
124 Heatwole, *Chrisman's Boy Company: A History of the Civil War Service of Company A, 3rd Battalion, Virginia Mounted Reserves*, (Bridgewater: Mountain and Valley Publishing, 2000), p. 10.
125 Weaver, Jeffrey and Patti Weaver. *The Reserves*, (Lynchburg: H. E. Howard, 2002), p. 314.
126 Heatwole, *op. cit.*, p. 19.
127 "Co A, 3D Bat. Virginia Reserves", *rootsweb.com*, August 2, 2004.
128 Weaver and Weaver, *op. cit.*, p. 319.
129 Heatwole, *op. cit.*, p. 14.
130 Tucker, *Brigadier General John D. Imboden*, (Lexington: University of Kentucky Press, 2003), p. 200.
131 *Ibid.*, p. 206.
132 Weaver and Weaver, *op. cit.*, p. 315.
133 Good, *Shadowed by the Massanutten*, (Broadway, Virginia: W. A. Good, 1992), pp. 496-497.
134 Tucker, *op. cit.*, p. 227.
135 Heatwole, *op. cit.*, p. 39.
136 Tucker, *op. cit.*, p. 234.
137 Heatwole, *op. cit.*, p. 43
138 *Ibid.*, Addendum to "Chrisman's Boy Company"
139 *Ibid.*
140 *Ibid.*
141 *Ibid.*, pp. 60-61.
142 *Ibid.*, p. 67.
143 *Ibid.*, p. 72.
144 Weaver and Weaver, *op. cit.*, p. 319.
145 Heatwole, *op. cit.*, p. 75.
146 "Virginia Confederate Pension Records", Onlinecatalog. Library of Virginia, *exlibris-group.com*, September 6, 2016.
147 Heatwole, *op. cit.*, p. 78.
148 *Ibid.*
149 1870 U.S. census for McLean County Illinois, p. 23, NA.
150 "Elmer E. Hillyard" *findagrave.com*, September 9, 2016.
151 1910 U.S. census for Rockingham County, sheet 15B, NA.
152 "James Hillyard", *ancestry.com*, September 6, 2016.
153 "Bethlehem Stone Church", *researchonline.net*, September 3, 2016.
154 *Ibid.*
155 "Confederate Pension Application of James D. Hillyard", Library of Virginia Online Catalogue. *exlibrisgroup.com*, September 3, 2016.
156 *Ibid.*
157 Kenzer, Robert. "Civil War Pensions", Virginia Department of the Humanities, *encyclopediavirginia.org*, March 9, 2010.
158 *Ibid.* September 13, 2012.
159 Heatwole, *op. cit.*, p. 85.
160 "James D. Hillyard", *findagrave.com*, July 3, 2016.
161 1910 U.S. census for Rockingham County, Virginia, sheet 9A, NA.
162 1930 U.S. census for Rockingham County, Virginia, sheet 14B, NA.

163 1940 U.S. census for Rockingham County, Virginia, sheet 3A, NA.
164 "Ernest Hillyard", *findagrave.com*, September 9, 2016.
165 "Mattie Hillyard", *findagrave.com*, September 17, 2016.
166 Hillyard, Eugene, personal conversation with author on July 31, 2004.
167 Hillyard, Ernest E. and Catharine A. Zigler, marriage certificate in the possession of the author.
168 1920 U.S. census for Rockingham County, Virginia, sheet 16A, NA.
169 *Ibid.*, sheet 16B, NA.
170 "Hillyard, Hazel R.", *findagrave.com*, September 17, 2016.
171 "Hillyard, James F.", *findagrave.com*, September 17, 2016.
172 "Hillyard, Reba I. Miller", *findagrave.com*, September 17, 2016.
173 "Hillyard, Isaac", *findagrave.com*, September 17, 2016.
174 "Hillyard, Hazel R.", *findagrave.com*, September 17, 2016.

Chapter VIII

1 USR of John R. King. NA.
2 King, Letter to Lenore Hamilton, Undated; courtesy of Elizabeth Foster.
3 King, "Reminiscences of Washington County." February 10, 1921; courtesy of Elizabeth Foster.
4 Cordell, *The Medical Annals of Maryland*, (Baltimore: Williams & Wilkins Co., 1903), p. 562.
5 King, Letter to Lenore Hamilton. Undated; courtesy of Elizabeth Foster.
6 King, "Reminiscences of Washington Co", February 10, 1921; courtesy of Elizabeth Foster.
7 "Boyd's Business Directory for Maryland, Hagerstown", *whilbr.org*, November 5, 2015.
8 The Southern Claims Commission, claims filed in Washington County, Maryland, NA.
9 Williams, *op. cit.*, p. 367.
10 "Soldier's Welcome", *Herald & Torch Light*, p. 3A, (Hagerstown: 5 July 1865).
11 "Reconstructing The Region", *www.crossroadsofwar.org*, The Catoctin Center for Regional Studies. October 29, 2015.
12 CSR of Charles G. W. Macgill, Davidge MacGill, James MacGill and William D. MacGill, *fold3.com*, November 5, 2015.
13 Beath, *History of the Grand Army of the Republic*, (New York: Bryan, Taylor & Co., 1889), p. 25.
14 *Ibid.*
15 Myers, *The Self-reconstruction of Maryland*, (Baltimore: Johns Hopkins Press, 1909), p. 31.
16 *Ibid.*, p. 31.
17 *Ibid.*, pp. 31-32.
18 *Ibid.*, p. 35.
19 *Ibid.*, p. 35.
20 "Union County Convention", *Herald & Torch*, p. 3, (Hagerstown: September 27, 1865)
21 *Ibid.*
22 Beath, *op. cit.*, p. 26.
23 "Boys in Blue", *Herald & Torch Light*, p. 3C, (Hagerstown: October 18, 1865).
24 "Meeting of the Soldier's Legion", *Herald & Torch Light*, p. 3B, (Hagerstown: October 25, 1865).
25 "Primary Meeting of the Unconditional Union men of Hagerstown", *Herald & Torch Light*, p. 2, (Hagerstown: May 23, 1866).
26 *Ibid.*
27 "Loyal Union League", *Herald & Torch Light*, p. 3, (Hagerstown: May 30. 1866).
28 "Boys in Blue Meeting", *Herald & Torch Light*, p. 3C, (Hagerstown: October 3, 1866).
29 *Ibid.*
30 Kennedy, Robert C. "Andrew Johnson's Reconstruction and How It Works", *harpweek.com*, October 28, 2015.
31 "Boys in Blue Meeting", *Herald & Torch Light*, p. 3C, (Hagerstown: October 3, 1866).
32 Beath, *op. cit.*, p. 27.
33 "Meeting of the Soldier's Legion", *Herald & Torch Light*, p. 3B, (Hagerstown: October 25, 1865)
34 Beath, *op. cit.*, p. 11.
35 *Ibid.*, p. 36.
36 "The Grand Army of the Republic and Kindred Societies", *www.loc.gov*, The Library of Congress. September 13, 2011, October 6, 2015.
37 *Ibid.*
38 Beath, *op. cit.*, p. 488.
39 *Ibid.*, p. 488.
40 *Ibid.*

41 *Ibid.*, p. 30-31.
42 *Ibid.*, p. 31.
43 *Ibid.*, p. 30.
44 *Ibid.*
45 "Gen. John R. King Ill", *The Sun*, p. 14, (Baltimore: February 15, 1913).
46 "Wood's Baltimore City Directory for 1868–1869", p. 792. *archive.org*, University of Maryland. December 4, 2015.
47 *Ibid.*, p. 290.
48 "Wood's Baltimore City Directory for 1871 and 1872", p. 335, 896 and p. 335, 923. *archive.org*, University of Maryland, December 4, 2015.
49 "Wood's Baltimore City Directory for 1873 and 1874", *archive.org*, p. 327, 898 and p. 317, 890. *archive.org*, University of Maryland. December 4, 2015.
50 "Soldiers' and Sailors' Grant and Wilson Campaign Club", *Herald & Torch Light*, p. 2, (Hagerstown: February 19, 1873).
51 "Political Appointments", *Herald & Torch Light*, p. 2, (Hagerstown: September 9, 1874).
52 "Wood's Baltimore City Directories for 1875 and 1876", p. 321 and p. 347. *archive.org*, University of Maryland, December 4, 2015.
53 "Wood's Baltimore City Directory of 1885" *archive.org*, University of Maryland, December 4, 2015.
54 Untitled. *Herald & Torch Light*, p. 3, (Hagerstown: April 11, 1889).
55 "History of U.S. Customs", *customsmuseum.org*, November 21, 2015.
56 *Ibid.*
57 "Captain King Promoted", *The Sun*, p. 12, (Baltimore: October 4, 1902).
58 "Port Baltimore; Flag British", *The Sun*, p. 9, (Baltimore: February 6, 1901).
59 *Ibid.*
60 "Yacht Lady Evelyn Of Baltimore Can Fly British Flag", *The Sun*, p. 9, (Baltimore: February 12, 1901).
61 "Good Words For Oystermen", *The Sun*, p. 12, (Baltimore: October 3, 1898).
62 "Named After Chief Marine Clerk", *The Sun*, p. 10, (Baltimore: September 11, 1897).
63 Howard County, Maryland. Deeds, 11: 197. Phillip C. Baltzell to David Hays, deed, 27 September 1851; 12:420. Rosalie E. Morris to David Hays, deed, September 25, 1852; George C. Morris Attorney to David Hays, deed, May 5, 1853; John I. Snyder Trustee to David Hays, deed, October 6, 1859; Sarah A. Hamilton to David Hays, deed, December 27, 1859; Sarah A. Slemmer to David Hays, deed, May 30, 1861, *mdlandrec.net*, December 27, 2015.
64 Friedman, S. Morgan. "Inflation Calculator", *westegg.com*, January 10, 2018.
65 Annie M. Snyder and John R. King, Deed of Marriage Settlement to John J. Snyder and Mary E. Snyder. 2 June 1874, (filed May 23 1874), Howard County, Maryland. Liber 33, folios 443-447. *mdlandrec.net*, December 27, 2015.
66 King, Letter to Lenore Hamilton, Undated; courtesy of Elizabeth Foster.
67 1880 U.S. census for Howard County, Maryland, p. 54, NA.
68 "United States 1890 census of Union Veterans and Widows of the Civil War", *familysearch.org*, November 9, 2013.
69 "Port Paragraphs", *The Sun*, p. 9, (Baltimore: January 18, 1899).
70 "Marriages", *The Sun*, (Baltimore: May 19, 1899).
71 King, Personal papers, Undated; courtesy of Elizabeth Foster.
72 "United States census, 1900", *familysearch.org*, December 6, 2013.
73 Howard County, Maryland, Deeds, 57: 588-590, Eliza H. Dickey Trustee to Annie M. King Trustee, deed, September 16, 1891; *mdlandrec.net*, September 21, 2012.
74 *Ibid.*, p. 589.
75 Howard County, Maryland, Deeds, 13: 326-327, George C. Morris, attorney and others to David Hays, deed, 5 May 1853; *mdlandrec.net*, December 27, 2015.
76 *Ibid.*, p. 331.
77 *Ibid.*, p. 331.
78 Callcott, *Mistress of Riverdale: The Plantation Letters of Rosalie Stier Calvert*, (Baltimore: Johns Hopkins University Press. 1991), p. 118.
79 *Ibid.*, pp. 237-238.
80 *Ibid.*, p. 239.
81 *Ibid.*, p. 238.
82 *Ibid.*, p. 237.
83 *Ibid.*, p. 238.
84 Howard County, Maryland. Deeds: 17: 193-195. Beale Spurrier, Trustee to George Calvert, deed. 5 May

1832. *mdlandrec.net*, December 27, 2015.
85 Calcott, *op. cit., p*. 366.
86 *Ibid.*, p. 386.
87 Rasbey, Laurie. "View Tree for William Spurrier", *genealogy.com*, December 24, 2015.
88 *Ibid.*
89 Maryland Bicentennial Commission, Maryland Historical Society, highway sign at Waterloo, Maryland.
90 Rasbey, Laurie. "View Tree for William Spurrier", *genealogy.com*, December 24, 2015.
91 "Spurrier's Tavern/Waterloo", Maryland Historical Marker. *waymarking.com*, December 31, 2015.
92 Calcott, *op. cit.*, p. 252.
93 Warfield, *The Founders of Anne Arundel and Howard Counties, Maryland*, (Baltimore: Kohn & Pollock. 1905), p. 342.
94 Brooks, *Darby's Universal gazetteer, or a new geographical dictionary*, (Philadelphia: Bennett & Walton. 1827), p. 864.
95 "Grand Army of the Republic History", *suvcw.org*, December 20, 2015.
96 "The Grand Army of the Republic and Kindred Societies", *loc.gov/rr/main/gar/garintro*, Library of Congress. September 13, 2011, October 6, 2015.
97 *Ibid.*
98 Beath, *op. cit.*, p. 490.
99 *Ibid.*
100 *Ibid.*
101 King, "Personal Memoir of September 15, 1925", p. 2; courtesy of Elizabeth Foster.
102 "GAR Encampment Over. Capt. John R. King Is Department Commander", *The Baltimore Sun*, p. 7, (Baltimore: February 23, 1900).
103 "The President Invited. Promises to Attend the Antietam Monument Dedication", *The Sun*, p. 10, (Baltimore: March 30. 1900).
104 King, "Personal Memoir of September 15, 1925", p. 2; courtesy of Elizabeth Foster.
105 "The Grand Army of the Republic and Kindred Societies", Library of Congress. *loc.gov/rr/main/gar/national*, September 13, 2011, December 20, 2015.

Chapter IX

1 "William R. King", *Herald & Torch Light*, p. 3, (Hagerstown: October 9, 1872).
2 "At Home", *Herald & Torch Light*, p. 3, (Hagerstown: September 20. 1882).
3 "U.S.S. *Swatara*", *wikipedia.com*, May 19, 2014, September 26, 2015.
4 "History of Baltimore Polytechnic Institute", *www.bpi.edu,* January 25, 2013.
5 "Passed Assistant Engineer", *Herald &Torch Light*, p. 3, (Hagerstown: September 20, 1894).
6 "Lieut. King Describes Polytechnic's Growth", *The Sun*, p. 7, (Baltimore: June 20, 1921).
7 "Board Fond of King", *The Sun*, p. 12, (Baltimore: December 13, 1900).
8 "Lieut. King Describes Polytechnic's Growth", *The Sun*, p. 7, (Baltimore: June, 20, 1921).
9 "Board Fond of King", *The Sun*, p. 12, (Baltimore: December 13, 1900).
10 *Ibid.*
11 *Ibid.*
12 *Ibid.*
13 1900 U.S. census for Baltimore City, Maryland, p. 189A, NA.
14 "Lieut. King Describes Polytechnic's Growth", *The Sun*, p. 7, (Baltimore: June 20, 1921).
15 *Ibid.*
16 *Ibid.*
17 "Pardons Lieut. King", *The Sun*, p. 12, (Baltimore: September 29, 1904).
18 *Ibid.*
19 "Lieut. King Describes Polytechnic's Growth", *The Sun*, p. 7, (Baltimore: June 20, 1921).
20 1910 U.S. census for Baltimore, Maryland, p. 8A, NA.
21 *Ibid.*
22 "Comptroller Holds Up Schoolbook Bill", *Baltimore American*, p. 16, (Baltimore: March 17, 1906).
23 *Ibid.*
24 "Poly Team Weakened", *The Sun*, p. 9, (Baltimore: April 30, 1915).
25 *Ibid.*
26 "Lieut. King for School", *The Sun*, p. 14, (Baltimore: September 11, 1908).
27 *Ibid.*
28 "Poly Graduates 128", *The Sun*, p. 6, (Baltimore: June 14, 1917).

29 *Ibid.*
30 *Ibid.*
31 *Ibid.*
32 "Lieut. King For School", *The Sun*, p. 14, (Baltimore: September 11, 1908).
33 *Ibid.*
34 "Lt. W. R. King Resigns As Principal Of B.P.I", *The Sun*, p. 3 & p. 18, (Baltimore: June 18, 1921).
35 *Ibid.*
36 *Ibid.*
37 *Ibid.*
38 "Lt. W. R. King Resigns As Principal Of B.P.I", *The Sun*, p. 3 & p. 18, (Baltimore: June 18, 1921).
39 "Former 'Poly' Dean Burial on Tuesday", *The Sun*, p. 4, (Baltimore: January 14, 1923).
40 Stricklin, Barbara M., Baltimore Polytechnic Institute, Letter to the Author of January 3, 2014.

Chapter X

1 Prechtel-Kluskens, Claire. "A Reasonable Degree of Promptitude: Civil War Pension Application Processing, 1861–1865", *archives.gov*, January 12, 2016.
2 *Ibid.*
3 *Ibid.*
4 Glasson, *Federal Military Pensions in the United States*, (Oxford, England: Oxford University Press, 1918), p. 266.
5 Archuleta, Brandon Jason. "Rise of the Policy Subsystem: Re-evaluating Civil War Pension Policy", *usma.edu*, January 13, 2016.
6 Prechtel-Kluskens, *op. cit.*
7 Costa, *The Evolution of Retirement: An American Economic History*, (Chicago: University of Chicago Press, 1998), p. 198.
8 *Ibid.*
9 Prechtel-Kluskens, *op. cit.*
10 "The Pension Bureau; Abstract of the Annual Report of Honorable Joseph H. Barett", *nytimes.com*, August 31, 1864. January 17, 2016.
11 "The Pension Bureau; Report of Commissioner Barrett", *nytimes.com*, January 31, 2016.
12 Costa, *op. cit.*, p. 199.
13 *Ibid.*
14 Archuleta, *op. cit.*, p. 13.
15 "Dependent and Disability Pension Act", *en.wikepedia.org*, July 21, 2015, January 13, 2016.
16 Archuleta, *op. cit.*, p. 32.
17 Costa, *op. cit.*, p. 200.
18 *Ibid.*
19 Archuleta, *op. cit.*, p. 33.
20 Costa, *op. cit.*, p. 201.
21 Prechtel-Kluskens, *op. cit.*
22 *Ibid.*
23 *Ibid.*
24 "Captain King Promoted", *The Sun*, p. 12, (Baltimore: October 4, 1902).
25 *Ibid.*
26 "Louis Emory McComas", Biographical Directory of the U.S. Congress, 1774–present. *bioguide.congress.gov*, January 29, 2016.
27 "Captain King Promoted", *The Sun*, p. 12, (Baltimore: October 4, 1902).
28 "Spedden Shipbuilding, Baltimore Maryland", *shipbuildinghistory.com*, January 29, 2016.
29 "Captain King Promoted", *The Sun*, p. 12, (Baltimore: October 4, 1902).
30 "Captain John R. King", *The Sun*, p. 14, (Baltimore: October 5, 1902).
31 "Theodore Roosevelt: The President Seeks Endorsement for Former Civil War Officer as a Pension Agent", Gallery of History Direct. *www.historyforsale.com*, January 20, 2016.
32 "Captain King Promoted", *The Sun*, p. 12, (Baltimore: October 4, 1902).
33 Friedman, Morgan. "The Inflation Calculator", *westegg.com*, January 13, 2018.
34 Howard County, Maryland. Deed. Annie M. King to Estelle B. Storm and Rosalie A. Storm. October 2, 1902. Liber JHO 76, folio 8-10. *mdlandrec.net*, January 20, 2016.
35 "Captain King Elected", *The Sun*, p. 7, (Baltimore: May 30, 1906).
36 Baltimore City Deeds. Henry Duffy to John R. and Annie M. King. November 28, 1908. Liber 2466. folio

60. *mdlandrec.net*, January 20, 2016.
37 "To Reappoint General King", *The Baltimore Sun*, p. 14, (Baltimore: October 6, 1906).
38 "Baltimore as a pension depository", *The Sun*, p. 4, (Baltimore: December 3, 1907).
39 *Ibid.*
40 *Ibid*
41 *Ibid.*
42 "More Pensions for Widows", *The Sun*, p. 2, (Baltimore: April 18, 1908).
43 Friedman, Morgan. "The Inflation Calculator", *westegg.com*, January 13, 2018.
44 "Gen. John R. King Confirmed", *Baltimore American*, p. 9, (Baltimore: February 1,1911).
45 Death Certificate for Mary Elizabeth Adams, Accession No. MSA SC 5458-103-8071, Maryland State Archives. Certified copy in possession of author.
46 "Questions and Answers About TB", *cdc.gov*, Center for Disease Control. December 21, 2012 February 4, 2016.
47 "Alvin Phillips Adams", *findagrave.com*, December 11, 2015.
48 "Alvin Phillips Adams. World War I Draft Registration Card", *familysearch.org*, February 3, 2016.
49 Death Certificate for Anna L. King. Accession No. MSA SC 5458-103-10921. Maryland State Archives. Certified copy in possession of author.
50 "Ex-Prisoners Of War To Meet", *Boston Globe*, p. 4, (Baltimore: August 6, 1904).
51 *Ibid.*
52 "Blackmar Elected. Boston Man New Commander. John R. King Next in Line", *Baltimore Sun*, p. 2, (Baltimore: August 19, 1904).
53 *Ibid.*
54 "Grand Army Turns Down Blue and Gray Reunion", *The Atlanta Constitution*, p. 1, (Atlanta: August 19, 1904).
55 "New Jersey Grand Army. John R. King to Speak at the Camp Fire Tonight", *Baltimore American*, p. 2, (Baltimore: June 22, 1905).
56 *Ibid.*
57 *Journal of the Proceedings of the 39th Encampment of the Grand Army of the Republic, Denver, Colorado, September 7 and 8, 1905*, (Boston: Griffith-Stillings. 1905), pp. 76-79.
58 *Ibid.*, p. 56 and p. 101.
59 "The Grand Army of the Republic and Kindred Societies", Library of Congress. *loc.gov*, September 13, 2011. December 20, 2015.
60 "General Blackmar Dies", *chicagotribute.com*, 17 July 1905, February 6, 2016.
61 "General W. W. Blackmar Dead", *nytimes.com*, 17 July 1905, February 6, 2016.
62 *Ibid.*
63 "Capt. J. R. King Head of G.A.R", *Baltimore American*, p. 14, (Baltimore: July 18, 1905).
64 "Gen. W. W. Blackmar Dies", *chicagotribune.com*, p. 4, (Chicago: July 17, 1905); February 6, 2016.
65 "Capt. J. R. King Head of G.A.R", *Baltimore American*, p. 14, (Baltimore: July 18, 1905).
66 "Capt. John R. King Issues First Order", *Baltimore American*, p. 3, (Baltimore: July 20, 1905).
67 "Gen. John R. King In Boston", *The Sun*, p. 5, (Baltimore: July 23 1905).
68 "General King To The G.A.R", *Baltimore American*, p. 13, (Baltimore: September 8, 1905).
69 "Journal of the Proceedings of the 39th Encampment of the Grand Army of the Republic; Denver, Colorado, September 7 and 8, 1905", *op. cit.*, p. 56.
70 *Ibid.*, p. 57.
71 *Ibid.*, p. 57.
72 *Ibid.*, p. 57.
73 *Ibid.*, p. 58.
74 *Ibid.*, p. 58.
75 *Ibid.*, p. 60.
76 *Ibid.*, p. 67.
77 "General King To The G.A.R", *Baltimore American*, p. 13, (Baltimore September 8, 1905).
78 "Journal of the 39th National Encampment of the Grand Army of the Republic. Denver, Colorado, September 7 and 8, 1905", *op. cit.*, p. 60.
79 *Ibid.*, p. 260.
80 *Ibid.*, p. 260.
81 *Ibid.*, p. 72.
82 "Dead Not Forgotten", *Baltimore Sun*, p. 9, (Baltimore: May 28, 1906).
83 Beath, *op. cit.*, p. iii.
84 "Capt. John R. King Elected. Union Memorial Commission To Select Site and Design", *The Sun*, p. 7, (Baltimore: May 30, 1906).

85 "Maryland Manual. Union Soldiers and Sailors Monument Commission", Archives of Maryland Online. *aomol.net*, November 23, 2011.
86 "Capt. John R. King Elected. Union Memorial Commission To Select Site and Design", *The Sun*, p. 7, (Baltimore: May 30, 1906).
87 "To Union Men Only. Monument Not To Be In Memory Of All Maryland's Fighters", Anonymous Letter to the Editor. *Sun*, p. 14, (Baltimore: March 26, 1906).
88 Matthews, H. H. "Union and Confederate Monuments", Letter to the Editor. *Sun*, p. 7, (Baltimore: April 16, 1906).
89 King, John R. "Marylanders in the Civil War", Letter to the Editor. *Sun*, p. 7, (Baltimore: April 26, 1906).
90 Broadwater, Luke. "Baltimore City commission recommends removal of two Confederate monuments", *Baltimoresun.com*, January 14, 2016. February 21, 2016.
91 "Maryland Manual. Chickamauga-Chattanooga Battlefield Commission", Maryland Archives Online. *aomol.net*, November 23, 2011.
92 "The Laws of Maryland", p. 68. *google.com*, November 23, 2011.
93 "Battle Flag Commission", Maryland Manual, 1904. vol. 116, p. 193. Archives of Maryland Online. *aomol.net*, November 23, 2011.
94 Riggs, *Report of the Adjutant General of Maryland, 1906–1907*, vol. 1908. (Baltimore: Geo. W. King, 1908), preface.
95 "500 Maryland Veterans Going to Gettysburg", *Frederick Post*, p. 7, (Frederick, Maryland: June 11, 1913).
96 "A Presbyterian, Republican and Civil War Veteran Denounces Bill To End State Subsidies", *The Sun*, p. 6, (Baltimore: March 4, 1918).
97 *Ibid.*
98 Beath, *op. cit.*, p. 18.
99 *Ibid.*, p. 20.
100 "Loyal Legion Holds Banquet. Captain King Tells of Retreat of Union Soldiers", *The Sun*, p. 7, (Baltimore: January 3, 1908).
101 *Ibid.*
102 "Loyal Legion Urges Defense", *The Sun*, p. 5, (Baltimore: January 8, 1915).
103 *Ibid.*
104 "Loyal Legion Elects. Annual Meeting Held at Belvedere Hotel", *Baltimore American*, p. 16, (Baltimore: May 7, 1920).
105 *Ibid.*
106 King, Memoirs of September 15, 1925; courtesy of Elizabeth Foster.
107 1910 U.S. census for Baltimore, Maryland, p. 8A, NA.
108 USR of Harrison E. King. *fold3.com*, July 26, 2014.
109 *Ibid.*
110 Merriam-Webster Dictionary, *merriam-webster.com*, March 2, 2016.
111 Washington County, Maryland, Deeds, James I. Hurley and Sophia A. Hurley to Harrison E. King. November 15, 1880. Liber 80. folio 100. *mdlandrec.net*, January 20, 2016.
112 1880 U.S. census for Pittsburgh, Pennsylvania, p. 52, NA.
113 Washington County, Maryland. Deeds. James I Hurley and Sophia A. Hurley to Harrison E. King. November 15, 1880. Liber 80. folio 100. *mdlandrec.net*, January 20, 2016.
114 Washington County, Maryland. Deeds. Harrison E. King to Samuel M. Bloom. July 18, 1884. Liber GBO 86. folio 152. *mdlandrec.net*, January 20, 2016.
115 1900 U.S. census for Cleveland City, Cuyahoga County, Ohio, p. 189A, NA.
116 1910 U.S. census for Osceola County, Florida, p. 4B, NA.
117 "United States Veterans Administration Pension Payment Cards, 1907–1933", *familysearch.org*, November 9, 2013.
118 "Obituary Notice. Harrison Eader King", *The Sun*, p. 13 (Baltimore: October 5, 1919).
119 "Married. McLaughlin-King", *Herald Freedom & Torch Light*, p. 2F, (Hagerstown: October 23, 1861).
120 "Horses Stolen", *Herald & Torch Light*, p. 3A, (Hagerstown: August 31, 1864)
121 1870 U.S. census for Hagerstown, Maryland, p. 102, NA.
122 1880 U.S. census for Hagerstown, Maryland, p. 3, NA.
123 Washington County, Maryland Deeds. Julia C. McComas to Samuel Z. and Mary A. McLaughlin, May 27, 1891. Liber 97, folio 222. *mdlandrec.net*, January 20, 2016.
124 1900 U.S. census for Hagerstown, Maryland, p. 139A, NA.
125 "Maryland Marriages, 1866–1970", index, *familysearch.org*, November 1, 2013.
126 "Maryland Births and Christenings, 1650–1995", *familysearch.org*, November 2, 2013.
127 1870 U.S. census for Hagerstown, Maryland, p. 78, NA.

128 "Maryland Births and Christenings, 1650–1995", *familysearch.org*, November 2, 2013.
129 "Body's Business Directory of Maryland of 1875, Hagerstown", *whilbr.org*, March 8, 2016.
130 Washington County, Maryland. Deeds, John L. Sadler to Samuel L. King. December 14, 1872. Liber WMcKK5. folio 324. *mdlandrec.net*, January 20, 2016.
131 1880 U.S. census for Hagerstown, Maryland, p. 18, NA.
132 "Committee of Arrangements, Potomac Lodge No 31, Odd Fellows", *Herald & Torch Light*, p. 2, (Hagerstown: April 14, 1869).
133 "Grand Lodge of Maryland, Independent Order of Good Templars", *Herald & Torch Light*, p. 2, (Hagerstown: November 22, 1871).
134 "Grand Lodge of Good Templars", *The Sun*, p. 1, (Baltimore: November 25, 1872).
135 "Samuel L. King Presided", *Herald & Torch Light*, p. 2, (Hagerstown: April 8, 1874).
136 "Samuel L. King On Standing Committee", *Herald & Torch Light*, p. 2, (Hagerstown: March 12, 1873).
137 "Temperance Alliance", *Herald & Torch Light*, p. 2, (Hagerstown: May 19, 1875).
138 "Samuel King the Oldest Member of St. Paul's Methodist Church", *Herald & Torch Light*, p. 5, (Hagerstown: November 16, 1893).
139 1940 U.S. census for Hagerstown, Maryland, p. 116, NA.
140 "Samuel Liles King, Jr", *The Morning Herald*, p. 20, (Hagerstown: July 22, 1948).
141 "Maryland Marriages, 1666–1970", *familysearch.org*, January 10, 2016.
142 "Carrie E. Show King", *The Morning Herald*, p. 15, (Hagerstown: 29 December 1945).
143 1900 U.S. census for Trenton Ward 2, Mercer, New Jersey, p. 4A, NA.
144 1920 U.S. census for Pittsburgh Ward 11, Allegheny County, Pennsylvania, p. 18B, NA.
145 1930 U.S. census for Pittsburgh, Allegheny County, Pennsylvania, p. 5A, NA.
146 1930 U.S. census for Pittsburgh, Allegheny County, Pennsylvania, p. 5A, NA.
147 "Samuel Liles King, Jr", *The Morning Herald*, p. 20, (Hagerstown; 22 July 1948).
148 Polk, *Baltimore City Directory for the year commencing April 1, 1914*, (Baltimore: R. L. Polk, 1914), p. 2665.
149 Bruce, *The Warehouse Manual and General Custom House Guide*, (New York: Hamilton, 1862), pp. 61-62.
150 "City Office for John R. King", *Baltimore American*, p. 16, (Baltimore: February 20, 1920).
151 *Ibid.*
152 Baltimore City, Maryland. Deeds, John R. and Annie M. King to William H. Marcus, December 10, 1915; Liber 3017. folio 241. *mdlandrec.net*, January 20, 2016.
153 "Deaths", *Baltimore Post*, p. 10, (Baltimore: May 5, 1917).
154 Death Certificate for Annie Maria King, May 4, 1917, File No. D4992, Baltimore City Department of Health, Bureau of Vital Statistics. Certified copy in possession of author.
155 "Has New Pennsylvania Plan. W. W. Emmart Would Connect Existing Railroad Stations", General King Scores Road", *Baltimore Sun*, p. 4, (Baltimore: May 8, 1917).
156 *Ibid.*
157 "Line Up Against the Smoke", *Baltimore Sun*, p. 6, (Baltimore: August 4, 1921).
158 *Ibid.*
159 "The Municipal Band, Dancing On the Streets and Community Singing Highly Praised", *Baltimore Sun*, p. 6, (Baltimore: July 30, 1915).
160 *Ibid.*
161 "Things He Prizes", *Baltimore Sun*, p. 6, (Baltimore: March 15, 1930).
162 King, "Reminiscences of Washington County", February 10, 1921; courtesy of Elizabeth Foster.
163 *Ibid.*
164 *Ibid.*
165 "Old Fashioned Fourths", *Baltimore Sun*, p. 8, (Baltimore: July 5, 1925).
166 "General King At Greenmount", *Baltimore Sun*, p. 7, (Baltimore: May 31, 1906).
167 *Ibid.*
168 *Ibid.*
169 "A Tribute From General King", *Baltimore Sun*, p. 10, (Baltimore: September 28, 1928).
170 *Ibid.*
171 "Grand Army of the Republic Debate Over Monument", *Baltimore American*, p. 3, (Baltimore: August 18, 1906).
172 "Silver Given Gen. King", *Baltimore Sun*. p. 11, (Baltimore: August 18, 1906).
173 "GAR Blocks Joint Civil War Reunion", *Washington Post*. September 13, 1929. *genealogybank.com*, November 2, 2013.
174 *Ibid.*
175 "GAR Group Quits Parade Because Confederate Flag Is Carried", *New York Times*, p. 4, (New York: June 15, 1931).

176 *Ibid.*
177 "Confederate Flag Breaks Up Parade", *Washington Post*, p. 2, (Washington, D. C.: June 15, 1931).
178 "Colonel John R. King, Past Commander-in-Chief of the Maryland Grand Army of the Republic Denounces The Proposed 'Wet Parade' on Memorial Day As A Desecration of An Anniversary To The Nation", *Baltimore Sun*, p. 6, (Baltimore: April 15, 1919).
179 "Mayor Against Wet Parade", *Baltimore Sun*, p. 20, (Baltimore: April 16, 1919).
180 "Wet Parade Postponed", *Baltimore Sun*, p. 16, (Baltimore: April 17, 1919).
181 "General John R. King Expresses The Hope That Memorial Day May Not Be Selected As The Date For The Reception To Our Boys From France", *Baltimore Sun*, p. 10, (Baltimore: May 25, 1919).
182 "City Arms Extended To Returning Heroes, 29th Division Parade Starts Today", *Baltimore Sun*, p. 18, (Baltimore: May 31, 1919).
183 "Veterans Honor Dead", *Baltimore Sun*, p. 4, (Baltimore: May 31, 1919).
184 "Challenges Mr. Klecka's Percentage", *Baltimore Sun*, p. 6, (Baltimore: September 8, 1919).
185 "Captain King's Fine War Record", *Baltimore Sun*, p. 10, (Baltimore: April 18, 1918).
186 "Colonel King Replies To A 'Senile' Critic", *Baltimore Sun*, p. 6, (Baltimore: April 22, 1918).
187 "John A. King Is Awarded Purple Heart", *Baltimore Sun*, p. 24, (Baltimore: September 15, 1932).
188 *Ibid.*
189 1920 and 1930 U.S. census for Baltimore City, Maryland, p. 4A and p. 22A, NA.
190 "Obituary, John R. King", *Baltimore Sun*, p. 11, (Baltimore: March 5, 1934).
191 Death Certificate for John Rigdon King, March 4, File No. 989976, Baltimore City Department of Health, Bureau of Vital Statistics. Certified copy in possession of author.
192 "John R. King Dead; Ex-Head of G.A.R.", *New York Times*, p. 31, (New York: March 4, 1934).
193 King, John Rigdon. "John Rigdon King's Last Will and Testament", March 15, 1934, *familysearch.org*, October 26, 2015.
194 King, John R. Speech Read Before the Commandery of the State of Maryland Military Order of the Loyal Legion January 7, 1915; courtesy of Harper's Ferry National Park Service.

Bibliography

Books

Alexander, J. H., "Southern Loyalist" in *Our Country, in its Relations to the Past, Present and Future,* p. 44, edited by Almira Lincoln Phelps (Baltimore: John D. Troy, 1864)

Andreas, A., *The History of Chicago: From 1857 until the fire of 1871* (Chicago: Andreas, 1888)

Armstrong, Richard L., *7th Virginia Cavalry* (Lynchburg: Howard Publishing Co., 1992)

Basler, P. Basler, ed., "Lincoln to McClellan, May 24, 1862, 4 P.M.," *Collected Works of Abraham,* vol. V (New Brunswick: Abraham Lincoln Association, 1953-55)

Bates, Samuel, *History of the Pennsylvania Volunteers* (Harrisburg: B. Singerly, 1869-1871)

Bates, Stockton, ed., "The Poetical Works of David Bates," (Philadelphia: Claxton, Remsen & Haffelfinger, 1870)

Beath, Robert B., *History of the Grand Army of the Republic* (New York: Bryan, Taylor & Co., 1889)

Bell, Herbert Charles, *History of Leitersburg District-Washington County, Maryland* (Bell: Leitersburg, 1898)

Boyce, C. W., *Brief History of the 28th Regiment New York Volunteers, First Brigade, First Division, Twelfth Corps, Army of the Potomac* (Buffalo: Mathews Northup Co., 1896)

Boyd, Belle, *Belle Boyd in Camp and Prison* (New York: Blelock & Co., 1866)

Boyd, William H., *Boyd's Business Directory of Maryland, 1875* (Washington D. C.: William H. Boyd, 1875)

Brooks, Richard, *Darby's Universal Gazateer, or a new geographical dictionary* (Philadelphia: Bennett & Walton,1827)

Bruce, Hamilton, *The Warehouse Manual and General Custom House Guide* (New York: Hamilton, 1862)

Callcott, Margaret Law, ed., *Mistress of Riverdale: The Plantation Letters of Rosalie Stier Calvert* (Baltimore: Johns Hopkins University Press, 1991)

Camper, Charles and J. W. Kirkley, *Historical Record of the First Maryland Infantry* (Washington, D. C.: Gibson Brothers, 1871)

Chapla, John D., *Forty-Eighth Virginia Infantry* (Lynchburg: H. E. Howard, 1989)

Clark, C., *The History of the 39th Regiment Illinois Volunteer Veteran Infantry in the War of the Rebellion* (Chicago. Veterans Assoc., 1889)

Clark, William, *History of Hampton Battery F, Independent Pennsylvania Light Artillery* (Pittsburgh: Werner Co., 1909)

Comstock, H. E., *The Pottery of the Shenandoah Valley Region* (Chapel Hill: University of North Carolina, 1994)

Cordell, Eugene Fauntleroy, *The Medical Annals of Maryland* (Baltimore: Williams & Wilkins, 1903)

Costa, Dora L., *The Evolution of Retirement" An American Economic History, 1880-1990* (Chicago: University of Chicago Press, 1998)

Current, R., *Lincoln's Loyalists: Union Soldiers in the Confederacy* (Lawrenceville: Princeton University, 1992)

Davis, Charles E. Jr., *Three Years in the Army, the Story of the Thirteenth Massachusetts Volunteers from July 16, 1861 to August 1, 1864* (Boston: Estes & Lauriat, 1894)

Davis, William C., *Stand in the Day of Battle: The Imperiled Union, 1861-1865* (New York: Doubleday, 1983)

Douglas, Henry Kyd, *I Rode with Stonewall* (Chapel Hill: University of North Carolina Press, 1940)

Driver, Robert J., *First Virginia Cavalry* (Lynchburg: H. E. Howard, 1991)
Dyer, Frederick H., *A Compendium of the War of the Rebellion* (Des Moines: Dyer Publishing Co., 1908)
Foote, Shelby, *The Civil War: A Narrative* (New York: Vintage Books, 1974)
Garrison, Webb and Cheryl Garrison, *The Encyclopedia of Civil War Usage* (New York: Castle Books, 2009)
Glasson, William Henry, *Federal Military Pensions in the United States* (Oxford: Oxford University Press, 1918)
Goldsborough, W. W., *The Maryland Line in the Confederate Army* (Baltimore: Guggenheimer & Co., 1900)
Good, William Algeron, *Shadowed by the Massanutten* (Broadway, Virginia: W. A. Good, 1992)
Gopsill, J., *Gopsill's Harrisburg Directory* (Jersey City: John H. Lyon, 1863)
Gott, Kendall D., *Where the South Lost the War: An Analysis of the Fort Henry-Fort Donelson Campaign, February, 1862* (Mechanicsburg: Stackpole Books, 2003)
Hall, Henry and James Hall, *Cayuga in the Field. A Record of the 19th New York Volunteers* (Auburn: Truair Smith, 1873)
Heatwole, John L., *Chrisman's Boy Company: A History of the Civil War Service of Company A, 3rd Battalion, Virginia Mounted Reserves* (Bridgewater: Mountain & Valley Pub., 2000)
Henderson, G F. R., *Stonewall Jackson and the American Civil War* (New York: Konecky & Konecky, 1898)
Journal of the Proceedings of the 39th Encampment of the Grand Army of the Republic, Denver, Colorado, September 7 and 8, 1905 (Boston: Griffith-Stillings, 1905)
Kelbaugh, Ross J., *Introduction to Civil War Photography* (Gettysburg: Thomas Publications, 1991)
Keller, R., *Roster of Civil War Soldiers from Washington County* (Baltimore: Clearfield, 2008)
Kercheval, Samuel, *A History of the Valley of Virginia* (Woodstock: John Gatewood, 1850) King, John R., "A Brief History of the Sixth Maryland Regiment, Maryland Infantry Volunteers, Third Division, Sixth Army Corps, 1915." *Military Order of the Loyal Legion of the United States.*
Lamon, W., *Recollections of Abraham Lincoln, 1847-1865* (Lincoln: University of Nebraska, 1994)
Magin, Irvin D., *Shenandoah County Gazateer & Historical Geography* (Stephens City: Commercial Press, 1991)
Marvin, Edwin E., *The 5th Regiment Connecticut Volunteers: A History Compiled from Diaries & Official Reports* (Hartford: Wiley, Waterman & Eaton, 1889)
Matchett, R., *Matchett's Baltimore Directory* (Baltimore: Matchett, 1849)
Matchett, R., *Matchett's Baltimore Directory* (Baltimore: Matchett, 1851)
Mayhue, Justin T., *Firefighting in Hagerstown* (Charleston: Arcadia Publishing Co., 2004)
McDonald, William N., *A History of the Laurel Brigade* (Baltimore: Sun Job Printing, 1907)
McElroy, A., *Philadelphia Directory for 1867* (Philadelphia: C. Sherman & Co., 1867)
Moore, Thomas, *The Poetical Works of Thomas Moore* (London: Longman, Orme, Brown, Green and Longmans, 1841)
Myers, William Starr, *The Self-reconstruction of Maryland* (Baltimore: Johns Hopkins Press, 1909)
Newcomer. C., *Cole's Cavalry or Three Years in the Saddle* (Baltimore: Cushing & Co., 1895)
New York, *Annual Report of the Adjutant General of the State of New York for the year 1900: Registers of the 39th, 40th, 41st, 42nd and 43rd Regiments* (Albany: James B. Lyon, 1901)
Pfanz, Donald, *Richard S. Ewell: A Soldier's Life* (Chapel Hill: University of North Carolina, 1998)
Phelps, Almira Lincoln, ed., *Our County, in its Relations to the Past,Present and Future* (Baltimore: John D. Toy, 1864)
Phisterer, Frederick, *From New York in the War of the Rebellion* (Albany: J. B. Lyon Co., 1912)
Plummer, Kenneth M., *A History of West Virginia Wesleyan College* (Nashville: Parthenon Press, 1965)
Polk, R. L., *Baltimore City Directory for the year commencing April 1, 1914* (Baltimore: R. L. Polk, 1914)
Proceeding of the 30th Encampment of the Department of Maryland (Baltimore: N. C. Killam, 1906)
Reidenbaugh, Lowell, *33rd Virginia Infantry* (Lynchburg: H. E. Howard, 1987)
Riggs, Clinton L., *Report of the Adjutant General of Maryland, 1906-1907,* vol. 1908 (Baltimore: Geo. W. King, 1908)
Roper, John Herbert, *Repairing the March to Mars: The Civil War Diaries of John Samuel Apperson* (Macon: Mercer University Press, 2001)
Ruffner, Kevin Conley, *Maryland's Blue and Gray* (Baton Rouge: Louisiana State University Press, 1997)
Scharf, John Thomas, *The History of Western Maryland* (Philadelphia: Louis H. Everts, 1882)
Schiller, Friedrich, *Schillers's Complete Works* (New York: P. F. Collier & Son, 1902)
Seilhamer, George Oberkirch, *Biographical Annals of Franklin County, Pennsylvania* (Chicago: Genealogical Publishing Co., 1905)
Shepherd, H., *History of Baltimore, Maryland from its Founding As a Town to the Current* (Baltimore: S. B. Nelson, 1898)
Smith, Tunsall, ed., *Richard Snowden Andrews Lieutenant-Colonel: Commanding the First Maryland Artillery, Confederate States Army Memoir* (Baltimore: Sun Job Printing Co., 1910)
Speer, Lonnie R., *Portals to Hell: Military Prisons of the Civil War* (Lincoln: University of Nebraska Press, 1997)

Stewart, J. Alger, *Descendants of Valentine Hollingsworth* (Louisville: K. P. Morton, 1924)
Taylor, Richard, *Destruction and Reconstruction: Personal Experiences of the Late War* (New York: D. Appleton & Co., 1879)
The American Heritage Dictionary (Boston: Houghton Mifflin Co., 1982)
Tucker, Spencer C., *Brigadier General John D. Imboden* (Lexington: University of Kentucky Press, 2003)
Turner, George H., *Record of Service of the Michigan Volunteers in the Civil War* (Kalamazoo: Ihling Bros. & Everard, 1905)
United States Navy Department, *Official records of the Union and Confederate Navies in the War of the Rebellion* (Washington: Government Printing Office, 1894-1922)
United States War Department, *War of the Rebellion: A compilation of the official records of the Union and Confederate armies,* (Washington: Government Printing Office, 1886-1901)
Vandiver, Frank E., *Mighty Stonewall* (New York: McGraw Hill, 1957)
Voorhees, Catharine Durant, *The Memoirs of Civil War Brigadier General Giles Waldo Shurtleff* (Bloomington: Author House, 2013)
Warfield, Joshua Dorsey, *The Founders of Anne Arundel and Howard Counties, Maryland* (Baltimore: Kohn & Pollock, 1905)
Warner, Ezra J. Jr., *Generals in Blue: Lives of the Union Commanders* (Baton Rouge: Louisiana State Press, 1964)
Weaver, Jeffrey and Patti Weaver, *The Reserves* (Lynchburg: H. E. Howard, 2002)
West Virginia, *Annual Report of the Adjutant General of the State of West Virginia for the year ending December 31, 1865* (Wheeling: John Frew, 1866)
Williams, Thomas J. C., *The History of Washington County, Maryland* (Chambersburg: Runk & Titsworth, 1906)
Wilmer, L., J. H. Jarnett and George W. R. Vernon, *History and Roster of Maryland Volunteer War of 1861-5* (Baltimore: Guggenheim, Weil & Co., 1898)
Wit., *Wit and Wisdom: Jokes, Conundrums, Sentiments and Aphorisms* (London: Ward & Lock, 1860)
Woods, John W., *Wood's Baltimore Directory* (Baltimore: Woods, 1860)
Woods, John W., *Wood's Baltimore Directory* (Baltimore: Woods, 1864)
Woods, John W., *Wood's Baltimore Directory* (Baltimore: Woods, 1865)
Woods, John W., *Wood's Baltimore Directory* (Baltimore: Woods, 1886)

Magazines

Clair, Eleanor, "Good Night," *The Peterson Magazine* (Philadelphia: C. J. Peterson, August, 1859)
Francis, Harritt E., "Sister Mary," *Godey's Lady's Book and Magazine,* p. 1 (Philadelphia:Louis A. Godey, August 11, 1859)
Ghost, White, "Teddy Ragan," *Henry DeMarsan's New Comic and Sentimental Singer's Journal* (New York: Henry DeMarsan, 1868)
Green, Fletcher M., "A People at War: Hagerstown, Maryland, June 15-August 31, 1863," *Maryland Historical Magazine*, vol. 40, issue 4, p. 257 (Baltimore: Maryland Historical Society, 1945)
Hays, E. H., "Stanza," *The Pocket Magazine of classic and polite literature,* vol. VI, p. 51 (London: John Arliss, 1820)
Johnson, Findley, "For M," *Peterson Magazine,* p. 96, (Philadelphia: C. J. Peterson, August, 1859)
Mayhew, Henry and Mark Lemon, eds., "Husband's Revenge," *Punch,* p. 89 (London: Bradbury & Evans, March 1, 1856)
Ristine, James, *Godey's Lady's Book and Magazine,* vol. 94, p. 136, p. 271, p. 502 (Philadelphia: Louis A. Godey, 1877)

Newspapers

American Sentinel, Westminster, Maryland
Baltimore American, Baltimore, Maryland
Baltimore Post, Baltimore, Maryland
Frederick Post, Frederick, Maryland
Hagerstown Mail, Hagerstown, Maryland
Harold Freedom, Hagerstown, Maryland
Herald of Freedom & Torch Light, Hagerstown, Maryland
Herald & Torch, Hagerstown, Maryland
Herald & Torch Light, Hagerstown, Maryland
Maryland Free Press, Hagerstown, Maryland
Morning Herald, Hagerstown, Maryland

New York Times, New York City, New York
Reading Times, Reading, Pennsylvania
Shenandoah Herald, Woodstock, Virginia
The Atlanta Constitution
The Boston Globe, Boston, Massachusetts
The Daily Mail, Hagerstown, Maryland
The Daily News, Frederick, Maryland
The Baltimore Sun, Baltimore, Maryland
The Staunton Spectator, Staunton, Virginia
The Weekly Courier, Fayetteville, North Carolina
Torch Light, Hagerstown, Maryland
Washington Post, District of Columbia
Weekly Chronicle, Hagerstown, Maryland

Public Documents

Frederick County, Virginia Deeds.
Maryland Bicentennial Commission
Maryland State Archives, Hall of Records, Annapolis
National Archives, Washington, D. C.

Family and Personal Papers

Hillyard, Eugene, personal communication of July 31, 2004
Hillyard, Eugene and Catharine A. Zigler, marriage certificate
King, John R., "A Brief History of the Sixth Maryland Regiment, Maryland Infantry Volunteers, Third Division, Sixth Army Corps, 1915." *Military Order of the Loyal Legion of the United States*, Courtesy of the Harper's Ferry Rare Book Collection, National Park Service.
King, John R., Personal Memoirs of September 15, 1925.
King, John R., Letter to Lenore Hamilton circa 1930.
King, John R., Personal Papers, undated.
King, John R., "Reminiscences of Washington County, Maryland."
Smith, Bryon C., personal communication of October 21, 2012.
Smith, Bryon C., personal communication of October 30, 2012.
Strickland, Barbara M., letter to the author of January 3, 2014.

Internet Sources

www.ancestry.com (September 6, 2016)
www.antietam.com (January 28, 2014)
www.antiquemedicines.com (April 7, 2014)
www.aomol.msa.maryland.gov (February 28, 2014)
www.aomol.net (November 23, 2011)
www.archives.gov (January 12, 2016)
www.archive.org (December 4, 2015)
www.baltimoresun.com (February 21, 2016)
www.beyondthecrater.com (March 4, 2015)
www.bioguide.congress.gov (January 29, 2016)
www.bpi.edu (January 25, 2013)
www.cdc.gov (February 4, 2016)
www.chicagotribute.com (February 6, 2016)
www.chroniclingamerica.loc.gov (April 18, 2015)
www.cincinnaticwrt.org (February 13, 2015)
www.civilwardailygazette (August 5, 2014)
www.civilwartalk.com (August 26, 2014)
www.civilwarathome (August 18, 2012)
www.civilwarreference.com (June 29, 2012)
www.civilwartrust.org (May 3, 2013)
www.civilwar.vt.edu (November 28, 2014)

www.civilwarwili.net (January 11, 2013)
www.crossroadsofwar.org (October 29, 2015)
www.customsmuseum.org (November 21, 2015)
www.distancebetweencities (May 3, 2013)
www.distancecalculator.globefeed.com (October 25, 2014)
www.distance-cities.com (January 2, 2015)
www.dlxs.richmond.edu (November 28, 2014)
www.dmna.ny.gov (April 5, 2014)
www.ehistory.osu.edu (February 28, 2015)
www.elmwoodhistoriccemetery.org (January 11, 2013)
www.encyclopediavirginia.org (March 11, 2015)
www.en.wikipedia.org (July 21, 2015)
www.etymoline.com (January 20, 2015)
www.exlibris-group.com (September 6, 2016)
www.familysearch.org (August 6, 2016)
www.findagrave.com (September 17, 2016)
www.fold3.com (August 7, 2016)
www.frenchfamilyassoc.com (July 4, 2016)
www.genealogy.com (December 24, 2015)
www.geocoaching.com (August 25, 2014)
www.google.com (November 23, 2011)
www.gracewin.org (September 13, 2012)
www.handley-regional.org (January 23, 2014)
www.harpweek.com (October 28, 2015)
www.harrisburgpatriotnews.pa.newsmemory.com (May 8, 2014)
www.heraldmailmedia.com (May 14, 2015)
www.heritagecenter. com (August 21, 2016)
www.historyncus.edu (January 14, 2015)
www.historyforsale.com (January 20, 2016)
www.historynet.com (October 22, 2014)
www.hscc.carr.org (March 1, 2015)
www.iagenweb.org (October 6, 2012)
www.ilga.gov (February 25, 2015)
www.illinoisgenweb.org (January 8, 2014)
www.jtsamuels.com (February 17, 2015)
www.learnnc.org (December 27, 2014)
www.linkedin.com (May 8, 2014)
www.loc.gov (December 20, 2015)
www.madhouse.com (January 30, 2013)
www.mdarchives.state,md.us (March 5, 2015)
www.mdlandrec.net (January 20, 2016)
www.merriam-webster.com (March 2, 2016)
www.msa.maryland.gov (April 17, 2012)
www.ncmuseumofhistory.org (November 28, 2014)
www.ncpedia.org (November 28, 2014)
www.newtownhistorycenter.org (July 24, 2016)
www.nps.gov (February 13, 2015)
www.nytimes.com (February 6, 2016)
www.obelin.edu (January 9, 2004)
www.pa-roots.org (March 18, 2014)
www.perseus.tufts.edu (October 6, 2012)
www.poetryfoundation.org (August 12, 2016)
www.presidency.ucsb.edu (March 7, 2015)
www.press.jhu.edu (March 19, 2014)
www.*researchonline.net* (September 3, 2016)
www.reynoldahouse.org (November 28, 2014)
www.richmondregister.com (March 1, 2015)
www.rootsweb.com (May 30, 2012)
www.shipbuildinghistory.com (January 29, 2016)

www.sixthmarylandinfantry.org (February 21, 2015)
www.slate.com (August 1, 2016
www.suvcw.org (December 20, 2015)
www.thefreedictionary.com (September 17, 2012)
www.thirteenthmass.org (June 28, 2012)
www.ushistory.org (June 3, 2015)
www.usma.edu (January 13, 2016)
www.washcolibrary (April 1, 2014)
www.waymarking.com (December 31, 2015)
www.westegg.com (January 13, 2018)
www.whilbr.org (November 5, 2015)
www.wikipedia.org (August 17, 2016)
www.winchesterhistory.org (December 20, 2012)
www.wlu.edu (February 18, 2015)
www.youseemore.com/handley (September 29, 2012)
www.zionhagerstown.org (March 21, 2014)

U.S. Bureau of the Census Records at the National Archives, Washington, D. C.

1850 U.S. Census for Frederick County, Virginia
1850 U.S. Census for Hagerstown, Maryland
1850 U.S. Census for Washington County, Maryland
1850 U.S. Census for Winchester, Virginia
1850 U.S. Census for Wayne County, Michigan
1860 U.S. Census for Baltimore City, Maryland
1860 U.S. Census for Boonsboro, Maryland
1860 U.S. Census for Brooklyn, New York
1860 U.S. Census for Fauquier County, Virginia
1860 U.S. Census for Frederick County, Virginia
1860 U.S. Census for Funkstown, Maryland
1860 U.S. Census for Hagerstown, Maryland
1860 U.S. Census for Martinsburg, Virginia
1860 U.S. Census for Mountjoy, Adams County, Pennsylvania
1860 U.S. Census for Oakland County, Michigan
1860 U.S. Census for Rockingham County, Virginia
1860 U.S. Census for Schuylkill County, Pennsylvania
1860 U.S. Census for Sharpsburg, Maryland
1860 U.S. Census for Stephensburg, Virginia
1860 U.S. Census for Washington County, Maryland
1860 U.S. Census for Winchester, Virginia
1870 U.S. Census for Allentown, Pennsylvania
1870 U.S. Census for Antietam, Maryland
1870 U.S. Census for Blair County, Pennsylvania
1870 U.S. Census for the District of Columbia
1870 U.S. Census for Frederick County, Virginia
1870 U.S. Census for Hagerstown, Maryland
1870 U.S. Census for Harrisburg, Pennsylvania
1870 U.S. Census for Lancaster, Pennsylvania
1870 U.S. Census for Loudoun County, Virginia
1870 U.S. Census for Martinsburg, Virginia
1870 U.S. Census for McLean County, Illinois
1870 U.S. Census for Montgomery County, Maryland
1870 U.S. Census for Philadelphia, Pennsylvania
1870 U.S. Census for Rockingham County, Virginia
1870 U.S. Census for Tallahassee, Florida
1870 U.S. Census for Washington County, Maryland
1870 U.S. Census for Winchester, Virginia
1880 U.S. Census for Frederick County, Virginia
1880 U.S. Census for Hagerstown, Maryland

1880 U.S. Census for Hancock, Maryland
1880 U.S. Census for Howard County, Maryland
1880 U.S. Census for Loudoun County, Virginia
1880 U.S. Census for Mifflin County, Pennsylvania
1880 U.S. Census for Pittsburgh, Pennsylvania
1880 U.S. Census for Rockingham County, Virginia
1900 U.S. Census for Baltimore City, Maryland
1900 U.S. Census for Cleveland, Ohio
1900 U.S. Census for Columbus, Ohio
1900 U.S. Census for Hagerstown, Maryland
1900 U.S. Census for Hancock, Maryland
1900 U.S. Census for Harrisburg, Pennsylvania
1900 U.S. Census for Howard County, Maryland
1900 U.S. Census for Lancaster, Pennsylvania
1900 U.S. Census for Loudoun County, Virginia
1900 U.S. Census for Mercer, New Jersey
1900 U.S. Census for Rockingham County, Virginia
1900 U.S. Census for Steuben County, New York
1910 U.S. Census for Baltimore, Maryland
1910 U.S. Census for Hancock, Maryland
1910 U.S. Census for Osceola County, Florida
1910 U.S. Census for Rockingham County, Virginia
1910 U.S. Census for Washington County, Maryland
1920 U.S. Census for Baltimore, Maryland
1920 U.S. Census for Pittsburgh, Pennsylvania
1920 U.S. Census for Rockingham County, Virginia
1930 U.S. Census for Baltimore, Maryland
1930 U.S. Census for Pittsburg, Pennsylvania
1930 U.S. Census for Rockingham County, Virginia
1940 U.S. Census for Hagerstown, Maryland
1940 U.S. Census for Rockingham County, Virginia